WHO LOSES, WHO WINS

WHO LOSES, WHO WINS

THE

JOURNALS

OF

KENNETH ROSE

VOLUME TWO

1979–2014

EDITED BY D.R. THORPE

WEIDENFELD & NICOLSON

First published in Great Britain in 2019 by Weidenfeld & Nicolson
an imprint of The Orion Publishing Group Ltd
Carmelite House, 50 Victoria Embankment
London EC4Y 0DZ

An Hachette UK Company

3 5 7 9 10 8 6 4 2

A CIP catalogue record for this book is available from the British Library.

ISBN (hardback) 978 1 4746 1058 2
ISBN (ebook) 978 1 4746 1060 5

Typeset by Input Data Services Ltd, Somerset

Printed and bound in Great Britain by Clays Ltd, Elcograf S.p.A.

MIX
Paper from
responsible sources
FSC   FSC® C104740
www.fsc.org

www.weidenfeldandnicolson.co.uk
www.orionbooks.co.uk

In memory of
Penelope Hoare

CONTENTS

Preface ix
Acknowledgements xix

So we'll live,
And pray, and sing, and tell old tales, and laugh
At gilded butterflies, and hear poor rogues
Talk of court news, and we'll talk with them too –
Who loses and who wins, who's in, who's out.

King Lear, Act 5, Scene 3

PREFACE

'What sort of diary should I like mine to be?' pondered Virginia Woolf. 'I should like it to resemble some deep old desk, or capacious hold-all, in which one flings a mass of odds and ends without looking them through.'[*] Such was the approach adopted by Kenneth Rose for seventy years, after he began recording the events of his life in 1944. The six million words that followed are kept in 350 boxes in the Bodleian Library, Oxford, to which institution he bequeathed the bulk of his estate. 'After the writer's death,' observed Jean Cocteau, 'reading his journal is like receiving a long letter.'[†] This 'long letter' took me two years to read and to photostat relevant material, followed by a further two years of selecting the text and supplying footnotes and linking passages.

Unlike Kenneth's early mentor Harold Nicolson, who observed ruefully, as the three volumes of his diaries were such a success when published by his son Nigel between 1966 and 1968 that he was now famous for a book that he did not realise he had written, Kenneth always intended that his journals would one day be his legacy.[‡] Of one thing he was absolutely clear: no entry should be rewritten in the light of later developments. 'A diary', wrote Tony Benn, 'is not trying to establish a reputation, but to give people an idea of what you thought at the time.'[§]

It was owing to Tony Benn – then Anthony Wedgwood Benn, later 2nd Viscount Stansgate, before campaigning successfully for the right to disclaim his peerage, and a compulsive diarist from the age of fourteen – that Kenneth began recording his experiences. The two were contemporaries in the 1940s at New College, on the same staircase in the Garden Quad. After

---

[*] Diary, 20 Apr. 1919.

[†] Diary, 7 June 1953.

[‡] Nigel Nicolson allowed K.R. to read the complete Harold Nicolson diaries from 1948 to 1952 when Nicolson was writing his life of George V. 'Reading the unpublished diaries shows me how skilful Nigel has been in separating his nuggets of gold from a considerable amount of dross.' K.R., Journal, 14 June 1976.

[§] *Daily Telegraph*, 30 Sept. 1995. Benn's published diaries eventually ran to eight volumes.

Hall one evening the pair, in customary undergraduate style, were putting the world to rights in Benn's room. The next day Kenneth visited Benn and noticed that his friend was colouring in a large sheet divided into twenty-four squares, representing hours. It was clear that this was a generalised record of the previous day. Kenneth asked Benn what the colours meant. Benn explained that black was when he was asleep, red was when he was working, and blue was when he was enjoying himself. Kenneth could not help noticing that the hours from 9 p.m. to midnight were at that moment being coloured in yellow. He asked what that colour represented. 'Oh that', replied Benn frankly, 'was a waste of time!' However, it was not a waste of time for Kenneth, who that very day resolved also to discipline himself to write up the events of his life, a task he maintained thereafter until a few days before his death on 28 January 2014. Bernard Donoughue, sometime Labour minister, a regular and accomplished diarist himself, acknowledged that 'the itch and urge to record life's events, however trivial, can never be fully suppressed'.* So it was with Kenneth.

Despite the many prize-winning histories that he wrote, Kenneth, like Sir Walter Scott, left as his posthumous *magnum opus* a journal. The editor of Scott's journal, Eric Anderson, wrote of Scott: 'he numbered among his friends almost all the great men of his day; his public was the entire civilized world'.† It is an apt description too of Kenneth at the height of his powers. William Shawcross described his journal as 'the most detailed, amusing and accurate account ever of the post-war world of the English Establishment'.‡ His close friend, Lord Carrington, was able to read much of the journal in its original form. He recorded his impressions:

> During his long and distinguished journalistic career, Kenneth Rose had the opportunities to meet, formally and informally, most of the interesting and influential figures of the time. All welcomed and trusted him, for he was the most discreet of men. The diaries, chronicling the events of previous generations, give a unique glimpse of the personalities and preoccupations of the statesmen of that time. Harold Macmillan and Rab Butler, among other figures, are shown in a different and more informal way than their biographers have done and the differences in their approach to politics and each other are amusingly revealed. The cast of characters is long and varied: the arts, politics, business and many powerful Americans

---

* *Westminster Diary* (I.B. Tauris, 2016), p. ix.
† *The Journal of Sir Walter Scott* (Canongate Classics, 1998), p. xxiii.
‡ *Sunday Telegraph*, 2 Feb. 2014.

and Europeans. They are a fascinating insight into the concerns of their time and those most involved. They are entertaining and funny, and, to those of us engaged in public affairs, offer a glimpse of that aspect of the people and events of the time, of which we know very little.

•

Hints are given as to the content of the journals in the thirty-six years of the 'Albany' column. Such a distinctive achievement attracted admiration, envy and parody. When Duff Hart-Davis was Literary Editor of the *Sunday Telegraph*, he organised a competition in which readers were invited to submit parodies of the paper's regular features. Cod versions of 'Albany' far outnumbered any others. The winning entry included the memorable line, 'Few other junior liberals, I imagine, ride a dromedary before breakfast.'*

In retrospect, the most interesting diarists, from Samuel Pepys to Jock Colville and later, are those who are not in high executive office themselves, but are on what Colville described as 'the fringes of power', which also applied to three of Kenneth's contemporary diarists, Harold Nicolson, Chips Channon and James Lees-Milne. It is a fitting description of Kenneth. The abiding interest of his life was in what that observer of statecraft F.S. Oliver described as 'the endless adventure of ruling men'. The unique quality of Kenneth's journals lies in the sheer range of those ruling men and women. It includes major political figures, eminent academics, fellow historians and biographers, the aristocracy and the Royal Family, opera singers and conductors, bishops and public-school headmasters. The worlds of science, medicine, commerce, industry and business are less well represented and he had no acquaintances among sportsmen, 'personalities' and people famous for being famous.

His friendships with members of the Royal Family were wide-ranging. After the war, when still in his twenties, he was a frequent guest of Princess Marina, the widowed Duchess of Kent, at her home Coppins in Iver, Buckinghamshire, and through her he came to know the young Duke of Kent, with whom he was to enjoy a lifetime of musical visits, including three trips to the Wagner Festival at Bayreuth. Princess Margaret was a figure for whom he felt much sympathy through her many difficulties. She particularly enjoyed his capacity for making people laugh.

The two royal figures whom he knew best, a unique combination, were the Duke of Windsor (he attended the last dinner party the Duke gave in January 1972 in Paris) and the Queen Mother, who was to give him so many

---

* *The Times*, 6 Feb. 2014.

insights into the character of King George V when Kenneth was researching his life of the monarch. From both figures he received intimate details of primary historical importance about the Abdication Crisis and its aftermath, duly recorded in his journals.

He was also well known and trusted in the world of the royal courtiers over the years. His many friendships also extended to foreign royalty, so much so that when he once asked his secretary at the *Sunday Telegraph*, 'Get me the King,' she had to ask, 'Which King?'*

Kenneth knew particularly well the political giants in the Conservative, Labour and Liberal parties, conversing intimately with the Churchill and Eden families, and all the prime ministers from Harold Macmillan onwards. When Hugh Gaitskell died unexpectedly in January 1963, his widow Dora advised his successor as Leader of the Opposition, Harold Wilson, to get to know Kenneth, as then he would find out so much of what was going on in the political world. Their friendship struck a spark from the beginning, partly owing to their respective West Yorkshire backgrounds of Huddersfield and Bradford, the latter described by J.B. Priestley as 'the right sort of town'.

Kenneth never asserted his Jewishness, and there were some close friends who did not know he was Jewish until the address given at his memorial service by Lord Waldegrave in the Chapel of the Most Excellent Order of the British Empire in St Paul's Cathedral. Though not a religious figure, he was drawn to the Anglican Church and its place in the nation's history. He noted the dates of major festivals in his diary, and attended many at St Mary Abbot's Church, Kensington.† Kenneth counted many of the higher clergy as friends: archbishops such as his fellow Reptonian, Michael Ramsey; Donald Coggan, at one stage Bishop of his home city of Bradford, before archiepiscopates at York and Canterbury; and Robert Runcie, with their joint links in Guards regiments. He had, though, no belief in an afterlife. In his letter to Harold Nicolson on the death of his wife Vita, he wrote: 'I wish I could write words of comfort to ease your pain. But to those of us denied a bright and tidy image of immortality there is no real consolation.'‡

Oxford and Cambridge loom large in the journals, with acute observations of the activities of so many of the key figures of post-war academic life: Noel Annan, Isaiah Berlin, Robert Blake, Asa Briggs, Alan Bullock (Kenneth contributed financially to the foundation of Bullock's St Catherine's College,

---

* Charlotte Hofton to the editor, 2 June 2015.
† The lady vicar of St Mary Abbot's conducted his funeral at Kensal Green. He had wanted no one to attend, as a memorial service would follow later. Nevertheless, Lord and Lady Waldegrave, Graham C. Greene, Sir John Nutting and D.R. Thorpe did attend.
‡ 3 June 1962.

Oxford), F.R. Leavis, Jack Plumb, A.L. Rowse, John Sparrow, A.J.P. Taylor and Hugh Trevor-Roper, recording their achievements and feuds in the enclosed world of the Senior Common Room and High Table. Of All Souls he observed that though the Fellows changed, the guests remained the same.

The world of the public schools, in a transitional and sometimes difficult age for those institutions, also features strongly in the journals. There are uninhibited accounts of the difficulties they faced, both politically and financially. After returning from war service, Kenneth initially taught at Eton when Kenneth Wickham, a housemaster and history beak, was unexpectedly indisposed for eighteen months after an operation. Claude Elliott, the Head Master, moved quickly to secure Kenneth's services, though the latter never saw this as a long-term career. He could be sharp with the sophisticated and independent-minded boys. 'You boys, you boys, I don't know why I bother to teach you,' he once told his division in exasperation. 'Sir, you need the money,' came the reply. 'The money I get here doesn't keep me in cigars,' was his response, an episode of which Claude Elliott disapproved when he heard of it, though it rather impressed the pupils.* Of one of his students, Antony Armstrong-Jones, Kenneth wrote in a report, 'Armstrong-Jones may be good at something but it is nothing that we teach at Eton.'†

As with bishoprics, deaneries and ambassadorships, Kenneth always seemed to have advance notice of forthcoming headships; sometimes, it was said, even before governing bodies had finally made up their minds. There are perceptive portraits of Sir Robert Birley and his successor as Head Master of Eton, Anthony Chenevix-Trench, who departed the Cloisters prematurely. Kenneth asked that devoted son of Eton, Harold Macmillan, his views on the sort of man to succeed Chenevix-Trench as Head Master. 'Preferably someone in Holy Orders,' replied Macmillan, 'so that if he does not do very well at Eton he can always be made a Bishop.'‡

Eton became in many respects a substitute alma mater for Kenneth: not just annual fixtures such as the Fourth of June celebrations and cricket versus Harrow at Lord's, but the whole ambience of the lotus years of that enchanted valley, as he described it. Many of his closest friends, such as the Hon. Giles St Aubyn, a fellow Bayreuth pilgrim, Wilfrid Blunt, Hubert Hartley and Hubert's formidable wife, Grizel Hartley, were part of the fabric of the College over many years, and of Kenneth's life. Grizel Hartley's observant humour

---

* The late Hon. Giles St Aubyn to the editor, 27 Sept. 2014.
† Ibid.
‡ Journal, 17 Aug. 1969. Interestingly, a question he put to the former Prime Minister whilst Chenevix-Trench was still in office.

particularly pleased him. When a haughty mother told Grizel that she hoped her daughter would marry a Moor, Grizel replied, 'What, like Desdemona?' He agreed with Grizel Hartley when she wrote, 'At Eton, the very stones cry out names.'[*]

Kenneth was not unaware of the idiosyncracies of Eton's ways, and when some years later he received a letter from the College offering him the very rare opportunity to become an honorary Old Etonian (an accolade he shared with the Queen Mother), his initial reaction was that it must be a practical joke. Only when he examined the envelope and saw that it bore a second-class stamp did he accept that the offer was genuine.[†]

He numbered among his close associates the leading diplomats and ambassadors of the day; a small number of businessmen, especially Lord King, who transformed British Airways, and Victor Rothschild, who spanned many worlds and who was Kenneth's last biographical subject; banking titans, especially those at Coutts; military figures from Field Marshal Bernard Montgomery, who later wrote to him after the war saying he did not recall him then as the two of them were on somewhat different levels; his fellow colleagues in the Welsh Guards during the war; artistic figures such as Salvador Dalí and Lucian Freud; broadcasting moguls and his fellow journalists; many of the greatest composers and musicians of his time, including Benjamin Britten, Sir Malcolm Sargent, Sir Georg Solti, Wagner's grandsons, Wieland and Wolfgang, and Sir William Walton; literary and publishing figures of note, especially his own mentor, Lord Weidenfeld, John Betjeman, Norman Douglas of *South Wind* fame, Lady Antonia Fraser, Anthony Powell and C.P. Snow. Like Harold Macmillan, he considered Snow's novel *The Masters* to convey acute insights into human nature. His journals and letters are punctuated with shrewd assessments. He much admired Arnold Bennett, noting that 'other novelists had written about industrial life – Dickens, Disraeli, Mrs Gaskell. For them it was something new and terrifying. For Bennett it was home.'[‡] Of Henry James, he noted that nothing important ever happens, but he holds the attention of the reader for 500 pages.[§] He thought H.G. Wells's *The New Machiavelli* 'quite his best novel'.[¶]

London clubland – he was a member of the Beefsteak and Pratt's – mattered

---

[*] Ibid., 12 May 2010. P.S.H. Lawrence (ed.), *Grizel: Grizel Hartley Remembered* (Michael Russell, 1991), p. 110.

[†] K.R. to the editor, 11 Jan. 2011.

[‡] Journal, 28 June 1984.

[§] Letter to Sir Philip Magnus, later Magnus-Allcroft, 4 Feb. 1964.

[¶] Journal, 8 Oct. 1949.

greatly to him. He called the Beefsteak 'the sixth form of the Garrick'.* In
the legal world, two of his longest-standing friendships were with Lord Goddard, the Lord Chief Justice (though, unlike Goddard, Kenneth was always
resolutely opposed to capital punishment), and Lord Shawcross, who was
the leading British prosecution counsel in the post-war Nuremberg Trials.
He was with Sir Brian Horrocks when Horrocks received the surrender of
Heligoland in 1945.

He had an eye for quirky details, recording that whenever Lord King,
Chairman of the Belvoir Hunt, saw a fox he shouted out, 'Charles James'!
At a Gentleman versus Players match at Lord's Kenneth noted that a bishop
was asked to remove his pectoral cross, as it was dazzling a batsman. He had
close links to many of the oldest families in the land, and friendships with
prominent Americans and Europeans. His interests were legion and in many
cases unexpected. He was fascinated by astronomy and eclipses and was a
regular at the Hastings Chess Congress. His *Times* obituary recalled that 'it
was not a party unless Kenneth Rose was there'.†

J.M. Keynes wrote of Edwin Montagu, the Liberal politician: 'I never knew
a male person of big mind who was more addicted to gossip than Edwin
Montagu. He could not bear to be out of things.'‡ The same applied to Ken-
neth, who once confessed: 'I find it difficult to let a good story pass me by.'§
When an acquaintance once disparaged 'gossip' to Kenneth, he responded:
'The cobbler must not criticise leather.'¶

Kenneth was not a mere fair-weather friend, but was especially support-
ive to those who fell into difficulties, notably Jeremy Thorpe and Jonathan
Aitken. Sarah, Duchess of York, to whom he wrote his last letter, was also
someone for whom he made much time. He was very good with children and
observant of their ways, noting how Sarah's daughters said grace before their
nursery tea, though when they called him 'Ken' he commented that the only
person to do likewise was Sybil, Marchioness of Cholmondeley.

Without family commitments and with no dependants as a lifelong bachelor, Kenneth was immensely generous to institutions that he loved – Repton,
New College, the Welsh Guards, Eton College, the London Library, his two
clubs and the Bodleian Library. When by chance he heard from a headmaster
of Repton that a promising pupil would not be able to stay on after O-Levels

---

* Journal, 7 Oct. 1990.

† 31 Jan. 2014.

‡ *The Collected Writings of John Maynard Keynes* vol. X, *Essays in Biography*, 1933 (Mac-
millan/CUP for the Royal Economic Society, 1972), p. 42.

§ Journal, 6 Sept. 1966.

¶ Ibid., 12 Dec. 1965.

owing to his parents' financial difficulties, he privately undertook to pay the school fees himself, anonymous philanthropy he repeated on more than one occasion over the years. Many of his friends who fell on hard times he helped with thousands of pounds, never wanting repayment. Politically he was a Whig, not a Tory, always preferring Gladstone to Disraeli. He never drove a car, owned a computer or a mobile phone. As an author of highly regarded books, his main characteristic was his thoroughness. His famous book on Lord Curzon and his circle was published in 1983, but he had begun researching it in the late 1940s.

•

Kenneth Vivian Rose was born on 15 November 1924 (a birthday, as he noted, that he shared with Nye Bevan, who was born in 1897), the second son of Dr Jacob Rosenwige, a distinguished surgeon of 348 Wakefield Road, Bradford and his wife Ada, née Silverstein. His mother trained as a pharmacologist and served in the Voluntary Aid Detachment in both world wars. His parents 'anglicised' their names to Jack and Ada Rose, a practice not uncommon at the time of covert, and at times not so covert, anti-Semitism. Kenneth's elder brother, Toby, who died of cancer in his early thirties in April 1953, also followed his father into the medical profession after wartime service in the Royal Navy, becoming an expert on the treatment of infantile paralysis. Kenneth endowed a medical prize at St Catherine's College, Oxford, for biological sciences in memory of his brother. This family background led Kenneth to publish a monograph on William Harvey, the discoverer of the circulation of the blood, in 1978.

Kenneth went to Repton School in September 1939. 'I remain grateful to all those who taught me so well and for the friendship and laughter of those days,' he later wrote of his schooldays. A precursor of his later career came in the form of his editorship of *The Reptonian*. A stalwart of the debating society, in February 1941 he proposed the motion that 'In the opinion of this House, communism is the only solution to the present social and economic chaos in Europe.' Not surprisingly, the motion was lost by eighty votes to fifteen. Unlike many of his contemporaries, he was never a 'professional' old boy and later declined offers to become President of the Old Reptonian Association. When his research into Lord Curzon's life took him to nearby Kedleston, he strained for a glimpse from the train of the needle-sharp spire in whose shadow Reptonians have lived for centuries. 'On the platform of Derby Station, too, at certain times of the year were piles of trunks labelled "Repton via Willington". Sometimes I have felt a little glow of nostalgia for my schooldays, but have generally preferred them to remain a distant prospect.'*

Though Kenneth had enjoyed Repton, his scholarship to read Modern History at New College in 1942 introduced him to a world that broadened his horizons. His time there fell into two phases, as he went away on war service with the Welsh Guards before returning to complete his degree. The contemporaries he met became lifelong friends – Lord Altrincham, later John Grigg; Tony Benn; Sir David Butler, the pre-eminent psephologist; Richard Ollard, historian and author; Sir John Smith, later MP for the Cities of London and Westminster, an eminent diarist himself;† and the distinguished biographer and author Philip Ziegler. Kenneth learned much from these friendships. Tony Benn and John Grigg, in that order, were the first two hereditary peers to disclaim their titles on 31 July 1963 following the passage that day of the Peerage Act that was eventually the means by which the Earl of Home became Prime Minister as Sir Alec Douglas-Home in October that year. It happened that Kenneth dined with John Grigg and Tony Benn on the evening they both disclaimed, an arrangement made some days before, none knowing what an historic day it would be. Oxford remained an important part of the rest of his life and he delighted in recording details of the university.

Kenneth remained immensely proud that he was able to experience action in the later stages of the war in the Welsh Guards, though his preliminary spell at Staff College saw him suffer bullying and anti-Semitic prejudice. He never forgot the support he was given at this time by Matthew Ridley, the 4th Viscount.

Kenneth was a latter-day Thomas Creevey (1768–1838), an observer of the doings of others rather than a participant. Creevey's fame derived from the extensive letters he wrote to his stepdaughter, Elizabeth Ord. No contemporary was a more important historical source on the appearance, looks and activities of royal personages and the most important political figures of his age. Kenneth was greatly influenced by this example. He also derived intense pleasure from the political diary of Sir Edward Hamilton (1847–1908), Gladstone's Private Secretary, which he kept from 1880, when he joined the secretariat in Downing Street, until 1906. The work comprises fifty-four volumes, now in the British Library. Creevey and Hamilton were, in their

---

* K.R., *One Boy's War, 1939–1942* (printed privately, 2006). *The Reptonian*, Mar. 1941 (no. 462, vol. LXII).

† The John Smith diaries, kept in Eton Coll. Library, contain many insightful references to K.R. over the years. The author is grateful to Sir John Smith's widow for privileged access to these closed volumes.

different ways, model influences on Kenneth. Dudley Bahlman's notice of Sir Edward Hamilton in the *Oxford Dictionary of National Biography* describes him as possessing 'diligence, accuracy, discretion, tact, and above all an ability to write clear summaries of complex questions',[*] attributes that were echoed in Kenneth's style and practice, something he had gleaned from his work, including intelligence matters, for the British Council in Rome and Naples from 1948 to 1951.

Kenneth's last years were blighted by recurrent cancer, though he died following a serious fall at home. The last person to visit him in hospital was the Duke of Kent, who was to read the lesson at his memorial service on 8 May 2014, a few weeks after he had gone to Paradise 'by way of Kensal Green'.[†] Lord Carrington reminded the congregation of Kenneth's lucid, elegant prose by reading a passage from his masterpiece, the life of King George V, which characteristically illuminated his careful scholarship.

---

[*] Vol. 24 (OUP, 2004), p. 785.
[†] G.K. Chesterton, 'The Rolling English Road'.

ACKNOWLEDGEMENTS

My greatest debt is to Kenneth, who entrusted me some years ago with the task of editing his journals and letters. We had spoken a lot about what this would entail and he had been hoping to work with me, at least initially, on the vast project. Sadly, his sudden and unexpected death at the age of eighty-nine in January 2014 prevented this. However, much preliminary work had been done.

I am indebted to many people for their help and advice on so many aspects, particularly his executor, Lord Waldegrave of North Hill, who has supported me constantly throughout the process of selecting material from the 350 boxes in the Bodleian Library. My publisher at Weidenfeld & Nicolson, Alan Samson, and his team, Celia Hayley, Linden Lawson and Simon Wright, have been a mine of information and valued advice regarding editing the text, the publishing house being not only Kenneth's, but also a specialist in publishing some of the most important diaries of the twentieth century. The late Graham C. Greene, who has been a mentor to me for over thirty years, has again been a valuable source of encouragement. I am very grateful to Sir Eric Anderson for reading the complete text in typescript and for his valuable comments.

My work would not have been possible without the skilful assistance of Richard Ovenden, Librarian of the Bodleian, and his dedicated team: Theodora Boorman, Dr Chris Fletcher, Michael Hughes and Oliver House.

I value greatly the support given to me by His Royal Highness the Duke of Kent, a friend of Kenneth's for over sixty years.

Other friends, colleagues, godchildren, secretaries, authors and publishers whose support has been invaluable include:

Tomás Almeida, Lady Anderson, Christopher Arnold, Jane Birkett, the late Tony Benn, Michael Bloch, Sir David Butler, Peter Catterall, Hannah Cox, Professor David Dilks, Christopher Everett, Helen Ewing, David Faber, Sarah Fortune, Lady Antonia Fraser, Cary Gilbart-Smith, Dean Godson, Field Marshal Lord Guthrie of Craigiebank, Marie-Louise Hamilton, Duff Hart-Davis, Charles Hastings, Louise Hayman, Professor Dr Simon Heffer,

Lord Hennessy of Nympsfield, Charlotte Hofton, Robert Holroyd, Graham and Vanessa Jones, Robert Lacey, Nicolas Marden, Michael Meredith, Charles Moore, Ferdinand Mount, the late John Julius Norwich, Sir John Nutting, Daniel Poole, Lady Prudence Penn, Angela Reed, the late Brian Rees, Natasha Rees, Viscount Ridley, Professor Jane Ridley, Professor Dr Andrew Roberts, the late Hon. Giles St Aubyn, Nicholas Shakespeare, the Hon. William Shawcross, Anthony Shone, Stephen Shuttleworth, Anton Smith, Lady Christian Smith, Rachel Smyth, Christopher Spence, Paul Stevens, the Hon. James Stourton, Joanna Taylor, Robert Tyerman, David Twiston Davies, Hugo Vickers, Professor Geoffrey Warner, the late Lord Weidenfeld, Tom Wheare, Nicholas Winston, the Revd John Witheridge, Ruth Winstone and Philip Ziegler.

The Carrington estate has given permission for the inclusion of Lord Carrington's description of Kenneth Rose.

1979

Margaret Thatcher became the UK's first female Prime Minister on 4 May 1979. Jeremy Thorpe went on trial at the Old Bailey charged with conspiracy and incitement to murder on 8 May. In his first Budget on 12 June the Chancellor of the Exchequer, Geoffrey Howe, cut the standard rate of income tax by 3p and reduced the top rate from 83 per cent to 60 per cent. On 22 June Jeremy Thorpe was cleared of the charges. On 27 August Lord Mountbatten, his fifteen-year-old nephew and a boat boy were assassinated by a Provisional IRA bomb placed on his fishing boat in Donegal Bay, County Sligo, the Dowager Lady Brabourne dying of her injuries the next day. The Times was published for the first time in almost a year after a long dispute on 13 November. Minimum Lending Rate was raised to 17 per cent on 15 November. On 7 December Lord Soames was appointed transitional Governor of Rhodesia to oversee its move to independence.

5 May 1979

The names of Margaret Thatcher's Cabinet are announced. The best news is that Peter Carrington[*] becomes Foreign Secretary: we had feared that it might go to Ted Heath, who quite rightly has not been given a job. As I forecast last October, Quintin Hailsham[†] returns to the Woolsack and Peter Rawlinson[‡] bides his time outside the Government. Ian Gilmour[§] does not go to Defence but to the FO as No. 2 to Peter, and with a seat in Cabinet as Lord Privy Seal. All very satisfactory.

---

[*] 6th Baron Carrington (1919–2018), Conservative politician. Foreign Secretary 1979–82; Sec. Gen. of NATO 1984–8; Father of the House of Lords 2007–18.

[†] Quintin Hogg, Baron Hailsham of St Marylebone (1907–2001), Conservative politician. MP for Oxford 1938–50 and for St Marylebone 1963–70; Lord Chancellor 1979–87.

[‡] Sir Peter Rawlinson, Baron Rawlinson of Ewell (1919–2006), barrister, Conservative politician and author. MP for Epsom 1955–78; Att. Gen. 1970–74; Att. Gen. for Northern Ireland 1972–4.

[§] Sir Ian Gilmour, Baron Gilmour of Craigmillar, 3rd Bt (1926–2007), Conservative politician. Sec. of State for Defence Jan.–Mar. 1974; Lord Privy Seal 1979–81.

8 May 1979

Supper party at George Weidenfeld's.[*] Have some agreeable talk with Lady Falkender,[†] who is modest and not at all politically aggressive. I please her by quoting Selwyn Lloyd[‡] on the relative merits of Harold Wilson and George Brown.[§]

Clarissa Avon[¶] tells me that she has always hated the Windsors, and thought it 'wicked' of Winston to destroy the evidence about the Duke's apparent readiness to become a German stooge in 1940. Later in the evening George asks me whether I would consider writing the official life of Anthony Eden, with all the papers. Apparently, Martin Gilbert,[**] who had been asked to undertake it by Clarissa, is odd and neurotic and with all his work on Churchill may not continue with it. It would be a heavy task.[††]

9 May 1979

Desperately sad newspaper photographs of poor Jeremy Thorpe[‡‡] arriving at the Old Bailey for his trial. The sustained euphoria of the past months seems suddenly to have vanished as he faces reality.

12 May 1979

I have much talk on Royal topics with Edward Ford.[§§] He tells me that Tommy Lascelles[¶¶] used to say that there were three sexes: male, female and

---

[*] Baron Weidenfeld (1919–2016), publisher and philanthropist; founded the publishing firm Weidenfeld & Nicolson with Nigel Nicolson in 1949. He published all K.R.'s books and was instrumental in securing K.R.'s Journals for the house.

[†] Marcia, Baroness Falkender (b. 1932), head of Harold Wilson's political office.

[‡] Baron Selwyn Lloyd (1904–78), Conservative politician. Foreign Secretary 1955–60; Chancellor of the Exchequer 1960–62; Speaker of the House of Commons 1971–6.

[§] Baron George-Brown (1914–85), Labour politician. MP for Belper 1945–70; First Sec. of State 1964–6; Foreign Secretary 1966–8; deputy leader of the Labour Party 1960–70.

[¶] Clarissa Eden, Countess of Avon (b. 1920).

[**] Sir Martin Gilbert (1936–2015), historian. Official biographer of Sir Winston Churchill.

[††] When Martin Gilbert gave up the task, the Countess of Avon invited Sir Robert Rhodes James to write Eden's life. This biography appeared in 1986, but, for various reasons, did not please her. Subsequently she asked me to write the life of Eden, which appeared in 2003.

[‡‡] (1929–2014), Liberal politician. MP for North Devon 1959–79; leader of the Liberal Party 1967–76. In 1979 he stood trial at the Old Bailey on charges of conspiracy and incitement to murder arising from a previous relationship with a stable boy called Norman Scott. Thorpe was acquitted but his reputation was ruined.

[§§] Sir Edward Ford (1910–2006). Assistant PS to George VI 1946–52 and to Elizabeth II 1952–67. In 1992 he wrote to the Queen's PS commiserating that in the fortieth year of her reign the Queen had endured an *annus horribilis*, a phrase she used on 24 Nov. that year in a speech.

[¶¶] Sir Alan Lascelles (1887–1981). Assistant PS to George V and Edward VIII, of whom he was

Royalty. After King George V had received a minister, he would send for Stamfordham[*] or Wigram,[†] tell them what had passed and assumed that a memorandum would be prepared for the archives. King George VI did not bother to do that. So the Private Secretary would get hold of the PM on his way out, give him a drink and listen to what he had discussed with the Sovereign. This worked well with Winston (who would drink anything) and with Wilson (who liked a glass of brandy), but Charteris[‡] would complain that he could get nothing out of the teetotal Callaghan. Edward would like to have had all conversations between Sovereign and PM taped.

Why is there a gulf between Tommy Lascelles and the Queen Mother? King George VI always used to consult her on important matters. But Lascelles thought her judgement bad and she came to know of this. Tommy always used to tell Edward <u>never</u> to discuss politics with the Queen Mother. Edward thinks one of the Queen Mother's strongest qualities is her belief in an indivisible unit: the Family. Although Princess Margaret could be very tiresome, Edward never once heard the Queen Mother rebuke her in front of others. Always a terrible fuss on Royal tours over presents. All would be arranged, and then Prince Philip would say: 'I don't see why we should give ------ anything.' So Edward would then have to carry the undistributed present with him for the rest of the day.

17 May 1979

I am deeply shocked by the evidence given in the Thorpe trial that the *Sunday Telegraph* is paying Peter Bessell,[§] the chief prosecution witness and an obvious crook, £25,000 for his memoirs if Jeremy is acquitted, but £50,000+ if he is found guilty. It is monstrously immoral. Should I resign from the paper?

23 May 1979

There are two significant points in the report of yesterday's proceedings in the Thorpe case:
(a) Scott admits that he claimed to be having a homosexual affair with J.T. at a time when he had met him only once and talked to him for no more than five minutes.

a harsh critic; PS to George VI 1943–52 and to Elizabeth II 1952–3.
[*] Arthur Bigge, Baron Stamfordham (1849–1931). PS to Queen Victoria 1895–1901 and to George V 1910–31. His grandson, Michael Adeane, was PS to Elizabeth II 1953–72.
[†] Clive Wigram, 1st Baron Wigram (1873–1960), PS to George V 1931–6.
[‡] Sir Martin Charteris, Baron Charteris of Amisfield (1913–99), PS to Elizabeth II 1972–7; Provost of Eton 1978–91.
[§] (1921–85), Liberal MP for Bodmin 1964–70.

(b) George Carman,* J.T.'s counsel, said to Scott: 'You knew when you went
    to the House of Commons in 1961 that Mr Thorpe at that time had
    homosexual tendencies, didn't you?' That is an admission by J.T. of pro-
    found importance. If he admits to having had 'homosexual tendencies'
    in 1961, it will strengthen the belief that he had a homosexual affair with
    Scott, which he has always denied.

Anthony Gilbey† thinks J.T. is bound to be convicted. I bet him £80–£20
against conviction.

27 May 1979

I go to stay with Rab and Mollie Butler‡ at Great Yeldham, Essex. The
eighteenth-century house, Spencers, stands in a fine wooded park.

Victor Rothschild§ and William Waldegrave¶ come over for a drink.
William does not seem at all intimidated by his first days in the Commons
and has several old friends with whom to share jokes.

Mollie is working out the wages of a new couple and comes in to ask:
'What is the difference between gross and net?' How lucky she is to have a
former Chancellor of the Exchequer to answer her question.

Rab talks to me about Eden. 'There was something of the statesman about
him. He was a wonderful diplomatist. He listened to all the Sirs at the Foreign Office, and no man could ever wear a grey suit better.'

He then discusses Selwyn Lloyd. 'After the General Election of 1951,
Winston asked me to be Chancellor of the Exchequer. I told him that I
thought the job would go to Oliver Lyttelton.** But Winston said that Oliver
was too identified with the City. So I was appointed. I at once rang Selwyn and
asked him to become my No. 2 at the Treasury. Selwyn replied that Anthony
had just asked him to go as <u>his</u> No. 2 at the Foreign Office. It changed his

---

* (1929–2001), leading barrister who successfully defended Jeremy Thorpe.
† 11th Baron Vaux of Harrowden (1940–2014), accountant, countryman and Conservative
Party worker.
‡ Richard Austen Butler, Baron Butler of Saffron Walden (1902–82), Conservative politician;
m. (2) 1959 Mollie Courtauld (née Montgomerie). President of the Board of Education 1941–4;
Minister of Education 1944–5; Chancellor of the Exchequer 1951–5; Leader of the House of
Commons 1955–61; Home Secretary 1957–62; Foreign Secretary 1963–6.
§ 3rd Baron Rothschild (1910–90), zoologist and public servant. Victor Rothschild was the
subject of K.R.'s last biography in 2003, *Elusive Rothschild: The Life of Victor, Third Baron.*
¶ Baron Waldegrave of North Hill (b. 1946), Conservative politician. Minister of Agriculture,
Fisheries and Food 1994–5; Chief Secretary to the Treasury 1995–7; Provost of Eton since
2009.
** 1st Viscount Chandos (1893–1972), businessman and Conservative politician. Sec. of State
for the Colonies 1951–4; first Chairman of the National Theatre 1962–71; its Lyttelton Theatre
is named after him.

career. He was a wonderfully loyal adjutant. He gave complete satisfaction. Eden liked him because he was industrious; because he had no ambition to displace Eden as Foreign Secretary; because he was discreet and would never betray the secrets of Eden's life. He was a good stolid speaker too.

'His ambition grew with the years. Although, as Macmillan said, he was essentially a middle-class lawyer from Liverpool, I never thought him vulgar. He acquired grandee habits from Eden. And Macmillan treated him as a favourite, perhaps even spoilt him a little by lending him Chequers. It gave Selwyn a flavour for landed acres and political intrigue. He also began to drink rather a lot. It made him feel a gentleman: it was rather the thing to do. But it did not affect either his capacity for work or his judgement.

'When Macmillan dismissed him as Chancellor in 1962, he suspected that I had had a hand in it. This was quite untrue. Macmillan told me that Selwyn was fussy and dilatory: "He gets on my nerves."

'When Macmillan resigned in 1963, Selwyn supported Alec Home as his successor. Alec made him Leader of the House. He learned its problems and was conciliatory. So it paved the way for his election as Speaker. He felt that this restored his reputation after his humiliating dismissal by Macmillan. He once told me: "This is my vindication." He enjoyed having a place once more in London society. He appointed an extra deputy, so that he was not tied to the House as much as his predecessors.

'His married life, which ended in divorce, was unfortunate. His wife told me: "I could not bear him wearing a sweater in bed: pyjamas yes, but not a sweater."'

Rab is critical of Mrs Thatcher for having abolished the Price Commission immediately on coming into office – yet just before a whole string of inevitable price rises.

He praises Alec Home, in spite of the premiership – 'The greatest gentleman in the land.'

31 May 1979

Peter Walker[*] tells me that on one of Churchill's birthdays, Macmillan made a little speech of congratulation in the House of Commons as Prime Minister. He was followed by Harold Wilson, who tried to match Macmillan's long association with Churchill. 'In the war,' he said, 'I joined the Cabinet Office . . .' Loud whisper from Macmillan: 'I thought he was in Bomber Command.'

---

[*] Baron Walker of Worcester (1932–2010), Conservative politician. MP for Worcester 1961–92; holder of several Cabinet posts under Edward Heath and Margaret Thatcher.

2 June 1979

Dine with Jeremy and Marion Thorpe at Orme Square. Jeremy talks freely of the trial. He finds it physically exhausting, and always goes to bed for two hours on returning from the Old Bailey. Archbishop Michael Ramsey[*] has sent a nice letter of encouragement to Jeremy.

Jeremy is deeply upset by Michael Hartwell's[†] decision to buy Bessell's memoirs – and to pay him double if Jeremy is convicted. 'How can I ever go to the Other Club again, when Michael is Secretary?' He is now inured to all the nasty articles written about him by Bron Waugh,[‡] but will never forgive him for saying that the memorial to Caroline on Coddon Hill should be removed. As always with Jeremy, cheerfulness keeps breaking in.

4 June 1979

Solly Zuckerman[§] tells me that Mountbatten,[¶] who exasperates him, has an absolute fixation on the Prince of Wales and brings him into every conversation and speech. Even when talking recently to a conference in Strasbourg on arms limitation, he branched off into Worlds College[**] – and so to his successor as President, the Prince of Wales.

7 June 1979

Dine with George Weidenfeld. Clarissa Avon promises to let me see her Suez diaries. She says: 'Anthony's friends are dead. So I have reverted to my own friends of twenty-five years ago.' An amusing story from her of how Winston came to the airport in 1952 to say goodbye to Anthony, who was desperately ill and flying to the United Sates for an operation. Winston assured him: 'Don't worry, I will not let them bring in commercial television while you are away.'

8 June 1979

Astonished to receive a huge envelope from the Master of the Royal Household containing an invitation to a supper party and concert at Windsor

---

[*] Baron Ramsey of Canterbury (1904–88), Bishop of Durham 1952–6; Archbishop of York 1956–61; 100th Archbishop of Canterbury 1961–74.

[†] Baron Hartwell (1911–2001), Chairman of the *Daily Telegraph* and founder of the *Sunday Telegraph*.

[‡] Auberon Waugh (1939–2001), journalist; elder son of Evelyn Waugh.

[§] Sir Solly Zuckerman, Baron Zuckerman (1904–93), public servant and scientific adviser during World War II.

[¶] Louis, 1st Earl Mountbatten of Burma (1900–79), naval officer and last Viceroy of India 1947.

[**] UWC, United World Colleges, the educational movement founded by Kurt Hahn in 1962.

Castle on 21 June. It is the first such event I have ever been asked to; in the middle of Ascot week.

Jeremy Thorpe is declining either to call witnesses or to give evidence himself. The inferences to be drawn from this are:

(a) He is guilty.
(b) He hopes that the bad character of those who have given evidence for the prosecution will persuade the jury not to find him guilty.
(c) He avoids having to make a public admission of homosexual behaviour.
(d) He at least has the advantages of (c) whether found guilty or acquitted.
(e) He accepts that his public career is at an end.

21 June 1979

To the Queen's concert and supper party at Windsor. Like a good Victorian I travel down by train: at 100 mph to Slough, then round the Eton curve in a rattler. I walk up to the State entrance of the Castle. Pass up a huge staircase, then through a series of dazzling rooms glowing with Van Dycks and Grinling Gibbons. There seem to be about 200 of us: the entire cultural establishment. The Queen, in glittering silver, and Prince Philip, in the Windsor uniform, receive each guest. I have a genial smile of recognition from the Prince.

Little round supper tables and spindly gilt chairs are grouped at either end of the vast St George's Hall, with plenty of space in the middle. We stand drinking and talking for about forty-five minutes. The hospitality is prodigious.

I ask Arnold Goodman[*] about the probable outcome of the Thorpe case. He replies that he has heard that the jury, which failed to reach a verdict again today, is divided eight to four. The inference is that eight are for conviction and four for acquittal. Were it the reverse, the minority would have agreed to acquit. A minority will insist on pressing for an acquittal, but rarely for a conviction.

Supper is excellent. The first dish is in the centre of each little table: an excellent fish mousse with slices of smoked salmon and a rich mayonnaise. We help ourselves to the two other courses from a buffet: a cold chicken dish and salads, then apricot mousse and cream. Footmen serve white wine, followed by a delicious claret. I have Edna Healey next to me, warm and affectionate as always. Opposite is Denis Healey.[†] On my other side is Ted

---

[*] Baron Goodman (1915–95), lawyer and political adviser.
[†] Baron Healey (1917–2015), Labour politician. Sec. of State for Defence 1964–70; Chancellor of the Exchequer 1974–9; deputy leader of the Labour Party 1980–83.

Heath. Considering the stern things I have sometimes written about him in my column, he is exceptionally genial and friendly.

At the end of supper we are ushered into the Waterloo Chamber. At the far end, on a flower-banked platform, is the English Chamber Orchestra, with Rostropovich[*] as conductor and soloist. The programme is just the right length: Elgar's Serenade for Strings, Haydn's Cello Concerto in C, Handel's 'Arrival of the Queen of Sheba', and Tchaikovsky's Variations on a Rococo Theme. Rostropovich is a master of grimace and gesture, and no cello would be so bold as to argue with him.

The party begins to thin a little at about 12.45. I am driven back to London by William Rees-Mogg.[†] Gillian Rees-Mogg[‡] tells me that the Queen does not like her guests to mention the excellence of the food when they write to thank her, saying 'They should tell that to my chef.'

22 June 1979

I hear on the 5 p.m. news that Jeremy Thorpe and his co-defendants are acquitted on all charges. He does not ask for costs, others do and are refused. I ring Orme Square with my good wishes and leave affectionate messages for both Jeremy and Marion. But it is an occasion more for relief and thanksgiving than for celebration.

27 June 1979

Philip Ward[§] tells me of a conversation reported to him of the present Queen and Princess Margaret in the Royal Box at the Coronation of 1937:

'Why isn't Uncle David here?'
'He abdicated.'
'Why?'
'He wanted to marry Mrs Baldwin.' [¶]

18 July 1979

I hear of a memorable put-down of Pamela Hartwell[**] by Katie Macmillan.[††] It

---

[*] Mstislav Rostropovich (1927–2007), Russian cellist and conductor.
[†] Baron Rees-Mogg (1928–2012), editor of *The Times* 1967–81.
[‡] Lady Gillian Rees-Mogg (b. 1939), company director.
[§] Maj.-Gen. Sir Philip Ward (1924–2003), Welsh Guards officer, Lord Lieutenant of West Sussex 1994–9.
[¶] Lucy Baldwin, Countess Baldwin of Bewdley (1869–1945), activist for maternity health; wife of Stanley Baldwin, three times Prime Minister.
[**] (1914–82), wife of William Berry, Baron Hartwell; society hostess.
[††] Katharine Macmillan (1921–2017), Viscountess Macmillan of Ovenden.

was soon after Katie had become a Vice-Chairman of the Tory Party. Pamela said to her: 'There are too many middle-class people running your party these days.' Katie: 'I am not sure I would know how to recognise a middle-class person, not being a Smith from Birkenhead.'

31 July 1979
Lunch with Harold Wilson at the Travellers' Club, the Athenaeum being closed. He is smart and spry in a well-cut, very dark brown suit, with neatly starched cuffs and elaborate cufflinks. A portrait of the great Duke of Wellington in Garter ribbon looks down on his fellow Knight Companion of the Order.

The main purpose of our meeting is to talk about 'The State of Israel in British Politics',[*] to be published by Weidenfeld. He has just finished a stint in the Cabinet Office, going through his own prime-ministerial papers for the Six-Day War period. He is happy for me to write an 'Albany' note on this. I am able to tell Harold about Curzon's correspondence with Balfour about Zionism, the blot of ink made by Balfour as he signed the Balfour Declaration, and Walter Elliot's[†] leaking of Cabinet discussions on Palestine to his mistress Baffy Dugdale,[‡] who in turn told it all to Chaim Weizmann.[§] 'But he was such an ugly man,' Wilson exclaims naïvely.

Some talk of anti-Semitism, especially Ernest Bevin's.[ſ] Wilson has heard of the relish with which Bevin, on becoming Minister of Labour and National Service in 1940, boasted that he would call up all the East End Jews. 'Real working-class anti-Semitism', says Wilson. I suggest it is more a characteristic of the lower-middle class, and he agrees.

I think Wilson must rank among the most egotistical of all public men I have ever met. He never pauses for a moment in his autobiographical odyssey: I sometimes manage to change the direction of the flow, but never to halt it.

---

[*] *The Chariot of Israel* by Harold Wilson was published by Weidenfeld & Nicolson in 1981 and was described by Philip Ziegler as his best book, as it was 'the one least affected by the urge to prove himself right'. Philip Ziegler, *Wilson: The Authorised Life of Lord Wilson of Rievaulx* (1993), p. 510.

[†] Dr Walter Elliot (1888–1958), prominent Scottish Unionist politician in the inter-war years. Sec. of State for Scotland 1936–8.

[‡] Blanche ('Baffy') Dugdale (1880–1948), author and Zionist; wrote a biography of Balfour in 1936.

[§] (1874–1952), Israeli statesman; first President of Israel 1949–52.

[ſ] (1881–1951), trade unionist and Labour politician. A key figure in the founding of the Transport and General Workers' Union in 1922. Minister of Labour 1940–45; Foreign Secretary 1945–51.

One of the hardest jobs he has ever done was as an assistant to Beveridge.*
'We had no pocket calculators in those days, though we did have slide rules.'
Beveridge, he says, was immensely conceited: he thought he would become
Chancellor of the Exchequer.

Wilson was responsible for Coggan's[†] appointment to be Archbishop of
Canterbury in 1974. Coggan said to him: 'I feel I should have to retire in
1979, when I am seventy. What can a man do in five years?' Wilson replied:
'Well, how much do you suppose that a man in my chair can do in five years?'
At the end of the interview, Coggan said that he would have to say his prayers
and ask his wife.

On Selwyn Lloyd's election as Speaker, Wilson tells me that the Shadow
Cabinet voted 12 to 8 in favour of Selwyn and against Boyd-Carpenter[‡] when
the Speakership became vacant in 1971. On Denis Healey, he says: 'Once a
man has been a Communist, his mind runs on intellectual tramlines.'

Wilson says that although he never does any work during his holiday at
his little house in the Scilly Isles, he would very much like to read my book
on the Cecils, particularly what I have written on Balfour. So, of course, I
offer to give him a copy, and suggest that as he has a car and driver (and detective) waiting for him outside the club, he drives me to my flat and collects
the book there and then. So he comes to my flat, peers with interest at my
books and at a few sheets of my King George V manuscript while I inscribe
a copy for him.

1 August 1979

I ask Arnold Goodman whether Harold Wilson ever tried to become head of
an Oxford or Cambridge college. Arnold says that Wilson would have liked
it, but only a grand one, like Trinity, Cambridge.

8 August 1979

Robert Wade-Gery[§] to dine. As a Deputy Secretary to the Cabinet, he is
finding his work something of a burden. He has to attend several Cabinet
committees and full Cabinet meetings, when foreign affairs are on the

---

* William Beveridge, 1st Baron Beveridge (1879–1963), economist. Master of University
Coll., Oxford 1937–45; Chairman of the Inter-Departmental Committee on Social Insurance
and Allied Services 1941–2, which led to the Beveridge Report of 1942.
† The Most Revd and Rt Hon. Baron Coggan of Canterbury (1909–2000), Bishop of Bradford
1956–61; Archbishop of York 1961–74; Archbishop of Canterbury 1975–80.
‡ John, Baron Boyd-Carpenter (1908–98), Conservative politician. Minister under Churchill,
Eden, Macmillan and Douglas-Home.
§ Sir Robert Wade-Gery (1929–2015), High Commissioner to India 1982–7.

agenda. On Friday, for instance, he will attend the Cabinet discussing Mrs Thatcher's new plan for Rhodesia put forward at the Commonwealth PMs' Conference in Lusaka. At Cabinet committees Christian names are used, but in Cabinet only the names of the offices: at both Mrs Thatcher is addressed as Prime Minister.

I ask Robert whether a Cabinet Secretary ever 'adjusts' Cabinet minutes after consultation with the Prime Minister. He says that the PM never sees the draft minutes, but that a good Cabinet Secretary knows what is in her mind and may act accordingly.

Junior ministers are treated like dirt both by their own ministers and by senior civil servants. The PM has ruled that if a senior minister cannot attend a Cabinet committee, he shall not be represented by a junior minister.

Robert thinks that the Government's present monetary policy will lead not only to unemployment, but also to bankruptcy of small businesses. 'The crunch will come', he says, 'when the friends of ministers begin to tell them that they are on the verge of bankruptcy.' There is also a further deterioration in Anglo-Soviet relations.

27 August 1979

I hear the tail end of a news bulletin which appears to be an obituary of Dickie Mountbatten. Then the full story emerges. During his holiday at Classiebawn in County Sligo, he has been killed by an IRA bomb planted in his little fishing boat. One of his grandchildren has been killed, as well as a young boat boy. John and Patricia Brabourne and Doreen Brabourne seriously injured.[*] It is a horrifying tale, and yet perhaps not the sort of end which Mountbatten would have scorned after eighty years of full life.

28 August 1979

The news from Sligo is that Lady Brabourne has died and that Patricia Brabourne is still unconscious. A day of brilliant sunshine, contrasting with the wave of national grief.

5 September 1979

I watch the Mountbatten funeral at Westminster Abbey on TV; it is all too

---

[*] John Knatchbull, 7th Baron Brabourne (1924–2005), Oscar-nominated film producer. Patricia Knatchbull, 2nd Countess Mountbatten of Burma (1924–2017), elder dau. of Lord Mountbatten. Doreen Knatchbull, Dowager Baroness Brabourne (1896–1979), Anglo-Irish aristocrat.

much, with endless troops and ceremonial. The final camera shot is of Nelson on his column.

8 September 1979

Xandra Trevor-Roper[*] tells me that Hugh[†] is to take the title Lord Dacre of Glanton for his life peerage. Glanton was his birthplace. Hugh later tells me that when the PM's offer of a peerage arrived, he teased Xandra by saying that he did not think men of letters ought to take honours. She replied: 'But think of all the people it will annoy.' What a pair.

18 October 1979

Party given by George Weidenfeld for Henry Kissinger.[‡] Talk to Harold Wilson, who tells me he has just read the copy of *The Later Cecils* which I gave him. It is characteristic of him that he proves this not by quoting from the book but by saying: 'And I will tell you exactly where it is: on the fourth shelf, six down from the left – isn't that so, Mary?' Harold shows exceptional passion on Hugh Dalton[§] – 'A bully and a coward.'

30 October 1979

A remark to me by David Eccles[¶] on Ted Heath: 'I knew him in the days when he didn't even know how to tip a waiter.'

9 November 1979

Jack Plumb[**] tells me that he thinks Diana Spencer[††] will marry the Prince of Wales. I wonder whether Johnnie's divorce, not to mention Raine's,[‡‡] would be an obstacle. But Jack is very emphatic. Perhaps I shall hear more when I stay at Althorp next month.

---

[*] Alexandra Trevor-Roper, Lady Dacre (1907–97), dau. of Earl Haig; god-dau. of Queen Alexandra.

[†] Hugh Trevor-Roper, Baron Dacre of Glanton (1914–2003), Regius Professor of Modern History at Oxford University 1957–80.

[‡] (b. 1923), US National Security Advisor 1969–75; US Sec. of State 1973–7.

[§] Baron Dalton (1887–1962), Labour politician. President of the Board of Trade 1942–5; Chancellor of the Exchequer 1945–7.

[¶] 1st Viscount Eccles (1904–99), businessman and Conservative politician. Minister of Education 1959–62; Paymaster General and Minister for the Arts 1970–73.

[**] Sir John Harold Plumb (1911–2001); Professor of Modern History at Cambridge University 1966–74; Master of Christ's Coll., Cambridge 1978–82.

[††] Lady Diana Spencer (1961–97), later Princess of Wales.

[‡‡] John ('Johnnie') Spencer, 8th Earl Spencer (1924–92), equerry to George VI 1950–52 and to Elizabeth II 1952–4. Raine Spencer, Countess Spencer (1929–2016); her three marriages accorded her five titles.

15 November 1979
Listen to the news of the PM's statement in the Commons today that Anthony Blunt* was a Russian spy.

16 November 1976
The papers write of nothing except the PM's statement yesterday, unmasking Anthony Blunt as a Russian spy.

24 November 1979
Alan Barker[†] says that the two front-runners to succeed Michael McCrum[‡] as Head Master of Eton are Eric Anderson[§] of Shrewsbury and Peter Pilkington,[¶] Headmaster of King's School, Canterbury. Walter Hamilton[**] is likely to play a part in the choice: it was he who secured McCrum's appointment to Eton.

3 December 1979
An exacting few hours finishing my review of the Hugh Gaitskell biography by Philip Williams;[††] it has more or less wasted the weekend. Even now I wonder if the review is not too irreverent, but Gaitskell was such a prig.

17 December 1979
To Chatham House for the presentation of the Bentinck Prize by Ted Heath. Instead of the few perfunctory words that are usual on such an occasion, he delivers a long set speech on the Common Market, containing a thinly veiled attack on the supposed triviality of Mrs Thatcher's approach to community problems. Over a drink afterwards I have some agreeable and useful talk with him. One never knows whether he is going to be friendly or prickly: tonight he is amiability itself. He is reading Mary Soames's life of her mother Clementine Churchill. Ted deplores the parochialism of the

---

* (1907–83), art historian. Surveyor of the King's and later the Queen's Pictures 1945–74; stripped of his knighthood after it was revealed that he had spied for Russia.
† (1923–88), master at Eton 1947–53 and 1955–8; Headmaster of the Leys School, Cambridge 1958–75; Headmaster of University School, Hampstead 1975–82.
‡ (1924–2005), Head Master of Eton 1970–80.
§ Sir Eric Anderson (b. 1936), Head Master of Eton 1980–94; Rector of Lincoln Coll., Oxford 1994–2009; Provost of Eton 2000–09; editor of the journal of Sir Walter Scott 1972.
¶ Baron Pilkington of Oxenford (1933–2011), Headmaster of King's School, Canterbury 1975–86 and High Master of St Paul's School 1986–92.
** (1908–88) Headmaster of Westminster 1950–57; Headmaster of Rugby 1957–66; Master of Magdalene Coll., Cambridge 1967–78.
†† (1920–84) *Hugh Gaitskell: A Political Biography* was published in 1979.

British Press. As a result he finds it difficult to get British newspapers abroad.

We talk about politicians' insatiable desire for honours. Only this morning he had a letter from a former Tory MP telling him that he was writing to ask Mrs Thatcher for an honour, and suggesting that Ted might also add his voice. Ted admits: 'If I had paid more attention to demands for honours, it might have changed the course of history.' It is true that Ted antagonised some of his supporters by withholding honours, but that was only one symptom of his failure to appreciate the character and desires of MPs. He was not re-elected leader owing to recommending few honours, but because he had alienated himself from them by aloofness, arrogance and impatience. Honours alone would not have won their allegiance.

18 December 1979

To the Italian Embassy for an evening party. Harold Wilson is amiable, but muddled. He says to Mary: 'You remember Kenneth Rose of the *Observer*? No, I mean the *Sunday Telegraph*. He would never write for a Trotskyite paper like the *Observer*.' His book on Israel, he tells me, is going well.

19 December 1979

Talk to Harold Macmillan, who is returning to Walter Scott's novels. He has been reading the Kissinger memoirs: 'I was fascinated by all 1,400 pages of it, but it is rather shocking that so much recent history has come out so soon. In any case, the cost of books is today so daunting that the shorter the better.'

Visit Leeds Castle. Geoffrey Lloyd* at seventy-seven looks far younger and retains immense vigour. The Chairmanship of the Trustees of Leeds Castle consumes much of his time. Much political gossip. Geoffrey is amused by Harold Macmillan but deplores all the publicity which Macmillan allowed to be given to his annual shooting parties. 'It did the Conservative cause in Birmingham no good at all.' Nor was Macmillan really a man of the world. He handled the Profumo† case badly. 'Baldwin would have elicited the truth

---

* Baron Geoffrey-Lloyd (1902–84), Conservative politician. MP for Birmingham Ladywood 1931–45, Birmingham King's Norton 1950–55 and Sutton Coldfield 1955–74; Minister of Fuel and Power 1951–5; Minister of Education 1957–9.

† John Profumo (1915–2006), Conservative politician. Sec. of State for War 1960–63; his political career ended after his relationship with Christine Keeler was revealed. Under cover of Parliamentary Privilege, the Labour MP George Wigg brought up the issue in the House of Commons on 21 Mar. Profumo, under pressure from Martin Redmayne, the government Chief Whip, denied to the House of Commons the next day that he had had an affair with Keeler. However, on 4 June he wrote to Harold Macmillan admitting he had lied to the House, and resigned from Parliament. For the next forty-three years he worked at Toynbee Hall in the East End of London; he was appointed CBE in 1975 for this charitable work.

from Jack by speaking to him like a father to his son, while Churchill would have browbeaten him into telling the truth.' There was a streak of hardness in Winston. He once said to Geoffrey: 'Is Woolton* any good?' And that was the man Winston had chosen to run the whole wartime food policy.

* Frederick Marquis, 1st Earl of Woolton (1883–1964), businessman and statesman. Minister of Food 1940–43; Chairman of the Conservative Party 1946–55.

1980

Industrial problems continued in the UK. Workers at the British Steel Corporation went on a nationwide strike on 2 January. Margaret Thatcher announced on 14 February that state benefits to strikers would be cut by half. Robert Runcie was enthroned as Archbishop of Canterbury on 25 March. Zimbabwe became independent of the UK on 18 April. On 5 May the SAS stormed the Iranian Embassy after it had been taken over by Iranian Arab separatists, freeing all the hostages. Inflation rose to 21.8 per cent on 16 May. The economy slid into recession in June. Death of C.P. Snow on 1 July. Former Prime Minister Harold Macmillan criticised Mrs Thatcher's economic policies on 15 October. Ronald Reagan was elected President of the US on 4 November. On 10 November Michael Foot was elected leader of the Labour Party. On 18 December opinion polls gave Labour a lead of twenty-four points.

7 January 1980

Train to Cambridge to spend two days working in the archives at Churchill College. Stay with Jack Plumb in the Master's Lodge at Christ's.

In the evening I dine with Jack and half a dozen dons in the Senior Combination Room. Somebody tells the story of the old Duke of Gloucester* dining at Magdalene, where his son William was an undergraduate. He was silent at first, but he eventually spoke and High Table fell silent too. 'Tell me,' he asked, 'what do you Fellows *do*?'

I have some private talk with Jack about the Royal Family. He still nurses a grievance against the courtiers for being so obstructive (and I suspect socially scornful) when Jack was making the TV *Royal Heritage* series. 'The trouble was that they all wanted to take part in it themselves, and we would not let them.'

---

* Prince Henry, Duke of Gloucester (1900–74), third son of George V and Queen Mary.

14 January 1980

Tea at Univ.* with Arnold Goodman. Martin Gilbert, he tells me, has abandoned his proposed official life of Anthony Eden, owing to pressure of his other work. Arnold says that so few people liked Eden, it is not easy to find a sympathetic biographer.

24 January 1980

I ask Hugh Trevor-Roper who is likely to succeed him as Regius Professor of History at Oxford. He says that Hugh Thomas† has been mentioned, 'because he is Mrs Thatcher's historian'. I reply: 'And whose historian were you?' This knocks him literally speechless, a rare state in which to find Hugh.

6 February 1980

Lunch in the Cholmondeley Room at the House of Lords before Jean Barker is introduced as Lady Trumpington.‡ Rab Butler talks to me about his choice of Anthony Howard,§ former editor of the *New Statesman*, as his official biographer. 'We considered William Rees-Mogg, but he was too busy. Geoffrey Lloyd urged that you should do it. Another possibility was Peter Goldman.'¶ I don't really think I should have the energy or inclination to write a big book on Rab, but I would quite like to have been consulted.

The ceremony of introduction goes well. As it is followed by a debate on Russia's invasion of Afghanistan I stay on for a couple of hours, until Gladwyn Jebb** makes everybody remember it is teatime.

13 February 1980

See Ted Heath in his large untidy office in the Norman Shaw block near Scotland Yard. He tells me something of his recent visit to South America. He was saddened to see in Brasilia that our Embassy is no more than a bungalow, in contrast to the huge Palladian Embassy built in Rio. Ted believes in

---

* University Coll., Oxford, where Lord Goodman was Master.
† Baron Thomas of Swynnerton (1931–2017), historian. Trevor-Roper's successor was Sir Michael Howard.
‡ Baroness Trumpington (b. 1922), Conservative politician.
§ (1934–2010), journalist, broadcaster and writer. Editor of the *Listener* 1979–81 and of the *New Statesman* 1972–8; obituaries editor of *The Times* 1993–9.
¶ (1925–87), defeated Conservative candidate at the Orpington by-election, Mar. 1962. Dir. of the Conservative Political Centre 1955–64; Dir. of the Consumers' Association 1964–87. Goldman was Rab Butler's ghostwriter for his memoirs and he also wrote Iain Macleod's biography of Neville Chamberlain, 1961.
** Sir Gladwyn Jebb, 1st Baron Gladwyn (1900–96), British representative at the UN 1950–54; Ambassador to France 1954–60.

showing a diplomatic presence. In Gothenburg before Christmas, he arrived from Stockholm on the day it was announced that our Consulate-General was to be severely cut in strength. The effect on the business community was appalling. Two-thirds of the names in the telephone directory there are English or Scottish. Gothenburg is in fact known as Little London. The same day he was shown a big new building going up: the Soviet Consulate-General with a staff of eighty-eight.

Ted says that he and Alec Home have always insisted that any member of our Diplomatic Service who wants to get to the top must be interested in trade. 'As political ministers take over so many ambassadorial functions, the ambassador must concentrate on trade.'

He tells me something I had not known about his time at No. 10. Although the entire house had been renovated while Macmillan lived temporarily at Admiralty House, dry rot soon afterwards broke out at No. 10 and spread from one room to another. This did not, however, prevent Ted from entertaining. The most memorable party, he thinks, was for William Walton's sixtieth birthday, attended by the Queen Mother. Ted had asked Walton what piece of music he would most like to have written in the whole of music. Walton replied that it was Schubert's B flat trio; so it was played.

I ask Ted what he had thought of Rostropovich's playing at the Windsor concert in the summer. He says that the Haydn Cello Concerto was excellent, but that no man can both play and conduct the Tchaikovsky Variations on a Rococo Theme.

21 February 1980

Rab Butler tells me that Ted Heath should concentrate on Europe and hold aloof from domestic issues. He recently told Terence Maxwell, Austen Chamberlain's[*] son-in-law, that he, Rab, had things in common with him. I suppose he has in mind: 'He always played the game and he always lost it.'

18 March 1980

Talk to Jock Colville[†] about the new book on Henry, Duke of Gloucester by Noble Frankland.[‡] Jock tells me that in the years 1951 to 1953, he used to

---

* Sir Austen Chamberlain (1836–1937), politician. Chancellor of the Exchequer 1903–5 and 1919–21; leader of the Conservative Party in the House of Commons 1921–2; Foreign Secretary 1924–9. Awarded the Nobel Peace Prize after the Treaty of Locarno in 1925.

† Sir John Colville (1915–87), Assistant PS to Neville Chamberlain 1939–40, to Winston Churchill 1940–41 and 1943–5 and to Clement Attlee 1945; PS to Princess Elizabeth 1947–9; joint PPS to Winston Churchill 1951–5.

‡ (b. 1922), historian. Dir. Gen. of the Imperial War Museum 1960–82; his biography *Prince*

be sent once a week by Winston to tell Queen Mary all the political news. At their last meeting, Queen Mary was very ill in bed but bejewelled and bewigged. She said to Jock: 'I wish you to take a very important message to Mr Churchill. It is this. I know that Harry is not very bright, but I nevertheless want the Prime Minister to do something for him . . .' Here her mind wandered, but she eventually continued: '. . . like making him Ranger of Richmond Park'.

30 March 1980

Film on television of last week's enthronement of Robert Runcie[*] as the new Archbishop of Canterbury. Extraordinary that this essentially Anglican ceremony should be cluttered up with Roman Catholics and Presbyterians, not merely attending as guests, but taking part in the service.

7 April 1980

An example of the Queen Mother's tact. When Quintin Hailsham stayed at Royal Lodge not long after his wife Mary's tragic death,[†] he should have been given the grandest of rooms. But it has two beds in it, and the Queen Mother realised it would make him feel unhappy. So he was given a smaller room with a single bed.

16 April 1980

Solly Zuckerman comes in for a drink. He dined at Windsor last night. Princess Margaret rather spoilt things by her habit of monopolising people. 'She has a bit of a brain, but is destroyed by drink, frustration and an awareness of her unpopularity.'

Solly has some tapes of long talks with Mountbatten and now has page after page of transcripts. He opened one talk by praising Mountbatten to the skies and rehearsing all his achievements. Mountbatten purred. Then Solly continued: 'Which makes it all the more remarkable that your contemporaries loathe you.' Poor Mountbatten was very taken aback.

Solly once stayed with Mountbatten at the President's House at Delhi a few years after independence. As the President went by in state with his mounted escort, Mountbatten said ruefully: 'There were more of them when I was Viceroy.' Solly replied: 'Don't forget that half of yours went to Pakistan.'

Henry, Duke of Gloucester was published in 1980.
[*] The Most Revd Robert Runcie, Baron Runcie MC (1921–2000), Archbishop of Canterbury 1980–91; the first Archbishop of Canterbury to have borne arms for his king and country.
[†] Lady Hailsham (1919–78) had been married to Lord Hailsham for thirty-four years when she died in front of him in a horse-riding accident in Sydney.

17 April 1980

Talk to King Constantine* at his office in Grosvenor Street, near Claridge's. We begin with the Olympics. He won a Gold Medal in the Dragon Class of the sailing regatta at Naples during the Rome Olympics of 1960. He was elected to the International Committee in 1963.

He thinks that President Carter and Mrs Thatcher moved too fast in trying to secure a boycott of the Olympics in Moscow. They should have consulted the Olympic Committees privately, to avoid the appearance of their being bullied by Governments.

'In 1964 I proposed that there should be a permanent Olympic stadium in Greece, instead of moving from country to country every few years. I did this on financial grounds. Of course, Greece was my country! But I also advocated that the Olympic centre should be "Vaticanised", i.e. it should be divorced from the Government of Greece, like the United Nations in New York, and that there should be no display of national flags or playing of national anthems. Thus, even if the colonels were still in charge, they would not gain any political advantage from the presence of the Olympics. But my proposals were rejected. Now the Olympic movement is perpetually embroiled in politics. If America boycotts the Moscow Games, Russia will boycott the 1984 Los Angeles Games.'

The King thinks that it is unwise of Carter to deploy the full force of US foreign policy in trying to gain the release of the hostages held in Tehran. The invasion of Afghanistan by Russia is an infinitely more serious matter.

24 May 1980

Peter Ramsbotham[†] gives me an account of his sacking from the Washington Embassy by David Owen[‡] in 1977. He had hoped to remain there, although he retired two years later. Indeed, he would have done so had Tony Crosland[§] lived and remained Foreign Secretary. On Crosland's death, Callaghan appointed David Owen to the Foreign Office, and Owen put his friend Peter Jay[¶]

---

* King Constantine II of Greece (b. 1940), last King of Greece 1964–73.
† 3rd Viscount Soulbury (1919–2010), Ambassador to the US 1974–7; Governor of Bermuda 1977–80.
‡ Baron Owen (b. 1938), politician and physician. Labour Foreign Secretary 1977–9; leader of the Social Democratic Party 1983–7.
§ Anthony Crosland (1918–77), Labour politician. MP for South Gloucestershire 1950–55 and for Great Grimsby 1959–77; Foreign Secretary 1976–7; author of *The Future of Socialism*, 1964.
¶ (b. 1937), economist and broadcaster. Ambassador to the US 1977–9.

in the Washington Embassy. Peter Ramsbotham was not entirely surprised to be superseded. He had been appointed to Washington in the very last days of the Heath Government and at the time wondered whether he should not have asked Harold Wilson about his future. Wilson nevertheless kept him in Washington, although rumours reached Peter that he was not considered a good representative of the Labour Government.

David Owen was apparently taken aback by the outcry at Peter's removal. On the night of Jay's appointment, Owen left for Tehran. Tony Parsons,[*] our Ambassador to Iran, later told Ramsbotham that Owen had sat in the Embassy garden trying to write a suitable letter to Peter, but tearing up draft after draft. Eventually he completed a letter and sent it to Peter. It was an extraordinarily emotional document in praise of Jay. 'I didn't care at all what he thought of Jay, but I was fed up at being called an unsuccessful stuffed shirt of an ambassador.'

Peter was tempted to retire in a huff. Instead, he sensibly asked Callaghan what future appointment he could expect. Permanent Under-Secretary. No, Palliser[†] had it. Government representative at the BBC. No, Greenhill[‡] had it. Government representative on the board of BP. No, Greenhill again. Then Palliser suggested Bermuda. Peter was inclined to turn it down out of hand, but decided to give it a try for two years and accepted. He is paid by the Bermudan Government and his salary is tax-free, so at least he can save a little money. When he retires at the end of this year, he will become a director of Lloyds Bank and of the Commercial Union. To show their affection for the Ramsbothams, American friends subscribed a handsome sum as a tribute. This Peter has given to the Folger Library,[§] the richest source of Shakespeare folios, to strengthen Anglo-American ties. It is used each year to endow a lecture.

29 May 1980

To *Tristan und Isolde* at Covent Garden with Prince Eddie.[¶] Jon Vickers[**] is

---

[*] Sir Anthony Parsons (1922–96), Ambassador to Iran 1974–9; UK Permanent Representative to the UN 1979–82.

[†] Sir Michael Palliser (1922–2012), Permanent Under-Sec. at the Foreign Office 1975–82.

[‡] Sir Denis Greenhill, Baron Greenhill of Harrow (1913–2000), Permanent Under-Sec. at the Foreign Office and head of the Diplomatic Service 1969–73.

[§] A research library on Capitol Hill, Washington DC, holding the world's largest collection of the printed works of William Shakespeare. It contains eighty-two copies of the 1623 First Folio.

[¶] Prince Edward, Duke of Kent (b. 1935) knew K.R. for sixty years and read the lesson at his memorial service.

[**] (1926–2015), Canadian heldentenor, renowned for his Otello, Tristan and Peter Grimes.

almost too powerful and melodramatic as Tristan, but Berit Lindholm[*] is a comely and melodious Isolde.

During the interval, Eddie gazes down into the stalls and says: 'I wonder who that pretty blonde is, next to my cousin Tino.' We soon know, for Tino comes up to the box with his companion, the wife of the night's conductor Zubin Mehta.[†] Someone says: 'No wonder he is taking the score so fast!'

17 June 1980

Two stories about Maurice Bowra.[‡] After a performance by the Oxford University Dramatic Society he commented: 'It was as good as a play.' And at a wedding, when asked if he was 'bride' or 'bridegroom', he replied: 'I don't know. I have slept with both.'

24 June 1980

Prince Eddie sends me an amusing story. A French minister was recently asked how his country managed to build such things as power stations so quickly, whereas in England they were held up by planning inquiries, etc. 'Ah,' he replied, 'you see when we decide to drain a swamp, we don't consult the frogs first.'

The Rector of St George's, Hanover Square, W.M. Atkins,[§] tells me that he has an unexpectedly large congregation on Sundays for a non-residential district: they are mostly refugees from the new Series 3 services of the Church of England elsewhere.

25 June 1980

Lunch at the Beefsteak. Edward Ford says he is a great enthusiast of the cartoons of H.M. Bateman:[¶] 'I should like to see a Bateman cartoon of the man who smoked Dutch cigars in Havana.' Edward also shows me his gold ring. It was given by A.J. Balfour to Mary Lyttelton, his grandmother's sister. He tells the story of the occasion when Lloyd George, on behalf of the two Houses of Parliament, presented A.J.B. with a Rolls-Royce on his eightieth birthday. In

---

[*] (b. 1934), Swedish soprano, renowned for her Isolde, Brünnhilde and Elektra.

[†] (b. 1936), Indian conductor.

[‡] Sir Maurice Bowra (1898–1971), classical scholar and academic. Warden of Wadham Coll., Oxford 1938–70; Vice-Chancellor of Oxford University 1951–4.

[§] Prebendary W.M. ('Bill') Atkins (1911–2003), scholarly High Churchman, Rector of St George's, Hanover Square, for forty-five years. When he had completed forty years in the parish, the Bishop of London asked if he had thought of retirement. 'No,' he replied, 'I have never regarded this as a temporary appointment.'

[¶] (1887–1970), cartoonist noted for his series 'The Man Who . . ', featuring exaggerated reactions to social gaffes, such as 'The Man Who Lit His Cigar Before the Royal Toast'.

his speech of thanks, Balfour said: 'When I was Home Secretary . . .' Lloyd George interrupted: 'You were never Home Secretary.' A.J.B.: 'Oh, wasn't I? Well, Foreign Secretary, then.'

He also tells the story of Winston at Balmoral in the early 1950s. He was awaiting the result of a nuclear test on a new bomb, and said to the Queen: 'By this time tomorrow, we shall know if it is a pop or a plop.'

27 June 1980

Robert Blake* is to edit the *Dictionary of National Biography* in succession to Bill Williams.† At one time I should have coveted the post, but I now see that much of one's time would have been spent rewriting and checking other people's work: a glorified sub-editor, in fact.

2 July 1980

Charles Snow‡ has died. He was always most kind and encouraging to me. I felt affection for him.

15 July 1980

Lunch with Peter Tapsell.§ He tells me: 'I am never able to see a play through to the end, as there is always a three-line whip at 10 o'clock. One day I must find out what happens in the last scene of *Hamlet*.'

16 July 1980

Party at Speaker's House for encouragement of business sponsorship of the arts. The first time I have been here since Selwyn's day. George Thomas¶ envelops one with Welsh charm and later makes an enchanting little speech of welcome. It prompts Norman St John-Stevas** to say: 'If you had not gone on the stage, you could have had a great future in politics!'

---

* Baron Blake of Braydeston (1916–2003), historian. Provost of Queen's Coll., Oxford 1968–87; biographer of Disraeli 1966; editor of the *DNB* 1980–90.

† Brig. Sir Edgar 'Bill' Williams (1912–95), Chief Intelligence Officer to Gen. Montgomery in the North African campaign; co-editor of the decennial supplements to the *DNB* 1949–80; Warden of Rhodes House, Oxford 1952–80.

‡ Baron Snow (1905–80), writer, civil servant, Labour politician and scientific administrator. His most famous novel, *The Masters* (1951), was the third in the eleven-volume sequence *Strangers and Brothers*.

§ Sir Peter Tapsell (1930–2018), Conservative politician. MP for Nottingham West 1959–64 and for Louth and Horncastle 1966–2015; Father of the House of Commons 2010–15.

¶ 1st Viscount Tonypandy (1909–97), Labour politician. Speaker of the House of Commons 1976–83.

** Baron St John of Fawsley (1929–2012), Conservative politician. MP for Chelmsford 1964–87; Minister for the Arts 1973–4 and 1979–81; Leader of the House of Commons 1979–81.

27 July 1980

William Rees-Mogg tells me that his boy Jakie,[*] aged eleven, plays the stock market and is a very real holder of shares in GEC. He went to the annual meeting and voted against the accounts on the grounds that the dividend was not big enough. The Chairman did not notice his hand was up, but Arnold Weinstock[†] did, and solemnly announced that the vote in favour of the accounts was not unanimous: 'Mr Rees-Mogg dissents.'

The boy has four bank accounts. When he went to open his fourth, at Lloyds, the manager patronisingly asked him why he had chosen that particular bank. Jakie replied: 'Because I like your picture of a horse – and you give half a per cent more interest than the others.' He will obviously end up as an extreme revolutionary Marxist!

8 August 1980

I see the old film *Goodbye, Mr Chips*, with Robert Donat,[‡] modelled on and made at Repton the year before I went. It is immeasurably sentimental, yet not displeasing.

19 August 1980

Robin Mackworth-Young[§] returns the text of my *King George V* up to 1914. He gives me copyright permission for all I need and kindly praises my writing. He says that Harold Nicolson[¶] ignored a memorandum by Balfour apparently admitting that he would not have been willing to form a Government had Asquith resigned over contingent plans to create peers.

10 September 1980

Dine with Martin Gilliat[**] at Buck's. We eat potted shrimps and grouse. He is still rather exhausted by all the organisation of the Queen Mother's eightieth birthday celebrations. 'I was so tired that I hardly knew what was going on. Although she herself was wonderfully appreciative in public, she was rather unenthusiastic in private: "It has all been blown up by the Press."' The PM, who sent her a huge birthday card signed by all the Cabinet, is giving her a birthday dinner on 11 November. I ask Martin whether that is not an odd

---

* Jacob Rees-Mogg (b. 1969), Conservative politician. MP for North East Somerset since 2010.
† Baron Weinstock of Bowden (1924–2002), businessman.
‡ (1905–58), film and stage actor; he won the Oscar for best actor for his role as Mr Chips.
§ Sir Robert Mackworth-Young (1920–2000), Royal Librarian 1958–85.
¶ Sir Harold Nicolson (1886–1968), diplomat, author, diarist and National Labour MP for Leicester West 1935–45.
** Sir Martin Gilliat (1913–93), PS to the Queen Mother 1956–1993.

day to choose, with memories of the Great War. He says the point was considered, but it is now many years since that particular date was revered.

18 September 1980

Oliver van Oss* tells me that when somebody wanted to burn an effigy of Hitler at Eton to celebrate the end of the war, the Provost, Henry Marten,[†] objected: 'After all, the fellow's dead.' Oliver appreciates Marten's generosity of character but nevertheless thinks that there would have been nothing distasteful about burning an effigy of Hitler.

13 October 1980

A cocktail party given by Julian Amery[‡] at 112 Eaton Square to mark the publication of his father's diaries, which alas are all too dull. Harold Macmillan is there and makes a neat little speech about Leo's[§] qualities of devotion and patriotism. Harold confesses how he is still haunted by the slaughter of the Great War.

For the rest of the party Macmillan sits in a chair with Bob Boothby[¶] next to him, talking to each other with entire amiability. This, I am afraid, evokes knowing sniggers.

David Dilks** thinks Leo Amery to be one of the most astute and most underestimated twentieth-century statesmen. Winston, by contrast, never saw the coming menace of Japan when he was Chancellor, so left us unprepared.

Jock Colville tells me that when he was seven he heard the shots which killed Henry Wilson[††] in June 1922.

---

* (1909–92), schoolmaster at Eton 1930–59, Lower Master 1959–64, Acting Headmaster 1963; Headmaster of Charterhouse 1965–73. A civilised and cultured force in independent education, he was instrumental in commissioning John Piper to design stained-glass windows for Eton Coll. Chapel.

† (1872–1948), Provost of Eton 1945–8 and private tutor to Princess Elizabeth.

‡ Baron Amery of Lustleigh (1919–96), Conservative politician. Son-in-law of Harold Macmillan. MP for Preston North 1950–66 and for Brighton Pavilion 1969–92; Sec. of State for Air 1960–62; Minister of Aviation 1962–4, in which he played an important role in the development of *Concorde*.

§ Leopold Amery (1873–1955), Conservative politician. Sec. of State for the Colonies 1924–9; a crucial figure in the appointment of Stanley Baldwin in 1923 and Winston Churchill in 1940.

¶ Sir Robert Boothby, Baron Boothby of Buchan and Rattray Head (1900–86), Conservative politician. The Queen Mother described him as 'a bounder but not a cad'.

** (b. 1938), Professor of International History at Leeds University 1970–91; Vice-Chancellor of Hull University 1991–9.

†† FM Sir Henry Wilson, 1st Bt (1864–1922) was assassinated outside his home at 36 Eaton Place, London, by two IRA gunmen as he returned from unveiling a war memorial at Liverpool Street Station.

21 October 1980

Talk to Richard Thorpe, the Charterhouse master, who has written an able
book on Austen Chamberlain, Curzon and Rab Butler, *The Uncrowned Prime
Ministers*. For Curzon he has drawn on my *Superior Person*, with generous
acknowledgements. I write to Colonel Terence Maxwell, Austen's son-in-law:
'I think Richard Thorpe's *The Uncrowned Prime Ministers* an admirable piece
of work: ingenious in theme, illuminating in conception, unpretentious in
tone and perceptive in judgement. Such few errors as I noticed are trivial: for
one of them Harold Macmillan was responsible.'

29 October 1980

Jim Lees-Milne[*] sends me the first volume of his life of Harold Nicolson.
He is angry that the *Sunday Times* should have chosen only the passages
describing one of Harold's homosexual affairs. I must confess that I too was
shocked when I saw the paper yesterday. Nor do I think it is at all well written: too slangy.

7 November 1980

Read the diaries of Leo Amery. All the personal touches have been excised,
leaving interminable and not always accurate accounts of political manoeu-
vre, e.g. he remains convinced wrongly that it was he who prevented Curzon
becoming PM in 1923. Sometimes, however, when his advice is not followed,
he adds later: 'It did not seem to make much difference.' That is endearing.

8 November 1980

A useful morning in the new Bodleian Library on the papers of Geoffrey
Dawson.[†] An excellent account by Stamfordham of all the talks he had
during the replacement of Bonar Law by Baldwin in 1923. But the best find is
serendipity itself: a letter from Tom Jones[‡] to Dawson, asking him, as a Fellow
of Eton, whether the school can take Ribbentrop's boy, Rudolf.[§] Ribbentrop
thought that thus his son would be able to learn English ways 'and pass them
on to the Hitler Youth'. Dawson replied that the boy was too old (fifteen) and
the school full.

---

[*] (1908–97), architectural historian, biographer and diarist. Secretary of the Country Houses
Committee of the National Trust.
[†] (1874–1944), editor of *The Times* 1912–19 and 1923–41.
[‡] Thomas Jones (1870–1955), Assistant and then Deputy Cabinet Secretary 1916–30.
[§] Joachim von Ribbentrop (1893–1946), Foreign Minister of Germany 1938–45; hanged after
the Nuremberg Trials. His son Rudolf (b. 1921) was educated at Westminster School when he
could not be admitted to Eton.

Arnold Goodman, whom I see later in the day, tells me that when he was one of Laurence Olivier's sponsors at his introduction into the House of Lords, the actor insisted on no fewer than three dress rehearsals!

13 November 1980

I always find Oliver Franks* warmly agreeable, in spite of his reputation as a cold fish. Tonight he tells me what a considerate guest he always found the Duke of Windsor in Washington. But there was one occasion when the Duchess told Franks: 'David always has a glass of milk before going to bed.' All the Embassy servants had gone to bed. But Oliver recalled that his children had their own fridge and there he found enough milk for the Duke.

18 November 1980

I meet Bob Runcie, the new Archbishop of Canterbury, at the Church of England Children's Society. He greets me by saying how much he liked my book on the Cecils. As Bishop of St Albans he was Robert Salisbury's† diocesan Bishop. I recall to him how Robert refused to relinquish his patronage of Church livings. 'Yes,' Runcie replied, 'it was one of those occasions on which my radical sympathies were obliged to triumph over my Conservative prejudices!'

The Archbishop also says that he enjoyed my teasing of Archbishop Blanch‡ of York about the new Alternative Prayer Book. A few minutes later, when he is asked to inscribe a Prayer Book for the Children's Society, Runcie asks, 'Is it the real one?' He then draws my attention to some of the unusual services it contains, including one for the commemoration of abbots. I look it up in the index and find that it immediately precedes 'Affliction, support in' and 'Angels'. Some talk of Runcie's love of pig-keeping. He is still a tenant of a farm at which he keeps his herd of Berkshires. It makes a small profit which he spends on going to Glyndebourne. It has also brought him much reverence from the American state of Iowa, home of the hog, as well as many abusive letters from the anti-farming lobby. He says of the *Church Times*: 'It is a duty to read it, but a sin to enjoy it.' And he recalls the American lady who said to him during a Swan Hellenic Mediterranean cruise: 'Is there still a sin problem in Port Said?'

---

* Sir Oliver Franks, Baron Franks of Headington (1905–92), Provost of Queen's Coll., Oxford 1946–8; Ambassador to the US 1948–52; Provost of Worcester Coll., Oxford 1962–76; Chairman of the inquiry into the Falklands War 1982.
† Robert Gascoyne-Cecil, 6th Marquess of Salisbury (1916–2003), Conservative politician. MP for Bournemouth West 1950–54.
‡ The Rt Revd Stuart Blanch, Baron Blanch (1918–94), Archbishop of York 1975–83.

23 November 1980

Finish reading Jim Lees-Milne's first volume of the life of Harold Nicolson.
There is far too much about his homosexuality, including the names of his
lovers. How tiresome, even hateful, his wife Vita could be, endlessly pan-
dering to his social prejudices. Harold thought it very 'bedint'* of Nigel,† his
son, to be a major and an MBE. Unbelievable that he should be emotionally
flattened every time he was separated from her.

27 November 1980

Martin Gilbert, whose recent book of companion documents on Churchill
I have just revised, tells me what I already suspected, that Michael Hartwell
has become violently hostile to the whole Churchill project. He has let it be
known that the *Sunday Telegraph* does not propose to serialise the last two
volumes, covering the war and the post-war years.

2 December 1980

Robert Wade-Gery gives me his estimate of some members of the Cabinet.
Mrs Thatcher, he says, can manage on four hours' sleep a night, so never
skimps the work on her papers. Peter Carrington, the Foreign Secretary,
gets up every morning at five and works at home till seven-thirty. So he too
manages on little sleep, but less well than the PM. The strain may affect his
health. Willie Whitelaw,‡ the Home Secretary, doesn't read his papers, but
has the gift of absorbing what he needs orally from his officials. Ian Gilmour,
No. 2 at the Foreign Office, in Peter's absence presents the FO case to Cabinet elegantly and clearly. But he cuts no ice. He will not battle like Peter.
Quintin Hailsham, Lord Chancellor, although increasingly infirm physically, remains clear in mind. Even on subjects not his own he can detect flaws
and bad points. Humphrey Atkins,§ Northern Ireland Secretary, nice, kind,
humane and ineffective.

Much talk on the machinery of Government. Ministers of State and parliamentary secretaries do little in the way of taking decisions: they merely

---

* 'Bedint' was a word, possibly coined by Vita Sackville-West, meaning tasteless, especially
regarding bourgeois aspirations to aristocratic behaviour.
† (1917–2004), writer and publisher. Conservative MP for Bournemouth East and
Christchurch 1952–9; co-founder with George Weidenfeld of Weidenfeld & Nicolson.
‡ William Whitelaw, 1st Viscount Whitelaw (1918–99), Conservative politician. Lord President of the Council 1970–72; Sec. of State for Northern Ireland 1972–3 and for Employment
1973–4; Chairman of the Conservative Party 1974–5; Home Secretary 1979–83; Lord President and Leader of the House of Lords 1983–8.
§ Sir Humphrey Atkins, Baron Colnbrook (1922–96), Sec. of State for Northern Ireland
1979–81.

absorb valuable Civil Service staff and their time. Most of their duties ought to be transferred to civil servants. Paul Channon,* Minister of State for the Civil Service, is an exception. He, not Christopher Soames,† runs the department.

But the real problem is the burden carried by Cabinet ministers – (a) the department, (b) the Commons, (c) constituencies, and (d) official entertainment. It reminds me of Selwyn Lloyd's remark that by the end of the evening one cannot remember what was discussed – not because of drink, but because of exhaustion.

Robert also tells me a story of when he was entertaining a White House official at the Athenaeum with Robert Armstrong,‡ Secretary of the Cabinet. Armstrong, pointing to Arnold Goodman, told the official: 'That man is the greatest fixer in England.' A few minutes later Arnold rolled across the room and said to Armstrong: 'Could you spare me a minute, Robert?' and led him away.

Stormont Mancroft§ telephones me this evening to relate a sad episode at the House of Lords this afternoon. A taxi drew up at the peers' entrance and the red-coated attendant opened the door. Inside was Patrick Gordon Walker,¶ dead. There was then an unedifying dispute as to where the body should be taken, and by what means.

6 December 1980
Nicky Gordon-Lennox** tells me that Maître Blum†† is convinced that Dickie Mountbatten, during a visit to the Duchess of Windsor in Paris, stole some of the Duke of Windsor's papers; there could, she has insisted, have been no question of misunderstanding.

26 December 1980
Read Harold Evans' forthcoming *Downing Street Diary, 1957–1963*.‡‡ As

---

* Baron Kelvedon (1935–2007), Conservative politician. MP for Southend 1959–97; Sec. of State for Transport 1987–9.
† Baron Soames (1920–87), Conservative politician and son-in-law of Winston Churchill. Minister of Agriculture, Fisheries and Food 1960–64; Ambassador to France 1968–72; European Commissioner for External Relations 1973–7; Governor of Southern Rhodesia 1979–80.
‡ Baron Armstrong of Ilminster (b. 1927), Cabinet Secretary 1979–87.
§ 2nd Baron Mancroft (1914–87), Conservative politician. Minister without Portfolio 1957–8.
¶ Baron Gordon-Walker (1907–80), Labour politician. MP for Smethwick 1945–64 and for Leyton 1966–74; Foreign Secretary 1964–5; Sec. of State for Education and Science 1967–8.
** Lord Nicholas Gordon-Lennox (1931–2004), Ambassador to Spain 1984–9.
†† Maître Suzanne Blum (1898–1994), legal adviser to the Windsors in Paris.
‡‡ Sir Harold Evans, 1st Bt (1911–83), Harold Macmillan's Press Secretary 1957–63.

Harold Macmillan's Press man at No. 10 he writes of my scoop of the top
Civil Service changes in 1962 – and of how he suspected that Bill Deedes,*
then Minister without Portfolio in the Cabinet, had leaked them to me. It
was in fact Charles Snow.

Some good insights into Macmillan, who <u>did</u> care what the Press said
of him. Of course, a book like his gives a false impression: as if Macmillan
was constantly brooding over newspaper criticism. Similarly, to read Lord
Moran's† diary one might think that Winston thought of nothing but his
health.

---

* Baron Deedes of Aldington (1913–2007), Conservative politician and journalist. MP for
Ashford 1950–74; Minister without Portfolio 1962–4; editor of the *Daily Telegraph* 1974–86.
† John Wilson, 2nd Baron Moran (1924–2014), Ambassador to Hungary 1973–6 and
to Portugal 1976–81; High Commissioner to Canada 1981–4: biographer of Sir Henry
Campbell-Bannerman (1973).

1981

Margaret Thatcher reshuffled her Cabinet on 5 January. The funeral of Princess Alice, Countess of Athlone, the last surviving grandchild of Queen Victoria, took place on 9 January. Inflation fell to 16.1 per cent on 16 January. The Labour Party Conference changed the election of party leader to an electoral college system: 40 per cent trade unions, 30 per cent constituencies and 30 per cent MPs. The engagement of Prince Charles and Lady Diana Spencer was announced on 24 February. Unemployment stood at 2.4 million on 21 March. An attempt was made to assassinate Ronald Reagan on 30 March. The Social Democratic Party was formed by the Gang of Four, Roy Jenkins, David Owen, Bill Rodgers and Shirley Williams, on 26 March. The Liberal Party and the SDP formed an Alliance on 16 June. The Toxteth riots erupted in Liverpool on 5 July and there were further riots throughout the country on 10 July. The wedding of Prince Charles and Lady Diana Spencer at St Paul's Cathedral on 29 July was watched on television by more than thirty million viewers. On 18 September opinion polls showed the SDP–Liberal Alliance in the lead. Shirley Williams won the Crosby by-election for the SDP, overturning a Conservative majority of almost 20,000. President Sadat of Egypt was assassinated on 6 October. Opinion polls showed Mrs Thatcher to be the most unpopular postwar Prime Minister on 19 December.

6 January 1981

Cabinet changes. Norman St John-Stevas is sacked, having rightly spurned an offer to retain responsibility for the arts, though in an inferior post as Minister of State.

Give Jack Plumb dinner at Claridge's. He seems desperately worried about the political outlook, which he sees solely in terms of how a left-wing Government will confiscate his money. He is certain that Wedgwood Benn*

---

* Anthony Wedgwood Benn, later Tony Benn (1925–2014), Labour politician. The first peer to renounce his title (2nd Viscount Stansgate) under the Peerage Act of 1963. MP for Bristol South East 1963–83 and for Chesterfield 1984–2001; Sec. of State for Industry 1974–5; Sec. of State for Energy 1975–9; President of the Stop the War Coalition 2001–14.

will one day come to power. Again and again he returns to the topic of his possessions: wine, silver, furniture and Sèvres china.

7 January 1981
Talk to Norman St John-Stevas. He is deeply upset, not so much by his sacking from the Cabinet as by an apparent implication in an interview given yesterday by the Prime Minister that he was dismissed for leaking Cabinet secrets. He asks my advice. I reply that when public men are aggrieved by the newspapers, wireless or TV, I generally counsel them to do nothing; but that in this case he should (a) write a short, stern letter to Mrs Thatcher demanding a retraction, and (b) simultaneously let it be known that he has done so, though without publishing the terms of his letter to her. This he does, and in the course of the day it becomes known that the PM has entirely withdrawn her innuendo.

The Government's economic policy is very unpopular. Whatever its monetarist virtues in reducing inflation, it lacks all semblance of human concern; what the Cabinet needs is not a change of policy but a public relations exercise.

9 January 1981
Hugh Leggatt[*] tells me that Norman St John-Stevas told him Ian Gilmour was also going to be sacked by the PM, but that Peter Carrington threatened to resign if she persisted. I am sceptical, but what I do think is that an Old Etonian baronet is harder to sack than a man of obscure background like Norman.

14 January 1981
To see King Constantine in his office in Grosvenor Square for a gossip at 9.45. He thinks the outlook in Greece is not encouraging. It is quite likely that Andreas Papandreou[†] and his leftist allies will win the next election. 'You can imagine what sort of a Government it will be. The left will try to take Greece out of the EEC; but even if Greece does remain, it will not prove a happy experience to that race of individuals.'[‡]

I talk to Tino about the Prince of Wales. He speaks of him with affection and sympathy. 'It is said that the most difficult role is Vice-President of the United States, but being heir to a throne is worse. I remember when I was

---

[*] Sir Hugh Leggatt (1926–2014), art dealer.
[†] (1919–96), Prime Minister of Greece 1981–9 and 1993–6.
[‡] Greece had joined the EEC on 1 Jan. 1981.

Crown Prince, I went to Norway. Crown Prince Olaf, as he then was, said to me, "Ours is a waiting game." The wait can be almost indefinite.'

26 January 1981

I read Stephen Roskill's life of Beatty.[*] Something of a disappointment. The author is essentially an historian rather than a biographer and his style has become ungainly with age. He is proud to have discovered the prolonged affair which Beatty had with the wife of Bryan Godfrey-Faussett, King George V's naval equerry. But instead of dealing with it in a separate chapter he includes little bits of their love letters chronologically interspersed with the naval narrative. How extraordinary that Beatty never succeeded in winning the decisive battle in the North Sea for which he yearned – although he was presented with chance after chance. The reasons – Jackie Fisher's[†] building programme, which sacrificed armour to speed; poor British gunnery, particularly at night; appalling lack of skill in signalling; and the failure of the Admiralty to pass on its excellent intelligence.

14 February 1981

Rohan Butler[‡] takes me to All Souls for China tea and plum cake. He tells me Bismarck's remark on Gladstone: 'He cuts down trees. I plant them.'

Rohan wrote to congratulate Alec Home on becoming PM on the day Alec was to renounce his title and he received back the last letter Alec wrote to be signed 'Home'.

Rohan is rather shocked at the widespread disloyalty of Tories to Mrs Thatcher – even Peter Carrington.

16 February 1981

George Thomas, the Speaker, asks me to his private apartments for a drink. He then takes me out to supper in his car. He is the first Speaker to fly a pennant on his car: the parliamentary portcullis with a mace. He says it is invaluable in traffic. He has a nice woman driver who carefully arranges a rug over his silk stockings in this icy weather. On the way he tells me how he enjoyed preaching at Eton recently. He also tells me that his predecessor, Selwyn Lloyd, was at heart a spiritual man.

---

[*] Stephen Roskill (1903–82), naval officer and historian. David Beatty, 1st Earl Beatty (1871–1936), First Sea Lord 1919–27.

[†] Adm. of the Fleet John Fisher, 1st Baron Fisher of Kilverstone (1841–1920), First Sea Lord 1904–10 and 1914–15.

[‡] Dr Rohan Butler (1917–96), historian. Fellow of All Souls 1938–84.

18 February 1981

I hear that Vice-President Bush[*] insists on sitting in the right corner seat when being driven in his car. This is not for reasons of protocol, but because a computer has worked out that he stood just a little less chance of assassination there than elsewhere in the car.

24 February 1981

The Times, of all papers, announces this morning that the Prince of Wales will today be betrothed to Lady Diana Spencer. Robin Day[†] asks me to go on *The World at One* programme to talk about possible residences for the couple. I decline.

Watch the Prince of Wales and Lady Diana Spencer being interviewed on TV. She comes over with much charm yet strength of character. Yet there is something sad about a girl of nineteen being led into Royal captivity.

26 February 1981

Martin Charteris to lunch at Claridge's. He is delighted by the Prince of Wales's engagement to Diana Spencer: 'It solves a lot of problems.' I am surprised that he shares the popular view of the Prince's future – appointment as Governor General of Australia. I maintain that even if the Prince's appointment won general approval in Australia (which I doubt), it would remove him from Great Britain for two or three years; and it is here that he primarily belongs, both for his own sake and for that of the monarchy. Martin now comes round to my view on this. 'Yes,' he says, 'we always maintained that if it came to a conflict of interests between Great Britain and the Commonwealth, Great Britain must come first.'

We discuss what remains to the Queen apart from the choice of Prime Minister and withholding or assenting to a dissolution of Parliament. Bagehot's[‡] three rights – to be consulted, to encourage and to warn – still hold the field. The Queen felt strongly about Harold Wilson's resignation Honours List, but felt she could not remonstrate with him, much less turn it down. Instead, Wilson was merely asked whether he really wanted to recommend so many more names than his predecessors had done; and whether they were the names which on reflection he would still wish to put forward. To both questions he replied yes, and there the Queen felt that her right to

---

[*] George Bush (1924–2018), Vice-President of the US 1981–9; President of the US 1989–93.
[†] Sir Robin Day (1923–2000), political broadcaster and commentator. Presenter of *The World at One* on Radio 4 1979–87.
[‡] (1826–77), economist and essayist. Author of *The English Constitution* (1867).

interfere had ended. The Queen took a similar line of non-interference when Wilson submitted Marcia Williams' name for a peerage.

Philip Moore,* the present Private Secretary, has the good brain of the Civil Service but he is slow and cautious. At Sandringham or Balmoral, when the Queen is anxious to leave for a shooting lunch with just enough time to make it, Moore will bring in a basket of papers and laboriously go through each one with her. Martin took far more on his own shoulders and did not hesitate to make jokes. But he admits that his more relaxed style would never have been possible if Michael Adeane† had not laid the foundations.

I ask him how well Edward Ford would have done as Private Secretary. Martin: 'He would not have got on well with Prince Philip.' Martin also describes how Edward came to consult him on whether or not he should accept the post of Assistant Private Secretary at the Palace in 1946 when both were serving in the army in Palestine. In the course of a walk on Mount Carmel, Martin said to Edward: 'Don't touch it.' Edward disregarded his advice and accepted the post. Then Martin changed his mind, followed him to the Palace, and in time superseded him.

28 February 1981

Read Jock Colville's *The Churchillians* for a *Sunday Telegraph* review. How he makes the Churchill industry work for him. I conclude that a Private Secretary like Jock has no more right to break confidences than a doctor like Moran, whom he has constantly disparaged. The only difference is that Jock has allowed not one year but sixteen to elapse before publishing his indiscretions. Loyalty, like reason, is sometimes a matter of dates.

4 March 1981

Roy Jenkins‡ describes to me how Dick Crossman§ once came to see him at his own request in the role of candid friend. He told Roy that he was at heart the inheritor of Nye Bevan's¶ Welsh radicalism, but that he was handicapped

---

* Sir Philip Moore, Baron Moore of Wolvercote (1921–2009), PS to Elizabeth II 1977–86.

† Baron Adeane (1910–84), PS to Elizabeth II 1953–72.

‡ Baron Jenkins of Hillhead (1920–2003), Labour Party, SDP and Liberal Democrat politician and biographer. Minister of Aviation 1964–5; Home Secretary 1965–7; Chancellor of the Exchequer 1967–70; President of the European Commission 1977–81; Chancellor of Oxford University 1987–2003.

§ Richard Crossman (1907–74), Labour politician. MP for Coventry 1945–74; his three-volume *Diaries of a Cabinet Minister* was published posthumously (1975) following a failed legal attempt by the government to block publication.

¶ Aneurin Bevan (1897–1960), Labour politician. MP for Ebbw Vale 1929–60; as Minister of Health and Housing 1945–51 Bevan was the architect of the National Health Service.

by his close links with the Establishment. Roy bore all this for two hours. He ended up by driving Dick Crossman home in his own car, leaving it unlocked and having its radio stolen.

15 March 1981

William Waldegrave tells me that at Eton, sitting under the board recording the names of the winners of the prestigious Newcastle Scholarship, he conceived two ambitions: to win it and to be one of the few winners whose name took up two lines on the board. He achieved the first, but Chenevix-Trench[*] omitted the 'Hon.' before his name, so it could all be crammed into a single line. The Newcastle, which began as a divinity scholarship, then became one for classicists, and is once more a test of divinity: there are not enough classicists of the required standard.

William also says that when Edward du Cann[†] was being run as a possible successor to Ted Heath for the party leadership, there was little opposition to him on the Conservative benches in the Commons. 'They would all have welcomed a seat on one of his bucket-shop boards.' It was the Lords which objected to him on grounds of financial laxity.

18 March 1981.

Lunch at White's. On the way home I run into Michael Adeane and tell him that I have just been lunching beneath d'Orsay's[‡] portrait of Wellington, with the Garter painted over the wrong shoulder. Michael: 'That's what comes of being painted by a foreigner.'

1 April 1981

Lunch with Alec and Elizabeth Home in the House of Lords.

Alec tells me a story about his relations with the Russians. At the United Nations in New York he once had a meeting with Khrushchev[§] at the Waldorf Astoria. He saw Khrushchev off at the front door of the hotel, but had to take a second lift down from his apartment as the first lift was full. So Mr K emerged first into the street, where a hostile crowd shouted:

---

[*] Anthony Chenevix-Trench (1919–79), Head Master of Eton 1963–9; he was asked to leave because of his enthusiastic attitude to caning.

[†] Sir Edward du Cann (1924–2017), Conservative politician. MP for Taunton 1956–87; Chairman of the Conservative Party 1965–7; Chairman of the 1922 Committee 1972–84.

[‡] Alfred, Count d'Orsay (1801–52), portrait painter. He painted his portrait of Wellington in 1845.

[§] Nikita Khrushchev (1894–1971), First Secretary of the Communist Party of the USSR 1953–64.

'Go home.' He shouted back: 'How can I go home without my Lord?'

When Elizabeth Home took Mme Gromyko* in tow during a London visit, she asked the Russian if she wanted to go shopping for clothes. Mme Gromyko replied, 'I am too great. I have no number.'

7 April 1981
Dine at the Beefsteak. Oliver van Oss outraged by the praise heaped on the Lyttelton/Hart-Davis letters – 'Why, I wrote <u>much</u> better letters to George Lyttelton than Hart-Davis ever did.'† He also tells a story of Chambers‡ at Eton, when a beak announced for the calendar that a Corps field day would be held on a certain day. One of the chaplains objected: 'But that is Ascension Day.' Beak: 'Field day was fixed first.'

8 April 1981
Lunch with Julian Faber§ at the Savoy Grill. He tells me that someone wrote to Harold Macmillan recently to suggest that he might care to resign as Chancellor of Oxford and make way for another man. 'Certainly,' he replied, 'if I could be sure that I would be succeeded by an older man.'

15 April 1981
Martin Gilliat tells me that Princess Margaret says that Clarence House staff are killing her mother by making her do too many engagements. But her doctors take an entirely contrary view: without a diverting programme she <u>would</u> die.

16 April 1981
Always a connoisseur of Harold Macmillan stories, Peter Carrington tells me of the occasion last year when he accompanied Macmillan to the twenty-fifth anniversary of the signing of the Austrian Treaty in Vienna.

At the British Embassy Macmillan referred scornfully to the American Secretary of State, Edmund Muskie,¶ having burst into tears when his wife

---

* Lydia Gromyko (1911–2004), teacher. Wife of Andrei Gromyko (1909–89), Chairman of the Presidium of the USSR 1985–8.
† The Hon. George Lyttelton (1883–1962), noted Eton housemaster. Sir Rupert Hart-Davis (1907–99), publisher and former pupil of Lyttelton. *The Lyttelton-Hart-Davis Letters* were published to great acclaim in six volumes between 1978 and 1984. The cover of the paperback volumes bore K.R.'s comment: 'One of the most urbane, civilised and entertaining correspondences of our time.'
‡ Chambers is the Eton term for the mid-morning meeting of masters, usually in School Hall.
§ (1917–2002), CO in the Welsh Guards, where K.R. served under him.
¶ (1914–96). US Sec. of State 1980–81.

was publicly accused of drunkenness. The Ambassador unwisely intervened and said to Macmillan: 'Well, what would you have said, Mr Macmillan, if Lady Dorothy had been accused of drunkenness?' Macmillan: 'I should have said, "You ought to have seen her mother."'

25 April 1981

Train to Cambridge at 9.35 to stay with Jack Plumb at Christ's. His other house guest is Princess Margaret with a lady-in-waiting. A large luncheon party in the Master's Lodge. When all the luncheon guests have disappeared back to London, I am left alone with Princess Margaret. Since I last saw her she has lost a lot of weight, and is now slim, elegant and exceptionally pretty, though with something of the Queen's firm mouth and jaw. As always, she behaves most amiably to me. Although Jack had not intended that I should be with her for the whole of the afternoon, she insists on sweeping me off to King's for a choir practice – even making room for me between her and the lady-in-waiting in the back of her car. King's Chapel is closed to visitors, so there we are in that enchantingly illuminated Xanadu, just our little party from Christ's, with the Provost, Bernard Williams.[*] It is indeed a rare privilege, like being alone in the Parthenon.

The choir sings gloriously, particularly a solo treble. PM admits to me that although she likes the music of church services, she finds the ritual very tedious. Tea with Bernard Williams in the Provost's Lodge. Bernard tells me that in the early days of Wolfson College, Isaiah[†] was much pestered to provide a crèche. He reluctantly agreed in principle, but there were demands for it to contain an ever-increasing number of children. Isaiah at last said in exasperation: 'Can't we give them transistor sets, as in India?' This remark was considered in very bad taste.

Back at Christ's Princess Margaret is very critical of Shirley Williams, Bernard's first wife, of course, for attempting to abolish the grammar schools – and says that the Queen Mother also feels strongly about it.

She tells me how deeply hurtful she finds the attacks of the popular Press on her for supposedly neglecting her duties. 'I cannot help being nervous in public, but always try to do my best.'

She is full of confidences. Her recent visit to Greece was treated as a

---

[*] Sir Bernard Williams (1929–2003), moral philosopher. Provost of King's Coll., Cambridge 1979–88.

[†] Sir Isaiah Berlin (1909–97), philosopher and historian of ideas. Founder President of Wolfson Coll., Oxford 1966–75.

political occasion by the Greeks. 'I had to do a lot of what my mother calls "playing dumb".'

Princess Margaret still regards Queen Mary with fear and dislike. 'I remember her warning us not to play with window blinds, or we would end up like the poor sightless King of Hanover.'*

Her most interesting remark on King George V is that her mother, who came from a home where nobody quarrelled, was appalled by the family storms that swept over York Cottage – and did much to relieve the tension of those cramped rooms.

Only once does PM mention Tony Snowdon.† As a former cox of the Cambridge Boat Race VIII, he asked the current VIII one year to come to Kensington Palace for a drink before going on to their traditional dinner at the Savoy on the night of the Boat Race. First, he cleared away everything breakable from the drawing room: china, silver, fragile pieces of furniture. When the VIII arrived they turned out to be quiet, beautifully mannered and drinking only orange juice.

Jack later tells me that Bernard would much prefer to have been Warden of All Souls: he is embroiled in terrible rows here with the students. Jack has some members of the university to come in after dinner to meet Princess Margaret. Owen Chadwick,‡ Master of Selwyn College, greets me: 'Ah! What a chapter you wrote on Linky!'§ He is writing a life of Hensley Henson,¶ then a book on Vatican policy during the war.**

27 April 1981

A registered letter from the Queen Mother, thanking me for the flowers that I sent her on her wedding anniversary yesterday: three beautifully penned pages in her own hand, phrased with a warmth and precision that few could

---

* King George V of Hanover (1819–78), last King of Hanover. Lost the sight of one eye in an accident in 1828, and the sight of the other eye in 1833.
† Antony Armstrong-Jones, 1st Earl of Snowdon (1930–2017), photographer and film-maker. Husband of Princess Margaret 1960–78.
‡ (1916–2015), Master of Selwyn Coll., Cambridge 1956–83; Dixie Professor of Ecclesiastical History at Cambridge University 1958–68; Regius Professor of Modern History 1968–83; Vice-Chancellor of the University 1969–71; President of the British Academy 1981–5.
§ Lord Hugh Cecil, Baron Quickswood (1869–1956), one of the subjects of K.R.'s *The Later Cecils* (1975).
¶ The Rt Revd Hensley Henson (1863–1947), Dean of Durham 1917–20; Bishop of Hereford 1918–20; Bishop of Durham 1920–39.
** Owen Chadwick's life of Hensley Henson appeared in 1983 and his book *Britain and the Vatican during the Second World War* in 1986.

match. What an astonishing lady even to think of undertaking such a task in her eighty-first year.

5 May 1981

Princess Margaret telephones to thank me for my explanatory notes on the Coburg and Brunswick families. She says I have made it clear where Dickie Mountbatten's relationship tables failed to do so. 'I simply couldn't understand them.' She is much amused when I tell her of the farmer who told Dickie how impressed he had been by the book – 'I use your system to record the breeding of my pedigree herd!'

16 May 1981

The Dean of Windsor, Michael Mann,* accompanies Prince Eddie and myself to the Festival Hall to hear the Bach Choir's performance of Beethoven's *Missa Solemnis*, in which Katharine Kent[†] is singing.

He has the specialised humour of the lifelong public schoolboy. He says that on being appointed Dean of Windsor, he received a letter from the Conduct, Roger Royle,[‡] at Eton, saying: 'I hope that your being a Harrovian won't make any difference.' Mann replied: 'See Psalm 121, verse 1.' This reads: 'I will lift up mine eyes unto the hills: from whence cometh my help.'

The Dean tells me, somewhat indiscreetly, that the Queen shares his dislike of the new Prayer Book, although Prince Philip does like it.

18 May 1981

Describing his recent journey to South Africa on a cargo boat, of all vessels, Harold Macmillan comments: 'And the wonderful thing was that I had a completely new audience for my stories!'

19 May 1981

Prince Eddie has some interesting remarks to make on State Visits. In other countries, the host always accompanies the State Visitors everywhere. Here, however, they are handed over to officials, except for the meeting at Victoria Station and the State Banquet at Buckingham Palace. Neither the Queen nor any other member of the Royal Family sees them off when they leave England. This is done by Chips Maclean,[§] as Lord Chamberlain.

---

* The Rt Revd Michael Mann (1924–2011), Dean of Windsor 1976–89; Chairman of the Governors of Harrow 1980–88.
† Katharine, Duchess of Kent (b. 1933), wife of Prince Edward, Duke of Kent.
‡ The Revd Canon Roger Royle (b. 1939), Conduct at Eton 1974–9.
§ Sir Charles Maclean, Baron Maclean of Duart and Morvern (1916–90), Lord Chamberlain

5 June 1981

Ted Heath tells me of one of his visits to Windsor just after Arnold Wein-stock had won the 200th running of the Derby, and so beating the Queen's horse. Ted said to the Queen and Prince Philip: 'Of course, if it had been a sailing race, we should all have hung back so that the Queen could have won it.' Prince Philip retorted: 'Like hell you would!'

9 June 1981

Discuss with Peter Thorneycroft* the forthcoming by-election at Warring-ton, when Roy Jenkins will stand as a candidate against Labour in order to test the strength of his Social Democratic Party. Peter says: 'None of us must utter a word of commendation of Roy, as that would be utterly fatal to his chances.'

10 June 1981

Much pride taken by David Nicolson,[†] industrialist and Euro-MP, in his early naval career. He met his wife on the Normandy beaches after D-Day; she was a nurse. He tells me about Ian Paisley[‡] at the European Parliament. He was at first annoyed to see himself seated between an Italian Fascist and an Irish Republican, then said: 'Oh well, Christ was crucified between two thieves.'

27 June 1981

Read the immortal scene from Dickens' *Martin Chuzzlewit* in which Mrs Gamp quarrels with Betsy Prig after supping off pickled salmon and a salad.[§]

16 July 1981

Johnnie Spencer tells me that he wanted to wear his Greys uniform when Diana marries the Prince of Wales, but that Diana herself objected. She thought it would detract from her own appearance. This is most extraordi-nary, like something from *King Lear*.

---

to Elizabeth II 1971–84.
* Baron Thorneycroft (1909–94), Conservative politician. President of the Board of Trade 1951–7; Chancellor of the Exchequer 1957–8; Chairman of the Conservative Party 1975–81.
† Sir David Nicolson (1922–96), company chairman; MEP 1979–84.
‡ Baron Bannside of North Antrim (1926–2014), loyalist politician and Protestant religious leader in Northern Ireland. First Minister of Northern Ireland 2007–8.
§ The quarrel occurs in Chapter XLIX ('A Cause of Division Between Friends').

24 July 1981

My train to Yorkshire breaks down at Peterborough. In the following one an hour later I find Denis Healey. We have some good talk. He says he would love to retire from politics, but I suspect that this is simply the reaction of a tired man at the end of a parliamentary session. Today he was up at six preparing a debate in the Commons this morning on the Brandt Report.* Now he is on his way to Leeds for (a) a meeting with some engineers about redundancy, (b) his own reselection process as an MP, (c) an interview on the TV, then (d) sleep back to London. He has a perceptive observation about Tony Wedgwood Benn: 'Part of his trouble is that he is a second son whose elder brother was killed in the war. So he has to strive to shine in his father's eyes.' I tell him that I will give him any help he would like in his fight with Benn for the deputy leadership of the Labour Party, but that I think silence on my part would be the truest kindness. Denis replies: 'Yes, Peter Thorneycroft stabbed me in the back with a stiletto by praising me publicly.'

28 July 1981

Supper party at the Belgian Embassy at seven before the firework display in Hyde Park to celebrate tomorrow's wedding of the Prince of Wales. The talk is of the cancellation by the King and Queen of Spain of their visit to London because the Prince of Wales and his bride are flying out to join the Royal Yacht at Gibraltar. Obviously the Foreign Office has failed to deter the Palace from such a stupid scheme, which can only help the old Franco fascists and undermine the democratic Anglophile Juan Carlos. Tonight Ian Gilmour tells me that neither he nor Lord Carrington was consulted: the decision was taken, or at least endorsed, entirely by Palace officials.

29 July 1981

Day of the Prince of Wales's wedding. I read in the papers that there were casualties in the crowd at the fireworks last night, including several miscarriages. I see all the processions on TV, followed by the service in St Paul's. The bride looks quite charming, accompanied by tiny girls with flowers in their hair. When the cameras focus on her hand with the wedding ring, it looks as if she is addicted to biting her fingernails. The Queen Mother looks pale. Johnnie Spencer is really the hero of the hour: without a stick he walks the whole length of St Paul's with Diana on his arm. Later, accompanying the Queen back to the Palace, he waves vigorously to the crowds. The service is

---

* The Brandt Report by the Independent Commission was chaired by Willy Brandt (1913–92), Chancellor of the Federal Republic of Germany 1969–74, to review international development.

well done, though I do not care for a new anthem – the music of tin cans – or a pretentious new setting of the National Anthem. Why not leave well alone? It falls to the Revd Harry Williams[*] to pray for the first time for the Princess of Wales. One slight hitch when Diana transposes the Prince's names in the response – 'Philip Charles' instead of 'Charles Philip'. I hope it does not invalidate the whole ceremony.

8 August 1981

On the Royal Wedding I hear that it was originally arranged that in the carriage procession from St Paul's back to the Palace, Johnnie Spencer should drive with his former wife (and of course Diana's mother), Mrs Shand Kydd.[†] But when told this at a meeting in Buckingham Palace, Johnnie pulled such a long face that the Queen said: 'Oh, all right then, you can drive with me,' which much to his delight he did.

The Spencers were given fifty seats for St Paul's. When Johnnie showed Diana his draft list, she crossed out all the family who had not bothered to come to the weddings of her sisters! One day she will be very formidable.

12 August 1981

The Prince of Wales's visit to Egypt this week as part of his honeymoon cruise in the Royal Yacht has annoyed all the other Arab countries, who of course do not like Egypt's flirtation with Israel. It is the second Royal visit to Egypt recently. When Prince Philip was in Cairo, President Sadat, who does not normally dine at foreign embassies, telephoned the British Ambassador one evening and said he would like to come to dinner to meet the Prince. He later said to the Ambassador: 'This is the first time I have been inside your Embassy. The nearest I ever got to it before was when I was with Nasser,[‡] looking for a way to blow it up.'

18 August 1981

Jack Plumb tells me that the Palace forgot to ask Gordon Richardson[§] to the Prince's wedding. He should have been here as Governor of the Bank of England; but that was not all. He lent the Bank to the Prime Minister for her to give a lunch to the assembled statesmen from abroad immediately after the ceremony at St Paul's.

---

[*] The Revd Harry Williams (1919–2006), Dean of Trinity Coll., Cambridge 1958–69.
[†] Frances Shand Kydd (1936–2004), mother of Diana, Princess of Wales; charity worker.
[‡] Gamel Abdel Nasser (1918–70), President of Egypt 1956–70.
[§] Sir Gordon Richardson, Baron Richardson of Duntisbourne (1915–2010), Governor of the Bank of England 1973–83.

6 October 1981

The second and final volume of Jim Lees-Milne's life of Harold Nicolson arrives. It makes quite a lot of use of my Journal notes I sent Jim, including an account of his eightieth birthday dinner at Sissinghurst.

Lunch with Julian Faber at the Savoy. He tells me his father-in-law is getting confused. A few months ago he telephoned Lady Diana Cooper and said: 'What's all this I hear about your going to marry the Prince of Wales?'

9 October 1981

Duke Hussey* has been staying with Philip Moore at the Private Secretary's house at Balmoral. He reports that rumours of Princess Diana's boredom are accurate: the Prince goes out at nine to shoot or fish and she does not see him again until seven. Dukie wonders if he will make a sufficiently good king: he thinks not. The Prince is too immature, and the contrast with the firm style of the Queen will be most marked.

12 October 1981

Watch the first two-hour instalment of *Brideshead Revisited* on TV. It has been heralded by a deluge of publicity. The most striking feature is its fidelity to the book. Oxford is beautifully done: I can recall just such sunlit vistas opening up. But the final impression is that *Brideshead* remains too mawkish a novel on which to spend so much effort. The homosexual element is made more explicit than in a casual reading of the book.

15 October 1981

At the Tory Party Conference at Blackpool. Charlie Morrison† was in the room when the PM telephoned Paul Channon offering him a sideways ministerial move in the recent reshuffle rather than promotion. When Paul instantly accepted, Mrs Thatcher put down the telephone and said to Charlie: 'I don't know what we would do without people like Paul.'

8 November 1981

Remembrance Sunday. See the Cenotaph ceremonial on TV, with Eddie dressed as a Scots Guardsman. Michael Foot, as Leader of the Opposition, cuts a deplorable figure. He wears a short green topcoat, tartan tie and brown

---

* Marmaduke 'Dukie' Hussey, Baron Hussey of North Bradley (1923–2006), Chairman of the Board of Governors of the BBC 1986–96.

† The Hon. Sir Charles Morrison (1932–2005), Conservative politician. MP for Devizes 1964–92. Channon was moved as Minister of State at the Civil Service Dept. to a similar post for the Arts.

shoes; gawps about him and fidgets throughout; and does not bow after laying his wreath.

9 November 1981
Walk through the park in brilliant sunshine to give Prince Eddie lunch at Claridge's. Talk of the Cenotaph ceremony yesterday, and of Michael Foot's demeanour, which now threatens to become a political issue.

Tonight he has to speak at the Royal Geographical Society, and asks if I have a suitable joke. I tell him the story of the woman who came back from India saying that the best thing she saw was the Aga Khan by moonlight.[*]

11 November 1981
At a meeting this morning between the Speaker and the Clerks of the House of Commons there was a disagreement. The Speaker proposes to call on Ian Paisley MP to explain his conduct in the House on Monday next; last Monday he shouted abuse at the PM from a side gallery of the House, then fled before he could be called to order. The Clerks say that the Speaker has no power to do such a thing. But the Speaker sees no reason why he should not create a precedent. Not so earlier in his Speakership. There was once a tied vote. As George Thomas, according to precedent, agrees to give his casting vote in favour of the status quo, a Member, Neil Kinnock,[†] shouted out: 'Vote Labour, George.'

23 November 1981
Alan Urwick[‡] and I have lunch with King Hussein of Jordan.[§] We drive up in the official car, which is stopped three times at barriers manned by fearsomely armed soldiers, every kind of rifle, pistol and automatic weapon.

The King joins us in his garden. This morning he took the passing-out parade of Jordan's Sandhurst, but has since changed into a tweed jacket, cavalry twill trousers and open-necked grey shirt. He carries himself with the same dignity that I used to admire in Emperor Haile Selassie.[¶] His voice is rather guttural, but his command of English impeccable. He speaks softly and is infinitely courteous in his manner. We talk of Harrow and Sandhurst. During his recent visit to London he spent his only free evening dining at

---

[*] A title formally recognised by the Viceroy of India in 1887.

[†] Baron Kinnock of Bedwelty (b. 1942), Labour politician. Leader of the Labour Party 1983–92.

[‡] Sir Alan Urwick (1930–2016), Ambassador to Jordan 1979–84.

[§] (1935–99), King of Jordan 1952–99.

[¶] (1892–1975), Emperor of Ethiopia 1930–74.

his old house at Harrow. Sandhurst he describes as 'a turning point in my life', and quotes with approval its motto, 'Serve to lead'. He tells me that the custom of the adjutant riding his horse up the steps of the Royal Military Academy at the end of a passing-out parade began when in 1927 a furious adjutant chased a sloppy-looking platoon of cadets into the Old Building.

Much talk throughout the meal, interrupted only when the King is called to the telephone to talk to Juan Carlos of Spain. Alan later says that after his return to the dining room, Hussein spoke far more freely, having heard from Juan Carlos that I was to be trusted absolutely.

The King desperately wants our Queen to repay the State Visit he made to London fifteen years ago, a point which Alan has several times made to the Foreign Office, but the Foreign Office thinks it would give unnecessary offence to Israel. In general we keep off relations between Jordan and Israel.

When we take our leave after lunch, the King clasps my right hand with both of his when we say goodbye.

Alan Urwick later tells me that Christopher Everett,[*] after serving in the Diplomatic Service 1957–1970, was appointed in 1970 to be Headmaster of Worksop. In 1975 he became Headmaster of Tonbridge. At Worksop there was an Arab boy. When Everett complained of his bad English essays, the boy replied: 'Ah, but English is not my first language. Now, if I were to write in Arabic, my essays would be <u>much</u> better.' So Everett told the boy to write his next essay in Arabic – and corrected all its mistakes himself no less severely.[†] He had served in Beirut.

27 November 1981

Robin Mackworth-Young writes that he will 'have to take instructions' on my chapter about King George V and the Tsar in view of its critical approach to both the King, and, even more, Stamfordham. He therefore asks for full source references of the chapter.

6 December 1981

Read Thomas Hardy's *The Dynasts*, and at last trace the quotation I want to use in my George V chapter on 1914–1918.

'I have beheld the agonies of war
Through many a weary season; seen enough

---

[*] (b. 1933), Diplomatic Service 1957–70; Headmaster of Worksop Coll. 1970–75 and of Tonbridge School 1975–89.

[†] The boy is now a doctor in New York. Christopher Everett to the editor, 25 Jan. 2017.

To make me hold that scarcely any goal
  Is worth the reaching through so red a road.'
What magnificent stuff it is.

7 December 1981

When I am talking to Isaiah Berlin, a man comes up to him, peers into his face, then says, 'Sorry, wrong man.' There can have been nothing like it since a stranger walked up to the great Duke of Wellington, held out his hand and said: 'Mr Jones, I believe.'

8 December 1981

Enchanting Christmas letter from Grizel Hartley.* She thinks the characters in TV's *Brideshead Revisited* are so common that it ought to be called *Maidenhead Revisited*.

15 December 1981

Derek Hill† was asked to go to the Palace recently to discuss a commission. He thought that at last he would paint the Queen. But no, it was to paint the corgis.

16 December 1981

Lunch with Prince Eddie at Buck's. I find him there at the bar with Denis Thatcher, a most amiable man. Forgetting he is not a work of fiction out of *Private Eye*, I expect him to say, 'What is a Press reptile like you doing here?'‡

Eddie is of course delighted to be awarded the Garter. He will wear his father's robes when he has located them.

---

* Hubert Hartley (1896–1977) and his wife Grizel (1900–87), K.R.'s close and long-standing friends from his days teaching at Eton, where Hubert was a housemaster.
† (1916–2000), portrait and landscape painter.
‡ Denis Thatcher's fictional letters *Dear Bill* (supposedly to Bill Deedes) were published by *Private Eye* 1979–90.

1982

1982 was the year of the Falklands War. On 21 January miners accepted the National Coal Board's offer of a 9.3 per cent pay increase. Unemployment on 26 January was recorded at over three million. Rab Butler died on 8 March. On 19 March the Argentinians landed on South Georgia, precipitating war. Roy Jenkins won the Hillhead by-election for the Social Democratic Party. On 2 April the Argentinians invaded the Falkland Islands. The Royal Navy task force set forth for the Falkland Islands on 5 April from Portsmouth. The Royal Marines recaptured South Georgia on 25 April. The Conservatives returned to the top of the opinion polls on 30 April. Pope John Paul II visited Britain on 28 May. The Battle of Goose Green commenced on 28 May. President Ronald Reagan addressed a joint session of Parliament. The Falklands War ended on 14 June after the Argentinians surrendered. Prince William was born on 21 June. Roy Jenkins was elected leader of the SDP on 2 July. The Mary Rose, *the flagship of Henry VIII which sank in 1545, was raised from the Solent on 11 October.*

4 January 1982

Dine with Martin Gilliat at Buck's tonight. He tells me a little story about the Queen Mother. When the Duke of Edinburgh had a big sale at Sotheby's last year to raise money for the Duke of Edinburgh's Award Scheme, the Queen Mother was asked to contribute. She said: 'I don't know that I have anything we can get rid of.' Eventually she gave a Seago painting. It fetched £14,000, bought by the Westminster Bank. Today she lunched with the directors of the Bank, who presented it back to her.

12 January 1982

Dine at the Beefsteak. John Ure[*] tells me that when he was Ambassador to Cuba Fidel Castro used to send him splendid New Year presents: a net of live lobsters and a suckling pig in a coffin.

---

[*] Sir John Ure (b.1931), Ambassador to Cuba 1979–81, Brazil 1984–7 and Sweden 1987–91.

17 January 1982

Jeremy and Marion Thorpe to lunch. They are in tolerably good spirits, having been snowed up in Devon. He tells me that he is thinking of writing to Michael Hartwell to express his sympathy about Pam's recent death, but wants to begin: 'Although certain events have made it impossible for us to meet . . .' I tell him that letters of condolence, like those of apology, should be unqualified. He will never forgive Michael for having made a deal with Peter Bessell by which he was to receive £50,000 for his memoirs if J.T. was convicted, but only £25,000 if J.T. was acquitted. It was a horrible, immoral contract. But what J.T. will not recognise is that several jurors admitted in interviews after his trial that the exposure of this contract made them suspect Bessell's evidence and so they acquitted J.T., otherwise he might have been found guilty and sent to prison.

18 January 1982

To Cambridge to stay with Jack Plumb at Christ's. As on my last visit, he has Princess Margaret as a fellow guest for lunch. This morning he took her to see the Pepys Library.

PM: 'Who was Pepys? Some sort of journalist, wasn't he?'

J.P.: 'No Ma'am, he was Secretary to the Admiralty.'

PM: 'Oh, I see, a sailor.'

Robert Rhodes James, MP for Cambridge, is at the lunch, with other Cambridge figures. He is much less austere, not to say pompous, than on other occasions when we have met. He has just completed a book on the Prince Consort: 'It is difficult to do this', he says, 'without hating Queen Victoria – just as Elizabeth Longford* after writing about Queen Victoria ended by hating the Prince Consort.'

At my end of the table we talk of Sir Geoffrey Keynes,† now in his ninety-fifth year. All seem agreed on his vanity and pederastic tastes, including his camping holidays in Norfolk, usually with a young man or a boy. At Houghton‡ one day Sybil Cholmondeley§ told her son Hugh¶ that Geoffrey Keynes was coming to lunch. Hugh replied: 'Well,

---

* Elizabeth Pakenham, Countess of Longford (1906–2002), historian. Biographer, particularly of prominent nineteenth-century figures.
† (1887–1982), surgeon and author; younger brother of J.M. Keynes.
‡ The family home of the Cholmondeleys in Norfolk.
§ Sybil Sassoon, Marchioness of Cholmondeley (1894–1989), Superintendent of the Women's Royal Naval Service 1939–45; she was the one person K.R. did not mind calling him Ken.
¶ Hugh Cholmondeley, 6th Marquess of Cholmondeley (1919–90), Lord Great Chamberlain of England 1968–90.

whoever he brings this year, I hope he will be in <u>long</u> trousers.'

20 January 1982

Lunch with Peter Carrington. He is disenchanted with the PM. When Ian Gilmour left the Government, Peter wanted to promote Douglas Hurd[*] to being No. 2 in the FO, or some independent post such as Minister of Transport. But she said impatiently – and stupidly – that she didn't want 'all those FO people'. I am amazed that Peter does not have enough influence with her on that sort of matter. He adds that she is a bad judge of people in general.

Two others come in for Peter's criticism. He thinks Philip Moore, the Queen's Private Secretary, to be dull and stupid: 'He causes me endless trouble.' He is also worried at the wilful way in which Hailsham is once more behaving as Lord Chancellor – affecting not to hear what he does not want to hear. There is rising resentment in the Lords, and it would be a tragedy for Quintin if he lost his job as a result of this.

Dine at Claridge's as George Thomson's[†] guest at the Thirty Club, composed mainly of newspaper and broadcasting tycoons. An obviously well-heeled crowd. George is a very generous and genial host. He is, of course, hugely delighted to be a Knight of the Thistle, and only sorry when he went to the Lords that he could not have been Lord Thomson of Dundee; but Lyon would not let him have the whole of Dundee. So he had to be Lord Thomson of Monifieth.

21 January 1982

John Grigg,[‡] in an article in *The Times*, announces that he is joining the Social Democrats. As one would expect, his reasons are utterly unconvincing, with that exaggerated humility of which he is such a master. Only a few weeks ago, when we lunched at the Charing Cross Hotel, he demolished Shirley Williams with well-reasoned disparagement.

Lunch with Dukie Hussey at Brooks's. Although Dukie has stayed at Balmoral with Philip Moore, he thinks him a disastrous Private Secretary to the Queen: boring and cautious. He will almost certainly be succeeded

---

[*] Baron Hurd of Westwell (b. 1930), Conservative politician. Diplomatic Service 1952–66; Home Secretary 1985–9; Foreign Secretary 1989–95.
[†] Baron Thomson of Monifieth (1921–2008), Labour MP for Dundee East 1952–72; Sec. of State for Commonwealth Affairs 1967–8; EEC Commissioner 1973–7; Chairman of the Independent Broadcasting Authority 1981–8.
[‡] 2nd Baron Altrincham (1924–2001), writer, historian and politician.

by Robert Fellowes rather than William Heseltine:* a reversion to the independent aristocrat.

29 January 1982

Paul Johnson,† writing on the Press in the *Spectator*, says that 'the only effective column at the moment is the splendidly eccentric "Albany" written
by Kenneth Rose in the *Sunday Telegraph*. Rose knows a lot of people, is a
first-rate scholar, and very industrious. So his column tells me things I don't
know and things I want to know, a vital qualification.'

10 February 1982

I mention my anxiety about Windsor's possible attempt to censor my chapter
on King George V's failure to offer asylum and hospitality to the Tsar and
his family in 1917. Leslie Rowse‡ says that I ought to do whatever Windsor
wants: a most uncharacteristic attitude on his part.§

17 February 1982

Tom Stoppard¶ tells me how fascinated he is by Noël Coward's diaries, now
being serialised in the *Daily Mail*. I find them repetitive and sometimes sad,
but then I have never liked the highly charged emotional world of the theatre.

24 February 1982

Just as former members of the Think Tank talk endlessly of Victor Rothschild, so stalwarts of the BBC forever talk of John Reith.** When Mrs
Thatcher came to the BBC in 1980 in the company of Ian Trethowan,†† then
Director General, she stopped in front of the bust, patted it, and said: 'They
don't make them like that now.'

---

* Robert Fellowes, Baron Fellowes (b. 1941), PS to Elizabeth II 1990–99. Sir William Heseltine
(b. 1930), PS to Elizabeth II 1986–90. Hussey was thus anticipating the succession wrongly.
† Paul Johnson (b. 1928), historian and journalist.
‡ A.L. Rowse (1903–97), historian and Shakespearean scholar. Of working-class Cornish
origins, he won a scholarship to Christ Church, Oxford, in 1921 and later became a Fellow of
All Souls.
§ K.R.'s worries were unfounded. In the end the Queen said: 'Let him publish' after which
Martin Gilliat, the Queen Mother's PS, said to K.R.: 'Your chances of an MVO have just floated,
out to 20–1!'
¶ Sir Tom Stoppard (b. 1937), playwright and screenwriter.
** 1st Baron Reith (1899–1971), Dir. Gen. of the BBC 1927–38. He introduced the former King
Edward VIII as 'Prince Edward', before standing aside to allow Edward to make his Abdication
broadcast. Served in the wartime governments of Neville Chamberlain and Winston Churchill. The BBC's Reith Lectures were instituted in 1948 in his honour.
†† Sir Ian Trethowan (1922–80), Dir. Gen. of the BBC 1977–82.

When Reith turned up informally to see the old BBC studio in Edinburgh he was shown round by the commissionaire. As he left he said: 'Now, don't forget to turn the lights out.'

4 March 1982
An immensely satisfying letter from Robin Mackworth-Young, telling me of the Queen's favourable decision on my chapter about King George V and the Tsar. I will write an equally understanding reply. Robin tells me that my text was in general much admired, though my judgement on the King and Lord Stamfordham over the events leading to the death of the Tsar may have been considered a little strong, but he conceded that it is a judgement I am perfectly entitled to make.

Lunch with Alec and Elizabeth Home in the House of Lords. At the next table is Mannie Shinwell,[*] in his ninety-eighth year, but bright as a button.

Alec describes how he once had to entertain a party of Oriental visitors, so took them to hear Maria Callas in *Tosca* at Covent Garden. The old Duke of Gloucester was also in the party, even more bored than the visitors. As Callas flung herself over the battlements, he said in his loud, high-pitched voice: 'Any chance of her really being dead, then we can all go home.'

9 March 1982
Spend the morning at the National Gallery. First, the conservation department, where I see recently acquired pictures being cleaned. Then the scientific department on pigment analysis and the measuring of colour changes over the years. Then a press conference given by Noel Annan.[†] One good epigram: 'The more visitors you have, the greater the dirt.' And on his wish to find a benefactor of £1 million: 'One never knows. One day at King's I received a letter offering the college the *Adoration of the Magi* by Rubens.'

A stab of sadness when I emerge from the Gallery: 'RAB DIES' on the newspaper placards.

What a contrast with a later Foreign Secretary. I hear tonight that at an official dinner George Brown was so drunk that he fell asleep. He then woke up and shouted to his Private Secretary to telephone and find out the score of some football match that was being played that evening. Meanwhile Harold

---

[*] Emanuel Shinwell, Baron Shinwell of Easington (1884–1986), trade union official and Labour politician. Minister of Fuel and Power 1945–7; Sec. of State for War 1947–50; Minister of Defence 1950–51.

[†] Baron Annan (1916–2000), military intelligence officer and author. Provost of King's Coll., Cambridge 1956–66; Provost of University Coll., London 1966–78; Vice-Chancellor of London University 1978–81.

Wilson looked on indulgently. Some years later Harold Wilson was asked if he remembered the evening. 'Yes,' replied Harold Wilson, 'the score was 2–1.' What an absolutely characteristic story of both politicians.

16 March 1982
Letter of thanks from Mollie Butler for both my letter and what I wrote about Rab in my column.

17 March 1982
Read R.L. Stevenson's *Weir of Hermiston*, an unfinished novel about a Scottish judge of overbearing temperament and his radical son. Superbly done.

23 March 1982
Dine with Terence and Diane Maxwell.* Diane tells me that her father was offered an earldom, but declined it as he had neither a country house nor a fortune, so he was given the Garter instead.

Norman St John-Stevas would passionately like the Speakership after George Thomas. I tell him how discreet he would have to be. He replies: 'There are the weekends.'

29 March 1982
On the subject of a successor to Harold Macmillan as Chancellor of Oxford University, Geoffrey Warnock† thinks that all the obvious politicians are too controversial. So it may be best to elect a judge. When Macmillan stood, Warnock voted for Oliver Franks. Geoffrey also tells me that so loathed was Evelyn Waugh at Hertford that when he died the college passed a resolution that it should not be represented at his funeral.

Send off another 100 or so pages of *KGV* to Windsor.

Very disturbing news: Argentina invades the Falkland Islands.

3 April 1982
Parliament sits at 11 a.m.: the first such Saturday assembly since Suez in 1956, which I attended. Hear a rather rattled Mrs Thatcher on the wireless, followed by an unusually confident Michael Foot. Nigel Fisher‡ makes rather an ass of himself by urging that Argentina should not be allowed to take

---

* Diane Maxwell (1912–99), dau. of Sir Austen Chamberlain.
† Sir Geoffrey Warnock (1923–95), Principal of Hertford Coll., Oxford 1971–88; Vice-Chancellor of Oxford University 1981–5.
‡ Sir Nigel Fisher (1913–96), Conservative politician. MP for Hitchin 1950–55 and for Surbiton 1955–83; biographer of Iain Macleod (1973).

part in the Football World Cup as a punishment – although I expect that it exactly reflects what the man in the street is thinking.

5 April 1982
It is announced on the 1 o'clock news that Peter Carrington has resigned as Foreign Secretary as a result of the Argentine humiliation. It is a deplorable blow to the Government – and to the nation.

Rab Butler's memorial service at Westminster Abbey. I sit in the South Transept, opposite Mrs Thatcher, who occupies a choir stall. Two places away from her is Peter Carrington, listed of course in the service booklet as Secretary of State for Foreign and Commonwealth Affairs, who reads the lesson with grave dignity. Admirable bidding prayer by the Dean, Edward Carpenter.[*] Why must we always have Cardinal Hume[†] taking part in every great Anglican occasion. Admirable address by Harry Williams, including an allusion to John Robinson's *Honest to God*, for which Rab had such contempt. At the end of the service, a little group of ex-Prime Ministers: Macmillan, Home, Wilson and Callaghan. Heath is in China.

6 April 1982
Enoch Powell complains that his name was not in *The Times* list this morning of those attending Rab's memorial service; nor was mine, though it did appear in the *Telegraph*. Enoch tells me how savage and bitter he is about the incompetence of the Foreign Office in general and of Peter Carrington in particular. When I ask him whether he hates all Foreign Secretaries to disparage them thus, he replies: 'Yes, especially when they are down.'

8 April 1982
Poor Nicky Gordon-Lennox is deeply depressed by the universal attacks on the FO for its supposed failure over the Falkland Islands and Argentina – whereas it is the politicians who are to blame for thinking that we can police the world, even in 1982.

12 April 1982
Nicky Gordon-Lennox tells me that in spite of the Falklands crisis, all the usual FO doors remained locked throughout the weekend and Nicky had, with his colleagues, to use some small side entrance.

---

* The Revd Dr Edward Carpenter (1910–98), Dean of Westminster 1974–85; biographer of Archbishop Geoffrey Fisher (1991).
† His Eminence Basil Hume (1923–99), Cardinal Archbishop of Westminster 1976–99.

14 April 1982

George Morpeth* tells me that the Duchess of Windsor is already beginning to go a bit gaga. When he lunched there she said: 'What was the name of my first husband?'

George also says that when Dorothy Macmillan, tiring of life with Bob Boothby, returned to Harold Macmillan there was no emotional reconciliation or apology. The doorbell rang, and there she was with her suitcase. She said: 'Are there any letters?'

16 April 1982

To Windsor. Katharine Graham† lectures in St George's Chapel on 'Fairness in the Media'. Rather woolly. I have some pleasant talk with the new Head Master of Eton and his wife, Eric and Poppy Anderson,‡ excellent and sensible Scots, who tell me they have heard much of me from Martin Charteris.

29 April 1982

Acute political tension over our advance on the Falklands Islands: Michael Foot, having at first been unwontedly brave, now has cold feet. Tony Benn wants us immediately to withdraw all our task force.

4 May 1982

Nicky Gordon-Lennox is as gloomy as I am about the outcome of the Falklands crisis. I cannot share any of the rejoicing at our having sunk an old Argentinian cruiser: the more we wound Argentina's pride, the more they will refuse to budge from the Falkland Islands. It is Thatcherism at its worst. An hour after talking to Nicky I listen to the news and the horror of HMS *Sheffield* having been sunk.

18 May 1982

Peter Carrington to lunch at Claridge's. The last time he lunched with me here he was Foreign Secretary and all the hotel waiters hovered round the table in a state of near-ecstasy. Today, with Peter in the political wilderness, I notice a just perceptible lowering of the temperature.

Peter is bitter that the dispute with Argentina over the Falkland Islands

---

* George Howard, 13th Earl of Carlisle, Viscount Morpeth 1963–94 (b. 1949), academic and commentator on Baltic affairs.

† (1917–2011), American publisher. Chair of the Board of the *Washington Post* 1973–93.

‡ Poppy (later Lady) Anderson (b. 1935), Governor, now Emeritus, of the RSC. In fact she hailed from Skipton, Yorkshire.

has left the Conservative Party at the mercy of the hard-headed jingoists. For the time being he is not going to the House of Lords, where anything he said would be meticulously analysed; if he did not speak, that too would be interpreted as hostile to the Prime Minister. She did in fact try to persuade him not to resign, although there is hardly any issue on which they agreed. 'Unlike me, she likes a fight over everything.'

Peter has had something like 1,000 letters since his resignation, with only perhaps a dozen that were hostile. Every Cabinet minister wrote, except the one man whose bacon he saved by resigning: John Nott,* the Minister of Defence. 'When I first became a Cabinet minister, it was a pleasure to dine with any of one's colleagues. Now there are only three: Jim Prior,† Willie Whitelaw and Quintin Hailsham.'

An amusing reminiscence of dining with Queen Juliana of the Netherlands in a magnificent room of the Palace in Amsterdam. When he expressed admiration, she said: 'Rembrandt painted a picture for this room.' Peter asked: 'Where is it?' The Queen: 'Oh, I don't know. It wasn't good enough.' It is now in the Royal Palace at Stockholm.

The Carringtons had Humphrey Atkins to lunch the other day, and also asked Ted Heath, who could hardly contain his glee at the difficulties of the Thatcher Government. Humphrey later told Peter it was the first time Ted had spoken to him for six years. Ted said to Peter: 'I suppose you will be going to the House of Lords to receive the plaudits for having behaved so honourably.' This may have been meant as a joke, but was delivered in sour and vicious tones. Afterwards Iona‡ commented: 'That man is corroded.' Peter is determined not to follow Ted's example in going on foreign tours in a semi-official way. Nor will he resume any of his directorships for the time being. But he may be pressed to accept the appointment of Secretary General of NATO (which Christopher Soames would like but will not get). Peter does not want the job; I have the impression, however, that he may feel obliged to undertake it.§

Peter says that during his last journey abroad as Foreign Secretary, he discovered that Begin,¶ Prime Minister of Israel, has a sense of humour. Peter said to him: 'One day you will <u>have</u> to negotiate with the PLO, just as we have

---

* Sir John Nott (b. 1932), Conservative politician. Sec. of State for Defence 1981–3.
† Baron Prior of Brampton (1927–2016), Conservative politician. MP for Waveney 1959–87; Sec. of State for Employment 1979–81; Sec. of State for Northern Ireland 1981–4.
‡ Lady Carrington (1920–2009) worked as a translator in World War II.
§ Lord Carrington was Sec. Gen. of NATO 1984–8.
¶ Menachem Begin (1913–92), Prime Minister of Israel 1977–83.

had to negotiate with terrorists – like Mugabe.[*] And of course there have been others.' Begin: 'You mean like me.'

20 May 1982
As all negotiations between us and Argentina seem to have failed, it looks as if an all-out invasion by our task force to recapture the Falklands is imminent.

21 May 1982
News of our landing in force on the Falklands: much air activity and the prospect of casualties.

26 May 1982
Depressing news from the Falklands: the Argentines have sunk two more of our ships. Most people in England thought that it would have been almost a walkover against a volatile and mildly humorous enemy.

Lunch with King Constantine at Claridge's. We discuss the Falklands. South America is less enraged with us than with the USA for giving us support. Tino says that of course it was wrong of Argentina to invade the Falklands. What they should have done was to land briefly, pack the British Governor off to England, withdraw their forces, and offer to negotiate. They would then have had a strong moral position. We agree how horrible it is to hear of a ship going down, possessing as it does a life of its own.

27 May 1982
Isaiah Berlin tells me a story of the late Duke of Gloucester at a gala performance of an opera at Covent Garden. Talking in the interval to some world-class singer, he enquired: 'And when did you last sing this role?' The man replied, rather puzzled: 'About four months ago.' Duke of Gloucester: 'What a good memory you must have.'

28 May 1982
Gloomy news: pictures of the ship sunk by the Argentines, HMS *Sheffield*. And a memorial service for the men of another ship sunk, HMS *Coventry*. Other depressing aspects of the conflict too. Then, ten minutes later, a news flash to say that we have captured one of the Argentine strongholds in the Falklands.

---

[*] Robert Mugabe (b. 1924), President of Zimbabwe 1987–2017.

29 May 1982

Derek Boorman* is critical both of the Press and TV people who deal with the Falklands, and of the Ministry of Defence's handling of the news. 'They are failed journalists with huge salaries.' He believes they have taken too contemptuous a view of our Argentine opponents. 'Instead of emphasising that 40 per cent are conscripts, they should emphasise that 60 per cent are regulars; Argentina has not run short of either planes or pilots; many of them have the spirit of polo players and racing drivers.' He is particularly furious at the press-concocted rumour that there is a deep division of opinion among the Chiefs of Staff. The other day a well-known journalist asked Derek to lunch. Derek replied that as he could not talk of military operations, such a meeting would cause problems both to guest and host. The journalist replied: 'You are doing your cause no good.' Your cause, not our cause.

Our paratroopers have captured Darwin and Goose Green on the way to retake the capital, Port Stanley. But sadly, the Commanding Officer of the Parachute Regiment, Lieutenant-Colonel 'H' Jones,† has been killed.

30 May 1982

I am sickened by papers such as the *Sunday Times* and the *Observer*, which on the Falklands issue arrogate to themselves the role of an independent and not always friendly critic of both political policy and military operations.

2 June 1982

Lunch with John Patten,‡ MP for Oxford. He has charm and style. Much talk on who is to succeed George Thomas as Speaker of the Commons. Norman St John-Stevas would be considered too indiscreet in his private life and perhaps in his conversation; Edward du Cann too encumbered by his past business life; Paul Channon, with his love of Westminster and knowledge of procedure, would be admirable in every way, but is too young at present. So that effectively leaves Bernard Weatherill,§ Chairman of Ways and Means: not a strong personality, but a nice man. To displace him there would have

---

* Lt-Gen. Sir Derek Boorman (b. 1930), Dir. of Military Operations at the Ministry of Defence 1980–82; Commander, British Forces in Hong Kong 1982–5.

† Lt-Col. Herbert Jones (1940–82), CO 2nd Bn Parachute Regiment during the Falklands War. He was killed at the Battle of Goose Green and awarded a posthumous VC.

‡ Baron Patten of Wincanton (b. 1945), Conservative politician. MP for City of Oxford 1979–83 and for Oxford West and Abingdon 1983–97; Sec. of State for Education 1992–4.

§ Baron Weatherill of North East Croydon (1920–2007), Speaker of the House of Commons 1983–92.

to be a very big figure indeed; otherwise three of the four offices of the Chair would be in Tory hands. Weatherill is proud of being a tailor, and carries a silver thimble in his pocket. He also likes to tell the story of how, as a new Member, he was in one of the recesses of the huge washroom when he heard one Knight of the Shires say to another: 'I'm told me tailor's boy is a Member now. 'Straodinary thing.'

9 June 1982
John Grigg tells me that Michael Foot is now absolutely besotted with admiration for Margaret Thatcher's handling of the Falklands crisis and the assault on the Argentine forces.

15 June 1982
Relief at the end of the fighting in the Falklands is tempered by news of Welsh Guards casualties: about forty Guardsmen killed when their landing ship was hit by a bomb.

17 June 1982
Jack Plumb tells me that it was Harold Macmillan who suggested to the PM that she should appoint a top, trusted civil servant to help her over the Falklands conflict. So she chose Michael Palliser, which put other contenders' noses out of joint.

21 June 1982
Dine at Brooks's when the news breaks that a son has been born to the Princess of Wales. Poor soul, with Gordonstoun, Outward Bound and Atlantic College looming ahead.*

22 June 1982
Willie Whitelaw tells me that the bombing of the ship in which so many Welsh Guardsmen lost their lives was a bad and unnecessary mistake. The men should have been landed by night. The reason that no officers were killed was that they had already gone ashore for an O-group.† Willie also expresses his deep hatred of Enoch Powell.

Peter Carrington was offered our Washington Embassy by Mrs Thatcher, but turned it down. 'I was not attracted by the job,' he told me. 'In any case, I

---

* K.R.'s fears were unfounded. Prince William received a traditional education at Ludgrove School, Eton and St Andrews University.
† Order Group.

might have had it only for a year' – an interesting reflection on Conservative election prospects.

When I ask William Waldegrave whom he would like to see as Speaker in succession to George Thomas, he instantly says: 'Paul Channon.'

William also gives me the origin of the nickname 'Red Robert' for Birley.[*] It was not owing to any manifestation of radicalism during his years as Head Master of Eton, but goes back to his post-war job with the Control Commission, in charge of German education. On his wall was a picture of Brahms.

Robert Wade-Gery tells me how Mrs Thatcher continues to use senior people, especially those at the Foreign Office, as doormats. I ask Robert why they don't stand up to her. He replies: 'Because she's a woman.'

23 June 1982

Robin Day comes to my summer party. He is enchanted by my old wooden wireless set. 'Has it Hilversum on the dial?' he asks. 'Yes, it has: two Hilversum stations.' He tells me, to my surprise, what a failure he thinks his life has been.

8 July 1982

Talk to Peter Carrington about the Falklands inquiry under the Chairmanship of Oliver Franks. He is furious at a piece in today's *Times* saying that he will be 'on trial' before the inquiry. He says that the report, when eventually it emerges, will stress that (a) our intelligence on Argentinian intentions towards the Falklands should have been better, and (b) our Embassy in Buenos Aires ought to have reported more fully to London.

14 July 1982

Talk to Dwin Bramall,[†] newly promoted to be Chief of the Defence Staff, a smallish, squat, grey-haired man of much charm. He learned painting at Eton under Wilfrid Blunt,[‡] who was grateful to him, for it made painting respectable in the eyes of Claude Elliott.[§] Dwin happened to be Captain of the XI.

---

[*] Sir Robert Birley (1903–82), headmaster and educational administrator. Headmaster of Charterhouse 1935–47; educational adviser to the military governor, Allied Control Commission, Germany 1947–9; Head Master of Eton 1949–63; Professor of Education at Witwatersrand University 1964–7, where he campaigned against apartheid.

[†] FM Edwin Bramall, Baron Bramall of Bushfield (b. 1923), Chief of the Defence Staff 1982–5.

[‡] (1901–87), art teacher. Curator of the Watts Gallery, Compton.

[§] Sir Claude Elliott (1888–1973), Head Master of Eton 1933–49, subsequently Provost 1949–65.

15 July 1982

Talk with Patrick Cormack* at his office in the Commons annexe. We discuss the future of the Speakership. Patrick is much in the confidence of George Thomas, who is likely to retire as Speaker of the Commons in early 1983. His successor will be a Conservative. Bernard Weatherill is the name most often mentioned.

16 July 1982

An extraordinary episode of a man who a few days ago penetrated all the security arrangements at Buckingham Palace and sat on the Queen's bed for ten minutes, with a bleeding hand and clutching a broken glass ashtray. No novelist would have dared to imagine such a thing.

17 July 1982

In the local grocery shop, I run into a very worried George Brown: 'I have written a strong article on the train drivers' strike for tomorrow's *Sunday Express*. But there are negotiations for a settlement, and I may have to alter it. Can I do so in time?' I say: 'That's what happens to you when you become a blackleg journalist.'

20 July 1982

Lunch with the Queen Mother at Clarence House. We have a long and vivacious talk. I am amazed that she should mind what the newspapers write about the Royal Family. She tells me, as if I had no connection with Fleet Street: 'I really think that the Press does more harm than all the Willie Hamiltons† put together.' It is rather touching that she should confide this to <u>me</u>.

I tell her the story of how Robert Birley came to be called Red Robert. 'Oh, that's very funny,' she says, adding that no good Head Master is ever popular.

On George V she says that she thought Dickie Mountbatten was rather a bounder in some ways, as when he drove his speedboat off Cowes and made a dangerous wash. I tell the Queen Mother that although he was most kind to me, I have discovered that not all his stories were accurate. Queen Mother: 'Of course, and there were so many of them!' The Queen Mother describes going to see Ramsay MacDonald at Chequers. 'He took us to see some of the little churches in the neighbourhood. Now darling Mrs Thatcher would

---

* Baron Cormack of Enville (b. 1939), Conservative politician. MP for Cannock 1970–74 and for South West Staffordshire 1974–83; author of historical works.
† ('Willie') Hamilton (1917–2000), Labour politician with strong republican views. MP for Fife 1950–87.

never do <u>that</u>! But then she has other great qualities such as PATRIOTISM – that's what we want!'

Dine with Harold Lever.* The most memorable part of the evening is talking to David Owen. He is much more agreeable and less arrogant than when he was Foreign Secretary. Harold Lever gives him some pertinent advice about the SDP: 'It is no use discussing political manoeuvres if you have no policies.' I ask Owen why Roy Jenkins said practically nothing about the Falklands War. Owen: 'He could not make up his mind. He is an old-fashioned Liberal. What the party needed to demonstrate was its PATRIOTISM!' Exactly what the Queen Mother had said to me a few hours earlier.

29 August 1982
Re-read John le Carré's wicked novel about Eton, *A Murder of Quality*, with its cruel portraits of Oliver van Oss and Grizel Hartley. What a revenge he took.

2 September 1982
Stay with Prince Eddie at Anmer House. He takes me over to Flitcham for a drink with charming old Sir William Fellowes,† the Agent at Sandringham from 1936 to 1964. He is full of interesting reminiscences. Although he saw little of King George V, he came to know Queen Mary well. One day she pointed out some hated ivy that had grown on a cottage wall. 'Who's responsible,' she asked him, 'the gardeners or the foresters?' He replied: 'I think the Agent.'

Vast amounts of game were given away. If ever King George VI heard of anyone with a misfortune, he would say: 'Send them some game.' Every stationmaster between Wolferton and Ballater was on the list. Keepers died rich men, and even the beaters made a lot out of it.

It is curious, he says, how King George V, even after moving to the big house in 1926, had York Cottage kept up till his death.

3 September 1982
Prince Eddie's views are thoughtful and sometimes unexpected. He does not share the general Conservative view that the Falklands Islands commemoration service in St Paul's was trendily unpatriotic.

---

* Baron Lever of Manchester (1914–95), Labour politician and barrister. MP for three successive Manchester seats 1945–79; Chancellor of the Duchy of Lancaster 1974–9.
† Sir William Fellowes (1899–1986), Agent to the Sandringham Estate 1936–64.

Later we drive over to Burnham Thorpe, where I am spending a couple of days with Solly Zuckerman. Solly in fine form. He describes how Gladwyn Jebb, staying with him at Birmingham for the Jewellers' Dinner, appeared at the top of the stairs, half dressed, and shouted: 'Solly, have you a spare KCMG?'

30 September 1982

Nico Henderson[*] tells me two good stories about Rab Butler when he was Foreign Secretary. During negotiations in Moscow he mixed up his own brief and a similar one prepared by the FO on what Khrushchev's position was likely to be. Having expounded the wrong one, he ended triumphantly: 'That is our position.' Khrushchev: 'But that's ours!'

And when taken to see Moscow University, Rab asked his guide: 'Does the university receive any State help?' The Russians thought that this elementary blunder concealed a penetrating and subtle question.

1 October 1982

Lunch with Nico Henderson at Brooks's. He now has an ingrained dislike of Mrs Thatcher, who during the Falklands campaign was believed to follow his advice, but in fact harangued him: 'What do you know of the British Empire?'

Nico will not readily forgive Gladwyn Jebb. Although a frequent visitor to the Paris Embassy when Nico was Ambassador, he secretly sent the FO a plan to reduce its grandeur and to turn part of it into flats.

He has two books in mind: one on the Foreign Secretaries he has known, another on the US politicians he has known. I advise him to include personal observations and anecdotes, thereby making it attractive for the general reader.[†]

5 October 1982

Jim Callaghan tells me of his being summoned to give evidence to the Falklands Commission.

He also tells me a story of Ernie Bevin. When a dinner was being given for King Haakon VII of Norway[‡] at Lancaster House, the first time it had

---

[*] Sir Nicholas Henderson (1919–2009), Ambassador to the Federal Republic of Germany 1972–5 and to France 1975–9; brought out of retirement by Margaret Thatcher to serve as Ambassador to the US 1979–82.
[†] Nicholas Henderson subsequently published *The Private Office* (1984); *Mandarin* (1994); *Old Friends and Modern Instances* (2000) and *The Private Office Revisited* (2001).
[‡] (1872–1957), King of Norway 1905–57.

been used for Government hospitality, Bevin said to his Principal Private Secretary, Frank Roberts:* 'See that it is properly furnished.' 'Suits of armour, perhaps?' enquired Roberts. Bevin: 'I told you to decorate it, not make it look like the first Act of '*Amlet*.'

6 October 1982

Dine with Peter and Iona Carrington in Ovington Square. How stylish of him to give a dinner party while the whole of the Conservative Party is having its annual Conference in Brighton. He is to be Chairman of GEC. Peter is still gloomy though. I say to him: 'You must be pleased to become Chairman of one of the great industrial companies in the world.'

'There are better things.'

'What?'

'Being Foreign Secretary.'

12 October 1982

Nico Henderson was at the PM's dinner at No. 10 last night for the Falklands operation. He sat next to General Jeremy Moore,[†] the land commander, who told him two interesting things: (a) one factor in the British victory was that the Argentinians, although they fought bravely, never counter-attacked, (b) our soldiers found a lot of beef on the islands: the Argentinians had obviously smuggled it through the naval blockade.

At the end of the dinner, Margaret Thatcher said: 'Shall we join the ladies?'

17 October 1982

Martin Charteris talks to me about the problems of choosing a new Head Master of Eton. Advertising does not necessarily bring the right candidates and could certainly attract the wrong ones. Instead, the Provost writes to about eight likely candidates to ask if they would care to be considered.

When Robert Birley was being interviewed by the Provost and Fellows he asked what his salary would be. Henry Marten passed him a slip of paper on which were written three figures, one under the other in descending order. The top two had been crossed out.

To choose the present Head Master, Eric Anderson, the Provost and a committee of Fellows met in Robert Armstrong's room at the Treasury to

---

* Sir Frank Roberts (1907–98), Ambassador to the USSR 1960–62 and to the Federal Republic of Germany 1963–8.

† Maj.-Gen. Sir Jeremy Moore (1928–2007), commander of the British land forces during the Falklands War. He received the surrender of the Argentine forces.

interview candidates. Then lunch at Brooks's on steak and kidney pudding. To the Treasury again, and a quick unanimous decision.

26 October 1982

Harold Wilson tells me that instead of writing his autobiography, he would have preferred a book of character sketches. 'But George Weidenfeld and my wife both said no.'

Talking of King George V, I ask Harold to guess who was his favourite Prime Minister –

'Baldwin?'

'No, MacDonald.'

'What did he think of Baldwin?'

'He thought he was lazy.'

'We could do with a lazy Prime Minister.'

27 October 1982

Dine Pratt's. Nigel Napier* tells me that whenever Princess Margaret saw Tommy Lascelles, she would say, 'There goes the man who ruined my life.'

Willie Whitelaw is also dining, furious at the contempt and discourtesy with which the Chairman of the Police Federation greeted him. There was even a police car outside blaring its siren as a gesture of support for the barracking. Willie has since had many letters from policemen apologising for the behaviour of their colleagues. He says how understanding the Queen was to him over the recent intrusion of a madman into her bedroom.

28 October 1982

Cocktail party given by the Luxembourg Embassy. Some invigorating talk with Alec Home. He tells me a remark of Linky's I have never heard before. He told Baldwin: 'If His Majesty's Government continues like this, a row of humble pies looms ahead.'

29 October 1982

Read *Stranger and Brother: A Portrait of C.P. Snow* by his brother Philip Snow.† It is full of odd sidelights on Charles. He thought he should have had both the OM and the Nobel Prize for Literature. Philip reveals that the character Lord Hillmorton from *In Their Wisdom* is based on Harold Macmillan.

---

* Sir Nigel Napier, 14th Lord Napier (1930–2012), Scottish soldier and courtier.
† (1915–2012), colonial administrator and Bursar of Rugby School.

31 October 1982

Work throughout the evening on the King's funeral for my biography, oblivious even to *Die Walküre* on the wireless. The story of the wreath in the shape of the King's pony left by an East End coster makes me weep and I end the book with this.

6 November 1982

To Cambridge, reading on the way that dear old Stephen Roskill is dead. Lunch with Hugh Trevor-Roper at Peterhouse. He complains to me of the parochialism of Cambridge. On noticing in *The Times* that a former Fellow of the college had died, Hugh told the porter to fly the college flag at half-mast. 'Yes,' the porter replied, 'just for today.' Hugh explained that it should be flown at half-mast until after the funeral. Porter: 'But the funeral is not in Cambridge.' In the same vein, a college cleaner, seeing some London telephone directories in the Master's Lodge, wanted to throw them out as rubbish. 'They are not Cambridge ones,' she said.

The Cambridge dons have no loyalty to a college, only to a faculty. They fight over the division of college offices only for the money. Hugh takes me round the college, including the old library, which has no books at all on its shelves. Apparently, many of them were stolen. So now what remains of the library is stored in packing cases.

Stay with Victor Rothschild in Herschel Road. Victor tells me that, invited by Edward VIII to stay at Fort Belvedere, he could not resist packing some writing paper and a face towel with the Royal cipher. When he arrived home he found that both had been discreetly removed.

Some talk of MI5. They had reason to think that Edward VIII when Prince of Wales was in too-close touch with Ribbentrop.

8 November 1982

To Toynbee Hall to hear Quintin Hailsham speak on the law. He makes some sharp remarks on the hounding of public men by the Press, citing the example of a judge, much criticised after a judgment, who died as a result of this.

'Should there then,' I ask him later, 'be some curb on what the Press may say of a judgement or a sentence?' Quintin: 'No, the judges must put up with it.'

1983

1983 was the year of Margaret Thatcher's second general election victory. On 9 January she visited the liberated Falkland Islands. Unemployment reached a record high of 3,224,715 on 3 February. The Liberal Party won the Bermondsey by-election on 24 February. Sir William Walton died on 8 April. The Budget on 15 March cut taxes by £2 billion. The one-pound coin was introduced on 21 April. Mrs Thatcher called a general election for 9 June. On 26 May the Conservatives were twenty-two points ahead of Labour in a MORI opinion poll. On 9 June Mrs Thatcher won a landslide victory with a majority of 144 seats over Michael Foot's Labour Party which won only 28 per cent of the vote. Tony Blair and Gordon Brown entered Parliament for the first time.

After her election victory Margaret Thatcher reshuffled the Cabinet. Michael Foot resigned as leader of the Labour Party on 12 June. Roy Jenkins resigned as leader of the SDP on 14 June and was succeeded by David Owen. The new Chancellor of the Exchequer, Nigel Lawson, announced public-spending cuts of £500 million on 7 July. Former Prime Minister Harold Wilson became a life peer on 21 July. Neil Kinnock was elected leader of the Labour Party on 2 October. Cecil Parkinson resigned as Trade and Industry Secretary on 14 October following revelations about his private life. US cruise missiles arrived at RAF Greenham Common in Berkshire on 14 November. The House of Lords voted to allow television broadcasts of its proceedings on 8 December. William Golding won the Nobel Prize in Literature on 10 December. The IRA bombed Harrods on 17 December.

19 January 1983

To the House of Lords for a friendly and not too crowded cocktail party given by John Hunt, the former Cabinet Secretary.* Chips Maclean tells me that there is an odd little controversy in the Palace. In the East Gallery some quite pretty early Victorian murals have come to light during redecoration,

---

* Sir John Hunt, Baron Hunt of Tanworth (1919–2008), Cabinet Secretary 1973–9, the first Roman Catholic holder of the office.

but they are to be covered up again, which is regretted by the non-experts. Chips adds that behind the panels of the Waterloo Chamber at Windsor there are still the Disney cartoons painted for the wartime pantomimes in which the Princesses took part.

20 January 1983

Nicholas Gordon-Lennox comes in for a drink. He tells me that Anthony Parsons, who on retiring as our man at the United Nations went to No. 10 as Mrs Thatcher's part-time adviser on foreign affairs, is having a hard time. One day, Parsons told Nicky, after the PM had asked him something, he replied: 'I am afraid I don't understand.' PM: 'You would if you had been here yesterday.' Parsons: 'But I only work three days a week.' The relationship is not likely to last.*

21 January 1983

Dine at Brooks's with Jim Lees-Milne and Derek Hill, the artist, and Michael Bloch.† Derek describes how Mountbatten was once invited to a Mitford family wedding, though he did not know them well. Told that at luncheon he would sit next to Pamela, he diligently enquired about her. When they sat down, he at once began: 'You are Debo's sister, you are called Woman in the family, you were married to Derek Jackson, etc., etc.' Pamela replied: 'How clever of you to know so much about me. But who are you?'‡

Michael Bloch is a protégé of Maître Blum, the Duchess of Windsor's lawyer and self-appointed guardian. A year or so ago we had a sharp exchange of letters when he wrote to deny my piece in 'Albany' that the Queen Mother had sent flowers to the Duchess of Windsor during her visit to Paris. Jim Lees-Milne warns me that he is therefore shy of me. But I put myself out to be agreeable, and we have some interesting talk. Bloch has since looked up my correspondence with the Duke and was impressed to find, attached to one of my letters: 'Make six copies of this.' It was the account from the Curzon papers of his visit to Japan as Prince of Wales. Bloch proposes to write at least one more book about the Windsors. Unfortunately for him, the best of the papers are beyond his reach. At the Duke's funeral at Windsor, Mountbatten and Prince Philip persuaded the Duchess to part with them. Within a day

---

* Parsons left the post in 1983.
† (b. 1953), author of several books on the Windsors; editor of the James Lees-Milne diaries (2000–08).
‡ Deborah Cavendish, Duchess of Devonshire (1920–2014), youngest of the six Mitford sisters; played a key role in the restoration of Chatsworth. Pamela Jackson (1907–94), second of the Mitford sisters; m. in 1936 Prof. Derek Jackson (1906–82), spectroscopist and jockey.

or two of her return to Paris, a truck drew up and whisked them away. They are now in the Royal Archives at Windsor and Bloch has been denied access to them: the only paper he was allowed to see is disobliging about the Duke.

23 January 1983

For all her ebullience, Jean Trumpington has been deeply wounded by an episode in the House of Lords. The Government Whips asked her to make a speech in a debate on the storage of information in computers: presumably there was a shortage of speakers. Although she knew nothing about the subject, she agreed, providing a speech was written for her. On receiving it, she sent it to Quintin Hailsham, asking if it made sense. She received a reply that it did. But throughout the delivery of the speech, Quintin sat on the Woolsack laughing, muttering and gesticulating. This put her off her stroke. As she left the Chamber, she paused by the Woolsack and said to Quintin, 'You made me feel very embarrassed.' Quintin replied: 'I meant to.' He seems to play the *enfant terrible* out of boredom, perhaps mischief or even malice. It was foolish of Jean to speak on a subject on which she was ignorant, but she had after all consulted Quintin first.

27 January 1983

Lunch at Lancaster House in honour of 'The Year of Small and Medium-sized Enterprises'. Peter Middleton,* who is shortly to become the new Permanent Head of the Treasury, tells me that letters from No. 10 are over-franked: not from the PM, but from the First Lord of the Treasury. That is characteristic of Mrs Thatcher. So too is the ruthlessness with which she has bagged all the best Treasury silver for No. 10.

28 January 1983

Alec Home tells me how Field Marshal Montgomery† once much admired a tree at the Hirsel and asked for some cuttings. When next they met, Monty said that they had not taken in his garden. It emerged that he had planted them upside down.

6 February 1983

I hear reports of the school where the Princess of Wales taught infants. She

---

* Sir Peter Middleton (b. 1934), Permanent Secretary to the Treasury 1983–91.
† Bernard Montgomery, Viscount Montgomery of Alamein (1887–1976), in World War II commander of the British Eighth Army in the Western Desert, the Allied invasion of Italy and of the Allied ground forces during Operation Overlord. C.-in-C. of the British Army of the Rhine and then CIGS.

is apparently not very clever and certainly without any of the intellectual resources needed in marriage to the Prince of Wales.

7 February 1983

John Grigg tells me that he lectured to the Political Society at Eton the other day, with Martin Charteris present. When John was questioned about his comments on the Queen nearly thirty years ago, Martin intervened to say: 'The monarchy has been much the better for what you said.'

John also asks me whether King George V took the pledge in 1915 on his own volition, or at the suggestion of Lloyd George: there is no direct evidence. I tell him that I think L.G. bounced him into it. John agrees with me.

17 February 1983

Willie Whitelaw tells me he is relieved to have overcome a Tory rebellion and to have got his amendments to the Immigration Bill through the Commons last night. 'Roy Hattersley* made the mistake of attacking me fiercely. That rallied our own side. He should have heaped praise on me.'

22 February 1983

Lunch with Oliver Millar† at Brooks's. He has an incisive mind and seems remarkably free from those nervous twitches which so often convulse courtiers; but then he is so much else.

He has little regard for Robert Rhodes James. 'I wanted to ask him about his forthcoming book on the Prince Consort, especially his influence on the arts, but all he wanted to talk about was his own political career.' When James said, 'I belong to the Ted Heath club,' Oliver replied: 'There can't be much of a waiting list for that.' James was much put out.

23 February 1983

Martin Gilliat to dine. He reads the whole of my supposedly controversial chapter on George V and the Tsar and says he finds it enthralling.

It is not easy to work for the Queen Mother. She complains to Martin either that he does not give her enough to do, or that he is killing her with overwork.

Already there is a queue of supplicants to write the official life of the

---

* Baron Hattersley of Sparkbrook (b. 1932), Labour politician, author and journalist. MP for Birmingham Sparkbrook 1964–97.
† Sir Oliver Millar (1923–2007), Surveyor of the Queen's Pictures 1972–88; Dir. of the Royal Collection 1987–8.

Queen Mother. To my surprise, Martin tells me that Duff Hart-Davis[*] is among them. I am less tempted by the task than I used to be.

26 February 1983
Read Siegfried Sassoon's diaries, 1915–1918. Like other poets of the Great War he has a command of lyrical beauty in describing the countryside behind the lines. By contrast the bitterness of his verse becomes oppressive. How well he knew the value of his MC, not least in the eyes of his men.

1 March 1983
I lunch with Michael Fraser, now Lord Fraser of Kilmorack,[†] who for many years ran the Conservative Party behind the scenes. We exchange stories about Rab. When Michael retired, there was a dinner at which Rab said: 'There is nobody I would rather say farewell to than Michael Fraser.' And at a Central Office meeting he noticed that Peter Goldman was wearing a Cambridge University Conservative Association tie. Rab: 'Ah, a CUCA tie. I designed it. It's unwearable, of course. But it looks good on you.'

My other neighbour is Geoffrey de Deney,[‡] a senior Home Office official, who used to be Rab's Private Secretary. He says that on an issue on which Rab could not make up his mind, the department prepared an elaborate document giving both sides of the question, and asked Rab to indicate his preference. It came back bearing the minute: 'An excellent and thoughtful piece of work, RAB.'

2 March 1983
Robin Mackworth-Young to lunch with me at the Charing Cross Hotel. We touch briefly on the episode of my chapter on the Tsar in 1917. I learn that Michael Adeane _is_ rather hurt at the light in which his grandfather, Lord Stamfordham, emerges; and that he has the support of others, including of course Philip Moore. But Robin affirms that I have been entirely fair in my text. In any case, the Queen has passed my version, and it is that which really matters.

I enquire what sort of a biography of the Prince Consort has been produced by Robert Rhodes James. Robin is cautious, but indicates that he thinks little of it.

---

[*] (b. 1936), author and journalist.
[†] Sir Michael Fraser, Baron Fraser of Kilmorack of Rubislaw (1915–96), Dir. of the Conservative Research Dept. 1959–64.
[‡] Sir Geoffrey de Deney (1931–2015), Principal, Home Office 1961–9; Clerk of the Privy Council 1984–92.

3 March 1983

Lunch with Jonathan Aitken* at 8 Lord North Street. He shares my affection for Selwyn Lloyd, who was his godfather. The most interesting years of Selwyn's career were those immediately after Macmillan had sacked him in 1962. He deliberately cultivated a public reputation for loyalty and magnanimity, while doing all he could behind the scenes to bring about Macmillan's downfall. And when Home succeeded Macmillan, Selwyn returned in triumph to the Cabinet with enhanced honour.

6 March 1983

Walk across the park to lunch with Mollie Butler at the Hyde Park Hotel. Mollie in brave spirits, though lonely without Rab. She describes how she was one day going through the cellar at their house in Essex to weed out the old wine that needed drinking. She came up with some champagne. 'You mustn't drink <u>that</u>,' Rab told her, 'it's <u>good</u> champagne.'

Tony Howard is making slow progress with his biography of Rab: he has only just reached his meeting Sydney,† whom he married in 1926.

Mollie went to Marlborough College the other day for the unveiling of a memorial to Rab. Archbishop Runcie and his chaplain took her back to London in his car. Runcie said: 'We are all wets here.'

8 March 1983

Peter Tapsell tells me that Norman St John-Stevas has no chance of becoming Speaker when George Thomas retires at the end of the present Parliament: 'Mrs Thatcher wants pliable people everywhere, even in the Speaker's Chair. So it looks like being Weatherill.' Peter goes on: 'It is typical of her to have chosen Robin Leigh-Pemberton‡ as Governor of the Bank. He is a nice enough fellow, but quite incapable intellectually of talking with other top international bankers and governors on equal terms.'

Work until 11.30 p.m. collating the source references for *KGV*. Reach 1914: 168 of the 410 pages. It is like writing a gigantic imposition.

---

* (b. 1942), Conservative MP for Thanet East 1974–83 and for South Thanet 1983–97. War correspondent in Vietnam and Biafra; Minister for Defence Procurement 1992–4; Chief Secretary to the Treasury 1994–5; biographer of Richard Nixon (1993). In 1999 Aitken was convicted of perjury and spent seven months in prison.

† Sydney Butler (née Courtauld) (1902–54), first wife of Rab Butler. It was said of her that 'she flew like an arrow'.

‡ Baron Kingsdown of Pemberton (1926–2013), Governor of the Bank of England 1983–93.

9 March 1983

Immensely sad to read that Alan Lennox-Boyd* was killed last night, crossing the Fulham Road after dining in Chelsea. How easily I can imagine that
happening in the euphoria of a happy evening with friends.

12 March 1983

When Andrew Devonshire,† the Duke of Devonshire, joined the SDP, the
Labour MP Eric Varley‡ said: 'He will bring to the party that common touch
which Roy Jenkins lacks.'

19 March 1983

Lunch with Harold Lever in Eaton Square. Nice talk with him about the
virtues of grammar schools. This is inspired by a terrible sentence in Susan
Crosland's§ life of her late husband, the Labour Minister of Education,
Anthony Crosland. He said to her one day: 'If it's the last thing I do, I'm
going to destroy every fucking grammar school in England.' Harold speaks
movingly of how much Manchester Grammar School meant to poor Jewish
boys. 'To them, those cold wet dirty streets were Paradise.'

22 March 1983

Hartley Shawcross,¶ after twenty years of independence from political ties,
joins the SDP. It is really very foolish of him, particularly as he is at heart a
Thatcherite.

31 March 1983

Lunch with Philip Ziegler** at Brooks's. The first draft of his life of Mountbatten is complete. 'I wonder what effect it will have on his daughters, for whom
he was the nearest thing to Jesus Christ.' Philip has found no evidence of

---

* 1st Viscount Boyd of Merton (1904–83), Conservative politician. Sec. of State for the Col-
onies 1954–59.
† Andrew Cavendish, 11th Duke of Devonshire (1920–2004), Conservative, then Social
Democrat and later cross-bencher in the House of Lords.
‡ Baron Varley of Chesterfield (1932–2008), Labour politician. MP for Chesterfield 1964–84;
Sec. of State for Industry 1975–79.
§ (1927–2011), American journalist; widow of Anthony Crosland, whose biography she wrote
(1982).
¶ Baron Shawcross (1902–2003), barrister, politician, businessman; leading British prosecuting counsel in the Nuremberg Trials, 1945. As his political pilgrimage drifted away from
Labour in the 1950s he was dubbed 'Sir Shortly Floorcross'. Shawcross and his family were
among K.R.'s longest-standing friends.
** (b. 1929), former diplomat and eminent biographer.

Mountbatten's supposed homosexuality. Since it was *Private Eye* which first made public such suspicions soon after Mountbatten's death, Philip asked the editor, Richard Ingrams,[*] what evidence he had. Ingrams replied that he had none: it was just malice. In any case, Philip adds, Mountbatten cared too much for his naval career to risk any homosexual entanglements, if that were in fact his inclination. He did, however, have a habit of touching people he liked, particularly the young of both sexes.

7 May 1983
Grizel Hartley tells me two stories about Rab Butler. When they were neigh-bours of the Butlers on Mull, they found Rab paddling in the sea with a thermometer in his mouth. 'I am', he explained, 'taking the temperature of the water.'

The second tale took place just before Rab ceased to be Master of Trinity. He said to Mollie: 'We have too many possessions to fit into our Essex house. We must sell some of them – that canteen of silver cutlery, for instance.' So a leading Cambridge jeweller was asked to take it away for valuation. The man telephoned the next day in embarrassment. 'I am sorry to have to tell you', he said, 'that every piece bears the crest of Trinity College.' The cutlery went with the Lodge.

17 May 1983
On the General Election on 9 June, Maurice Macmillan[†] forecasts a Conserv-ative majority of no more than 35. He would not be against St John-Stevas for the Speakership – 'after all, it is only boys'.

Poor old Harold Macmillan: his legs and eyes are both failing, but he does have a machine for projecting a whole page of a book onto a screen.

Maurice is not too happy about Alistair Horne's[‡] appointment as Harold Macmillan's official biographer.

27 May 1983
To Windsor for the unveiling by the Queen Mother of the restored Lutyens memorial to King George V. It has an air of a village fete about it: not too much police supervision, the band of the Irish Guards with its dopey mascot

---

* (b. 1937), co-founder and second editor of *Private Eye*.
† Viscount Macmillan of Ovenden (1921–84), Conservative politician and son of Harold Macmillan. MP for Halifax 1955–64 and for Farnham/South West Surrey 1966–84; Chief Secretary to the Treasury 1970–72; Sec. of State for Employment 1972–3; Paymaster General 1973–4.
‡ Sir Alistair Horne (1925–2017), biographer and historian.

dog, Cormac, once put on a Company Conduct Sheet for 'Conduct to the prejudice of good order and military discipline, contrary to Section 69 of the Dog Act 1955.' This was 'for failure to eat the sweets offered to him by Queen Elizabeth the Queen Mother'. There is a pretty little pavilion from which the Queen Mother makes a charming speech, appearing scarcely to glance at her text. Lots of old soldiers in Brigade ties and their wives in herbaceous hats. There is then a tea party in the Castle Hotel. But the QM takes a broad view of tea: it is sparkling white wine and little things on toast. Martin Gilliat tells me that the QM would like to talk to me. She looks younger than ever. When I tell her that my *KGV* will be published in a very few weeks, she claps her hands.

7 June 1983

Lunch at Clarence House. I am the last to arrive and find the others drinking in the garden. The Queen Mother, in blue, looks as well as I have ever seen her. I give her one of the first copies of *King George V*, which she at once looks through, then carries round to show everyone. 'I'll lend it to you,' she says to one enthusiastic guest, then adds: 'No, I won't, you can buy it for yourself.'

The Queen Mother announces: 'We are having a picnic today.' But it is not like anyone else's picnic. There is a long table set under the trees with comfortable folding chairs for the guests and a proper dining-room chair with arms for the QM; also a big red velvet footstool for her. As always, lovely silver and china: the handles of the toast racks are in the form of Royal coronets and there is my favourite claret jug, an eagle with ruby eye. Two footmen in black livery, one in red. The food is even more delicious than usual. We begin with asparagus, covered with scrambled egg; then chicken, then strawberries embedded in thick cream; then cheese. The QM eats a little of everything, except the cheese, and drinks claret. I have white wine.

I am on the QM's left, facing the Mall. Although we are not far from the garden wall, the noise of the traffic hardly seems to penetrate. The QM says how much she regrets that she can no longer visit South Africa, 'such a beautiful and mystical country', because of political pressure, and questions me closely on whether there has been any improvement in apartheid. I tell her some of the ways in which it has become less oppressive. She also talks of Field Marshal Smuts – 'a good egg', she calls him.

Some wartime reminiscences, particularly of Winston arriving late for lunch at the Palace one day, rather flustered and carrying a little despatch box. 'I bring you victory,' he announced. It was news of El Alamein.

We talk of the North-East, of which she has always spoken with affection. I compare today with the turn of the century, when John Burns* said: 'The tragedy of the working classes is the poverty of their desires.' The QM is much taken by this and wonders how a man of Burns's humble education could have made so inspired a remark.

Queen Victoria crops up in our conversation too, and I tell her of how spectacles were forbidden at court in those days. It does not surprise her at all. She says: 'Of course I make no bones about wearing them.' In fact, I don't think she has ever worn them in public: her speeches are typed for her in enormous letters on a special typewriter.

As we finish our coffee, the QM says: 'Let us go into the next room,' pointing to a circle of garden chairs. We linger for only a few minutes, as she has an appointment with the Prime Minister of Australia, Bob Hawke,† this afternoon. Many affectionate farewells, then she disappears into the house, *King George V* under her arm.

10 June 1983

The Conservatives win a landslide election victory with 397 seats, the largest number since Anthony Eden's 344 in 1955. Labour are reduced to 209 seats, their lowest number since 1935. The Liberal/Social Democrat Alliance wins only 23 seats, despite gaining 7.7 million votes. They will press for proportional representation, which of course the Conservatives and Labour will oppose.

3 July 1983

Dine with Arnold Goodman in Portland Place to meet Lucian Freud.‡ He told us that when he received the insignia of the CH from the Queen he felt some resentment against the courtiers, who in supposedly putting him at his ease managed to be both patronising and irritating. The painter's eye was amazed by the Queen's complexion – 'as if the lines had been drawn on her face'.

Apparently he is a compulsive gambler, who loses literally tens of thousands of pounds a year. Arnold pleads with him: 'I wish that whenever you

---

* (1858–1943), trade unionist. MP For Battersea 1892–1918; President of the Local Government Board 1905–14.

† (b. 1929), Prime Minister of Australia 1983–91.

‡ (1922–2011), arguably the foremost British twentieth-century portrait painter. He lived a few yards away from K.R. in Brunswick Gardens. Once K.R. pointed out to me a tramp-like figure walking past his house and asked me to guess who it was. He told me it was Lucian Freud and then added, 'Ah, did you once see Shelley plain?'

sell a picture, you would send me half to put away for you.' But Freud does not want any money in the bank. He lives simply and will not face the problem of old age or incapacity.

Freud reads the *Sporting Life* every day; also the *Sunday Telegraph*, for he asks me about George V's failure to rescue the Tsar. But he finds the *Daily Telegraph* priggish – 'though not as priggish as the *Guardian*'. He confesses that he owes a debt to the Royal Family. Through the intercession of our own Prince George, Duke of Kent,* Eddie's father, he became a naturalised British subject in 1939, when a schoolboy of seventeen, thereby avoiding internment as an enemy alien.

He tells me that he lives 'like a snake' – one large meal a day, if that. As far as his painting habits go, he likes returning to the same subjects again and again. I find it extraordinary that he should entrust me with these confidences. I would like to see him again, but I believe he rarely ventures out.

3 August 1983
The start of my visit to the Bayreuth Festival with Prince Eddie. Up at six and Eddie calls for me in his Jaguar at eight on the dot. We drive down to Dover for the cross-Channel ferry and so across Europe to Bayreuth; just twenty-nine years since we last did the same journey.

4 August 1983
Arrive Bayreuth in the late morning and under a downpour. Stay at the Hotel Anker, in the centre of the town. We have quiet rooms at the back overlooking the rooftops.

Into a black tie at three and drive up to the Festspielhaus. Inside the Festspielhaus the atmosphere is as austere as ever: gloomy neo-classical columns; steeply banked rows of the hardest seats in the world – and without arms. Of course, no carpets. I have brought rather a large cushion with me, bought in Kensington Church Street a few days ago. It proves to be one of the best investments I have ever made. *Parsifal* is entrancingly sung, although the sets are rather messy, especially the uneven floors. At the end there are boos for the producer and for the Kundry.

6 August 1983
Look at the shops. Every window has a bust or picture of Wagner, though

---

* (1902–42), the fourth son of George V and Queen Mary. He died in an air crash while serving with the RAF.

there are almost as many of Sir Georg Solti,[*] the prefix is punctiliously included, in an advertisement for Decca recordings.

Tonight we have *Die Meistersinger* in an old-fashioned familiar production by Wolfgang Wagner;[†] one could count each of the several thousand leaves on the tree in the final Act. But, in common with so many producers, he <u>will</u> insist on playful movement among the chorus – back-slapping and beer-drinking – even during the most wonderful solos. A robust Hans Sachs and a melodious Walther, but seeing Geraint Evans[‡] as Beckmesser at Covent Garden has killed the role for everybody else.

7 August 1983

The sun emerges and we set out to visit Rosenau, near Coburg, the birthplace of the Prince Consort. We find Rosenau set in a pleasant park with a lake. It is on a hill, a not very large house of yellowish ochre with a steep roof and gable windows; also a separate little round tower overlooking fine woods and a stream. It must have been quite a catch for Prince Albert to marry Queen Victoria from such a comparatively modest estate, although they were of course first cousins.

Tonight it is *Rheingold*, the first opera of the new *Ring* cycle produced by Peter Hall[§] and conducted by Georg Solti. It begins excellently with apparently naked Rhine Maidens swimming in a great deal of real water. But the rest of the production is indifferent, and at the end Peter Hall makes no appearance, apparently annoyed at having been booed at the end of the first cycle. Solti does appear, to a rapturous roar of acclaim. The Wotan was lacking in dignity; how one sighs for Hans Hotter.[¶] One cliché of the production is too much smoke, which fills the Festspielhaus. Curious how this supposedly sophisticated audience giggles at the toad hopping across the stage. Two huge and magnificent giant bouquets of flowers flung at the singers during curtain calls; such a difference from the austerity of 1954.

Georg and Valerie Solti[**] give a supper party after the performance. I find

* (1912–97), Hungarian-born conductor. Principal Conductor of the London Philharmonic Orchestra 1979–83.

† Wolfgang Wagner (1919–2010), German opera director. Grandson of Richard Wagner; Dir. of the Bayreuth Festival 1966–2008.

‡ Sir Geraint Evans (1922–92), Welsh bass-baritone, a celebrated Beckmesser, among his seventy roles.

§ Sir Peter Hall (1930–2017), founder of the RSC 1961; Dir. of the National Theatre 1973–88; Dir. of Glyndebourne Festival Opera 1984–90.

¶ (1909–2003), German operatic bass-baritone renowned for his Wotan and other Wagnerian roles.

** Lady Solti (b. 1937), television presenter; patroness of the World Orchestra for Peace.

myself sitting next to Ted Heath. He must be in what for him is a less surly mood than usual, for he says: 'Coming here on the plane today I read your much less elegant substitute on the "Albany" column. On the whole you do your column quite well.' He tells me that he never reads Bernard Levin,[*] to which I reply that Arthur Balfour, on being asked whether he read *The Times*, said: 'It is not a paper that I refrain from reading.' That does make Ted laugh. I add how glad I am to see him looking so well after his months of ill-health. He says: 'That's what my colleagues in the Commons tell me – but they don't mean it.'

Ted is interesting on the performance of *Rheingold*; the production was full of imperfections, but Solti bridged the gaps. He mentions one fault in particular: that the rainbow was upside down – 'as if the Union Jack were flying upside down'.

I am delighted to see Wolfgang Wagner again, white-haired and benign, with a *Tarnhelm* round his neck. Wolfgang is amusing on the technical problems of the day: 'When a Rhine Maiden wears contact lenses, she cannot see the conductor from under the water.' It is only fair to add that contact lenses are <u>all</u> that a Rhine Maiden wears nowadays.

8 August 1983

I am not reading English newspapers while abroad, but Eddie produces yesterday's *Sunday Telegraph*. In the list of bestselling books, I am number two in the non-fiction section, beaten only by Martin Gilbert's latest volume on Churchill.

Tonight it is *Die Walküre*. Sieglinde and Brünnhilde are splendid. The sets are unimpressive and a creaking stage does not help. The tree hut is quite good. But the mountain top is too angular, as if a railway cutting had been driven through it. The Valkyrie, however, are given a spectacular eminence. As usual, billows of smoke from the mountain top. One might call the production 'Smoke without Fire'.

9 August 1983

Lovely sunny day. Enchanted to find a quartet of three boys and a girl playing Mozart in the little square outside the hotel.

To *Tristan und Isolde* tonight, which proves a real delight. The sets are perfection, the prow of the ship in Act 1 being taken up in the real tree of

---

* (1928–2004), journalist, author and broadcaster.

Act 2, and again in the dead trees of Act 3. Daniel Barenboim* is no less a master of the orchestra than Georg Solti. The Tristan sings gloriously and the Isolde is equally superb. In the second interval I run into Ted Heath, who, in his melancholy way, eyes agitated with misery, describes the production as 'acceptable', and complains that the tempi are too slow. What a fellow.

10 August 1983

I meet Claus Moser,† who tells me that Wolfgang Wagner does not like Peter Hall's production at all, although he has to support it for economic reasons. One difficulty is that Peter Hall speaks little or no German, Wolfgang scarcely any English.

More talk of Ted Heath, whose criticism of that memorable *Tristan* grew more bitter with every Act. Why does he ever come? Nothing pleases him. Claus tells us that he once asked Heath, tongue in cheek, if he would like to conduct at Covent Garden. 'Oh yes,' Ted replied seriously. Claus: 'And what opera would you choose?' Ted: '*Fidelio*. It offers such a challenge to the conductor.'

On another occasion when Claus asked Ted to Covent Garden, he enquired at the end whether his guest had enjoyed it. Ted: 'An indifferent production, badly performed.'

Claus dined last night with Daniel Barenboim after *Tristan*. Two gushing Americans came up to him and said: 'Oh, Mr Barenboim, how we enjoyed the last Act.' Barenboim: 'And how did you enjoy the intervals?'

Tonight we have *Siegfried*. Alberich, Mime and Manfred Jung's Siegfried are all good, and Hildegard Behrens‡ superb as Brünnhilde. The sets somewhat messy, except for an ingenious tree from which Erda appears.

At the end of the opera, Valerie Solti takes us backstage to watch the curtain calls. Wolfgang Wagner arranges them. Rather too many of them as the audience melts.

---

* Daniel Barenboim (b. 1942), Argentine-Israeli pianist and conductor. Music Dir. of the Chicago Symphony Orchestra 1991–2006, of the Berlin State Opera since 1992 and of the Staatskapelle Berlin from 1992.
† Claus Moser, Baron Moser of Regent's Park (1922–2015), statistician. Chairman of the Royal Opera House, London 1974–87; Warden of Wadham Coll., Oxford 1984–93.
‡ Manfred Jung (1940–2017), German operatic tenor, renowned for his Wagnerian roles. Hildegard Behrens (1937–2009), German soprano renowned for Wagnerian roles and those of Richard Strauss.

11 August 1983

Some extraordinary things in the Bayreuth shops, including busts of Wagner made of marzipan.

Meet Bernard Levin in the street. He shares all our dismay at Ted Heath's graceless behaviour. When Bernard asked him how he had enjoyed one of the operas, Ted replied: 'I would not presume to give an opinion in the presence of such an authority as yourself.' Later, Eddie tells me that somebody at the Festspielhaus went up to Ted and asked: 'Are you Harold Wilson?' Ted replied: 'No, I'm Mr Heath – and much better.' That does show a gleam of humour.

News that Peter Hall has given a disobliging interview to *The Times* about Bayreuth and even Wolfgang Wagner. But none of us has actually seen a copy.

12 August 1983

Nice morning in the Wahnfried garden and a quiet lunch.

Then to our last opera, *Götterdämmerung*. The singing and the orchestra are very fine. So is one scene of Peter Hall's production: Waltraute, in a setting of black and gold. We dine for the only time in the Festspielhaus restaurant: expensive but not at all bad. Robert Armstrong joins us for wine in one of the intervals. He recalls how, when he was Ted Heath's Private Secretary, Ted would play deep, romantic music on his gramophone. And on the night the Commons passed his Common Market resolution, he played Bach's Prelude No. 1 on the piano. Robert also says that when he was Private Secretary to Roy Jenkins, Roy telephoned from London Airport, where he was off on some journey, to say that he had forgotten his handkerchiefs, and could some be sent on. Robert got on to No. 11 Downing Street, but there was only an au pair there, an Italian girl who did not speak English. Robert could not at first remember the Italian for handkerchief – until he recalled the libretto of Verdi's *Otello*!

17 August 1983

Robert Runcie is amusing on how he came to join the Scots Guards. As he took a good Cert. B. in the corps at Oxford when he was at Brasenose, it was suggested that he might like to join the Guards. So he did join and was not only brave, but happy. 'It was the sort of regiment where one was allowed to write a book.'

I tell him that Prince Eddie, contrary to the general Establishment view, admired his sermon in St Paul's for the Falklands service. Even more surprising, he tells me, is that the Queen Mother congratulated him on it. 'I really mean it,' she continued, 'it was exactly what was wanted.'*

29 August 1983

Harold Macmillan comes to lunch with Carol and Julian Faber. He wears the same old light-grey suit with a chalk stripe that I have seen for years and a Brigade tie.

He refers to my biography of King George V, but says that he can no longer read. So I promise him the first recording of it as soon as this has been done. He wonders whether I had such fun writing *KGV* as the Cecils. I ask him what I should write next. He says: 'There are two sorts of biography you can do. Either a minor figure like Addington,† with some new discoveries; but not many people will read it. Or a far better-known figure like Pitt the Younger, whom people want to read about again and again.' 'And Selwyn Lloyd?' I ask. 'Oh, dear boy,' he says, taking my arm, 'definitely of the Addington class.'

H.M. is having *David Copperfield* read to him at present. We also agree what a vigorous novel Trollope wrote in *The Way We Live Now*.

On the present Government, H.M. says: 'Mrs Thatcher has made some strange changes. I am told that one member of her Cabinet does something called "monitorism".'‡

He thinks that one of the worst things ever done by any Conservative Government is the change in the names of counties by Heath and Walker. This leads H.M. to talk of Peter Walker and his dilemma as a 'wet' member of the present Government: 'It is sometimes necessary in politics to sell one's soul to the devil. But one must exact a good price. Walker has not exacted a big enough price.'

He adds: 'Politicians today do not seem to enjoy themselves. We enjoyed ourselves even when out of office. There was so much to do – reading and writing and business and shooting.'

On College at Eton: 'When I was there it was like a nineteenth-century workhouse. Now, I am told, it is like the Savoy Hotel.'

1 September 1983

I give Oliver Millar lunch at the Charing Cross Hotel. Some talk about Robert Rhodes James's forthcoming life of the Prince Consort, which I am

---

* Lord Home of the Hirsel also admired Runcie's sermon. Lord Home to the editor, 8 Apr. 1991.
† Henry Addington, 1st Viscount Sidmouth (1757–1844), Prime Minister 1801–14. It was said of him that Pitt is to Addington as London is to Paddington.
‡ A pun on 'monetarism', the economic theory that excessive expansion of money supply is inherently inflationary.

sorry to say we are about to serialise in the *Sunday Telegraph*. Oliver says that an opportunity to write a definitive life has been missed. It is not only that R.R.J., as an MP, does not have the time to write such a book: he is too egotistical to take advice. O.M. asked him to lunch to tell him about certain papers in the Royal Collection which had never been used and which were most illuminating. 'But Robert Rhodes James simply delivered an unending monologue on his life, his family, his political career . . .'

2 September 1983

Denis Healey speaks rhapsodically to me of his holiday with Edna in Italy and Austria. He says: 'I am so glad at being out of the running for the leadership of the Labour Party. I don't need to go to Blackpool to solicit votes at the TUC Conference.'

17 September 1983

I tell Perina Fordham,[*] Rab's stepdaughter, of Rab's remark to me after the appointment of Anthony Howard as his biographer: 'We thought of you, you know.' Perina, who has been selling innumerable copies of my *KGV* at her Chelsea bookshop, appears shocked at such tactlessness: 'It's because Rab took such silly decisions that he never quite got to the top.' Mollie, Perina adds, is disenchanted with Howard's progress.

20 September 1983

I take Jim Callaghan to dine at the Hyde Park Hotel grill room. Audrey[†] is in hospital and he likes a cheerful evening. He is immensely proud of his connection with the sea. His grandfather was a ship's carpenter and his father in the Navy. Before World War I his father was offered two interesting appointments simultaneously: as a member of Scott's[‡] expedition to the Antarctic and as a sailor in the Royal Yacht *Victoria and Albert*. He chose the Royal Yacht and used to carry the future Duke of Windsor up the gangplank. Jim's mother married his father when she was nineteen; she was widowed at twenty when he was killed in an accident at sea. 'Sailing in *Britannia* with the Queen, I used to wonder what my father would have thought of it all.'

---

[*] Perina Fordham (b. 1933), dau. of Augustine and Mollie Courtauld, later Lady Butler of Saffron Walden (1907–2009); worked in the book trade.

[†] Audrey Callaghan, Baroness Callaghan of Cardiff (1915–2005), political campaigner and fundraiser.

[‡] Capt. Robert Falcon Scott (1868–1912), 'Scott of the Antarctic', who led two expeditions to the Antarctic and with his party was second to reach the South Pole on 17 Jan. 1912.

When Robert Menzies,[*] the PM of Australia, died, the Queen asked Jim if he would like to be Lord Warden of the Cinque Ports. He felt he could not take it on when still PM, so suggested the Queen Mother instead. At Balmoral the Queen said to him: 'Tell my mother after church.' So she said to the QM: 'The PM has something to say to you. You had better go into the library.' Jim told the QM about the Cinque Ports, and she was delighted to accept. She added: 'I am so relieved. When the Queen told me that you wanted to talk to me, I thought you were going to rebuke me for something I had said.'

Jim tells me that Philip Moore has twice asked him if he would ever care to be a Knight of the Garter. 'Do you think he was asking me on behalf of the Queen?' I reply that I am certain he was: so cautious a Private Secretary would never dare to ask on his own behalf. Jim says he will never take it, but I urge him to think again when he retires from the House of Commons.[†]

Jim shares my delight in the personality of the Queen Mother. At a lunch given by the Queen for heads of Common Market countries, she observed to Jim in a loud voice: 'I am glad we are in the Common Market. You see, they have so much to learn from us.'

We talk of the Queen. After Jim had helped Elizabeth Longford with her forthcoming book, he asked her not to use one of his remarks: 'She's a real pro.' But it is true. I ask Jim if he feels any awe when in the Queen's presence. 'No, not awe, but great respect.'

I mention Martin Charteris' remark to me: that he regretted Jim would not stop for a glass of whisky after the PM's weekly audience with the Queen in order that Martin could know what had been discussed. Jim: 'It was not that I don't drink whisky. I deliberately refused to talk to Martin about our audiences, which I regard as confidential between the Queen and her PM. Sometimes the Queen would talk to me of her family matters, for she has so few people to confide in.'

Referring to David Owen's demand that he should be invited to lay a wreath at the Cenotaph on behalf of the SDP, I ask Jim whether he does not think that the time has come to make it a non-political ceremony, with the Queen laying a wreath on behalf of the whole nation and the Commonwealth. He replied simply: 'No. It was a very proud moment when I laid my wreath. It should continue. In any case, the Commonwealth High Commissioners would not like to be excluded.'

Jim has not only an avuncular charm, but also an admirable sense of dignity at the position he occupies. As we finish dining, a Cypriot waiter comes

---

[*] Sir Robert Menzies (1894–1978), Prime Minister of Australia 1939–41 and 1949–66.

[†] Callaghan accepted the Garter in 1987.

up to our table with a large autograph book, opens it and asks Jim if he would add his name to a long list that occupies half a page.

'Look,' the waiter adds ingratiatingly, pointing to the last name, 'Dicky Davies.'*

Jim: 'And who is Dicky Davies?'

Waiter: 'He is a sports commentator on television.'

Jim turns over the page of the book, ignoring the blank page on the left, and signs in the middle of the page on the right, saying as he does so: 'Dicky Davies ought to have a page to himself.'

Lord Curzon himself could not have done better.

22 September 1983
Lunch at the Beefsteak. Bevis Hillier,[†] who is writing John Betjeman's life, tells me that not even in his cups will John Sparrow[‡] part with his letters from Betjeman; probably because they shared a salacious interest in little boys' muddy football shorts.

23 September 1983
To Harrogate for a day and night at the Liberal Party Conference. David Steel's[§] set-piece speech is full of left-wing claptrap and devoid of any economic reality: taxation would have to be prohibitive to support the inflated social services he demands.

1 October 1983
At a Leeds Castle weekend, I hear that Tony Howard <u>asked</u> Rab Butler if he could become his biographer, and he was told that he could: an extraordinary concession to someone who has never written a biography. Now Mollie is rather disillusioned at his slow pace. It is not entirely Tony's fault. He is waiting for the Treasury papers to become available under the thirty-year rule. That will be in 1986, so the book cannot possibly appear before 1988 at the earliest. Mollie also seems just a little disturbed at Tony's discovery of an early love affair of Rab's – he kept all the letters; but pleased to hear that Rab's first wife, Sydney, proposed to him. I gather that it has been suggested to Mollie that I should write an interim life of Rab. But that really would not do.

---

* (b. 1933), television presenter best known for presenting ITV's *World of Sport* 1968–85.

† (b. 1940), art historian, author and journalist.

‡ (1906–92), academic and barrister. Warden of All Souls Coll., Oxford 1952–77.

§ Baron Steel of Aikwood (b. 1938), Liberal then Liberal Democrat politician. MP for Roxburgh, Selkirk and Peebles 1965–83; and for Tweeddale, Ettrick and Lauderdale 1983–97. Leader of the Liberal Party 1976–88; and of the Liberal Democrats Mar.–July 1988.

Tony would surely resent it; and I think that Mollie might be a demanding and censorious taskmaster.

6 October 1983

Cecil Parkinson, Secretary for Trade and former Chairman of the Conservative Party, in deep trouble. He has got his former secretary with child and abandoned his promise to marry her; instead he is remaining with his wife. The PM has asked him not to resign.

8 October 1983

I have a drink with Denis Greenhill. He is proud to have joined LNER before the war, and has an LNER clock in his drawing room. He was once acting stationmaster at Great Ponton, near Grantham, and had to stand to attention on the platform as the Royal Train roared through.

We talk of the FO. Denis thinks highly of Antony Acland* and regrets that he must spend so much time appearing before Select Committees justifying the expense of embassies.

Denis describes an AGM of BP where he was a Government director. A shareholder got up to attack 'do-gooders who are fighting to reduce the lead content in petrol'. He continued: 'What we want are bigger dividends, not more expenses. I don't care if the next generation does have two heads.' Denis expected the man to be shouted down. Not at all. There was a roar of applause.

11 October 1983

There is much argument in the media as to whether Cecil Parkinson should resign from the Government. I think that he should, but others clearly think there is no need. What price the supposed Victorian values preached by his arch-protector, Mrs Thatcher?

13 October 1983

To Blackpool for the final twenty-four hours of the Conservative Party Conference. I do not book a room in an hotel, knowing that I can always stay at one of those dismal boarding houses smelling of fried eggs and cats. But then the Conference Office lets me have a room in the Imperial Hotel, reserved *en bloc* for the richer delegates. Such a nice girl fixes it for me. Such a joy not to have to venture out too much in this blustery weather.

---

* Sir Antony Acland (b. 1930), Permanent Under-Sec. of State for the Foreign Office 1982–6; British Ambassador to the US 1986–91; Provost of Eton 1991–2000.

Spend the mid-afternoon in the Conference Hall. First there is Cecil Parkinson, replying to the debate on trade. He comes onto the platform almost literally under the wing of the PM and receives a standing ovation, presumably as a tribute to his newly revealed talents as an adulterer. But at the end of a commonplace speech, the applause is muted. The PM sets the tone by clapping, but remaining seated.

Maurice Macmillan, always stimulating on such occasions, tells me that he does not think that Parkinson ought to resign. Those who do want him out, he says, fall into four categories:
1. Those who are jealous of his meteoric rise.
2. Those who don't want to have affairs with their secretaries.
3. Those who do have affairs with their secretaries and think that denouncing him will protect them.
4. Those who don't have affairs with their secretaries, but denounce him in case their constituencies think that they do.
The other debate is on immigration, with one or two nasty fascists, absurdly unintelligible.

Spend the rest of the day at the Imperial, amid frenzied speculation about Parkinson's future. It is generally agreed that his reception today hardly justifies his remaining in office.

Willie Whitelaw tells me of his happiness at being translated from the Home Office to the calm of the Upper House. Had the Conservatives been returned with a smaller majority, he would have had to remain in the Commons to support the PM. He says how tiresome Quintin Hailsham continues to be, claiming that he must remain on the Woolsack because there is nobody suitable to take his place.

14 October 1983

The papers this morning write of nothing else except Parkinson's future. As I am coming down to breakfast from the third floor, the lift stops at the second floor – at the very moment that Parkinson passes by. He looks ghastly, with a face the colour of liver. The lift stops at the first floor too, immediately opposite the door to the PM's suite; and there, in a black suit sitting on a chair, is Denis Thatcher, presumably awaiting his orders for the day.

Immediately after breakfast I hear a TV set in the lobby announce that Parkinson has resigned, apparently in response to further comments from Sara Keays, the secretary whom he got with child, printed on the front page of the late editions of *The Times*.

19 October 1983

David Jewell,* Headmaster of Repton, is rather pleased that Repton is one of the thirty-three public schools named in a recent book as having an effective old-boy network. He thinks that Rugby should not be in the list: it is a very bad school nowadays, although Brian Rees† may succeed in improving things.

He tells me a story of Archbishop Ramsey, who recently stayed at Repton. He told Jewell that he will hardly have arrived in heaven when he will hear a voice saying, 'RAMSEY!', and it will be Geoffrey Fisher.‡

We discuss the appeal. I will plan to give £4,000 for the new music school, preferably to be used for its library.

20 October 1983

When Veronica Wedgwood§ was awarded the OM, Hugh Trevor-Roper wrote to congratulate her, but she did not reply. When next they met, Hugh asked if she had received his letter. 'Yes,' she replied, 'but I did not answer it; because you know and I know that I didn't deserve it.'

21 October 1983

A gratifying and kind letter from Harold Macmillan at Birch Grove, dictated with a top-and-tail in his own shaky hand, advising me, following our recent talk, on what biography to write next. His four suggestions are the great Lord Salisbury, Balfour, Beaverbrook¶ and Field Marshal Alexander.** I think the best is Balfour – but would it sell? Even at ninety Macmillan has not ceased to be the man of business. The letter ends: 'Perhaps we might be able to persuade you to become a Macmillan author in the full sense.' They published my *KGV* in paperback.

25 October 1983

The annual party of Bruno Heim†† at Archbishop's House, Westminster. The

---

* David Jewell (1934–2006), Headmaster of Repton 1979–87 and Master of Haileybury 1987–96.
† (1929–2016), Headmaster of Rugby 1980–84.
‡ Baron Fisher of Lambeth (1887–1972), Archbishop of Canterbury 1945–61.
§ Dame Veronica Wedgwood (1910–97), historian who wrote under the name C.V. Wedgwood, renowned for *The Thirty Years War*, first published in 1938 and frequently reprinted.
¶ William Maxwell Aitken, 1st Baron Beaverbrook (1879–1964), newspaper proprietor and politician. Member of the War Cabinet 1940; Minister of Aircraft Production 1940–41.
** Harold Alexander, 1st Earl Alexander of Tunis (1891–1969), prominent FM in World War II noted for his North African campaigns against Rommel. Gov. Gen. of Canada 1946–52.
†† The Most Revd Bruno Heim (1911–2003), the Vatican's first Apostolic Nuncio to Britain.

comedian Jimmy Saville* is there, wearing a tracksuit with a Papal medal round his neck, accompanied by his agent and his photographer, and determined to squeeze every drop of publicity out of it. So he talks to nuns and to someone in a wheelchair immediately in front of where Bruno is receiving his guests. I am glad to say that most people turn their backs on this nauseating misuse of the occasion.

26 October 1983
Meet Peter Carrington for lunch at Wiltons. He is to accept the post of Secretary General of NATO. 'I don't quite see how I can refuse.' But he hopes there may be quite a lot of commuting from Buckinghamshire.

Story of Harold Macmillan at the door of No. 10 being abused by a big docker in the crowd. H.M. walked up to him and said, 'Well, you are entitled to your opinion (pause) I suppose.'

31 October 1983
Peter Rawlinson tells me that he has no hope of becoming Lord Chancellor under Mrs Thatcher. It is not so much that she finds his politics objectionable: indeed, he has rather right-wing views. But she dislikes him personally. Geoffrey Howe would seem to be the obvious successor to Quintin, as long as he does not harbour designs on No. 10.

13 November 1983
William Waldegrave tells me that at a meeting at No. 10 on local-government reform, at which Mrs Thatcher, on being told that the whole of the Tory Establishment would be against her, replied: 'Good.'

24 November 1983
In the London Library, Philip Ziegler tells me of his life of Mountbatten: 'I now know what I want to say, but there is a considerable gap between that and what Robert Armstrong, Secretary of the Cabinet, thinks proper.'

30 November 1983
Lunching in the House of Lords I see Mannie Shinwell, now in his hundredth year, at the next table, looking as spry as a man of sixty. When he reaches his centenary in October 1984 there is a plan to present him with a replica of the

---

* Sir Jimmy Saville (1926–2011), television personality, posthumously revealed to have been a serial sexual abuser.

crown which fell from the ceiling of the Lords a year or two ago onto the seat he happened <u>not</u> to be occupying that day.

5 December 1983, Letter to the Duke of Portland*

Thank you for your letter of 2 December and for your interesting suggestion that I should write a life of Sir Austen Chamberlain.

There seem to be two initial objections to this:

(a) Whenever he has intruded into my books on Curzon, on the Cecils and on King George V, I have found him able and honourable, but not interesting enough to live with for the three years or so it would take me to write his life.

(b) Would many people want to read, much less buy, a biography of so forgotten a statesman? I have to live by my pen.

Not long ago, as it happens, a History master at Charterhouse called D.R. Thorpe wrote a book entitled *The Uncrowned Prime Ministers: A study of Austen Chamberlain, Lord Curzon and Rab Butler*, all of whom had missed the supreme prize of all. He used Austen Chamberlain's papers at Birmingham University, and the result is that, combined with A.C.'s own memoirs and Charles Petrie's two-volume life, there is not much to add.†

I am, however, lunching with Harold Macmillan tomorrow, and will ask him what he thinks of the idea, both as statesman and publisher.

6 December 1983

Lunch with Harold Macmillan at Birch Grove. He now lives upstairs in what used to be his mother's bedroom and is on his own: at one end a narrow bed with pale-green pyjamas laid out on it, at the other a big log fire. Long windows looking out on the Sussex hills and trees, comfortable armchairs and endless tables loaded with papers, books, decanters, and a machine for playing recordings of books.

As I arrive Macmillan is talking to a young doctor, who soon leaves. 'I have all sorts of things wrong with me, but he will find a cure.' For a man approaching his ninetieth year, he looks in splendid shape. His sight is poor and scarcely improved by thick spectacles. But he is neat, almost dapper in appearance, with a double-breasted grey suit and Brigade tie, his moustache trimmed, every hair of his head beautifully brushed. His mind is simply

---

* Sir Victor Cavendish-Bentinck, 9th Duke of Portland (1897–1990), Ambassador to Poland 1945–7.

† Sir Charles Petrie, 3rd Bt (1895–1977), historian. His two-volume *The Life and Letters of the Rt Hon. Sir Austen Chamberlain, K.G., P.C., M.P.* was published in 1939 and 1940. David Dutton (b. 1950), historian; wrote *Austen Chamberlain: Gentleman in Politics* (1985).

dazzling, as quick and luminous as it has ever been; his memory prodigious. In telling a story he occasionally searches for a name but always finds it; and he remembers even such details of past talks as his comparison of Selwyn Lloyd to Addington.*

He has received the complete set of recordings of my *King George V*, but is awaiting a machine on which to play them. His own machine is specially made for the blind and my reels will not fit it. Alexander† is to solve the problem. He tells me of his renewed delight in *Jane Eyre*, which he has been playing recently.

To avoid stumbling on the stairs, he has had a lift installed. We go down into the dining room, which has fine mahogany doors. A silent housekeeper has put out both hot and cold food. Macmillan eats shepherd's pie and carrots (later returning to finish the entire dish), I have cold pheasant and salad. We drink champagne. When, in full flood of talk, he begins to open the second bottle, I say: 'I'm afraid I don't drink much in the middle of the day.' Macmillan: 'I drink all I can lay my hands on.' He is so engrossed in our conversation that pudding, cheese and coffee are left untouched.

As always, he touches on the Great War, and speaks with emotion of the Brigade. 'I saw the English in the trenches being killed one by one. How wonderfully brave they were.' He adds: 'If only the war had ended in 1916 or 1917, what slaughter we should have been spared. When I was Prime Minister, I so enjoyed watching the Birthday Parade. Our own drill is so much less stiff than that of foreign armies: really it is a ballet.'

During the Falklands campaign, the old war horse felt the smoke of battle in his nostrils again when he called on Mrs Thatcher and was asked for his advice. 'You see, nobody at No.10 had ever fought a war before. So I told her how to run it, with a small War Cabinet, and she wrote down everything I said in a small notebook.'

He had a similar experience the other day when Michael Heseltine,‡ as Minister of Defence, invited him to lunch with the Chiefs of Staff. Heseltine is one of the few members of the Thatcher Government for whom he has

---

* When I was researching the official life of Selwyn Lloyd, Harold Macmillan, then in his ninety-first year, told me that he thought Selwyn Lloyd was not dissimilar in many ways to Augustine Birrell (1850–1933), who was also born near Liverpool, started out as a Liberal politician, was called to the Bar and became a KC, then an MP and holder of various Cabinet posts.

† Alexander Macmillan, 2nd Earl of Stockton (b. 1943), Conservative politician and publisher.

‡ Baron Heseltine of Thenford (b. 1933), Conservative politician. MP for Tavistock 1966–74 and for Henley 1974–2001; Cabinet Minister under Margaret Thatcher and John Major; Deputy Prime Minister 1995–7.

respect. Norman Tebbit[*] is another. But he dislikes what he calls the New Men with whom the PM has surrounded herself. They have no interests between the higher technology and golf. And they don't enjoy themselves. They don't find politics fun. They don't lunch at the Turf Club.' On Mrs Thatcher: 'I worked for a united country. She is narrow and hard, a middle-class megalomaniac.' This reflects what he said of her at Coldharbour: her 'monitorism'.

On the Queen, Macmillan takes an affectionate but detachedly Whig view. 'I tried to interest her in politics, but she is only interested in the personalities of politics. I still see her sometimes. She is lonely and apprehensive about the future.' Here I detect his disappointment at not having been able to play Melbourne to her Queen Victoria. He admits to me that even with her Prime Ministers, the Queen maintains a reserve.

I quote Lady Ponsonby[†] on the Royal Family's 'cold egotism'. Macmillan agrees. Macmillan has known the Queen Mother for much of his life. 'But I still do not have the remotest idea of what goes on in her mind.' We laugh over her splendid extravagance and all those footmen when lunching in the garden. Macmillan: 'That is what happens when a poor woman marries a rich man. But when a rich woman marries a poor man, she makes a good frugal wife.' As always Macmillan relishes having married into the world of great noblemen, especially the Whigs.

We talk of war and generals. 'Montgomery was the Wellington of World War II, Alexander the Marlborough.[‡]' At Alex's HQ during the Italian campaign, when the US General Mark Clark[§] was behaving sluggishly, Macmillan asked Alex: 'Why don't you give him an order?' Alex replied: 'I can give no orders. Under my command are British, Americans, Italians, Canadians, Greeks, Brazilians, and nightly they all telegraph to their Prime Ministers complaining of me.' Had Alex had the powers of a supreme commander, Macmillan thinks the war could have been shortened by a year.

He describes a wartime exchange between John Waverley[¶] and Eddie Devonshire,[**] at a committee to decide whether British children ought to

---

[*] Baron Tebbit of Chingford (b. 1931), Conservative politician. Sec. of State for Employment 1981–3 and for Trade and Industry 1983–5; Chairman of the Conservative Party 1985–7.

[†] Lady Mary Ponsonby (1832–1916), courtier. Wife of Sir Henry Ponsonby (1825–95), PS to Queen Victoria 1870–1895.

[‡] John Churchill, 1st Duke of Marlborough (1650–1722), soldier and statesman. Victor of the Battle of Blenheim in 1704.

[§] Gen. Mark Clark (1896–1984), senior US army officer who served in both world wars.

[¶] John Anderson, 1st Viscount Waverley (1882–1958), Home Secretary 1939–40; Chancellor of the Exchequer 1943–5.

[**] Edward Cavendish, 10th Duke of Devonshire (1895–1950), soldier and politician. Under-Sec. for Dominion Affairs 1936–40.

be evacuated to Canada. Asked his opinion, the Duke replied: 'I would rather our children were brought up under Hitler than under Mackenzie King.'*

On Charles Snow: 'He sent me the proofs of *Corridors of Power* to read at a time when I was ill. I remember two absurd things about the book. One was when the Minister of Defence had to decide whether or not to make an atom bomb, without any reference at all to the Cabinet. The other was when a penniless man married the daughter of a rich nobleman and thus immediately could inherit a fine country estate and a big London house. I told Snow: 'The daughter of such a nobleman would get £30,000 and not a penny more. I know. I married one.' I mention how Charles Snow was fascinated by Pratt's, thinking that great affairs of state were discussed there instead of somebody talking about his woodcock. Macmillan: 'Yes, always those woodcock – except at Munich and Suez.'

Discussing again what book I should write next, I touch briefly on the Munshi.† This touches Macmillan's imagination and he muses aloud: 'Queen Victoria was at heart a romantic, a regency figure like Princess Margaret, who loved dancing and adored Lord Melbourne. Then she had to do all her business with Peel and Gladstone and hated it. Suddenly there was Disraeli, who flattered her and made her Empress of India. What fun! And so she brought over Indian servants and among them was the Munshi. Yes, there is certainly a book in it.' He is delighted when I tell him the episode of the Viceroy and the Indian Governors who returned the Munshi's Christmas cards. 'I am sure they must have been Whigs. They did not mind if they were not altogether respectful towards the Queen.'

He traces the decline of the great middle-class book market: 'First there were the big lending libraries like Boots and *The Times* and Harrods. As a young man in the publishing business I used to sell them thousands of our books in a day. Then it became respectable to use public libraries, and the lending libraries closed one by one. Now the public libraries are having their funds cut. And on top of it all, the middle classes have always grudged the price of a book in the shops.'

On David Dilks: 'He is skilful in the new school of History that arranges documents so well – like Martin Gilbert's factory for producing the life of Churchill.'

On Nigel Fisher: 'A dull writer. To write a biography of me, he potted my

---

* William Lyon Mackenzie King (1874–1950), Prime Minister of Canada 1921–6, 1926–30 and 1935–48.
† Abdul Karim, the Munshi (1863–1909), Indian attendant to Queen Victoria.

own six volumes. I didn't mind. It left the interesting parts to be done by somebody else.'

On F.E. Smith:[*] 'I am sure he had gypsy blood. He loved horses and had such skill with them. Yet he had never seen a horse until he came up to Oxford.'

On Julian Faber: 'I'm really rather frightened of him.'

On Marie-Lou de Zulueta:[†] 'She is very kind to me. Philip is very good with her.'

On Rab Butler: 'Sydney played Svengali to his Trilby.'[‡]

On Jim Callaghan: 'I am fond of him. He is like a ship's bosun.' And when I tell Macmillan about the episode of the autograph at the Hyde Park Hotel, he says: 'Ah yes, we Prime Ministers know our place!'

15 December 1983

William and Caroline Waldegrave give a dinner party for Harold Macmillan. Victor Rothschild is also a guest. None of us has very much to say except to stimulate the old man, who is as dazzling as ever.

Macmillan tells us how, as Chancellor of Oxford, he had to give an honorary degree to a Russian scientist. Behind the scenes in Moscow, he learned, there was a dispute as to whether he should be allowed to travel to England. His fellow scientists wished him to accept the honour, but the KGB wanted to keep him inside the USSR. It was eventually decided that he could come for the day, heavily escorted. He was met at Heathrow by the university officials on the morning of Encaenia, and rushed to Moss Bros for some formal clothes. Owing to a misunderstanding, these turned out to be evening dress, with a stiff shirt and tails. Then to Oxford, where he took part in the ceremony, conducted of course in Latin. That night he dined at Christ Church, where there was an elaborate Latin grace, and of course the Chancellor is in stick-up collars and bands. And so back to Russia. 'Now what impression, do you suppose, he took back to Moscow?', Macmillan continues. 'Why, that we are a country that wears nineteenth-century clothes and speaks scarcely anything but Latin.'

The Russian scientist leads us to relativity. Victor quotes Einstein: 'God

---

* (1872–1930), 1st Earl of Birkenhead, lawyer and Conservative politician. Lord Chancellor 1919–22, most renowned for his part in the Irish Treaty of 1921.

† (b. 1930), wife of Sir Philip de Zulueta, K.R.'s contemporary at both New Coll. and in the Welsh Guards. He served three Prime Ministers and was PS for Foreign Affairs to Sir Anthony Eden, Harold Macmillan and Sir Alec Douglas-Home.

‡ Svengali, fictional character in the novel *Trilby* (1895) by George du Maurier (1834–96), cartoonist and author. Trilby O'Ferrall is the heroine of the novel.

does not dice with the universe.' Macmillan: 'No, but Einstein did.'

Much to his surprise, Macmillan one day received a two-page telegram telling him that he had been awarded the Aristotle Onassis Prize, worth about £100,000. 'How wonderful,' he thought, 'I have four grandsons and each can now have a Purdey.' Then he turned over to the second sheet. 'As honorary President of the Fund, you will no doubt be only too pleased to contribute your prize to that noble cause.' Macmillan: 'It was what in one's private-school days one would call a swizz.'

When golden sovereigns were changed to paper money, Macmillan commented: 'One never then knew what to give one's loader.'

We talk of Duff Cooper.* Macmillan tells the story of how, in the Beefsteak Club, someone said to Duff: 'You are the worst Secretary of State for War we have ever had.' Duff: 'How can you say that in the presence of Jack Seely?'†

On Duff's resignation speech at the time of Munich, I recall that *The Times* called it 'a damp squib'. Macmillan: 'Yes, *The Times* is always wrong – and every twenty years or so publishes the next volume of its official history to demonstrate the fact!'

On Mrs Thatcher Macmillan reflects: 'Her first term of office was admirable. She met the emergency and won her Alamein. Now she is making mistakes.' He adds, with deep feeling: 'Oh, how I wish I were twenty-five again.'

21 December 1983

Lunch at the Beefsteak. Alistair Horne talks rather uneasily about his biography of Harold Macmillan. They have had long and difficult talks about the repatriation of the Cossacks and other dissident nationals at the end of the war.

Nico Henderson says that when there was a Press strike of national newspapers, the Queen did not know it, saying to him: 'I got my *Sporting Life* as usual.'

---

* 1st Viscount Norwich (1890–1954), diplomat and Conservative politician.
† John Seely, 1st Baron Mottistone of Mottistone (1868–1947), politician and soldier. Sec. of State for War 1912–14.

1984

On 1 February the Chancellor of the Exchequer, Nigel Lawson, announced that the halfpenny would be withdrawn from circulation. Death of Maurice Macmillan on 10 March. Tony Benn was returned to Parliament at the Chesterfield by-election on 1 March. The miners' strike began on 12 March. The last Bank of England £1 note was issued on 31 March. More than 100 pickets were arrested in violent clashes at collieries in Derbyshire and Nottinghamshire. WPC Yvonne Fletcher was shot by a gunman during a siege outside the Libyan Embassy in London on 17 April. The UK severed diplomatic relations with Libya on 22 April. On 18 June there was fighting between police and striking miners at Orgreave colliery, leaving sixty-four injured. British unemployment reached 3,260,000 on 1 June. It was announced on 20 June that O-Levels and CSE would be replaced by the GCSE from September 1986. On 26 July the Trade Union Act prohibited strikes without a ballot. The Princess of Wales gave birth to her second son, Prince Harry, on 15 September. On 12 October the Brighton hotel bombing by the Provisional IRA killed five people during the Conservative Party Conference. On 5 November 800 miners ended their strike. Ronald Reagan was re-elected President of the US on 6 November. British Telecom shares went on sale on 20 November. Mikhail Gorbachev of the Soviet Union visited Britain from 16 December.

3 January 1984

To Oxford to lunch with Isaiah Berlin at All Souls. We are joined by John Sparrow, not unamiable but rather heavy in manner. He describes how he was invited to lunch at Chequers by Mrs Thatcher in mistake for the John Sparrow* who was head of the Think Tank and who has just been knighted. Such mistakes are not unknown. Churchill infamously confused Irving Berlin with Isaiah Berlin in wartime.† The error was realised in time, so both John Sparrows were there.

---

* Sir John Sparrow (b. 1933), head of the Central Policy Review Staff 1982–3.
† Irving Berlin (1888–1989), American composer and lyricist. In the spring of 1944 Churchill invited Berlin to lunch, intending to talk with Isaiah Berlin, and asked him what was the most

Isaiah talks of Jews and anti-Semitism. With characteristic sharpness he describes it as 'disliking Jews more than is reasonable'. He also says: 'Some of my best friends are anti-Semites.' Both these remarks are made, as it were, in the inverted commas of irony; but they explain why some of his friends, such as Arnold Goodman, feel that he does not embrace Jewish causes openly or strongly enough.

Isaiah says that Jews play less of a part in British intellectual life than do their counterparts in other countries. On the continent of Europe, poor Jewish families struggle to provide the best possible education for their children, up to university level. In Britain, however, Jews follow the pattern of the social class to which they belong: so many of them go straight into business.

Why did Arnold Goodman, once so close to Harold Wilson, fall out with him? It happened when Wilson showed Arnold his notorious retirement Honours List. Arnold told him: 'These honours will do no good to their recipients, but will do lasting harm to you.' H.W.: 'Is that not rather an anti-Semitic remark?' Arnold: 'No. If you took a poll of British Jews on those they would wish to see honoured, they would vote for none of your candidates.' When the list was published unchanged, Arnold determined to have nothing more to do with Wilson.

There was one comic episode in the course of the above conversation between Arnold and Wilson. Arnold began by saying: 'I have many vices, but lack of frankness is not one of them.' But he had only got as far as 'vices' when Wilson nodded his head. Telling the story afterwards, Arnold said: 'He nodded too soon.'

Story of Lord Londonderry's[*] daughters, two of whom married Nazi sympathisers. Someone asked him when the third would marry. Londonderry: 'I am saving her for the Chief Rabbi.'

Also an account of Winston's visit to All Souls between the wars. He was treated guardedly, like some caged beast, and seated in the SCR with his own decanter of whisky. He was not at ease until someone asked him whether there was going to be a war. This provoked him to paint a picture of terror in London, with the population struggling to escape from the bombs, while animals escaped from the Zoo and roamed the streets. He went on to express his contempt for the Cabinet and even more for Stanley Baldwin – 'that epileptic corpse'.

---

important work he had done for the Allies lately. Berlin replied: 'It should be a *White Christmas*, I guess.'

[*] Sir Charles Vane Tempest-Stewart, 7th Marquess of Londonderry (1878–1949), Sec. of State for Air 1931–5; leading member of the Anglo-German Fellowship, and as such known as 'Londonderry Herr'.

Jack Plumb comes to dine. Tonight he is querulous and ill-tempered. He pours scorn on my affection for the Church of England and refers to Hugh Dacre with venomous dislike, and complains how much his holiday with Princess Margaret in the West Indies will cost him.

4 January 1984

When I tell Nicky Gordon-Lennox that I am having a note in my column on Sunday, on the PM's putting inverted commas round 'Chequers' on her Christmas card, he says: 'You have already lost your CVO with the Tsar. Now bang goes your CBE.'*

11 January 1984

I go to the Middlesex Hospital to see A.J.P. Taylor, who is recovering from being knocked down by a car in Soho. He looks haggard and exhausted, with red-rimmed eyes and a slight tremor. But he is pleased to see me. He is amused when I tell him that his eulogy of my *KGV* in the *Observer* pushed me up the bestseller list above his own memoirs. I ask him why he says so little of Isaiah Berlin in them. 'Because he stands for nothing. He is genial, but simply makes amusing remarks about other people.'

14 January 1984

Claus Moser recently took the Waldegraves to the ballet at Covent Garden. The other guests were the Gloucesters and Hugh Casson.† William tells me: 'Casson drew a lovely drawing of the set for the little Gloucester boy,‡ but didn't offer to do so for anyone else. I should have liked one myself. But I saw by the end of the performance that the boy had covered it with his own drawings of Centurion tanks and bomber planes.'

18 January 1984

Talk to William Waldegrave about last night's debate on 'rate-capping', in which he wound up for the Government. He had rather a rough ride, not least with Ted Heath, who voted against the Government without telling the Whips – and he himself a former Chief Whip. After the debate William said to Ted in a friendly way that he was sorry they found themselves on opposite sides. Ted: 'You didn't do well, did you?' There can surely be no

---

* K.R. was in fact awarded a CBE in 1997.
† Prince Richard, Duke of Gloucester (b. 1944), m. to Birgitte, Duchess of Gloucester (b. 1946), sponsor of two Royal Navy ships and patron of St Paul's Cathedral School. Sir Hugh Casson (1910–99), architect, artist and writer; Dir. of Architecture at the Festival of Britain in 1951.
‡ Alexander Windsor, Earl of Ulster (b. 1974), formerly an officer in the King's Royal Hussars.

more graceless man in politics. William, having made a pleasant reference in his speech to being a former junior soldier in Ted's army, is wounded by such nastiness.

21 January 1984
Talk to Zara Cazalet.* She asked Jim Callaghan what he most missed in ceasing to be Prime Minister. He replied: 'My audiences with the Queen.'

26 January 1984
There is criticism of the Queen's Christmas broadcast, led by Enoch Powell. There was no specific Christian utterance in the speech, which extolled the spirit of the Commonwealth and showed especial favour to Mrs Gandhi.† I talk to Martin Charteris about it. He says (a) it is the first time in thirty years that it has gone wrong, (b) the speech <u>was</u> sent to No. 10, even though not strictly covered by ministerial responsibility, and the PM made no comment on it, and (c) it would be better if the Queen returned to texts of anodyne sentiments expounded in memorable language, with which I agree.

13 February 1984
Michael Bloch gives me an authentic account of the financial settlement made on the Duke of Windsor at the time of the Abdication. On becoming King, Edward VIII had inherited a life interest in Balmoral and Sandringham. At the Abdication he could not simply sell this life interest to George VI. For if the Duke of Windsor had then died, the life interest would have passed to the Duchess of Windsor. Instead there was a 'mock' sale at the valuations which Michael found in the Wigram papers:

    Sandringham £146,000
    York Cottage £5,000
    Balmoral and Birkhall £90,000
    Settled contents of houses <u>£15,000</u>
      £256,000

This total was not paid to the Duke, but put into a trust fund, from which he was allowed £5,000 p.a. But this £5,000 was made part of the settlement of £25,000 p.a. which George VI made to his brother. The Duke also agreed to take on the payment of £5,000 of pensions to those on the

---

* (1917–2004), widow of Peter Cazalet, horseracing trainer; friend of the Queen Mother, who often visited the family home, Fairlawne in Kent.
† Indira Gandhi (1917–84), Prime Minister of India Jan. 1980–Oct. 1984, when she was assassinated.

Royal estates. He therefore received £25,000 less £5,000 of pension payments.

Frances Donaldson is certainly wrong in her biography of Edward VIII in claiming that (a) the Duke received £60,000 p.a., and (b) that the two estates were together valued at £1 million.*

24 February 1984
Poor Brian Rees resigns as Headmaster of Rugby on grounds of health.[†] How I feel for him.

29 February 1984
In India with Robert Wade-Gery, who tells me the story of Victor Rothschild being called upon by two Whitehall Permanent Secretaries soon after his appointment as head of the Think Tank. He replied: 'Well, one was intelligent and the other was sober.'

6 March 1984
We drive out to Kingsway Camp, about ten miles north of Delhi, to see the graveyard of the Raj: the little park near the site of the Durbar where the statues of George V and his Viceroys are being stored. That of the King-Emperor himself rises above the surrounding trees. It has been removed from the memorial designed by Lutyens in Princes' Place, New Delhi, where the stone baldachin rises from a circular basin, which is now empty of water. Robed and crowned, George V gazes out over the Durbar field from his high pedestal. Round him in a semicircle are some of his Viceroys, all in the robes of the Star of India. This little park must be the only place in India where there is scarcely an Indian to be seen: just the gardener and his dog.

Between this graveyard and the Durbar field is a little eminence on which stands an obelisk. It bears the inscription, in English on one side, in Urdu on the other:

> Here on the 12th day of December 1911 His Imperial Majesty King George V, Emperor of India, accompanied by the Queen Empress in solemn Durbar, announced in person to the Governors, Princes and Peoples of India his Coronation celebrated in England on the 22nd day of June 1911, and received from them their dutiful homage and allegiance.

---

* Lady Donaldson of Kingsbridge (1907–94), biographer. In *Edward VIII* (1974) she qualified these claims by stating on p. 292: 'Informed guesses put the figure for Sandringham and Balmoral at £1 million pounds and the yearly income paid by George VI to his brother at £60,000.'
† The story was more complex. See 'The Head Who Toppled', *Sunday Telegraph*, 23 June 1991.

10 March 1984

Got up at six to see the dawn light on the Taj Mahal. Later in the day I spend some time on the hotel roof gazing at the Taj. In the full glare of midday, it becomes hard and unromantic; then dissolves into a luminous haze in the evening sun. I finish reading Paul Scott's moving novel *Staying On*,[*] with the prospect of the Fort and the Taj Mahal spread out before me.

14 March 1984

In the afternoon to the original Viceregal Lodge, now the Institute for Advanced Study. It was built by Lord Dufferin[†] in the late 1880s, an enormous Elizabethan pile of grey stone: a Himalayan Hardwick, as it were. The rose garden was laid out by Curzon, the terraces by Minto,[‡] Irwin added an annexe. It was here that Mountbatten showed Nehru, early in May 1947, the first draft plan for the partition of India.

The house is approached by a long steep hill. It must have been a fearful grind for the rickshaw boys: cars of course were not allowed, except for a very few grandees. There is a huge old oak in the garden, and I pick up an acorn or two to see if they will grow in London. I also see a sundial bearing the quaint legend: 'Madras or Railway Time is 12 minutes fast of Simla Mean Time.'

The vast entrance hall, panelled in teak, is like the nave of a cathedral, a fine broad staircase leading up to an open gallery. There I am shown the viceregal rooms, still containing some handsome pieces of furniture and portraits. Downstairs, in what I suppose used to be the ballroom, the names of the Viceroys are still painted on the wall at intervals, but their armorial bearings have gone.

21 March 1984

I meet Karan Singh.[§] We talk of Mountbatten. I say that his reputation was on the wane when he was killed. But that this martyrdom has revived a less critical approach to his character and career. Karan Singh: 'One could say the same thing of Gandhi. He always insisted that India should never be

---

[*] Paul Scott (1920–78), novelist, renowned for his tetralogy *The Raj Quartet*, to which his Booker Prize-winning *Staying On* (1977) was a coda.

[†] Sir Frederick Temple Hamilton-Temple-Blackwood, 1st Marquess of Dufferin and Ava (1826–1902), Viceroy and Gov. Gen. of India 1884–8.

[‡] Gilbert Elliot-Murray-Kynynmound, 4th Earl of Minto (1845–1914), Viceroy and Gov. Gen. of India 1905–10.

[§] (b. 1931), MP for Udhampur 1967–84; member of India's Upper House of Parliament, the Rajya Sabha, 1996–2012.

divided; and when it was his reputation faded. But with his death it became difficult to criticise him.'

26 March 1984

Dine with Princess Margaret, after which she absorbs her usual stiff ration of whisky. She talks of *KGV*, but has not yet read it all – 'I am still on Antonia Fraser's* *Charles II.*' The old hostility to Queen Mary re-emerges: 'Did Mummy ever tell you what Queen Mary told her when she married? She said that Mummy should not have friends, as it could be embarrassing.'

When I mention the Balmoral custom of KGV in asking his family to watch him finishing dressing, as if he were Louis XIV at Versailles, she says: 'Papa liked that, too.'

Princess Margaret still resents that she was not allowed to share the Queen's History tutorials with Sir Henry Marten. 'I was told that it wasn't necessary. I have often reproached Mummy with this.'

2 April 1984

Talk to Katie Macmillan. She tells me an amusing vignette of the old man's ninetieth birthday party at Birch Grove after he had accepted an earldom. Ex-Speaker George Thomas, now Lord Tonypandy,† greeted Harold with the words: 'Fancy you and me joining the aristocracy!'

Arnold Goodman tells me that at Harold Macmillan's ninetieth birthday party Mrs Thatcher was placed at a distant table between Alexander Macmillan and Julian Amery. Furious, she never spoke a word to either.

4 April 1984

Hatchards gives an Author of the Year party on the Martini Terrace of New Zealand House. Delighted to see Asa Briggs‡ there. As neither his *Social History* nor my *King George V* is on the display of books, we take it out on Hatchards by drinking much champagne.

Asa Briggs gives me a sparkling account of Harold Macmillan's speech at the Balliol dinner recently, attended by all Heads of Houses. Harold said: 'It is extraordinary that this dinner should take place at all. For the Vice-Chancellor and the Master of Balliol never agree except when the two offices

---

* Lady Antonia Fraser (b. 1932), historian, biographer and writer of detective fiction. Dau. of Frank and Elizabeth Pakenham, 7th Earl and Countess of Longford, and wife of Harold Pinter.
† 1st Viscount Tonypandy (1909–97), Labour politician. Speaker of the House of Commons 1976–83.
‡ Baron Briggs of Lewes (1921–2016), historian. Provost of Worcester Coll., Oxford 1976–91; Chancellor of the Open University 1978–94.

are held by one person. And this leads to another question: having agreed to entertain us all here tonight, how have they shared the cost?'

Also at this Balliol dinner, Asa saw Roy Jenkins and Julian Amery glaring at each other like two dogs with their hackles up.

I do not know many people at the Hatchards party but some pleasant talk with Alec and Elizabeth Home. And I meet for the first time Jan Morris,[*] whose books I much admire, particularly those on Victorian imperialism.

18 April 1984, Letter to Lord Annan

I am more touched than I can say by the kindness and generosity of your letter about my *King George V.* I well recall all the encouragement you gave me when my book on Curzon came out, and now you have put me doubly in your debt. What particularly delights me is that you have appreciated its humorous side. All the reviewers have written well of it, but apparently only a few have enjoyed the jokes. Knopf are about to publish it in New York and the previews so far are respectful, even enthusiastic, but awfully solemn.

Harold Nicolson had to overcome several Bloomsburian prejudices in writing his official life of the King: shooting and stamp-collecting. The result is nevertheless majestic, the model of an authorised biography. But he was writing with Queen Mary and George VI breathing down his neck; this would explain the several occasions on which he smoothed over certain awkwardnesses. What surprised me more was his reluctance either to venture outside the Royal Archives or to interview many survivors of the reign. From his diaries, which Nigel allowed me to consult in full, it seems that he never once even tried to talk to any of the children about their father. This is astonishing. I found the Queen Mother a mine of information.

19 April 1984

Edward Ford talks to me about George VI. Edward says that his outbursts of temper – or gnashes, as they were called in the family – were probably epileptic. He was never angry with someone to their face, but always to others, e.g. he would say to Edward: 'I could shoot that bloody man Attlee.'

Edward says: 'The thought of Sandringham used to make me ill, and once I did fall ill as soon as I arrived for a shooting party, but the King was kind and sent me encouraging little notes of enquiry. Owen Morshead[†] never knew how to handle the King – he treated him as if he were soothing a fractious child. Tommy Lascelles said it was best to ignore the King's outbursts.

---

[*] (b. 1926), historian; renowned for the *Pax Britannica* trilogy.
[†] Sir Owen Morshead (1893–1977), Royal Librarian 1926–58.

22 April 1984

I see the film *Chariots of Fire*. It has two themes. The first runner, based on Harold Abrahams,[*] is determined to win an Olympic medal as an answer to the anti-Semitism he encounters at Cambridge. The second, a Scot, Eric Liddell,[†]is equally ambitious, but refuses to run on a Sunday. Yet it is a far from cosy film. Brilliant vignette of an anti-Semitic master of a Cambridge College by John Gielgud.

24 April 1924

Philip Ziegler is still locked in argument with Robert Armstrong about the text of his life of Dickie Mountbatten.

Lunch with Julian Faber at the Savoy Grill. He tells me two interesting things about Harold Macmillan.

(a) He is bringing out his North African diaries, 1943–1945.

(b) He will shortly leave Birch Grove to spend several months at Chatsworth. Andrew Devonshire told Julian that he never got on well with his own father and has looked on Harold Macmillan as his surrogate. At Chatsworth, Julian says, the old man will be much better cared for than at Birch Grove. But he hopes to come back for Encaenia in June.

26 April 1984

I hear that when it was not still publicly known who would be the new Archbishop of Westminster, Abbot Hume (as he then was) put a lot of money on himself with Ladbroke's at 25–1, and won enough to redecorate part of the Cathedral. When the Cardinal was a boy in Newcastle he was known to bet.

1 May 1984

Michael Adeane dies at seventy-three. I am sad, for I liked his pleasant talk and dry humour. Jock Colville, Baba Metcalfe[‡] and Martin Charteris all told me that Michael 'thought Kenneth had got it wrong about the Tsar in his book on King George V'. Nevertheless, he said he thought it a good book. And the only time I saw him since the book appeared, lunching one day at the Beefsteak, he was as warm and friendly as ever, though he made no mention of it. He cannot have been pleased at some of the criticism I wrote

---

[*] Harold Abrahams (1899–1978), athlete; winner of the 100m in the 1924 Olympic Games.

[†] Eric Liddell (1902–45), missionary and athlete; winner of the 400m in the 1924 Olympic Games.

[‡] Lady Alexandra Metcalfe (née Curzon) (1904–95), wife of Edward Dudley ('Fruity') Metcalfe (1887–1957), equerry to King Edward VIII.

of Stamfordham. I do rather wish he had discussed this with me. One may spare children in a biography, but surely not grandchildren.

Martin Charteris thinks we are agreed on Michael's virtues: modesty, loyalty, tact, humour. His failings according to Martin: (a) he stayed too long, (b) he was over-cautious, and (c) he hated discussion, especially in committee.

4 May 1984

Take the 3.30 train to Derby, where David Jewell meets me and drives me to Repton. Walk round the playing fields, where my young trees flourish. David stops briefly to rebuke a boy and a girl, both pupils, walking hand in hand.

'Overt signs of affection are frowned on.' The beauty of Repton strikes me afresh. Intellectually the school flourishes, with the highest number of Oxford and Cambridge awards in any one year.

9 May 1984

I have dinner with Tony Snowdon. I have hardly seen him for many years, but it was as if we have been close friends since Eton. 'Hello, Sir,' he begins and repeats the joke throughout the evening. He says I have not changed since those days; nor in fact has he, although I notice how stiffly he moves after sitting down for an hour – the result of polio. He says of Eton: 'You were very much loved,' a compliment I deny.

Tony will never go to any reunion – Eton, Cambridge, etc. He is even shy of sitting at the communal lunch table in the House of Lords. Nor would he ever go alone to a restaurant. When we talk of watches, he shows me his: costing only £7 at Marks and Spencer, with beautiful hinges on the watch strap.

6 June 1984

3.30 train to Godalming to talk to the boys at Charterhouse on KGV as a constitutional monarch at their political society, named in honour of the Old Carthusian William Beveridge.* I take the precaution of asking to have every possible window open, as this keeps my audience awake. It all goes as well as I have ever known on one of my school visits.

Richard Thorpe, rather like Edward Adeane† in appearance, looks after me. We have some talk on Selwyn Lloyd, whose life he is hoping to write.

---

* Sir William Beveridge, 1st Baron Beveridge of Tuggal (1879–1963), economist and social reformer. Master of University Coll., Oxford 1937–44; best known for the Beveridge Report, *Social Insurance and Allied Services*, 1942.
† The Hon. Edward Adeane (1939–2015), lawyer. PS to the Prince of Wales 1979–85.

After the talk, before dinner in the Common Room, I am given whisky by an agreeable housemaster and his wife, Graham and Vanessa Jones,[*] in a house commanding a fine view of playing fields and distant hills. Also an economist called Jim Bayliss,[†] who laughs noisily at his own jokes.

Richard Thorpe tells me that Walter Sellar,[‡] co-author of *1066 and All That*, used to be a housemaster here. During the war new boys were measured at the beginning and end of the term. Sellar was surprised to note that one of them began the term at 4 feet 8½ inches tall and ended it at 4 feet 8¼. He began his report: 'This boy is settling down nicely.'

10 June 1984

A huge party for Walter Annenberg[§] at Eton: drinks in the Head Master's garden, then lunch in Election Hall.

Martin Charteris is hoping to revive the habit of portraits of leaving boys, but parents are unwilling to fork out the money. I must commission Derek Hill to paint one of a boy selected by Martin.

Giles St Aubyn[¶] tells me that Rugby has run downhill under Brian Rees, both academically and in the number of boys. Peter Pilkington has refused the vacant Headmastership; nor is his immediate wish for a bishopric, which carries a salary of only £16,000.

12 June 1984

Prince Eddie tells me that he is being given the use of the Royal Yacht to visit Turkey on a trade mission. He says that the Duke of Gloucester is to make his maiden speech in the House of Lords tomorrow during an anti-smoking debate. I for one think it cranky of him. The Royal Family must not become scolds.

I am amazed to hear that little Nicky,[**] now a day boy at Westminster, walks to and from the school each day unguarded.

---

[*] Graham Jones (b. 1944), economist and schoolmaster. Headmaster of Repton 1987–2003. Vanessa Jones (b. 1939), secretary to the Charterhouse Headmaster 1973–80.
[†] James Bayliss (b. 1945), economist and schoolmaster.
[‡] (1898–1951), schoolmaster at Fettes and Charterhouse and humorous writer. His most famous work is *1066 and All That* (1930).
[§] (1908–2002), American publisher, philanthropist and diplomat. US Ambassador to the UK 1969–74.
[¶] The Hon. Giles St Aubyn (1925–2015), biographer of Queen Victoria (1991) and Edward VII (1979) and long-serving housemaster at Eton. They first met when K.R. became an Eton master, and kept up with one another for the rest of their lives.
[**] Lord Nicholas Windsor (b. 1970) was later educated at Harrow and Harris Manchester Coll., Oxford, where he read Theology; Patron of the Society of King Charles the Martyr.

14 June 1984

Some talk of diplomatic life with Nico Henderson. So many official visitors at the Paris Embassy showed little consideration for the staff, but not Wedgwood Benn, who was always polite and charming. Some would say, 'I might as well have another drink, as I pay for them.' In fact, a large lump of an ambassador's salary is deducted by the Government as part of his *frais*: an intolerable imposition. When Lord Cromer* was in Washington he challenged the Treasury on this, and after many threats he won. But it established no precedent.

Julian Bullard[†] is bitter not to have become Permanent Head of the Foreign Office in succession to Michael Palliser, and would like to become head of an Oxford College. And Michael Palliser is no less aggrieved not to have received the customary peerage on his retirement. The PM's dislike of the FO has also cost Nico his peerage: she cannot reward Nico, whom she does respect, without appearing to give a double snub to Palliser.

15 June 1984

Lunch at the American Embassy in Regent's Park. It is in honour of Walter Annenberg. The Queen Mother is one of the guests. Although the QM only returned last night from her annual visit to France, she is as lively and amusing as I have ever known her; and without a trace of that distant nervousness she showed at a recent London Library party. Of course, she knows everybody who is here today very well and is entirely at her ease. How enchantingly cool she looks on this hot day, in diaphanous blue.

Before moving in to lunch, we drink on the terrace in the sunshine. Claus Moser says there is betting in the opera world on whether George Christie[‡] will receive a peerage or a knighthood in tomorrow's Birthday Honours List. Having seen the list at the office this morning, I tell him it will be a knighthood. 'Ah,' he says, 'then I must make no more bets.' Claus still seems a little nervous about how Oxford will receive him as the new Warden of Wadham: he hopes to spend a lot of time in London, but doesn't want to be found out. Arnold Goodman quoted John Maud's[§] advice: 'Whenever I have to go

---

* Sir Rowland Baring, 3rd Earl of Cromer (1918–91), banker. Ambassador to the US 1971–4.
† Sir Julian Bullard (1928–2006), Ambassador to the Federal Republic of Germany 1984–8; Pro-Chancellor of Birmingham University 1989–94.
‡ Sir George Christie (1934–2014), Chairman of Glyndebourne Opera 1956–99; oversaw the building of a new opera house, 1992–4.
§ John Redcliffe-Maud, Baron Redcliffe-Maud (1906–82), diplomat; Master of University Coll., Oxford, 1963–76.

to London, I make a point of standing about in the main quad for several minutes before I leave.'

From the Queen Mother I have a warm 'How very nice to see you again,' both when she arrives and when she leaves. I have some spirited talk with her in the drawing room after lunch. She seems rather worried that the Tories have lost the by-election at Portsmouth to the SDP – what she calls the Socialist-Democrats. She puts it down to unemployment and says that the solution is to bring back National Service. We also talk of Harold Macmillan. 'Before the war he was very left-wing – not that we used the horrible phrase then – and wrote a book called *The Middle Way*.' I can discern no real affection for him in what she says. Perhaps he has still not been forgiven for his 'left-wing' views.

17 June 1984

Motor down to Glyndebourne with William and Caroline Waldegrave. It pours with rain on the way down, then the evening clears and we have a sumptuous picnic on the grass. We see Ted Heath, but manage to avoid him: he has behaved venomously to William over Government policy, even trying to incite William's Bristol constituents against him.

18 June 1984

Waterloo Day; and that other fateful anniversary of the Guards' Chapel in 1944.

Peter Carrington to lunch at Claridge's. He leaves for Brussels on Sunday to take up his appointment as Secretary General of NATO. Not at all happy at present. He must live in an hotel for the first three months, and then move to the unlovely villa of Joseph Luns,* his predecessor. Peter has asked for another house, but everything requires the agreement of so many countries, of which the meanest and stickiest is Britain. As he pointed out, a new house is equivalent in cost to half an inch of an airfield runway. Nor has NATO a plane for his use. He will be able to commute, but only by British Airways.

In recent weeks Peter has made a tour of the NATO capitals, where he generally found the Heads of State to be more impressive than the Prime Ministers. Peter enjoyed King Juan Carlos' description of the Spanish army: 'It is like an elephant: difficult to get moving, and once it has got moving difficult to stop.'

---

* (1911–2002), Dutch politician. Sec. Gen. of NATO 1971–84.

26 June 1984

Alexander Macmillan to lunch at the Charing Cross Hotel. His firm is about to take a decision to reprint my *Superior Person* in paperback. He says Harold Macmillan is enjoying his prolonged stay at Chatsworth, although the company is not as varied as he would wish. Debo says: 'We ought to put him on show and charge extra.' He is being pestered by Garter King of Arms about his motto and supporters. His war diaries are also causing him worry as Nikolai Tolstoy[*] is about to attack them for not being more forthcoming about the repatriation of Cossacks and others who wore German uniform. Alexander rightly says: 'What my grandfather did may not in retrospect have been the best solution, but it seemed reasonable at the time.'

9 July 1984

Part of York Minster destroyed by fire: a terrible tragedy. It is said to be a divine thunderbolt, only a few hours after the consecration of the supposedly heretical Dr Jenkins[†] as the new Bishop of Durham.

12 July 1984

British Academy dinner in Middle Temple Hall. The usual agreeable half-hour of drinks first. I talk to Eric Anderson, now working on an edition of Percy's Reliques.[‡] Owen Chadwick makes a good speech. Greeting Hugh Casson, he quotes Gainsborough's last words: 'We are all going to heaven and Van Dyck is of the company.' What Owen does not realise until I tell him afterwards is that he is standing a foot or two in front of a Van Dyck of Charles I.

16 July 1984

Edward Ford tells me that the Queen is shocked that Michael Adeane left in-structions that there should be no memorial service. She thinks it is because he was an atheist; in fact, he just wanted to avoid fuss.

4 August 1984

Train to Bath, to stay with Owen Lloyd George.[§] Owen tells me the story of

---

[*] Count Nikolai Tolstoy (b. 1935), Anglo-Russian author, campaigner regarding the forced repatriation of Soviet citizens during and after World War II.
[†] The Rt Revd David Jenkins (1925–2016), Bishop of Durham 1984–94.
[‡] *Reliques of Ancient English Poetry* (1765) by Bishop Thomas Percy (1729–1811), Bishop of Dromore. Anderson's edition was published in 1988.
[§] Owen Lloyd-George, 3rd Earl Lloyd-George of Dwyfor (1924–2010), Capt. in the Welsh Guards; cross-bench peer 1968.

a man whose death was concealed to avoid death duties; so with the conniv-
ance of the family doctor he was put into the deep freeze. Then the doctor
died. When the time had elapsed for death duties to be paid, the family took
the body out of the deep freeze, thawed him and sent for the new doctor.
A conscientious young man, he examined the corpse, and observed that
although it was December, there were raspberries in the stomach. 'Oh, that's
quite all right,' the doctor was assured, 'we have a deep freeze.'

A.J. Sylvester, Lloyd George's Secretary, comes to lunch.* Owen lent him
my *KGV* and he wants to meet me. Now in his ninety-fifth year, he is still
spry and active, immersed in a two-year war with his local Water Board.
As recently as 1977 he received a 'supreme award' for ballroom dancing. He
wears a homburg hat that must surely date back to before the war: perhaps
even the one he wore when taking part in the historic game of golf at Cannes
between L.G. and Aristide Briand,† with René Massigli‡ now the only other
survivor.

He has a splendid contempt for much supposedly true history, which he
calls 'mush' and pronounces 'moosh'. He also expresses a similar disgust
at the conduct of L.G.'s second wife, Frances Stevenson,§ who 'ran through
all his money, then tried to sell his pocketbook to Beaverbrook'. A.J.'s place
in history is probably to have been the first man to have taken a shorthand
note of Cabinet proceedings. He speaks of all the services great and small
he performed on L.G.'s behalf: from extracting secret papers from the War
Office for his memoirs to securing him a room of his own in the House of
Commons – 'even though it resembled a mortuary'. Owen also tells me that
when he went over to see L.G. at Churt in 1944, at 9 p.m. the old man turned
not to the BBC news on the wireless, but to 'Lord Haw-Haw.'¶

11 August 1984

Tony Quinton** gives a large luncheon party in the hall of Trinity, Oxford.

---

* Albert James Sylvester (1889–1989), Principal PS to Lloyd George 1923–45.
† (1862–1932), Prime Minister of France for eleven terms; co-Laureate of the 1926 Nobel
Peace Prize. On 9 Jan. 1922 Briand, who had never played golf before, accepted Lloyd George's
challenge to a match after a bibulous lunch at Cannes Golf Club; photographs of his undignified efforts appeared in the French press the next day and led to his resignation.
‡ (1888–1988), French politician and diplomat.
§ Frances Lloyd-George, Countess Lloyd-George of Dwyfor (1888–1972), personal secretary
of Lloyd George, whom she married in 1943.
¶ William Joyce (1906–46), known as Lord Haw-Haw, made Nazi propaganda broadcasts to
the UK during World War II. He was hanged for treason.
** Antony Quinton, Baron Quinton of Holywell (1925–2019), political and moral philosopher.
President of Trinity Coll., Oxford 1978–87.

We have some talk on a successor to Harold Macmillan as Chancellor – not that the old man shows any sign of budging. William Waldegrave favours Isaiah Berlin.

John Patten is very interesting on how badly women's colleges have done in Schools. This is because the best girls now go to men's colleges, as do the best men dons. So the women's colleges end up with less good men dons and less good men undergraduates.

Philip Goodhart* rejoices that in Ian Gow† we shall have the first whole-hearted Unionist to be Secretary of State for Northern Ireland. He also says: 'When David Steel gets up to speak in the Commons, 500 MPs on all sides of the House get up to go.'

16 September 1984

Michael Duff‡ recently went to the ballet with the Queen Mother. At supper she said: 'My footman is so lucky. He went to the first night. I couldn't get in.'

23 September 1984

I talk with Jock Colville about the Royal Family and other matters. Jock is at last going to publish the diaries he kept during his years as Private Secretary to Neville Chamberlain. He also wants to publish the diary he similarly kept when Private Secretary to the present Queen as Princess Elizabeth in 1947-9. So he sent them to the Queen the other day for her approval. She replied in a long letter in her own hand, admitting that there was nothing specific to which she could object, but nevertheless asking him not to publish them. Tommy Lascelles left his own diaries to his daughters,§ who now want to publish them. If the Queen allows Jock to publish his, there could be no objection to Tommy's; and the Queen is very much against their being published. It does seem extraordinary that so 'correct' a Private Secretary should have kept a diary while in the Queen's service: a right which is denied to every footman or other official. The legal position is not clear. The two executors were Edward Ford and Michael Adeane, who not long before Tommy's death persuaded him to deposit the diaries in the Royal Archives

---

* Sir Philip Goodhart (1925–2015), Conservative politician. MP for Beckenham 1957–92; Under-Sec. of State for Northern Ireland 1979–81.

† (1937–90), solicitor and Conservative politician. MP for Eastbourne 1974–90, when he was killed by an IRA bomb.

‡ Sir Michael Duff, 3rd Bt (1907–80), Lord Lieutenant of Caernarvon 1960–74 and of Gwynedd 1974–80.

§ Lavinia Lascelles (b. 1923), m. Maj. Edward Renton, then Gavin Maxwell. Caroline Lascelles (b. 1927), m. Anthony Lyttelton, 2nd Viscount Chandos.

in Windsor. But what does 'deposit' mean? Can the daughters, to whom they were left in Tommy's will, claim them back? And if so, would there be any legal objection to publication, as opposed to merely displeasing the Queen? Duff Hart-Davis, who is bringing out a book of Tommy's early letters and diaries, may know.

At one moment Jock was asked by Windsor to write a life of Edward VIII. Then Frances Donaldson produced her book, so the idea was dropped.

Some sidelights on the Queen Mother: he thinks that the Press exaggerated Mountbatten's influence on the Royal Family in general and on Prince Charles in particular. Queen Mary thwarted Mountbatten's attempt to make the family name Mountbatten. Queen Mary went to Winston, who persuaded the Cabinet to tell the Queen that it would never do.

Princess Margaret once said to Jock: 'The two men who have ruined my life are Tommy Lascelles and Winston Churchill, who would not let me marry Peter Townsend.' Jock replied: 'I don't know about Tommy, but Winston did not want to repeat the mistake of 1936.' Princess Margaret was not pleased by this.

Before the birth of the first child of the Prince and Princess of Wales, Jock reminded the Prince that after the row in Scotland over the Queen calling herself Queen Elizabeth II, Parliament decided that all future kings were to be called by the highest number of their names, whether in England or Scotland. So if they called the infant James, he would one day have to rule as King James VIII.

12 October 1984

Fearful news of a bomb blast at the Grand Hotel, Brighton, in the early hours of this morning: the work of the IRA. Many killed and injured, but the PM escapes.

Later comes the news that Tony Berry[*] has died in the explosion. What irony: had he been sent to prison the other day for drunken driving, he would be alive today. I shall long remember our happy talk only a couple of days ago.

16 October 1984

Duff Hart-Davis to lunch at the Charing Cross Hotel. On Tommy Lascelles' papers, he emphasises how exceptionally discreet he was in writing about other members of the Royal Family, except Edward VIII. But his hatred of

---

[*] Sir Anthony Berry (1925–84), Conservative MP for Southgate, later Enfield Southgate, 1964–84.

the Windsors, which is now known to the Queen, may provoke a complete Royal ban on the whole of his Palace diaries.

18 November 1984

Richard Thorpe tells me that he is definitely going to write Selwyn Lloyd's life. He has been invited to do so by the family and executors. Graham C. Greene* will publish the biography at Jonathan Cape. He will have exclusive access to the vast collection of Lloyd papers at Churchill College, where I advised the family to deposit them. He hopes to get an Archives Fellowship at Churchill College for a term in order to work on the papers. I hope he can manage to combine so much research with teaching at Charterhouse.

2 December 1984

Brigadier Geoffrey Hardy-Roberts,† Master of the Royal Household from 1967 to 1973, used to worry at the difficulty of keeping food hot when served on gold plate. But the Queen told him: 'People come here not to eat hot food, but to eat off gold plate.'

4 December 1984

At a British Council lunch, the former Foreign Secretary‡ makes a jolly speech. He recalls an ABCA pamphlet in the war entitled: 'What we are fighting for.' It was stamped across the top: 'The information in this pamphlet must not be revealed to unauthorised persons.'

I enjoy some talk with Michael Foot. We agree that Harold Laski's§ untruthfulness and snobbery have concealed his considerable importance as an economics teacher.

5 December 1984

Lunch at the Savoy given by the *Spectator* for presentation of the Parliamentarian of the Year Awards. Jo Grimond¶ makes an avuncular speech of introduction. The winners produce some characteristic remarks. 'I feel

---

* (1936–2016), publisher. MD of Jonathan Cape 1962–90; nephew of Graham Greene.

† Brig. Sir Geoffrey Hardy-Roberts (1907–97), British Army officer, Conservative politician, Master of the Royal Household 1967–73.

‡ Michael Stewart, Baron Stewart of Fulham (1906–90), Labour politician. MP for Fulham 1955–79; Foreign Secretary 1965–6 and 1968–70.

§ Harold Laski (1893–1950), economist and political theorist. Professor at the London School of Economics 1926–50.

¶ (1913–93), Liberal politician. MP for Orkney and Shetland 1950–83; Leader of the Liberal Party 1956–67 and May–July 1976.

like a man helping police with their inquiries,' said Malcolm Rifkind* when named 'Member to Watch'. And Jack Cunningham,† named as 'Debater of the Year', said: 'The Government have given us a large goal to shoot at.' Tam Dalyell‡ was named 'Troublemaker of the Year'. But he didn't turn up!

I sit next to a Government Whip, Peter Lloyd,§ MP for Fareham. As a young man, before he got into Parliament, he presided over a Bow Group dinner for Harold Macmillan. Harold asked him if he was a candidate, whether he had a job, and did he go to this job every day, and stay all day? The answer was in the affirmative to all questions. When Harold came to make his speech, he said: 'You have a wonderful Chairman. He has a job, and he goes to his office every day and all day, and I'm sure that when he gets home in the evening he has no servants!'

---

* Sir Malcolm Rifkind (b. 1946), Foreign Secretary 1995–7.
† Jack Cunningham, Baron Cunningham of Felling (b. 1939), Labour politician. MP for Copeland 1983–2005; Minister of Agriculture, Fisheries and Food 1997–8; Minister for the Cabinet Office 1998–9.
‡ Tam Dalyell (1932–2017), Labour politician. MP for West Lothian 1962–83 and Linlithgow 1983–2005; known for the 'West Lothian' question' on whether non-English MPs should vote on English-only matters.
§ Sir Peter Lloyd (b. 1937), Conservative politician. MP for Fareham 1979–2001.

1985

23 January saw the first televising of a debate in the House of Lords. Margaret Thatcher was publicly refused an honorary degree by Oxford University on 29 January. The miners' strike ended after one year on 3 March. Mikhail Gorbachev became Soviet leader on 11 March. George Brown died on 2 June. Unemployment fell to 3,178,582 on 4 July. The wreck of RMS Titanic *was located by a Franco-American expedition on 1 September. Riots broke out in Handsworth, Birmingham, on 9 September and two people died on 10 September when a post office was petrol-bombed. Conservatives fell to third place in an opinion poll, with the SDP–Liberal Alliance in the lead. Riots in Brixton on 28 September led to fatalities. Neil Kinnock attacked the Militant Tendency in a speech at the Labour Party Conference in Bournemouth. The Conservatives returned to the lead in the opinion polls on 15 October. On 1 November unemployment had fallen by 70,000. On 15 November an Anglo-Irish Agreement was signed at Hillsborough Castle. On 5 December it was announced that unemployment had fallen for the third month in succession.*

15 January 1985
Dine at Pratt's. Harold Macmillan is holding forth: 'We are going to be televised in the House of Lords on Wednesday and all the bishops are <u>very</u> excited.' So is he!

29 January 1985
Oxford University turns down a proposal to give Mrs Thatcher an Hon. DCL by 738 to 319: a tremendous blow. They cannot all be Socialists.

3 February 1985
John Patten is furious with Harold Macmillan, who only now comes out in

support of Mrs Thatcher. As Chancellor of Oxford University he should have tried to stifle the hostile vote before it took place. I agree.[*]

16 February 1985

In reading about the Duke of Windsor, I keep coming across an odd assertion: that in 1936 the then Duke of York was so reluctant to accept the Crown, that the Government and the Royal Family considered whether it should not be offered to Prince George, Duke of Kent, not least because he had a male heir. It sounds unlikely to me, for if the Duke of York did not want to become King, would the Crown not have gone to the next brother, Prince Henry of Gloucester?[†]

3 March 1985

Lunch with John Lisburne.[‡] Sir Robert Mark,[§] the former Commissioner of Police, has told John that the collapse of the miners' strike has long been predictable. From the moment Scargill[¶] won the 1974 strike, the police have been plotting redress. In 1974, Mark went to the then Home Secretary, Roy Jenkins, to persuade him that the police must be reorganised and made more mobile to prevent such a happening in the future. Jenkins, although a Labour Home Secretary, agreed. Ten years later the police were ready for Scargill.

4 March 1985

The coal strike collapses after having lasted about a year. A satisfactory defeat for Scargill.

---

[*] Another interpretation of this controversial event is held by some at Oxford. 'Macmillan had suggested the honorary degree to Geoffrey Warnock, the Vice-Chancellor, knowing that a nonagenarian Chancellor would not be denied, but also with impish mischievousness, that the proposal would be controversial. He thus lit the blue touch paper and then retired to watch the subsequent fireworks.' D. R. Thorpe, *Supermac: The Life of Harold Macmillan* (2010), p. 655.

[†] K.R. often thought about this issue over the years, especially as at one stage he was considered as a biographer of the Duke of Kent. Various historians, especially Dermot Morrah (1896–1974), had mooted this possibility, noting that the Duke of York, the future George VI, was initially left in the dark as to developments. K.R. accepted that initial informal consideration may have been given, but that, if so, it was soon abandoned, not only on legal grounds, but on the basis that one Abdication was a major constitutional crisis and that any further standing aside by the Duke of York and the Duke of Gloucester would have been totally unacceptable.

[‡] John David Malet Vaughan, 8th Earl of Lisburne (1918–2014), officer in the Welsh Guards; called to the Bar in 1948; later a businessman.

[§] Sir Robert Mark (1917–2010), Commissioner of the Metropolitan Police 1972–7.

[¶] Arthur Scargill (b. 1938), President of the National Union of Mineworkers 1982–2002.

23 March 1985

I hear that Bishop John Bickersteth,* Clerk of the Closet to the Queen, is something of a trendy bishop. At Sandringham he tried to convince the Queen Mother that the World Council of Churches was a good thing, but she remained sceptical. This annoyed Bickersteth. When he preached next day, he introduced a passage into his sermon saying that the WCC was a much-maligned body, and he turned and looked at the Queen Mother as he did so. The QM trembled with rage.

27 March 1985

To the film of E.M. Forster's *A Passage to India*. It is all I had feared.

4 April 1985, Letter to Sir David Scott†

I have spent a month in India, an admirable country, except for the habitual sloth of its inhabitants. The faded glory of Simla was particularly memorable, the houses with names like Balmoral. The Viceregal Lodge has been turned into a kind of All Souls, where studious academics turn out dismal treatises on the rupee and other intimidating topics. In its library I spotted one of my biographies, and felt the same pride as Dr Johnson on being told that Catherine the Great was reading *Rasselas* on the banks of the Volga!

I was once more overwhelmed by the genius of Lutyens' New Delhi, at once the Versailles and Valhalla of British rule. In the basement I came on all the viceregal portraits, safely insulated from republican eyes. They included Gerald Kelly's‡ State portraits of George VI and Queen Elizabeth, but were labelled: 'Artist unknown.' How Kelly would have minded. When elected President of the Royal Academy he wrote to the Head Master of Eton asking for a whole holiday in his honour. 'No,' replied Robert Birley.

There has, incidentally, been a new life of Birley, called *Red Robert*. It is an inappropriate title given him by a stupid OE general who saw what he thought was a portrait of Karl Marx in Birley's office in post-war Berlin. It was in fact a portrait of Brahms. The only revolutionary thing Birley ever did was to abolish the bowler hat at Charterhouse.

From the sublime to the ridiculous. I ran into Harold Wilson outside the Houses of Parliament this afternoon, and was delayed a good ten minutes while he tried out passages from his forthcoming autobiography on me. I

---

* The Rt Revd John Bickersteth (1921–2018), Bishop of Bath and Wells 1975–87; Clerk of the Closet to the Queen 1979–89.
† Sir David Scott (1919–2011), Ambassador to South Africa 1976–9.
‡ Sir Gerald Kelly (1879–1972), portrait painter. President of the Royal Academy 1949–54.

thought of Emerson's* remark: 'The louder he talked of his honour, the faster we counted our spoons.'†

Then I saw Peter Carrington, which restored my faith in mankind. What a nice man. As you know, he is going off to be Secretary General of NATO, with a house in Brussels, plus bodyguards.‡ So he is brushing up his French, he tells me, with a young lady. Can you imagine Austen Chamberlain or Lord Curzon doing anything so daring?

11 April 1985

Martin Gilliat to dine. He tells me the Queen Mother disapproved of Philip Ziegler's life of Lady Diana Cooper, and that she never cared for either of the Mountbattens. She felt that Dickie was rather an outsider vis-à-vis the real Royals such as Princess Marina, so rarely entertained them.

Martin thinks it terribly wrong that the Duchess of Windsor has never become HRH. 'I hope that before she dies, my employer may come to see the lack of charity in this attitude.' I have never heard him express a stronger opinion.

17 April 1985

At 11 o'clock to Marlborough House for a conference addressed by Prince Philip on Commonwealth veterans. What an oppressively ornate house, with horrible pink wall covering and far too much gold. I suppose the Commonwealth Secretariat like it.

Prince Philip speaks briskly, but joins the growing number of people who say disinterested when they mean uninterested.

18 April 1985

Lunch with Julian Faber at the Savoy. Some good talk on Harold Macmillan. As a boy at Summer Fields he was miserable and homesick. A friend tried to comfort him by saying, 'Your predicament is difficult but not desperate.'

23 April 1985

Lunch with Robert Armstrong. He tells me that when he was Rab Butler's Private Secretary he once went to Bad Godesberg with him. Rab said that since Chamberlain's flight there in 1938 he had never carried an umbrella.

---

* Ralph Waldo Emerson (1803–82), American essayist and poet.
† The phrase originated in the life of Samuel Johnson by James Boswell (1740–95), Scottish biographer.
‡ When I visited Lord Carrington at his home in London at this time, bodyguards were in evidence. He introduced me to one, saying 'This is the man who shoots the man who shoots me.'

Rab used to take immense trouble over his letters to MPs, each a little different from the others, and one or two withheld for further thought. He had a highly developed political touch.

Churchill once asked Rab, as Chancellor, why we had to eat <u>Canadian</u> cheddar. Rab replied with a lengthy brief on dollars, etc. Winston eventually said: 'I only asked.'

30 April 1985
Richard Thorpe, the Charterhouse master, comes to dine. I give him a lot of my notes and talks on Selwyn Lloyd. He tells me that at Charterhouse people joked about when Oliver van Oss would bring up two of his favourite subjects – Leonardo da Vinci and his own lengthy career at Eton – when dining in the Common Room. One senior master, a close friend of OVO, and something of an 'all-licensed fool', said one evening: 'Well, Oliver, there's one thing the Mona Lisa will be grateful for, you can't claim she was in your house at Eton!'

31 May 1985
King Simeon of Bulgaria* comes to tea. As always, he is agreeable and intelligent, though I do wish he would not call me 'Sir'. Today he looks tired and nervous, playing endlessly with a string of worry-beads and with a heavy gold-linked bracelet on his wrist. When offered a piece of chocolate cake, he says: 'No, I must not, though I see it smiling at me.'

We talk of the Duke of Windsor. The King always found him exceptionally kind: 'In his last years he seemed to return to his German roots and always spoke German to me. Until then he had used English.'

11 June 1985
Staying with the Carringtons in Brussels. Peter's official Rolls-Royce takes me to the NATO headquarters. The car is heavily armoured and there is always a bodyguard in the front next to the driver. Peter says: 'Of course, the one way to be absolutely inconspicuous in Brussels is to go about in a green Rolls-Royce with two wireless aerials!' The car cost half a million dollars.

NATO HQ is even more soulless than the EEC building, like a prefabricated military hospital. Peter has tried to cheer up his box of an office with some V&A pictures. There is a notable absence on his desk of those horrible model nuclear missiles and other such trophies. But he does have a

---

* King Simeon II of Bulgaria (b. 1937), King 1943–6 when the monarchy was abolished; 48th Prime Minister of Bulgaria 2001–5.

case containing six toy soldiers: three of the 1st Prussian Guards in 1815 and three Grenadiers of the same year; they were allies at Waterloo.

I hear that Mrs Tebbit,* wife of the Industry Minister, still paralysed after the Brighton Grand Hotel bomb outrage, is being helped with her considerable medical expenses by both the PM and the Duke of Westminster.†

Peter Carrington tells me that when Harold Macmillan went to Austria to sell books, the journalists instead wanted to ask him about international affairs. One exasperated questioner at a Press conference burst out with:

'Don't you realise, Mr Macmillan, that U Thant‡ is going to Geneva to end the Vietnam War?'

Long pause.

Macmillan: 'How very good of him.'

27 June 1985

Dine Martin Gilliat at Brooks's. He looks very tired. He is worried about the strain which the forthcoming tour of Canada will put on both him and the Queen Mother. 'The telephone number at the very top of my list is Kenyon, the undertaker.'

29 June 1985

William Clark§ is dead. A bitchy obituary in *The Times*, contrasting his supposed patrician style of a flat in Albany and the Athenaeum with his supposed humble background. But is either premise true? He went to Oundle, which is hardly a board school.

30 June 1985

Gillian Rees-Mogg tells me that her boy Jacob at Eton asked the Head Master, Eric Anderson, whether he could start a Conservative Society. The HM said not under that name. So it is to be called the Stockton Society, and old Harold Macmillan is delighted.

2 July 1985

Read Patrick Devlin's new book on the trial of Dr John Bodkin Adams,¶

---

* Margaret Tebbit, Baroness Tebbit of Chingford (b. 1934), a former nurse; permanently paralysed in the Brighton Grand Hotel bombing in 1984.

† Maj.-Gen. Sir Gerald Grosvenor, 6th Duke of Westminster (1951–2016).

‡ (1909–74), Sec. Gen. of the UN 1962–71.

§ (1916–85), economist; press secretary to Anthony Eden during the Suez Crisis.

¶ Dr John Bodkin Adams (1899–1983), GP, tried and acquitted of the murder of one of his patients, 160 of whom had died in suspicious circumstances between 1946 and 1956. Lord

the Eastbourne doctor, over which he presided. It really seems to have been animated by spite towards Reginald Manningham-Buller[*] and surely sets a bad precedent: a judge who relives a case in print and finds an acquitted defendant more or less guilty.

10 July 1985
Buffet lunch on the terrace of the House of Lords. It is a charming spectacle, with little white steamers scuttling along the water and the Archbishop's flag flying over Lambeth.

Quintin Hailsham agrees with me that it was wrong of Patrick Devlin to try the Bodkin Adams case again in print, and imply that he was guilty. But, he adds, 'It is a jolly good read.' He also says of the case: 'It is the only one in which I personally knew the judge, leading counsel on both sides – and the prisoner, whom I had met dining out in Sussex.' Quintin mentions that, like Alec Home, he refuses to have security guards, in spite of a former prisoner having come to his house to try to murder him.

9 August 1985
In the *TLS* Michael Howard[†] reviews some books on the dropping of the atom bomb on Hiroshima in 1945. He dwells on the huge casualties we might have encountered had the landing in Malaya in September 1945 taken place: probably my own life among them.

17–18 August 1985
The Prince of Wales is a fellow guest with me of John King[‡] at Strathnaver for the first couple of days. He had come to fish alone, except for the three detectives who discreetly guard him day and night. In such remote surroundings he loses all trace of tension and nervousness. He comes in from fishing in the late afternoon. Through the window I see him pause for a few minutes, gazing out on the sunlit hills, looking both alone and lonely.

Leaner, taller and more handsome than I recall. A very firm handshake. 'I have heard so much about you and read so much of yours.' He plunges at

---

Devlin's book on the case was called *Easing the Passing: The Trial of Doctor John Bodkin Adams* (1985).
[*] 1st Viscount Dilhorne (1905–80), lawyer and Conservative politician. Lord High Chancellor 1962–4.
[†] Sir Michael Howard (b. 1922), military historian, Regius Professor of Modern History at Oxford University 1980–89.
[‡] Baron King of Wartnaby (1917–2005), dubbed 'Mrs Thatcher's favourite businessman'. Chairman of British Airways 1981–93.

once into *KGV* and asks whether I worked in the Royal Archives. When I explain how I had Harold Nicolson's unused transcripts of papers from the Royal Archives, he says: 'How clever!'

Much talk about the Windsors, not least the inglorious reign of Edward VIII. He has twice been to their house in Paris and was struck by how Royal an atmosphere they made, with all the kingly relics of the Duke's past. 'It is horrible to think of the Duchess lying there, very nearly dead, and being kept alive at great expense.' Yet it was Maître Blum who, when his boy William was born, sent him a christening set which had belonged to the Duke of Windsor. Prince Charles adds that it was only recently he became aware of the gold cup given to him at his christening by Queen Mary: it had originally been given by King George III to a godchild. This casts an interesting light on how difficult it must be for the Royal Family to keep track of their enormous treasure house of possessions. Prince Charles thinks that the Windsors <u>did</u> have Queen Alexandra's jewels, and wonders if they will ever return to England.

We discuss the Duke's character, and I point to the evidence that he never really wanted to be King. 'But, of course,' I add, 'there is no way in which the heir to the throne can renounce his rights before he succeeds.' Prince Charles: 'Oh yes there is. He can marry a Catholic – almost as serious a matter as trying to go to a Papal Mass!' This is very sharp of him: if a member of the Royal Family marries a Catholic, he or she loses the right of succession, by the Act of Settlement of 1701.

On Philip Ziegler's life of Mountbatten, he would have liked much more detail. This I find surprising. He tells me a characteristic story of KGV he heard from the Queen Mother. The King was standing dangerously in the road somewhere, perhaps at a shoot, and Queen Mary warned him to take care. 'Why should I?', he replied. 'It's the King's Highway, isn't it?' The Prince says that he is a dedicated diarist, who also likes to illustrate it if there is time. 'It always amazes me that people seem to remember exactly what I said to them years ago.' I ask him if this prompts him to be discreet. 'No, I gave that up several years ago!'

Prince Charles would love to live in Marlborough House. 'I grit my teeth with rage whenever I go to some Commonwealth event there. But what can one do? Once the people get inside a building it is impossible to throw them out.' His face suffuses with anger when he recalls 'the contempt shown by architects to blokes like myself who criticise their efforts'. His present passion is a study of classical architecture.

For someone who read History at Cambridge and has taken an interest in it since, I am surprised that he has never heard of the *Dictionary of National Biography* or of the practice begun by Queen Victoria and continued by

Edward VII and George V of having a minister in attendance at Balmoral.

In spite of widespread rumours that the Prince is a vegetarian and cranky about his food, I see no sign of any excessive worry on his part. He eats meat, but does put honey in his tea.

We have some talk on current problems. John King is most interesting on this: 'The Prime Minister relies too much on Denis, who was never more than the director of a small company. So he read the balance sheet of Rolls-Royce, and without wider knowledge said that the company was bust. It wasn't. Margaret Thatcher admires such leaders of private enterprise as Laker and Maxwell,* but not ICI or GEC.' In all this I think that John is giving a lesson to the impressionable Prince, so that he will not be attracted only to the colourful figures in the business world. Certainly the Prince appears to agree with him. On the French, Charles says: 'They are individually charming, but collectively unscrupulous.'

On the morning of his departure, the Prince does not leave until well past 10 o'clock, having earlier arranged to do so sharp at 9. Instead he sits about gossiping. He carries down his own suitcase. Then a little procession of two Range Rovers leaves for Balmoral – 'the only place where I have time to read and see my friends'. His detectives seem tough but friendly. One of them cheerfully examines my little wireless, which has gone dead – and gives me a new Royal battery for it.

3 September 1985

Four o'clock, tea with Arnold Goodman at his flat in Portland Place. Find him reading George Bernard Shaw's collected musical criticism. He thinks Mrs Thatcher has made a mistake in not recalling Cecil Parkinson to the Cabinet after his resignation two years ago for having got his secretary with child. He compares it with Mr Gladstone's rejection of Charles Stewart Parnell after the Kitty O'Shea scandal† – 'It would have ensured the settlement of Ireland if a man of Parnell's gifts had continued to lead the Irish Party at Westminster.' I disagree. Even without Parnell Gladstone carried Home Rule through the Commons but was defeated in the Lords. Parnell would never have swayed the opinion of the Upper House. Arnold adds that those

---

* Sir Frederick Laker (1922–2006), airline entrepreneur. Robert Maxwell (1923–91), media proprietor and Labour MP for Buckingham 1964–70. He died in mysterious circumstances after falling from his yacht in the Atlantic Ocean.

† Charles Stewart Parnell (1846–91), Irish nationalist politician. Katharine O'Shea (1846–1921), wife of Capt. William O'Shea (1840–1905), Catholic Nationalist MP for County Clare, divorced by him citing Parnell as co-respondent. She married Parnell, whose political career was ruined.

Conservatives who put pressure on the PM not to recall Parkinson may have been acting as much from self-interest as from a high standard of morality. If Parkinson were not recalled, there would be one more Cabinet post available to the current candidates.

18 September 1985

The garden is suddenly a blaze of red roses. I put in about 100 snowdrop bulbs. Jean Trumpington to dine. She relates how when she went to take her leave of the Queen as a Baroness-in-Waiting on being promoted to be Under-Secretary in the Department of Health and Social Security, the Queen said of the PM: 'She stays too long and talks too much. She has lived too long among men.'

20 September 1985

Dine with Jonathan Aitken and other friends in Lord North Street to meet ex-President Nixon.* After dinner – an avocado, roast beef and a pudding – Jonathan welcomes Nixon, who talks for about twenty minutes on his world tour, then answers questions. He is lucid, incisive and humorous: more of a statesman than Reagan.† He rightly claims credit for unfreezing relations with China, and he pays a memorable tribute to Great Britain's role in India and the Far East, with its legacy of good administration and the English language. The ex-President is asked whether he thinks Edward Kennedy will ever be President. 'No,' Nixon says, 'he hasn't the class.' He talks with exceptional knowledge, perception and humour. Whatever traces of the Watergate scandal may cling to him, Nixon does possess that indefinable quality one may call statesmanship.

I talk to John Connally,‡ the former Governor of Texas. He shows me how he cannot turn one hand where it was struck by a bullet when he was travelling in the same car as J.F.K. on the day the President was assassinated. The episode used to haunt him with nightmares.

23 September 1985

Ted Heath most affable at a dinner in Tite Street. I tell him how impressed I was by Nixon. Ted agrees and says it was absurd for him to be disgraced

---

* Richard Nixon (1913–94), US President 1969–74.
† Ronald Reagan (1911–2004), US President 1981–9.
‡ John Connally (1917–93), Governor of Texas 1963–9; seriously wounded when President Kennedy was assassinated. In 1966 he said: 'I am convinced beyond doubt that I was not struck by the first bullet.'

over Watergate. When Ted was in China soon afterwards, Zhou Enlai* said to him: 'This is ridiculous isn't it? After all, we all tap our opponents' telephones.' Ted: 'No, not in England. It is much simpler there. The two-party headquarters are opposite each other in Smith Square, and as the staff of both use the same pub, each party knows the other's secrets.'

When Ted mentions that someone has invited him to breakfast, I tell him how agreeable it is at the Hyde Park Hotel and ask him whether he would like to come one morning. He says he cannot bear breakfasting out. This, I tell him to his delight, shows that he could never be mistaken for a Liberal.

5 October 1985

In 1968, when Christopher Soames was about to take up his post as Ambassador to France in order to bring Britain into the Common Market, he was asked to lunch with the Foreign Secretary, George Brown – at Brown's Hotel, as it happened. Christopher told him: 'I have been told that you have several times tried to resign. Now I have a vested interest in your support at the Foreign Office, so don't resign again.' Brown replied: 'No, I won't. I will not see you out, but I am likely to see you in for much of your time in Paris.' That very evening he resigned in a fit of pique, and Harold Wilson accepted his resignation. So Christopher had to work with Michael Stewart, who showed his ineptness when Christopher asked him for a meeting by inviting him to lunch in the Strangers' Dining Room in the Commons: all confidential talk was thus impossible.

Christopher tells me a curious tale of how luck can make or mar a career. As a young MP he was appointed Financial Secretary to the Admiralty at the same time as Tam Galbraith became the Civil Lord. Each was allocated a young Private Secretary and told it didn't matter which one they chose. Galbraith took the one called Vassall,† who was later unmasked as a Soviet spy. Galbraith's unguarded but innocent letters to Vassall ruined his political career and may even have been a factor in his early death. Christopher says that something of all this would surely have rubbed off on him had he been unlucky enough to have chosen Vassall as his first Private Secretary.

---

* (1898–1976), first Premier of the People's Republic of China 1949–76.
† Sir Thomas ('Tam') Galbraith (1917–82), Scottish Unionist politician. MP for Glasgow Hillhead 1948–82. When Galbraith died unexpectedly, Roy Jenkins, who was looking for a viable constituency to fight, was rung up by a secretary who said simply: 'Galbraith is dead.' Jenkins thought he was referring to the American economist J.K. Galbraith (1908–2006) and sent off a letter of condolence to the supposed widow. John Vassall (1924–96), civil servant.

Christopher's years at the Admiralty with Mountbatten convinced him that he was a much over-rated man who bullied the First Sea Lord, Selkirk,[*] and took any credit that was going.

Also a story of Frank Longford[†] walking through Soho with a friend. He says: 'Now you see this place here? It used to be a vulgar spot with a brothel and a sex shop and all sorts of other undesirable things. And now look: it is a nice healthy massage establishment.'

6 October 1985

Talk with Mary Soames. Martin Gilbert is considered very untrustworthy by the Churchill family. One episode was when, having been given complete access to papers and photographs for the purpose of the official life only, he produced an illustrated short biography full of young Winston's inherited photographs – without asking permission. The money for the biographical volumes has now almost run out – and that for the companion volumes has run out altogether.

She is most interesting on the burning of the Graham Sutherland portrait of Winston by Clemmie. 'For twelve years we lied about it, maintaining that it was safe and sound. But on the death of my mother we insisted on an announcement being made between her funeral and the memorial service.' So the storm broke, died away and that was apparently the end of it. Then Mary heard that Harold Wilson was saying the Soames family still had the picture and would one day produce it, when it would become immensely valuable. Perhaps Wilson did not realise the implications of what he was saying: that they were deliberately defrauding the Treasury by concealing an asset of Winston's estate – or rather Clemmie's – on which they should have paid death duties. At a party one evening, Mary bearded Wilson on this, and even gave him, as a sign of good faith, the name of the odd-job man who carried out the actual burning.

21 October 1985

Cecil Parkinson tells me that his former mistress has recently sold her memoirs to the *Daily Mirror* – on condition that they should be published during the Conservative Party Conference. He is deeply upset by the episode. His harassed and self-pitying air convince me that those Tories who persuaded

---

* George Douglas-Hamilton, 10th Earl of Selkirk (1906–94), First Lord of the Admiralty 1957–9.
† Frank Pakenham, 7th Earl of Longford (1905–2001), social reformer and Labour politician. Leader of the House of Lords and Lord Privy Seal 1964–8; Sec. of State for the Colonies 1965–6.

the PM not to bring him back into the Government during the recent reshuffle were right.

25 October 1985

Read *Cecil Beaton* by Hugo Vickers.[*] It has a horrible fascination tinged with pity: all those emotional entanglements which caused him such misery, all that posturing and affectation. He scarcely ever read a book either, and had no real sense of humour.

14 November 1985

Lunch with Julian Faber at the Savoy Grill. He talks of Harold Macmillan, who he thinks is neglected at Birch Grove: just the retired gardener's wife comes in to look after him. Both the garden and the house are looking rather neglected. Carol has tried to persuade her father to live in London during the winter, but he refuses. Fortunately, Philip de Zulueta[†] keeps a kindly eye on him.

17 November 1985

Edward Adeane tells me that Cyril Alington,[‡] when asked how he prepared a sermon to be preached before the King and Queen, said: 'As if it were for Lower Chapel at Eton, with the difficult bits left out.'

16 December 1985

Lunch with Prince Eddie at Buck's. He is delighted to have been awarded the Garter on the occasion of his fiftieth birthday in October, but is worried that his father's Garter robes have gone astray. They were stored at Hampton Court and an intensive search for them is under way.

We talk of the recent book purporting to reveal not only all the innermost secrets of Freemasonry,[§] but also allegations of corruption among Freemasons in local government, the police, etc. Eddie thinks that the book has on balance done good, by enabling the Freemasons to demonstrate that they are neither wicked nor barbaric. When I mention that Michael Adeane asked me to become a Mason many years ago, which I declined to do, Eddie is surprised, as he did not think that Michael was ever a Freemason.

---

[*] Hugo Vickers (b. 1951), royal biographer, broadcaster and journalist.
[†] Sir Philip de Zulueta (1925–89), civil servant and businessman.
[‡] (1872–1955), cleric, educationalist and author. Headmaster of Shrewsbury 1908–16; Head Master of Eton 1916–33.
[§] *The Brotherhood: The Explosive Exposé of the Secret World of the Freemasons* (1983) by Stephen Knight (1951–85), investigative author.

24 December 1985

Marie-Lou de Zulueta tells me a charming story of Prince Charles when a small boy. One day he came barging into Boy Browning's* room, and heard him talking on the telephone to the Queen. So he asked: 'Who is the Queen?' Boy explained that it was his mother, but Charles simply did not believe that she could be both his mother <u>and</u> Queen. Next day, however, he admitted that Boy Browning had been right. 'How do you know?' Boy asked. 'I asked the policeman.'

31 December 1985

'A letter from Sandringham,' the postman says brightly when I answer his ring at the door. It is from Princess Margaret, thanking me for *Kings, Queens and Courtiers*.† She writes with genuine warmth and interest, explains those episodes which the book lightly criticises, is delighted by my hits at Tommy Lascelles and Cecil Beaton, confides something of her inner thoughts, and adds a warm dash of praise. I am touched by the spirit of her response to the book.

---

* Lt-Gen. Sir Frederick Browning (1896–1965), senior British Army officer who saw action with the First Allied Airborne Army during Operation Market Garden in Sept. 1944; Comptroller and Treasurer to HRH Princess Elizabeth 1948–52.
† K.R.'s *Kings, Queens and Courtiers: Intimate Portraits of the Royal House of Windsor from its Foundation to the Present Day* was published in 1985. He described it as 'a self-indulgent book which I hope may perhaps add a footnote or two to history'.

1986

1986 was the year of the 'Big Bang' deregulation of the financial markets. Michael Heseltine resigned as Secretary of State for Defence over the Westland helicopter affair on 9 January. On 20 January Britain and France announced plans to construct the Channel Tunnel. Inheritance Tax replaced Capital Transfer Tax on 18 March. Buckingham Palace announced the engagement of Prince Andrew to Sarah Ferguson on 19 March. The Duchess of Windsor died on 24 April and was buried at Frogmore five days later. The millionth council house was sold to its tenants, seven years after the right-to-buy scheme began. GCSE examination courses replaced GCE O-Level and CSE courses in September. The completed M25 London Orbital Motorway of 122 miles was opened by Margaret Thatcher on 29 October. Harold Macmillan died on 29 December at Birch Grove.

3 January 1986

My Christmas holiday was brief, but I did escape to Sussex for two days and worshipped in a tiny village church. I ground my teeth over the Alternative Prayer Book, Rite A, such a vapid, fustian liturgy, with an artificial bonhomie utterly lacking in grace or euphony. At least we were spared the New Jerusalem Bible. It describes how the newborn Jesus was laid in a manger not 'because there was no room at the inn', but 'because there was no room in the living space'. Our bishops have gone quite insane.

Dine with Peter Thorneycroft at Northbourne one of the days. Julian and Carol Faber are there and have brought Harold Macmillan, an irony in itself. For in 1958, when Peter resigned as Chancellor of the Exchequer in protest against Macmillan's inflationary expenditure, the Prime Minister described his departure as no more than 'a little local difficulty'.

The old man is sitting glumly in the corner of a sofa and I am asked to cheer him up. He is soon on his very best form, although he has markedly shrunk and grown frailer since I last saw him. When asked how he enjoyed his return to No. 10 the other day to dine with the Queen and all the other ex-Prime Ministers, he says: 'Oh, it was terrible. No. 10 used to be a gentle-man's house. Now it is like Claridge's.'

When he was told that Isaiah Berlin at a recent dinner had talked first about God and then about the Prime Minister, H.M. said: 'Not much dif-ference, really.' Then, as so often with the old conjurer, he comes up with an entirely new story. 'Dickie Mountbatten once sent John Wyndham[*] a volume of family history he had compiled. With the book came a letter: "Dear John, You may care to have this book, which shows that we are both descended from King Edward VI. Yours ever, Dickie." John replied: "Dear Lord Mount-batten, I think there must be some mistake. My grandfather was a bastard. Your sincerely, John Wyndham."'

10 January 1986
John King thinks that Michael Heseltine's dramatic resignation from Cab-inet yesterday displays the same erratic judgement as swinging the mace in the House of Commons:[†] a demonstration of how unsuitable he would be as PM.

11 January 1986
Stimulating gossip with Nico Henderson. He does resent Mrs Thatcher's slight in not having given him a peerage. But he says, quite correctly: 'How terrible to see all those old Labour people, attacking wealth and privilege, while sitting in the House of Lords bars all day boozing away at the taxpay-ers' expense.' Harold Macmillan put it in a different way: 'Such a wonderful place for an old man: you cannot walk twenty yards without finding a bar and a lavatory.'

On Antony Acland's appointment to be our man in Washington, Nico says: 'I don't want to sound callous, but being a widower could be a positive advantage for him. To be an extra man is one of the most lovable of all qual-ities in the United States.'

16 January 1986
I had a drink at Pratt's and found Harold Macmillan sitting in front of the fire with pipe and glass, like the old crofter he sometimes pretends to be. He was half asleep, but he soon roused himself, and I had half an hour of

---

[*] (1903–69), science-fiction writer, one of whose best-known works is *The Day of the Triffids* (1951).

[†] On 27 May 1976 Heseltine seized the mace after a particularly heated debate in the House of Commons.

entertaining talk. He was following Heseltine's resignation with scandal-
ised delight and has asked to meet him to hear of things at first hand. He is
pleased to see Mrs Thatcher in trouble, yet magnanimous enough to admire
the skill with which she handles her Cabinet.

He talks of his contemporary at Eton and the Grenadiers, Harry Crookshank.* Once, in the Great War, he was buried alive by a shell, but was
eventually dug out and returned to duty the next day. 'Nowadays,' Harold says,
'he would have been sent to a psychiatric hospital and gone mad.' Crookshank
was known as Lazarus, because he had taken up his bed and walked. Then his
spirit weakens, and he says: 'Old age is a terrible thing, a terrible thing.'

21 January 1986

Long committee meeting at the London Library, during which we decide to
accept the more aesthetic but less practical scheme for providing extra room
for books in St James's Square.

Afterwards Roy Jenkins earnestly engages me in talk about my account of
the change of PMs in 1923, wondering whether Curzon's peerage was really
the only factor in his rejection.

22 January 1986

I meet Princess Margaret, pretty and animated. She wears pale blue with a
touch of turquoise which matches her eyes. I receive a warm greeting: 'How
tolerant you were of my letter about your latest book.' She goes on to talk of
Cecil Beaton's jealousy of Tony Snowdon, and his drawling at her at the time
of their engagement: 'Thank you, Ma'am, for removing a dangerous rival.'
Princess Margaret continues: 'After we were married, Tony wanted to give
up photography. We all thought this was wrong. So Lillibet and I worked on
him for a year and eventually succeeded. He returned to photography.' How
interesting that she refers to 'Lillibet'. Before it has always been 'The Queen'.

24 January 1986

Leon Brittan† resigns as Secretary of State for Trade, brought down by
Michael Heseltine as part of the imbroglio over Westland helicopters. Things
must now look doubtful for Mrs Thatcher at the next election, though memories are short.

---

* Harry Crookshank, 1st Viscount Crookshank of Gainsborough (1893–1961), Conservative
politician. MP for Gainsborough 1924–56; Minister of Health 1951–2; Leader of the House of
Commons 1951–5.
† Leon Brittan, Baron Brittan of Spennithorne (1939–2015), Conservative politician. MP for
Richmond, Yorkshire 1983–8; Home Secretary 1979–81; European Commissioner 1993–9.

25 January 1986

Prince Charles tells me he has been reading my *King George V* on the way to Australia: 'I not only loved the book, but loved the King more and more.'

The Prince and Diana are going to Klosters for a skiing holiday in a chalet with friends next week and are terrified that Press photographers will make life unendurable for them. 'But we had the editors to lunch one by one and I think that did some good.'

We return to the Windsors and he repeats his horror of the Duchess's being kept alive 'by teams of expensive doctors and nurses'. Prince Charles says that the only thing the Duke left him in his will was a collection of kilts: 'But as my great-uncle was such a tiny man, none of them fit me!'

He says: 'Well, goodbye, Kenneth. I shall look forward to seeing what you have to say in the *Sunday Telegraph* this weekend,' adding, a reference to current labour problems, 'if it's printed!'

Walking down Kensington High Street a few days ago I noticed two small boys, one black and the other white. The white one was eating a doughnut, and suddenly held it out to the black boy to take a bite. Children are utterly unconscious of colour, and I suspect would remain so throughout life if it were not for the busybody intervention of politicians and the race-relations industry.

6 February 1986

Lunch at the Beefsteak. Oliver van Oss is mysterious about the circumstances in which Brian Rees left the Headmastership of Rugby, albeit with compensation of £60,000.

16 February 1986

I am at a lunch at which Harold Macmillan is one of the guests. He looks in far better shape than when I last saw him in Pratt's, with a fuller face and brighter eyes. He drinks champagne before lunch. He is delighted to have voted against the Government on the Shops Bill in the Lords the other day, defeating certain clauses of the measure by a single vote. He explains that it is a deceptive piece of legislation. The first part, to which he does not object, allows Sunday trading. The second part, which offends him, removes the previous protection given to shopworkers by Winston Churchill's Shop Hours Bill of 1910–11. Harold says: 'It is absurd to claim that there is a free contract between the employed and the employer. I know. My grandfather was a shop assistant who came south and eventually found work in Cambridge at £30 a year. One cannot call that a free contract. He worked a twelve-hour day. If he had given up his job, he would either have starved or had to beg or applied

for Poor Law relief – unthinkable in a proud Highland Scot.' Harold is annoyed with the bishops for opposing the Bill on its Sunday trading clauses,
but not on its withdrawal of projection: 'I suppose they all went off to the
Athenaeum.'

He deplores the mess made by Neil Kinnock in his attack on Mrs Thatcher
over the leaked Solicitor General's letter in the Westland helicopter affair.
'How well someone like John Simon[*] or Asquith would have done it: a quiet,
calm unfolding of events, and then TWO UNANSWERABLE QUESTIONS!'

Gaitskell, he continues, was also a formidable debater, but he had two
faults. Although he knew which two unanswerable questions to ask, he could
not resist asking four more; and he would also go on speaking too long, so
that Harold did not (to his relief) have time for a full answer. 'I would answer
the four easy questions, then the debate had to end.'

He asks me to come and sit with him after lunch. On the Falklands, he
sees why Mrs Thatcher is unwilling to negotiate with Argentina: 'After all,
she won the election on the Falklands, and once one begins to negotiate, one
must eventually give them up. I would rather have saved Malta, which is now
a Soviet base.'

He says that since he was wounded in the Great War seventy years ago, he
has never had a day free from pain. On No. 10 he says: 'It used to have nice
wooden floors on which my grandchildren used to roller-skate. I had a notice
put up: "No roller-skating on Cabinet days!"'

17 February 1986

Dine with Philip and Marie-Lou de Zulueta. Just the three of us. Story of
Winston on one of his last birthdays before his death. Odette Pol-Roger[†]
usually sent him a case of twelve bottles for his birthday; but this time it
was only six. Churchill went round the presents, and Anthony Montague
Browne[‡] tried to keep him away from the champagne. But he was wheeled
up to it at his insistence, and with his stick he counted the bottles: 'One, two,
three . . .' When they ended at six, he said: 'Oh well, I suppose she thought
they would see me out.'

When Harold Macmillan was asked what he thought of Cliveden becoming an hotel, he replied: 'It always was one.'

---

* 1st Viscount Simon (1873–1954), leader of the National Liberals 1931–40. The first politician
to serve in the three great offices of State: Home Secretary 1915–16 and 1935–7; Foreign Secretary 1931–5; Chancellor of the Exchequer 1937–40; he was also Lord Chancellor 1940–45.
† (1911–2000), grand dame of her family's champagne house.
‡ Sir Anthony Montague Brown (1923–2013), PS to Winston Churchill 1952–65.

22 February 1986

My next biographical subject is to be the Rothschilds.* In Oxford to look at Rothschild letters in the MS collections. I have no time to see how my St Catherine's cedar tree is faring, but go straight to the Bodleian. Quite a lot of Rothschild material in the papers of Sir William Harcourt.† I also look at the Bibliothèque Nationale catalogues, which reveal a great mass of stuff.

How I love those dim dusty shelves, and the thrill of opening a box of papers or letters for the first time: in search of what Lytton Strachey‡ called 'the delicious bickerings of political intrigue'.

Tea with Arnold Goodman at Univ. He goes carefully through my draft contract with Weidenfeld for the Rothschilds, and concludes that it is a generous one from my point of view.

27 February 1986

At Eton Eric Anderson takes me to see the leaving portrait of the music scholar Stephen Layton§ by David Hill, which I commissioned, now hanging in the Head Master's study.

16 March 1986

Lunch at Chevening with Geoffrey Howe. Chevening is austerely elegant, built of red brick and stone. First a tour of the house, with its fine library. Geoffrey says: 'We do have your *King George V*, but it is out at the moment' – as if it were the Tooting Bec municipal lending library. He also shows me a first edition of Adam Smith's *The Wealth of Nations*. On the wall of another room is the manuscript of my favourite poem by Thomas Macaulay, 'A Jacobite's Epitaph'.¶ The bookcases are not worthy of the books – ugly painted brown wood.

Robert Carr** is one of the guests. He tells me how, many years ago, when their house was bombed by terrorists, Alec Home lent them Dorneywood.

---

* In the end this project became a biography of Victor Rothschild, *Elusive Rothschild: The Life of Victor, Third Baron* (2003).
† (1827–1904), lawyer, journalist and Liberal statesman. Home Secretary 1880–85; Chancellor of the Exchequer 1886 and 1892–95.
‡ (1880–1932), biographer, critic and founding member of the Bloomsbury Group; best known for *Eminent Victorians* (1918).
§ (b. 1966), Dir. of Music at the Temple Church 1997–2006; Dir. of Music at Trinity Coll., Cambridge 2006; Artistic Dir. of the City of London Sinfonia 2010.
¶ Thomas Babington Macaulay, 1st Baron (1800–59), historian and Whig politician. Secretary at War 1839–41; Paymaster General 1846–8; author of *The History of England from the Accession of James II* (5 vols, 1848–61).
** Baron Carr of Hadley (1916–2012), Conservative politician. Home Secretary 1972–4.

But nobody had warned the staff. So they had to fork out money for some shopping to be done before they could even have a meal.

20 March 1986

Baba Metcalfe telephones me to ask if I have any news of Kedleston's future. On this, her eighty-second birthday, she gives me a hair-raising account of a recent visit to Uganda for the Save the Children Fund. I really do admire that old battleaxe.

21 March 1986

Baba Metcalfe on the telephone again to tell me that she has just heard from Pat Gibson,* the outgoing head of the National Trust, that the Trust is to acquire Kedleston with an endowment from the National Heritage Fund. She is ecstatic about it.

26 March 1986

Give Mollie Butler lunch. Anthony Howard's book on Rab is going well as a political history – 'But where is the magic? I wish you had done it.' I don't. I think Mollie would have been very demanding and perhaps censorious.

14 April 1986

To the *Economist* in St James's Street for a party to celebrate the completion of Norman St John-Stevas' edition of Walter Bagehot in fifteen volumes. Norman introduces me to Margaret Thatcher, who is exceptionally friendly; speaks warmly of the *Sunday Telegraph* in general and of my 'Albany' column in particular; and uses my name in conversation with the practised ease of an American Senator. She is having the burden of deciding how much support to give President Reagan in his bombing of Libya with US planes from British bases; and tonight there is a tricky vote in the House of Commons on the Government's unpopular Shops Bill. Yet she appears to have no more pressing occupation than to talk to me. She also makes a witty speech about Bagehot.

Greeted warmly by Robert Runcie. And while I am talking to Jim Callaghan, Harold Wilson joins us and I hear again of their visit to Russia and the Bolshoi.

---

* Patrick Gibson, Baron Gibson of Penn's Rock (1916–2004), Chairman of the National Trust 1977–86.

15 April 1986

Michael Bloch tells me that he is bogged down in his biography of the Duke of Windsor: Weidenfeld want the book too soon. He also says that the Duchess may be dead in a few days, having developed water on the lungs. But, of course, she has fooled us all before. She has received a pension of £5,000 a year from the Queen's personal funds since the Duke's death in 1972. Michael is amused by the right-wing views which the Duke expressed in a letter to the Queen in June 1970, immediately after the Tory victory in the General Election. The Duke implied that although the Queen couldn't openly hold political views, he was sure she would agree with him. The Queen's reply is in the Duke's papers. She made no allusion to this part of her uncle's letter.

17 April 1986

A few minutes' talk with Harold Macmillan. He is in high glee over the Libyan Crisis and praises the PM's fortitude in backing President Reagan. 'I would bomb Libya every week.' That comes oddly from the man of whom it was said at the time of Suez, 'First in, first out.' But I suppose an epigrammatic mischief is permissible in one of his years and fame.

Harold Wilson also tells me that he not only supported Mrs Thatcher in this, but has long appreciated her personal kindness to him. During his serious illness a few years ago, she was the first to send him flowers. She also offered him a car and driver.

18 April 1986

I see some of the lesser-known corners of St George's Chapel, Windsor. There is the King's Chapel where King George VI is buried, with stained glass by John Piper and a plaque with the words: 'I said to the man who stood at the gate of the year . . .'* It is here that the Queen Mother will also be buried.

I also see the beautifully restored Private Chapel next to the Deanery.

23 April 1986

Jock Colville tells me that at Arnold Goodman's party he too talked to Harold Macmillan, who blamed Harold Wilson for President Reagan's imbroglio with the Libyan leader Colonel Gaddafi.† Had Wilson not sought to save £2 million by withdrawing two battalions of British troops in Libya,

---

* The King quoted these lines from a poem by Minnie Louise Haskins (1875–1957) in his Christmas broadcast in 1939. The poem was read at the Queen Mother's funeral in 2002.

† Mohammed Abu Minyar Gaddafi (1942–2011), Libyan revolutionary leader.

the dynasty of King Idris* would still be reigning there. That night, Jock challenged Callaghan on this at the Other Club. Callaghan said it was all the fault of the then Chancellor of the Exchequer, Roy Jenkins, who was also dining. 'Roy went very red,' Jock said.

24 April 1986

The Duchess of Windsor dies, as Michael Bloch predicted she would. I have happy memories of our meetings in Paris and fitful correspondence.

Lunch with Nico Henderson at Brooks's. He tells me that he was not the initial choice to be our Ambassador in Washington. Peter Rawlinson was first considered, and Nico thinks that he could have been excellent.

We talk about Queen Victoria and John Brown.† I cannot believe that Queen Victoria was the mistress of John Brown, except in the other sense.

The Duchy of Cornwall is producing a great deal of money for the Prince of Wales. It will be £1.25 million this year, and £2 million the next. This will need some careful handling if the radicals begin to criticise it. When I mention that Nico must be the first Lord Warden of the Stannaries not to be a peer, he replies: 'Walter Raleigh.'

28 April 1986

Telegram from the Lord Chamberlain, David Airlie,‡ inviting me to the Duchess of Windsor's funeral at St George's Chapel tomorrow. His office must be the most confused in England. Michael Bloch tells me that although the list of guests desired by the Duchess was revised by Maître Blum each year and sent to the British Embassy in Paris, the final one sent to the Lord Chamberlain was a very old one, with most of the people on it now dead. Fortunately, this was spotted in time. Michael also tells me that at the memorial service for the Duchess in Paris, the lesson was read by John Fretwell,§ the British Ambassador, on the theme of persecution.

29 April 1986

To Windsor for the Duchess of Windsor's funeral. I wear a dark suit, not morning dress, under a black overcoat. The nave contains few guests, all of us facing a curious row or rather semicircle of stalls, like a Wagnerian opera. I am in the front row. Michael Bloch sits further along the same row.

---

* El Sayyid Muhammad Idris (1889–1983), King of Libya 1951–69.
† (1826–83), personal servant of Queen Victoria.
‡ Sir David Ogilvie, 13th Earl of Airlie (b. 1926), Lord Chamberlain of the Royal Household 1984–97.
§ Sir John Fretwell (b. 1930), Ambassador to France 1982–7.

The service, with much processional pageantry, is beautiful but deliberately excludes emotion. After the service, when talking to Robert Runcie in the Cloisters, I ask him when he last attended the funeral of a person whose name was nowhere mentioned from beginning to end. He says: 'No, never.'

The plain coffin passes within a foot or two of me, followed by the tiny group of mourners: the Queen, Prince Philip, the Queen Mother and the Prince and Princess of Wales. I see Baba Metcalfe and Diana Mosley[*] afterwards.

Overall it was an odd occasion: all the grandeur and pageantry of a Royal funeral, yet with a cold heartlessness. No hospitality whatever was offered to the mourners: not so much as a glass of sherry or a cup of tea.

30 April 1986

Lunch with Victor Rothschild at New Court. He then hands me over to the bank's archivist for a brief survey of what I may see for my book on the Rothschild family. There are some rich veins of personal letters, not least a correspondence with Disraeli.

Dine with James Stourton[†] at the Dolphin Square Brasserie, of which he is part owner. Back to Brunswick Gardens, where I discuss with James the possibility that he might care to replace Giles St Aubyn as my literary executor. Giles does not really know the world of my Journals, lives in Guernsey and is incurious, and above all is my own age. James is intelligent, alert, hard-working and nice. All this, of course, presupposes that I do not live to edit my own Journals. Even if I do, James might care to help with them.

4 May 1986

Edward Ford tells me that he used to suggest to the Queen that she might publicly heal the breach with the Windsors by inviting them for a day or two of Ascot races, where they would be swallowed up in the other guests. But the Queen said no.

5 May 1986

I have a couple of days at Blagdon with Matthew Ridley.[‡] Princess Margaret is a fellow guest. Matthew has taken Princess Margaret to a military entertainment in Newcastle. They return in high spirits with Princess Margaret

---

* Diana, Lady Mosley (1910–2003), one of the Mitford sisters; m. Sir Oswald Mosley in 1936 at the home of Joseph Goebbels, with Hitler as guest of honour.

† The Hon. James Stourton (b. 1956), art historian. Chairman of Sotheby's UK 2007–12.

‡ 4th Viscount Ridley (1925–2012), Lord Lieutenant of Northumberland 1984–2000; Lord Steward 1989–2001.

singing Geordie songs and swaying to their rhythm. She says: 'What a curious class difference there was. The officers didn't mind shouting and making
fools of themselves in front of their wives. But the Other Ranks did mind,
and sat glassy-eyed in front of their wives.'

8 May 1986

John Nutting,[*] the son of Anthony Nutting and a barrister, is junior prosecuting counsel in the Old Bailey trial of the IRA people accused of blowing
up the Grand Hotel, Brighton. He says the case against them is overwhelm-
ing, largely through fingerprints.

11 May 1986

I have an interesting talk with Princess Margaret. 'Seven years ago, when
the Duchess of Windsor was thought to be dying, I asked if I need go to the
funeral. The Queen said of course not, so I didn't go the other day. I really
don't know why Mummy went. It is such nonsense that there was a feud
between Mummy and the Duchess. She didn't know Mrs Simpson. What she
resented was Edward VIII giving up the throne.'

I also hear that the bad-tempered corgis that the Queen Mother warned
me not to touch are now dead.

The Princess adds: 'Journalists have learned how to pick up police messages on the wireless at Balmoral, so they always know where to follow us. We
regard them as our enemies.'

17 May 1986

I visit Peter Pilkington at King's, Canterbury. The pupils I meet are all very
friendly and forthcoming. One girl tells me excitedly that she is much looking forward to next week's Greek play in which one of her boyfriends appears
throughout 'wearing nothing but a golden jockstrap'. All very different from
Repton in my day!

27 May 1986

I hear that the Queen found she had an unexpectedly free evening recently
and that Philip was away. So, on the spur of the moment, she decided to give
a little dinner party. 'And wasn't I lucky?' she said. 'I asked about a dozen
people at twenty-four hours' notice and by great good fortune they were all
free to come!'

---

[*] Sir John Nutting QC, 4th Bt (b. 1942), barrister. Senior Treasury Counsel 1988–95; eldest
son of Sir Anthony Nutting (1920–99).

30 May 1986

Ted Heath has spent £100,000 on his new home in the Close at Salisbury
Cathedral. But the locals don't like him. When someone asked him if he had
played on the Cathedral organ, he replied: 'You don't think I would play on
such a poor instrument?'

4 June 1986

Dine with Katie Macmillan in Warwick Square. A splendid dinner cooked
by Katie. When talking about food, I mention how, when we were children,
chicken was a great luxury; yet today it is the cheapest form of meat. 'Yes,'
said Katie, 'I remember when Andrew Devonshire addressed an election
meeting, somebody shouted: "Get back to Chatsworth, with your chicken."'
How things have changed. Why, the other day I met a Duchess on a <u>bus</u>!

7 June 1986

A few days ago I went to lunch at the Belgian Embassy. It was in honour of
the Queen Mother, who was about to make a short private visit to Brussels.
Afterwards she sat on a sofa, with the Ambassador on one side of her, I on
the other. At one stage she said: 'Tell me, Ambassador, on which side were
the Belgians at Waterloo?'

In a more serious vein, the Queen Mother told me how annoyed she was
by all the newspaper stories – though not mine – at the time of the Duchess
of Windsor's death, accusing her of a vendetta against them both. What so
few of her critics do not realise is that the withholding of the style of HRH
from the Duchess of Windsor was not a Royal whim on the part of George
VI, much less of Queen Elizabeth, but an Act of Government initiated by the
Cabinet and carried out by Letters Patent under the Great Seal. Socially, of
course, there <u>was</u> a boycott of the Windsors.

26 June 1986

Summer drinks party in the garden of the American Embassy in Regent's
Park. Some particularly good talk with Eric and Poppy Anderson. The collection of Eton leaving portraits is growing. Martin Gilliat has now followed
my example by commissioning Derek Hill to paint a boy, and there are
others. I later talk to Derek about this. He is charging Martin exactly what
he charged me – £500.

Eric tells me that the Patronage Secretary at No. 10 asked Eric some time
ago if Peter Pilkington would make a good bishop. Eric said a very good one
indeed. But the Crown Commissioners have obviously decided that public-
school headmasters may not become bishops. I later hear that Robert Runcie,

who also recommended Peter, was told not to send names of public-school heads in future.

Eric wonders whether I would like to join the Samuel Johnson Society, but I plead that I cannot manage any more clubs or, like Browning, I shall dinner away my life.

Jim Callaghan very avuncular. He has just completed his memoirs, to be published by Collins. We are joined by Michael Heseltine, who surprises Jim by proclaiming that the Conservatives will win the next General Election. By then Jim will be in the House of Lords.

3 July 1986

I give Robert Runcie one of our occasional lunches at the Savoy. ('Dost thou think, because thou art virtuous, there shall be no more cakes and ale?') I have known him fitfully since Oxford days, and in the army, where he was an intrepid tank commander in the Scots Guards. He is a good, decent man, but like so many prelates will insist on offering worldly solutions to problems like South Africa or unemployment for which there is no specific Christian remedy. So in general we do not speak of such things, but rather of the state of the Church and other human comedies.

The moment we sit down he comes out with an episode he has been saving up for me. It was told to him by a Canon of Windsor at the Duchess of Windsor's funeral. Some official that morning happened to look at the labels on the wreaths arranged round the cloisters, to which public and Press would have access after the service. One read: 'You would have made a swell Queen.' A Guardsman was summoned with a pair of clippers to remove it.

10 July 1986

To the Royal Garden Party at Buckingham Palace. I meet Michael Mann, who tells me why the Duchess of Windsor's name was not mentioned at her funeral service in St George's, Windsor. The absence of her name was at her own request, Michael tells me. She wanted the same service as the Duke's, omitting only the proclamation of his styles and titles. But she was mentioned by name at the committal service at Frogmore.

15 July 1986

I ask Angus Ogilvy* if it is true that the sale of the Duchess of Windsor's jewels has been entrusted to Sotheby's. He says that every auction house wants them, and that no decision has been reached. But the Queen thought

---

* Sir Angus Ogilvy (1928–2004), businessman and husband of Princess Alexandra.

it very courteous of Maître Blum to ask if she had any objection to a public sale. Of course, the Queen has no objection: she does not feel identified with the Windsors.

17 July 1986

John Grigg writes awful rubbish in *The Times* today, claiming that the Queen has a perfect right to criticise publicly Mrs Thatcher's anti-sanctions stand on South Africa. He cannot see how her duties as our Queen far outweigh those as Head of the Commonwealth.

I hear that Bob Boothby has died.

Philip and Marie-Lou de Zulueta give a large luncheon party in the Institute of Directors, formerly the United Service Club in Pall Mall. I hear that Grizel Hartley is deeply shocked by Wilfrid Blunt's references to his own homosexuality in the second volume of his autobiography. What a sheltered life she must have lived at Eton.

I also hear that the Queen was furious with Jock Colville for even suggesting that he might publish the diaries he kept when her Private Secretary before her accession.

21 July 1986

Today would have been my brother Toby's sixty-fifth birthday.

A curious storm caused by an allegation in the *Sunday Times* that the Queen is at loggerheads with the PM over Mrs Thatcher's refusal to join the black Commonwealth in imposing sanctions against South Africa. The newspaper claims to have received its information from a highly placed source in the Palace, and there is speculative chatter about the Queen's circle of 'unofficial advisers'.

I talk to Martin Charteris about all this. He thinks the culprit may be Michael Shea,* the Palace Press Officer. 'The trouble with PROs is that they are inclined to believe that their principals think as they do.' He continues: 'What we really need is an anti-Press Officer.'

One trouble of course is that nobody can 'advise' the Queen on Commonwealth matters. But whatever her views on the Commonwealth, she must not allow them to interfere with the workings of our own Constitution or with the established relationship between Sovereign and Prime Minister.

Martin Gilliat and Alastair Aird† were utterly exhausted by the visit to

---

* Michael Shea (1938–2009), Press Sec. to Elizabeth II 1978–87.
† Capt. Sir Alastair Aird (1931–2009), courtier.

Walmer,* though the Queen Mother herself never wilted for one moment. On a day crowded with engagements, which she allowed to run beyond the planned time, she arrived back at the Lord Warden's apartments at Walmer with an hour to spare before going to a cocktail party. Rest? Not at all. She said: 'I have always wanted to see the cellars of the castle. Let's explore them now.'

Jim Callaghan exposed to much good-natured teasing after the tender carrying him and others during a House of Commons regatta sank in the Thames. 'It came as a shock to him to learn that he could not walk on the water . . .'

20 August 1986

I hear that both Macmillan and Callaghan have been consulted about what the Queen should do in the event of a hung Parliament after the next General Election.

Also that Michael Shea, the Queen's Press Officer, had a reputation when in the Diplomatic Corps for being left-wing. That would explain his anti-Thatcher briefings.

21 August 1986

When George Harewood† was taken prisoner in the war, King George VI said to one of his friends in the same regiment: 'Don't worry. The Germans are such snobs that George will be well looked after.'

22 September 1986

Party at midday in the City for Martin Gilbert's new volume of the Churchill life. He is not pleased by the criticism of the reviewers (including myself) that there is little new and that he is a compiler not a biographer. Heinemann have insisted on one more volume only, 1945–1965.

I ask Martin whether he has used the diaries kept by Winston's private office. He is evasive.

25 September 1986

Philip de Zulueta has agreed to review Robert Rhodes James's life of Anthony

---

* Walmer Castle, the official residence of the Lord Warden of the Cinque Ports, a post held by Queen Elizabeth the Queen Mother.
† George Lascelles, 7th Earl of Harewood (1923–2011).

Eden for the *Spectator*. The author did not bother to interview either Philip himself or Freddie Bishop,* which is quite extraordinary.

5 October 1986
Read Evelyn Shuckburgh's† *Descent to Suez: Diaries 1951–1956*. Intensely interesting, particularly on Eden's vanity and volatile character.

15 October 1986
Jim Callaghan tells me a story of New York. Mrs Iphigene Sulzberger,‡ aged about ninety, used to be taken out for a drive every day, but had to stop from time to time for relief. Special arrangements were made for this in advance, the 'comfort stations' including a funeral parlour. During a halt there a funeral was in progress, and Mrs Sulzberger signed the book of condolence as a courtesy. A few weeks later she received a letter from a lawyer enclosing an enormous cheque. The deceased person had left instructions that his vast estate was to be divided up among those who came to his funeral – and almost nobody except Mrs S. turned up. As Jim says: 'Unto her that hath . . .'

21 October 1986
Dine at Pratt's. Talk with my neighbour about Anthony Eden. During the war he was in a Brigade Headquarters in Berlin during the Potsdam Conference of 1945, where Winston and Eden came to dine. When Winston asked how the men would vote, he was told that they admired Winston as a war leader, but thought less of him as a potential post-war PM. Winston was annoyed by this, but Eden thought it a warning as to what would happen at the polls.

30 October 1986
George Weidenfeld gives a lunch for Evelyn Shuckburgh on the publication of his Foreign Office diaries, *Descent to Suez*. I sit next to Alec and Elizabeth Home. Both are in good spirits, although Alec has hurt his knee in a fall. Elizabeth tells me the story of when Alec's brother Henry was in prison and someone applied to Alec when he was at the Scottish Office for permission

* Sir Frederick Bishop (1915–2005), Principal PS to Eden 1956 and Macmillan 1956–59; Dir. Gen. of the National Trust 1971–5.
† Sir Evelyn Shuckburgh (1909–94), Principal PS to Anthony Eden 1951–4; Ambassador to Italy 1966–9.
‡ Iphigene Sulzberger (1892–1990), a key figure in the development of the *New York Times*, of which she was a director.

to make a special visit. 'No,' said Alec. 'But you allowed William to do so,' Henry's friend insisted. Alec: 'He was an old boy.'*

31 October 1986
Martin Gilliat to dine. While staying at the Castle of Mey, the Queen Mother asked him what he was reading. When he told her it was Wilfrid Blunt's second volume of autobiography, covering his years as an art master at Eton, she asked to borrow it. When she returned it, she wrote how enormously she had enjoyed it. This surprised Martin. He feared she might have been shocked or upset both by the admission of his homosexuality (though never with boys) and his courageous defence of his brother Anthony Blunt.

7 November 1986
By train to Canterbury to talk to the sixth-form pupils at King's School on 'The Queen as Constitutional Monarch'. I am taken for a drink with the new Dean, John Simpson,[†] former Archdeacon of Canterbury, a quiet, alert, humorous and most agreeable man. Simpson bears out what I have earlier heard: that Hewlett Johnson,[‡] the Red Dean, was a punctilious Dean. During one of his absences in Russia, the Chapter thought he had overstayed his permitted number of days away. But no: there he was in his stall for Evensong, with a few hours only to go.

The new Headmaster, Canon Anthony Phillips,[§] comes to collect me for the lecture. It seems to go well, with some penetrating questions at the end.

I tell them the true story of King George V's supposed retort on his deathbed, 'Bugger Bognor.' In 1929, on the day the King was about to leave Bognor after his convalescence, a delegation of the local council appeared and asked the King's Private Secretary, Lord Stamfordham, whether they could commemorate his recovery at Bognor by calling it Bognor Regis. Lord Stamfordham told them that he would ask the King, which he did. The King, who was still not feeling too well, exclaimed: 'Oh, bugger Bognor.' Lord Stamfordham returned to the delegation. 'His Majesty', he announced, 'has been graciously pleased to accede to your request.'

I also mention how the Court Circular at times can yield up an unwitting joke. It was announced from Windsor in April 1915 that the Royal Household

---

* The Hon. Henry Douglas-Home (1907–80), ornithologist and broadcaster. The Hon. William Douglas-Home (1922–92), playwright, had himself been in prison.
† The Very Revd John Simpson (b. 1933), Dean of Canterbury 1986–2000.
‡ Hewlett Johnson (1874–1966), Dean of Manchester 1924–31 and Dean of Canterbury 1931–63. Known as the 'Red Dean' because of his political views.
§ The Revd Canon Anthony Phillips, Headmaster of King's School, Canterbury 1986–96.

would become teetotal for the remainder of the war. This was immediately followed by the statement: 'The Earl of Rosebery and the Hon. A.J. Balfour have left the Castle.'

Then to dine with the Headmaster and others. He describes how, on his first day at Canterbury, he gave what he thought was a considered address to the teaching staff on the ideals of education and the virtue of an ancient institution such as King's. When he had finished, a senior master rose to his feet. 'Yes, Headmaster,' he said, 'that is all very well, but what is your policy on lost property?'

The Headmaster also describes an occasion when he was Chaplain at St John's College, Oxford, when Harold Macmillan was gently baiting the President, Sir Richard Southern.* 'Of course, nobody reads the Old Testament in Oxford nowadays,' said Harold. 'I suppose it is because you don't like such sentences as "Thou shalt not commit adultery."'

10 November 1986

Talk to Gladwyn Jebb about Eden. Randolph Churchill once told Gladwyn that Eden had said to him: 'I can't get on at all with Gladwyn. He treats me like an equal.' To which Randolph replied: 'How kind of Gladwyn, for intellectually he is certainly your superior.'

13 November 1986

I ask Martin Charteris whether there is any truth in the rumour I have heard: that the Princess of Wales is having tuition in English literature and other matters at Eton from Eric Anderson. He tells me it is so, although officially it is being denied.

19 November 1986

Julian Amery tells me that when Ian Harvey had to resign as Under-Secretary at the Foreign Office, and also as an MP, after being found with a Guardsman under the bushes in St James's Park, Harold Macmillan could scarcely understand his foolishness. 'Why didn't he put the Guardsman into his official car and drive him home?' A Private Secretary said: 'But Prime Minister, Under-Secretaries do not have official cars.' A few days later there came an edict from No. 10. In future Under-Secretaries <u>were</u> to have official cars.

---

* Sir Richard Southern (1912–2001), President of St John's Coll., Oxford 1969–81.

12 December 1986

Nicky Gordon-Lennox tells me that his boy Anthony* has been elected to Pop at Eton. On the first morning he set out from his house in all his finery, when a small boy shouted from an upper window: 'Fascist!'

20 December 1986

Mollie Butler talks to me. She is reading the proofs of Anthony Howard's life of Rab. It is causing her much distress. Every single act of his political career is subjected to a niggling and sometimes hostile exegesis. 'Rab and I must have been mad not to ask you to write it.' And, of course, I remember one of the most famous of all Rabisms – 'We thought of you, you know.'

28 December 1986

Hugh Dacre is in his last year as Master of Peterhouse. He quotes with glee the remark of one Fellow immediately after his election: 'They thought they were electing a Tory and found that they have elected a Whig.' He is watching from afar (though apparently well supplied with information) the manoeuvres in selecting his successor. There are two parties: those who want a weak Master and those who want a strong Master. Those who want a weak Master say: 'A college is like a ship. To steer it needs only a touch on the tiller.' Those who want a strong Master say: 'Yes indeed, a college is like a ship. But a touch on the tiller is not enough. There are sometimes barnacles to be scraped off the hull and weevils to be fumigated from the woodwork.' So the two parties grow further apart. All internal candidates have apparently been eliminated.

29 December 1986

Breakfasting at Chicheley this morning, where I am staying with Johnnie Nutting, we talked of Harold Macmillan. Tonight at home I turn on the midnight news and hear that he has died at the age of ninety-two. This fills me with deep sadness and I recall all the glittering conversations of his that I have enjoyed over the years.

---

* Anthony Gordon-Lennox (b. 1969), founder of AGL Communications; CEO since 2009.

1987

1987 was the year of Margaret Thatcher's third general election victory. Harold Macmillan was buried in the churchyard of St Giles's in the village of Horsted Keynes on 5 January. The Church of England's Synod voted on 26 February to allow the ordination of women. The jewellery of the late Duchess of Windsor was sold at auction for £31 million on 3 April, six times the expected value. On 11 May Mrs Thatcher called a general election for 11 June which gave the Conservatives a majority of 102, compared to the 144-seat majority at the 1983 election; Roy Jenkins and Enoch Powell both lost their seats.

Margaret Thatcher's third term as Prime Minister began with news on 18 June of the biggest monthly fall in unemployment since 1948. Conservative support reached 50 per cent in a MORI poll on 25 June. Agreement was reached between Britain and France on the Channel Tunnel on 29 July. David Owen resigned as SDP leader when its members voted to merge with the Liberals on 6 August. On 17 August Rudolf Hess was found dead in his cell at Spandau Prison. Sixteen people died in the Hungerford Massacre on 19 August. An Australian court lifted the ban on the publication of Spycatcher *on 23 September. The Great Storm hit Britain on 15–16 October, causing extensive damage. On 17 November the government announced that the Poll Tax would be introduced in April 1990. Death of Duncan Sandys on 26 November.*

6 January 1987

Jonathan Aitken immensely interesting on his trial at the Old Bailey on a charge under the Official Secrets Act. The judge was wildly biased on his side. Jonathan also helped his own defence by going to earlier cases to study the prosecuting counsel. 'I made up my mind not to be too exact, not to be trapped.'

Quintin Hailsham has said of the trial about secrets and MI5 in Australia: 'Now I know what a kangaroo court is.'

8 January 1987

Katie Macmillan talks of her father-in-law's funeral the other day. She felt very sorry for the PM, who didn't like Harold – nor he her – but felt that she ought to attend the funeral. She did not return to Birch Grove for the lunch. She does not know what will happen eventually to Harold Macmillan's papers, but thinks they may be sold to America. I beg her to try to keep them in England and I write out a list of our PMs since Rosebery, with the places where their papers have been deposited.

At the memorial service at Westminster Abbey, the two lessons are to be read by the two sons-in-law, Julian Amery and Julian Faber. This is wrong. It should be the Prince of Wales and the PM for such a great national figure.

In the Cecil tradition, Katie says, her brother David Ormsby Gore brought up his children to make conversation during meals, however young they were and however intimidating the guests. When Harold Macmillan came to our Washington Embassy, little Francis Ormsby Gore* was seated next to Philip de Zulueta. After a little silence he said: 'Sad about Adam, isn't it?' P. de Z: 'Which Adam?' Francis: 'The Garden of Eden one.'

9 January 1987
Prince Edward under much public pressure as he contemplates leaving the Royal Marines in the middle of an exceptionally tough training course. Why should he devote the best years of his life to a yobbo regime? I gather that there was an element of deliberate humiliation of him on the training course. The same was true when he played rugby at Cambridge, so much so that he eventually gave up the game.

Nico Henderson talks to me about President Reagan's claim that he wants to establish good relations with Iranian moderates. The wisecrack in America is that 'An Iranian moderate is an Iranian who has run out of ammunition.'

The death is announced of Wilfrid Blunt. I am immensely sad. How I admired his courage and high spirits, his modesty and industry and versatility in so many fields.

21 January 1987
Dine with Leslie Rowse in an upper room at the Athenaeum. I am agreeably placed next to Robert Lacey,† full of sparkling talk. He is most interesting on how certain pressures were put on him by the otherwise helpful Mountbatten, who acted as intermediary on behalf of both the Queen and Eden with

---

* David Ormsby Gore, 5th Baron Harlech (1918–85), Conservative politician. MP for Oswestry 1950–61; Ambassador to the US 1961–5. Francis Ormsby Gore, 6th Baron Harlech (1954–2016), Conservative Member of the House of Lords until the House of Lords Act (1999).
† (b. 1944), historian and author of several bestselling biographies, including those on Henry Ford and Elizabeth II.

a strong request to remove an alleged remark in his book *Majesty* by Prince Philip that was critical of Eden's handling of Suez. Here Lacey gave in. But he refused to take out a passage told him by Jock Colville: that when Eden had a bile-duct operation in Boston in 1953, with Winston out of action through a stroke, Rab Butler could not be trusted with the acting premiership in case he refused to relinquish it on Eden's return. So Bobbety Salisbury was brought in. Robert also describes how, when he went to lecture at Gordonstoun, Prince Andrew* was detailed to show him round the school. In his study was a copy of Robert's book on the Queen, 'but I shall not read it,' he explained. And when in the course of the talk Robert said that the Royal Family did not like being written about, the young Prince nodded his head vigorously in agreement.

23 January 1987
Quintin Hailsham tells me that although he hates gambling, he was annoyed when Archbishop Fisher said that Premium Bonds were immoral. This provoked Quintin into going out and buying the maximum number allowed.

27 January 1987
I hear that when Valerie Solti, wife of Sir Georg, took her daughter† down to begin her first term at King's School, Canterbury, laden with musical effects, she said to the housemaster: 'Her harp is coming down later with the maestro.' The housemaster replied: 'I didn't know one could get a harp into a Maestro.'

10 February 1987
To Westminster Abbey for the memorial service for Harold Macmillan. The usually gloomy interior is brightly illuminated for TV: there are television screens down the nave on which we can see what is taking place in the quire. It is curious that whereas the congregation do not rise for the Prime Minister (nor need they do in a church), they do so for the Mayor of Westminster. The Prince of Wales looks rather worn. The Archbishop of Canterbury is in a horribly bright violet-coloured cape and mitre, preceded by a huge crucifix and candles. I can imagine Harold in Pratt's saying, 'Really, it was as if the Reformation had never taken place!' Rather too military a flavour to the service, with the band of the Grenadier Guards at full blast. Julian Faber reads the first lesson, too fast; Julian Amery, in a grey tailcoat of all things,

---

* Prince Andrew, Duke of York (b. 1960), second son of the Queen and Prince Philip.
† Gabrielle Solti (b. 1970), Head of South Hampstead Junior High School.

gives a passable imitation of Winston Churchill when he reads his. Quintin Hailsham wears a grubby brown muffler round his neck. Alec Home very competent, but not quite inspired in his address. Rather touching to see three little great-grandchildren carrying Harold's insignia of the Order of Merit on a cushion. Philip Goodhart later says to me of Runcie: 'He looked a right Nancy.'

21 February 1987
Talk to Peter Carrington, who tells that he was pressed to stand for the Chancellorship of Oxford, but thought it would be wrong for a non-university man to do so. He was amused by Ted Heath's deviousness in getting his doctor (the Medical Officer of Peter's Grenadier battalion) to telephone Peter to find out if he was a candidate. 'I assumed it was Ted's way of telling me not to.'

25 February 1987
James Stourton calls for me at nine and we drive to Cambridge in bright sunshine. We call on Dadie Rylands* before I give him lunch at the Arts Theatre. Next month it will be sixty years since he was first elected a Fellow of King's, and he has occupied the rooms in the Gibbs Building ever since, a Bloomsbury time capsule immortalised by Virginia Woolf in *A Room of One's Own*. Dusty donnish souvenirs jostle with relics of Bloomsbury. His library is impressive: a second Folio Shakespeare given to Dadie by Victor Rothschild. None can match the love of English literature and drama he has inspired in generations of his pupils.

9 March 1987
Prince Eddie tells me that the future of the Royal Masonic Hospital at Ravenscourt Park is still a running sore. Eddie sensibly thinks it should be sold and the money used to provide a health service for Freemasons through BUPA, etc. This would be on the lines of the closure of the Royal Masonic Junior School in 1970 and the Royal Masonic Senior School in 1977, both in Bushey. Eligible sons of Freemasons were then educated privately at public schools near their homes. Eddie has received some very unpleasant letters about the hospital, which accuse him of conniving at the disposal of valuable assets. This has wounded him.

---

* George Rylands (1902–99), literary scholar and theatre director; Fellow of King's Coll., Cambridge 1927–99.

12 March 1987

Decide not to go down to Oxford to vote for a new Chancellor. Ted Heath has no manners, Roy Jenkins is too smug a radical and Robert Blake does not have the stature.

15 March 1987

Jim Prior tells me that when Macmillan resigned in 1963, Martin Redmayne* as Chief Whip asked him whom he preferred to be PM. Jim said Rab Butler. 'Oh,' Redmayne replied in a disappointed voice, 'but if Alec Home stood, would you be satisfied?' Jim answered non-committedly that Alec was a nice fellow. 'I am sure', he said, 'that Redmayne put me down as a supporter not of Rab, but of Alec.'

16 March 1987

I hear the result of the election for the Oxford Chancellorship:

Jenkins 3,249
Blake 2,674
Heath 2,348

I am surprised that Heath was beaten so soundly: probably the result of too much zeal on the part of the Conservative Whips in what should not be a party-political contest. There was also a characteristic intervention by Norman St John-Stevas, who urged his fellow Catholics to vote for Heath because in 1972 he had three cardinals to dine at No. 10.

18 March 1987

A letter from Brian Rees, hoping that his biography of Edward German will be a success, as 'the wolf is rather close to the door'. I must see if I can find some tactful way of helping him.[†]

18 April 1987

Lunch with Arnold Goodman at his new home in Headington. Clarissa Avon is there, whom I always like to see. Clarissa plays the same role in Arnold's life that Ann Fleming[‡] used to do: a provocative, right-wing critic and stimulant. When we tease Arnold about the dullness of his forthcoming memoirs

---

* Martin Redmayne, Baron Redmayne of Rushcliffe (1910–83), Conservative politician. MP for Rushcliffe 1955–64; Chief Whip 1959–64.

† K.R. in the end gave Brian Rees direct financial help in his difficulties.

‡ Ann Fleming (1913–81), society hostess.

if he includes such chapters as 'How I founded the Open University', he says, 'You both take class attitudes.'

23 April 1987
Jim Callaghan is made a Knight of the Garter. I look up the notes of a conversation we had in September 1983. He said he would never take the Garter, if offered, but I urged him to think again when he retired from the Commons. He will not in fact stand at the next election.

26 April 1987
Jack Plumb invites me to what he says is his last Princess Margaret weekend before he retires as Master of Christ's.

I sit next to Princess Margaret at the dinner. We talk of the Queen Mother – 'Mummy' – and of her wedding anniversary today. I say: 'It was an event which changed the course of English history.' She says: 'I think you underestimate my father.' Years ago I would have been abashed by this. Now I argue the point. 'They were a partnership, and with a partner other than Queen Elizabeth it would not have been at all as effective.' Princess Margaret accepts this. She goes on to describe her father's sheer guts and determination: 'When he found out how much he suffered from his stammer, he went out in search of a cure and overcame it.'

I ask Princess Margaret if she knows whether the Queen has accepted the Abdication table of King Edward VIII from the Windsors' house in Paris. At first she does not know what I mean by the Abdication table. Then she realises: 'Oh yes, now I know, all those brothers sitting round the table <u>blubbing</u>.' After dinner we walk round the garden, and Princess Margaret sings: 'Oh come into the garden, Maud,' in a pleasantly light voice!

13 May 1987
John King dined last night with Cecil Parkinson at the Savoy: a rather joyless gathering, it turned out. John thinks that if Mrs Thatcher wins the election – this morning the odds are 10–1 on – Cecil will return to the Cabinet as Minister for Energy,* at least as a start. It is the portfolio given to those who are not in entire favour with the PM, e.g. Peter Walker and Tony Benn.

19 May 1987
I am much disturbed by a letter from Brian Rees which tells me that he is flat

---

* A correct prediction by John King.

broke. I shall have to send him some money, and try to raise some for him elsewhere.

The Foreign Office telephones to ask if I can come to see Janet Young[*] at five. We have tea in her lovely room that once housed the Secretary of State for India, and she tells me that in the event of a Tory victory she will decline to remain in the Government. Although Janet says there is no friction with the PM, I suspect that her demotion from the Cabinet, with no prospect of returning to it, must have coloured her decision. If the Conservatives are returned she thinks that Whitelaw, Lawson, Howe and Hurd are likely to remain in their present posts. The Woolsack poses a problem: Quintin may not wish to move, and the best successor, Lord Mackay of Clashfern,[†] does not find favour with English judges. She hopes that Jean Trumpington will not be dropped and that Cecil Parkinson will not be brought back.

Walk up through St James's Park for a drink with Victor Rothschild. He thinks that the election result will be closer than expected and suggests that we bet on a hung Parliament. Victor reaffirms his promise that he will help me in writing about him in my Rothschild book.

21 May 1987

I send Brian Rees £1,000.

Pleasant lunch with Julian Faber and David Montagu[‡] in the City. I ask David where Ted Heath's money comes from. He thinks there may not after all be a lot of it. In London he receives his house in Wilton Street either free or at a low rent from the Grosvenor Estate. And his house in the Close at Salisbury does not belong to him. There were 300 applications for the lease (at a controlled rent to the Church Commissioners) and Ted somehow emerged at the top of the list.

Jacky d'Avigor-Goldsmid[§] once told David that Ted when he was PM was doing himself much harm by failing to entertain or even recognise his backbenchers. So David told Ted this. A few weeks later Jacky told David that Ted had asked him to a drink at No. 10. David: 'Who else was at the party?' Jacky: 'Oh, it wasn't a party. Just me.'

---

[*] Janet Young, Baroness Young of Farnworth (1926–2002), Conservative politician. The first female Leader of the House of Lords 1981–3; Lord Privy Seal 1982–3.

[†] James Mackay, Baron Mackay of Clashfern (b. 1927), Lord Chancellor 1987–97.

[‡] David Montagu, 4th Baron Swaythling (1928–98), Chairman of Rothmans International 1988–98.

[§] Maj.-Gen. Sir James d'Avigdor-Goldsmith, MC, 3rd Bt (1912–87), Conservative politician. MP for Lichfield and Tamworth 1970–74.

25 May 1987

John King telephones. He is not too impressed by the Conservative election campaign.

27 May 1987

I send a copy of Brian Rees's sad letter to Edward Adeane, who expressed interest in helping him. Brian taught him at Eton.

Read Bruce Chatwin's *On the Black Mountain*. A dazzling novel about life on a Welsh farm. I am enraptured by it. Bruce is indeed a great novelist.

31 May 1987

Read William Golding's *An Egyptian Journal*. He spins out a tour of two or three weeks along the Nile into a book of 200 pages: much of it contrived, arch and modestly conceited. What I would call a publisher's book.

8 June 1987

Dine at White's with John King. After dinner we watch the election news on the TV in the billiards room. Watch David Owen and Neil Kinnock being interviewed: Owen concise and excellent, Kinnock a tedious little Welsh windbag. A Labour victory would be a real disaster for the country.

11 June 1987

General Election day.

It is announced that Philip Ziegler is to write the official life of Edward VIII. I wonder that there is much left to say.

I vote for Brandon Rhys Williams,* a Welsh Guards man, in the General Election, which for once I have not followed closely. Turn on the wireless about midnight and listen for an hour or so. A Conservative victory is assured. I am sorry poor old Roy Jenkins has been defeated, though surely a merciful release for him. Delighted that Shirley Williams has been unable to unseat Robert Rhodes James at Cambridge. David Owen very dignified at the collapse of the SDP–Liberal Alliance.

What a triumph for common sense that the electorate was not swayed by the slick TV campaign of Kinnock, compared so favourably by every political commentator with that of Thatcher. How satisfactory, too, is the failure of Labour to annexe the red rose as its party symbol and vote-winner.

---

* Sir Brandon Rhys-Williams (1927–88), Conservative politician. MP for Kensington South 1968–74 and for Kensington 1974–88; MEP 1973–84.

12 June 1987

The final result of the General Election is an astonishing victory for Mrs Thatcher: an overall majority of 102. I had forecast 37. Enoch is out: a commanding, though not a particularly likeable parliamentarian.

Pleased to see in an advance copy of the Honours List in the office that Dadie Rylands has been made a Companion of Honour.

13 June 1987

The Queen appoints Princess Anne to be Princess Royal.

The main Cabinet changes are announced in the evening. Quintin is replaced as Lord Chancellor by Michael Havers and John Biffin also goes.* Peter Walker becomes Secretary of State for Wales. Tebbit retires to the back benches. According to John King, he will leave politics altogether quite soon in order to look after his wife, paralysed in the Brighton bomb attack. Paul Channon is demoted from Trade and Industry to Transport, but remains in the Cabinet. Cecil Parkinson is brought back as Energy Secretary after a period of penance for his extra-marital activity.

14 June 1987

Harold Macmillan leaves only £42,000. I suspect that he made over his money to his grandchildren too soon, was left with little himself and so put some of the financial burden of his last years on to Katie – that is what she has always claimed.

In Oxford. Look in at the Ashmolean and enjoy seeing old favourites such as Uccello's *Hunt in the Forest.*

Sit in the garden at New College for a while. What a lot the gardener at Buckingham Palace could learn about peonies and herbaceous borders from it. Mildly annoyed to see the lovely eighteenth-century windows in the Garden Quad still plastered with Labour and SDP election posters – one in the windows of my old room. It should be forbidden on aesthetic, not political grounds.

15 June 1987

Lunch in the boardroom of Sotheby's with Angus Ogilvy. Also James Stourton, Harold Lever and Jim Prior. Harold Lever thinks that the Labour Party in its present form will never again return to power. Jim Prior is more sceptical, and so am I. The wheel always turns in the end.

---

* Michael Havers, Baron Havers (1923–92), barrister; Lord Chancellor June–Oct. 1987.
John Biffen (1930–2007), Conservative politician. Lord Privy Seal 1983–7.

17 June 1987

Bruce Chatwin thanks me for the letter I wrote praising his novel *On the Black Hill.* He says that he learned much from me, which really does please me – he is a far more inspired writer than me. Bruce tells me something of how he worked as a farm labourer in Wales. Mucking out a barn of antique filth when exactly one week before he had been having a drink with Jackie Onassis!

19 June 1987

Paul Channon talks about his move from Trade and Industry to Transport and does not imply in any way that it is a demotion. But he talks of the anxious hours between a call from No. 10 in the morning and seeing the PM in the afternoon. What he learned later is that the PM asks to see only those who are to be given jobs; those about to be dismissed are asked by the Private Secretary whether or not they wish to see the PM.

20 June 1987

Prince Eddie is very upset by a Church of England report on Freemasonry, which condemns it. An added cause of annoyance is that the report was sent to him only after the Press had received it – and accompanied by a patronising letter. 'I may need your help in refuting it,' he says.

22 June 1987

I give Peter Attenborough,* Headmaster of Charterhouse, lunch at Overton's. A youngish man, serious without being solemn. We talk about the Robert Birley memorial lecture, an annual series, I am to give, and he approves of my general theme: the pursuit of historical truth and the demolition of myths.

As an undergraduate he was at Peterhouse, but retains no great affection for the college since the occasion when he was asked to preach in chapel on the commemoration of benefactors. His greeting was a rebuke from the then Master that he had not brought a square with him. 'As you are breaking a university rule by not wearing one, we must run across the road in order not to be seen.' The Master abandoned him in the ante-chapel, where Attenborough waited to be conducted to his stall. Instead the curtain dividing the ante-chapel from the chapel itself was closed and the service began. Attenborough nervously peered through the curtain and by good fortune caught the eye of the Bishop of Ely, who saw him to a stall. After the service, the

---

* Peter Attenborough (b. 1938), Headmaster of Sedbergh School 1975–81 and of Charterhouse 1982–93.

Dean, Edward Norman, came up to him and said: 'Where were you before the service started?' At the dinner which followed, nobody accompanied him from Hall to the Senior Combination Room. He vowed he would never return, but has done so occasionally.

23 June 1987

Robert Runcie tells me he has a new chaplain. 'The old one[*] has gone, against my wishes, to Eton – a very corrupting place.'

On the same day by chance Douglas Hurd tells me that he has made quite a little nest of Etonians in the Home Office – himself, Douglas Hogg (Under-Secretary) and Timothy Renton (Minister of State).[†]

27 June 1987

Harold Lever tells me that in the election of Callaghan as leader of the Labour Party after Wilson's resignation in 1976, he voted for Roy Jenkins in the first round – a tribute to their shared belief in our joining the EEC; for Denis Healey in the second round – to build up his paltry vote in order to save his face; and for Callaghan in the third because that was the man Harold always wanted as the new PM.

1 July 1987

I give Professor John Honey[‡] of Leicester University lunch at Overton's. He talks on his favourite theme – public-school history. I ask him what he knows of the circumstances in which Brian Rees was sacked at Rugby. He says it was (a) drink, and (b) importing a young man to live with him in the HM's house – Dr Arnold's – and provocatively informing the governors of this, thereby leaving them no option but to remove him.

8 July 1987

To York House, where I have a brief talk with Prince Eddie about the controversy over the future of the Royal Masonic Hospital. He then drives me

---

[*] The Revd John Witheridge (b. 1953), Chaplain to the Archbishop of Canterbury 1984–7; Conduct at Eton 1987–96; Headmaster of Charterhouse 1996–2013. Runcie told Witheridge that he should have gone to an urban priority area where there was important work to be done, not Eton. Witheridge replied that there was also important work to be done in urbane priority areas.

[†] Douglas Hogg, 3rd Viscount Hailsham (b. 1945), Conservative politician. MP for Sleaford and North Hykeham 1979–97; Minister of Agriculture, Fisheries and Food 1995–7. Timothy Renton, Baron Renton of Mount Harry (b. 1932), Conservative politician. MP for Mid Sussex 1974–97; Minister for the Arts 1990–92.

[‡] Prof. John R. de S. Honey (1933–2001), educationalist and author of books on public schools.

to Covent Garden for Richard Strauss's *Die Frau ohne Schatten*. We park the car in the courtyard of Bow Street police station. There is a notice stuck up. It once read: 'Beware falling masonry.' This had been changed to 'Beware falling Masons.'

The opera is very Wagnerian and robustly sung, particularly the spectacular end of the second act and the whole of the third. We have supper afterwards with Gwyneth Jones,[*] who sang the part of Barak's wife.

14 July 1987

Douglas Hurd asks me what book he should give to the Cabinet Library. I strongly suggest *An End to Promises*, about his years as Ted Heath's Political Secretary.

16 July 1987

Matthew Ridley and Philip de Zulueta to lunch to celebrate the forty-fourth anniversary of our joining the army at Pirbright.

Prince Eddie thanks me for my note on Freemasonry and Christianity, which he says was most helpful.

17 July 1987

I dine with Edward Ford. We discuss the recent Freemasonry controversy. Edward is not an enthusiast, but he did join the Old Etonian Lodge at the behest of Michael Adeane so that it was not always Michael who had to accompany George VI to Masonic meetings.

Martin Charteris says of his directorship of the Savoy Hotel Group: 'I never open my mouth during the board meetings and never shut it during the luncheons that follow!'

18 July 1987

Much talk with Clementine Beit[†] about David Pryce-Jones's life of Unity Mitford,[‡] which gave offence even to those members of the Mitford family who were robustly anti-Nazi. Andrew Devonshire asked Clementine to intercede with George Weidenfeld for the removal of certain passages – one of which apparently compared Unity to a prostitute in her relations with Hitler. George complied.

---

[*] Dame Gwyneth Jones (b. 1936), dramatic soprano renowned for her Wagner and Richard Strauss roles.

[†] Clementine, Lady Beit (1915–2005), a cousin of the Mitford sisters.

[‡] David Pryce-Jones (b. 1936), author and commentator. His biography of Unity Mitford (1914–48), socialite and devotee of Hitler, was first published in 1976.

I hear that soon after Christopher Soames's arrival in Paris as Ambassador, the owner of one of France's most famous vineyards determined to ingratiate himself by sending two cases of wine. But, not knowing of Christopher's experienced palate, the wine grower thought he would economise by offering the vintage of an inferior year.

Soames acknowledged the present with politeness. To show his gratitude, he wrote, he proposed to make it the main wine at an Embassy dinner, to which he would ask other friends in the wine industry; and he hoped that his correspondent would come too. By return of post the embarrassed donor replied that he would of course be delighted to come. He added that, by some administrative error, the wrong wine had been sent to the Embassy. As a replacement several cases of the renowned 1929 vintage were already on their way to the British Embassy.

24 July 1987
Saddened to hear the news of the death of Grizel Hartley in her eighty-eighth year. She will be remembered with affection by generations of Eton boys and their parents for her distinctive character as a housemaster's wife and for her courage and good humour during her last years of failing health. One day, I hope, somebody will collect Grizel Hartley's letters, remarkable for their content and calligraphy alike.*

4 August 1987
Read *August and Rab†* by Mollie Butler. Rather a naïve little book, though entertaining. Mollie implies that Peter Goldman more or less wrote *The Art of the Possible* for Rab.

14 August 1987
Lunch with Victor Rothschild in Cambridge. He insists on sending car and driver for me. He still broods angrily on his treatment by Labour MPs and others during the Peter Wright‡ episode. He wants to send a letter to the *Listener* denying certain insinuations that appeared in a recent article there, but I dissuade him. Already people are becoming tired of it all, and he should not stoke the dying flames. Victor is particularly aggrieved at charges of having connived with Wright to produce a book. 'I knew he was at work on it as long

---

* This was accomplished by Peter Lawrence (1913–2005), who edited and published *Grizel: Grizel Hartley Remembered* (1991).
† August Courtauld (1904–59), Arctic explorer, was Mollie Butler's first husband.
‡ (1916–95), principal scientific officer for MI5 and author of *Spycatcher* (1987), which the British government attempted to ban.

ago as 1980, and warned MI5 of what he was doing. Far from encouraging him to write his book, I managed to suppress it for seven years.'

I tell Victor that any book which I write on the Rothschild family must include a full vindication of him, though of course I would wish to deal fully with all other aspects of his life. I tell Victor what shocked me in reading the Wright book was the damage that can be done to the reputation of innocent people. But Victor says that the civil servants are never behind in such matters. As Harold Wilson once observed of Burke Trend:[*] 'There are no fingerprints on his dagger.'

2 September 1987

Arrive in Yalta, which looks very pretty: white stucco houses and rich green gardens against a background of mountains. But we soon realise we are in Russia: endless formalities with currency and passports. A tedious episode, not made any better by the notices that greet everyone on going ashore: 'You are welcome.'

The Vorontsov Palace in Alupka is an ugly nineteenth-century Gothic castle on its land side, a Moorish building as it faces the sea. It was here that Churchill stayed for the Yalta Conference of 1945. The Gothic dining room, of extraordinary gloom, was where the Foreign Ministers conferred in 1945. The architect of all this mess was apparently Edward Blore,[†] who also did Buckingham Palace.

18 September 1987

I write to Mary Soames about Christopher's death. Alas, how often I have to write such letters.

Then Mary herself telephones to ask me to the funeral in the country on Monday afternoon, telling me that the Camroses[‡] would be delighted if I lunched first with them at Hackwood. As it is a private funeral, I am touched by her sweet thought. She sounds very much in control of herself and again tells me how much Christopher enjoyed my letters.

---

* Sir Burke Trend, Baron Trend of Greenwich (1914–87), Cabinet Secretary 1963–73; Rector of Lincoln Coll., Oxford 1973–83.
† (1787–1879), antiquarian draughtsman; the Alupka Palace was built between 1828 and 1846, a mixture of Gothic Revival and Moorish Revival.
‡ Seymour Berry, 2nd Viscount Camrose (1909–95), Conservative politician and newspaper proprietor. MP for Hitchin 1941–5. Joan, Viscountess Camrose (1908–1997), hostess and landscape gardener.

21 September 1987

Train to Basingstoke, where I am invited to lunch at Hackwood (once Curzon's home) before going on to Christopher Soames's funeral at Odiham. Joan and Seymour are at the front door under the portico, so warm in their welcome. The house is charmingly arranged. Hackwood is less imposing than I had supposed, though substantial and dignified. I know most of the other guests, including Ted Heath and Clarissa Avon. Ted Heath is in exceptionally good humour. I say: 'I never saw you climbing the spire of Salisbury Cathedral with the Prince of Wales.' He replies that the last time the Prince came he climbed only to the stone parapet, and even then his knuckles were quite white clinging to the rail. Ted asks me to lunch at his house in the Close one day and to see the Cathedral.

Drive in somebody's Rolls to All Saints, Odiham, where the town itself is stiff with police and journalists. Rather a nice vicar greets everybody at the door. I suppose there are about 200 people there – I see Mr Mugabe, the Prince and Princess of Wales, Roy Jenkins, Jack and Valerie Profumo and John King.

There are three lessons, each read by one of Christopher's sons;[*] a prayer by William Temple; an unusual passage from *Pilgrim's Progress*; the prayer for the Order of St Michael and St George. Harrowing to see the coffin carried out, covered in white lilies.

25 September 1987

Jean Trumpington calls for me with her ministerial car and driver at 12.15 to drive down to Eton for Grizel Hartley's memorial service. I give her lunch at a restaurant off the hill going up to the Castle at Windsor. Then we walk down to College Chapel in the sunshine. Meet Martin Charteris on the steps. The order of service has such a pretty engraving of lilies on the front instead of the traditional cross. Johnnie Henderson, Monty's ADC,[†] reads one lesson well, Martin the other even better, with an almost theatrical ring of the voice. The choir is superb, not least in the anthem by John Ireland, 'Greater Love Hath No Man'. I recall Oliver van Oss's imaginary anthem suitable for a Confirmation service in College Chapel when all the parents are present – 'Sooner Shall the Camel'. The new Conduct, John Witheridge, whose move to Eton so discomfited Robert Runcie, reads beautifully, especially 'all the

---

[*] The Rt Hon. Nicholas Soames (b. 1948) Conservative and Independent politician. MP for Crawley 1983–97 and for Mid Sussex since 1997. The Hon. Jeremy Soames (b. 1952), businessman. The Hon. Rupert Soames (b. 1959), businessman.

[†] (1920–2003), banker and racehorse owner.

day long of this troublous life.' A hymn by Cyril Alington and the Founder's Prayer. Opposite where I sit, high on the wall, is a statue of the Founder, King Henry VI, a sceptre in one hand, an orb in the other: that no less than the Eton roar of voices, so strong and confident, moves me.

Jean tells me at tea in School Hall that there was a late house martin in College Chapel yesterday. Martin Charteris said it was Grizel come to see the arrangements.

26 September 1987

I talk to Peter Attenborough, Headmaster of Charterhouse, about my forthcoming Birley lecture. He agrees with me that both Hugh Dacre's and William Rees-Mogg's lectures must have been impenetrable to the boys; so I will change my subject to 'Writing About Royalty' – a striking title with many jolly stories about KGV.

Malcolm Sargent's* flat, in which I spent many happy hours, is on the market for £110,000, but that only covers a lease of seventy-six years.

1 October 1987

Dennis Walters MP† confirms that Peter Goldman, who has just died, not only ghosted Rab Butler's *The Art of the Possible*, but also Iain Macleod's‡ life of Neville Chamberlain which almost prompted Anthony Eden to take legal action.

5 October 1987

To Charterhouse to give the Sir Robert Birley memorial lecture. Met at the station by Peter Attenborough. How well I know his house from the time of Brian Rees.

Richard Thorpe chairs the meeting in the Lecture Theatre. My lecture on KGV goes well and the applause goes on and on. Then talk to a dozen of the senior boys, who seem bright and agreeable. Only one of them professes Labour sympathies.

Lunch with the Attenboroughs. Richard Thorpe is there among other guests. He has almost completed his life of Selwyn Lloyd.

I rather took to Charterhouse, which looks exactly how Greyfriars would be.

---

* Sir Malcolm Sargent (1895–67), conductor, organist and composer.
† Sir Dennis Walters (b. 1928) Conservative politician. MP for Westbury 1964–92.
‡ (1913–70), Conservative politician. Sec. of State for the Colonies 1959–61; Chairman of the Conservative Party 1961–3; Chancellor of the Duchy of Lancaster 1961–3; Leader of the House of Commons 1961–3; Chancellor of the Exchequer June–July 1970.

10 October 1987

Story of John Russell, arriving home on leave from one of his embassies, and sending a telegram to somebody in the Foreign Office, asking him to telephone instructions to his house in Kent so that his hunting clothes would await him at Dover. By mistake the telegram went to Alec Home, Secretary of State. His only comment was: 'Nice to know how the other half lives!'

16 October 1987

Staying at Peter Carrington's in Brussels I hear horrifying tales of the storm early this morning in Britain. Many thousands of trees blown down and damage to innumerable houses.

Peter speaks with irritated admiration of Mrs Thatcher, not least her physical energy. At the Lusaka Conference, Peter describes her as 'rabbiting on at 1.30 in the morning'. He announced he was going to bed. PM: 'Oh, <u>poor</u> Peter, are you tired?' He was up at six the next morning. So was she. The only time he found her really rattled was during the Westland affair.

18 October 1987

Breakfast with all the Sunday papers. Peter Carrington talks of Christopher Soames, at whose memorial service he is to give the address. He is not finding it easy. Neither at Eton nor in the Coldstream did he make friends. It was Peter who not only sent him to Rhodesia, where he won much glory, but who also persuaded a reluctant Mrs Thatcher to give him a seat in the Cabinet. Christopher liked buccaneers who stood up to him, like his eldest son Nicholas.

Peter is amused by Roy Strong's* lust for publicity. When the public spotlight was on the V&A during the appointment of a new Director to replace Roy, he complained to Peter how utterly exhausted he was by all his TV appearances. Peter therefore offered, as Chairman of the Trustees of the V&A, to do all the TV programmes for the next three days. 'No, no,' an anxious Roy Strong replied, 'I can manage perfectly well.'

Peter tells me some interesting things about King Baudouin of Belgium,† who, in spite of a political crisis, is flying to Oxford for the day tomorrow to receive an honorary degree. When Peter told Mrs Thatcher that the King was to be honoured by Oxford, she replied: 'More than they did for me.'

We drive to Bruges. I am overwhelmed by the beauty of the town,

---

* Sir Roy Strong (b. 1935), art historian. Dir. of the National Portrait Gallery 1967–73; and of the Victoria and Albert Museum 1973–87.

† (1930–93), fifth King of the Belgians 1951–93.

particularly when seen from our boat trip along the canals. There is a splendid white building which used to be the British Consulate, and endless tiny houses, too, of much charm. As in Oxford and Cambridge, the juxtaposition of stone and brick, trees and sky, is irresistible. I buy some lace handkerchiefs for friends.

We go to a concert in the evening. The Place Royale looks enchanting as we drive through it. We hear Bruckner's noisy and lengthy Third Symphony. During the applause at the end, Peter says: 'Let's go now before they do it all over again.'

20 October 1987

Lunch at the House of Lords with Jean Trumpington. I give her a handkerchief of Bruges lace bearing her initial. She drops it on the floor, and as I retrieve it I have to remind her what happened to Desdemona.

Dine with George Weidenfeld. Ralf Dahrendorf,* former Director of the LSE and now Warden of St Antony's College, Oxford, is a fellow guest. He tells me of the advice given to Arnold Goodman on becoming Master of Univ., which Arnold passed on to him: 'Do not make any changes until you have won the trust and support of the Fellows. That will be in your last term.'

22 October 1987

By chance I meet Arnold Goodman and I tell him Ralf Dahrendorf's story. Arnold adds that when he became Master of Univ., Rab Butler advised him 'to have nothing to do with the dons'.

27 October 1987

Michael Havers retires as Lord Chancellor on grounds of health after only a few weeks in office. It was a job on Mrs Thatcher's part to get him a substantial pension for life. His successor has long been mentioned for the job: Lord Mackay of Clashfern.

5 November 1987

Dine with Philip Ziegler in Brooks's. The purpose is to talk about his authorised life of King Edward VIII. It was he who suggested it to the Queen, not vice versa. 'I cannot avoid bringing out the triviality on both sides of the family,' he says, 'but there will not be much about him after 1945.'

---

* Sir Ralf Dahrendorf, Baron Dahrendorf of Clare Market (1929–2009), sociologist and political scientist. Dir. of the London School of Economics 1974–84; Warden of St Antony's Coll., Oxford 1987–97.

He asks why Edward suddenly began to loathe Winston in the middle of the Great War. Was it because Winston failed to protect Prince Louis of Battenberg from anti-German attacks? I suggest that the Prince of Wales simply absorbed the Grenadier view of Winston.

Philip says that the Duke of Windsor did send a letter of condolence to Princess Marina on the death of Prince George in 1942. In a letter to Queen Mary which Philip has seen, the Duke of Windsor told her that he was about to do so, and would also send Marina a copy of the memorial service for Prince George in the Bahamas.

On another vexed point, Philip says that the Duke did abandon Fruity Metcalfe in Paris in 1940. It is true that Frankie Donaldson reports this without direct quotations from Fruity's letter. But the letter does exist; it could not be quoted because Baba Metcalfe would not allow it.

Philip is lunching with the Queen Mother tomorrow, but has been unable to secure a longed-for talk with her beforehand – only a few minutes after lunch. He asked Alastair Aird whether there might be a chance of another session with her. He replied: 'Frankly no. She hates talking about the past.' I lend Philip various letters, diary extracts and papers that may be of some use to him. We agree that Mountbatten would seemingly gratefully accept correction of his well-worn stories – but within a very few weeks would revert to his original versions.

25 November 1987

To the annual Highland Park whisky lunch at the Savoy. I sit next to a serious Labour MP for Dunfermline, Gordon Brown.* I later talk to Willie Whitelaw about the supposition that the Queen has opened the Order of the Garter to women in order to give it to Mrs Thatcher. Willie says that the Queen will surely not do so as long as Mrs Thatcher is in office: there are not many precedents for it, except Austen Chamberlain, Eden and Churchill (the last two of whom had earlier refused it). In any case Ted Heath would have to be given it before Margaret.

28 November 1987

Martin Gilliat says that Philip Ziegler would like to write the Queen Mother's official life after Edward VIII.

But after his book on Diana Cooper, this is a remote possibility. The Queen Mother herself will not even consider the problem. She does not want a book

---

* (b. 1951), Labour politician. Chancellor of the Exchequer 1997–2007; Prime Minister 2007–10.

about herself written at all if she can help it. If it were left to Martin I should be invited to do it. What seems most likely is that Robert Blake will be asked to find a capable young biographer who does not know her.[*]

8 December 1987

Shocked to read in this morning's *Times* that Gary Bennett,[†] the New College don, has committed suicide. He was widely accused of having written the anonymous Preface to the new Crockfords' Clerical Dictionary attacking the character and lack of leadership of Archbishop Runcie. He had in fact publicly denied that he was the author. Was he not telling the truth and felt remorse? Or was he simply depressed by the accusation?

I have John King and Mary Soames to dine. Mary is in black, still very sad and with the added blow of Jock Colville's recent death, suddenly on a platform at Winchester Station. She describes one of the few rows that Jock ever had with Christopher. Even as the wife of our Ambassador in Paris, Mary insisted on continuing to curtsey to the Duchess of Windsor, as she had done before to please her father. 'I regarded it as a point of honour.' The trouble was that junior wives in the Embassy were specifically told by the FO not to curtsey. But when the Windsors dined at the Embassy they would not see Mary curtsey, as she greeted them with Christopher at the foot of the stairs. When she and Christopher took Prince Charles to call on the Windsors at the house in the Bois, she explained to him why she would curtsey, and he seemed to accept it.

9 December 1987

I talk about Edward Halifax[‡] with Isaiah Berlin. He says that the War Cabinet in the summer of 1940 voted only by a narrow majority not to put out peace feelers to the Germans. In favour were Halifax and Chamberlain; against were Winston, Attlee and Bevin. Winston was dismissive of Halifax to Isaiah: 'Grovel to the Indians, grovel to the Italians, grovel to the Germans.'

15 December 1987

Dine with Clarissa Avon at her flat in Bryanston Square. An agreeable little party. Clarissa gives us two forks for the fish: very rarely done nowadays.

---

[*] As previously noted, the task was eventually assigned to William Shawcross.

[†] Gareth Bennett (1929–87), Anglican priest and academic.

[‡] Edward Wood, 1st Earl of Halifax (1881–1959), Conservative politician. Foreign Secretary 1938–40; Ambassador to the US 1940–46.

What lovely pictures and books she has: Eden was one of the last Prime Ministers with civilised values.

28 December 1987

Tony Lambton* telephones from the Villa Cetinale to tell me how much he is enjoying my *Kings, Queens and Courtiers* and to repeat his invitation for me to stay in Italy in 1988. He tells me one interesting light on Mountbatten's assassination in Ireland. For weeks before it happened, MB could not get any local boatmen to take him out: they must have heard that something was being plotted against him. Yet MB was foolhardy and refused to take precautions.

---

* Anthony Lambton (1922–2006), briefly 6th Earl of Durham, Conservative politician; cousin of Sir Alec Douglas-Home.

1988

On 3 January Margaret Thatcher became the longest-serving British Prime Minister of the century, having been in office for eight years and 244 days. On 14 January unemployment fell for the eighteenth successive month. On 3 January David Steel announced that he would not stand for the leadership of the new Social and Liberal Democratic Party; the merger of these two parties occurred on 2 March, which meant that the Liberal Party ceased to exist after 129 years. The Chancellor of the Exchequer, Nigel Lawson, announced that the standard rate of income tax would be cut to 25p and the maximum rate from 60p to 40p. On 23 April the former Archbishop of Canterbury, Michael Ramsey, died. In May the first sixteen-year-olds sat the new GCSE examinations. On 2 June President Reagan began his visit to Britain. The Church of England announced on 5 July that women priests would be ordained from 1992. On 28 July Paddy Ashdown was elected the first leader of the Liberal and Social Democratic Party. George H.W. Bush was elected President of the US on 8 November. On 12 December thirty-five people were killed in the Clapham Junction rail crash. A Pan Am flight exploded over Lockerbie on 21 December, killing 270 people; the Queen recorded an addition to her Christmas broadcast to take account of this.

5 January 1988

I had an interesting talk with Anthony Powell* about the origin of his character Widmerpool in *A Dance to the Music of Time*, often supposed to be based on Reggie Dilhorne. Tony lets drop a cryptic hint: that Widmerpool, a non-Etonian (which rules out Reggie Dilhorne), comes in the fourth volume of his memoirs. I skim through the volume: could he mean C.P. Snow?

12 January 1988

Brian Rees comes for a meal. At last he has got a job: helping to run a Government-aided scheme at Notting Hill that puts the unemployed into

---

* (1905–2000), novelist; *A Dance to the Music of Time* was published between 1951 and 1975.

small businesses. He pours out a long tale of bad luck. He is very grateful for the help and support from friends. We talk of Eton days. He says that one of Claude Elliott's unfulfilled ambitions as Head Master was to have a printed card for replying to parents: 'Dear Sir or Madam, I have your communication. Go to hell. C.A.E.'

19 January 1988
Dine at St Antony's, Oxford, with Ralf Dahrendorf, who as always is most agreeable and amusing. He tells me that when Roy Jenkins was elected Chancellor the first thing he asked was, 'Where is my room?' 'We had to tell him that he did not have a room, and that he was not expected to appear in Oxford very often.'

28 January 1988
Some days ago I asked Richard Thorpe to dine with me so that he could bring up the typescript of his biography of Selwyn Lloyd. He produced an amusing remark told him by Olwen Carey Evans[*] in the course of his researches. When Olwen was a little girl she was kept waiting in the village shop in Criccieth. 'Don't you know who I am?', she enquired indignantly. 'I am Lloyd George's daughter.' The shop girl replied, 'Aren't we all, dearie?'

19 March 1988
I spend much of the day reading the typescript of Richard Thorpe's life of Selwyn Lloyd. He has been exceptionally thorough both in research and in talking to over 400 people who knew Selwyn. He has digested the material well and writes with clarity.

20 March 1988
George Weidenfeld is very enthusiastic about publishing eventually the Journals I have been keeping.

5 April 1988
At Strathnaver with Mary Soames as a fellow guest. She says that Winston talked very freely in the family circle. But when he said something very secret, he would add: 'I label this.' So Mary knew the date of D-Day in June 1944 and was surprised when it did not happen – postponed for twenty-four hours because of the weather.

---

[*] Lady Olwen Carey Evans (1892–1990), wife of the surgeon Sir Thomas Carey Evans; author of *Lloyd George Was My Father* (1985).

He loved gambling at the tables and lost large sums. Walking away from the Casino in Monte Carlo after losing disastrously, he said to his equally unlucky friend: 'I shall write an article and get it all back. As for you ...' The friend waited for Winston to say that he would pay his debts too. But Winston continued: 'As for you, I advise you to do the same.'

Clemmie hated Brendan Bracken,* even though she recognised how he had stood by Winston in the pre-war years. She hated to be called Clemmie by him (or even by President Roosevelt) and would not have him to stay until Winston insisted. She once said, 'Because of the way the Tories treated my father before the war, I can never be a wholehearted Conservative.'

Mary tells me that the French take precedence very seriously. Mary used always to consult the Quai d'Orsay before a dinner party about placement at the British Embassy. Once there was a guest list that included ambassadors, cardinals and Academicians. The Quai d'Orsay replied: 'You cannot give this luncheon.'

Christopher Soames's farewell present to the Paris Embassy was to replace the missing books from Duff Cooper's library. When Mary lights up a 'Hamlet' whiff, John King says: 'I bet your father didn't smoke many of those.'

17 April 1988

Dine with John King to meet the Prime Minister and Denis Thatcher. After dinner I am put on a sofa next to the PM. She looks in splendid form, beautifully dressed, not a hair out of place, utterly relaxed in spite of a testing debate in the Commons tomorrow night during which a group of Tory backbenchers will vote against parts of a Social Security Bill. She is hopeful of continuing good relations with China. We talk about Curzon. 'He was a shallow thinker, was he not?' I explain that perhaps his imperialism solidified too early, but I emphasise how enlightened he was about colour and other sensitive topics.

Emboldened by her friendliness, I ask the PM why she appointed David Jenkins to be Bishop of Durham. 'I learned that he was an outstanding theologian and Durham of course has a long tradition of such men.' She regularly reads her Bible, 'especially the Old Testament'. It upset her very much when Edward Boyle† told her a few weeks before his death that he had lost his faith.

She remains in favour of the death penalty, 'especially for those who murder policemen'. We argue about her wish to reintroduce National Service;

---

* 1st Viscount Bracken (1901–58), Conservative politician. Minister of Information 1941–5.
† Baron Boyle of Handsworth (1923–81), Conservative politician.

and she concedes that it prevents the Regular Army from concentrating on its own efficiency.

I am much impressed by her clarity of thought and robustness of expression. The only quality she seems to lack is humour.

25 April 1988
A piece of bad news. Jean Trumpington rings to say that Alan has died. It has come suddenly and unexpectedly.

27 April 1988
Raine Spencer telephones to ask me to lunch at Althorp. She talks at length about the Prince of Wales's marriage. She much admires the public qualities of the Prince, especially his concern for the inner cities. But she thinks the Princess of Wales has a difficult life. 'They don't look to me like two people in love. They have different bedrooms and she never seems to want to touch him. When he says, "Give me a kiss" she does not respond.' She has no artistic side to match his, which is a further gulf.

28 April 1988
Richard Thorpe comes to hear my comments and corrections on his Selwyn Lloyd biography. We talk at length about the difficulty of referring to Selwyn's homosexual tendencies. It has to be in code.

Interested to hear that Philip Ziegler has outsmarted Ben Pimlott[*] for the official Harold Wilson biography.

13 May 1988
Lunch with Angus Ogilvy at St James's Palace. We spend much of the time discussing Prince Eddie's wish that I should do a memoir of Princess Marina. Of course, I cannot refuse so old a friend. But Angus thinks there is nothing much to be written about her. 'She did not have an interesting life. She painted but did not read much. When she first came to England, it was thought that it was to marry the Prince of Wales, but I don't know who jilted whom. She found herself a foreigner in a not very welcoming circle, and was lonely. Her marriage to Prince George blossomed late. She felt herself very Royal and hated curtseying to the Queen Mother.

---

[*] Prof. Ben Pimlott (1945–2004), Labour historian. Biographer of Hugh Dalton (1985); Harold Wilson (1992) and Elizabeth II (1996). See D.R. Thorpe, obituary, the *Independent*, 14 Apr. 2004.

16 May 1988

To St Paul's School, Hammersmith, to talk on the writing of Royal biography. A three-line whip has gone out to all historians and the head of History has bagged Peter Pilkington's study for a small lunch party with senior boys. I talk to an intelligent boy called George Osborne.*

24 May 1988

Rupert Soames asks me what I think of the Waleses' marriage and I am circumspect. We both agree that whatever the tensions, it has got to last. Rupert thinks it unwise for Diana to have been sent to Eric Anderson at Eton so that he could educate her intellectually. 'It is not a question of their acquiring each other's interests, but of tolerating them.'

29 May 1988

Alexander Macmillan tells me that Alistair Horne has been asked to rewrite some of his life of Harold Macmillan, putting in more anecdotes and removing some history. It is to be in two volumes, published at an interval. I ask why not together. 'Because he hasn't yet finished Volume Two!'

19 July 1988

Buckingham Palace Garden Party. A lovely summer day, so wear a grey suit instead of tails. A long gossip with Denis Healey. We discuss the changing class of the Conservative Cabinet. He says: 'Now that the landowners have gone, there is a continuous spectrum from the grammar-school boys in Parliament down to the yobbos on the football grounds.'

21 July 1988

Philip Ziegler tells me that he asked the Queen if he could write an authorised biography of Edward VIII. He produced a variety of reasons, but it was the weakest of them that persuaded her – Edward VIII would otherwise be the only monarch not to be the subject of an official life. Other comments he makes: during the row over money for the Duke of Windsor, the Duke told his brother he had only £92,000 when in fact it was at least £800,000. And York Cottage is not 'a glum little villa', as Harold Nicolson described it, but enormous.

---

* (b. 1971), Conservative politician. MP for Tatton 2001–17; Chancellor of the Exchequer 2010–16.

27 July 1988

Julian Amery tells me that during a well-contested election at Preston North in October 1964, he remembered that there was a French Carmelite nunnery in the constituency. So he called on the Mother Superior, and so charmed her with French and flattery that she agreed to allow the nuns to vote. 'Which way will they vote?', he tactfully enquired. 'There are fifteen nuns,' replied the Mother Superior. 'Fourteen of them are Conservatives. The fifteenth will be doing penance that day.' Julian scraped in by fourteen votes – 20,566 to 20,552.

2 August 1988

Mollie Butler tells me she has written to Roy Jenkins to say that she thinks him and myself the two best living writers of English prose. I jokingly reply, 'Why bring Roy into it?'

6 August 1988

Much talk with Peter Thorneycroft on the absurd resolutions of the bishops at the Lambeth Conference in Canterbury. First, they say that violence is justified in some political circumstances. And when the Northern Ireland bishops at once protest against this encouragement of the IRA, they pass another resolution that says in effect: 'Violence is justified, but not in Ireland.'

7 August 1988

To Canterbury for the closing service of the Lambeth Conference. It is rather moving to see from how many corners of the earth the bishops have come, and easy to see why Robert Runcie has striven to paper over the cracks of dissent on such subjects as the ordination of women in order to keep intact the Anglican communion. No representative of either the Queen or the Government.

23 August 1988

Alec Home tells me that his father-in-law, Cyril Alington, when Head Master of Eton, at the Eton v. Winchester cricket match of 1921 sat next to the Wykehamist at lunch who had scored 248 of their first innings total of 313. Alington's way of putting him at his ease was to say: 'Just the number of Spartans who held the pass at Thermopylae.'

25 August 1988

Grey Gowrie* tells me of his recent visit to Chequers, when the PM showed him the stained-glass windows bearing the arms of former PMs. There was none for Ted Heath: 'I suppose he doesn't believe in that sort of thing,' Grey said. PM: 'Not at all. He thinks he is going to come back!'

8 September 1988

Alexander Macmillan tells me that Andrew Devonshire is paying at least some of the costs of the action for libel which Toby Aldington[†] is bringing against Count Tolstoy: the result of Tolstoy's book which implicated Toby in the enforced repatriation of Cossacks and the Russian nationals at the end of the war. As Harold Macmillan's nephew by marriage, Andrew feels he has a duty to protect the reputation of his uncle and Toby.

14 September 1988

John King is worried about the Prince of Wales's marriage. 'The difference in age of twenty and thirty-two is OK. So is sixty and seventy-two. The dangerous period is twenty eight and forty.'

6 October 1988

To the Festival Hall for a Karajan[‡] concert: Schoenberg's *Verklärte Nacht*, Op. 4 and Brahms' First Symphony. Karajan is fearfully battered. He has to be hoisted up the two or three stairs at the side of the auditorium, then gropes his way to the podium clutching a rail of arms held out by the violas and violins. To conduct he leans against a padded bar. But what magic he draws out of his well-drilled Berlin Philharmonic Orchestra. The Schoenberg is dreamily lyrical, the Brahms as brisk as a military march. Karajan is a master of gesture: the faintest salutation to the audience and they go wild with delight.

8 October 1988

Julian Faber tells me that the Macmillan family are deeply wounded by a passage in Alistair Horne's life of Macmillan that is being serialised in the

---

* Grey Ruthven, 2nd Earl of Gowrie (b. 1939), Conservative politician. Minister for the Arts 1983–5; Chairman of Sotheby's 1985–94; Chairman of the Arts Council of Great Britain 1994–8.

† Sir Toby Low, 1st Baron Aldington of Bispham (1914–2000), Conservative politician and businessman.

‡ Herbert von Karajan (1908–89), renowned Austrian conductor; Principal Conductor of the Berlin Philharmonic 1956–89.

Sunday Times. It describes how Sarah Macmillan[*] discovered before marriage that she was pregnant and was pressed by Lady Dorothy to have an abortion, otherwise 'it will ruin your father's career'. On no better authority than Bob Boothby, Horne also adds that it was this abortion (which left her sterile) rather than the revelation that Bob was her father which led her to drink and ultimately to suicide. I am astonished by his hurtful story, largely irrelevant to Macmillan's career – and, according to Julian, untrue. The family have persuaded Horne to delete it from further editions of his book. But Carol Faber also wants to write a letter to the *Sunday Times.* What do I think? It is a difficult problem. If Carol says nothing, those who have read the serial may think it is true and quote it in the future. If she writes a letter, it will focus attention on it. On the whole I just prefer silence.

19 October 1988

Letter from Brian Rees, enclosing a copy of his Robert Birley memorial lecture at Charterhouse on his father-in-law's work in South Africa. Brian is now working as a fork-lift truck driver. Oh dear.

8 November 1988

Katie Macmillan tells me a story of Moucher Devonshire[†] sitting next to King George V when he came to lunch. They had enormous table napkins. As Moucher tied hers round her neck she said to the King: 'It's like being in bed.' Everybody except the King was very shocked.

9 November 1988

I discuss with Katie Macmillan Volume One of Alistair Horne's life of Harold. It seems to me to be a portrait of a man with no attractive characteristics except courage. Katie says that her own mother, Lady Harlech,[‡] called him 'damp hands' and could never bear to shake them. This may have had something to do with the wounds he received in the Great War. Katie thinks that alcoholism in the family comes not only from the Cavendishes: the Macmillans were equally vulnerable. On the book in general, Katie thinks that Alistair Horne simply does not know H.M.'s world.

George Bush is elected President of the USA.

---

[*] (1930–70), youngest dau. of Harold and Lady Dorothy Macmillan. See D.R. Thorpe, *Supermac: The Life of Harold Macmillan*, pp. 99–100, which provides evidence that Sarah was Macmillan's dau. and not Robert Boothby's, as was sometimes supposed.

[†] Mary Cavendish, Duchess of Devonshire (1895–1988), Mistress of the Robes to Elizabeth II 1953–67.

[‡] (1891–1980), dau. of the 4th Marquess of Salisbury.

Mollie Butler tells me a lovely Rabism. Johnnie Nutting told her that at a shoot at Stanstead, Rab shouted down the table to her: 'We must remember to ask some interesting people for the next shoot.'

Some interesting talk with Toby Aldington about his impending libel suit against Count Tolstoy over the repatriation of the Cossacks and Yugoslavs in 1945. It will probably be settled out of court. Certainly, there was no conspiracy with Macmillan. If Toby was seemingly ruthless in the orders he issued, it must be seen against the background of Yalta – and a natural distaste at that time for anybody wearing German uniform.

10 November 1988
Philip du Zulueta is annoyed with Alistair Horne's book on Macmillan. Horne correctly quotes Philip as saying that Clarissa's influence on Anthony when in office was 'disastrous'; and that she stirred him up when he needed calming down. What Horne does not quote is what Philip said next: that for the last twenty years of Anthony's life in retirement she proved the most wonderful wife.

12 November 1988
I see a TV video of the Prince of Wales's programme attacking modern architecture. He has a lively and sensitive mind, but his comments are often unfair. He does not show any good modern buildings and fails to see that nobody nowadays can afford spaciousness in the middle of the City of London. On rural architecture, he also underestimates the cost of stonemasonry.

I finish reading Alistair Horne's first volume on Harold Macmillan. He is more at home on political and military affairs than on H.M.'s character.

18 November 1988
Talking of Bishop Jenkins of Durham, Katie Macmillan says to me: 'One should not unsettle the faithful.' That is the essence of the matter.

21 November 1988
Steven Runciman* tells me that when it was decided that Prince Charles should go to Gordonstoun, Princess Marina said to Prince Philip: 'How like you to send him to the only German school in Britain.' The Queen Mother, overhearing this, said to Princess Marina: 'I have always wanted to say that,

---

* Sir Steven Runciman (1903–2000), historian; author of a three-volume *History of the Crusades* (1951–4).

but didn't dare.' And he adds that it was Princess Marina, not Mountbatten, who was the marriage broker between the Queen and Prince Philip.

28 November 1988
The Queen was talking one day to one of her courtiers about the intruder into her bedroom in 1982 at the Palace. She said: 'Of course, it was easier for me than it would be for anybody else. I am so used to talking to strangers.'

13 December 1988
I have a chat with Robert Runcie. He shrewdly comments: 'The real problem of the BBC is not pornography or violence or bias. It is trivialisation.'

28 December 1988
Lunch with Arnold Goodman in Headington. The general Oxford opinion is that the rejection of the PM for an honorary degree has led to a falling-off in contributions to the latest big appeal. I am not surprised.

30 December 1988
I meet up with Brian Rees, so resilient in the midst of all his setbacks. His talk is as good as ever. I like his story of G.M. Trevelyan, with whose son Charles* Brian used to stay at Wallington. Brian had just gone up to Trinity and the old man asked him: 'Are you reading History because you want to know, or because you think it easy?'

Brian has got another literary project under way, which is encouraging. He is editing the papers of his father-in-law Sir Robert Birley for the publishers John Murray.† He has discovered from the papers that Robert Birley wrote King George VI's last Christmas broadcast, in 1951.

---

* Charles Trevelyan (1909–64), Fellow of King's Coll., Cambridge 1947–64.
† *History and Idealism: Essays, Addresses and Letters by Robert Birley*, ed. Brian Rees (1990).

1989

Shortly after the Clapham Junction and Lockerbie disasters, a British Mid-land Boeing crashed onto the MI at Kegworth on 8 January, killing forty-four people. The Abbey National Building Society offered free shares to its five and a half million members on 11 January. Sky Television began broadcasting the first satellite TV service in the UK on 5 February. The Poll Tax was intro-duced in Scotland on 1 April. Ninety-four football fans were crushed to death during the FA Cup semi-final at the Hillsborough Stadium in Sheffield on 15 April. Margaret Thatcher completed ten years as Prime Minister on 4 May. Unemployment fell below two million on 18 May for the first time since 1980. Laurence Olivier died on 11 July. On 20 August the pleasure cruiser Mar-chioness collided with a barge on the River Thames, killing fifty-one people. On 26 September Nigel Lawson resigned as Chancellor of the Exchequer, to be replaced by John Major, while Douglas Hurd became Foreign Secretary. The Social and Liberal Democrats were renamed the Liberal Democrats on 16 October. Labour had a 10 per cent lead over the Conservatives in a MORI poll on 19 October. The General Assembly of the Church of England voted to allow the ordination of women on 7 November. Mrs Thatcher visited Berlin on 10 November, the day after the fall of the Berlin Wall. The House of Commons was televised for the first time on 21 November. Sir Anthony Meyer challenged Mrs Thatcher's leadership of the Conservative Party on 23 November; Mrs Thatcher won the subsequent ballot on 5 December, but sixty Conservative MPs did not vote for her. The Romanian leader Nicolae Ceaușescu and his wife Elena were executed on 25 December.

3 January 1989

I give Roger Holloway[*] dinner at the Ark. He has taken on two stimulating posts: Appeals Director of the Imperial Cancer Research Fund and one of the clergy at St Margaret's Westminster. On Christmas Eve he administered the chalice to Enoch Powell. We discuss the sad Garry Bennett episode.

---

[*] The Revd Roger Holloway (1933–2010), Anglican priest.

Roger has heard that at New College a few days before, the talk turned on the best way to commit suicide; it was agreed that a hosepipe attached to the car exhaust was the most effective.

4 January 1989

John King tells me that he is flying up to Lockerbie, in Scotland, to attend a memorial service for the victims of the Pan Am crash. Everything about this is wrong. John and British Airways should not be identified with a crash, particularly of a rival airline; nor should the Prime Minister milk publicity out of it by attending; nor should the Press generate an emotional orgy. I also think it wrong that Paul Channon, who must attend as Transport Minister, is flying up in John's private plane, not in an official plane.

5 January 1989

Frank Johnson[*] to dine. He is most interesting about his youthful literary tastes of the 1960s. Unlike his rebellious contemporaries, he liked Harold Nicolson and Jim Lees-Milne. He rightly felt that Jim did not make the best of Harold's life because Jim was uninterested in politics; however inept as a politician, Harold had it in his bones. Biography leads us to talk about Selwyn Lloyd, in the news because of Richard Thorpe's forthcoming life.

16 January 1989

Thelma Cazalet-Keir[†] has died. With her sense of history, she once said that when King George VI visited the wrecked Chamber of the House of Commons in 1941, he was the first Sovereign since Charles I to enter it.

Martin Gilliat to dine at Claridge's. He says that the two front-runners for Provost of Eton are Nicky Gordon-Lennox and Antony Acland.

He tells me of a gaffe made by Ludovic Kennedy[‡] when he met the Queen Mother recently at somebody's house. He told her he had been busy the previous weekend writing her obituary.

17 January 1989

A young man called Andrew Roberts[§] comes to see me. He has read my *DNB* notice on Edward Halifax and wants to write a new biography of him. So I lend him my file of correspondence on the *DNB* notice, as well as one or two

---

[*] (1943–2006), journalist. Editor of the *Spectator* 1995–9.
[†] Thelma Cazalet-Keir (1899–1989), Conservative politician. MP for Islington East 1931–45.
[‡] Sir Ludovic Kennedy (1919–2009), author, broadcaster and journalist.
[§] (b. 1963), historian and journalist. Author of biographies of Lord Halifax (1991) and Lord Salisbury (1999), and military histories.

other documents. He seems a bright fellow, short, fair-haired in his twenties. He got a First at Cambridge. I like his self-confidence.

18 January 1989
To the Royal Fine Art Commission in St James's Square before lunch, where the Prime Minister introduces a report on the state of London. Norman St John-Stevas is amusing in his introduction. After the speech we move into another room for drinks, and Norman brings me up to the PM, who apparently has been knocking the stuffing out of some guests who want her to restore the Greater London Council.

I ask the PM what restoration is taking place at Marlborough House. This provokes her into some splendidly indiscreet remarks about its tenants, the Commonwealth Secretariat, and indeed about the Commonwealth itself. 'How did they come to occupy it?' she asks. 'Was it under Queen Mary's will?'* She says: 'Why should we spend all that money restoring the building for them?' I suggest that the Secretariat should continue to occupy its smaller, temporary premises and that Marlborough House should become the home of the Prince of Wales. She likes the idea of the Prince there. 'If, as we all hope, the Queen lives as long as Queen Victoria, then we shall need a fine house, not only for the Prince of Wales, but also for his sons.' She adds that it was she who suggested that the Prince should establish his offices in St James's Palace to get him away from Kensington Palace: not good to live over the shop. It proved convenient, too, by moving the Lord Chamberlain to Buckingham Palace.

20 January 1989
Edward du Cann tells me that his relations with Ted Heath remain frosty. He said to Ted one day recently: 'How are you?' Ted replied: 'In the best of health – and that will not please the Tory Party.'

23 January 1989
Dine at Eton with Michael Meredith. A sumptuous meal. The only others are Eric and Poppy Anderson, so we have an exhilarating few hours. First a tour of School Library, for which Michael has collected an impressive array of books and documents. Tonight he has laid out several tables of them that he knows will interest me. They include some Curzon letters. I give Michael a copy of *KGV* for School Library, also some letters of George Bernard Shaw,

---

* The tenancy was negotiated by the Earl of Home when Commonwealth Secretary. See D.R. Thorpe, *Alec Douglas-Home* (1996), pp. 158 and 353.

Evelyn Waugh, Max Beerbohm, Lord Curzon, Anthony Eden, Monty and Evelyn Waugh. Some talk about the Prince and Princess of Wales. Whatever the state of their marriage, it <u>has</u> to work. Eric gave her tutorials at one time, but I am not sure he made much headway. Who is to be Provost? No new names.

12 February 1989

Jim and Audrey Callaghan come for lunch. How warm-hearted they are. Jim is amusing on Clem Attlee's offering him his first ministerial post as Parliamentary Secretary for Transport. 'I give you two pieces of advice. Remember that you are now a member of the 1st XI not the 2nd XI. And if you are going to negotiate with a man tomorrow, don't insult him today.' Jim resists my contention that Clem was a great man. 'No, he preferred Frank Longford to me as First Lord of the Admiralty!'

13 February 1989

I meet Willie Whitelaw at a party at the US Embassy in Regent's Park. I tell him that his 'retirement' role in the House of Lords should be to curb the Government's excessive restrictions on personal liberty and the makings of a nanny state – the latest phase is that we should eat no cucumber or Brie and boil our eggs for ten minutes. He does not dissent.

Caroline Waldegrave speaks of Ted Heath with a mixture of pity and irritation. When the Waldegraves went for a meal at Ted's house in Salisbury, it looked like the room of a museum – not a sign of life or personality in it. And he could not even remember the name of one of his guests, the New Zealand High Commissioner's wife, introducing her as 'Miss New Zealand'. His mean-minded attacks on Mrs Thatcher irritate both William Waldegrave and Douglas Hurd. One day they may have to say so publicly.

14 February 1989

Alistair Horne to lunch at Bertorelli. He is amiable but rather nervous. I am interested in the difficulties he has had with the Palace in writing his book on Macmillan. Not surprisingly, he was forbidden to print certain letters from the Queen to Macmillan, including an account of how she found the deposed ministers after 'the night of the long knives'* in July 1962. What amazes me is that he was not even allowed to record the obvious: that the Queen wrote to Macmillan in her own hand.

---

* A major reshuffle in which Harold Macmillan removed seven members of his Cabinet.

At a dinner at White's, David Windlesham* comes to sit next to me after dinner and pours out a long saga of misery at the attacks made on him for his report† on the TV film of the Gibraltar shootings of IRA members. But what did he expect? He was bound to be attacked either by the left for being a former Tory minister or by the right for his indulgence towards TV investigative journalism. He is sending me a copy of the report so that I can judge for myself. He finds a crumb of comfort in a nice letter he has had from Geoffrey Howe to neutralise Geoffrey's public condemnation of his report.

15 February 1989

Graham C. Greene, the publisher at Jonathan Cape, gives a pleasant dinner party in a private room at the Garrick to celebrate the publication of Richard Thorpe's life of Selwyn Lloyd. The guests include Alec Home, Jack Profumo, Peter Walker, Michael Fraser, Donald Logan,‡ who was with Selwyn at the first Sèvres meeting during the Suez Crisis, Anthony Shone, his nephew, and some of the publishing people.

Alec is tremendously spry for his years in spite of being a little bent. Peter Walker tells some amusing anecdotes of Selwyn. As PPS to Selwyn, Peter would take notes at committee meetings. Then Selwyn would interrupt the proceedings: 'Peter, do some filing.' This meant he had to go to a filing cabinet and extract a bottle of whisky and some glasses.

Jack Profumo tells me of his adoption for Stratford-upon-Avon for the General Election in 1950. Eden, who was speaking for him outside the Shakespeare Memorial Theatre, was shouted at by a heckler. 'How can we have a man called Profumo in Shakespeare's constituency?' Eden replied: 'Would you like us to change his name to Prospero?' It is, Jack adds, the only joke Eden ever made.

17 February 1989

Lunch with the Queen Mother at Clarence House, with some members of the Household. Queen Elizabeth, in a simple little green flowered frock and large diamond spray, gives me that lovely greeting of leaning back, tilting her head and holding out her hand with a dazzling smile. The drawing room seems somewhat larger: it has swallowed up the adjacent little room where I

---

* David Hennessy, 3rd Baron Windlesham of Windlesham (1932–2010), Conservative politician. Lord Privy Seal and Leader of the House of Lords 1973–4; Principal of Brasenose Coll., Oxford 1989–2002.
† The Windlesham-Rampton Report on 'Death on the Rock', 1989.
‡ Sir Donald Logan (1917–2009), Assistant PS to Selwyn Lloyd 1956–8; prepared Selwyn Lloyd's account of Suez for posthumous publication.

had tea with Tony Snowdon a day or two after the birth of his first child. The room also looks more shipshape than when I last lunched, with a huge bunch of red roses given to the QM as a Valentine.

When asked what I should like to drink, I decide to follow Queen Elizabeth and have gin and Dubonnet. While Ralph Anstruther is preparing it, she bustles up and supervises him: 'Put plenty of gin in it, or it tastes too sweet. And is there enough ice in it?' Meanwhile an old radiogram in the corner is pouring out favourites of the 1940s.

The QM draws me to the two armchairs by the fire, facing the windows, for a talk about Princess Marina. Her theme is that she was so 'foreign' and never really became one of the team. But the QM very much admired the way in which she brought up the children – 'and she was very devout, you know'. I mention that in her papers she expresses disappointment that the Prince of Wales took so little notice of her in the 1920s when she was in London. 'Yes, he liked a different sort of woman.'

Later we talk about foreign affairs and she says: 'I am glad you believe that we did so much for India. Nehru didn't really like us.' The QM has much praise for Alec Home, Peter Carrington and also Selwyn Lloyd – 'a particularly good egg'. But when Shirley Williams comes up in conversation, the QM lowers her glass below the table in that celebrated gesture of disapproval.

During the last few minutes of our talk in the dining room, while continuing to talk to me, she feeds biscuits to one of her corgis.* As we go out, it rolls over on its back for me to scratch it, but I am too old and hard to fall for that perilous pastime.

The Queen Mother also mentions the sadness of Michael Mann's impending retirement as Dean of Windsor. She has been listening to candidates for the vacancy preaching in 'my chapel – where of course we have the old Prayer Book'. They are then asked to lunch afterwards at Royal Lodge – 'It is easier for them than to be asked to the Castle.' I get the impression that none of them so far have come up to scratch.

15 March 1989

I have lunch with Richard Beaumont.† We discuss the ethics of machine-gunning survivors of torpedoed enemy ships in wartime, recently resurrected as a topic of concern in the *Sunday Telegraph*. I describe how Mountbatten

---

* When I had an audience with the Queen Mother at Clarence House while researching Alec Home's life for the official biography, she tossed biscuits from time to time to the attendant corgis, who plucked them expertly out of the air. 'We could do with them in the slips for England,' she quipped.

† Sir Richard Ashton Beaumont (1912–2009), Ambassador to Iraq 1965–7 and Egypt 1959–73.

once told me that he was machined-gunned by the Germans after the *Kelly* had been sunk – 'but that was war'. Richard says that Mountbatten once complained that not even he could get his men to machine-gun Germans in the water. When this was reported to Churchill he said: 'That is the German in Dickie.'

25 March 1989

Read Peter Rawlinson's memoirs *A Price Too High*. It is understanding on Ted Heath, but quietly ferocious on Thatcher, who denied him the Woolsack.

30 March 1989

I have a gossip with Princess Margaret. She tells me – as she has done before – how she asked the Queen to allow her not to attend the Duchess of Windsor's funeral. The Queen gave her permission, though I have the impression that it was given with reluctance.

When I mention my own meetings with the Duke, she asks what we talked about. I tell her it was about Oxford and the Welsh Guards, adding how he wanted to be Colonel of the Regiment. 'How like him,' Princess Margaret says. 'Could he not see when he gave up being King he could not continue to have all that went with it?'

31 March 1989

I take very much to Shane Alexander,[*] Field Marshal Alex's son, whom I meet at a lunch. He tells me a characteristic story of his father's modesty. Somebody came up to the Field Marshal in Piccadilly when he was on leave: 'I do admire you so much, let me shake you by the hand.' Afterwards Alex said to a friend: 'I wonder whom he mistook me for.'

25 April 1989

Prince Eddie to lunch at Claridge's. He is unwillingly in the news today. On Saturday, as President of the Football Association, he is to represent the Queen at the Hillsborough disaster memorial service. This has prompted an hysterical and synthetic outburst on the part of Liverpool, who are demanding the presence of the Queen in person, or at least one of her children. Liverpool's whining self-pity has long been nauseating. But Eddie is, as one would expect, calm and good-humoured in the face of likely insulting behaviour.

Eddie asks me for something light to include in his speech when presenting

---

[*] Shane, 2nd Earl Alexander of Tunis (b. 1935), Lord in Waiting Jan.–Mar. 1974.

the prizes at Wellington College. I will send him one or two anecdotes, including Dr Warre[*] at Eton being asked if he knew all the boys – 'No, but they all know me.'

2 May 1989

Dine with Alan Clark[†] at the Beefsteak. He is most entertaining on the fear inspired by the PM among her ministers. She conveys her disapproval in a minute to the peccant minister's Private Secretary. The usual victim is Geoffrey Howe. This would not matter very much except that the rebuke is copied to the Private Secretaries of any other department that may have an interest in the matter. So all Whitehall knows. The only man who stands up to Thatcher, Alan says, is Nigel Lawson. Here is a conversation he heard while attending Cabinet: PM: 'Am I alone in thinking so-and-so?' Nigel: 'Only you can know, PM, whether you are alone. And if you are, only you will know how to deal with it.'

3 May 1989

Such a sweet letter from the Queen Mother, to whom I sent flowers on her wedding anniversary. It includes a sentence of historical importance: 'When one remembers the innocent happiness of that day, perhaps it was a good thing that one had no inkling of the tremendous burden that was to descend on my husband's shoulders.'

13 May 1989

To Cambridge to stay with Jack Plumb at Christ's for Princess Margaret's visit. Princess Margaret tells me that on Noël Coward's seventieth birthday he was to have lunched with the Queen Mother at Clarence House, but she was unwell. So the Queen came to take her place. She gave Noël a little silver box, suggesting that it could be used for toothpicks. 'Alas, Ma'am,' he replied, 'a lost cause.'

In the small drawing room. When the Queen Mother hears martial music she moves swiftly to the window overlooking the road by the side of Clarence House and pulls back the heavy net curtains, explaining to me that they are a protection against blast. The small crowd on the pavement stare at the apparition in amazement that turns to delight and begin to wave to her. She

---

[*] The Revd Edmond Warre (1837–1920), Head Master of Eton 1884–1905.

[†] (1928–99), Conservative politician known for his flamboyance. Minister of State for Trade 1986–9; Minister for Defence Procurement 1989–92. The three volumes of his diaries were published between 1993 and 2002.

waves happily back. It is a full guard of honour of the Scots Guards, pipes
and Regimental Colour, on the way to greet President Bush at Buckingham
Palace. As Giles St Aubyn remarks to me later, she must have seen it thousands of times, yet her excited enjoyment of the spectacle never fades.

We go into lunch, where I am put on her right and Giles on her left. The
QM mentions that she is going to Oxford shortly as patron of an appeal, and
asks whether there are any German Rhodes Scholars nowadays. I suspect
that there are not, but am not certain. Nor does Giles know. 'I have caught
both of you out!' she exclaims in triumph.

It leads us to discuss our relations with Europe. She expresses strong admiration for Mrs Thatcher's determination to concede no sovereignty to the
EEC.

Giles tells her about his book on Queen Victoria, which leads to talk about
the Royal Mausoleum at Frogmore. I ask her about the Duchess of Kent's[*]
more elegant mausoleum nearby. 'Oh, you must come to Royal Lodge and
see it.' Giles asks whether he is right in thinking that she (the Queen Mother)
was the last member of the family to live at Frogmore House. 'Yes,' she says,
'soon after we were married. You see, there is never enough room for my
family to live in.'

Some talk of biography, and I say I regret that Philip Ziegler is writing
another life of the Duke of Windsor. Queen Mother fervently agrees – 'It
has been raked over so often.' She goes on: 'I wonder whether he really liked
England. I am certain, however, that he did want to come back as King.'
That is a most important historical statement, and sheds much light on her
relationship with the Windsors.

The QM confides to Giles how much she dislikes the pound coin. 'So
when I put something in the collection at church, it is always a Scottish
banknote.'

As we take our leave after this exceptionally happy party, the Queen
Mother says: 'It's lovely to reminisce.'

8 June 1989

Lunch with Tony Snowdon. I call for him at his house in Launceston Place,
which is in the hands of builders. The noise is driving him mad. As we walk
round to the Launceston Place restaurant, he points out to me how few
houses have retained their authentic Regency ironwork and sash windows.
He has tried in vain to get the worst developments improved.

---

[*] Princess Victoria of Saxe-Coburg-Saalfeld, Duchess of Kent (1786–1861), mother of Queen
Victoria.

Tony loves Italy. 'Did you know,' he asks in his enthusiastic way, 'that clothes are Italy's third biggest industry, after cars and tourism?'

He has always had a passion for Marmite. He was once arrested for shoplifting in the shop of a Moscow hotel. The detective saw something bulging in his pocket: it was his personal jar of Marmite.

He is delighted I am writing about his Brighton exhibition this weekend, and goes to a lot of trouble to see that I have the photograph of the 'Doge Kennel' I want to reproduce.

12 June 1989
I hear that Princess Marina went to some engagement, a Women's Institute. She was told that they were all teetotal, so they <u>ate</u> the King's health in cake.

29 June 1989
I meet Harold and Mary Wilson at Jonathan Aitken's house in Lord North Street. Mary tells me that she has recently been putting all her letters from John Betjeman in an album. He was immensely kind to her and critical only in the gentlest manner. While writing one of her poems, she took a particular liking to two stanzas but felt they did not quite fit in with the others. So she consulted John, and he replied: 'Take them out, they are weak Swinburne.'*

3 July 1989
To Peterhouse for a talk with Henry Chadwick, the new Master. We sit in two high armchairs in the tall-ceilinged entrance hall. Speaking of the Church of England, Chadwick says that 'the work of three decades is in process of being hopelessly destroyed' – the reconciliation of Canterbury and Rome. As a member of the Anglican-Roman Catholic International Commission since 1969, he blames this on the Papal demand for 'universal jurisdiction'. Too much Vatican centralisation has led to a huge drain of priests from the Church of Rome, perhaps 40 per cent. The present Pope, John Paul II,† is personally authoritarian. But he has always been exceptionally courteous to Chadwick, who has lunched four times at his table. 'But as answers are longer than questions, I got little to eat.'

I go on to see Dadie Rylands for lunch. I ask him what the Queen said to him when investing him with the Companion of Honour. First she asked him where Othello came from, and he answered 'Mauretania'. Then she described going to a performance of it at which the woman in front of her had

---

* Algernon Charles Swinburne (1837–1909), poet, playwright, novelist and critic.
† (1920–2005), Pope 1978–2005.

fainted. The Queen continued: 'Of course, much of it is set in Cyprus.' Dadie: 'She had been well briefed.'

14 July 1989

Lunch with Martin Charteris. He describes his own first interview with the Queen, then Princess Elizabeth, at Clarence House. He had an appointment a 11.30, so went at 11.15 and spent a few minutes discussing the job with Boy Browning. At about 11.25, Browning rang through to the Princess on the intercom and said: 'Ma'am, Martin Charteris is here. Shall I send him up?' 'Yes,' came the Princess's clear voice, 'at 11.30.'

Martin's distrust of Jim Callaghan springs from the occasion when the Queen was to address both Houses of Parliament, and wished to emphasise her attachment to a United Kingdom. So various governments worked on a draft which Martin polished. It was then slightly altered to avoid offending Scottish sentiment, and finally approved by the PM, Callaghan. But the Queen's declaration, 'I cannot forget that I was crowned Queen of the United Kingdom' did offend some in Scotland. Callaghan then disowned the speech.

On his own successor as Provost at Eton, Martin confesses that he would have liked Nicky Gordon-Lennox, but he is satisfied with Antony Acland. 'The most important role of the Provost', he adds, 'is to appoint a good Head Master – and I don't think I have failed with Eric Anderson.'

15 July 1989

Pamela Hicks[*] tells me that the sense of being Royal or not being Royal persists in the family in curious ways. When Dickie Mountbatten once asked the King for a photograph of himself with the Queen Mother, he enquired whether it was for Dickie or Edwina. If for Dickie, the photograph would be signed 'Bertie and Elizabeth'; if for Edwina, 'George RI and Elizabeth R'.

16 July 1989

Ralph Anstruther describes to me how Bishop Herbert,[†] an enthusiastic shot, arrived at a shoot only to find that he had brought the case containing his crozier. But he was philosophical about it – 'Not as bad as if I had gone to a Confirmation with a shotgun.'

---

[*] Lady Pamela Hicks (b. 1929), younger dau. of Earl Mountbatten of Burma, lady-in-waiting to Elizabeth II 1953–4.
[†] The Rt Revd Percy Herbert (1885–1968), Bishop of Norwich 1942–59.

22 July 1989

John King talks to me of the impending Cabinet reshuffle, in which Lord Young[*] is likely to be replaced by Nick Ridley[†] at the Department of Trade and Industry. The PM once asked John whether he thought Lord Young would make a good Chairman of the Party. John said: 'No, he's too North London.' The PM bridled at this, thinking it was an anti-Semitic remark. In a way it was, yet John thinks Young too urban to unite the party in the country.

29 July 1989

Poor Toby Aldington confident of winning his libel action against Count Tolstoy, but fears that he will be unable to recover his astronomical costs. He is furious that Nigel Nicolson is backing Tolstoy.

David Shaw[‡] tells me that Geoffrey Howe has insisted on being given an official residence – Dorneywood, at present occupied by Nigel Lawson – as compensation for his violent demotion from the Foreign Office to the Leadership of the House. Apparently, he sold his London flat during the stock market boom, then lost much of it in the Great Crash of October 1987. So he has nowhere to live. It sounds extraordinarily improvident for any politician, particularly a former Chancellor.

9 August 1989

Dukie Hussey thinks that Geoffrey Howe behaved disgracefully in leaking to the Press the details of his effective demotion from Foreign Secretary to Lord President and Leader of the House of Commons – not least that the PM offered him the Home Office without telling Douglas Hurd of her intention. Douglas alone has emerged with credit, having said nothing.

Seeing the PM at a function the other day, two things mildly shocked me: the air of toadyism everywhere the PM goes, and the number of otherwise respectable guests who produce cameras and pursue her from garden to marquee, some even asking her for her autograph. I have a sense it will not last.

22 August 1989

I take Clarissa Avon to lunch at Claridge's. She has had a miserable August

---

[*] Baron Young of Graffham (b. 1932), Conservative politician. Sec. of State for Employment 1985–7; and for Trade and Industry 1987–9).

[†] Nicholas Ridley, Baron Ridley of Liddesdale (1929–93), Conservative politician. Sec. of State for Trade and Industry 1989–90.

[‡] David Shaw (b. 1950), Conservative politician. MP for Dover 1987–97.

in what for her has been an empty month, so is delighted to be taken out. In her dry manner she gives little away, but she remains bruised by the harsh verdicts on Anthony in political biographies. Robert Rhodes James's life of Anthony did not satisfy her and she thinks she might commission another.*

31 August 1989
I hear that Princess Anne and Mark Phillips† are to separate. Yet another erosion of the mystique of monarchy. And Peter Scott‡ is dead. As long ago as 1939 I recall his paintings of ducks and geese in so many of the studies at Repton.

3 September 1989
Tony Lambton tells me that Ian Gilmour had intended to join the Labour Party. Harold Macmillan heard of this and sent for him. 'What is this I hear about your wanting to join the Labour Party?' 'Well, the Conservatives are so awful.' 'Yes, they are,' replied Harold, 'so you should do what I did. Join them and reform them from inside.' So Ian did.

6 September 1989
A long and cheerful letter from Brian Rees. He is not only writing a book about Robert Birley, but has been asked to write a history of Stowe School by the governors. So he keeps his head above water. I do admire his courage and industry.

13 September 1989
To the National Portrait Gallery for George Weidenfeld's seventieth birthday party: a tremendous crush, but quantities of Buck's Fizz. Nigel Nicolson makes a charming speech. He describes how in the early days of Weidenfeld and Nicolson ('I was Spencer to his Marks') they asked Jonathan Cape to lunch at Claridge's in order to pick his brains about publishing. Cape gave them two pieces of advice: (a) books on South America never sell, and (b) any book about Mary Queen of Scots sells a lot. So they went back to the office and commissioned Antonia Fraser, then Pakenham, to write her life. I have some talk with Ted Heath, and he tells me that he has been invited to conduct

---

* In 1990 the Countess of Avon, who had helped me with my biographies of Selwyn Lloyd and Alec Douglas-Home, invited me to write a new life of Anthony Eden. *Eden: The Life and Times of Anthony Eden, First Earl of Avon, 1897–1977* was published in 2003.
† Capt. Mark Phillips (b. 1948), husband of Princess Anne 1973–92; gold medallist at the 1972 Munich Olympic Games in the team three-day event.
‡ Sir Peter Scott (1909–89), ornithologist, conservationist and painter.

at the Leningrad Conservatoire, the first foreigner ever to be asked. I tell him to drop politics and master Elgar's First Symphony. I wonder whether Mrs Thatcher ever gives parties with string quartets at No. 10. 'No,' says Ted, 'music is not one of us.'

15 September 1989

Tony Lambton telephones from Italy. He has heard that the Queen vetoed a knighthood for me because of what I wrote about King George V and the Tsar.

Audrey Callaghan[*] tells me how outraged she is that the Great Ormond Street Hospital for Children now has to hold flag days to keep going. 'I thought that sort of charity belonged to the past.' I wonder with her whether people do not like giving money in the street for a good cause.

8 October 1989

I am sad to read of the death of the cricketer Norman Yardley[†] at the age of seventy-four. How the news brings back memories of those happy cricket festivals at Scarborough long ago.

10 October 1989

Peter Carrington is furious with the Church of England in general and Bob Runcie in particular. He has received a rude letter from the Bishop of Buckingham, Simon Burrows,[‡] telling him that as he has failed to fill a living in his gift, the patronage has passed to the Bishop. This has happened in spite of Peter's having several times asked Runcie to suggest a suitable candidate without once getting a reply.

In cheerier mood, Peter tells me that after one Labour Budget, he said to Harold Lever, then Financial Secretary to the Treasury: 'With a budget like that, you will bankrupt us all.' Harold replied: 'It would take more than that Budget to bankrupt me!'

12 October 1989

Poor Toby Aldington is having a terrible time under cross-examination

---

[*] Audrey Callaghan was Chairman of the Board of Governors of Great Ormond Street Hospital 1968–72; Chairman of the Special Trustees 1983–90. The playwright J.M. Barrie (1860–1937) gave the rights of *Peter Pan* to the hospital in perpetuity. A bronze statue of Peter Pan stands in a garden outside the hospital; the ashes of both Lord and Lady Callaghan were interred by this statue.

[†] (1915–89), Yorkshire cricketer who captained England 1947–50.

[‡] The Rt Revd Simon Burrows (1928–2015), Bishop of Buckingham 1974–94.

in the libel case he is bringing against Count Tolstoy, who accused him of sending Cossacks and others to their deaths when he was a young Brigadier at the end of the war.

16 October 1989

An evening party at the House of Commons to celebrate the publication of Denis Healey's memoirs *The Time of My Life*. He inscribes a copy for me. His speech is worthy of a latter-day Charles James Fox.* There is a special welcome, for instance, to the former Governor of the Bank of England, Gordon Richardson – 'luxuriating in the problems of his successor'. And on Nigel Lawson: 'He has problems similar to those that I faced as Chancellor. Throughout I was sustained by the loyalty of the Prime Minister, Jim Callaghan. I would strongly advise Nigel to choose a Prime Minister like him.'

19 October 1989

Lunch with Nico Henderson at Brooks's. We talk of Rab, always a favourite theme. When Rab came to stay at the Paris Embassy, Nico's Private Secretary made various suggestions to Rab of things to do – Shopping? No. A walk? No. A visit to Versailles? No. At last the Private Secretary said, 'What about a visit to the best Impressionists?' Rab: 'The best Impressionists are in my house.'

26 October 1989

John King telephones me at about seven to discuss the political bombshell announced this evening: Nigel Lawson's resignation as Chancellor in protest at the PM's retention of Sir Alan Walters† as her economic adviser at No. 10. It raises the question of why the PM did not sacrifice Lawson before – and indeed why she needs an economic adviser at No. 10 at all. It will erode her reputation considerably. And she has ensured the worst of both worlds, for now Walters has resigned too. John Major moves from the FO to the Treasury, and Douglas Hurd achieves a lifelong ambition by becoming Foreign Secretary.

27 October 1989

As expected, there is a stock-market slump after Nigel Lawson's resignation. Noel Annan sends me a copy of *Hansard* in which he compared Walters to

* (1749–1806), Whig statesman. Britain's first Foreign Secretary Feb.–Sept. 1806.
† Prof. Sir Alan Walters (1926–2009), economist. Chief Economic Adviser to Margaret Thatcher 1981–3 and 1989.

Harold Laski. He put the question in the Upper House two days before the
resignations: perceptive of him.

30 October 1989
To George Weidenfeld's for a cocktail to mark the publication of Sarah Bradford's life of King George VI.

Nigel Nicolson is a tremendous partisan of Count Tolstoy in his case with
Toby Aldington. Nigel will give evidence on Tolstoy's behalf that he protest-
ed at the time against the repatriation of Yugoslavs. Elizabeth Longford says
that the Queen Mother should have seen Sarah Bradford and helped her with
the book.

3 November 1989
To Cambridge. I lunch with Owen Chadwick at the Garden House Hotel.
He tells me two good stories about Noel Annan. When Owen was sitting
for his Tripos Finals, he noticed that the man in front of him was elegantly
dressed and much at his ease. While Owen chewed his pen, the paragon
began writing with effortless fluency and did not stop until the papers were
collected. 'Ah,' Owen thought, 'a certain II.i.' In fact, Noel took a starred
First.

Noel also complained to Owen when Provost of King's that he had no
time to write. 'Why?' 'Because we are such a rich college and it takes time to
look after so much money.'

9 November 1989
Andrew Roberts, writing a life of Lord Halifax, telephones to ask if I can help
on one point. Nowhere in Halifax's papers is there the slightest reference to
the Abdication, though he was in the Cabinet at the time. That is indeed
strange.

10 November 1989
Dine with Derek Boorman at his house in Eaton Mews. Two of the fellow
guests are Prince Andrew and his wife Sarah, Duchess of York.* She is
striking in a flamboyant way: red-haired, tall, and very friendly in a slightly
frenzied way. Within minutes she is calling me Kenneth and continues to do
so again and again throughout the evening. She is writing about Osborne on

---

* (b. 1959), former wife of Prince Andrew; charity patron. K.R. became a great help to the
Duchess of York and her two daughters, and when he died on 24 Jan. 2014 the sole surviving
Christmas card on his chimneypiece was from the Duchess of York and her children.

the Isle of Wight, and asks if I can help her. I say of course, and promise to send her anecdotes about the house which are not well known. As she says, everybody has read Queen Victoria on Osborne, but few know what it was like to be a guest there. The nicest side of Fergie comes out when she tells me of a visit to the convalescent house there: 'It was so sad. All the patients are shut in from 5 p.m.'

Prince Andrew is amiable. He tells us of his day: teaching his men how to escape from an underwater hatch in the morning, then doing a broadcast on a charity, then judging a photographic competition.

15 November 1989

Dine with Martin Gilliat. He tells me that the Queen Mother has read Philip Ziegler's *Edward VIII* in page proof. She thought he had included too many extracts from intimate family letters.

27 November 1989

Grey Gowrie gives a party at Sotheby's for his fiftieth birthday. Much attention focuses on Sir Anthony Meyer,* MP for Clwyd North West, who is challenging Mrs Thatcher for the leadership of the Tory Party next week. He has not a hope of winning, but the contest may damage the party by revealing a loss of enthusiasm for Mrs Thatcher. Intense efforts are being made for him to withdraw.

12 December 1989

Victor Rothschild tells me that during grace in Hall at Trinity College, Cambridge, one night before dinner, Bertrand Russell† said to him: 'Why do they continue to have this sort of rubbish nowadays?'

27 December 1989

Dukie Hussey tells me that when Mrs Thatcher visited Salzburg, she was taken to the much-praised production of *Così fan Tutte*. At the end of the first Act she said how outraged she was by 'this most immoral opera'.‡

---

* 3rd Bt (1920–2004), soldier, diplomat and Conservative politician, best known for standing against Margaret Thatcher for the Tory leadership in 1989.

† 3rd Earl Russell (1872–1970), philosopher, social critic and Nobel Laureate in Literature 1950.

‡ A view which was shared by one of its great interpreters, the conductor Herbert von Karajan (1908–89).

31 December 1989

Alexander Stockton tells me that his grandfather took a huge gamble in bringing out a new edition of Grove's *Dictionary of Music*. It could have cost the firm £6 million, but it turned out to be a money-spinner.*

---

* *The New Grove Dictionary of Music*, twelve years in the making, was published in twenty volumes in 1980. It was particularly successful in America, where it was launched by Leonard Bernstein (1918–90). Its second edition in 2001 ran to twenty-nine volumes. See D. R. Thorpe, *Supermac: The Life of Harold Macmillan*, p. 592

1990

On 18 January the first MORI poll of the year gave Labour a twelve-point lead over the Conservatives. The UK and Argentina restored diplomatic relations after eight years. Nelson Mandela was released from prison in South Africa after twenty-seven years on 11 February. On 25 March the Archbishop of Canterbury, Robert Runcie, announced his decision to retire at the end of the year. The Labour lead in a MORI poll had extended to twenty-three points on 19 April. Victor Rothschild died on 20 March. On 11 May inflation was at 9.4 per cent, the highest rate for eight years. The Social Democratic Party was wound up on 3 June after nine years. The destruction of the Berlin Wall began on 13 June. George Carey, Bishop of Bath and Wells, was named as the new Archbishop of Canterbury on 25 July. An IRA bomb killed the Conservative MP for Eastbourne, Ian Gow, on 30 July. The historian A.J.P. Taylor died on 7 September. The pound sterling joined the Exchange Rate Mechanism on 8 October. The Liberal Democrats won the by-election for the Eastbourne seat of Ian Gow on 18 October; Geoffrey Howe, Deputy Prime Minister, resigned on 1 November over the government's European policy, and on 13 November made a dramatic resignation speech in the House of Commons. On 14 November Michael Heseltine announced that he would challenge Margaret Thatcher for the Tory leadership; she failed to win an outright victory in the first ballot on 20 November, and on 22 November announced her resignation after having been Prime Minister for eleven years and leader of the Conservative Party for fifteen years. On 27 November John Major was elected leader of the Conservative Party and became Prime Minister, the youngest to that date of the twentieth century. On 1 December Channel Tunnel workers from Britain and France met forty metres beneath the English Channel seabed, the first land connection between Britain and mainland Europe for 8,000 years.

1 January 1990
I telephone William Waldegrave to congratulate him on becoming a Privy Counsellor.

2 January 1990

Robert Armstrong tells me that when Harold Macmillan came back to No. 10 to see Alec Home, he took the old man into the Cabinet Room. Harold leaned on his stick and said: 'Ah, how well I remember sitting there talking on the phone to President Kennedy during the Cuban Missile Crisis.' Robert goes on: 'I didn't have the heart to tell him that it was in fact not at No. 10, but in Admiralty House.'

8 January 1990

I dine at Pratt's with Ralph Carr-Ellison.* He tells me that when Monty visited St Aubyn's prep school some years ago, one of the boys took photographs of him. He asked Monty where he should send them. Monty replied: 'Field Marshal Montgomery, England, will do.' Then he paused and added: 'Better put Hampshire as well.'

10 January 1990

I hear that when Henry Kissinger was speaking at Conrad Black's† annual dinner, he began with the usual formal list of guests – 'Your Excellency,' etc. When he came to 'Your Eminence,' he turned and added, 'Not you, Conrad.'

16 January 1990

I hear that Harold Wilson, when PM, summoned all the university Vice-Chancellors to No. 10 and harangued them. Ted Short, Secretary for Education, chipped in: 'Just what I said in my last speech, Prime Minister.' Harold: 'Really? I didn't know you had two speeches, Ted.'

19 January 1990

I go to a concert given by the New College choir at St John's, Smith Square. The music is glorious. Princess Margaret is there and gives a party afterwards. She is in fine form and tells me that she has just packed off the choirboys to Oxford. 'Some of them', she said, 'were almost completely obscured by their frilly ruffs, like little pink cutlets!'

25 January 1990

Willie Whitelaw takes me to the Carlton. He deplores the fact that the new Conservative MPs will never dine out, but use only the Commons; nor can

---

* Sir Ralph Carr-Ellison (1925–2014), businessman and television executive; Lord Lieutenant of Tyne and Wear 1984–2000.

† Baron Black of Crossharbour (b. 1944), former newspaper publisher, cross-bench peer.

he persuade them to make the Carlton Club the centre of Conservatism it used to be.

27 February 1990

To Lambeth Palace for a very nice party given by Robert Runcie for Owen Chadwick's new life of Archbishop Michael Ramsey. Robert looks exhausted, which is hardly surprising after a tour of Pakistan and Bangladesh, accompanied by perpetual dissension in Church affairs.

Robert tells me that in the Lords recently he introduced the measure allowing the Archbishop latitude to give a dispensation from the rule that divorced men may not be ordained. 'Which way did you vote?' he heard one Tory peer ask another. 'With the Scots Guards, of course,' was the reply.

I hear from another guest that when Runcie is accosted by a bore, he says: 'Do you mind if I put my spectacles on? I cannot quite hear you.'

Owen Chadwick is modesty itself. Nowhere does his Michael Ramsey biography designate its author as a member of the Order of Merit.

4 March 1990

My story about Peter Walker's impending resignation has been put at the top of the front page of the *Sunday Telegraph*. I am sorry that nothing has been left of my remarks about Peter's success as Secretary for Wales.

In the course of the morning Peter Walker issues a statement confirming that he is to retire, probably in a couple of months. It is the big story of the week; another blow for Mrs Thatcher.

6 March 1990

After my Peter Walker story and the further setback to Tory morale, the Stock Exchange suffered a fall of about twelve points yesterday. Much comment on my story in other papers.

Woodrow Wyatt's[*] annual Tote lunch at the Hyde Park Hotel. Alun Chalfont[†] tells that many people are doing their best to block the chances of Richard Harries,[‡] Bishop of Oxford, as the next Archbishop of Canterbury. 'All those sanctimonious broadcasts,' he adds.

---

[*] Baron Wyatt of Weeford (1918–97), Labour MP for Birmingham Aston 1945–55; reporter on the BBC's *Panorama* while out of Parliament; MP for Bosworth 1959–70; later a fervent supporter of Margaret Thatcher; Chairman of Horserace Totalisator Board 1976–97.

[†] Alun Gwynne Jones, Baron Chalfont (b. 1919), (former Labour) politician and historian. Minister of State for Foreign and Commonwealth Affairs 1968–70.

[‡] The Right Revd and Rt Hon. the Lord Harries of Pentregarth (b. 1936), Bishop of Oxford 1987–2006; Gresham Professor of Divinity 2008–12.

18 March 1990

Jean Trumpington tells me that a Tory peer had said to her in the Lords: 'How can you be so civil to Robin Cook?'* Jean: 'He's much nicer than he looks.' Tory peer: 'That's what he says about you.'

21 March 1990

A terrible day. Victor Rothschild has died, very suddenly of a heart attack. In spite of William Waldegrave's warning to me that Victor's health was precarious, I am deeply shocked. Even in his eightieth year he seemed vigorous.

Marie-Sygne Northbourne† tells me that the Pope, soon after his election, asked for a swimming pool to be built in the Vatican. He was politely told that it was too expensive. He replied, 'Well, it will be cheaper than another Papal election.'

23 March 1990

Jim Callaghan, talking of Michael Stewart and Victor Rothschild, says: 'I hate going to the House of Lords nowadays. A friend one sees there one day is dead the next.'

28 March 1990

Ten past nine train to Birmingham for the presentation by Clarissa Avon of Anthony Eden's papers to the University of Birmingham Library. I share a carriage with John Eden,‡ most agreeable.

Delighted to see Diane Maxwell, who has come over from Shropshire. The Neville and Austen Chamberlain papers are housed at Birmingham also. The display of selected documents is most interesting. I notice that Anthony Eden's diary refers to taking out his son Simon§ from Eton for <u>luncheon</u>. When I show this to Mary Soames, she says: 'But I always say luncheon.'

Ted Heath gives a good speech. Travel back to London with the MP Peter Tapsell. He thinks it significant that Robert Rhodes James was not at the ceremony, and surmises that he has not been asked because Clarissa did not

---

* (1946–2005), Labour politician. Foreign Secretary 1997–2001.

† Lady Northbourne (b. 1937), Chair of Kent Opera 1980–89.

‡ Sir John Eden, the Rt Hon. Baron Eden of Dinton (b. 1925), nephew of Sir Anthony Eden; Conservative politician. MP for Bournemouth West 1954–83.

§ (1924–45), eldest son of Sir Anthony Eden, killed on active service in Burma. His name is on the 1939–45 war memorial in the cloister at Christ Church, Oxford, above the inscription: *All these were honoured in their generations and were the glory of their time.*

like his biography of Anthony. I do not mention that Clarissa might commission another life. Peter says that Mrs Thatcher 'should retire as soon as possible with dignity and honour'.

31 March 1990

I hear an extraordinary story. A friend wanted to put his girl down for the sixth form at Marlborough. A master said they took girls only if they were on the pill. The girl in question was fifteen. The father indignantly withdrew her name. A sign of the times?

Talking of schools, I also hear how pathetic Chenevix-Trench could be. He once said at Eton that he felt like a pony entered for the Grand National.

3 May 1990

I have dinner with the Waldegraves. I talk to John Major, Chancellor of the Exchequer, who has a cheerful honesty about him. I ask him when he does his overnight boxes. Apparently, both in the evening *and* in the early morning. 'Much of it is not really necessary, but of course it makes one feel so important as one unlocks a red box.'

9 May 1990

Clarissa Avon tells me a perfect story about the garden at No. 10 and Harold Macmillan. A few days after becoming Prime Minister, he was standing at the window of the Cabinet Room with a visitor and said: 'Hasn't Dorothy done wonders with the garden.' Of course, it was all the work of Clarissa.

20 May 1990

I am asked to take part in an elaborate and supposedly secret BBC rehearsal of what will happen when the Queen Mother dies. A car comes for me at 3.30 and delivers me to BBC TV headquarters, where supposedly the news of the QM's death from a heart attack at Royal Lodge has been received twenty minutes or so earlier. Elizabeth Longford has similarly been summoned and we discuss the QM's life and influence between newsreels of her life. The absurdity of it all is that it is a BBC exercise in logistics. We are not recording for the day, so there is no incentive to tell one's best stories of her. Indeed, we might just as well have read a page from the telephone directory. It lasts rather more than two hours, but is quite moving in its way.

12 June 1990

Dine with Martin Charteris at Eton. Drive down with Clarissa Avon in Hugo Vickers' car. He has brought all my books to be inscribed.

I take Martin my Luxmoore* watercolour of Upper School, which I never display, and which will enrich Eton's own collection. Martin takes me to an upper window of the Brewhouse Yard exhibition to catch a glimpse of the new bridge from Fellows' Eyot to Luxmoore's Garden. Its drawback is to make the garden too accessible and un-secret.

22 June 1990
Richard Thorpe writes from Charterhouse to say that Alec Douglas-Home has appointed him to be his official biographer. I am pleased for him. He is an able man. I will give him all the help I can.

28 June 1990
Jane Buccleuch† tells me how a little godson asked her: 'Is it possible for a *man* to be Prime Minister?'

29 June 1990
A nice party given by Philip Goodhart. One of his little grandsons goes round with plates of smoked salmon, pushing them under one's nose in a determined way. I ask him whether he will act as a waiter at one of my parties. He goes away, comes back and says; 'It will cost you a pound.'

2 July 1990
To the Athenaeum, where Quintin Hailsham is giving a party for his memoirs, *A Sparrow's Flight*. An odd book, full of majestic pronouncements and petty grievances.

12 July 1990
A tremendous political row blows up about an interview Nick Ridley has given to the *Spectator*, criticising German economic ambitions in Europe as well as an EEC dominated by 'non-elected political rejects'. It is amazingly indiscreet.

13 July 1990
Will Nick Ridley have to resign? Last night I thought it possible that he would brazen it out; this morning I am not so sure. A comparison between

---

* H.E. Luxmoore (1841–1926), schoolmaster at Eton 1864–1908.
† Jane Scott, Duchess of Buccleuch (1929–2011), a model for Norman Hartnell; paved the way for disabled people to serve as MPs, including her husband, the 9th Duke, who had been paralysed in a hunting accident.

Chancellor Kohl* and Hitler is implied, fortified by a brilliant cartoon on the cover of the *Spectator* by Nicholas Garland† – Nick running away after daubing Hitler hair and a moustache on a poster of Kohl.

14 July 1990

The morning news says that the PM has left it to Nick Ridley whether to resign or not – and he has not yet done so. At 1 p.m. it seems that he has passed the buck back to the PM by stating that he will resign only if she says it would be harmful to the Government for him not to do so. His resignation comes at 6 p.m., with little backbench support for him, though perhaps more in the country.

I hear that the boys at the Dragon School, Oxford, call the new Head-master St George. Why? Because he killed the Dragon.

19 July 1990

I give David Dilks lunch at Bertorelli. He tells me that the administrative burden of his present job prevents him from writing Volume Two of his biography of Neville Chamberlain.

When David was editing Alec Cadogan's‡ Foreign Office diaries, he found disobliging references to both Eden and Macmillan so asked them whether they wished them deleted. Macmillan said please take them out. But Eden said the complete text would one day be published and readers would think that he had requested or insisted on the cuts; so he told Dilks to leave them in.

25 July 1990

George Carey, Bishop of Bath and Wells, is the surprise appointment to suc-ceed Robert Runcie as Archbishop of Canterbury. I rather took to him when he preached in Wells Cathedral at midnight Mass last Christmas. Delighted it is to be neither Habgood of York nor Sheppard of Liverpool.§

---

* Helmut Kohl (1930–2017), Chancellor of Germany (the Federal Republic until 1990) 1982–98.
† Nicholas Garland (b. 1935), political cartoonist.
‡ The Rt Hon. Sir Alexander Cadogan (1884–1968), Permanent Under-Sec. for Foreign Af-fairs 1938–46.
§ The Most Revd and Rt Hon. the Lord Carey of Clifton (b. 1935), Archbishop of Canterbury 1991–2002. The Right Revd Lord Sheppard of Liverpool (1929–2005), Bishop of Liverpool 1975–97; England Test cricketer 1950–63.

30 July 1990

Deeply shocked to hear on the 1 p.m. news of the murder of Ian Gow by
the IRA: they blew up his car with a bomb at his home in Sussex. It was
always jolly to see him at Friston with Hartley Shawcross: a good, brave and
honourable man, one of the few politicians in recent years to resign on a
matter of principle.

1 August 1990

There was evidently quite a betting coup over the appointment of George
Carey to succeed Robert Runcie as Archbishop. Some home affairs correspondents got wind of it shortly before the announcement and told senior
colleagues. Ladbrokes was offering Carey at 20–1 or even 25–1. So they
plunged and made a killing. People who were not told the secret revealed the
plot in disgruntled anger.

26 August 1990

On his relations with Ted Heath at No. 10, Robert Armstrong tells me that it
was never easy. For the party which Ted gave for William Walton's seventieth
birthday, he asked Herbert Howells[*] to compose a grace, and asked Robert,
his Principal Private Secretary, to find some suitable words. This Robert
did, and the piece became the standard grace for dinners at No. 10. Robert
wanted to publish it – and perhaps get some royalties for himself and the
composer – but Ted wouldn't allow it.

Another story concerns the launch by Ted of an appeal for St Paul's
Cathedral. Robert was asked to produce a draft speech. After consulting
various authorities, he wrote what he thought rather a good little speech and
sent it up to Ted in an official box. It came down unmarked and presumably unread. The same thing happened during the next two days, so Robert
assumed that Ted had liked the speech and wanted to make no alterations.
On the morning of the ceremony Robert drove with Ted to St Paul's. In the
car Ted asked Robert if he had prepared a speech. Robert gave it to him. Ted
glanced at it and then said: 'This is awful, I am not going to use it. But I will
make my own notes on the back of it.' Robert felt very abashed. In St Paul's
Ted stood up and gave his speech, word for word of what Robert had written.
It was his idea of a joke.

Robert also talks to me about his father, Sir Thomas Armstrong,[†] who
was born on 15 June 1898 and educated at the school of the Chapel Royal,

---

[*] (1892–1983), composer known for his large output of Anglican church music.
[†] (1898–1994), Principal of the Royal Academy of Music 1955–68.

St James's. For years he liked to tell the story of how he had not only sung at the funeral of King Edward VII, but had been the soloist in Mendelssohn's 'Oh, for the wings of a dove'. Out of curiosity Robert looked up the order of service, but found that Mendelssohn's piece was not in it. He simply thought that his father's memory was at fault. Then somebody sent him a copy of the *Graphic* for May 1910. It included a picture of ten of the small boys from the Chapel Royal singing in the King's bedroom at Buckingham Palace as he lay in state. It is well known that Queen Alexandra was reluctant to part with her husband's body, and put it on show in the bedroom for several days after his death and had the choir of the Chapel Royal sing her favourite pieces, including that by Mendelssohn. Old Sir Thomas recognised himself as one of the ten boys in the picture.

27 August 1990

William Waldegrave tells me that when someone expressed surprise to Harold Macmillan that the Iranians had done surprisingly well in the long war against Iraq, he replied: 'Of course they did well. They shot all their generals before they began.'

William also tells me that during his early days as a minister he was sent for by the PM. Pointing to the portrait of Sir Robert Walpole in the Cabinet Room, he mentioned modestly that he was descended from him. All Mrs Thatcher said in a level voice was: 'He looks better now he has been cleaned.'

2 September 1990

Katie Macmillan tells me that she tried to persuade Harold Macmillan that I, not Alistair Horne, should write his life. She felt that Alistair did not understand the Cavendish world.

10 September 1990

John Simpson, the Dean of Canterbury, likes the new Archbishop, George Carey, but does not think him clever. 'He is very evangelical in a folksy way, not an austere Calvinist. Can he manage a traditional established Church?'

16 September 1990

I mention to Arnold Goodman how unfair it is to saddle Hugh Dacre for all time with his blunder in thinking the Hitler diaries to be genuine: against this must be set much historical writing of the finest quality. Arnold says that Rupert Murdoch, an invariable optimist, telephoned him a week or two before publication of the diaries in the *Sunday Times* to say that he had the greatest journalistic scoop of all time. Arnold had doubts: for in all the many books and diaries about Hitler there was never a mention of Hitler's diaries – or of his going off to write his diaries. He was further dubious when Hugh was interviewed in Germany over the diaries. The interviewer spoke in English: if Hugh had been able to read the Hitler diaries at sight, surely he should have been able to be interviewed in German?

18 September 1990
Ted Heath tells me that when William Walton's arrangement of the National Anthem was played before the first production of Britten's *Gloriana* at Covent Garden in 1953, the Queen turned to Prince Philip in the Royal Box and said: 'Are they allowed to do this to it?' Princess Margaret passed it on to Walton, who was dejected.

28 September 1990
Brian Rees tells me that he is working at Stowe on the school history, and meanwhile also standing in for a storeman-cleaner. 'I can't help smiling when doing some of the basic jobs to think I was once interviewed for the Headmastership there.' Surely he could find some more exacting and better-paid job?

1 November 1990
Geoffrey Howe has resigned as Lord President of the Council because of a conflict of views between him and the PM on Europe. He is the last member of her original Cabinet of 1979. I do not think it will make much difference to the stability of the Government. Geoffrey was already an impotent passenger, demoted and consoled with the empty distinction of being Deputy Prime Minister.

Peter Carrington tells me that when Ted became PM he once said to Peter: 'Of course, you live near my house now,' i.e. Chequers. Peter replied: 'No, Ted. You lodge temporarily near my house.'

8 November 1990
I talk to Willie Whitelaw about Michael Heseltine's challenge to Thatcher for the party leadership. He tells me that he no more trusts Heseltine's judgement than he did Quintin Hailsham's when Macmillan retired.

13 November 1990
Speculation mounts about Mrs Thatcher's future after Geoffrey Howe's vitriolic resignation speech in the Commons this afternoon. I catch a TV programme of Howe's resignation speech in the evening, less effective than I

had expected, partly because he makes too much use of notes: premeditated malice.

15 November 1990
Lunch at the Beefsteak, buzzing with anti-Heseltine sentiment.

18 November 1990
Jean Trumpington tells me two stories going the rounds at Westminster. 'The party is in danger of throwing away a diamond in order to wear costume jewellery.' And of Howe's resignation speech: 'It took Elspeth Howe* ten minutes to write it and Geoffrey Howe ten hours to deliver it.'

20 November 1990
Intense speculation about Mrs Thatcher's future after the result of the first ballot of Tory MPs for a leader:

Mrs Thatcher 204

Michael Heseltine 152

Abstentions 16

As the PM has not won a big enough majority under the rules to remain leader, she must either resign or go forward to another ballot a week today. The closeness of the contest makes her long-term survival doubtful.

22 November 1990
Support for Mrs Thatcher appears to be crumbling even inside the Cabinet, though she seems determined to battle on.

To Westminster Abbey for the memorial service for Elizabeth Home, who died in September. All the old warriors are there: Callaghan, Carrington, Heath, Hailsham. Alec very bent on a stick, but with a smile of greeting for old friends. Martin Charteris gives a good address. Denis Thatcher walks in alone. Can Margaret have resigned already or is she merely embroiled in a battle to save herself? I walk out of the Abbey with William Waldegrave, who tells me that she has resigned and the newspaper placards already blazen the news. So Michael Heseltine has toppled her. But he must now face another ballot, opposed by both Douglas Hurd and John Major. As William and I turn right to go along the Abbey railings to the Palace of Westminster, Heseltine is coming the other way. William gives him a curt nod.

---

* Baroness Howe of Idlicote (b.1932), cross-bench life peer.

23 November 1990

Heseltine, Hurd and Major set for a three-cornered contest, to be decided next Tuesday and Thursday. Waldegrave is for Hurd. A fair chance that either of the newcomers will defeat Heseltine.

24 November 1990

Tory leadership battle in full spate. Douglas Hurd, taxed with his patrician Eton background, replies: 'I was a scholarship boy there.' Major seems to be the most likely winner at this stage. Anything would be better than Heseltine.

25 November 1990

The Sunday papers suggest that Hurd appears to be slipping, so the final contest is likely to be between Heseltine and Major.

27 November 1990

Martin Charteris tells me that the moment he decided to announce his impending retirement as Provost of Eton was at a party there, when some beaks asked him, 'What changes would you like to see at Eton?' He replied, 'None,' then realised it was time to go.

Soon after 6.30 I hear the result of the second-round ballot of Tory MPs for a new leader:

John Major 185

Michael Heseltine 131

Douglas Hurd 56

The second two at once concede defeat, so there will be no third ballot on Thursday. The new leader, and the new PM, will be John Major. I am sorry for Douglas.

29 November 1990

The Cabinet changes are announced. Norman Lamont is to be Chancellor, a reward for managing Major's leadership campaign. Heseltine taken into the Government as Secretary for the Environment, Kenneth Baker[*] to the Home Office and Chris Patten to be Chairman of the party. Malcolm Rifkind to Transport. Parkinson has resigned.

2 December 1990

I begin to read Andrew Roberts' biography of Edward Halifax in proof. The early part is loosely written with too many adverbs. The latter part on Munich

---

[*] Baron Baker of Dorking (b. 1934), Conservative politician. Home Secretary 1990–92.

is admirable and shows how Halifax stood up robustly to both Chamberlain and the Nazis.

7 December 1990
Andrew Roberts comes to collect the proof copy of his life of Halifax. It makes a strong case for his policy as Foreign Secretary: playing for time in order to rearm, even at the expense of appearing to grovel to the Nazis. He accepts cheerfully my comments on his style; if not I should have wasted many hours annotating his pages – as he says, 'Like Halifax in the red ink of a Secretary of State.'

News comes later in the day of the Order of Merit for Mrs Thatcher and a baronetcy of all things for Denis Thatcher.

12 December 1990
John Grigg tells me that the clock of St James's Palace is stuck at ten to three.*

13 December 1990
Brian Rees dines with me tonight, talking very freely of his life. He begins by telling me what I never suspected until the abrupt end of his career as Head Master of Rugby, that he has always been homosexual. He hastens to add that through his entire career as a schoolmaster he has never made any sexual approach to a boy, much less had sexual relations with one. He pours out his troubles to me since his wife Julia's death in 1978 and his departure from Rugby. He says that Rugby was a tenth-rate school when he arrived and he left it a third-rate school. The *Sunday Telegraph* are wanting to interview him about his fall from grace for a generous fee. He says that being homosexual gave him an insight into boys' minds – 'I saved two or three from suicide' – and sharpened his love of music. By 1983 he had become unsettled by a combination of factors. He missed Julia and had nobody to lean on. As well as running Rugby, he was Chairman of the Independent Schools Information Service. He found relief in drink, but only once had a real problem at the school. This was aggravated by the exhaustion of a fundraising trip to South Africa.

The next thing Brian knew was that he was being summoned to a meeting of the governors. It went badly. Pat Dean, former UK Ambassador in Washington, was the Chairman. They concentrated on his having had a young Canadian (who had no connection with the school) staying in the

---

* Like the clock at Grantchester in the poem 'The Old Vicarage, Grantchester' by Rupert Brooke (1887–1915).

Head Master's house. The governors were implacable. 'Until you have been up against the Establishment,' said Brian, 'you don't know what it's like.'

They browbeat him into resigning with a pay-off of £87,000, of which £30,000 went in tax: and, of course, it left him with no home. Brian says he has nothing to be ashamed of in his life. He has been a good schoolmaster, and raised five nice children. He says that the fee from the *Sunday Telegraph* would be most welcome, but he has to think what his children would say. Nor does he want to endanger his present jobs, particularly writing the history of Stowe School.

He will think about it. After we part, I wonder whether it would not be better if he wrote us a long chapter of autobiography on all this?

17 December 1990

Peter Thorneycroft says of Mrs Thatcher's departure: 'It is strange that she never saw it coming – but they never do.'

I also hear that Daniel Macmillan, Harold's brother, always used to say: 'If a man tells you that his word is his bond, take his bond.'

1991

The government introduced Tax-exempt Special Savings Accounts on 1 January to promote personal saving. On 16 January the final phase of the M40 through Oxfordshire was opened, giving the West Midlands a direct motorway link to London. The Gulf War ended on 28 February with the defeat of Saddam Hussein. The Provisional IRA launched a mortar attack on 10 Downing Street, blowing in all the windows of the Cabinet Room during a Cabinet meeting. The British scientist Tim Berners-Lee introduced World Wide Web, the first web browser, on 26 February. On 22 March John Major announced the abolition of the Poll Tax. George Carey was enthroned as Archbishop of Canterbury on 19 April. On 22 May the breakthrough in the North Rail of the Channel Tunnel was achieved; the final breakthrough in the South Rail tunnel took place on 28 June. On 6 August the first website went online. On 11 October John Major outlined his vision of a 'classless' Britain. Robert Maxwell was found dead off the coast of Tenerife on 5 November.

2 January 1991
There is an attempt to de-select Peter Tapsell in his Lincolnshire constituency for having run Michael Heseltine's campaign to evict Mrs Thatcher. I expect he will survive.

3 January 1991
Talk to Peter Pilkington about the impending appointment of a successor to Graham Leonard[*] as Bishop of London – not Peter himself, alas. But he has heard that there was a proposal to 'proceed by consecration', i.e. to appoint someone in Holy Orders but not a bishop. In the end, this was rejected.

Runcie is said to favour Andrew Graham, Bishop of Newcastle,[†] a quiet and

---

[*] The Rt Revd Mgr and Rt Hon. Graham Leonard (1921–2010), Bishop of London 1981–91; became a Roman Catholic priest in 1994.

[†] The Rt Revd Andrew Graham (b. 1929), Bishop of Newcastle 1981–97.

scholarly bachelor. Another candidate is David Hope, Bishop of Wakefield.*

Long talk on the telephone with Robert Runcie, who retires as Archbishop of Canterbury on 31 January. 'I don't mind retirement,' he says, 'but the process of retirement is exhausting, with dinners given by the bishops, the City, Downing Street, the orthodox people, etc.' He is to live in St Albans as an assistant bishop with a canon's stall 'where I can say my prayers'. He adds, 'I hope to recover some of my scholarly interests.' When Harold Wilson appointed him to St Albans, he said that it lay 'halfway between Oxford and Cambridge'.

On the subject of his Falklands sermon in St Paul's, Robert says that Mrs Thatcher thanked him for it. She never expressed any displeasure to him about it, 'though her henchmen felt they had to have it in for me'. He emphasises that she always maintained a friendship with him. 'The service could have been better. A Christian service should not leave you sad. That in St Paul's did not have enough assurance of the Gospel at the end.'

24 February 1991
I see a large twig lying on the pavement. Someone had attached a label to it that read 'Special Branch.'

26 February 1991
Wanda Boothby† telephones me out of the blue. There is to be a blue plaque to Bob outside No. 1 Eaton Square. Wanda misses Bob very much. When they married she said to him: 'Remember, I will never divorce you!' She is depressed about the life of Bob by Robert Rhodes James which is soon to appear. In what she says was a light-hearted decision Bob agreed that Robert Rhodes James should be his biographer. But, so far, he has not talked to her about Bob, but merely used Bob's papers. I think James similarly shunned personal reminiscences when he wrote Eden's life. She talks of Bob with deep emotion, but admits that their marriage was sometimes stormy.

28 February 1991
Victory in the Gulf War, but it is essential that Saddam Hussein‡ should be seen to be beaten and his army destroyed.

---

* The Rt Revd and Rt Hon. David Hope, Baron Hope of Thornes (b. 1940), Bishop of Wakefield 1985–91; Bishop of London 1991–5; Archbishop of York 1995–2005.

† Wanda Sanna, Lady Boothby (b. 1933), second wife of Lord Boothby.

‡ (1937–2006), President of Iraq 1979–2003.

3 March 1991

Sir Richard Southwood,* Vice-Chancellor of Oxford, a man of much charm, tells me that he has been taking soundings in Oxford on whether the university would now give Mrs Thatcher an honorary degree. He finds that her enemies remain implacable.

4 March 1991

Lunch at White's with Peter Carrington, who is furious with Jenkins, the Bishop of Durham, for saying that a military parade to welcome home our soldiers in the Gulf would be 'obscene'. Peter rightly asks why the Bishop cannot use some other word such as 'untimely' or 'inappropriate'.

5 March 1991

Johnny Henderson tells me that Bill Williams gave a Press conference on Monty's behalf when the Germans surrendered in May 1945. An American correspondent in the vast Press Corps said: 'You know, this is the greatest thing since the Crucifixion.' Bill replied: 'Yes, but it only took four of you to record it in those days.'

20 March 1991

At a dinner, Peter Brooke† tells me, when Roy Hattersley was very quarrelsome, Peter tried to lower the temperature by asking if anyone could guess which member of the Cabinet had played cricket at Lord's. (In fact, it was Tom King, Secretary for Defence, when a boy at Rugby.)‡ Robin Butler,§ Secretary of the Cabinet, said: 'I have been so conditioned by my present job, I almost said Mrs Thatcher.'

21 March 1991

Richard Thorpe is seeing the Queen Mother at Clarence House next week to talk about Alec Home and he asks me about the protocol of his audience. I advise him not to take notes, but to work out in advance how he would like

---

* (1931–2005), Linacre Professor of Zoology at Oxford University 1979–93 and Vice-Chancellor 1989–93.

† Baron Brooke of Sutton Mandeville (b. 1934), Conservative politician. MP for the Cities of London and Westminster 1977–2001; Sec. of State for Northern Ireland 1989–92; Sec. of State for National Heritage 1992–4.

‡ Baron King of Bridgwater (b. 1933), Conservative politician. MP for Bridgwater 1970–2001; Sec. of State for Defence 1989–92.

§ Baron Butler of Brockwell (b. 1938), Principal PS to Margaret Thatcher 1982–5; Cabinet Secretary 1988–98.

the talk to go; also to have plenty of questions or topics in reserve. And watch out for the corgis!

22 March 1991
The end of the Poll Tax, which brought down Mrs Thatcher as much as did her abrasive personality.

24 March 1991
To Cambridge, where I have lunch with Dadie Rylands in King's. Dadie is re-reading Mrs Gaskell's life of Charlotte Brontë, which we both agree is a wonderful biography.

I later meet Jakie Astor* at the Fitzwilliam Museum and he drives me to his house near Royston for tea. He tells me: 'I once spent half an hour with Harold Macmillan waiting for a train at Plymouth. As we talked together, he speculated on which Prime Ministers had been cardinals and which warriors: he and Winston, he claimed, were the only two to be both.'

25 March 1991
Four o'clock. Richard Thorpe, writing Alec Home's official life, comes to talk about him. I am able to give him some personal recollections and details of obscure but useful secondary sources such as Charles Douglas-Home's life of Evelyn Howick.†

Richard has already had some good reminiscences from Alec himself. Alec Home once asked Andrei Gromyko to shoot at Douglas in Lanarkshire. Gromyko asked: 'Is it private land?' Alec replied that it was. Gromyko told him that it would be wrong for a good Communist to shoot on private land. Alec had a brilliant solution: 'I will lease it to Lanarkshire County Council for the day.' That eased Gromyko's conscience.

While Richard was staying at the Hirsel, they watched a TV film of Saddam Hussein in plain clothes, patting the head of a child hostage from England. Alec: 'He's a rum one. He's wearing an Eton Rambler's tie!'

8 April 1991
The new Archbishop, George Carey, is to have pop music at his enthronement in Canterbury Cathedral on 19 April. Oh dear, I feared as much.

---

* Maj. Sir John Jacob Astor (1918–2000), Conservative politician. MP for Plymouth Sutton 1951–9.
† Charles Douglas-Home (1936–85), editor of *The Times* 1982–5. Evelyn Baring, 1st Baron Howick of Glendale (1903–73), Governor of Kenya 1952–9.

I write to John Major, a keen cricket follower, to suggest another honour for Jim Swanton,* who received the OBE as long ago as 1964.

22 April 1991
Rosemary Wolff† tells me that Peter Carrington is disenchanted with Mrs Thatcher, who refers to the present Cabinet as the B-team. There has always been something socially insecure about Mrs T. When Rosemary was staying with the Carringtons one weekend, the Thatchers came over from Chequers to dine. The other women wore simple shirts and long skirts; Mrs T. came dressed as for a State Banquet at the Palace. What a class-conscious nation we are. Rosemary also tells me that when Ted Heath visited grand houses, they treated him like an RAF officer billeted on them during the war.

27 April 1991
Peter Thorneycroft has written to Mrs Thatcher telling her that she is placing her niche in history at risk by waging a vendetta against John Major and his Government. Her behaviour, in fact, closely resembles that of Ted Heath after Mrs T. had defeated him for the leadership. She is demented enough to hope that John Major will lose the next election, and that the Tories will bring her back as their leader.

8 May 1991
Norman St John-Stevas telephones to apologise for not having been able to give me advance news of his appointment as Master of Emmanuel College, Cambridge, which is announced in the papers this morning. How he continues to fall on his feet.

19 May 1991
I have heard so much about the devastation of Dresden caused by Allied bombing on the night of 13/14 February 1945 that I am surprised to find it a very beautiful city, though battered in places. At Chequers on 23 February 1945, Jock Colville asked Sir Arthur Harris,‡ C.-in-C. Bomber Command, what the effect of the raid on Dresden had been. 'Dresden?' Harris replied. 'There is no such place as Dresden.' Happily, this is no longer the case in 1991. From my cabin window I gaze across the river to some handsome, sombre

---

* E.W. Swanton (1907–2000), cricket writer and commentator.
† (1926–2003), political hostess and a leading figure in the group around Edward Heath when he was leader of the Conservative Party and Prime Minister.
‡ 1st Bt (1892–1984), known as 'Bomber' Harris.

government offices. But it is on the other bank that the full glory of baroque Dresden bursts on one.

What masks the bomb damage is the enormous number of trees lining the streets of Dresden: an estimated fifteen million of them. There are fine parks and the Hercules Allee, an imposing avenue that resembles the long walk at Windsor.

The Frauenkirche,* or Church of Our Lady, is a small mountain of broken stone, with only the tower intact. A poignant memorial to the bombing that reminds the English visitor of the fate suffered by so many of our City churches; or the apse of the Guards' Chapel that for years was all that remained after its destruction with heavy loss of life that dreadful Sunday morning in June 1944.

The rebuilt Opera House and Royal Palace (still in splints) are splendid buildings worthy of the Kings of Saxony.

14 June 1991

I see an advance copy of tomorrow's Honours List in the office. A peerage for the historian Robert Skidelsky.† Robert Rhodes James receives a knighthood as an MP, not as an historian. Only a CVO for Philip Ziegler, instead of the KCVO given to Harold Nicolson and Jack Wheeler-Bennett‡ as biographers of a Sovereign.

20 June 1991

Dine with the Old Etonian Association committee to say goodbye to Martin Charteris as Provost. They give him a panel of stained glass blown out of a window in College Chapel by a German bomb on Founder's Day 1940: the face of an Apostle nicely framed, with a silver label inscribed 'To a much-loved Provost'.

22 June 1991

Bob Runcie, talking about cricket in a radio interview, describes how as an

---

* The Frauenkirche was rebuilt after the reunification of Germany, and the Duke of Kent was President of the British Dresden Fund. He attended a service at the Frauenkirche on 13 Feb. 2014 with the President of Germany to mark the 70th anniversary of the bombing of Dresden.
† Baron Skidelsky of Tilton (b. 1939), historian. Appointed Professor of International Studies at Warwick University in 1978 and Professor of Political Economy in 1990; author of a biography of Oswald Mosley (1975) and a three-volume biography of John Maynard Keynes (1983; 1992; 2000).
‡ Sir John Wheeler-Bennett (1902–75), historian and authority on Germany in the inter-war years; his official biography of George VI was published in 1958.

undergraduate at Brasenose he was one day carrying a cricket bag, with a volume of Plato under his arm. He met Isaiah Berlin, who was delighted: 'This is what we all stand for, what we all stand for.'

26 June 1991
A guest at the National Theatre of Mary Soames. The party includes Jack Profumo, who tells me what a tyrant everybody found David Margesson* as Chief Whip. Jack infuriated him by voting against Chamberlain in the Norway debate in May 1940 only a few weeks after being elected MP for Kettering.

27 June 1991
I talk to Robert Fellowes and touch briefly on King George V and the Tsar. Robert: 'You musn't blame Philip Moore too much. He thought you had got it wrong.' K.R.: 'No, he knew I had not got it wrong. He merely thought it was inconvenient.' Robert: 'Where I work there is not much difference between the two!'

2 July 1991
John Tooley,† whom I always like, asks me whether I have subscribed to the Repton Appeal. I tell him I have given £15,000, adding, 'On condition not a penny is spent on science or sport.'

6 July 1991
I hear that Wittgenstein liked solving mechanical problems. One day he had an appointment to see Isaiah Berlin. At the door he was startled to be greeted by a maid, who said: 'Thank goodness you have come.' She showed him to the kitchen where the fridge had broken down. She had mistaken him for the mechanic. Wittgenstein sat down, stared at the fridge for some time until he had discovered how it worked, mended it, and left – without seeing Isaiah.

10 July 1991
Clarissa Avon is reading Robert Rhodes James's life of Bob Boothby. Clarissa is so dissatisfied with Robert Rhodes James's life of Anthony that she wants it to be done again. She is thinking of asking Richard Thorpe, whom she helped over his life of Selwyn Lloyd and his current project on Alec Home.

---

* The Rt Hon. David Margesson, 1st Viscount Margesson (1890–1965), Conservative politician. Government Chief Whip 1931–40.
† Sir John Tooley (b. 1924), Gen. Dir. of the Royal Opera House 1970–88.

19 July 1991

I receive with delight Peter Lawrence's[*] edition of Grizel Hartley's letters, including several from me. It is beautifully printed and produced. Her invincible courage and cheerfulness, even during those last years, move me deeply.

23 August 1991

I visit Abbotsford, the home of Sir Walter Scott. There is an enchanting little library with an upper gallery – like the reading room of the London Library, though of course smaller and prettier. Glass cases full of memorabilia: the clasp of Napoleon's cloak, in the form of bees, picked up on the field of Waterloo; a pair of narrow spectacles; a complicated clasp knife given to Sir Walter in Sheffield in return for one of his visiting cards. Ebony furniture presented to Scott by George IV; suits of armour and Jacobite relics. I could well spend hours here.

28 August 1991

I hear that when de Gaulle was succeeded as President of France by Pompidou he said: 'It's like being cuckolded by one's chauffeur.'

2 September 1991

I start reading Jim Lees-Milne's biography of Harold Nicolson. Far too big a book; and how Bloomsbury stinks.

13 September 1991

Hartley Shawcross still thinks he could have become leader of the Labour Party – and eventually Prime Minister – had he not loyally declined to stand against Herbert Morrison.[†] Not long ago he had a letter from an ex-MP who told him that Harold Wilson had said: 'Hartley could have been PM had he played his cards right.'

21 September 1991

Duncan Davidson[‡] tells me that he is still sometimes teased for having been a page at the Coronation in 1953. 'Did you not faint at a rehearsal?', somebody asked him recently. He says: 'Yes, one of the bishops made an indecent suggestion to me.'

---

[*] (1913–2005), schoolmaster at Eton.
[†] Baron Morrison of Lambeth (1888–1965), Labour politician. Home Secretary 1940–45; Deputy Prime Minister 1945–51; Foreign Secretary Mar.–Oct. 1951.
[‡] (b. 1941), businessman; founder of Persimmon, the house builders.

22 September 1991

During the London visit of Bulganin* and Khrushchev in 1956, there was a lunch given by Selwyn Lloyd at which the FO interpreter got drunk. He produced remarks like this: 'Mr Khrushchev says how happy he is to be here, though he no doubt misses the forced labour camps of Siberia.' Richard Thorpe was told the full story by Tony Lambton, who was present, and describes the event in his biography.†

27 September 1991

Dinner party for Jim and Audrey Callaghan. Jim tells me that, walking out of Westminster Abbey after the memorial service for Elizabeth Home, he found himself next to Ted Heath. It was the morning Mrs Thatcher had resigned and Ted turned to Jim and said: 'I had better compose my features so that the photographers will not record my true feelings.'

As Foreign Secretary, Jim was able to secure the release of Denis Hills, an English teacher, from imprisonment at the hands of Idi Amin‡ of Uganda. This was not so much because Jim was Foreign Secretary, but because he was an MP for Cardiff, where Amin had trained for the Commonwealth Games in 1958 in the swimming events.

Mrs Thatcher would not allow Antony Duff§ to brief Neil Kinnock on matters of security. So Jim fixed an informal meeting at his house in Sussex where the two men could talk.

4 October 1991

To the Foreign Office in the morning for the unveiling by Douglas Hurd of a bust of Ernest Bevin. He makes a nice little speech in which he specially greets me as one who 'keeps an affectionate eye on our doings'. What a good friend he is.

1 November 1991

At twelve noon to New College for a meeting with the Warden, Harvey McGregor, and the Fellow in charge of the gardens, Robin Lane Fox,¶ about

---

* Nikolai Bulganin (1895–1975), Soviet politician. Minister of Defence 1953–5; Premier of the Soviet Union 1955–8

† See D.R. Thorpe, *Selwyn Lloyd* (1989), pp. 203–4.

‡ (c.1925–2003), President of Uganda 1971–9.

§ Sir Antony Duff (1920–2000), Dir. Gen. of MI5 1985–88.

¶ Harvey McGregor (1926–2015), barrister and Warden of New Coll., Oxford 1985–96. Robin Lane Fox (b. 1946), classicist and gardening writer; Fellow and Tutor in Ancient History at New Coll. 1977–2014.

my benefaction of £20,000 for the restoration of the Mound off the Garden Quad. McGregor is most welcoming and shows me with pride the whole of the renovated Warden's Lodging, an enormous range of rooms. The work has been done with much taste and elegance, and I am pleased that the college should house its Warden so sumptuously.

We climb up to the top of the Mound, and Robin Lane Fox says that he has long wanted to reshape it, to remove a few dead or ugly trees, and to build two or more flights of steps that lead to an arbour. He radiates enthusiasm, and there and then extracts a promise from the Warden that if my £20,000 (which will become £25,000 with a tax rebate) does not stretch to all he wishes, the college will make up the deficit.

20 November 1991

Lunch with Graham Jones, the Headmaster of Repton, at the East India Club in St James's Square. We discuss my benefaction of £15,000. The present Repton appeal does not cover the library, which is mostly for computers and that sort of thing. But the chapel does come within its orbit. So Graham suggests that part of the money could be used to commission a modern sculpture.

26 November 1991

Dine at the Spanish Embassy in honour of Ted Heath. Ted is in good humour. He says: 'I have the utmost difficulty getting into Kenneth's column these days.' He refers curtly to 'Thatcher' and tells me that he has never had a single conversation with her since she became Prime Minister, and that is twelve years ago.

15 December 1991

Arnold Goodman tells me that when he taught at Downing College, Cambridge, he said good morning to F.R. Leavis each day for two years. Leavis never replied or even acknowledged Arnold's presence.

1992

1992 was a much-anticipated general election year. On 17 January the first MORI poll of the year showed the Conservatives three points ahead of Labour on 42 per cent. On 1 February President George Bush and the Russian President Boris Yeltsin met at Camp David and declared that the Cold War was over. The Maastricht Treaty on the integration of Europe was signed on 7 February. On 6 March Parliament passed the Further and Higher Education Act, allowing polytechnics to become new universities. On 11 March John Major declared that the general election would be held on 9 April. Buckingham Palace announced on 19 March that the Duke and Duchess of York were to separate after six years of marriage. The editors of Punch *let it be known that the magazine would close on 8 April. Opinion polls showed a narrow lead for Labour, suggesting a hung Parliament; the final MORI poll before the general election on 7 April gave Labour a 1 per cent lead. At the general election on 9 April the Conservatives were re-elected for a fourth successive term; their majority was reduced to 21 seats, but they won over 14 million votes, the highest number ever in a general election. Margaret Thatcher and Michael Foot retired from the House of Commons.*

On 13 April Neil Kinnock resigned as leader of the Labour Party; on the same day the Princess Royal announced her divorce from Captain Mark Phillips. Betty Boothroyd was elected Speaker of the House of Commons on 27 April, the first woman to hold the post. Margaret Thatcher took her place in the House of Lords on 30 June. On 17 July John Smith was elected leader of the Labour Party. The government suspended the UK's membership of the European Exchange Rate Mechanism on 16 September, 'Black Wednesday'. Interest rates were cut to 8 per cent on 16 October. Bill Clinton was elected President of the US on 3 November. The Church of England voted to allow women priests on 11 November. £50 million worth of damage was caused at Windsor Castle in a major fire on 20 November; the Queen described her year as an annus horribilis *on 24 November. On 9 December the separation of Prince Charles and the Princess of Wales was announced. Princess Anne married Timothy Laurence at Crathie Church on 12 December.*

8 February 1992

Charles Guthrie* describes to me the scene in the VIP Lounge at Heathrow Airport one day. The only other two people there with him were Ted Heath and Boris Becker,† neither of whom knew who the other was.

He also says that at the lying-in-state of King George VI, the Chiefs of Staff did a vigil with reversed swords. Charles was asked to supervise the arrangements and took along a Welsh Guards Regimental Sergeant-Major. Mountbatten turned up in full fig, and said to the RSM: 'How do I look?' RSM: 'Terribly sloppy, Sir.' The other Chiefs of Staff were enchanted by this.

19 February 1992

Lunch with Derek Hill at Boodle's. He tells me that when he asked one of the Mitford sisters whether it was true that Unity, on being allowed back to England during the war, went to work among East End Jews to make amends, Diana replied, 'I hope not: she's been through enough already.'

25 February 1992

Prince Eddie tells me that when Philip Hay‡ was about to become Private Secretary to Princess Marina in 1948, he was asked to see Tommy Lascelles at the Palace. Walking down a passage, they passed Anthony Blunt. When Blunt was out of earshot, Tommy said to Philip: 'That man is a Soviet spy, you know.'

9 March 1992

An amusing story Victor Rothschild once told me of how he had a six-volume nineteenth-century novel. Four of them had pretty gold fillets on the boards, two had not – though these two volumes, unlike the other four, did have the author's signature on the flyleaf. Victor sent the two to have gold fillets put on them with the other four to copy from. The two came back, beautifully adorned and identical to the other four: these also now had signatures!

27 March 1992

I give Paul Potts§ dinner at Geales. The Conservative election campaign, he says, is going very badly and amateurishly. There is no fire in it. 'William

---

* FM Sir Charles Guthrie, Baron Guthrie of Craigiebank (b. 1938), head of the British Army 1994–7; Chief of the Defence Staff 1997–2001.

† (b. 1967), German No. 1 professional tennis player.

‡ Sir Philip Hay (1918–86), Treasurer to the Duke and Duchess of Kent 1962–86.

§ (b. 1950), editor-in-chief of the Press Association 1996–2006.

Waldegrave always answers the questions put to him like a gentleman. That is a mistake.' One trouble is that the Tories are determined not to recognise how much Mrs T. has done for the country; if they did, it would arouse much enthusiasm. An example of the bad administration: Norman Tebbit is the best speaker the Tories have got. Yet for a meeting at Newcastle he had to drive himself up – and in a car without a telephone. He should be master-minding the Tory campaign.

2 April 1992
Owen Chadwick talks of the new life of Geoffrey Fisher, which I must read. One passage shocked Owen. At the Coronation, a group of prelates and Church leaders were lined up to receive Holy Communion. Fisher deliberately missed out the Moderator of the Church of Scotland.

9 April 1992
General Election day. The papers forecast a hung Parliament, with the prospect of Kinnock just scraping in as PM. I prefer to be optimistic, remembering 1970. There may again be a last-minute swing to the Tories in the marginal constituencies. I vote for Dudley Fishburn,* our excellent MP in Kensington.

To Claridge's for the election party given by Leonard Wolfson.† Arnold Weinstock tells me that he had a colt born today, so telephoned at 11.30 a.m. to have its name registered as Election Day.

Mrs Thatcher and Denis turn up, straight off Concorde from New York. She very sprightly, he unwontedly discreet. As the results start coming in, it looks as if the Tories may after all squeak home. Poor Chris Patten loses his seat in Bath, however, but makes a dignified speech to a howling mob of Labour supporters. I settle down to a 'midnight' breakfast with Clarissa Avon and Arnold Goodman. The election continues to go the way of the Tories, though far from a landslide.

10 April 1992
The Tories emerge with a majority of 21: what a blessing not to have Kinnock,

---

* (b. 1946), Conservative politician. MP for Kensington 1988–97.
† Baron Wolfson of Marylebone (1927–2010), businessman and Chairman of the Wolfson Foundation.

Kaufman,* Hattersley or the rich hangers-on like Harold Pinter and John
Mortimer.†

14 April 1992

John Major completes his reshuffle of middle-ranking and junior offices.
Jonathan Aitken to be Minister of State for Defence.

King George V welcomed the result of the General Election of 1931 with
the hope that the country would 'now have a little peace and less worries',
feelings which could be equally applied to last Thursday's result.

18 April 1992

I have a talk with Anthony Nutting. He describes trying to brief Winston on
the 'cod war' with Iceland. But the PM was not interested. Anthony swears
that he could hear the BBC Light Programme coming out of the old man's
hearing aid.

When Anthony resigned over Suez, Field Marshal Templer‡ was exceptionally unpleasant to him. He told Anthony that he ought to resign from
Boodle's: if Anthony didn't, he would resign himself. Anthony didn't; nor in
the end did Gerald Templer.

Eden wanted him to take on Robert Cranborne§ as a PPS to please Bobbety.
But Anthony didn't want him and pleaded that a mere Parliamentary Under-
Secretary ought not to have a PPS.

Anthony tells me about his difficulty in clearing his book on Suez, *No
End of a Lesson*, with the Cabinet Office, particularly over collusion with
France and Israel. He told Burke Trend: 'Instead of writing a book, I could
have made a statement in the House of Commons.' Burke Trend replied: 'If
you had made a statement in the Commons, you would have had to show it
first to the Cabinet Office – as if it were a book.' At which Anthony exploded:
'WHAT!' Burke was quite wrong. MPs cannot be subjected to Cabinet or
Cabinet Office censorship.

---

* Gerald Kaufman (1930–2017), Labour politician. MP for Manchester Gorton (formerly
Manchester Alnwick) 1970–2017; Chair of the Culture, Media and Sport Committee 1992–
2005; Father of the House of Commons 2015–17.
† Harold Pinter (1930–2008), playwright, awarded the 2005 Nobel Prize in Literature. Sir John
Mortimer (1923–2009), barrister, dramatist, screenwriter and author.
‡ FM Sir Gerald Templer (1898–1979), CIGS 1955–8 and Eden's chief military adviser during
the Suez Crisis.
§ Robert Gascoyne-Cecil, 7th Marquess of Salisbury (b. 1946), Conservative politician. MP
for Dorset South 1979–87; Leader of the Opposition in the House of Lords 1997–8; Chancellor
of Hertfordshire University since 2005.

30 April 1992

I give Prince Eddie lunch at Green's. He is much concerned to find a member of the Royal Family to succeed him as Grand Master Mason of England. He has now done the job for twenty-five years.* He tried young Prince Edward, who was not interested – he cares only for the theatre. Eddie is proud of how he has opened up Freemasonry to public scrutiny and abolished the bloodcurdling oaths that made it seem ludicrous.

10 May 1992

The Times has a nasty, sly, sarcastic article on the Freemasons, adorned with a picture of Prince Eddie and two others in their aprons and ornate collars. It is not easy to look dignified in such adornments.

16 May 1992

Tony Lambton tells me that during the war he was visiting a country house in Sandbach, well stocked from its own farm, and asked if he could bring Lord Woolton with him. So that the Minister of Food should not see how well fed they were, the ham, the butter, etc. were all hidden away and only meagre rations were on show. The visitors arrived. But Lambton had made a mistake. It was not Lord Woolton, but Lord Wilton.†

29 May 1992

I hear that things are very bad again financially for Brian Rees. I send him £300 to pay for the groceries. But what are his children doing for him?

Diane Maxwell asks me about the progress of David Dilks's second volume of Neville Chamberlain's life. I say that he is wedded to administration for years to come and suggest that she asks him to find a clever youngish historian to take over the papers and complete the task.

30 May 1992

I hear that John Major, in spite of professing to be the simple man, has a yearning for grandeur. He has police outriders, which Mrs Thatcher never had. And he is now to get a powerful official plane. Mrs Thatcher never minded what sort of plane she had; but if it went too fast, she would certainly see that it reduced its cruising speed in order to save petrol.

---

* The Duke of Kent became Grand Master in 1967. In 2017 he had completed fifty years in the post.
† Seymour Egerton, 7th Earl of Wilton (1921–99); having inherited the title at the age of six he was a peer for seventy-two years.

5 June 1992

Story of Macmillan at the enthronement of Bob Runcie as Archbishop of Canterbury from Peter Pilkington. Macmillan drew Peter's attention to Cardinal Hume and said: 'He looks like the landlord who has come to see if the tenants are keeping the place in good repair.'

11 June 1992

Robert Salisbury has withdrawn co-operation from Robert Rhodes James's proposed biography of Lord Salisbury, the 3rd Marquess, because of the vulgarity of his book on Bob Boothby. A young historian such as Andrew Roberts would be a good replacement.[*]

12 June 1992

In Germany. Standing in the spray of the Reichenbach Falls, I thrilled to the greatest legend of detective fiction: the fight to the death between Sherlock Holmes and Professor Moriarty, re-enacted in 1968 by Paul Gore-Booth.[†]

Nuremberg offers a succession of contrasts and paradoxes. From the fine medieval castle perched above a sea of red roofs, descend on foot down cobbled lanes with window boxes of scarlet and pink geraniums, expecting at every turn to meet Hans Sachs, the cobbler, or Beckmesser,[‡] the town clerk, or do I mean Geraint Evans? Then to the best mechanical toy in the world: the Männleinlaufen, or ancient church clock, out of which emerge at noon the Seven Electors of the Holy Roman Empire. Three times they pass before the Emperor Charles IV in single file, three times they bow before disappearing from sight.

I was pleased to see that the concrete podium, or pulpit as it was called, from which Hitler addressed his Nuremberg rallies has been allowed to crack and crumble. It looks satisfyingly shabby.

I have always loathed those symbolic displays of pagan power. But the law courts where the Nazi leaders were tried for their war crimes stand four-square behind their clean stone façade. With chilling irony, they back onto a Jewish graveyard.

9 July 1992

To the National Theatre to see Alan Bennett's play *The Madness of George III*

---

[*] *Salisbury: Victorian Titan* by Andrew Roberts was published in 1999.
[†] Baron Gore-Booth (1909–84), diplomat.
[‡] Characters in Wagner's opera *Die Meistersinger von Nürnberg*.

as the guest of Mary Soames. The play is a triumph, with Nigel Hawthorne[*] in a sustained tour de force as the King. Supporting actors and production are excellent. It is moving too. I note that when there are lines in the play about a united Royal Family, the audience laughs rudely. This would not have been so a year or two ago.

11 July 1992

Solly Zuckerman says that Dadie Rylands was once invited to become Provost of King's, but declined. On the wartime bombing of Germany, Solly says that he was amazed that amid the ruins the population was (a) so clean, and (b) so unhostile. That was my experience too. Their faces were blank.

13 July 1992

Robin Day tells me that he was once invited to Encaenia at Oxford by Roy Jenkins, who made an impressive entry preceded by six beadles with silver wands. Robin said to him afterwards: 'If the monarchy should ever fail, we now know where to find a President.' Roy (unsmilingly): 'I am too old.'

17 July 1992

To Glyndebourne. I have a few words with George Christie. The opera is *Jenufa* by Janáček. A girl has an illegitimate child, which so shames her mother that she murders it, but is detected and carried off to prison. It is performed with harrowing intensity: altogether too emotionally demanding.

18 July 1992

I hear that Gerald Berners[†] took a present of caviar, scent, etc. to Diana Mosley when she was in Holloway Prison during the war. Through some bureaucratic regulation he was not allowed to see her – perhaps she had used up her quota of visits – but he was told he could present the parcel to the head wardress. The woman apologised for having to open it in case it contained contraband. Then she exclaimed: 'Oh, her ladyship *will* be pleased.'

27 July 1992

Former Prime Ministers and their spouses give a dinner for the Queen and the Duke of Edinburgh at Spencer House. There is a large reception beforehand for others, to which I am invited. I speak to both the Queen and

---

[*] Sir Nigel Hawthorne (1929–2001), actor, renowned for his portrayal of Sir Humphrey Appleby in *Yes Minister* and its sequel *Yes, Prime Minister*.
[†] Gerald Tyrwhitt-Wilson, 14th Bt Berners (1883–1950), composer.

the Duke, who talk freely. The Queen tells me she was much amused by the attempt of Winston Churchill during the war to call a dreadnought HMS *Oliver Cromwell*. Jim Callaghan says: 'I must confess I should have done the same.' I ask the Queen whether she still has to approve the names of all the new warships. 'Oh yes,' she tells me, 'and New Zealand ships too. That is not so easy, as they often have Aboriginal names.'

Most fascinatingly of all, the Queen tells me of her diary, which she keeps without fail. 'And how much do you write, Ma'am?' I ask, not adding, 'We diarists!' She replies: 'About so much,' spreading out her hand, from thumb to little finger, i.e. about six inches. 'But I have no time to record conversations, only events.' Nor, she says, does she dictate, finding it inhibiting.

John Major equally amiable. We talk of his reading habits and I promise him a copy of *KGV* if he would like it – 'Oh, yes please,' he says, 'as long as you autograph it.'

Prince Philip greets me with warmth and we talk about Australian pictures: he bought several by Sidney Nolan and William Dobell.*

Poor Mary Wilson, who looks tragically haunted, with poor mindless Harold in tow (Prince Charles said to Clarissa Avon that he really ought not to be taken out now), almost bursts into tears when I tell her how much I like her poetry. 'Alas, I have no time for it nowadays,' she says. 'But I do treasure all those letters John Betjeman sent me.'

Ted Heath, alone and unwelcoming. The Royal Standard flies above Spencer House as well as above Buckingham Palace.

12 September 1992

Denis Greenhill full of interesting stories when I talk to him about his memoirs, *More by Accident*, which I have just read in proof. Rab Butler, up in Mull, and talking to an FO official on the telephone: 'I'm very pleased with all you down there.'

A less agreeable light on Rab when he went to see the US Secretary of State, Dean Rusk:† 'This is a matter that has been worrying everyone, up to the Prime Minister – or should I say down to the Prime Minister.' Rusk was much put out by this disloyal reference to Alec Home.

---

* Sir Sidney Nolan (1917–92), Australian artist, particularly of subjects from Australian history. Sir William Dobell (1899–1970), Australian artist.
† (1909–94), US Sec. of State 1961–9. Harold Macmillan, with his predilection for nicknames, used privately to refer to Rusk as 'the biscuit man'.

30 September 1992

John Lisburne tells me that the Princess of Wales, visiting a housing estate, when told that there was a shortage of men there, replied: 'There you are. It's the story of our lives.' That is really irresponsible of her.

27 October 1992

To Covent Garden for Verdi's *Otello*. Georg Solti conducts with wonderful vigour and precision. Both Plácido Domingo and Kiri Te Kanawa are excellent.* Rather fussy crowd scenes, as always nowadays. No wonder Covent Garden runs a deficit with so crowded a stage. John Major, who is in the party, remarks musingly: 'Iago is someone we could do without. I wonder if there is one here tonight.'

4 November 1992

The Government survives defeat over the Maastricht Treaty by only three votes. How reckless of the anti-Europe Tory rebels to risk letting in a Labour Government.

25 November 1992

The Queen Mother comes to open the new wing of the London Library. She unveils a plaque in the inner room, has a drink and a chat with people, and presents a certificate of life membership to Andrew Devonshire. The QM is in marvellous form, and nicely dressed in deep turquoise with white gloves. We talk of the Sickert exhibition and her own Sickert picture of George V, which she allowed me to use on the cover of my biography, and is delighted when I tell her that the photographer of George V and his racing manager at the Grand National in 1927 complained that the artist had merely copied his work – and received in return a postal order for 17s and 6d.

26 November 1992

At an evening party in Cleveland Row I talk to Margaret Thatcher. She asks me why my column is called 'Albany'. I explain how I proposed living there in 1961 but changed my mind because it was so gloomy. She fervently agrees. She was apparently lent some rooms there on ceasing to be PM and found it depressing. I tell her of the joys of London gardening, which fires her with enthusiasm: I can almost see the sap rising in her.

---

* Plácido Domingo (b. 1941), world-renowned Spanish tenor and conductor. Dame Kiri Te Kanawa (b. 1944), operatic soprano from New Zealand.

27 November 1992

Today's papers are full of the Queen's decision to pay income tax and to support other members of the Royal Family out of her own private funds.

1 December 1992

To the unveiling of a blue plaque to Malcolm Sargent outside Albert Hall Mansions, where he lived. Delighted to see Donald Coggan, who tells me that he ministered to Malcolm Sargent during his last illness in 1967. One day they said goodbye to each other, for Malcolm was expected to live only a few hours more. That night on TV Donald was amazed to see Malcolm in white tie and tails making a farewell, but non-conducting appearance at the Proms. He died a day or two later. We have much gossip about Yorkshire.

2 December 1992

I hear that somebody was to entertain Georg and Valerie Solti to dinner and telephoned his secretary to ask if there was anything he could not eat. The answer came back: 'No flies.' The host was puzzled by this and rang back to enquire again. This time he got Solti himself, who told him that what he meant was nothing that flies. As a boy in Hungary he used to have to kill ducks and chickens and now cannot bear to eat them.

To a dinner at Claridge's at which both President Nixon and President Reagan are present, which betokens a confident host. I have a talk with Nixon and tell him how grateful I was that he wrote me a long letter in his own hand after reading the copy of *King George V* I sent him after our meeting at Jonathan Aitken's house. He laughs, takes my arm, and says: 'Hang on to it. It's valuable.' After dinner he gives a brilliant *tour d'horizon* of international affairs without a note. 'Russia is poor in goods, but rich in spirit,' he says. 'The United States is rich in goods, but poor in spirit.' Intellectually, few Presidents have surpassed him.

Dukie Hussey tells me that when he met Nixon shortly after he took office, Nixon made three points to him: (a) there would be no problem with Russia – they were in touch on the hotline; (b) there would be detente with China; (c) the most difficult problem would be the Middle East, and on that he could venture no prognostication.

5 December 1992
Princess Anne is to marry again. Her fiancé is a former equerry to the Queen called Tim Laurence.*

8 December 1992
The other day Peter Carrington asked Margaret Thatcher: 'Why are you so nasty to John Major when you made him?' She afterwards complained that Peter had been rude to her.

9 December 1992
I hear on the wireless the PM making a Commons statement on the impending separation of the Prince and Princess of Wales. No divorce; no constitutional implications; no reason why Diana should not be crowned Queen (at which point there is a gasp from MPs, who obviously do not accept this). No financial rearrangements affecting the Civil List, as the Waleses live on the Duchy of Cornwall income.

All this needs digesting. They should have remained under the same roof: anything less is on the slippery slope that could lead to abdication or disestablishment. And how the two boys will play their parents off, one against the other. Almost at once the telephone repeatedly rings with requests for articles and TV and radio interviews, including one from Canada. Turn them all down.

10 December 1992
I read Queen Victoria's journals about Crathie Church, where Princess Anne is to remarry on Saturday. The editor wants the whole of my column this week to be on the Royal Family. I think we are already at saturation point.

11 December 1992
Ironic that all these events should take place in the anniversary week of the 1936 Abdication. John King says that Diana should now do no more public engagements. I tell him that he underestimates her public appeal and that the country would not stand for her to be driven out of public life, however cunning and spiteful she may be in her attitude to Charles.

13 December 1992
Arnold Goodman calls. We talk, of course, about the Wales affair. He does

---

* Vice-Adm. Sir Timothy Laurence (b. 1955), Fellow of St Antony's Coll., Oxford 1999; company director.

not care for Charles's 'empty pretensions to be an intellectual', nor for his unforgiving character. 'Of course, Diana has deliberately and publicly humiliated him – and incidentally made Morton[*] a millionaire. So it is not surprising that he hates her and has not the generosity of spirit to offer a reconciliation. But that is the only ultimate solution if the monarchy is to survive beyond the Queen's reign.'

How will Diana now behave? After all, the separation was at her insistence. Will she now lead a quiet and dignified life that could one day lead to a reconciliation? Almost certainly not. She wants to make it difficult for Charles to become King, and to ensure that she will be the nemesis.

14 December 1992

I hear that Antony Acland is already in receipt of 'good advice' from various quarters about Eton: 'Have nothing to do with the beaks, who when they dine talk shop in a corner. Better with the boys: easy, talkative and amusing.'

15 December 1992

Michael Crick[†] of BBC *Newsnight* is running a campaign to have all reserved documents such as those on the Abdication brought within the thirty-year rule, instead of the present hundred-year rule. Do I agree? Certainly about the Abdication papers. There is surely nothing new to be learned. In any case, although it was not initially realised, the correspondence from the Secretary of State for India to the Viceroy, all openly available in the India Office Library, tells all that needs to be known. Somebody told Crick it would kill the Queen Mother. That is nonsense.

I take Prince Eddie to lunch at Green's. He is unusually gloomy, much worried about talk of emasculating the Royal Family in the wake of current troubles. He of all members of the family has led an exemplary life and resents the sneers.

17 December 1992

Jim Callaghan confirms my impression of him as a traditionalist when he says that the trouble with the Royal Family began when the Queen allowed TV cameras into her homes, as opposed to her palaces. How I agree. Letting daylight in on magic, as Bagehot warned.

Philip Ziegler seems a little disturbed about his forthcoming book on Harold Wilson in the wake of Ben Pimlott's 800-page biography. Philip

---

[*] Andrew Morton (b. 1953), journalist; author of *Diana: Her True Story* (1992).
[†] (b. 1958), journalist, broadcaster and author.

alone has seen the archives, but Pimlott managed to get Marcia Falkender to talk to him; Philip thought she would not do so.

Peter de la Billière,[*] speaking to the boys at Harrow the other day, told them: 'When I was at Harrow, queer meant highly eccentric, gay meant a rattling good party, and only generals had aides.'

21 December 1992

Raine Spencer told me how tiresome Johnnie found the Prince of Wales when he came to Althorp. After two hours talking about rainforests and other environmental themes, he showed no sign of stopping. So Johnnie said he had to telephone and went out. Raine found him lying on his bed and he said: 'I'm not down to dinner for two more hours of rainforest.' Raine eventually persuaded him to come down for a bit. Johnnie, like so many courtiers at heart, was wary of the Royal Family. He used to say: 'I worked for the King. But like all of us, we went to the shop, we bought a flag, we waved it, but we didn't get any closer.'

25 December 1992

Christmas Day. The Queen's broadcast, at the end of a difficult year, is admirable and beautifully delivered.

---

[*] Gen. Sir Peter de la Billière (b. 1934), Dir. Special Forces 1979–83; C.-in-C. British Forces Middle East 1990–91.

1993

The European Single Market was created on 1 January. British newspapers carried reports on 10 January that the Princess of Wales wanted a divorce from the Prince of Wales. Bill Clinton was sworn in as President of the US on 20 January. The Bank of England lowered interest rates to 6 per cent on 26 January, the lowest since 1978. A MORI poll on 25 February showed that 80 per cent of Britons were dissatisfied with the way John Major was running the country. On 29 April the Queen announced that Buckingham Palace would open to the public for the first time. On 7 May the Conservatives lost the Newbury by-election to the Liberal Democrats. Kenneth Clarke succeeded Norman Lamont as Chancellor of the Exchequer on 27 May. William Golding, Nobel Laureate, died on 19 June. A high-speed train made the first journey from France to England through the Channel Tunnel on 20 June. The Conservatives lost the Christchurch by-election to the Liberal Democrats on 29 July. The UK Independence Party was formed on 3 September. The Princess of Wales announced her withdrawal from public life on 3 December.

11 January 1993

James Stourton to dine at the Ark. We talk, as everybody does these days, of the marital disasters of the Royal Family and the Queen's agreement to pay tax on her private money.

12 January 1993

Lunch with John Whittingdale,* the youngish Conservative MP who was Margaret Thatcher's Political Secretary. An agreeable Wykehamist, much amused by my speculation in my piece on Sunday that Jack the Ripper had been at Winchester.

He tells me that of all the presents given to her and Denis, they kept what they wanted but auctioned the rest among the staff once a year. Among the

---

* (b. 1959), Conservative politician. MP for Maldon 1992–2010; Sec. of State for Culture, Media and Sport 2015–16.

objects sold one year was a glass bowl containing a glass apple and pear, given by President Mitterrand:* horribly ugly, it fetched only £1. All the money went to charity.

13 January 1993

Confirmation that the Princess of Wales has been feeding details of her marital failure to the tabloid Press has driven all other news off the front pages. Probably anorexia has a harmful effect on character. Divorce now looks probable.

14 January 1993

Read the text of the pirated telephone call between Prince Charles and Camilla Parker Bowles:† nothing really obscene, but a sad longing for each other. The publication of all this may bring popular sentiment once more in favour of the Princess. The Prince has put himself in the same position as Edward VIII.

To a party given by Jonathan Aitken in Lord North Street to celebrate the publication of his life of Richard Nixon.

21 January 1993

Call for Martin Gilliat at St James's Palace and take him to lunch at Green's. Outside in the courtyard, vans are unloading the possessions of the Prince of Wales, carried there from Kensington Palace after his separation from Diana. He is to live in David Airlie's house, until now used only for entertaining.

5 February 1993

Catch the 12.50 train to Windsor for Oliver van Oss's memorial service in College Chapel at Eton. The lessons are good and well read by Peter Attenborough, Headmaster of Charterhouse, and by Antony Acland, the Provost. An elderly congregation. It is in fact a joint Eton-Charterhouse event. I ask someone if they have seen Peter Attenborough in School Hall, where there are tea and sandwiches. 'No,' is the reply, 'he has gone back to Charterhouse to crush a mutiny.'

---

* François Mitterrand (1916–96), President of France 1981–95.
† Camilla, Duchess of Cornwall (b. 1947); m. Charles, Prince of Wales in 2005.

10 February 1993

Talk with David Gilmour,[*] who is working on Curzon's papers for his biography, interrupted only by lunch at the Ark. We talk about Roy Jenkins and his books. Although Roy is a close friend of the Gilmours, David is critical of his methods as an historian. Roy once came upon David at work on his Curzon book, with my own biography and David Dilks's study of Curzon's time in India open before him. Roy said: 'I see you follow my own practice of writing your own books by copying from other people's.' This is certainly not true of David. It is not only laziness on Roy's part, but his books are dated. Because Curzon was something of a figure of fun in Lloyd George's Cabinets, Roy assumes he was a similar figure of fun in India, which he most certainly was not.

17 February 1993

Now that Victor Rothschild has died I have decided that my Rothschild book should be a biography of him.[†] When I tell Noel Annan, he says: 'You are going to have a hell of a time with Victor's life.' I rather agree. When I have handed in the typescript I shall probably go abroad.

I ask Alec Guinness whether he has ever met Dick White, the Smiley voice is so similar. Alec says he has very occasionally met him, but never studied him as a prototype for Smiley.[‡]

2 March 1993

Richard Thorpe gives me dinner at the Oxford and Cambridge Club in that cavernous and elegant dining room. Good food. Richard will soon be fifty and wonders how much longer he should go on teaching at Charterhouse. He is not only well into his biography of Alec Home, but he <u>has</u> been invited by Clarissa Avon to write a new life of Anthony Eden, which she says she will regard as the official life – using many papers which Robert Rhodes James did not see, as well as her own detailed Suez diary. He does not know why she so dislikes Robert Rhodes James's book: David Carlton[§] did a far more savage biography. It seems to me that Richard will diminish Anthony's

---

[*] Sir David Gilmour, 4th Bt (b. 1952), author; biographer of Curzon (1994) and Rudyard Kipling (2002).

[†] This was published as *Elusive Rothschild: The Life of Victor, 3rd Baron* in 2003.

[‡] Sir Dick White (1906–93), British intelligence officer. George Smiley is a fictional character created by John Le Carré; Sir Alec Guinness (1914–2000) played the part in two television adaptations of Le Carré novels.

[§] Dr David Carlton, senior lecturer in International Studies at Warwick 1975–1992; author of *Anthony Eden: A Biography* (1981).

reputation on the 1938 resignation, but make his Suez policy more appreciated.

He now has two authorised Prime Ministerial biographies in hand and tells me that Alec Home jokingly refers to the Eden project as his 'overtime'. But there are many advantages. Alec has already been telling him a lot about Anthony and when he interviews people he can talk about both subjects. He would be well advised to take early retirement and concentrate on writing and research full-time.

16 March 1993

Frank Johnson is pleased I have come round to agreeing with him that Major's Government is utterly incompetent. Even the PM's new scheme for supposedly awarding honours on a wider social basis is all nonsense of course.

17 March 1993

Isaiah Berlin and I have an interesting talk on modes of address. Among the oddities, I quote the example of Harold Macmillan writing to A.L. Rowse as 'My dear friend' – not wanting to use either Leslie or Rowse. Isaiah says that he always rather disapproved of Harold's writing to him 'Dear Isaiah Berlin'. When I tell him that when John Major writes to me he tops and tails the letter 'My dear Kenneth . . . Yours ever, John', Isaiah agrees that the PM wants to be liked too much.

22 March 1993

This evening Prince Eddie's Private Secretary, Roger Walker,* telephones me. Robert Fellowes has asked him to find out whether I am still writing a life of Prince George, Duke of Kent. This is a purely independent enquiry. I tell him that I am not, and sketch in a little of the background. I wonder why the Queen is interested.

Roger also gives me an interesting piece of news. The Australian Government wants its own Unknown Warrior of the Great War. The body will have to come from France, as Belgium does not release the remains of the dead. Our own Unknown Warrior is not in fact unknown: one or two people know his identity. If Australia, Canada will probably follow.

5 April 1993

I hear how cunning the Princess of Wales is. The other day she discovered when the Prince would be in his new quarters in St James's Palace, then

* Roger Martineau-Walker (b. 1940), PS to the Duke and Duchess of Kent 1990–93.

turned up and told him she had come to see if he was comfortable. She even insisted on looking at his bedroom, and saying that it needed a small table which she would find for him. The Prince is terrified of her.

Martin Charteris tells me: 'If the Queen had taken as much trouble over the bloodlines of her son's wives as she has over her horses and dogs, she would have avoided a lot of trouble.'

6 April 1993

I have lunch with Peter Inge.* He is most revealing on the PM's visit to Bosnia. With an intense wish to be liked, Major wanted to take out all sorts of 'comforts' for our troops – from turkeys to tapes. Peter had to point out that if he did that, he ought to do no less for our troops in Northern Ireland. Similarly, when the PM wanted to write to the parents of the only British soldier to be killed in Bosnia so far, Peter asked if he was prepared also to write to the parents of every British soldier killed in Northern Ireland.

On the run-down state of the army, and such minor problems as colonelcies of regiments, Peter cannot constitutionally approach the Queen. He gets round this by writing to Robert Fellowes, knowing that his letters will be shown to the Queen.

Peter is worried about the investigation into the alleged shooting of Argentine prisoners of war by paratroopers during the Falklands campaign. There may be something to it: people are not always on their best behaviour in a bloody battle. It seems to me that the prolonged investigation by Scotland Yard, against the wishes of the Falkland Islanders, is an unpleasant form of national self-mutilation.

9 April 1993

A feast of Good Friday music: St Matthew Passion, Mozart's Requiem and the Good Friday music from *Parsifal*.

Charles Guthrie telephones me from Germany for a talk about Bosnia. He is interesting on the ramifications of this. For us to intervene, four conditions must be met: (a) it must be a moral cause; (b) it must be in our national interest; (c) we must be certain of success; and (d) we must have public opinion behind us. In the Gulf we had all four. In Bosnia, nothing except (c) is certain.

---

* FM Sir Peter Inge, Baron Inge of Richmond, North Yorkshire (b. 1935), CGS 1992–4; Chief of the Defence Staff 1994–7.

15 May 1993

I have a talk with Peter Wilmot-Sitwell* about the Royal Family. We are agreed that the Queen is good with ministers, ambassadors and representatives of the Commonwealth, but not with her children or indeed many other people. She appoints weak Private Secretaries when somebody of the stamp of Peter Carrington is needed.

28 May 1993

John Major has dismissed Norman Lamont as Chancellor of the Exchequer and has not offered him the consolation of a CH.

31 May 1993

I hear that Martin Gilliat died peacefully in hospital on 27 May. His death has hit me hard.

4 June 1993

Eric Anderson is to become Rector of Lincoln College, Oxford. I recall that Robert Birley missed the Mastership of Balliol for some absurd reason, so telephone Brian Rees. Yes, Birley drove cross-country from Canterbury, lost his way, so failed to attend a vital meeting with the Fellows.

The Queen Mother was at Martin Gilliat's funeral yesterday in the Chapel Royal, St James's. It must have been private. No list of mourners in the papers. I should like to have been there. Continue to think of Martin, particularly the jokes.

11 June 1993

Wrestle with the intricacies of parliamentary procedure as I write about Norman Lamont's resignation and the former convention that an ex-minister did not use such an occasion to attack another MP. The House of Commons is like a run-down school in need of a brisk matron. Thank God I am not an MP.

Talk to Robin Lane Fox about the New College Mound. The archaeological survey has been completed and now we have full planning permission. He is putting in steps of Yorkshire stone – thirty-nine of them, of course. The work should be finished by the first week in August. Meanwhile I shall look at it tomorrow.

---

* (b. 1935), Chairman of S.G. Warburg 1990–94.

12 June 1993

To Oxford in the afternoon. First to New College to look at the Mound. It pours with rain, but from what I can see it is a huge improvement on the old black copse. Robin has left me a copy of the archaeological review, full of interesting background material.

18 June 1993

I have dinner with Hartley Shawcross. The most interesting reminiscence is that he now regrets that William Joyce, Lord Haw-Haw, whom he prosecuted for treason, was hanged on a technicality. He had, after all, applied to become a naturalised German.

21 June 1993

Andrew Roberts says that Robert Salisbury would like someone to write an authoritative biography of his great-grandfather, the Prime Minister. Should he undertake it? Yes, very much so. It would establish his reputation.

To Ian Gilmour's annual garden party at Old Isleworth. Simon Phipps[*] reminds me of the story of the notice outside College Chapel at Eton – 'Visitation of the Blessed Virgin Mary, Preacher: The Visitor'.

7 July 1993

Matthew Ridley reminds me that it is fifty years to the day since we joined the army together.

8 July 1993

To St Martin-in-the-Fields for the memorial service for Martin Gilliat. I am shown to a seat in the front row of the gallery that gives me a commanding view of the whole church. There is scarcely a seat unoccupied. The courtiers act as ushers, so trim and sleek. Ted Heath is given a seat behind Norman St John-Stevas.

The Queen Mother is in black and white and leaning on a stick, but quite animated and cheerful in spite of the death of Ruth Fermoy[†] a couple of days ago.

Martin Charteris gives an admirable address with several good lighter

---

[*] The Rt Revd Simon Phipps (1921–2001), Bishop of Lincoln 1974–86. The Visitor of Eton is the Bishop of Lincoln.

[†] Ruth Roche, Baroness Fermoy (1908–93), close friend of the Queen Mother; maternal grandmother of Diana, Princess of Wales.

touches – 'He was as generous in pouring out his own drink as Queen Elizabeth's.'

The regimental march of the Royal Green Jackets and the Eton Boating Song: the two institutions he loved best.

13 July 1993
I see the new Queen Elizabeth Gates in Hyde Park for the first time. They are unbelievably coy and meretricious, and entirely unworthy of their name. Sub-standard Disneyland or Festival of Britain 1951.

14 July 1993
Lunch with Jeremy and Marion Thorpe in Orme Square. They have been asked by Michael Bloch to give him their approval and help for a biography of Jeremy, assuring them that it will enhance Jeremy's reputation. As Michael has already done much digging into Jeremy's past and interviewed many of his friends and acquaintances (though Mark Bonham Carter,* Jo Grimond and David Steel have refused), the Thorpes are faced by a *fait accompli*. Bloch has assured them that he has no intention of approaching Norman Scott, which gives them confidence. Jeremy, too unwell to write his own memoirs, is attracted by the idea of once again occupying the political stage, if only in print. He wants Bloch to include all those episodes in which Jeremy rubbed shoulders with the great. So I think Bloch will be taken into their confidence – even though they could not hope to control or censor the text of the book.†

As for Jeremy's health, it seems no worse; and his colour is fresher than when I last saw him. Marion remains a cheerful saint.

22 July 1993
George Tonypandy tells me that as Speaker he declined to accept Selwyn Lloyd's ruling that the Speaker did not need to scrutinise a Member's personal statement on resignation before delivery.

Robert Fellowes supports Princess Diana's wish to be publicly in the swim. As it happens, the night of the Prime Ministerial dinner at Spencer House saw the final breakdown of the marriage. The Princess of Wales asked to see the Queen before dinner to tell her she wanted a separation from Charles. The Queen was in a hurry to dress, so told her the discussion would have to be resumed at the Palace at the end of the evening. That is what happened and

---

* Baron Bonham Carter (1922–94), publisher and Liberal politician; won the safe Conservative seat of Torrington by 219 votes in 1958.
† *Jeremy Thorpe* by Michael Bloch was published in 2014, a fortnight after the subject's death.

the marriage bust. In the meantime the Queen had to sit through dinner with the Prime Ministers and even talk to me. Amazing how in the circumstances she remained so composed and cheerful. The Waleses, by comparison, were red-faced and agitated, as I noted at Spencer House at the time.

9 August 1993

In Berlin. I visit the Olympic Stadium, hugely expanded by Hitler for the 1936 Olympic Games. It is spacious but ugly, with grotesque naked statues. Across the top of a neoclassical portico is carved, in German, the motto: 'The sacred concept of perfection is a reminder from the beginning of time.'

The Olympic Stadium itself is shabby and in places crumbling. I stand on Hitler's tribune, surrounded by the ghosts of Chips Channon and other Nazi sympathisers. Nearby is a Coca-Cola dispenser.

Jesse Owen's[*] name is carved on the list of Olympic winners. The Olympic bell is just outside the stadium. On it is carved, in German, 'I summon the youth of the world'. Also in bas-relief, a German eagle with the five Olympic rings in its claws; swastikas; and a reproduction of the Brandenburg Gate. In the nearby Olympic swimming pool soldiers' children are bathing.

11 August 1993

Tony Lambton is disappointed by Alan Clark's diaries: not at all as good as those of Chips Channon.

To the National Theatre to see *Arcadia* by Tom Stoppard. It is fearfully pretentious and some of the jokes are designed to shock the suburban audience with f-words. Also the actors do not speak their lines clearly and some of the text is lost.

22 August 1993

To Lincoln's Inn to dine with Arnold Goodman on his eightieth birthday. Clarissa Avon has chosen the menu and arranged the seating plan: two big tables and about thirty smaller ones. A good dinner with mousse, halibut, sorbet and fruit. Two Rothschild wines.

Champagne before dinner. Peter Tapsell tells me a characteristic story of Ted Heath. When staying with Peter in the country, Ted looked at a portrait of Peter and said to him: 'It must be by a woman.' It was. Peter: 'How do you know?' Ted: 'She has made you much better-looking than you are. Only a woman would flatter you.'

Isaiah Berlin says that at New College in 1946 the two undergraduates

---

[*] James Cleveland Owens (1913–80), four-times Olympic gold medallist at the 1936 Games.

who were most respectful to the dons were John Grigg and Anthony Benn. Isaiah adds, with emphasis: 'You were <u>not</u>!' He also says that Alan Bullock[*] minded very much not having served in the Armed Forces during the war.

23 August 1993
Eric Anderson tells me that the Fellows of Eton are likely to choose a new Head Master in mid-November. He has told them that he does not wish to recommend a name, but, if asked, he will give his opinion on any particular candidate. All very correct.

30 August 1993
To bed to the noise of the Notting Hill Carnival, like a Bullingdon dinner.

2 October 1993
Read a few chapters of C.P. Snow's *Corridors of Power*. Not as good as *The Masters*, but what novel of his is?

11 October 1993
In Oxford I see the renovated Mound at New College. The broad stone steps to the top of the Mound look superb, a majestic and lasting adornment to the college from whatever angle: even from the windows of the old library. At the Warden's suggestion, with which Robin Lane Fox and myself agree, the paved top of the Mound is to be extended by a foot or two. I ask for some branches to be cut, giving a view of Magdalen Tower and perhaps of the city wall.

Over a late lunch, Robin mentions that he has been approached to see if he would like to be considered as HM of Eton. He would not. The task would be considerable. He thinks that even under Eric Anderson the school is still too rooted in the past, with archaic dress, long holidays, outdated attitudes. Someone else to be approached is Charles Swallow:[†] former Headmaster of a comprehensive school and before that a Harrow schoolmaster; historian, and racquets champion; aged fifty-five.

11 November 1993
To Cambridge at the invitation of Norman St John-Stevas to see the Princess

---

[*] Baron Bullock (1914–2004), historian. Master of St Catherine's Coll., Oxford 1962–81; Vice-Chancellor of Oxford University 1969–73.

[†] (b. 1938), schoolmaster at Harrow 1961–73; Headmaster of Grace Comprehensive School, Potters Bar 1973–84.

of Wales lay the foundation stone of the new buildings at Emmanuel. Norman is exuberant, and trembles on the brink of going too far when in his speech of welcome he says that the massed photographers have come to take pictures of <u>him</u>. It is so like him, too, that a cloud of balloons in the Emmanuel colours of blue and pink is released at the moment the stone is laid. I notice that his own name is in letters no smaller than those of the Princess.

The Princess shows no trace of her supposed nervous disorders, and has matured physically. During the buffet lunch, Norman comes down to lead me up to her, which is a kindly courtesy. She at once says, 'Ah yes, you used to come to Althorp.' We chat about those times, and how Barbara Cartland's* false eyelashes once fell into Prince Eddie's stew during a shooting lunch! We also talk about Ruth Fermoy and the forthcoming memorial concert. Princess Diana could not possibly have been more friendly.

Enjoy some talk with Michael McCrum. He is in his last year as Master of Corpus, Cambridge, having been elected in 1980, the year he ceased to be Head Master of Eton. He was Vice-Chancellor 1987–1989. He thinks that Eton is electing its new Head Master this week. His own choice would be John Lewis, Master-in-College 1975–1980, then Principal of Geelong Grammar School, Australia. He thinks the salary would be about £80,000. When Michael went from Tonbridge to Eton, he took a drop in salary of £2,000 and he annoyed Eton housemasters by saying that his drawing room was half the size of the one he had had at Tonbridge. He is appalled by the decline in academic standards at Cambridge.

Graham C. Greene gives his annual party of the Museums and Galleries Commission in the Wallace Collection. As he says, it is the least known of London galleries. Very few of those he asks have been here for years – and they are all museum men and women. Admire the gold boxes with Jean Trumpington – particularly one of white enamel decorated with peacock features. Also look at Poussin's *Dance to the Music of Time* and think of Tony Powell and the inspiration he drew from it.

15 November 1993

William Waldegrave tells me that when he was Ted Heath's Political Secretary, he would be rung up out of the blue by peppery colonels who would say: 'What we want as Prime Minister is not an old queer like Heath, but a fine upstanding gentleman like Jeremy Thorpe.' At that very moment, William had on his desk the Home Office files on Jeremy's private life.

---

* Dame Barbara Cartland (1901–2000), author of romance novels; step-grandmother of Diana, Princess of Wales.

He also tells me that when he went to Wiltons the other day and asked for a purée of Brussels sprouts with his fish, he was told they never made a purée of Brussels sprouts. 'But I often used to have them when I lunched with Lord Rothschild.' 'Yes,' came the reply, 'but we only did it for Lord Rothschild.'

18 November 1993

To Buckingham Palace at six for a party and concert in memory of Ruth Fermoy. It is all very well done. The guests include nice Norfolk people, musicians and country clergymen.

Antony Acland tells me that he and the Fellows of Eton are taking their time choosing a new Head Master, although they must complete the task by December so that the Head Master can give notice to his old school.

24 November 1993

I catch a train to Sunningdale to have tea with Sarah, Duchess of York. I am met at the station and driven quite a short distance to her home. Two frisky Dalmatian dogs. All the rooms I see have several pictures of Prince Andrew. Pleasantly untidy with books and papers. The Duchess's writing table has about a hundred objects on it: I am not sure it does not surpass Queen Mary's ninety-seven. The telephone hardly stops ringing during my visit. Her two sweet little girls[*] join us and we have nursery tea in the dining room. They are enchanting and very well brought up by a Welsh nanny from Anglesey. They put their hands together and say grace. When one of them begins to get down before the other has quite finished she is made to get back and begin all over again. There is a vast spread on the table of sausage rolls, sandwiches and a chocolate cake. Also a pretty sauce boat with ketchup. I have the impression that she misses Andrew dreadfully.

Fergie is naturally sensitive about her position in the Royal Family. 'The Queen has been marvellously kind,' she says. 'And the Queen Mother said kind words about my Everest expedition for the disabled – "It makes us so small."'

She insists on sending me back to London by car: in fact there seems to be almost a shuttle service.

25 November 1993

Dine with George Tonypandy at the House of Lords. He describes preaching at Eton as the guest of Martin Charteris. 'Is chapel compulsory?' George asked. Martin: 'It is today.'

---

[*] Their Royal Highnesses Princess Beatrice of York (b. 1988) and Princess Eugenie of York (b. 1990).

When I use the phrase the First Commoner, George punctiliously points out the Speaker ceased to be so in 1919, when Speaker Lowther[*] asked for the Speaker's precedence to be changed. After the Royal Family, it is now the Archbishop of Canterbury, the Lord Chancellor, the Archbishop of York, the PM and the Lord President of the Council, then the Speaker; and the PM is nowadays always a commoner. Such a warm and comfortable evening.

26 November 1993
I ask Martin Charteris whether he knows who is to be the new HM of Eton. He says he does not. But what he does know is that (a) Hammond, Headmaster of Tonbridge, received a letter telling him that he has not been successful and (b) the name of the successful candidate will not be announced until next week. This probably means that he is overseas, which points to John Lewis, Principal of Geelong. I decide to take a chance and predict Lewis in my 'Albany' column.

Martin adds that he thinks there is no chance of a reconciliation between Charles and Diana.

1 December 1993
To the Atlantic Richfield dinner at Claridge's. Former President George Bush is one of the speakers. He makes a very good remark: 'Former Presidents have to promise not to criticise the current President for a year. Well, we only have fifty days to go!'

3 December 1993
The Princess of Wales announces that she is to cease all public engagements in the New Year. She implies that media attention has led her to do this. I think it is a step towards divorce, and a decision to be welcomed. She should never have allowed the broken marriage to lead to official separation: now she has done so, public engagements on her part lose their authority. As there can never be a reconciliation, the sooner they are divorced the better. Then Charles can start to pick up the pieces before the end of the Queen's reign.

13 December 1993
Robert Armstrong is impressed that I successfully forecast the new HM of Eton, and asks me if Martin Charteris had told me. I honestly reply that he didn't – and indeed, that he had told me that he didn't know. But I did

---

[*] James Lowther, 1st Viscount Ullswater (1855–1949), Speaker of the House of Commons 1905–21.

deduce, from his telling me that the announcement was to be delayed for a few days, that the successful candidate lived at a distance. Robert, who is a Fellow of Eton, was impressed by John Lewis, not least when he was asked if he thought he could be both a successful HM and also a happy man. Lewis took his time in answering: he was not to be rushed.

Some interesting talk with Robert about Cabinet papers. Norman Brook[*] kept a secret file on Suez, including records of collusion, which he later burned. 'I would have kept it in a very secure place, but I should never have destroyed it.'

Robert does not think that the notebooks in which the Cabinet Secretary records Cabinet discussions as they occur should be readily released to researchers. Ministers will speak more freely if their remarks are not noted verbatim – though Crossman and Benn have breached this convention. It is much better if general conclusions are printed and circulated at once, though without attributing opinions to individual ministers. 'I kept notebooks as a tool of Government, not for the convenience of historians.'

15 December 1993

Rupert Allason MP[†] to dine at Shepherd's restaurant. He writes about intelligence matters under the name of Nigel West. Rupert seems to think that I was in MI5, and I do not disabuse him.

16 December 1993

I talk to George Carey, the Archbishop of Canterbury, for the first time since the Christmas midnight service at Wells Cathedral. He remembers the occasion well and we have a pleasant talk. He is larger physically, as well as intellectually, than he appears in the largely hostile Press, with none of that hesitancy and clumsiness he displays when being interviewed.

---

[*] 1st Baron Normanbrook (1902–67), Cabinet Secretary 1947–62.
[†] (b. 1951), military historian and Conservative politician. MP for Torbay 1987–97. He is thought to have lost his seat for failing to tip a pub waitress a week before the election. As a result, fourteen waiters who had planned to vote for Allason switched to the Liberal Democrats. Allason lost by twelve votes.

1994

The Duchess of Kent converted to Catholicism, the first member of the Royal Family to do so for more than 300 years. The first women were ordained as priests in the Church of England on 12 March. Opinion polls showed that Conservative support had fallen to 26 per cent on 29 April; the Conservatives lost 429 seats in council elections on 5 May. The Channel Tunnel was opened on 6 May. John Smith, the Labour leader, died unexpectedly at the age of fifty-five on 12 May. Tony Blair won the Labour Party leadership election on 21 July. On 18 August Labour had a thirty-three-point lead over the Conservatives in the opinion polls. The Sunday Trading Act came into full effect on 26 August. The Provisional IRA declared a ceasefire on 31 August. The Criminal Justice and Public Order Act on 3 November lowered the age of consent for male homosexual acts from twenty-one years to eighteen. The first UK National Lottery draw took place on 19 November. The first meeting between the British government and Sinn Fein for more than seventy years was held on 9 December.

2 January 1994

Princess Margaret tells me how busy she has been for the past week or two destroying much of the Queen Mother's old correspondence and the battered attaché cases in which it has been kept. PM suggested to the Queen Mother that she should read out what seemed to her to be interesting, then ask the QM whether or not it should be destroyed. 'I have already filled two big sacks, and the servants are so pleased at my cleaning up the mess.' This is terrible news. Later I discuss it with Prue Penn,* who is as shocked as I am. PM has already told her that the papers include all Arthur Penn's letters to the QM, going back even before her marriage to the Duke of York. Prue realises how much more valuable it would be for the QM's ultimate biographer to read both sides of the correspondence.

PM tells me that Tony Snowdon and she used to ask Noël Coward to dine

---

* Lady Prudence Penn (b. 1926), Lady-in-Waiting to the Queen Mother.

à trois, in order to have his wit to themselves. But Noël asked for a bigger party: he needed an audience.

Prue, when alone with me, talks of Christmas at Sandringham. Charles confessed to her that there was so much pressure on him to marry. Prue wanted to tell him at the time to call it off, even at a late stage.

Later PM says to me: 'I could never go to India. They would hate to see the daughter of the last Emperor.' What nonsense: they would be enchanted, as they are when Baba Metcalfe goes.

12 January 1994

Much absurd gush in the papers about Katharine Kent's conversion to Catholicism, not least a leader in *The Times* implying that the Queen gave her 'complete approval'.

I talk to Oliver Everett[*] about Princess Margaret and the Queen Mother's papers. He is shocked at this private destruction. As he has business to do with PM on some other matter, he will delicately raise the issue.

22 January 1994

Read Adam Sisman's[†] *A.J.P. Taylor,* an exceptionally well-constructed, penetrating and amusing biography.

21 February 1994

I talk to Guinevere Tilney[‡] about the row between Margaret Thatcher and Norma Major, who has publicly worn a diamond necklace given by a Gulf ruler to Margaret and deposited under the rules at No. 10. I don't see why Norma should not have done so. But Guinevere says it was tactless of her to do so when Margaret loved it so much. Even so, I think it was both undignified and unkind of Margaret to complain – and feeble of John Major to agree that his wife should wear it no more.

5 March 1994

Nigel Jaques,[§] the former Eton housemaster, writes: 'I have this evening been told of the death (drowned in a far country) of my last house captain, who

---

[*] (b. 1943), diplomat; Librarian, Royal Library 1985–2002.

[†] (b. 1958), historian; biographer of A. J. P. Taylor (1994), Hugh Trevor-Roper (2011) and John le Carré (2015).

[‡] Dame Guinevere Tilney (1916–97), President of the National Council of Women 1961–8; UK Representative on the UN Committee on the Status of Women 1970–73; adviser to Margaret Thatcher 1975–83.

[§] (b. 1935), Eton schoolmaster.

arranged my farewells, and left the house with me last summer. It gives one an idea of what it was like for housemasters in 1914–1918, when such news came every week.'

6 March 1994

Michael Bloch brings round the first two chapters of his biography of Jeremy Thorpe. His relations with Jeremy Thorpe continue to fluctuate; Marion regards him with constant suspicion. Michael asks Jeremy's old friends all about him, and some then tell an alarmed Jeremy.

I am not at all pleased with Dominic Harrod* for having revealed to Michael that Jeremy had a retainer from the *Sunday Telegraph* of £500 a year – £5,000 a year in today's currency. This I arranged in December 1962 at the instigation of Michael Hartwell. It is a breach of confidence on Dominic's part to have told Michael of this business relationship. Dominic must have realised this, for he asked Michael not to tell me that he had spoken to him about it.

Later in the day I read the opening chapters. They are good, revealing the world of fantasy in which Jeremy dwelled from youth: the belief he inherited from his father, for instance, that he had a claim on the dormant barony of Thorpe. There was not a scrap of evidence, yet Jeremy clung to it – and used the Thorpe crest, to which he was not entitled. Even today, Michael says, Jeremy mistakenly thinks he may be given a peerage.

I tell Michael not to assume or imply that all schoolmasters are homosexual. He suggests that Leggy Lambart† and Wilfrid Blunt had romantic passions for their Eton pupils. I tell him that I suspect Lambart was sexless and that Wilfrid was certainly chaste as far as his pupils were concerned.

16 March 1994

It has been announced that Charles Guthrie is to succeed Peter Inge as Chief of the General Staff. Charles telephones this morning, and we discuss what I can usefully write in my column on Sunday. He is the last C-in-C BAOR – the first was Monty, which leads him to tell me that he was inspected by the Field Marshal at Sandhurst.

17 March 1994

To Jonathan Aitken's house in Lord North Street to hear President Nixon

---

* (1940–2013), journalist and broadcaster.
† Julian Lambart (1893–1982), master at Eton 1919–45; Lower Master 1945–59; Vice-Provost 1959–67.

speaking. As on his previous visit, he is full of interesting remarks:

'There are only two people who think that Gorbachev will make a comeback: Gorbachev and his wife.'

'Those who lead revolutions are not good nation-builders.'

'The Republicans should not allow the scandal of the Clintons[*] to nullify Presidential policy on bigger themes.'

'Khrushchev had the fastest reaction time of anyone I have met.'

'Russia is still a world power – the only power that can destroy the USA with 28,000 nuclear weapons.'

14 April 1994

I have some interesting talk with the Home Secretary, Michael Howard,[†] a pleasant and friendly man. He was Selwyn Lloyd's personal assistant for the 1964 General Election when Michael was starting his pupillage after Cambridge, and thought him a shrewd and under-rated man.

21 April 1994

I give John Grigg lunch at Bertorelli. I tell him how much I have enjoyed and admired his history of *The Times*.[‡] What has caused him anguish is the utter mess made of distributing the book by the publisher. Though well paid for writing it, he will make little from the royalties.

29 April 1994

Advance publicity of Tim Card's new book on Eton[§] has led to a flood of articles on William Cory's[¶] involvement with boys and Anthony Chenevix-Trench's love of beating. One of Chenevix-Trench's many victims has come out with a savage attack in an article in the *Evening Standard* on beating.

I receive an anonymous letter addressed to 'Albany column', giving details of 'Homosexual housemasters at Eton, 1970–1978'. The author will be disappointed if he thinks I will print it.

---

[*] The Whitewater scandal, an investigation into the real-estate investments of Bill Clinton (b. 1946), US President 1993–2001, and his wife Hillary Rodham Clinton (b. 1947), later US Sec. of State 2009–2013.

[†] Baron Howard of Lympne (b. 1941), Conservative politician. Home Secretary 1993–7; leader of the Conservative Party 2003–5.

[‡] *The History of the Times: Volume VI, The Thomson Years 1966–1981* (1993).

[§] *Eton Renewed: A History from 1860 to the Present Day* (1994).

[¶] William Johnson Cory (1823–92), Eton schoolmaster 1845–72, when he was forced to resign owing to the closeness of his relations with boys.

6 May 1994

To Clarence House for lunch with the Queen Mother. As it happens, it is the anniversary of the accession of King George V. She greets me warmly and thanks me for sending her my printed lecture on Harold Nicolson. We are quite a small party. Having had drinks in the room to the left of the entrance hall – tumblers of gin and Dubonnet dispensed by Alastair Aird – we eat in what used to be the drawing room, with the portrait of the QM by Augustus John. The QM is fully restored to health now and looks no older than ten years ago and does not even carry a stick. She talks in that light, distinctive, emphatic voice. We eat a succession of rich and ambrosial dishes: scrambled egg and prawns with a sauce, chicken with delicious vegetables, hot black cherries with a superb ice and cheese. After I have taken a sliver from a blue cheese, the butler whispers to me, 'Do take some cream cheese from the Home Farm at Windsor, Sir,' which I do. It is bright-yellow and very tasty. We drink claret from an eagle covered in white enamel. Throughout lunch four corgis sprawl on the carpet and occasionally scratch the door to be let out.

After lunch I have some talk with the QM, who says that she will have nothing to do with the Channel Tunnel – being opened at that very minute by the Queen.

9 May 1994

I have dinner with William Waldegrave at the House of Commons. He has put an end to the system by which ministers and MPs and civil servants, travelling by air on official business, put the 'air-mile' credit they received from the airlines to their own personal use. Now the credit goes to the Treasury. The civil servants have taken this well, but the ministers and MPs are furious at being robbed of a perk.

12 May 1994

My secretary telephones me: 'Did you know that John Smith is dead?' I am absolutely horrified, thinking it is John of Smith Square. But a moment later she explains that it is the leader of the Labour Party.* I feel like the heroine in Evelyn Waugh's *A Handful of Dust*, when she learns that the John who has been killed is not her lover, but her son. But I am also very saddened at the death of one of the better current politicians.

---

* John Smith QC (1938–94), Labour politician. Leader of the Labour Party 1992–4; MP for Monklands East 1970–94. Sir John Smith (1923–2007) was a contemporary of K.R. at New Coll.; Conservative MP for the Cities of London and Westminster 1965–70; Lord Lieutenant of Berkshire 1975–8.

13 May 1994

The papers are awash with tributes to John Smith, the leader of the Labour Party and a knight in shining armour. His death has subdued all political party passions.

17 May 1994

To Harrow School for the opening of a Lord Byron exhibition. It is curious to take a Tube from Baker Street in the rush hour and to emerge half an hour later in a small nineteenth-century town surrounded by green fields. The exhibition is well done, not least Byron's schooldays at Harrow. I ask a boy who is peering into a case of documents beside me if he knows how Byron died. 'Wasn't he drowned?' the boy replies, confusing him with Shelley. I meet the Headmaster, Nicholas Bomford,* a genial man, who kindly says to me: 'Are you not the man who brought King George V to life?'

19 May 1994

I give Richard Ryder† lunch at the Caprice. He is pursuing a list of books presented, as is traditional, by current Cabinet ministers to the No. 10 library, but some of his colleagues are cagey about their intentions. 'The House of Commons', he tells me, 'is full of embittered people who all want to be Prime Minister. There used to be Knights of the Shires without ministerial ambitions, who only wanted to serve. Far better.'

29 May 1994

I hear a story about Henry Kissinger, who, having been given a length of English cloth for a suit by Margaret Thatcher, took it to a London tailor. 'I am sorry,' the tailor told him, 'but there is not quite enough for a suit.' So he tried a Paris tailor: same result. Finally, he tried a tailor in Tel Aviv. 'Certainly, Mr Kissinger, with this cloth we can make a suit and a spare pair of trousers.' 'How can you manage that?' 'You are not such a big man in Israel.'

2 June 1994

I have an amusing talk with Roy Jenkins on ambition at a dinner in Jesus College, Oxford. He says: 'I never wanted to be Foreign Secretary.' I say: 'No, but you would like to have been asked.' He laughs. He would never have done so five years ago.

---

* (b. 1939), Headmaster of Uppingham School 1982–91; Headmaster of Harrow 1991–9.
† Baron Ryder of Wensum (b. 1949), Conservative politician. Government Chief Whip 1990–95.

7 June 1994

Charles Moore* gives me lunch at the Savoy Grill. We are joined by Frank Johnson. He shares my annoyance with John Major at the abolition of the Military Medal in favour of an all-ranks Military Cross. What Major cannot grasp, having no experience of army life, is that a corporal would rather have an MM than an officer's MC.

9 June 1994

To Peter Thorneycroft's funeral at St Peter's, Eaton Square. I am rather shocked by both the interior of the church and the service – as near Roman Catholicism as makes no difference. There are painted statues of the Virgin Mary, incense, holy water and candles. The priest who takes the service strikes a discordant note by referring to Peter's 'sense of sinfulness', whatever that means; and he does not mention that Peter began life with a regular commission in the Gunners, of which he was very proud. I do not take Communion.

Prince Eddie is about to go to Poland on an official visit. This is of deep interest to him, as there was once some talk of his father becoming King of Poland. He will try to find any papers there may be on the subject.

I ask Nico Henderson, who was Ambassador to Poland from 1969 to 1972, if he can recall anything of it. He cannot remember much, but he thinks that Prince George went to Poland to see the prominent Polish family the Potockis.

Nico has received a raspberry from Princess Margaret about his diaries, for revealing Royal conversations. I say that the content of the conversations is harmless enough, but that the Prince of Wales may now feel that he cannot talk privately even with an ambassador. Nico does not disagree with me.

11 June 1994

With Princess Margaret for a weekend at Henham Hall, near Macclesfield. PM does not smoke and drinks barley water throughout the day until six, when she has a whisky and water. Surprisingly, PM does not get on with Peter Carrington. 'He won't tell me anything about foreign affairs.' On Suez PM says: 'We were all against it except Mummy, who liked Eden. I could never bear him.'

PM is much exercised by all the changes in the litany. '"The reason that the old Prayer Book is never used", I told the Archbishop, "is because it is never taught."'

---

* (b. 1956), editor of the *Daily Telegraph, Sunday Telegraph* and the *Spectator*; author of the authorised biography of Margaret Thatcher (2 vols, 2013 and 2015).

12 June 1994

Before Sunday lunch I have a stimulating talk with Sir Bernard Lovell,[*] a charming, resilient old boy, immensely proud of his radio telescope and experimental station nearby at Jodrell Bank. I ask him whether he will take our little party to see it this afternoon if PM will agree. She does, having been there as long ago as 1960. So we go over in the afternoon.

Lovell explains that to save money when constructing it, he bought for £1,000 each from the breakers' yard two racks from the fifteen-inch guns of HMS *Revenge*. He also describes the measures taken to prevent the telescope being blown over, as nearly happened during the 1975 hurricane. It takes five years to paint the whole telescope. PM happily snaps away with her camera. She tells me she is relieved we do not have to go out onto the catwalk.

13 June 1994

Princess Margaret, other members of our party and myself leave at 1.15 from Manchester Airport, where a large aircraft of the Queen's Flight is waiting for us. PM complains that the part where we sit, although more comfortable than the cabin aft, is noisier. A steward offers us boiled sweets, then coffee and drinks. PM does the crossword, I read. As we land I look out on unfamiliar territory. 'Where are we?', I ask. 'We have brought you to Belgium,' PM replies, laughing. It is in fact Northolt. From the window of the plane I see a row of senior RAF officers lined up, including a group captain. Also four police cyclists in yellow. I am put in the front of a Mercedes – why that make of German car? – with PM in the back. I am rather annoyed to see the brusqueness with which the police wave all traffic into the side of the road.

PM describes how she met President Mugabe of Zimbabwe at Heathrow and drove him to Horse Guards Parade, where the Queen waited to receive him. But their car was held up by heavy traffic and was late. PM found the Queen trembling with the cold. We are soon at Kensington Palace, and a police car drives me home to Brunswick Gardens.

14 June 1994

Charles Moore writes warmly about my article on the destruction of the Guards' Chapel to mark the fiftieth anniversary of the tragedy this week. One bizarre touch I discovered is that the flying bomb grazed a building in Victoria which deflected it directly on to the Guards' Chapel. The building was the HQ of MI5.

---

[*] (1913–2012), physicist and radio astronomer; first Dir. of the Jodrell Bank Observatory 1945–80.

17 June 1994

Edward Ford tells me the part he played in breaking the news of King George VI's death in 1952 to the Prime Minister and to Queen Mary. Tommy Lascelles had arranged with him that if he received a message 'Hyde Park Corner', it meant that the King was dead. Fortunately, Edward had gone through his pocket book a few days before the King's death and had come across the code (there were other phrases meaning different things, such as the death of Queen Mary). Otherwise he would not have known when Tommy Lascelles telephoned him from Sandringham and said: 'Hyde Park Corner'. It was not wise to choose the name of a place as the code words. When it was telegraphed to the Queen in Kenya, the intended news never got through to her: it was mistaken as the place of origin of an uncompleted message. Edward first went to No. 10, where he found Winston in bed working on a speech about foreign affairs. By his side was a lighted candle for his cigar.

'I have bad news for you, Prime Minister, the King is dead.'

'Bad news? The worst.'

Winston then said that he must talk to Eden, and Edward replied that he must go to break the news to Queen Mary. Edward went off to Marlborough House, where he saw Cynthia Colville* and asked her to tell Queen Mary that the King was dead. Lady Cynthia said that when she broke the news of the Duke of Kent's death to her in 1942, she had been rebuked for doing it too abruptly, and she proposed telling Queen Mary at first that the King was very ill. Edward insisted that she should tell Queen Mary the truth, which she did, alone of course. Then Queen Mary received Edward with the utmost composure.

20 June 1994

Lunch at the Foreign Office for Clarissa Avon on the occasion of the unveiling of the bust of Anthony Eden. I go up in the Foreign Secretary's lift, a swift and streamlined contraption compared to Curzon's birdcage. Many people connected with Eden are there. It was thoughtful of Clarissa to include Richard Thorpe, who is undertaking the new biography of Eden, among the guests.

Until last week nothing more inspiring than a bowl of dried flowers adorned the wall at the bottom of the grand staircase of the Foreign Office. Unveiling the bust, Clarissa Avon told us that his years in the Foreign Office had been the happiest of his life. 'When he returned here in 1951, it was like a man coming home.' Douglas Hurd paid tribute both as a former diplomat

---

* (1884–1968), Woman of the Bedchamber to Queen Mary.

who in youth had served under Eden, and as a Foreign Secretary who can boast both experience and the eye of an historian. 'He showed miraculous skill in picking up the pieces of the European Defence Community.'

Hurd's salute to Eden as the greatest Foreign Secretary since the war is nowadays an unfashionable view, not least when expressed under the gaze of Ernest Bevin's bust, halfway up the grand staircase. Yet it would be almost unchallenged but for the shadow of Suez that later eclipsed Eden's diplomatic triumphs.

After this tutorial in history, we lunched in the Victorian splendour of the Locarno Room, named after the treaty of 1925. In the following year Eden became Parliamentary Private Secretary to the architect of the settlement, Sir Austen Chamberlain.

21 June 1994

Foyles literary lunch for Nico Henderson's diaries. I am fortunate enough to sit next to Antonia Fraser, but the bitter pill is that I am asked as I sit down to propose a vote of thanks. I say that diplomacy is a continuation of war by other means. Not much laughter from the old pussycats up from Tonbridge and Esher! But more than Nico receives for his funnier anecdotes.

Give Christopher Northbourne* dinner at the Ark. He reminds me of George Lyttelton's address to new boys in his house at Eton: 'You are not as nice as your parents have led you to believe.' And his comment to a parent: 'You have brought me a charming boy. In five years he will leave here as a charming young man. But the years between are going to be hell for both of us.'

27 June 1994

Matthew Ridley telephones. He and Prince Eddie would like to give me a seventieth birthday lunch in the Cholmondeley Room at the Lords in November. I am very touched.

Matthew tells me that during the Lords debate on whether to lower the age of homosexual consent from twenty-one to eighteen, Jean Trumpington went up to a peer and said: 'Come on, let's go and vote for the buggers.' It was Lord Montagu of Beaulieu.†

---

* Christopher James, 5th Baron Northbourne (b. 1926), Chairman of Betteshanger Farms 1975–97; cross-bench spokesman for families and children in the House of Lords.
† Edward Douglas-Scott-Montagu, 3rd Baron Montagu of Beaulieu (1926–2015). His conviction and imprisonment for homosexual sex in 1954 eventually led to the setting-up of the Wolfenden Committee, which advised the decriminalisation of adult homosexual activity. The Sexual Offences Act of 1967 followed its recommendations.

Mary Soames has had two literary proposals from publishers – a revised edition of the life of her mother and an edition of the letters between her mother and father.* I wonder whether the Churchill market is not a little saturated.

28 June 1994

Lord Moran's controversial diary of ministering to Winston Churchill as his doctor was not an authentic day-to-day compilation, but was doctored later with the benefit of hindsight. Mary Soames says that one of Moran's faults was a determination always to show that he was in the know. Yet he was only at No. 10 or Chequers as a professional man. 'I do not ever remember Charles being asked to a lunch or a dinner just for fun.' Winston was deeply shocked when in 1951 Charles Moran asked to be made Minister of Health, claiming: 'You owe your life to me.' Winston replied: 'Any conman can say that.' Mary tells me that Jock Colville detected oddities in Charles Moran's text.

At the local library I manage to get hold of the official life of Moran, published by the Royal Society of Medicine,† which gives a clear account of how the diary came to be written. The biography is full of fascinating sidelights, too, on Moran's other activities. He was reluctant to charge influential patients such as Beaverbrook and Churchill. He suffered poor health. He asked Churchill for a peerage. When he was in ill-favour after the publication of his Churchill diaries, Frank Longford used to come and sit with him at the Other Club.

30 June 1994

London is buzzing with discussion of an interview given by the Prince of Wales on TV last night. Its most glaring indiscretion was to admit that he had committed adultery. He also said that he wanted to be Defender of Faiths rather than of The Faith: a path that would lead straight to the disestablishment of the Church of England. Perhaps the two most alarming statements, when taken together, were that (a) he has no plans to divorce, and (b) that his marriage has irretrievably broken down. How extraordinarily immature he is: all heart and no intellect.

---

* *Speaking for Themselves: The Personal Letters of Winston and Clementine Churchill*, ed. Mary Soames (1998).
† *Churchill's Doctor: A Biography of Lord Moran* by Dr Richard Lovell (1993).

1 July 1994

William Shawcross[*] tells me that Hartley is gently declining at Friston and is unlikely to come to London again. He is not apparently unhappy and his mind is clear – except that he asks the same questions over and over again. All this saddens me. Our friendship has lasted for more than forty years.

An amusing, affectionate card from Eric Anderson thanking me for my good wishes about his move to Lincoln College.

4 July 1994

Dine with Martin and Gay Charteris.[†] Martin mourns the abandonment or sale of the Royal Yacht *Britannia*; he loves her as much as he loves the Queen.

One important and encouraging piece of news. Eric Anderson has been tapeing the Queen Mother's reminiscences; so far there are five hours of them. What an inspiration.

6 July 1994

To Glyndebourne. The new opera house is agreeable enough outside except for a large and ugly tower. Inside it is superb: elegant, spacious, airy, comfortable seats, legroom, with tiers of boxes in the classical tradition. The acoustics are splendid. Well pleased with the opera: *Eugene Onegin*.

14 July 1994

I am so touched when William Shawcross tells me that he wants to give a party for my seventieth birthday. That will be a splendid way of gathering friends from the worlds of letters and journalism.

20 July 1994

John Fretwell tells me that members of the Foreign Office have been warned to tell me of no new appointments – 'Or if you must, warns the PUS's office, so that we know when the news is coming out.'

Cabinet reshuffle his evening. Apparently William Waldegrave is safe.

21 July 1994

In the Cabinet reshuffle, John Patten and Peter Brooke go, but William Waldegrave moves to Agriculture. Jean Trumpington also survives, which

---

[*] (b. 1946), son of Hartley Shawcross, writer, journalist and lecturer on international policy; author of the official life of the Queen Mother (2009).
[†] The Hon. Gay Charteris (1919–2017), second dau. of David, 1st Viscount Margesson (1890–1965), Chief Whip to four Conservative Prime Ministers.

is good. The biggest surprise is Cranborne to be Leader of the House of Lords with a seat in the Cabinet: he was much liked as Under-Secretary for Defence. I am pleased that Nicholas Soames is promoted to Minister of State for Defence, and even more so that Jonathan Aitken enters the Cabinet as Chief Secretary to the Treasury. I talk to Jonathan, who tells me that all three junior Defence Ministers have been promoted to the Cabinet together; Malcolm Rifkind, the Secretary of State, can be proud of his nursery.

10 August 1994

Nicholas Shakespeare[*] telephones from the *Evening Standard* to ask who is going to edit my Journals. I tell him that one day Weidenfeld & Nicolson would like to publish them, but no decision has been made about an editor. Or is likely to be for some time. The one quality one wants in an editor is that he should be younger than the diarist – or both diarist and editor might die at about the same time.

I read John Betjeman's letters, well edited by his daughter Candida Lycett Green.[†] They take his life up to 1951. He was very pro-Éamon de Valera[‡] when at our legation in Dublin during the war; though this was probably in Britain's interest.

25 August 1994

Robert Rhodes James talks to me about his plan to write a book on the constitutional influence of George VI.[§] He emphasises that it is not a response to Andrew Roberts' hostile portrait in *Eminent Churchillians*.

3 September 1994

At a concert in Brussels, after which I meet Ted Heath. I ask him what he thought of the Mahler symphony. He says: 'It is a rotten work, not worth doing, all that noise and all those chords. I once asked a very famous conductor why he had included it in his repertoire, instead of Haydn or Mozart. He replied that his orchestras were incapable of Haydn or Mozart – but could manage Mahler.'

Others I see include Young Winston.[¶] He tells me he has just made a speech

---

* (b. 1957), novelist and biographer.
† (1942–2014), author and maker of television documentaries.
‡ (1882–1975), Irish statesman. Taoiseach 1937–48, 1951–4, 1957–9; President of the Republic of Ireland 1959–73.
§ *A Spirit Undaunted: The Political Role of George VI* (1999).
¶ Winston Spencer-Churchill (1940–2010), son of Randolph and grandson of Winston; Conservative politician. MP for Stretford 1970–83; and for Davyhulme 1983–97.

in which he said: 'When people ask me why we are not good Europeans, I tell him to look at the war cemeteries of Europe.'

7 September 1994

I hear that the jaunty, irreverent tone of Andrew Roberts' *Eminent Churchillians* may have provoked Robert Salisbury to withdraw his permission for Andrew to write the life of the 3rd Marquess based on the archives at Hatfield. If this does happen, I shall write to Robert asking him to reconsider. Andrew's biography of Halifax was a perfectly respectable book.

12 September 1994

John Smith, former MP for the Cities of London and Westminster, and a contemporary at New College after the war, says that I should be a Fellow of the college. I point out to him that, having given a handsome benefaction for the Mound Garden, I could never accept an honorary Fellowship in case I were to be accused of buying it. John has been re-reading his Oxford diaries, which he is going to deposit at Eton. He once asked me to dine, saying that he was sure I would like to sit next to the daughter of a baronet. I said: 'What was the year of his creation?'

14 September 1994

Hugo Vickers calls for me at 3.30 and we motor down to see the Duchess of York at her home near Sunningdale. Soon after we arrive there is a thunderstorm and rain as heavy as I have seen in England. Fergie has been out riding with the children and comes in late and a bit dishevelled – also rather depressed. But she cheers up hugely throughout our visit.

The usual nursery tea, where I am greeted with shouts of 'Ken, Ken,' from Beatrice and Eugenie. There is the biggest, richest chocolate cake I have ever seen, and all sorts of other things such as crumpets, sausages, sardines and fish fingers.

Fergie has both sides of her correspondence with Andrew: when he was away she wrote to him every day. She also has the letters written to her by the Queen. She goes on: 'I also have Prince Philip's letters, telling me that I have let down The Firm. In one of them he wrote that he had been reading a book about Edwina Mountbatten, and that my conduct reminded him of hers.'

19 September 1994

Denis Healey tells me that he wonders whether he would not have been wise to become an Oxford don rather than a politician – although he did not miss becoming Prime Minister by much.

25 September 1994

I give Clare Hollingsworth* lunch at the Ark. She despairs of Chris Patten as the democratic champion of democracy in Hong Kong. The Chinese spit when mentioning his name. Lord MacLehose,† the former Governor, was sent out by the Government on a secret mission of guidance, but could make no impression on him.

27 September 1994

Long, exhilarating talk with Isaiah Berlin about Oxford's denial of an honorary degree for Margaret Thatcher. The problem began earlier when Hugh Dacre put up Ali Bhutto,‡ which proved controversial. Until then nobody had much minded who received an honorary degree though there were unsuccessful protests about Cecil Rhodes§ and President Truman.¶ Bhutto was denied it by seventy votes to seventy-two. Then two voters confessed that they were not entitled to vote. But it was too late – and in any case undesirable – to give Bhutto an honorary degree on a tie. From that time, it was decided not to give honorary degrees to active politicians, though Christopher Soames 'slipped through the net' for his settlement of Rhodesia.

Then came Thatcher's rejection in 1985. Margaret behaved very well. She telephoned the Vice-Chancellor, Pat Neill,** and said: 'I hope you didn't mind too much.'

As for Heath's defeat for the Chancellorship of Oxford, he minded very much. He thought that Robert Blake should have stood down, both as the lesser man and not to split the Conservative vote. As both Ted and Roy Jenkins were Balliol men, the Master, Anthony Kenny,†† invited Ted to tea and Jenkins to drinks after dinner. While Ted was having tea, someone appeared and told him that he had come second. He took it well: 'Oh, these things happen.' Then the man appeared again and said: 'I am sorry to have misled

---

* (1911–2017), journalist. The first war correspondent to report the outbreak of World War II; travelling from Poland to Germany she spotted massed German forces on the Polish border and three days later they invaded.

† Sir Crawford Murray MacLehose, Baron MacLehose of Beoch (1917–2000), Governor of Hong Kong 1971–82.

‡ (1928–79), Prime Minister of Pakistan 1973–7.

§ (1853–1902), Prime Minister of the Cape Colony in South Africa 1890–96; established the Rhodes Scholarships at Oxford University.

¶ Harry S. Truman (1884–1972), President of the US 1945–53.

** Patrick Neill, Baron Neill of Bladen (1926–2016), Vice-Chancellor of Oxford University 1985–9.

†† Sir Anthony Kenny (b. 1931), Master of Balliol Coll., Oxford 1978–89.

you. In fact you came third.' Ted has never since talked to Isaiah because he voted for Jenkins.

Isaiah says somewhat maliciously: 'Ted learned to live like a gentleman at Balliol.' He adds that Clarissa Avon always liked Ted, because he was loyal to Anthony.

2 October 1994

Read James Lees-Milne's *Mingled Measure: Diaries 1953–1972*. A curious blend of acute observation of people and places, self-absorption and malicious gossip. I dislike his occasional cruelties when writing about friends and his extreme right-wing views. But he has a Kilvert-like* touch in describing the countryside; has a vast knowledge of churches, houses and vicissitudes of families; and is the match of John Aubrey[†] in the spicy anecdote.

18 October 1994

I talk to King Constantine about Jonathan Dimbleby's[‡] book on Prince Charles. We agree that it cannot do the Prince any good and almost certainly will bring him into public contempt. It surprises Tino when I say that unless Charles and Diana divorce before the death of the Queen, Diana must become Queen Consort. The King cannot deny that Dimbleby's book was a gigantic error. It might have been worse had certain political passages not been removed from the earlier drafts, e.g. that the Prince was opposed to cuts in the Armed Forces. Yesterday the Prince took his two sons to a children's meet of the Beaufort: an error of judgement, not because foxhunting is necessarily cruel, but because over half the country thinks it is so – and he will one day have to reign without controversy over the entire nation.

26 October 1994

Richard Evans[§] tells me that he has never been offered a seat on the Governing Body of Repton, his old school, since he told the Chairman, in answer to a question, that he was sending his own boys to Eton. Repton, he rightly says, is now a regional school; and that is the reason it has such a low academic standard, as revealed in recent A-Level statistics. Richard was bold enough to tell the Chairman that Eton offered both a better education and

---

* Francis Kilvert (1840–1879), clergyman remembered for his diaries recording rural life.
† (1626–97), antiquary and writer, best known for his *Brief Lives*.
‡ (b. 1944), television and radio current affairs presenter; his biography of Prince Charles was published in 1995.
§ Sir Richard Evans (1928–2012), Ambassador to the People's Republic of China 1984–8.

opportunities to meet and make friends with cleverer and more interesting boys. That is brutal but true.

28 October 1994
Poor Jonathan Aitken has been accused of corruption by Mohamed Al-Fayed* because it seems that some of a large bill at the Ritz in Paris was paid for him by an Arab business associate. I hope he survives. He is not the sort of person to cadge, nor of course does he need to.

31 October 1994
Dine with Nigel Jaques at Brooks's. Having given up his Eton house, he is not known to the boys. When taking a junior division, one boy said: 'I think you taught my father, Sir.' Nigel confirmed this was so. Boy: 'Well, you haven't got on very far, have you, Sir?'

1 November 1994
Jonathan Aitken seems increasingly embroiled in whether he paid his own bill or had it paid for him by Arabs at the Ritz in Paris. Fayed seems determined to destroy him.

5 November 1994
Staying at Blagdon with the Ridleys. Princess Margaret is a fellow guest. She agrees with me that the Prince and Princess of Wales <u>must</u> divorce. 'But Charles simply won't listen to my advice. As I talked to him, I noticed his eyes roaming round the room.'

PM minded very much that the Dimbleby book about the Prince came out during the Queen's visit to Russia. The journalists covering the tour were only looking for disasters. 'When I talked to a journalist so that he could write a book about me, I made sure that he showed it to me before publication.'

PM returned recently to Royal Lodge to find the Queen Mother being interviewed by Eric Anderson, accompanied by a tape recorder. This leads me to say that when I talked to the QM several times at Clarence House for *KGV* I thought that even note-taking would upset her, so I prepared my questions carefully beforehand, then trusted to memory. PM: 'And then I suppose you rushed to the loo to write it all down?' Clever of her.

When I mention King George VI's habit of wearing his bearskin for a few days before the Trooping of the Colour, even when gardening, she says: 'Yes,

---

* (b. 1929), Egyptian business magnate.

I used to wear his bearskin too – and the crown.' From her expression I think I know what she wants to convey.

'People are very unkind about Dickie Mountbatten. He was quite harmless. My father used to prick his balloon and everyone would laugh – "Poor old Dickie."'

Her maid is the one who found a man in the Queen's bedroom and exclaimed: 'Bloody 'ell, what's going on 'ere?'

PM shares my dislike of the Festival of Remembrance each year at the Albert Hall and refuses to go. It is the mixture of sentiments that offends her.

She does not much like opera, preferring ballet. But she was impressed listening to a broadcast of *Rheingold* the other night.

As I am leaving tomorrow morning before PM will be up I say goodnight and goodbye. She says: 'Haven't we had a nice time.'

20 November 1994
Charles Guthrie tells me that he hates all the glitter of the State Opening of Parliament – it is in his capacity as a General to the Queen that he attends.

21 November 1994
To Brooks's for the dinner given for me by Prince Eddie and Matthew Ridley. After drinking some champagne we move to what must be considered one of the most beautiful rooms in London, with a single long table beautifully set out. We sit down and Matthew proposes my health in a charming little speech. He recalls how we joined the army on the same day in 1943, the beginning of our long friendship; how I dedicated a book to him, and other literary themes. In reply, I recall the link of the army and other Services that binds nearly all of us. I mention that Jean Trumpington was exposed to a greater peril than any of us – as one of Lloyd George's Land Girls. I end by saying how grateful, moved and humble I feel.

12 December 1994
Alexander Stockton tells me that when his grandfather went out to Algiers as Resident Minister during the war Winston said to him: 'You will wear uniform, of course.' Harold replied: 'No, there are too many generals there.' Winston: 'I see nothing between the baton and the bowler.'

15 December 1994
Christmas card from the Duchess of York with an enchanting photograph of her two little daughters playing with a dolphin. It is signed ('with love') by both Fergie and Andrew. Could this mean a reconciliation?

1995

On 20 January the first MORI poll of the year showed that the Conservatives had cut Labour's lead from thirty-nine points to twenty-nine. Neil Kinnock resigned from Parliament on 16 February to take up a role as a European Commissioner. Barings Bank collapsed on 26 February. The Queen and the Duke of Edinburgh visited Northern Ireland on 9 March for the first time since the IRA ceasefire. On 20 March the Queen arrived in Cape Town for the first royal visit to South Africa for nearly fifty years. The fiftieth anniversary of VE Day was celebrated across the UK on 8 May. Harold Wilson died on 24 May. On 22 June John Major resigned as leader of the Conservative Party, but not as Prime Minister, and sought re-election to assert his authority over dissidents. On 4 July John Major won the Conservative leadership election by 218 votes to John Redwood's eighty-nine. On 27 July the Conservative government's majority dropped to 9 seats as the Liberal Democrats won the Littleborough and Saddleworth by-election. The Conservative MP Alan Howarth defected to Labour on 7 October, cutting the government's majority to 7 seats. Alec Douglas-Home died on 9 October. On 20 November the Princess of Wales gave a candid interview on Panorama; *the Queen wrote to the Prince and Princess of Wales on 20 December urging them to divorce as soon as possible. The Conservative majority fell to 5 seats when Emma Nicholson defected to the Liberal Democrats on 29 November.*

7 January 1995

The *Spectator* contains a most indiscreet interview by Martin Charteris, including a remark that the Duchess of York is 'vulgar, vulgar, vulgar'. I am sure that he thought he was talking off the record. He will be tremendously embarrassed.

9 January 1995

An interesting talk with Hugh Dacre about the failure to give A.L. Rowse any sort of honour under the Crown. It springs from opposition from fellow academics, who maintain that Rowse has produced nothing of note for forty years. Those who have pleaded on his behalf – such as John Grigg and myself – are not academics, so carry no weight with the professionals. Rowse is hated in All Souls for his perpetual self-vaunting, even at breakfast: hence the failure of the college to elect him to a Distinguished Person Fellowship. The younger Fellows dislike him. He has also written insulting letters to people, many of whom he has thus unnecessarily alienated.

A good remark about All Souls: 'The Fellows change, but the guests remain the same.'

10 January 1995

To Pratt's for a drink. A barrister tells me that the Queen Mother came to dine in the Middle Temple one evening some years ago, when talk turned to Britain's entry to the Common Market. The conversation seemed to be somewhat at cross-purposes. It emerged that the Queen Mother thought they were talking about the future of Aintree. She also said: 'The Boots are coming to see me.' She meant the Wellington family. Talking of King George VI, she said: 'I have done my duty all my life and I shall soon be with my husband again.'

14 January 1995

To St Catherine's, Oxford, for the lunch given for Prince Philip, the Visitor. He is in an amiable mood, and mention of my tree by the new Master, Lord Plant,* leads to some interesting talk on replanting trees at Windsor.

After lunch we walk out to look at the two cedar trees – mine and a reserve put in by the college in case the transplanted one failed. They are about the same size, but unfortunately too close together. So one will have to come down. I offer to pay for this to be done. I am told that the money I gave for the Rose Medical Prize in memory of my brother Toby has fructified and is now enough for a scholarship or a bursary. Would I approve? Of course.

On my way home I look in at New College. The plants are beginning to grow round my steps on the Mound, and the effect is pleasing. It will be even better in May or June.

25 January 1995

A smartly dressed messenger from Buckingham Palace delivers a large white envelope. As I am signing for it I ask him who sent it. 'Sarah,' he replied. In the package are two charming letters from Fergie. One thanking me for what

---

* Raymond Plant, Baron Plant of Highfield (b. 1945), Master of St Catherine's Coll., Oxford 1994–9.

I wrote about her in my column after the Martin Charteris interview, the other in reply to my personal letter. With the world supposedly against her, she seems extraordinarily grateful for any support. Also enclosed is a copy of a letter of apology from Martin Charteris. Fergie has accepted his apology with warmth and understanding, so the matter seems to have been settled with good grace and dignity.

25 February 1995

Richard Luce, Vice-Chancellor of the University of Buckingham, has asked me to the ceremonies for conferring honorary degrees on Casper Weinberger and Lord Porter OM, the Nobel Prizeman.*

By train to Milton Keynes, where I am met by a car and driven to the Vice-Chancellor's house for coffee before the proceedings begin at 11.30. Denis and Margaret Thatcher are here, she as Chancellor of the university. Denis slopes off after a few minutes, I suppose to play golf on this lovely day. I am shocked by Margaret's appearance: thin, drawn, rather shrunk. She is as always elegantly turned out and friendly. But humour is not among her qualities. I am hugely taken by Casper Weinberger, whom I met briefly at Leeds when he received a degree from the Duchess of Kent a few years ago. He is a dynamo. He amazes me by saying that not only has he read my *KGV*, but that he reviewed it for a San Francisco newspaper.

We walk to the local church of St Peter and St Paul, full of young graduates and their parents. As each is given a scroll and a handshake from Mrs Thatcher in robes of blue and gold, a photographer snaps them. Nearly all are well dressed with shining shoes.

Richard Luce gives an excellent short address. In bestowing degrees Mrs Thatcher confines her Latin to the phrase '*honoris causa*'. Her predecessor, Quintin Hailsham, performed the whole rite in Latin. I wonder what the students make of her justification of the Falklands campaign and her admonishing them to be resolute. With Cap Weinberger an honorand, she could do nothing gentler.

Cap alone returns thanks. He takes up her belligerent theme, recalling how she used to say, 'The possibility of defeat does not exist.' I wonder if he knows that Thatcher borrowed it from Queen Victoria.

We lunch in a marquee off quail. Then with Lord Porter I go back to Milton Keynes and so to London by train. Porter, most genial and forthcoming, tells

---

* Sir Richard Luce, Baron Luce of Adur (b. 1936), Vice-Chancellor of Buckingham University 1992–6. Casper Weinberger (1917–2006), American Sec. of Defense 1981–87. George Porter, Baron Porter of Luddenham (1920–2002), awarded the Nobel Prize in Chemistry in 1967.

me that the Royal Society offers FRS to a Prime Minister only if he or she has held office at No. 10 for two or more terms.

26 February 1995
Barings have crashed again. What exactly happened in 1890? I consult Philip Ziegler's excellent book on Barings and my Rothschild files.

2 March 1995
Talk to John Witheridge, the Eton Conduct, who tells me of a forty-foot painting of the crucifixion done by a boy to hang in College Chapel at Easter. He confirms what I learned directly from Bob Runcie, that the then Archbishop disapproved of his going to Eton. Indeed, I recall that Bob did not really believe that Etonians had souls.

14 March 1995
Roy Harrod,* Maynard Keynes's original biographer in 1951, objected to Harold Macmillan's proposal to bring out an updated biography in the light of new material and including details of Keynes's homosexuality. Harrod wrote a threatening letter to Harold Macmillan, more or less saying, 'What about the relationship of Maynard and your brother Daniel?'† Nevertheless, the new biography by Robert Skidelsky did appear and last year we gave him the Wolfson Prize for Volume Two of his life of Keynes.

28 March 1995
The Court Circular again reports that the Prince of Wales has received the Prime Minister at St James's Palace. I ask the Palace Press Officer, Allan Percival,‡ at whose request this meeting took place. He says: 'By agreement, two or three times a year, to keep in touch.' It is all wrong.

30 March 1995
At a dinner at Spencer House for Shimon Peres,§ I sit next to Lord Mishcon.¶ As I know that he acts for the Princess of Wales, I ask him whether he has read the Dimbleby book. He has and thinks, 'It has done the Prince of Wales no good.' He continues: 'Some say it was a justified answer to Morton's book

---

* Sir Roy Harrod (1900–78), economist; official biographer of John Maynard Keynes.
† See D.R. Thorpe, *Supermac: The Life of Harold Macmillan*, pp. 594–6.
‡ (b. 1950), Press Sec. to the Prince of Wales 1993–6.
§ (1923–2016), Prime Minister of Israel 1995–6; President of Israel 2007–14.
¶ Victor Mishcon, Baron Mishcon of Lambeth (1915–2006), solicitor and Labour politician; his firm acted for Princess Diana in her divorce.

on the Princess, but it has had the opposite effect.' From her solicitor, that verges on the indiscreet.

Shimon Peres makes a boring speech ruminating about the chance of a peace treaty with Syria, but at least credits President Assad* of Syria with a sense of humour. Assad recently said to him: 'I can't understand why everyone says I'm surrounded by yes-men. Whenever I say "no" all the people around me say "no" too.'

Roy Jenkins drives me home. He muses on why so many couples do not marry nowadays but simply live together. I suggest it goes back to fiscal legislation when he was Chancellor. Curiously, he does not laugh.

1 April 1995

I have lunch in Bruton with Peter Morrison.† Denis Thatcher is also a guest. His talk and laughter seem rather forced. He says to me: 'Margaret thinks the buggers will get in at the next election.'

I watch the Boat Race with Peter: a Cambridge victory. We talk of the Prince of Wales, whose differences with Peter at the Department of the Environment are recorded in the Dimbleby book. Peter: 'He is unfit to rule. If he succeeds soon, he should abdicate as soon as possible in favour of Prince William, then go ahead with Camilla.' This view, unthinkable five years ago, is now commonplace.

23 April 1995

Anthony Shone, Selwyn Lloyd's nephew, telephones me from the Wirral to tell me that he was passing Marlborough House the other day and noticed a contractor's notice on the gates marked WALLIS. So she got there in the end!

25 April 1995

William and Caroline Waldegrave to dine at Bertorelli. The friendship of the Waldegraves for Jonathan Dimbleby has cooled considerably since he published his book on the Prince of Wales. He does not realise how much he has damaged the Prince's reputation. The Prince showed Caroline his correspondence with Dimbleby, in which she begged him not to include certain passages, but to no effect. Camilla Parker-Bowles was treated abominably in the book, but only after the Prince had admitted on TV to committing adultery with her. What has our Royal Family come to?

---

* Hafez al-Assad (1930–2000), President of Syria 1971–2000.
† Sir Peter Morrison (1944–95), Conservative politician. MP for Chester 1974–92; PPS to Margaret Thatcher July–Nov. 1990.

On Victor Rothschild, I wonder why he was so concerned about whispers of his association with Blunt in November 1979: hardly anything appeared in the Press. William: 'Journalists were deterred from writing about the possibility that Victor might have been a Soviet agent by the laws of libel. He wanted to clear his name so that these lies should not be published after his death.'

27 April 1995

I see Fergie again at Sunningdale. She talks about herself and her marriage and her relations with members of the Royal Family: an astounding succession of confidences to someone who likes her but has never been an intimate.

She realises she has made mistakes, and even, as Martin Charteris said, that she is vulgar. 'But if I am cheerful and noisy, it is not because I am over-confident, but because I am insecure.' She has adjusted to this in the face of hostility from all the Royal Family except the Queen. The worst enemies are 'all those failed officers who become courtiers. They are so boring, too, talking only about the best route from London to Sandringham.' Her children are the best link she has with the Queen. 'I have taught them to hug their granny when they see her.'

9 May 1995

An enchanting letter from the Queen Mother, written in her own hand, even though she is almost blind. 'At the moment the events leading up to the anniversary of VE Day bring back many memories of those now far-off days, though sometimes they seem very close, and how close we all were to each other then in this dear old country.'

15 May 1995

Robert Wade-Gery says he cannot remember a time when the Civil Service had less confidence in a Government or were more obstructive towards it.

30 May 1995

Robert Runcie to lunch at Claridge's, very spry and youthful. We begin with some talk about the war, and agree that at the time we did not perhaps appreciate just how concerned were our parents for our safety. He tells me a story about his training. A Regimental Sergeant-Major barked: 'Wake up man. You are marching like a Free Frenchman.' Company Sergeant-Major: 'He is a Free Frenchman, Sir.'

Robert agrees with me that the Prince of Wales must divorce to avoid even more catastrophic consequences. Coming from a former Archbishop of Canterbury that is something.

3 June 1995

I stay for the weekend with David* and Pamela Hicks. Pammy refers to Prince Charles as Charles Wales. Princess Alexandra told Pammy that she never argues with him, so terrible is his rage. He never consults the Queen. 'There has been a complete break.'

Pammy says that she sometimes writes to the Queen to tell her things of supposed interest. 'The only time she has ever replied was when I sent my sympathy after one of her dogs had been killed by a Clarence House corgi. She then wrote six pages.'

Prince William is tiresome, always attracting attention to himself. Hardly surprising when he is so spoilt by the tug-of-war of his parents, and by courtiers, servants and detectives.

9 June 1995

Kenneth Baker tells me that at his very first Cabinet meeting, Heseltine dramatically resigned, a startling introduction.

17 June 1995

To lunch with Denis and Edna Healey at their home at Alfriston, near Lewes. I am surprised by how spacious a place it is – large, well-kept gardens, a big house full of books: all comfortable and settled.

Edna consults me about various sources for her forthcoming book on Buckingham Palace. Denis describes the Queen Mother at dinner saying: 'Think of all that port going down people's throats whenever the loyal toast is drunk. How good for the nation's health!'

When Buckingham Palace was first opened to the public, the numbers took everyone by surprise. They had to send to Coutts for clerks to come and count all the money.

19 June 1995

The memorial service for Arnold Goodman at the Liberal Jewish Synagogue, St John's Wood. One of the most moving memorial services I have ever attended. It is a pleasant, airy synagogue with some remarkable differences from Orthodox practice: women unsegregated, hats for men optional and much of the service in English. Noel Annan, in a white-silk skullcap like a Pope, delivers an exemplary address, humorous, poignant and perceptive. Afterwards Isaiah Berlin says to me: 'I must book him for mine.' Jonathan Aitken as debonair and relaxed as ever in spite of being under renewed

---

* David Hicks (1929–98), interior decorator.

parliamentary pressure for his involvement in allegedly selling arms to the Middle East before he joined the Government. He is off to lunch with Henry Kissinger. The Hebrew parts of the service are haunting. Hebrew is surely the supreme language of melancholy, though not I think of rejoicing.

21 June 1995

The Carringtons are going for the weekend to Royal Lodge. Peter was, alas, rather shocked when he saw the Queen Mother at the Garter lunch on Monday: frail, very blind and in pain from her leg. Oh dear, I hope I am given one last sight of her at Walmer Castle in three weeks' time.

Increasingly Peter likes Jim Callaghan, who is apprehensive at having to eulogise Harold Wilson at his memorial service in Westminster Abbey shortly. 'Oh dear,' he said, 'all that obituary stuff has appeared.'

On current politics, Peter thinks that John Major is virtually finished. Lamont may challenge Major for the leadership this autumn, then Portillo[*] and Heseltine will do a deal, with Heseltine emerging as leader.

Story of Mrs Thatcher who, when she met Chairman Mao,[†] asked him out of politeness an initial question about what he thought of the world outlook. He spoke without interruption for twenty minutes. Mrs T. then interrupted him with a rap of her ring on the table. Chairman Mao said: 'I have not finished,' and continued for another twenty minutes. In the midst of the second instalment Peter passed her a note: 'Talking too much, as usual, Margaret.'

23 June 1995

Douglas Hurd is soon to resign as Foreign Secretary. I would have welcomed him as PM.

27 June 1995

John Redwood[‡] has resigned as Welsh Secretary to challenge John Major for the party leadership. He seems to have the most ghastly lot of supporters.

3 July 1995

Nico Henderson tells me a Rab Butler story I have not heard before. Robert Runcie, preaching at Trinity, took the crucifixion as his theme. Afterwards Rab said to him: 'Such a sad story.'

---

[*] Michael Portillo (b. 1953), former Conservative politician. Sec. of State for Defence 1995–7; television presenter, known for his series on great railway journeys.

[†] Mao Zedong (1893–1976), Chairman of the Communist Party of China 1943–76.

[‡] The Rt Hon. John Redwood (b. 1951), Conservative politician. Sec. of State for Wales 1993–5.

4 July 1995

The result of the Tory leadership contest announced. The PM is safe. Both the *Telegraph* and the *Sunday Telegraph* were virulently against him.

Major 218

Redwood 89

Abstentions 8

Spoilt Papers 12

In social terms the leadership contest saw John Major, born a class or two below Redwood, as the traditional liberal-minded gentleman; Redwood clings to lower-middle-class beliefs such as hanging.

12 July 1995

To the memorial service for Harold Wilson in Westminster Abbey. The Prince of Wales and King Constantine attend. George Tonypandy escorts Mary Wilson. The lessons read by the PM, the Speaker and Tony Blair, leader of the Labour Party. Jim Callaghan adequate but was obviously embarrassed at having to deliver a eulogy. One or two jokes – 'He was a brilliant party manager. There is nothing wrong with party management. It is how well one does it that matters.' And: 'Harold was an optimist who carried a raincoat.' I am glad a poem by Mary Wilson has been included, well read by David Attenborough.*

16 July 1995

To Coldharbour with Christopher Northbourne. Change into a black tie and we drive to Walmer Castle in the evening light to dine with the Queen Mother. There are no guards or spectators, just that delectable toy castle with the Lord Warden's flag flying from the turret. We are met by an ADC and taken up medieval stairs and along passages to the drawing room.

The Queen Mother looks wonderfully summery in pink, with pearls and a large ruby brooch. One or two hairpins are sticking out, which gives her an informal touch. The corgis are on guard. She raises her hands in welcome and says how lovely it is to see me again. We sit down for a minute or two, then she asks whether I have been here before. She then leads me onto the terrace with the view over to France.

The dining-room table, lit by candles, looks very pretty. In the centre is a large bowl of pink roses, each the size of a grapefruit. The table mats are of watercolours done by Prince Charles. There is my favourite eagle claret jug. At dinner the QM talks of the Cecils and 'your wonderful book'.

---

* Sir David Attenborough (b. 1926), naturalist and broadcaster.

After dinner the QM insists that we see the room where the Duke of Wellington died. And so we say goodbye to the most remarkable, enchanting woman of our time. She has had three full days of engagements on the eve of her ninety-fifth birthday, yet never flags for an instant.

9 August 1995

My third visit to Bayreuth with Prince Eddie, after 1954 and 1983. The English have been deterred this year by the rate of exchange: half of what it was twelve years ago.

Tonight's *Rheingold* is dominated by the majestic presence and singing of John Tomlinson as Wotan. Donner and Froh also do well; and although I like the voice of Siegfried Jerusalem as Loge, he lacks the elfin lightness of touch and mischief demanded by the role. A superb Alberich and Mime. All in all a superb cast. James Levine* conducts with magic precision. But the beauty of the 1954 production has burned into my soul.

10 August 1995

Walküre tonight. John Tomlinson's Wotan never flags for an instant: he must almost be in the Hotter class. During the second interval we are invited to a light supper by Wolfgang Wagner. We are invited to help ourselves from big dishes of cold meats, smoked salmon, salads. Wolfgang says that until the 1950s *Tristan* was the least popular of his grandfather's operas. He prefers the mellowness of the German brass to the sharp tones of the French.

12 August 1995

Tonight it is *Siegfried* with Wolfgang Schmidt† in the title role. He looks as though he has wandered out of a production of *Billy Budd*. A good description by Eddie of the forge scene – 'Siegfried potters about as if he is making a model aeroplane.' At the end of the opera there is applause for the singers, but only Tomlinson's Wotan is received in triumph.

14 August 1995

To *Götterdämmerung* by the old-fashioned hotel bus. Eddie, who is obsessed by the timing of the operas, tells me that this year's *Ring* was much on the slow side, not least in the scene with Siegfried and Brünnhilde, neither of

---

* Siegfried Jerusalem (b. 1940), German operatic tenor, renowned for his Wagnerian roles. James Levine (b. 1943), American conductor; Music Dir. of the Metropolitan Opera, New York 1976–2016.

† Wolfgang Schmidt (b. 1955), German operatic tenor.

whom has good voices, but their disparity of size – a wee Siegfried and a strapping Brünnhilde – dispels both majesty and magic. So too do their absurd costumes.

17 August 1995

Back in London, Eddie is disturbed by what I tell him of Princess Alice's unhappiness at having to leave Barnwell and of our conversation when I sat next to her at the Gloucesters'. Barnwell, with its big staff, costs £150,000 a year to run, and Richard simply could not afford it. Nor in recent years has Princess Alice had the strength to garden. Prince Eddie also has an eye on economy. As always, he likes talking about his Freemasons and laughs when I talk of seeing men with shallow attaché cases making their way up St James's Street, 'not obviously on their way to White's.' He receives quite a lot of mail about the Masons from people having rows with their neighbours, who blame it on 'a Masonic plot'.

19 August 1995

Today and tomorrow are celebrations for the end of the war fifty years ago. I am glad not to be taking part: that mixture of thanksgiving, patriotism and pageantry is too sentimental for my taste.

I visit Stowe with Edward Tomkins.* He was at Ampleforth as a boy, but became a governor of Stowe. First to the Corinthian Arch, with a striking view of the main buildings framed in it about half a mile away. A fine avenue, part of which was to have extended from Stowe to London, all on property belonging to the Dukes of Buckingham.† Inside the Palladian main building is a notice: 'Under the Marriages Act of 1949, the Blue Room, the Marble Hall and the Music Room are licensed for the solemnisation of marriages.' Indeed, there is one today, with tables set out for a wedding breakfast. In another room are boards bearing the names of boys who have won scholarships to Oxford and Cambridge – they include Noel Annan and Tony Quinton. No names after 1984. Was it because the school had few successes to record? I wonder how beneficial is the effect on the boys of living in such magnificent buildings: probably not a lot.

Edward tells me that an English nanny said to one of the Rothschilds: 'Drink up your Lafite or you will have no water.'

---

* Sir Edward Tomkins (1915–2007), Ambassador to France 1972–5.
† The line began with Richard Temple-Grenville, 1st Duke of Buckingham and Chandos (1776–1839), landowner and politician.

1 September 1995

Jean Trumpington gives me lunch at the Savoy restaurant. We have a table overlooking the river. Much Royal talk, for the VE and VJ celebrations have brought her many encounters. In Argentina, where she went for the FO, she heard good things about the Duke of York from our Ambassador. It seems that he was driving along when he saw a monument and asked what it was. He was told it was a memorial to the sailors who drowned on the cruiser *Belgrano* when sunk by our navy during the Falklands War. He said he wished to get out and pay his respects, which he did. The Argentinians were moved and impressed. Jean thinks this reflects well on Andrew, as indeed it does.

6 September 1995

Some lively talk at the Beefsteak with Roy Jenkins. He tells me how one day, finding himself with the Archbishops of Canterbury and York, Runcie and Habgood, he mentioned that he was going to the United States to give a lecture on Cardinal Newman.* Habgood turned to Runcie, as if Roy were not there: 'Do you think he knows anything about it?'

I tell Roy how pathetically grateful Habgood is for the £5,000 subscribed in York as a farewell present. Roy: 'Yes, and I notice that poor Runcie's address in St Albans is 26A something road, which is not very encouraging.'

10 October 1995

Robert Fellowes tells me that Sir Edward Ford once accompanied King George VI at a Buckingham Palace Garden Party. As the King was turning to go indoors he said to Edward: 'I forgot to thank the bandmaster.' Edward replied: 'Don't bother, Sir, I have done it myself.' The King: 'That is not the same thing at all.'

12 October 1995

To Baba Metcalfe's memorial service at the Chapel Royal, St James's. I sit next to Mollie Butler. Peter Carrington gives the address. He mentions the books on her father, Curzon, written by David Gilmour and myself.

Lunch at the Beefsteak. Sit next to Nigel Nicolson, who tells me such an interesting thing about my *KGV*. The Queen's Private Secretary, Philip Moore, was so annoyed at my having managed access to much Royal Archive material through Harold Nicolson's papers that Nigel was asked to hand over

---

* Cardinal John Henry Newman (1801–90), Catholic theologian; author of *Apologia Pro Vita Sua* (1864) and *The Dream of Gerontius* (1865).

all his father's KGV material. Rather weakly, he did so. But, of course, there is nothing of importance in the material which I did not publish.

14 October 1995

I am staying at West Wycombe Park with Sir Francis Dashwood.* There are Disraelian connections. Princess Margaret is also a guest. Looking at the bookcases, PM says that she has read most of Dizzy's novels; and that Moneypenny and Buckle† used to be a standard wedding present.

16 October 1995

To No. 11 Carlton House Terrace, once Mr Gladstone's house, for a party to mark Roy Jenkins' new biography of the Grand Old Man. He plays a recording of Mr Gladstone speaking: very indistinct but a resonant voice comes through. I can detect no trace of a Lancashire accent.

7 November 1995

I go to a Press conference at Burlington House given by David Hockney‡ before the private view of his show which opens tomorrow. He is cheerful. Comfortable, unpretentious, unexpectedly verbose. In answer to each question his sentences ramble on and on. There is scarcely a trace of Bradford in his voice: more a burr with a touch of California.

I then take a train to Eton to lunch with the Vice-Provost, Tim Card. The place never fails to enchant, and I stop to admire the autumn light on Fellows' Eyot and the river. Tim, remarkably like Oliver van Oss in build and vigour, has gone to some trouble to prepare a robust lunch. Eton gossip over lunch. Talk of the Fellows, some of whom are retiring. I say that William Waldegrave would love to be a Fellow. Tim: 'I think he would prefer to be Provost.'§ After lunch we see the excellent new exhibition on Eton and World War II in Brewhouse Gallery. Much about Linky v. Claude Elliott on air-raid shelters. Of the filmed interviews, Peter Carrington is most impressive when he describes how a tank crew lived together, and how two of his men had been unemployed – perhaps the root of Peter's Tory radical dislike of Thatcherism.

16 November 1995

Tony Lambton is horrified by the news that the Princess of Wales has

---

* Sir Francis Dashwood, 11th Bt (1925–2000), High Sheriff of Buckinghamshire 1976–7.
† Joint biographers of Disraeli.
‡ (b.1937), painter and stage designer.
§ Lord Waldegrave of North Hill became a Fellow of Eton in 2007 and Provost in 2009.

secretly negotiated an hour-long interview with the BBC, to be broadcast next Monday, without having informed the Palace. Obviously a tit-for-tat against the Prince. We shall be lucky if the monarchy lasts very long into the twenty-first century.

17 November 1995

Peter Pilkington telephones me in the evening to say that he will be in a list of 'working' peers to be announced tomorrow – as Conservative of course. How it will annoy all the other headmasters. I have heard elsewhere that John Lewis is not popular as HM at Eton – he displays no strength of personality – markedly so at the HMC.

20 November 1995

Dukie Hussey has been caused much embarrassment as the Chairman of the BBC, who was not even informed of tonight's television interview with the Princess of Wales; nor of course can he suppress it. The episode illustrates the impotence of his appointment – either he can sack the Director General or he can do nothing, with no other possible course of action.

21 November 1995

The Princess of Wales's TV interview seems to have been technically accomplished but horribly indiscreet – an admission of adultery with James Hewitt.*

22 November 1995

To No. 11 Downing Street for a cocktail party. The first person I see is Roy Jenkins, who tells me he has rarely been back here since ceasing to be Chancellor himself in 1970. He is proud of the collection of political cartoons of former Chancellors arranged by Jennifer on the top part of the staircase to the drawing room. But I think them vulgar and out of place there. We are both dismayed that the portraits of former Chancellors on the lower part of the staircase do not include Gladstone. I suggest that there must be a full-size one somewhere. Sure enough, we find it in the entrance hall: a Millais of Gladstone in Oxford DCL robes. It is a copy of the one in Christ Church given to Gladstone by his secretaries in 1895.

---

* (b. 1958), former Household Cavalry officer.

29 November 1995

I have a useful talk with my fellow Wolfson Prize judge, Averil Cameron.[*]
When she suggests that Roy Jenkins' book on Gladstone must be a strong
candidate, I say that I should prefer Colin Matthew's[†] edition of Mr Gladstone's diaries, with their superb introductory essays. She says that Roy
Jenkins would be very upset. I reply that his book, with no original research
and much borrowed from Matthew, is more a Whitbread Prize winner. In
any case, he has already acquired many of life's prizes.

4 December 1995

To Edinburgh for Alec Home's memorial service at St Giles Cathedral. St
Giles might almost be Roman Catholic or High Anglican: candles on the
Communion table, a large choir dressed in white with gold trimmings, processions, and for good measure a hymn by Cardinal Newman and a prayer
by Pusey[‡] (also a hymn by Cyril Alington.)

5 December 1995

To Frank Longford's ninetieth birthday party given by Antonia and Harold
Pinter. Nice to see all the family. Harold Pinter affably talks cricket with
me and I tell him of the remarkable career of Neville Cardus[§] as a protégé
of Cyril Alington. Endless speeches. When an unknown man gets up, I ask
Isaiah Berlin his name. 'I don't know. Some murderer, I expect.'

12 December 1995

I talk to Robert Runcie about the appointment of his old chaplain, John
Witheridge, to be Headmaster of Charterhouse.

21 December 1995

I give breakfast to Charles Guthrie at the Hyde Park Hotel. He tells me of the
four pieces of advice given by his RSM at Sandhurst:
1. Never get separated from your kit.
2. Never put your trust in the RAF.
3. Never march on Moscow.
4. Never become involved in the Balkans.

---

[*] Dame Averil Cameron (b. 1940), Warden of Keble Coll., Oxford 1994–2010.

[†] (1941–99), Professor of Modern History at Oxford University 1992–9; editor of the diaries
of Gladstone 1972–94; editor of the *DNB* 1992–9.

[‡] Edward Bouverie Pusey (1800–82), one of the leaders of the Oxford Movement.

[§] Sir Neville Cardus (1888–1975), writer and critic, especially on cricket and music, for the
Manchester Guardian.

The last of those rules we have broken. Of our 100,000 troops, 13,500 are in Yugoslavia and 15,000 in Ireland.

The army does not like the Prince of Wales. When Charles was received by him the other day, he complained of overwork, which is absurd. As for the Duke of York, is he a sailor or not?

It is revealed that the Queen has told Charles and Diana that they must divorce. Charles has let it be known that he wants to divorce – and will not remarry. No answer from Diana.

1996

*On 22 February the Conservative MP Peter Thurnham announced his resig-
nation from Parliament, reducing the Conservative Party's majority to 2 seats,
so since the general election the government lost 19 seats owing to resignations,
defections and by-election defeats. On 28 February the Princess of Wales
agreed to give the Prince of Wales a divorce, more than three years after their
separation. On 13 March a gunman killed sixteen children, their teacher and
himself in the Dunblane primary-school massacre – one of the young pupils
who escaped was Andy Murray, the future World No. 1 tennis player. On 17
April the Duke and Duchess of York announced their divorce. On 2 May the
Conservatives lost 578 seats in the local council elections. On 15 June a massive
IRA bomb devastated the centre of Manchester. The Prince and Princess of
Wales completed their divorce proceedings on 28 August and Diana, Princess
of Wales, lost her title of Her Royal Highness. On 30 November the Stone of
Scone was installed in Edinburgh Castle 700 years after it was removed by
Edward I.*

1 January 1996

I meet Princess Margaret at a house party in Sutton Courtenay, the village
where Asquith lived and is buried. She tells me: 'Very occasionally I sat next
to Winston Churchill, but when I talked to him, as we had been told to do,
he just grunted.'

8 January 1996

I talk to Miles Norfolk* about a CH in the New Year's Honours List for Archbishop Worlock.† It was not Miles who recommended him for it, 'but a group
of Staff officers rather than generals'. At one time Worlock was earmarked
to become Archbishop of Westminster, but, said Miles, 'He had no panache.'
He cultivated those in the Vatican who would help him – 'They were often

---

* Miles Fitzalan-Howard, 17th Duke of Norfolk (1915–2002).
† Archbishop Derek Worlock (1920–96), Archbishop of Liverpool 1976–96.

Irish, what I call the RASC of the Catholic Church. But it did Worlock no good.' 'I got Hume the job by talking to Archbishop Heim.* Worlock was disappointed but behaved well.'

The CH is in its way unique for a Catholic prelate. But Miles says that both Callaghan and Thatcher offered a peerage to Hume, who declined in order not to be drawn into party politics. 'He is astute and clever at playing the humble card. Only he could have persuaded the Queen to attend Vespers – she calls him "My Cardinal".'

9 January 1996
Graham C. Greene telephones to tell me he is to be the new Chairman of the British Museum in succession to David Windlesham. There was no formal ballot: the other trustees were consulted by David Attenborough, and Graham 'emerged'.

It is also announced this evening that Dukie Hussey is soon to retire as Chairman of the BBC. Graham says: 'The idea that he was a Thatcher crony is absurd. Douglas Hurd recommended him as a good man.'

The one foolish thing that Dukie did was to appoint John Birt† to be Director General without going through the usual advertising and consultation process. Graham had a blazing row with Nicky Gordon-Lennox after asking him: 'Why did you not legitimise Birt's appointment by advertising it?' Nicky replied: 'Because he was so obviously the best man.' That was a silly answer. Graham thinks that the man Dukie really wanted was Jonathan Dimbleby.

14 January 1996
Jean Trumpington has been told by the political correspondent of the *Glasgow Herald* that the Princess of Wales spent seventeen hours recording the notorious TV broadcast: she did each bit again and again until she had achieved the right degree of spurious sincerity.

19 January 1996
Four days before the first round of the Conservative leadership contest in November 1990, Margaret Thatcher made an official visit to Northern Ireland. As she walked into a room in Hillsborough, Peter Brooke, the Secretary of State, was watching the TV. The announcer was saying: 'Mr Douglas Hurd is to stand . . .' Peter at once turned the TV off – and so none of them heard

---

* Archbishop Bruno Heim (1911–2003), the Vatican's Apostolic Nuncio to Britain 1982–5.
† Sir John Birt, Baron Birt of Liverpool (b. 1944), Dir. Gen. of the BBC 1992–2000.

the next words '. . . should Mrs Thatcher be defeated.' What they did hear cast much gloom.

6 April 1996

Read Anthony Powell's *Temporary Kings*, the penultimate volume of *A Dance to the Music of Time* and one of the Widmerpool series I have never read before. I can barely finish it. So many convoluted relationships and so ill-written. Hugely inferior to Evelyn Waugh, and C.P. Snow for that matter.

3 May 1996

To the cinema at Notting Hill Gate to see Ian McKellen[*] in Shakespeare's *Richard III*. It has some resemblance to the original plot but is set in a Fascist or Nazi England of the 1930s. A lurid melodrama. Richard shouts: 'A horse, a horse, my kingdom for a horse' when his Bren gun breaks down. Everybody smoked throughout. I wonder why.

13 May 1996

Clarissa Avon telephones me for help in preparing an address to be given at Henry Colyton's[†] memorial service. I take the opportunity of asking her whether Arnold Goodman left her the Lucian Freud portrait of himself. No, he left it to Christopher Portman,[‡] whose affairs he managed and who is immensely rich. 'Such a waste,' Clarissa says. The money, about £400,000, went to Arnold's secretary. All Clarissa got were some volumes of Trollope, which she did not want. What a scandalous will: Clarissa did everything for him for years, yet he leaves her nothing.

Clarissa now lives in a part of Middleton Park near Bicester, rebuilt by Lutyens, as well as in Bryanston Square.

20 May 1996

I hear of David Cecil at New College, that behind those nervous flutterings lay a shrewd critical brain as a tutor. He was also unexpectedly witty at times. When one pupil asked him to define the difference between poetry and prose, he replied: 'Poets are better-looking.'

---

[*] Sir Ian McKellen (b. 1939), actor, the recipient of every major theatrical award in the UK.

[†] Henry Hopkinson, 1st Baron Colyton of Farway (1902–96), Conservative politician. MP for Taunton 1950–56.

[‡] 10th Viscount Portman (b. 1958), property developer.

29 May 1996

Robert Wade-Gery tells me that during the Falklands dispute, Al Haig,* the
US Secretary of State, came to a conference at No. 10. His delegation was
given the use of the Patronage Secretary's room, which was empty, it being a
Saturday. Haig was utterly bewildered by the flags pinned into large maps on
the wall of Britain and wondered what secrets they concealed. He was told
that they showed which bishops were in which dioceses, and for how long,
and where the next vacancies would be.

31 May 1996

Staying for the weekend with Paul Channon. Princess Margaret is a fellow
guest. When I tell her how the Royal burial ground at Frogmore is, in my
view, too accessible to the public, she says: 'I should like to be commemorat-
ed, but not buried.'†

PM says that Charles and Anne were well brought up, but the Queen was
too busy to bring up Andrew and Edward. She adds: 'How glad the family
will be to be rid of the wives, Diana and Fergie.'

10 June 1996

I read the diaries of Kenneth Williams.‡ He reveals a complicated character.
Although he writes endlessly about being homosexual, he is in fact a Puritan
with a horror of homosexual physical contact. With him it was almost entirely a matter of fantasy.

At one point he writes: 'I walked to the National Theatre – it is like a
terrible municipal housing estate and has nothing to do with theatre.' He
sees flaws in Anthony Powell's style: 'This writer is praised by critics for his
learning and his wit. His writing is full of literary pretensions and the narrative endlessly interrupted by authorial conceits.' Too true.

11 June 1996

Clarissa Avon tells me that the BBC are to do another TV film on Suez. She
is concerned to deny that Anthony was on drugs at the time and so incapable
of taking rational decisions. She has been to look at the medical records in
the Avon papers at Birmingham University, which bear her out. Nearer the
broadcast she will let me see them.

---

* Alexander Haig, US Sec. of State 1981–2.
† Princess Margaret was cremated at Slough Crematorium on 15 Feb. 2002, the fiftieth anniversary of her father's funeral, and her ashes were later interred in the George VI Chapel at St
George's, Windsor.
‡ (1926–88), comic actor.

To Oxford for the night. The undergraduates are coming out of the Examination Schools in their white ties, which sends a little shudder through me.

Walk to New College to look at the Mound. It is much less parched at the top than when I last saw it and a promising border of skimmia has been planted round the paved summit. The stone steps have weathered well and darkened.

25 June 1996

Marie-Lou de Zulueta complains about Robert Blake's *DNB* notice on Harold Macmillan. She says he has underestimated his influence on President Kennedy during the Cuban Missile Crisis, and was wrong to put down Macmillan's resignation in October 1963 to hypochondria.

5 July 1996

Peter Carrington sends his car to drive me to Bledlow. We motor to Garsington for a performance of Rossini's *Il Turco in Italia*. The opera is wonderfully lively. Usually I dislike slapstick, but tonight I roar with laughter. I am told that Leonard Ingrams* is still having trouble with the planning authorities about the future of his enterprise. A band of hostile villagers count the cars each night to strengthen their case against a renewal of the licence on environmental and disturbance grounds.

6 July 1996

How did George Carey come to be appointed Archbishop of Canterbury? I hear that the Crown Appointments Commission, heavily weighted with liberal Synod members, chose John Habgood of York and David Shepherd of Liverpool as the two required names to be submitted to the PM. The Commission then thought it unfair not to appear, at least, to give some freedom from the liberal wing of the Church, so they instead added George Carey of Bath and Wells to the list, believing that this would ensure Habgood's translation. Margaret Thatcher promptly chose Carey.

8 July 1996

Roger Bannister,† Master of Pembroke College, Oxford, tells me that Dr

---

* (1941–2005), merchant banker and founder of Garsington Opera 1989; the Festival moved to the Getty estate at Wormsley in 2011.
† Sir Roger Bannister (1929–2018), Master of Pembroke 1985–93. In 1954 he ran the first sub-four-minute mile.

Johnson was not as poor as has been asserted when an undergraduate at Pembroke: college accounts show he drank a lot.

10 July 1996
Some talk with George Weidenfeld. He wonders whether Andrew Roberts really would be suitable to edit my Journals in due course. That is precisely the thought that has been haunting me.

12 July 1996
The divorce of the Prince and Princess of Wales is officially announced. What a relief.

15 July 1996
Breakfast with Charles Guthrie at the Hyde Park Hotel. There we are joined by Prince Eddie, who becomes animated about the impending end of the Royal Yacht *Britannia*. Once she is out of commission it will take years to produce a new one, so time is short. Perhaps it would be best to aim at a new yacht by the year 2002, the Queen's Golden Jubilee. Modern ships require smaller crew, so it would not be prohibitively expensive.

17 July 1996
One interesting thing Jack Plumb tells me: when numbers were substituted for names in Cambridge examinations the number of women gaining Firsts rose sharply.

21 July 1996
I hear that members of the Prince of Wales's Trust resent being made to go down to meetings at Highgrove: not only the long double journey for busy men, but a lot of time being wasted being shown the garden and tasting cordials. The main trouble with the Prince is that he hates being told anything he does not wish to hear.

29 July 1996
Michael Heseltine makes a speech on our future in Europe in which he says: 'The mistake now would be to treat the City of London with the same apparent disinterest.' He means 'lack of interest': just the opposite of what he says. And he is Deputy PM.

5 September 1996

Ewen Fergusson[*] talks of Tony Crosland, whose Private Secretary he used to be. When Martin Charteris accompanied the Queen to the USA for the bicentenary celebrations in 1976, he was warned that Crosland had such a bad heart he could drop dead at any moment. He survived until February 1977, aged fifty-eight. In spite of his hatred of public schools, Crosland resented having gone to what he called 'a third-rate school' – Highgate.

As a loyal Rugbeian and the present Chairman of the Governors, Ewen deeply minds the way in which Brian Rees lowered the reputation of the school by his open indiscretions. Tom Howarth,[†] who was a governor of both Rugby and Charterhouse at the time, and whose idea it was that Rees should move to Rugby, knew all about them, but failed to pass the knowledge to Rugby. Howarth was subsequently asked to leave the Governing Body of Rugby.

7 September 1996

An extract from Humphrey Carpenter's[‡] new life of Robert Runcie in *The Times*, together with a letter from Robert bitterly regretting that he allowed himself to be so extensively tape-recorded. The letter begins: 'I have done my best to die before this book is published.' The extract includes the remarkable confession that most of his sermons and speeches were ghosted for him. Many were produced by Gary Bennett, of New College, who eventually committed suicide after the scandal of the Crockford's Preface, his revenge for having been consistently denied preferment. Another ghostwriter was Richard Chartres,[§] now Bishop of London. Poor Bob, he must feel betrayed. But what a chump to confide in Carpenter, who after all did an exceptionally frank biography of Benjamin Britten.

9 September 1996

Another chapter of the Runcie biography in *The Times*: astonishingly indiscreet comments on the Royal Family and their marital affairs. Also a sneer at 'the *Spectator* gang', who want to preserve the language of the old Prayer Book. The Scots Guards were unpleasantly snobbish to him when he first joined the regiment.

---

[*] Sir Ewen Fergusson (1932–2017), Scottish international rugby player and diplomat. Ambassador to South Africa 1982–4; and to France 1987–92.

[†] (1914–88), High Master of St Paul's School 1962–73; Senior Tutor, Magdalene Coll., Cambridge 1973–80.

[‡] (1946–2005), biographer and broadcaster.

[§] The Rt Hon. and Rt Revd Richard Chartres (b. 1947), Bishop of London 1955–2017.

17 September 1996

At Cetinale with Tony Lambton. He produces a proof copy of Richard Thorpe's life of Alec Home, which he is reviewing for the *Spectator*. He is annoyed that Thorpe never consulted him.* At first sight of the book I am impressed by his immense industry and the management of his material. I tell Tony that I hope he will not be too hard on Richard Thorpe in his *Spectator* review of his book on Alec Home. It would do Tony no good if he ignored its important light on political history.

27 September 1996

To tea with Clarissa Avon in Bryanston Square about an article which is to appear in the *Sunday Times* claiming that Eden lived on Benzedrine during the Suez Crisis. Clarissa knows this story to be a complete myth. She has looked at Anthony's papers in Birmingham, which disclose no support for it. She has also written to Freddy Bishop and Guy Millard,† his two surviving secretaries from that time, who also fail to confirm it. Freddie Bishop went on record to say that throughout the Suez Crisis Eden was 'remarkably calm and steady', and Guy Millard described the rumour about Benzedrine as 'complete nonsense motivated by the malice of his political opponents'.

Although Anthony was not an easy man to work with, Clarissa says that only twice did she see him shed tears: at Bobbety's funeral and when visiting the grave of his son Simon in Burma. Clarissa is very calm about the whole matter, but would value vindication of Anthony.

21 October 1996

Finish reading Ben Pimlott's book on the Queen, on which he came to consult me. It is rather dull, enlivened by the usual indiscretions from Martin Charteris and Edward Ford, also the unpublished passages from Jock Colville's diaries when he was Private Secretary to Princess Elizabeth. The most controversial, and inaccurate, sentence in the book is Pimlott's remark that the Queen's choice of Alec Douglas-Home to be PM in 1963 'must be considered the biggest political judgement of her reign'. Yet the only alternative for the Queen would have been to descend into the political arena as a partisan: to weigh Rab Butler's experience against his irresolution, Hailsham's intellect against his volatile temperament, Home's antipathy to economics

---

* After Lord Lambton had helped me with my life of Selwyn Lloyd, I wrote to him asking for his help with Alec Douglas-Home. He never replied.

† Sir Frederick Bishop (1915–2005), Principal PS to Anthony Eden and Harold Macmillan 1956–9. Sir Guy Millard (1917–2013), appointed PS for Foreign Affairs by Eden; Ambassador to Hungary 1967–9, Sweden 1971–4 and Italy 1974–6.

against his skill as a diplomat. She had to remain above the fray. What seems to have outraged Pimlott and other 'progressives' of course was not so much the Queen's dependence on Macmillan for advice (for which she had asked), as the advice itself. Had the recommendation been for Butler rather than a 14th Earl, not a dog would have barked.

Now that the Conservatives, like Labour, openly elect a new leader, the Queen entrusts the formation of a new government to that elected figure. Traditionalists may deplore this erosion of the Royal prerogative; realists recognise that by relieving the Sovereign of making a decision, it strengthens the monarchy.

The most fatuous comment in Pimlott's book: John Grigg's belief that if Australia became a republic, 'it would be largely the Queen's fault, for allowing herself to be known there only as an occasional visitor'.

25 October 1996

Gladwyn dies at the age of ninety-six and Miles[*] goes to the House of Lords. He deserves a little gilt in his life after so many crushing years in his father's shadow.

It is reported that the Chaplain of the House of Commons no longer prays for Diana, Princess of Wales. I talk to Robin Janvrin[†] at the Palace about any intention of dropping her from the Prayer Book. He gives an interesting answer. The divorce settlement said that she was to remain a member of the Royal Family, presumably as the mother of the ultimate heir. 'So nobody wants to prevent her from being prayed for.' If she is removed from the Prayer Book, it has to be done by Royal Warrant 'on advice.' The minister would be the Home Secretary, but Lambeth would of course have to be consulted.

26 October 1996

Tony Lambton has written an unkind and inadequate review of Richard Thorpe's book on Alec Douglas-Home for the *Spectator*. It would, I think, have been even more cruel had I not pointed out its merits to him at Cetinale; especially the important evidence of how the White House did down Hailsham for the premiership in October 1963.

---

[*] Miles Jebb, 2nd Baron Gladwyn of Bramfield (b. 1930), officer in the Welsh Guards; businessman.
[†] Sir Robin Janvrin, Baron Janvrin of Chalford Hill (b. 1946), PS to Elizabeth II and Keeper of the Queen's Archives 1999–2007.

31 October 1996

Somebody went to see the newly ennobled Peter Gummer, now Lord Chadlington,* at the Arts Council. 'Can I see Lord Chadlington, please?' Doorkeeper: 'Who's he?' Visitor: 'He's the Chairman.' Doorkeeper: 'I thought it was Mr Gummer, but he can't have lasted long, can he?'

3 November 1996

Peter Carrington describes an episode to illustrate Margaret Thatcher's utter lack of humour. At a lunch he said to her: 'Of course, we in the Tory Party are utterly loyal.' 'Of course.' 'So if John Major loses the next election, he will of course have to go?' 'Yes.' 'And be succeeded by Kenneth Clarke?' At which Margaret suddenly erupted in indignation; only then did she realise Peter had been teasing her. She would like Peter Lilley† to be leader.

7 November 1996

Tony Lambton telephones for one of his long, desultory conversations. The PM, he says, offered James Goldsmith‡ a peerage if he would abandon his Referendum campaign before the next General Election. 'Yes,' he replied, 'if it's a dukedom.'

16 November 1996

As I look through this morning's post, there is an OHMS white envelope marked 'Prime Minister'. I open it and find a letter from Alex Allan,§ the Prime Minister's Principal Private Secretary. It is an offer of the CBE, with the usual wording, 'The Prime Minister would be glad to know if this is agreeable to you.' I accept cordially.

20 November 1996

Peter Carrington gives a delightful little dinner party. I talk to Robin Butler, who is most interesting. He says that the Government of the country has virtually ceased in the run-up to the General Election. He likes John Major personally – and by inference thinks little of his ability as a PM. He is also

---

* Baron Chadlington of Deene (b. 1942), businessman; Chairman of the Arts Council 1991–6.
† The Rt Hon. Peter Lilley (b. 1943), Conservative politician. MP for St Albans, later Hitchin and Harpenden, 1983–2017; Sec. of State for Trade and Industry 1990–92; Sec. of State for Social Security 1992–7.
‡ Sir James Goldsmith (1933–97), financier and politician; founded the short-lived Eurosceptic Referendum Party.
§ Sir Alex Allan (b. 1951), senior civil servant. Principal PS to John Major 1992–7; British High Commissioner to Australia 1997–9; Chairman of the Joint Intelligence Committee 2007–11.

full of admiration for William Waldegrave and thinks Peter Lilley an exceptionally competent minister. He admires Blair and thinks that he will last
once elected as PM. I ask him when the Government is likely to announce
plans, if any, for a new Royal Yacht. Its cost would be negligible compared to
the billions lost by the Government each year through incompetence. Robin
says that the Government does not want to make itself even more unpopular
by announcing a supposedly large sum to be spent on the Royal Family, so
may slip it into a naval debate next year.

22 November 1996

With William Waldegrave I visit an ailing Leslie Rowse in Cornwall. His
secretary tells us that three days ago a letter arrived from the Prime Minister offering Leslie a CH. It would be good if it could be announced on
his ninety-third birthday on 4 December, as his doctors say he could die at
any time.

He drifts in and out of sleep, but makes wry comments. 'Blair? He is like
Gaitskell – high-minded. Not my cup of tea.' That alone is worth a CH.

William is not surprised by this news of the CH, for he has been pressing
for it and discussed it with Robin Butler very recently.

William tells Leslie that he has just been to see Margaret Thatcher: 'She
was very fierce about the Germans.' Leslie: 'She is quite right. They ruined
our world. She got her views on Germany and her history from me.'

Both William and I are glad that we made the effort. My pleasure in a
CH for Leslie is clouded by resentment that it should have been delayed by
successive Prime Ministers until the very last days of his life, the eve of his
ninety-third birthday. Not even John Major would have moved, I suspect,
without prodding from William.

4 December 1996

It is Leslie Rowse's ninety-third birthday, so I telephone his housekeeper in
St Austell to give him my best wishes. She says that he has recovered some of
his health since William and I went down to see him and has asked to go out
today in a wheelchair.

I do not understand BBC politics, but it seems that by the time Dukie
Hussey retired as Chairman the other day, he was no longer on speaking
terms with John Birt, the Director General. One cause was Birt's failure to
tell Dukie that the Princess of Wales was to give her infamous TV interview
in which she admitted adultery – not that Dukie could have stopped it, even
if he had wanted to.

10 December 1996

Norman St John-Stevas has been given rooms at Emmanuel on his retirement as Master, and also retains a place on the Governing Body. When Claus
Moser retired from the Wardenship of Wadham, he said he would accept no
Oxford invitations for a year. 'It didn't really matter,' Norman says, 'for he
received none.'

1997

1997 was a general election year which saw an end to eighteen years of Conservative government under Margaret Thatcher and John Major, and Tony Blair becoming Labour Prime Minister. On 16 January the Conservative government lost its Commons majority with the death of Iain Mills, MP for Meriden. The Labour Party promised on 20 January not to raise income tax if it won the general election. On 27 February the Labour Party won the Wirral South by-election, once, as Wirral, the safest of Conservative seats for Selwyn Lloyd. On 17 March John Major announced the general election for 1 May. On 18 March the Sun *newspaper, for many years staunchly Conservative, announced its support for Tony Blair and Labour. On 8 April Labour had a lead of fifteen points in a MORI poll; on 29 April the last MORI poll before the election tipped Labour for a sizeable win as they had 48 per cent of the projected vote. On 1 May the Labour Party under Tony Blair won a landslide victory over the Conservatives.*

After the general election a record 119 women were now MPs. On 6 May Gordon Brown, Chancellor of the Exchequer, announced that the Bank of England would assume independent responsibility for UK monetary policy, including interest rates. The government banned tobacco sponsorship of sporting events on 19 May. On 1 July Britain transferred sovereignty of Hong Kong to the People's Republic of China. On 2 July the first Labour Budget for nearly twenty years included a further £3 billion for education and healthcare. On 19 July the IRA declared a ceasefire. Labour lost the Uxbridge by-election to the Conservatives on 31 July. On 2 August John Major's Resignation Honours were announced, including the CH for Michael Heseltine. On 31 August Diana, Princess of Wales, was killed in a car crash in Paris and the Royal Family was criticised throughout the next few days for its response to her death; on 5 September the Queen made a live TV broadcast in tribute to the Princess of Wales. Sir Georg Solti and Mother Teresa died on 5 September. The funeral of the Princess of Wales took place on 6 September in Westminster Abbey – TV coverage on BBC 1 and ITV attracted an audience of thirty-two million people. On 22 September the former Speaker, Viscount Tonypandy, died. Isaiah Berlin died on 5 November. On 20 November the Queen and the Duke of Edinburgh celebrated their Golden Wedding anniversary. The Royal Yacht Britannia was decommissioned on 11 December after forty-four years' service. James Lees-Milne died on 28 December.

1 January 1997

Leslie Rowse's CH is announced in the New Year's Honours List. It has fallen to John Major to remedy the shameful neglect by his predecessors at No. 10 and to bestow on our leading Elizabethan historian the first recognition he has ever received from the Crown. Our friendship goes back to the years immediately after the war when I was an undergraduate at New College and he a Fellow of All Souls. He encouraged me in the pursuit of history, and taught me much that eye and ear might otherwise have missed. The best of his books are to be found among his earliest. *A Cornish Childhood*, published in 1942, may well endure the longest of all.

25 January 1997

I was shocked to hear that not long after Jeremy Thorpe had been acquitted of attempted murder conspiracy, he asked Marcia Falkender at No. 10 if she could arrange for him to receive a peerage.

Fergie sends me a copy of her book *My Story* with an acknowledgement of my friendship.

February 1997 began with confirmation of a development Kenneth Rose had not anticipated, the ending of his contract to write a weekly 'Albany' column for the Sunday Telegraph *after thirty-six years. Starting on 5 February 1961, he wrote nearly 1,700 columns, each of about 1,000 words. Overall, he worked for the* Telegraph *for forty-four years.*

11 February 1997

At 9 p.m. a special messenger brings a letter from Dominic Lawson.* 'I'm afraid I'm not in a position to amend the proposal I put to you in January.' He offers me an ex-gratia payment of £25,000; as much space as I want for a valedictory article; and the hope that I shall contribute articles in future to the paper. He also makes flattering remarks about my work.

Rather than writing, I decide it would be better to talk to him on the telephone, and we have an amiable exchange. We agree that I shall write my last column next Sunday, to be followed on 23 February by a valedictory

---

* The Hon. Dominic Lawson (b. 1956), journalist; editor of the *Sunday Telegraph* 1995–2005.

article. I also assure him that I shall not 'do a Worsthorne'* by disparaging him in the *Sunday Times*; nor will I elaborate on my retirement by intriguing journalists. 'Yes,' Dominic says, 'you are a gentleman.'

15 February 1997

My last day doing the 'Albany' column – though there will be a valedictory article next week. Dean Godson, chief leader writer on the *Daily Telegraph*, says that Conrad Black had told him Lawson had wanted me out 'as the column had gone on for too long'. Conrad apparently did not dissent.

18 February 1997

In the course of the evening, I receive many expressions of sympathy about my news – but I have lost my column and begin to feel symptoms of deprivation.

19 February 1997

Lunch with Peter Carrington at White's. I show him the draft of my valedictory article for the paper next Sunday. He rightly says that I should remove the phrase 'creative accounting' in referring to the *Telegraph*'s financial policy. I substitute: 'The relentless pressure of Conrad Black's balance sheet.'

21 February 1997

Letter from Dominic Lawson: 'Dear Kenneth, What a wonderful valedictory piece you have written for us. I am proud to be publishing it. Yours, as ever, Dominic.'

Jean Trumpington says that she is going to retire at the General Election, whichever way it goes. She is deeply sad at the prospect.

George Weidenfeld rings and asks my plans on retirement from the paper. Already I feel a certain relief at freeing myself from its constant pressure.

23 February 1997

My valedictory article appears in the *Sunday Telegraph* adorned by a montage of photos of my sitting with the Duke of Windsor, Emperor Hirohito† and Harold Macmillan. A leader article says that my Journals will be essential reading for anyone who wants to understand our times. Bill Deedes says

---

* Sir Peregrine Worsthorne (b. 1923), journalist, writer and broadcaster; editor of the *Sunday Telegraph* 1986–89.
† (1901–89), Emperor of Japan from 1926 until his death.

that he cannot wait to see them between hard covers. So at last the comedy is over.

21 March 1997

Up early on my Investiture day. A day of dazzling sun. The scarlet camellias are coming into flower in my garden. As it is such a nice day I walk down to Buckingham Palace through Green Park, calling in to leave a short coat at the Ritz, where I am lunching with the Queen Mother later, a function arranged by Matthew Ridley to celebrate my CBE. I pass a rather tousled young man on the path to St James's Palace: it is Prince William, who I expect has been to Buckingham Palace for a swim. Surely he should be shadowed by a detective.

Across the forecourt and inner quadrangle of the Palace, where 'recipients' (as we are known) and guests are herded in different directions. Up the grand staircase and into a long, wide gallery hung with Poussins and a Van Dyck of Charles I and his family.

The MBEs are at one end, the OBEs and CBEs at the other. There is still one more division to be made. The MBEs and OBEs each have little hooks attached to their coats or dresses to receive their insignia. We CBEs have a ribbon hung round our necks at the actual ceremony, so stand proudly hook-less. Everybody thus notices what the next person has or doesn't have: an odd little piece of anthropology.

Robert Fellowes comes up and asks me to have a drink in the Equerries' room afterwards. Robin Janvrin also greets me.

A hearty man in Brigade uniform shows how we are to enter the throne room, bow to the Prince of Wales (who is taking the Investiture in place of the Queen), advance a pace or two towards him so that he can hang the ribbon and badge round the neck, talk to him for a brief minute, shake hands, step back a pace or two, bow and withdraw.

It all goes smoothly after we have been lined up in alphabetical order and checked several times. What fun it would be if we were one out all the way down the line. As one recipient turns away from the Prince, in naval uniform, the name of the next is proclaimed from a little lectern.

The Prince beams and says: 'Well done, Kenneth.' I tell him I am lunching with the Queen Mother afterwards. 'Oh good, I shall be calling in to see her just before lunch.' Then the handshake. From 11 to 12.30 he keeps up a high standard of charm, interest and affability.

On leaving the Throne Room one is directed to a room in which a man removes ribbon and insignia from one's head, folds it, puts it into a black leather case stamped CBE, closes it, and hands it over, together with an envelope on how to order a video of the ceremony.

I go by car to the Ritz, where Prince Charles is already. He tells me that the head of Wimbledon asked whether he thought the Queen would come to open a new court. 'I doubt it,' Prince Philip replied, 'unless there are dogs and horses.'

Queen Elizabeth arrives at 1.15 and all the guests move to a corner of the marble hall for a drink. As we enter the dining room and move to a round table in the far-left corner overlooking Green Park, everybody in the room stands, which is touching. I sit on the Queen Mother's right. Matthew Ridley, our host, is on robust form. He tells the QM how we joined the army on the same day at Pirbright, when a sergeant-major greeted us by saying: 'Mussolini has heard of you lot. He's just abdicated.'

1 May 1997
General Election day, but I do not vote. Alan Clark will be safe in Kensington and Chelsea.

Another day of hot sunshine. The laburnums are just coming into blossom.

About 11 p.m. I look in on the election-night party given by Tom Stacey.[*] Then on to Covent Garden for Charles Moore's election-night party. Even as I arrive at about 11.45, it is obvious that Tony Blair has scored a landslide victory. Bruce Anderson[†] is particularly dejected. Of all the political correspondents, he alone forecast a Tory victory.

Andrew Roberts is there. He says that his biography of the great Lord Salisbury may take him as long as four years.

2 May 1997
Read of yesterday's crushing defeat of Tory hopes. No fewer than seven Cabinet ministers are out, including Portillo and William Waldegrave. Also Jonathan Aitken. I feel fortunate at having lost my column: it would have been tedious and unrewarding to learn even the names of the new Labour team.

Labour win 419 seats, more than in July 1945; the Tories only 165, fewer than in 1945; and the Liberal Democrats 46. Blair says that things can only get better. We shall see.

3 May 1997
There is a new young equerry at Clarence House. He says he is studying an Open University course on art, but does not like any twentieth-century

---

* (b. 1930), novelist, journalist and broadcaster.
† (b. 1949), columnist and former political editor of the *Spectator*.

works. Prue Penn said to him: 'But the house is full of lovely twentieth-century pictures,' adding, 'there is a whole roomful of Pipers.' Equerry: 'Are they Scots Guards pipers?' And when Prue told him that the Queen Mother was going to see some almshouses he asked: 'What sort of arms do they make there?'

Alas, Princess Margaret still continues to put the Queen Mother's correspondence in black bags for destruction – except for the very few that PM thinks ought to be preserved.

9 May 1997

The new Government is showing signs of the feverish itch that is only to be expected. The Prime Minister has announced that his Cabinet ministers are to call each other by their Christian names in Cabinet, not by their offices: the PM is to be Tony. And the language of the Queen's Speech is to become 'more lively'.

10 May 1997

In Scotland, I visit Glamis: a huge pink castle, far larger than I expected. None of the rooms is particularly beautiful or impressive, nor are the pictures and furniture. But the whole is the embodiment of family history. The three rooms occupied by Queen Elizabeth and King George VI during part of their honeymoon are typical: a jumble of furniture without elegance or beauty. Of course, an enormous billiard room lined with unreadable books; a drawing room like a children's playroom; an intimate chapel; several Macbeth-like halls and stairs; and everywhere memorabilia of the Queen Mother.

17 May 1997

Hot weather. I spend the day in the garden reading Max Egremont's *Under Two Flags: The Life of Sir Edward Spears.*[*] Well written and well balanced. Max is illuminating of the shady character of Spears in every phase of his life. Fascinating on how his closeness to de Gaulle in 1940 gave way to deep hatred over the Levant later in the war. The bloody-minded pettiness of de Gaulle is scarcely credible, even in a man determined to display his independence in exile.

---

* Max Wyndham 2nd Baron Egremont (b. 1948), biographer. Maj.-Gen. Sir Edward Spears (1886–1974), head of the British Military Mission in Paris 1917–20.

22 May 1997

Welsh Guards annual dinner. I talk to Charles Guthrie, who has formed a favourable view of the Labour Cabinet during the past three weeks. He had already, of course, made some contact with the Blair circle before the election and received a friendly reception. He particularly likes the Secretary of State for Defence, George Robertson,[*] who had expected to be made Secretary of State for Scotland. Charles took him to Bosnia, where he declared his admiration and support for our forces.

27 May 1997

Dukie Hussey's retirement from the BBC was handled as inelegantly as my own from the *Telegraph*. He retired as he said he would, when the BBC Charter had been renewed. As Cabinet Secretary, Robin Butler applied the rules with a rigid lack of generosity, according to Dukie, which he says cost him a whole year's salary. But he managed to keep his car for an extra six months. He also was able to take home with him a Graham Sutherland painting of the Pyramids which had been hanging in his office for ten years. Dukie says: 'There should be a club of the worst appointments of the Conservative years: Bob Runcie, Robin Leigh-Pemberton[†] and myself.'

1 June 1997

To Headington for tea with Isaiah Berlin. A sumptuous tea with delicious smoked-salmon sandwiches made with white bread – now almost outlawed by health faddists – and every sort of chocolate biscuit.

We talk of relations between the Queen and her Prime Ministers. The Queen is careful never to reveal what she thinks of each, although it is generally known that she and Margaret Thatcher had sharp disagreements on the importance of the Commonwealth. Isaiah now has an important piece of evidence. Both the Queen and Thatcher came to a gala at Covent Garden, but sat in different parts of the house. In the interval the Queen let it be known that she did not want to meet Mrs Thatcher – who was sent to an upper room for drinks, as was Isaiah. Thatcher then said she would like to say goodbye to the Queen, a request that was ignored.

I have dinner with Eric and Poppy Anderson at Lincoln College. Eric tells me that he has brought his recorded talks with the Queen Mother to an end.

---

[*] George Robertson, Baron Robertson of Port Ellen (b. 1946), Labour politician. Sec. of State for Defence 1997–9; Sec. Gen. of NATO 1999–2004.

[†] Sir Robert Leigh-Pemberton, Baron Kingsdown of Pemberton (1926–2013), Governor of the Bank of England 1983–93.

She never liked being questioned and Eric found she was repeating herself. 'She gave nothing away.' He asks me whether I would be interested in writing her official biography – in a way that leads me to think he would have some influence. I am not sure. How interesting would her influence on the King prove to be, and would I be able to discover this? How nice is she really behind the enticing façade? Would I be censored? Do I really want to devote my remaining years to earning money I don't really need and a KCVO that would come too late to give me pleasure?

I also hear a little about Tony Blair, whom Eric taught at Fettes. He was astute enough to write to all the senior civil servants who worked over the first weekend after the election victory and dropped in on the weekly Permanent Under-Secretaries' meeting. Eric and Poppy dined with the Carringtons to meet the Queen.

4 June 1997

The Queen will dine at Spencer House today with the entire Chapter of the Order of the Garter in an early celebration of her Golden Wedding. Established in 1438, the most coveted of all Orders has survived every vicissitude of political and social change. Alone of her subjects, Harold Macmillan refused the highest honour in the Queen's gift, on ceasing to be her Prime Minister. 'Publishers should not have the Garter,' was his whimsical explanation. It was designed to tease, yet not without sincerity, for he had grown up in the Edwardian age and respected its shibboleths.

7 June 1997

Jonathan Aitken's case for libel against the *Guardian* and a TV company is exciting much interest, not least because George Carman is determined to go for Jonathan's jugular vein. Jonathan can well refute charges that he acted for rich Arabs, but the episode of his hotel bill at the Ritz in Paris, allegedly paid by Arab friends while he was a minister, looks damaging. What may help him is that the judge, Oliver Popplewell,* is known to be suspicious of Carman's forensic flamboyance.

20 June 1997

I see in the papers that Jonathan Aitken and his wife are to divorce. Extraordinary that this should emerge in the middle of his libel case, which seems to be going well. Almost at once John King telephones me to say that not only is

---

* Sir Oliver Popplewell (b. 1927), Judge of the High Court of Justice, Queen's Bench Division 1983–99.

the case against the *Guardian* and another company not going well; Jonathan has thrown in the sponge as evidence is about to emerge that he has lied on oath. I am flabbergasted. Jonathan has exuded confidence throughout.

29 June 1997
Sadness at the handing over of Hong Kong to the Chinese.

13 July 1997
Sickening story in the papers that Diana has taken her two sons for a cruise with Mohammed Al Fayed in his yacht in the Mediterranean. Apparently, she justifies this by Fayed having been photographed with the Queen at the Windsor Horse Show, which he sponsors. Both events are unseemly and degrading. There are echoes of King Edward VII's liking for sailing with Sir Thomas Lipton,* the tea magnate. Edward was taunted by the Kaiser† for 'boating with his grocer' and Queen Victoria even wrote him a letter of admonishment: 'If ever you become King, you will find all these friends most inconvenient and will have to break with them all.'

15 July 1997
I mention to Robin Butler what Jim Callaghan once told me: that after an audience with the Queen he declined to talk to anybody about what had passed. Robin says that nowadays the general practice is for the PM to take his Private Secretary with him to the Palace, who does not attend the audience itself, but takes part in a discussion afterwards between the PM and the Queen's Private Secretary – but only on what action, if any, is to be taken as a result of the audience. That is what happened when Robin was Mrs Thatcher's Principal Secretary and Philip Moore was the Queen's Secretary. He calls it 'a threesome'.

Robin admits that when writing Cabinet minutes he sometimes paraphrases a view in order to make it more concise and intelligible.

21 July 1997
How absurd that every single street sign in Wales has to be in both Welsh and English. Hugely expensive, and because the Welsh always comes first, it takes the English-speaking motorist a second or so more to read – which could be dangerous.

---

* (1850–1931), owner of tea and rubber estates in Ceylon.
† Kaiser Wilhelm II (1859–1941), eldest grandchild of Queen Victoria; last German Emperor 1888–1918.

Peter Carrington is disgusted with Chris Patten for accusing Tory ministers of having sabotaged his plans for Hong Kong and for his virulent attacks on Geoffrey Howe and Percy Cradock.* 'It was quite wrong of him publicly to raise these issues. He will certainly never become leader of the Conservative Party.'

30 July 1997

To a Foyle's literary luncheon for Martin Gilbert's latest over-long book, *History of the World in the 20th Century: Volume 1, 1900–1933*. I sit next to young Winston. Winston was not happy at Eton, though he liked Giles St Aubyn. He nevertheless sent a telegram to Chenevix-Trench on the birth of his son Randolph,† asking for the child to be put down on a housemaster's list. There was a delay, then C.-T. wrote in an unfriendly way to say that the HM should not have been troubled with such a matter. By then there was no vacancy on the list of future housemasters, only on the general list. So Winston washed his hands of Eton and sent the boy to Harrow.

23 August 1997

I see in the *Daily Telegraph* that in the league table of A-Level results, Repton is 433rd out of 822 schools: appalling.

24 August 1997

Read the diaries of Siegfried Sassoon, edited by Rupert Hart-Davis. Some sharp vignettes, not least of Elgar, pompously refusing to contribute to Queen Mary's Doll's House. How I wish I had had that for my *KGV*.

31 August 1997

I am awakened by the telephone at 6.15. It is NBC from America. 'Have you heard the news? Princess Diana and Dodi Fayed‡ have been killed in a car crash a few hours ago. Will you take part in a programme on her?' I am astounded. Then I think very quickly. At such a moment only undiluted appreciation will serve, and I am not the man to do it off the cuff. So I decline. I also turn down a request for an article for the *Telegraph*.

I turn on the radio news and hear Bill Deedes, not very coherent, paying tribute to her anti-landmine campaign. A succession of bulletins that do

---

* Sir Percy Cradock (1923–2010), Ambassador to the People's Republic of China 1978–1983.
† Lt Randolph Spencer-Churchill, b. 22 Jan. 1965, two days before his great-grandfather Sir Winston Churchill died; newspapers announcing Sir Winston's death on 25 Jan. also carried the announcement of his great-grandson's birth.
‡ (1955–97), film producer.

not add much to details of the crash, except that the car was apparently being chased by paparazzi, and crashed into a tunnel by the Seine. Instant destruction.

Later in the day there is news that Diana's remains are being flown back to Northolt this evening. Annoyed to hear that the PM has said that her funeral arrangements must of course be for the family – but that <u>he</u> wants a national commemoration of Diana. It smacks of his cashing in on the event politically.

Australian Broadcasting asks me to discuss the constitutional implications of Diana's death. I reply that there are none.

1 September 1997

The full horror of Diana's death emerges. The Mercedes belonging to the Fayeds was being driven at 110 mph, apparently to shake off the paparazzi on motorbikes. Was that speed necessary? It later emerges that the driver was three times over the French drink limit.

National wave of emotion. Flowers piled outside gates of Kensington Palace and Buckingham Palace. Widespread hatred of the Press: paparazzi would have no role if their intrusive photographs were not bought by newspapers and seen by readers. I decline to write an article for the *Spectator*. Passions are running high and only uncritical acclaim for Diana will be acceptable to the reader. I also refuse to appear on BBC *Newsnight* to talk about what sort of a funeral would be suitable.

No novelist would have dared to produce a plot as lurid as that of Mohammed Fayed. He was determined to infiltrate the Royal Family. So he buys the Windsor house in Paris and contents, spending millions on restoration. The Royal Family are not interested, so he puts the whole collection of memorabilia on the market, to be sold by Sotheby's later this month. Then he helps bring together his son and Diana – with quite a high chance, it seems, of marriage; so he sees himself as the step-grandfather of the future King. Then the wheel of fortune spins again, and Dodi and Diana are killed together.

There is such nonsense about Diana being hounded by the Press, but nothing of how Diana manipulated the Press in her campaign against Charles.

2 September 1997

Sarah, Duchess of York, asks me whether I am writing to the Prince of Wales on Diana's death. I am not. Divorce makes it unnecessary.

Blair is clearly trying to make capital out of the funeral arrangements: No. 10 on behalf of the people v. the Palace and a stuffy Establishment.

Dominic Lawson talks to me about Diana's funeral. He thinks she was much closer to Catholicism than Anglicanism. He rightly emphasises that the public, in contrast to the Establishment, never hated her, and inclined to take her part against the wimpish Prince. He thinks that even in the funeral arrangements, there is a division between the Establishment way of doing things and the bending to popular demand.

3 September 1997

The country is in the grip of an intense emotional crisis over Diana's death: a manipulated grief that is turning against the Royal Family. It is not confined to London. The news says that there are traffic jams for miles around Althorp as people arrive 'to pay their respects'.

In the meantime I hear that Rudolf Bing* has died. I always found him the greatest fun, and I had something to do with securing a KBE for him.

More news on Diana's funeral from Dominic Lawson. Although the Queen does not care for Diana's favourite music, the Verdi Requiem, part of it is to be included in the service. Charles is insisting that the boys must follow the gun carriage. He was offered a lesson-reading, but he declined.

4 September 1997

Hysteria over Diana's death intensifies. Public and Press attacks on the Queen for remaining in seclusion at Balmoral instead of travelling south to display her grief. However much criticism the Prince of Wales has incurred during the past few days, it was wise of him to keep his two young sons at Balmoral until shortly before the funeral. As for the Queen, I do think that she, like me, has misjudged public opinion by insisting on not flying the Union Flag at Windsor at half-mast, because by tradition the flag on a fortress is never lowered. There is no flag at Buckingham Palace, at half-mast or otherwise.

5 September 1997

Letter from Colin Matthew inviting me to contribute to the new *DNB* an expanded version of my original *DNB* notice on Eddie Winterton.† It would be agreeable to have a notice included in the new *DNB*, particularly when invited by Colin, for whom I secured the Wolfson Prize as editor of the Gladstone diaries.

---

* Sir Rudolf Bing (1902–97), Austrian-born opera impresario; Gen. Manager of the Metropolitan Opera, New York 1950–72.

† Edward Turnour, 6th Earl Winterton of Shillinglee (1883–1917), Conservative politician. Chancellor of the Duchy of Lancaster 1937–9; Baby of the House when elected in 1904 for Horsham at the age of twenty-one; Father of the House at his retirement in 1951.

The Post Office announces that it will deliver no letters tomorrow 'as a mark of respect for Princess Diana'. All sport cancelled too.

Traffic jams all over London as people flock to the Royal Palaces to lay flowers in her memory: vast carpets of them. I see nice young people going past my window clutching little bunches. How has all this come about? Only last week the nation was observing with amused disrespect her dalliance with Dodi Fayed. And nobody dares mention the marriages she broke, particularly that of Will Carling, the England rugby captain.* 'What, have they canonised him?' an old cynic exclaimed on finding Disraeli's statue smothered in primroses a year or two after his death. Princess Diana has not had so long to wait.

Under pressure from the Government, the Press and the people, the Queen gives a short live memorial tribute to Diana on television. If only she had done so four days ago. As it is, she has been humiliated. Similarly, the Queen has agreed to fly the Union Flag at half-mast when she is not there: on her arrival the Royal Standard will be flown. What a revenge Diana has taken on the family that 'rejected' her.

6 September 1997

The day of Diana's funeral. The death is announced of Georg Solti and Mother Teresa: a nightmare for the newspaper editors, as it was on the day of Kennedy's assassination when C.S. Lewis and Aldous Huxley died on the same day.

Mohammed Fayed has put out a number of statements about Dodi's liaison with Princess Diana of unbelievable bad taste. They concern the couple's exchange of presents and Diana's supposed last words. Fayed has also asked the Spencer family to put into Diana's coffin a poem written to her by Dodi and engraved in silver.

The main TV commentator is David Dimbleby. Like all of his kind, he talks too much. One yearns for silence as the simple gun carriage escorted by Welsh Guardsmen moves silently through the park on a lovely day. It is painful to see the little Princes following their mother's coffin during the last stage of the journey from St James's Palace to the Abbey. William keeps his face down throughout, staring at the ground; little Harry bewildered but more robust.†

The service itself is a blend of the formal and the trendy. Diana's two

---

* Will Carling (b. 1965), captained England fifty-nine times.

† Prince William, Duke of Cambridge (b. 1982). Prince Henry of Wales, Duke of Sussex (b. 1984).

sisters, like her,* give their readings in what are by no means conventional upper-class tones. The Prince of Wales, who looks under torture, crosses himself as the coffin passes him. The PM, Tony Bair, is embarrassingly histrionic in reading the lesson. Elton John's song 'Candle in the Wind' is surprisingly attractive. Charles Spencer's† address is an angry attack on the Press for hounding Diana, which is acceptable; and a scornful dismissal of the Royal Family, which is not. In his view it seems that the two boys were primarily Spencers and scarcely members of the Royal Family at all. He is given a burst of applause by those outside which is taken up by those in the Abbey. I find this a horrible experience. Who is Spencer, with his troubled marital affairs, to appoint himself the Princes' guardian? And was Diana so wholly blameless and persecuted in her exposed life? Macaulay called Westminster Abbey a temple of reconciliation. I wish I could share his optimism. Then I watch the motor hearse on its long journey to Althorp, showered with flowers along the whole route. The service was born of compromise, like the Church of England itself; the spectacle brought solace to millions, but the damage to the monarchy is less easy to measure.

8 September 1997
The whole of this part of London is still choked with traffic as people arrive to gaze at Kensington Palace, many of them still leaving flowers. Helicopters making an awful din photographing the scene.

10 September 1997
The papers say that Kensington Gardens may have its name changed to the Princess Diana Gardens and become a shrine attracting hundreds of thousands of tourists. What a ghastly prospect. It should be left as an oasis of peace.

11 September 1997
Peter Pilkington says how much he agrees with me about Diana's funeral when we talk about it. He was as horrified as I was by the funeral address of Charles Spencer. 'I have preached many funeral sermons, but have always made it a rule not to parade division and hatred.' Peter puts down the mass hysteria, which is still continuing, to a rootless, undereducated urban population. Not that Peter has a lot to say for Prince Charles. 'He has compounded his personal failings by too much moralising. On the Duchy of

---

* Lady Sarah McCorquodale (b. 1955) and Jane Fellowes, Baroness Fellowes (b. 1957).
† 9th Earl Spencer (b. 1964), author and broadcaster.

Cornwall estates he is known for his high rents and expensive organic farming.'

15 September 1997
William Hague* attacks Blair for having made political capital out of Diana's death and funeral. He is right, but it is stupid to raise the issue a whole week later. It is now widely said that Hague's election as leader of the Conservative Party has been a mistake. I doubt whether he will last. Kenneth Clarke seems to me an obvious successor.

22 September 1997
Death of Speaker Thomas, Lord Tonypandy, an affectionate old friend.

1 October 1997
Derision in all the papers at Tony Blair's having had a photographer at the church service at Brighton for the Labour Party Conference – not just for his arrival and departure, but gazing heavenwards during the service itself. How low can one stoop in the quest for publicity?

11 October 1997
I re-read Tony Powell's *A Question of Upbringing*, the first novel in his *Dance to the Music of Time* series. It is incomparably better-written than all the later novels.

10 November 1997
The Times, instead of a photograph of the Royal Family on the balcony of the Home Office at the Cenotaph service yesterday has one of Tony Blair's parents and his own children – all wearing sweatshirts. New Labour indeed.

16 November 1997
Adam Nicolson's† book about the fire at Windsor Castle in 1992 and its subsequent restoration is brilliantly written. As good as anything his grandfather Harold wrote, and better than his father, Nigel.

---

* Baron Hague of Richmond (b. 1961), Conservative politician. Foreign Secretary 2010–14; First Sec. of State 2010–15; Leader of the House of Commons 2014–15.
† 5th Baron Carnock (b. 1957), author of books on history, landscape and literature; son of Nigel Nicolson.

17 November 1997

To Windsor by 9.30 to see the restoration. We are all given a copy of Adam Nicolson's book. Nigel is also here and I meet Adam for the first time: a charming fellow as well as an able writer.

The most spectacular work has been in St George's Hall, with an entirely new and lofty hammer-beam roof. The shields of Garter Knights have been repainted. I see those of the Kaiser (a black eagle) and the Emperor Hirohito (a chrysanthemum) and a lozenge shield for Mrs Thatcher. Both the Green and Crimson Drawing Rooms are simply dazzling with gold leaf. A huge kitchen with, surprisingly, a stag's head on the wall. The old Gothic tables are now topped by stainless steel. Rows of copper pans and kettles.

22 November 1997

How disgusting the way in which Blair has hijacked the Queen's Golden Wedding (as he hijacked Diana's funeral) by sharing her 'walkabout', waving to the crowds himself and shaking people's hands. He should have walked ten yards at least behind the Queen and Prince Philip.

24 November 1997

Astonishing news that the Princess of Wales never remade her will after the divorce. So the settlement of £17 million, left to her two boys, is subject to tax of £7 million. What on earth were her lawyers up to?

5 December 1997

I hear that Churchill had a German prisoner of war at Chartwell. On his birthday he went out to the garden and gave the prisoner a cigar. Would Hitler have done that?

8 December 1997

I hear a Radio 3 programme about Isaiah Berlin, who died last month. Like me, he disliked *Falstaff, Wozzeck* and *Peter Grimes* for their cruelty. I have hardly ever found anyone to agree with me that the humiliation of Falstaff in the final Act is detestable.

12 December 1997

How characteristic of the present Government that yesterday it decommissioned the Royal Yacht *Britannia* and invited the Sinn Fein leader Gerry Adams* to meet Blair at No. 10.

---

* (b. 1948), Irish Republican politician.

13 December 1997

I see my doctor at Holland Park surgery about my health problems. Walk away thinking of John Betjeman's poem 'Devonshire Street W1'.* One must simply go on – though it does limit one's horizons.

29 December 1997

Death of James Lees-Milne yesterday. I always enjoyed his company. He was absurdly diffident about his considerable literary skills. Curious how insensitive he was in his diary about the physical failings of the old. He loved only old buildings.

---

* The poem movingly describes the determination of a patient to carry on with his life for whatever time remains.

1998

Enoch Powell died on 8 February. Positions for BBC governors were advertised in Sunday newspapers on 1 March. The Good Friday Agreement between the UK and Irish governments was signed on 10 April. On 3 May European nations agreed on a single currency, the Euro. A £2 coin was issued in the UK on 15 June. The Omagh bomb on 15 August killed twenty-nine people. On 15 October the BBC lost the rights to broadcast Test cricket. On 19 November the US House of Representatives Judiciary Committee began impeachment hearings against President Bill Clinton. The Queen's Speech was interrupted by MPs and peers on 24 November when the Queen set out the government's plans to abolish the rights of 700 hereditary peers to sit and vote in the House of Lords. On 16 December President Clinton ordered American and British airstrikes on Iraq. On 19 December the House of Representatives impeached President Clinton.

2 January 1998

Some talk with Princess Margaret at Sutton Courtenay. She tells me she wept when she heard of Isaiah Berlin's death.

We talk of religion and she makes it plain that she dislikes Presbyterianism and Roman Catholicism with equal fervour.

Her father used to smoke Dunhill tobacco. 'Years later, Tony smoked the same tobacco, which was very evocative.'

Although Princess Margaret does not care for opera, she joins in the chorus of the Hebrew slaves from *Nabucco*. She goes on to describe how at the end of a performance of *Lucia di Lammermoor* Joan Sutherland* came up to be received: 'Oh, I'm always meeting you in my nightie.'

She says she was sorry when her son David† could not get into Eton. 'But going to Bedales worked out well. It gave him access to contemporary design.'

---

* Dame Joan Sutherland (1926–2010), Australian dramatic coloratura soprano.

† David Armstrong-Jones, 2nd Earl of Snowdon (b. 1961), furniture maker and Chairman of Christie's UK.

She refused to attend the decommissioning ceremony of the Royal Yacht *Britannia*.

14 January 1998

To Isaiah Berlin's memorial service in the Hampstead Synagogue. It is of ugly red brick with garish stained glass. It is evidently Orthodox: the men and women are separated. Not much of the service in English. Some lovely music – Isaac Stern* plays Bach. Also a Beethoven quartet. The Chief Rabbi, Jonathan Sacks,† preaches adequately. Noel Annan, whom I heard booked to give the address by Isaiah after Arnold Goodman's memorial service, is as always brilliant, moving and funny.

Dine at the Beefsteak. Graham C. Greene, only recently elected to the Beefsteak, tells me he was to have become Chairman of the Arts Council, but was vetoed by Mrs Thatcher.

3 February 1998

Dukie Hussey to lunch at the Ritz. The best food I have ever had here: crab cakes and a lobster sauce; a ragout of beef and venison; and a melting chocolate mousse.

We are at one on the spurious reputation for saintliness of Diana. She wanted to watch an operation at the Royal Marsden Hospital, of which Dukie was Chairman. Dukie was absolutely against it, but how to put her off? The solution was to find a patient who would refuse to give permission for any spectator to be present. This the administration managed to do and the news was broken to a sorrowful Diana.

5 February 1998

Charles Guthrie to dine at Green's. For a key man in the renewed crisis with Iraq over Saddam Hussein's refusal to allow UN inspection of nuclear and biological warfare weapons, Charles remains wonderfully calm and amusing. He has established a close rapport with Tony Blair, far more effective than with John Major. A prolonged air strike against Iraq would be hugely expensive and not necessarily decisive. In any case, any attack on him will rouse the whole of the Middle East against us.

11 February 1998

Dine with Martin Charteris. I hear from him that Nigel Jaques has been to

---

* (1920–2001), Ukrainian-born American violinist and conductor.
† Baron Sacks of Aldgate (b. 1948), Chief Rabbi 1991–2013.

Balmoral in the summer to tutor little Prince Harry in the hope that he will be able to get into Eton.

16 February 1998

I hear from former *Telegraph* colleagues how Dominic Lawson was away most of the week that began with Princess Diana's death. He came back to edit the paper, expecting to find it full of articles extolling Diana. Instead, almost every article was cool in the face of the almost universal hysteria whipped up by the tabloids and No. 10. Dominic was crestfallen, but it was too late to alter the paper.

18 February 1998

I listen to Elgar's Third Symphony, reconstructed from early drafts, bits and pieces. It has some noble moments and rhapsodic passages, but as Elie de Rothschild* said of Château Pétrus, 'C'est un gimmick.'

28 February 1998

The Government seems to have persuaded the Queen not only to allow a Bill to be debated, changing the line of succession so that a female firstborn takes precedence over all other children, but also to express approval of the content of such a Bill. That is quite wrong: with shades of King George V, Asquith and contingent guarantees over peerages.

5 March 1998

I hear from Andrew Roberts that the other day, at Conrad Black's house, the talk turned to the Cleveland Street scandal.† 'What sort of boys were they?' Conrad asked. Andrew: 'Telegraph boys.' Conrad: 'Sunday or Daily?'

7 March 1998

The *Sun* newspaper this morning has a story that the Royal Family are to make some drastic reforms. What really lies behind the story, true or not, is a tabloid-Downing Street alliance to diminish the Royal Family, a process that has continued relentlessly since Diana's death. What a posthumous revenge she has taken on the Royal Family she so hated and plotted to undermine.

　　I talk to Prince Eddie about the *Sun* story. Regarding money, the Queen

---

* Baron Élie de Rothschild (1917–2007), guardian of the French branch of the Rothschild family who ran the Château Lafite-Rothschild premier-cru claret vineyard 1946–74.
† The Cleveland Street scandal occurred in 1889, when police uncovered a male brothel. The government was accused of covering up the news to protect prominent patrons, including, it was rumoured, Prince Albert Victor, second in line to the throne.

now pays for most members of the Royal Family out of her own Civil List, so the cost does not fall directly on the Treasury. One reform Prince Eddie would welcome: a more simplified programme for Royal visits to the provinces: less ceremonial, smaller police escorts, and Lord Lieutenants not to wear uniform on visits to factories and other places.

18 March 1998
Jonathan Aitken arrested on a charge of conspiracy to pervert the course of justice and perjury. What a price he is paying for a silly little lie about who paid his hotel bill in Paris during a visit to his Arab friends.

20 March 1998
Lunch at the Beefsteak with Giles Shepard,* who is on one of the Royal Parks committees; he tells me that the Diana Memorial Committee is thought to have decided that part of Kensington Gardens should become a memorial garden to her. That is appalling news. It is likely to attract millions of visitors each year and ruin the comparative peace of the place. I don't suppose the Royal inhabitants will welcome it, either.

22 March 1998
The *Sunday Telegraph*, like all newspapers, has a showbiz flavour tempered by much nonsense about Mr Blair's 'Cool Britannia'.

1 April 1998
I gather it is generally reckoned that the principal problem facing the Royal Family is getting the Queen and Prince Charles to work more closely together. The Queen evidently has much longer audiences with Blair than those in the Thatcher and Major years.

5 April 1998
The papers are full of the attempted sale to a newspaper of the love letters written by Princess Diana to Major Hewitt of the Life Guards. This recalls a parallel with those written by Edward VII to Daisy Warwick† and her attempt to use them to blackmail King George V.

23 April 1998
Valerie Solti had much trouble with the Dean of Westminster, Dr Wesley

---

* (1937–2006), businessman; member of the Advisory Council for the Royal Parks 1993–8.
† Frances Greville, Countess of Warwick (1861–1938), socialite.

Carr,* in arranging Georg's memorial service at the Abbey, about what the service could and could not include, that she nearly withdrew it from the Abbey.

30 April 1998

Anthony Gilbey tells me he thinks Blair will change the name of the Order of the British Empire to something more in keeping with 'Cool Britannia' – perhaps the Order of British Endeavour, which would retain the same initials. He also tells me that the 'educated' accent which he and his friends use counted against him in his various law cases. Juries nowadays are almost entirely confined to those on low wages: the higher-paid know how to claim exemption.

1 May 1998

I go to the memorial service for John Wells[†] at St Paul's, Covent Garden, at twelve. The place is swarming with police because the Prince of Wales is expected. The speakers do not pitch up their voices and I miss quite a lot. Some jocular talk with Tony Snowdon on the way out. John Smith similarly asks: 'Whom are you representing?' I reply: 'Eton beaks who did not stay the course.'

19 May 1998

Richard Thorpe, writing his life of Anthony Eden in Oxford, where he is now a Fellow of St Antony's College, sends me a copy of a letter he has come across from Dean Acheson[‡] to Roy Welensky,[§] telling him that his Christmas in 1970 had been made by reading my Curzon book, *Superior Person*.

20 May 1998

I talk to Mollie Butler, such a young voice and mind, even at ninety. She still wants a new life of Rab, dissatisfied that Anthony Howard 'never really got under his skin'.

30 May 1998

Robert Rhodes James sends me the typescript chapters on George V from his new work on George VI. It contains scarcely anything new – but a great deal

---

* (b. 1941), Dean of Westminster 1997–2006.
† (1936–98), actor, writer and satirist. Like K.R., he taught for a time at Eton.
‡ (1893–1971), US Sec. of State 1949–53.
§ Sir Roland Welensky (1907–91), Northern Rhodesian politician. Prime Minister of the Federation of Rhodesia and Nyasaland 1956–63.

from my *KGV*, inadequately acknowledged. I disagree with him that Stamfordham gave the King the right advice in telling him to reject Asquith's demand for a contingent guarantee over the Parliament Bill; and that the King allowed a supposed dislike of Curzon to colour his choice of Baldwin as PM in 1923. How dogmatic he is on subjects of which he can know nothing. He says that the King's smoking had no effect on his illness of 1928–1929; but that the septicaemia began in his chest.

By chance, as I am reading the typescript Philip Ziegler telephones to ask whether he should answer a letter from Prince Eddie formally or informally: I say formally always safest. I tell him what I am reading. He says of Robert Rhodes James: 'His biography of Rosebery was a good book. Since then every successive one has been worse than the last.'

4 June 1998

Princess Margaret tells me about the proposed memorial garden to Princess Diana in front of Kensington Palace: 'Of course we don't want it. After all, she lived at the back of the house, not the front. It will be quite enough of a memorial to restore the grass in front which all these people trampled the week she died. And certainly no 300-foot fountain in the Round Pond!'

12 June 1998

Long talk with Edward Ford at dinner. I ask him how he came to be tutor to King Farouk.* Lord Killearn,† who took an avuncular as well as a proconsular interest in the young Farouk, asked Claude Elliott to find him a place at Eton. But Claude said no, just as he had said no to Ribbentrop's son. Farouk was too old, knew no Latin, and would not be able to follow the usual Eton curriculum. So Killearn asked whether Claude could detach an Eton beak to become his tutor. That too Claude turned down. But he did recommend Edward, who had done two spells of six weeks each teaching at Eton when other beaks were ill. Killearn saw Ford and sent him to see Vansittart‡ at the FO. Edward received the princely salary of £2,000 a year, £60,000 in the currency of today, as well as a farewell present of a jewelled gold cigarette case. Farouk expected to be first given the answers to any examinations; without these he failed miserably.

---

* (1920–65), King of Egypt and the Sudan 1936–52.
† Miles Lampson, 1st Baron Killearn of Killearn (1880–1964), Ambassador to Egypt and the Sudan 1936–46.
‡ Robert, 1st Baron Vansittart (1881–1957), Permanent Under-Sec. for Foreign Affairs 1930–38.

Edward also says Anthony Blunt should undoubtedly have been sacked from the Royal Household when his treason was first known.

29 June 1998
Johnnie Nutting tells me he will not charge Jonathan Aitken a penny for defending him in his forthcoming trial for perjury. They were exact contemporaries and friends at Eton, but did have a great row when, at the time of Suez, Jonathan told Johnnie that Anthony Nutting was a traitor. Johnnie says: 'I know I flew at him and I may have been armed with a poker.'

12 July 1998
The Queen Mother tells me she is not in favour of a memorial to Princess Diana in Kensington Gardens. But she goes on to emphasise that there was no break with the Queen – 'It was all made up by the Press.'

The QM is also strongly against the lowering of the homosexual age of consent from eighteen to sixteen, which is soon to be debated in Parliament. She has urged the Queen to speak to the PM about it.

18 July 1998
Max Egremont is now writing a life of Siegfried Sassoon. I ask him whether it was worth spending four years writing Spears's life. Max: 'It made no money, but showed I could write a biography of a difficult character. So for Siegfried Sassoon I have an advance of £100,000.' K.R.: 'The publisher will expect a lot of buggery for that.' Max: 'He shall have it.'

21 July 1998
Prince Eddie to lunch at Le Gavroche. He is utterly furious about the plans for a memorial garden to Princess Diana in Kensington Gardens – 'and I don't mind if it is known'.

22 July 1998
The House of Lords is buzzing with excitement at the debate this afternoon on whether the homosexual age of consent should be lowered from eighteen to sixteen. The Commons have already given a big majority to the change. The argument being touted in some parts of the Lords is that if kept at eighteen it will be widely flouted and cannot be enforced.

23 July 1998
The peers inflicted a heavy defeat on the homosexual lobby last night by

voting down the Government's lowering of the age of consent. So another conflict looms between the two Houses.

31 July 1998

The Court of Appeal has upheld an appeal by the family of Derek Bentley, hanged forty-five years ago for the alleged murder of a policeman, because of a flawed summing-up by Lord Chief Justice Goddard,* who is much reviled. Bentley is hailed as a martyr and a saint.

Although nearly half a century divided us in age, I knew Goddard well in the last twenty years or so of his life. Our table talk was largely about the law, in which I had taken a layman's interest since schooldays. He much commended Dickens for his knowledge of judicial procedure in the case of Bardell and Pickwick, which he would quote at length.

11 August 1998

John King, depressed by his indifferent health, talks to me of death. He wants to be buried rather than cremated – 'just in case there is a resurrection.' I do not attempt to disabuse him of his erroneous theology.

15 August 1998

I am amazed to see a headline in the *Daily Mail* in a newspaper scoop that says the Prince of Wales has written to the Chancellor of the Exchequer approving the proposed memorial garden to Princess Diana in Kensington Gardens. Why should the public be deprived of part of that lovely park to soothe the Prince's conscience? I make a point of sitting there for some time this afternoon: utter peaceful delight.

20 August 1998

Lunch with Edward Ford. He shows me some of the letters he has received from Robert Rhodes James about his book on George VI. I suspect it will be as dull as the earlier chapters R.R.J. showed me. He has had access to the papers of George VI and Tommy Lascelles, but can quote from neither directly. I am amazed that he agreed to write the book on such terms. It is forty years since Wheeler-Bennett published his official life, including extracts from the King's diaries. Since then nobody has published more of them – and now R.R.J. is also barred. But it is significant that, according to R.R.J., both the Queen and the QM became evasive when talking about Lascelles.

---

* Rayner, Baron Goddard (1877–1971), Lord Chief Justice 1946–58, known for his severe sentencing.

Edward says that he was 'against the Queen's marriage to Prince Philip and would have preferred Hugh Grafton'.* Another point that R.R.J. brings out is the King's difficulty in achieving intimacy with Attlee, but everybody had difficulty doing this.

21 August 1998
Michael Bloch tells me that James Lees-Milne left him the remaining volumes of his diaries to edit.†

29 August 1998
Every newspaper is full of the most appalling gush and counter-gush as the first anniversary of Princess Diana's death approaches.

3 September 1998
The railings round Kensington Palace are again surrounded by bunches of flowers in memory of Diana – but only a tiny fraction of the display a year ago. Most of the crowd seem to be foreigners. Few people have removed the wrapping paper of the flowers, so that their beauty is hidden: just a sea of white and grey, a sad sight on a golden summer evening.

20 September 1998
Train to Windsor, where the station has been developed to include several excellent cafés and shops while retaining some striking Victoriana and a fine mid-nineteenth-century locomotive.

Walk down to Eton to lunch with Tim Card, the Vice-Provost. We both talk about Eton's declining political role. The present Government contains only one Etonian, and that an Under-Secretary.‡

I ask whether I am correct in surmising that many boys in the school today speak with regional accents (as, of course, did Gladstone). Yes, says Tim, most of them. He is concerned with supervising the reading of lessons in College Chapel and finds that few can pronounce a word of, say, four syllables: one or two are usually omitted. And most speak in what Tim calls 'Estuary English'.

---

* Hugh Fitzroy, 11th Duke of Grafton (1919–2011), ADC to FM Earl Wavell, Viceroy and Gov. Gen. of India 1943–7; President of the Society for the Protection of Ancient Buildings.
† The Lees-Milne diaries eventually totalled twelve volumes.
‡ In the run-up to the 1959 election Harold Macmillan said: 'Mr Attlee had three Old Etonians in his Cabinet; I have six. Things are twice as good under the Conservatives.'

22 September 1998

I write to Jonathan Aitken, wishing him luck in his forthcoming ordeal.

Read extracts from Ted Heath's memoirs. He makes an awful nonsense of the chronology of the change of Prime Ministers from Harold Macmillan to Alec Home in 1963. His memory is fallible and his researchers obviously have not checked.

3 October 1998

I hear Prince Eddie talking to Michael Berkeley on his weekly radio programme on Radio 3 *Private Passions** about his choice of favourite music: a Chopin nocturne and the last scene of Jánáček's *Katya Kabanova*. He also says that his first visit to Bayreuth in 1954, 'without any preparation', hooked him for life.

20 October 1998

Serialisation of Woodrow Wyatt's scandalous diaries in the *Sunday Times* during the last three weeks makes me ponder my Journals. I think I am less malicious, and certainly I never record the sexual lives of others.

21 October 1998

Splendid news: the grandiose Government plan to spend £10 million making a memorial garden to Diana in Kensington Gardens has been abandoned because of fierce opposition from local residents and no enthusiasm from other parts of London and the country. So we shall be spared a Diana Disneyland and a 300-foot jet in the middle of the Round Pond. There may well be an improved children's park near the North Gates.

23 October 1998

I am flabbergasted to receive a handwritten letter from John Butterwick,[†] Chairman of the Old Etonian Association, telling me that I have been elected an honorary member. At first I think it some kind of practical joke, but when I see that there is a second-class stamp on the envelope I realise it is genuine! Apart from beaks, who are elected automatically after twenty years (i.e. non-Etonian beaks), the only other honorary OEs are two Head Masters, Michael McCrum and Eric Anderson, and the Queen Mother. I cannot imagine what I have done to deserve it. The only person I telephone is Giles St Aubyn. It

---

* K.R. listened to *Private Passions* on Sunday mornings whenever he could. When I appeared on the programme in June 2012 he rang within five minutes of it ending to discuss my choices.
† (b. 1923), Chairman of the OE Association 1986–99.

entitles me to wear an OE tie – but of course I shall never do so: OE braces perhaps.

3 December 1998

A first-class political row blows up. Robert Cranborne, without consulting William Hague, has negotiated a deal with Blair by which the Tory peers in the Upper House will allow Government business to go through in return for the retention of about ninety peers who would otherwise have suffered the fate of all the other hereditary peers and lost their seats. It is open to debate as to whether it is a good or a bad bargain. What cannot be doubted is that Cranborne has behaved deviously in not consulting Hague and that Hague is justified in dismissing Cranborne as Leader of the Opposition in the Lords. Curiously enough, Cranborne seems to have been given the choice by Hague of dismissal or resignation, and chose dismissal. I think he should have resigned, in the old Cecil tradition.

I talk to Peter Carrington about it. He tried to get Hague to agree to the Cranborne plan, but failed. Peter, however, does not attempt to defend the way in which Cranborne acted behind Hague's back in collusion with No. 10. He thinks it mad of Hague to refuse the deal and to cling to last-ditch opposition to Government legislation in the Lords unless Blair produces a long-term settlement for a Second Chamber. Peter says that Hague even wants to oppose Government Bills on second reading, which the country will not accept. Had Hague agreed to the Cranborne deal, at least the hereditary peers would have retained a toehold in the Lords. The Cranborne plan is in fact similar to the one Peter put forward when Leader of the Opposition peers in 1968; but it was scuppered by an unholy alliance between Enoch Powell and Michael Foot.

16 December 1998

Read *Speaking for Themselves: The Personal Letters of Winston and Clementine Churchill.* A monumental volume of 700 pages, impeccably edited by Mary Soames. I would have liked more family gossip. Clemmie could be formidable in urging W.S.C. on a course of action he found distasteful: often a matter of manners. Her health seems to have been deplorable, so that there were long separations while she sought a cure.

24 December 1998

The resignations of Peter Mandelson and Geoffrey Robinson* have dealt the Government a shattering blow. More will emerge of Robinson's secret loan to Mandelson of £373,000: was it an inducement for Mandelson to further Robinson's political career?† One satisfactory aspect is the exposure of 'sleaze' in the Government of the self-serving Blair.

My *TLS* review of Robert Rhodes James on King George VI. I have been more charitable than he deserves.

30 December 1998

The enforced resignation of Peter Mandelson rumbles on in the newspapers.

I read the first quarter or so of Herman Melville's *Moby Dick* and find its discursiveness and apocalyptic style and slow dialogue unappetising.

31 December 1998

New Year Honours. John Major accepts a CH from Blair for services to the 'peace process' in Northern Ireland. He should not have done so. Why should he have put himself in Blair's debt and given him a spurious reputation for magnanimity?

---

* Peter Mandelson, Baron Mandelson (b. 1953), Labour politician. MP for Hartlepool 1992–2004; Sec. of State for Northern Ireland 1999–2001; Sec. of State for Business and President of the Board of Trade 2008–2010. Geoffrey Robinson (b. 1938), Labour politician. MP for Coventry North West since 1976; Paymaster General 1997–8.

† Geoffrey Robinson denied any wrongdoing to the *Guardian*: 'Peter Mandelson, a friend of long standing, asked me for help in 1996. I was in a position to help through a loan and did so with the understanding that it would be repaid in full in due course. That is all there was and there is to it.'

1999

On 1 January the Euro was launched, but the Labour government stuck to the pound sterling. On 1 April a minimum wage was introduced in Britain, set at £3.60 for those over twenty-one and £3 for those under twenty-one. The first elections were held for the Scottish and Welsh Parliaments on 6 May. On 8 June Jonathan Aitken was sentenced to eighteen months in prison for perjury. The European Parliament elections were held, the Conservatives gaining 36 seats compared to Labour's 29. Cardinal Basil Hume died on 17 June. The marriage of Prince Edward and Sophie Rhys-Jones took place at St George's Chapel, Windsor, on 19 June. Construction of the Millennium Dome was completed on 23 June. William Whitelaw died on 1 July. Charles Kennedy was elected leader of the Liberal Democrats on 9 August. A solar eclipse across Europe on 11 August was witnessed by 350 million people. A MORI poll gave Labour a twenty-two-point lead over the Conservatives on 20 August. The Ladbroke Grove rail crash on 5 October claimed the lives of thirty-one people. The London Eye began to be lifted into position on the South Bank in London on 10 October. Millennium celebrations were held across the UK on 31 December.

2 January 1999
At Prue Penn's, Princess Margaret says the Queen told her that there were three miracles from the Windsor Castle fire:
1. No loss of life.
2. Many contents had already been removed for rewiring.
3. There was no wind.

6 January 1999
Announcement of the engagement of Prince Edward to the girl he has been living with for years, Sophie Rhys-Jones.* Speculation about a possible

---

* (b. 1965), wife of Prince Edward, Earl of Wessex.

dukedom. Sussex would be the most innocuous. All the others have military associations or disreputable memories.

13 January 1999
Lunch with Peter Carrington at the House of Lords. 'Were you disappointed not to be knighted?' Peter asks. I can quite sincerely say that I was not, but I do mention that the Royal Victorian Order would have been agreeable for my biography of King George V. Peter agrees that it is absurd to confine the Order to officially commissioned biographies of the Royal Family.

Quite a long talk on the telephone with Jonathan Aitken. He comes to trial in June. Johnnie Nutting thought earlier that he would get four years, but is now a bit more optimistic. Much may depend on the choice of trial judge. But that is not his only worry. He is facing imprisonment, divorce and bankruptcy – owing £2.5 million to the *Guardian* for legal fees. 'So I look to the three Fs: Faith, Family and Friends.'

23 January 1999
Repton announces that the local professional football team Derby County is to send up to six star apprentice players there a year, as boarders. It should help the 1st XI, if not the academic standard.

28 January 1999
Sussex University tell me that each of the two joint winners of the Rose Prize this year receive £125, entirely from the interest on the capital I gave the university.

2 February 1999
John Grigg asks me a political conundrum. When did Michael Heseltine come closest to becoming Prime Minister? Not at one of the elections for the leadership, but when the IRA launched a mortar bomb at No. 10 from Whitehall during a Cabinet meeting. Had the entire Cabinet been wiped out, Heseltine would have become PM, as he was not present for some reason.

3 February 1999
Antony Acland has been badly treated in not receiving a peerage. It used to be the traditional reward for a retiring Permanent Under-Secretary at the Foreign Office. But Mrs Thatcher did not like the FO in general and Michael Palliser as PU-S in particular. He received no peerage, though he was made a Privy Councillor. Since then Antony has been passed over, but others such as

Patrick Wright* have been made peers. Anthony is retiring in or about March 2000 when he will be seventy. Eric Anderson is to be the next Provost of Eton after Antony, and if he were to be made a peer it would deeply upset Antony. Such an honour, though, for a Provost of Eton cannot be high in Blair's list of priorities. If Antony were to be given a peerage for his FO work, then Palliser and Nico Henderson would also have to be considered. A complex scenario all because of Thatcher's prejudices about the FO.

10 February 1999

Dwin Bramall talks to me about Monty – 'a good leader, but an awful character'. He owed everything to the death of 'Strafer' Gott,† who had been nominated by Winston to command the Eighth Army but was killed on the way to take up his command when his plane was shot down by the Germans. Monty was then Winston's new choice. Years later, after the war, Lady Gott went up to Monty at some party and said: 'I am Strafer Gott's widow.' Monty looked through her and said: 'I have never heard of him.' It is too gruesome, but not uncharacteristic.

13 February 1999

Brian Rees sends me a copy of his life of Camille Saint-Saëns, on which he has laboured for years. I will try to seek some publicity for it. I do admire his industry and courage in the face of so many obstacles, worries and misfortunes.

14 February 1999

The art critic Brian Sewell‡ gave a talk at St Paul's School. Afterwards the High Master asked him what he thought of the boys. Brian replied: 'They make pederasty an incomprehensible vice.'

17 February 1999

Andrew Roberts has finished his life of Salisbury and received a letter of warm praise from Robert Cranborne. Cranborne's father is reading it at present and may prove more difficult. Andrew has already arranged a publishing party for 28 September at the National Army Museum. 'Write it down now,' he says, 'there will be lots of people you know.' I mischievously say: 'Yes, and you may know a few of them too.'

---

* Sir Patrick Wright, Baron Wright of Richmond (b. 1931), Permanent Under-Sec. at the Foreign Office 1986–91.
† Lt-Gen. William Gott (1897–1942); served in both world wars.
‡ (1931–2015), art critic and media personality.

23 March 1999

A cheery card from Jonathan Aitken, as if he were about to go on a Swan Hellenic cruise: 'I am in good spirits as Wormwood Scrubs beckons. Give me some tips for a reading list, please, as I'm going to have time in abundance for all those great works I should have read years ago.'

26 March 1999

Rather than write to Jonathan about him, I telephone with details of some of the lesser-known biographies, such as G.O. Trevelyan's *Macaulay*[*] and Lockhart's[†] life of Sir Walter Scott. Tell him that Austen Chamberlain found pleasure in reading it. And then there is Gibbon. Jonathan hopes to be able to take courses in theology and computer studies.

28 March 1999

Summer Time begins. I go to St Paul's Cathedral for the Palm Sunday matins. I have a seat at the front with the splendid vista of dome and choir before me. I give thanks that my medical prognosis is better. The singing is exquisite, especially of the *Lamentations of Jeremiah* by Sir Edward Bairstow,[‡] organist, chorus master and composer, born in Huddersfield with its rich choral tradition.

Afterwards I go down to the crypt to look at the Order of the British Empire Chapel.[§] A kindly verger opens it for me and shows me some of its features. He is pleased with one or two anecdotes about the history of the Order which he did not know and will doubtless add to his repertoire.

Home to lunch in the sun in the garden. The pink camellia is still smothered in flowers. But I am haunted by the horror of Yugoslavia and the conviction that Blair has blundered in tying himself to Clinton's coat-tails by committing British planes and troops. It is bizarre to find Blair stiffening Clinton in his NATO assault on Yugoslavia – and even calling in Margaret Thatcher for advice on how to run a war.

11 May 1999

Jonathan Aitken declares himself bankrupt. The good side to it is that Granada TV and the *Guardian*, which he foolishly and unsuccessfully sued

---

[*] Sir George Otto Trevelyan, 2nd Bt (1838–1928), statesman and author. Chief Secretary for Ireland 1882–4.

[†] John Gibson Lockhart (1794–1854), writer and editor; his life of Sir Walter Scott, his father-in-law, appeared in seven volumes.

[‡] (1874–1946), composer and organist.

[§] It was in this chapel that K.R.'s memorial service took place on 8 May 2014.

for libel, will not now get their £2 million legal costs; only ten days ago they rejected his offer of £840,000 put together by his wife and friends.

12 May 1999

To a party given by Richard Chartres, the Bishop of London, and Martin Charteris on behalf of the Prayer Book Society to celebrate the 450th anniversary of the Book of Common Prayer. Richard Chartres is charming. It is a very Trollopian evening.

19 May 1999

Mary Soames tells me that Roy Jenkins is writing a one-volume life of W.S.C.: apparently there is an inexhaustible demand for Churchill works, even today. Mary also tells me how angry she was with Robert Rhodes James. He agreed to her invitation to write a life of Christopher Soames and she gave him all the papers. Then R.R.J. changed his mind. He told me, but obviously not Mary, that he could not continue as he had found something discreditable, unspecified, about Christopher's war service. Mary very much approves of my mildly critical review of R.R.J.'s recent study of KGVI.

22 May 1999

I am more upset than I should have imagined at the death of Robert Rhodes James, aged sixty-six. I heard not long ago that he had cancer, but did not expect the end so soon. Whether from too many interests, unfulfilled ambition or drink, he never again wrote such a good biography as his life of Rosebery, though his edition of Chips Channon's diaries put us all in his debt. He was quirky in his use of material; equivocal about sources; ungenerous to those he had crossed, such as Andrew Roberts; self-important, as in his Preface to his book on Prince Albert. He always expressed a friendly interest, even admiration, in my work; but could make clumsy judgements, as in his last work, on George VI, when he attributed the success of my *KGV* to my dependence on Harold Nicolson. I think my review of his *KGVI* was nevertheless fair, though I worried at the time whether, for old times' sake, I should have made it warmer. Had I known he was nearing his grave, I should have done so.

25 May 1999

Philip Ziegler gives a neat talk on Royal biography at the Biographers' Club. He described how, when he consulted Tommy Lascelles on his biography of Edward VIII and asked how far he could mention sex and money, Tommy replied: 'Take away sex and money from Edward VIII, and what is left?' This contrasts with Tommy's advice to Harold Nicolson that he must omit anything discreditable in his official life of KGV.

1 June 1999

Andrew Roberts tells me that the untimely death of Robert Rhodes James will protect him from a bitchy review of his forthcoming life of Lord Salisbury. R.R.J. conceived a deep hatred for Andrew, as he said he was a fascist.

I recall the day exactly sixty years ago of the news of my scholarship to Repton, but also the news of the tragedy of the submarine *Thetis*.[*]

8 June 1999

Jonathan Aitken sentenced to eighteen months in prison for perjury and perverting the course of justice. He will be out in nine months.

15 June 1999

The use of St George's, Windsor, for the wedding of Prince Edward next Saturday is said to be because the Queen did not want the spotlight to shine on the quarrelsome Dean of Westminster, embroiled in controversy at the moment over his dismissal of the organist Martin Neary.[†]

19 June 1999

The day of Prince Edward's wedding, but I do not listen to the wireless broadcast. The Queen has made him Earl of Wessex and Viscount Severn. Why not Thane of Korda?

22 June 1999

Paul Johnson tells me that Roy Jenkins was much criticised at Oxford for not having attended the opening of the business school endowed by Wafic Saïd[‡] at a cost of £20 million – a stupendous benefaction. 'Roy is afraid of offending the left-wing.'

William Rees-Mogg, who has been re-reading my *Later Cecils*, has more reason than most to remember Linky. As a small boy, William sat for an Eton scholarship and the examiners put him on the list for election. Then Linky intervened and declared that a Roman Catholic could not be a King's Scholar. So William went to Charterhouse – and the Provost was henceforth

---

[*] The submarine HMS *Thetis* sank with the loss of ninety-nine lives during sea trials on 1 June 1939. She was salvaged and recommissioned as HMS *Thunderbolt*, but was lost with all hands on 14 Mar. 1943.

[†] (b. 1940), organist and choral conductor.

[‡] (b. 1939), entrepreneur and philanthropist.

excluded from interfering with elections to College. All this William relates with bitterness.

23 June 1999

To Rhodes House in Oxford for the Vice-Chancellor's lunch. I have the good fortune to sit next to Reg Carr,* Librarian of the Bodleian, so we are able to have some useful talk about my proposed benefaction. As well as the money and my papers, including the Journals, he would like my library as a whole. He mentions that the executors of Enoch Powell are preparing to offer his papers on long deposit, which means that they could one day be withdrawn, not very satisfactory regarding cataloguing which is so expensive.

When Reg showed the Queen round a Bodleian exhibition in Univ., the quad was full of cheering undergraduates. 'I suppose they are cheering you,' she remarked.

25 June 1999

Listen to part of Cardinal Hume's funeral at Westminster Cathedral on the wireless. The Duchess of Kent is representing the Queen. I am surprised. It should have been the ecumenically minded Prince of Wales.

13 July 1999

Sarah York sends a car and driver to take me down to Sunninghill Park for tea. A discreet entrance with the notice: 'Private. Crown Property.' A shrubby drive, then the house itself, much criticised when built by the Queen for the Yorks – justifiably so. A lot of guests, including Bishop Peter Ball,† the former Bishop of Gloucester, who resigned his see after some trouble with a boy many years ago; apparently the Prince of Wales has given him a house on the Duchy of Cornwall estate. He is a jokey man, I suppose a way of demonstrating his innocence. When I happen to ask him what he thinks of Richard Chartres, the Bishop of London, Ball smirks: 'He writes good limericks.' When I say: 'Is that not a frivolous answer?' he goes on smirking.

The two little Princesses, Eugenie and Beatrice, are as enchanting as ever, and not a bit put out by the incursion of so many strangers.

---

* Reginald Carr (b. 1946), Bodley's Librarian, Oxford 1997–2006.
† The Rt Revd Peter Ball (b. 1932), Bishop of Gloucester 1992–3; in Oct. 2015 he was sentenced to thirty-two months' imprisonment for indecent assault of eighteen young men; he was released in Feb. 2017.

19 July 1999

A long and amusing letter from Jonathan Aitken, in which he says that prison is no more Spartan than Eton in the 1950s. I spend an hour or so drafting a witness statement pleading that his library should not be sold by the trustee in bankruptcy since it contains 'the tools of his trade', as exempted by the Insolvency Act of 1886.

29 July 1999

Such a nice letter from Jonathan Aitken, dictated in Standford Hill Prison, typed out by his solicitor, thanking me for the 'magisterial witness statement' I wrote for him to try to prevent his library from being seized and sold by the trustee in bankruptcy. As there seems to be much more freedom of correspondence allowed to prisoners nowadays, I must write him a jolly letter.

21 August 1999

Prince Eddie calls, as always kind, modest, interested, dignified. I show him the most recent of Jonathan Aitken's letters to read and he marvels at his cheerfulness, courage and wit.

24 August 1999

I am touched to receive a copy of Andrew Roberts' life of Salisbury, inscribed: 'To Kenneth, in homage to a Master.' Almost embarrassed by this, but he does have a generous nature.*

26 August 1999

Write a long letter to Jonathan Aitken: really an 'Albany' column just for him. I don't suppose he will find many fellow prisoners to share it with. He has had a visit from Frank Longford. 'To have a visit from the senior Knight of the Garter is indeed an accolade: a cross between Holy Communion and receiving your house colours. I told the Channons about it at Kelvedon last weekend. Your account was hugely appreciated and they send you their warmest good wishes.'

9 September 1999

Michael Portillo has not yet decided whether to put in for Alan Clark's seat, Chelsea, with its huge Tory majority. Paul Channon says he would not be certain to be selected, particularly in view of his declaration that at Cambridge

---

* Kenneth is correct. Andrew Roberts inscribed my copy 'To Richard, with best wishes for *Eden*, with admiration and with my fondest regards.'

he had homosexual encounters.* And if he did become MP for the borough, he would not find it easy to dislodge Hague as leader.

14 September 1999
Andrew Roberts is still rather apprehensive about reviews of his life of Lord Salisbury, though with one exception they have so far been laudatory. Roy Jenkins, however, has been unpleasant in the *FT*: perhaps because Andrew was one of the judges who denied him the National Cash Register Prize (now called something else) for his book on Gladstone.

1 November 1999
Shocked and saddened by the sudden death at fifty-eight of Colin Matthew, editor of the *DNB*. I am more pleased than ever that I pushed his claims on the Wolfson Prize at the expense of Roy Jenkins' book on Gladstone, largely plagiarised from Colin's edition of Gladstone's diaries.

2 November 1999
Andrew Roberts' *Salisbury* is very well done and he deserves any prizes that are going. He has mastered a huge mass of archival material and has given the book a logical and pleasing architectural shape. Some delectable gossip too about honours and offices. Salisbury emerges as a cold and sometimes cruel man, but one who could not write an uninteresting sentence. What a burden of work he carried into old age. I like his reverence for Queen Victoria and corresponding contempt for the Prince of Wales. I get the impression that Andrew is rather disappointed in the sales.

When I mention how pleased I am to have denied Roy Jenkins for the Wolfson Prize in favour of the much-lamented Colin Matthew, Andrew tells me that he too dished Roy for the NCR Prize. 'Jenkins' *Gladstone* was all taken from Colin, and now Roy has the impudence to embark on a life of Churchill taken from Martin Gilbert.'

16 November 1999
Hugo Vickers telephones in a bate with the content of the Queen's Speech at the Opening of Parliament. He says that it contains not only the Government's forthcoming legislative programme, but also much contentious self-congratulation on its supposed achievements since coming to office. Hugo thinks this is unconstitutional. The Government can include what it likes, though this is an undesirable precedent.

---

* Portillo was selected as candidate for the seat, which he won in a by-election in Nov. 1999.

25 November 1999

Peter Carrington to lunch at the Ritz. Ted Heath has told Peter he is worried about the renewed investigation into 'Bloody Sunday' in Londonderry. Apparently, he once wrote a memorandum which is likely to be produced in evidence, in which he said that the earlier Widgery* investigation was not wholly judicial, but also political.

26 November 1999

Invitations have been sent out to the Millennium Dome celebrations on New Year's Eve. The letter proclaims that it will be opened by HM The Queen 'in the presence of the Prime Minister'. That is the way Blair deals with the monarchy.

5 December 1999

Read Anthony Powell's *Books Do Furnish a Room*. It is obviously based on Cyril Connolly and *Horizon*, but the publisher-author plot bores me.

11 December 1999

John King tells me that Marcus Kimball[†] has told him that when the Blairs stayed at Balmoral, they signed the visitors' book 'Tony Blair' and 'Cherie Booth QC'.[‡] She was not of course invited as Cherie Booth QC, but as the wife of the PM.

A beautifully wrapped parcel arrives from Sarah York, as well as a charming Christmas card of the children.

31 December 1999

Watch the opening of the Millennium Dome on TV with the Ridleys, though none of us is enthusiastic. The Queen is alone among the many thousands in wearing a hat, with a touch of remoteness from it all. The music is sub-pop. Blair soapy, Mandelson anxious, Heath supine. Fireworks display memorable, but far too long, and shameful that £1 million should have been spent on

---

* Sir John Widgery, Baron Widgery of South Molton (1911–81), Lord Chief Justice of England and Wales 1971–80, presided over the Widgery Tribunal into the events of Bloody Sunday in Jan. 1972.

† Baron Kimball of Easton (1928–2014), Conservative politician. MP for Gainsborough 1956–83.

‡ Cherie Blair, known professionally as Cherie Booth (b. 1954), barrister.

it. The Eiffel Tower in Paris by contrast is superbly illuminated. The Queen reluctant to cross arms with Blair for 'Auld Lang Syne'. So ends the twentieth century.*

---

* Though K.R. was not alone in believing that the real end of the century came a year later.

2000

Millennium celebrations took place throughout the UK on 1 January, the start of a century leap year. Vladimir Putin was elected President of Russia on 26 March. The novelist Anthony Powell died on 28 March. May Day riots took place in central London on 1 May and the statue of Churchill in Parliament Square and the Cenotaph were daubed with graffiti. Ken Livingstone was elected Mayor of London on 4 May. The Tate Modern was opened on 12 May. Donald Coggan, former Archbishop of Canterbury, died on 17 May. Tony Blair was heckled and slow-handclapped at the Women's Institute on 10 June. The Millennium Bridge across the Thames was opened on 10 June, but had to be closed when it started swaying. Robert Runcie, former Archbishop of Canterbury, died on 11 July. The Queen Mother celebrated her 100th birthday on 4 August. There were nationwide protests at high fuel prices on 8 September. The Conservatives were two points ahead of Labour in a MORI poll on 14 September. Wembley Stadium closed on 7 October, to be rebuilt for reopening in 2003. After settlement of the fuel crisis Labour regained a lead of thirteen points in a MORI poll on 23 October. The first resident crew entered the International Space Station on 2 November. The US Presidential election, Bush v. Gore, was left unresolved on 7 November. The Church of England introduced the Common Worship series of service books on 3 December. After complex recounts and court cases, George Bush was declared President of the US on 14 December. Arctic weather blighted Britain on 29 December. The Millennium Dome closed on 31 December.

1 January 2000

The papers are full of complaints about the organisation of the celebrations at the Millennium Dome last night: huge queues at the Tube stations, so that many guests arrived late or not at all; several thousand invitations not sent out in time; the 'river of fire' on the Thames a flop; the BA wheel out of action by order of the health and safety inspectors. There has never been an event which I am more pleased to have missed.

2 January 2000

Dominic Lawson in the *Sunday Telegraph* writes about the cavalier way in which he and other 'VIPs' were treated at the Dome, having been obliged to queue in the rain.

3 January 2000

Clear, cold, sunny day. Fill in the year 2000 on all the cheques in my cheque-book – and tell everyone else to do so. London still very dead.

11 January 2000

Peter Williams,* the Master of St Catherine's College, Oxford, tells me he accompanied the Prime Minister and a few businessmen to Tokyo. He was well prepared to listen as well as talk. But Williams was disturbed by how little sleep Blair allowed himself – albeit while also dealing with Northern Ireland from thousands of miles away. 'Margaret Thatcher needed only four hours' sleep and got them. Blair needs seven hours and gets only four.'

13 January 2000

Peter Carrington tells me that among the speakers at a Lords debate he initiated on Tuesday on foreign affairs were four ex-Foreign Secretaries, three ex-Chancellors, seven ex-Cabinet ministers and three Permanent Under-Secretaries. There were only three Government ministers present and the debate was replied to by an Under-Secretary. Not a word of the debate was reported.

14 January 2000

Good talk with Pammie Hicks. Years after Mountbatten had ceased to be Viceroy, he and Pammie went to stay with the President of India in Delhi. On the last day the President said: 'By the way, I have had the King of Afghanistan staying here. You must meet him.' So vast is Lutyens' palace that they had been unaware of a State Visit taking place elsewhere in the building.

21 January 2000

Eric Anderson writes to let me know that the memorial service to Martin Charteris, who died just before Christmas, is to be in College Chapel at Eton on 20 March, and that Gay has asked him to speak. Can I help? So I telephone with a few anecdotes. Eric laughs at Martin's remark to me: 'The Queen and

---

* Sir Peter Williams (b. 1945), physicist; Master of St Catherine's Coll., Oxford 2000–02.

I produce an excellent speech, then Prince Philip gets hold of it and rewrites it in German.'

24 January 2000

Hugo Vickers tells me that Prince Philip has now read and passed – without enthusiasm – his life of the Prince's mother.* He has annotated the typescript heavily, but objects to nothing of importance. Where P.P. wrote 'nonsense' in the margin about one episode, Hugo pointed out that what appears in the text was based on sixteen pages of Foreign Office documents.

31 January 2000

A message from David Windlesham, asking me to stay the night in the Principal's Lodgings at Brasenose after I have dined in the college next month as the guest of Richard Thorpe. It is kind of him.

Richard, who is now at Brasenose after his one-year Fellowship at St Antony's, working on his life of Eden, has discovered in the papers of Archbishop Geoffrey Fisher at Lambeth that Fisher was so opposed to Suez that he welcomed secret anti-Eden information from Rab Butler and William Clark, which he then passed on to William Haley, editor of *The Times*. What a horrible old man he was.

15 February 2000

To Oxford for a long talk with Richard Thorpe about his biography of Anthony Eden, followed by High Table dinner in Hall at BNC. I take him my files on Jim Cilcennin,[†] as well as some Eden anecdotes.

Richard speaks of Randolph Churchill's unpleasant behaviour to his cousin Clarissa on her marriage to Eden. He told her: 'I give Anthony two years to improve. If he fails to do so, I shall begin attacking again in the *Evening Standard*.' Two years to the day after the marriage, another poisonous article on Eden appeared.

Richard wonders how much Clarissa wants to guide his hand, though there is no sign of it yet. He would like to know what she so disliked about Robert Rhodes James's biography, which on the whole was favourable to Anthony. Another issue to be resolved is why Winston clung to office until 1955 – was it because he mistrusted Anthony's ability to be PM, or to allow Anthony to recover fully from his gall-bladder problems simply because he

---

* *Alice, Princess Andrew of Greece* (2000).
† James Thomas, 1st Viscount Cilcennin (1903–60), First Lord of the Admiralty 1951–6.

himself liked being PM?[*] Eden was not much liked by the King and Queen – he had been anti-Chamberlain and a friend of Edward VIII. Richard says that Macmillan always disliked Eden from the days when Eden was so far below him at Eton.

We dine agreeably in Hall, a charming building with portraits of Bob Runcie, William Golding and Field Marshal Haig.[†] Good food and wine. Sit next to David Windlesham, and at dessert I have Vernon Bogdanor,[‡] a Fellow of BNC and Professor of Government at Oxford.

20 March 2000

To Eton with Mary Soames for Martin Charteris' memorial service. Eton looks lovely in the pale sunlight. College Chapel absolutely packed. A clutch of Royals including the Prince of Wales in the stalls next to the Provost. The service has some very Charteresque touches. Antony Acland has a fine bearing and reads well. After the service Eric Anderson says to me: 'There will be more of Rose when I give another address at the St Margaret's service for Martin.' Gay Charteris very composed. A host of friends for tea in School Hall. A notable occasion but altogether too many ghosts.

Andrew Roberts telephones tonight to tell me he has had a letter from the Wolfson Foundation. He is to share this year's Wolfson Prize with someone else, as yet unknown. So he will receive £12,500. I am delighted for him. The industry alone is prodigious and the architecture of his book impressive. Had he not won the Wolfson, I doubt whether any other prize would have come his way. An 800-page biography of Salisbury, an almost unknown PM to the unhistorical reader, is not easy to promote. I write him a line of warmest congratulation, with a teasing postscript: 'Have you not thought of entering *Eminent Churchillians* for the Booker Prize for Fiction?'

24 March 2000

Eric Anderson sends me the text of his address at Martin Charteris' memorial service. It is full of plums: 'Maths was never Martin's strong suit,' and of meetings of the Provost and Fellows he would say, 'All I want to know is are we rolling in money or are we on the rocks?'

Johnnie Nutting tells me a story of Jonathan Aitken's arrival in prison. He was interviewed by a psychologist, who asked him: 'How big is your

---

[*] Lady Soames assured me that it was the third reason: her father could not bear the thought of leaving the stage.
[†] FM Sir Douglas Haig, 1st Earl Haig (1861–1928), C.-in-C. of the BEF on the Western Front 1915–18.
[‡] (b. 1943), Professor of Government at Oxford University 1996–2010.

immediate family?' 'Five.' 'And how many of those know you are in prison?' 'All of them.' 'And how many people not of your family know you are in prison?' 'Oh, I suppose about twenty million.' The psychologist put him down as a megalomaniac.

I dine at Christ's as a guest of Jack Plumb. At dinner I meet an honorary Fellow of the college, Jeffrey Tate,[*] the conductor and operatic director. He was born with spina bifida and bears his ailment with cheerful courage. We have some good talk about the famous Wieland Wagner production of the *Ring* at Bayreuth in 1954. He was once assistant to Pierre Boulez at Bayreuth and is to direct his own *Ring* at Cologne later this year.

The dinner has the appearance of an officers' guest night. Goronwy Rees[†] once told me that, on joining the army, he became at first a waiter in the sergeants' mess and observed that its rituals and shibboleths resembled those he had experienced on the High Table of All Souls.

29 March 2000

Death of Tony Powell yesterday at the age of ninety-four. I have written about him many times over the years. *A Question of Upbringing*, the first of his Proustian chain, is the best. He had a brilliant gift of writing about soldiers, particularly the Welsh. But some of his writing was diffuse and sloppy. Also he had a spiteful nature.

12 April 2000

Prince Eddie to lunch at Le Gavroche. He is worried about the future of English Freemasonry. When he retires there will be no Royal Grand Master Mason or any other senior Mason from the Royal Family for the first time since the eighteenth century. He had an hour with Prince Edward in his room at Buckingham Palace to try to persuade him, but failed.

There is to be a service of thanksgiving for the Queen Mother in St Paul's on 11 July. Eddie says that is a day Giles St Aubyn will be in London and we might all lunch.

16 April 2000

I give lunch to the Carringtons. I hear that the energy of the Queen Mother is deceptive. She goes out, gives every ounce of what she has, enchants everybody, but comes back exhausted. At one time she didn't mind whether or not she lives to be 100. Now she is determined to do so.

---

[*] Sir Geoffrey Tate (b. 1943), conductor; President of the UK Spina Bifida charity.
[†] (1909–79), Principal of Aberystwyth University 1953–7.

17 April 2000

Hugo Vickers tells me that the Royal Household now spend more time pleasing Tony Blair than they do the Queen.

3 May 2000

During an anarchist riot in London yesterday, the statue of Winston Churchill in Parliament Square was grotesquely vandalised, also the Cenotaph. How now, Mr Blair, and your sustained contempt for the forces of conservatism. I write a letter of sympathy to Mary Soames.

5 May 2000

Ken Livingstone elected Mayor of London. We shall all regret it. But the local-government elections have deprived Labour of several hundred seats.

Mary Soames thanks me for my message about the criminal vandalism in London, saying that she minded the damage to the Cenotaph most of all.

6 May 2000

I have lunch at Clarence House, just the Queen Mother, Prue Penn and myself, so we have a wide-ranging talk. Regarding Antony Acland's impending retirement as Provost of Eton, I express my sympathy that he has never received the peerage to which his role as PU-S at the FO entitled him. The QM did not realise that it used to be the standard reward until Mrs Thatcher's dislike of the FO changed the rules. I do not of course mention Martin Charteris' death: death is not a subject she welcomes.

We also touch on the ejection of most of the hereditary peers from the Lords: QM makes her feelings all too clear.

She asks me whether I like the poetry of Ted Hughes,[*] and I truthfully reply not very much. She seems surprised by this.

15 May 2000

Lunch with Edward Ford. We discuss whether the Queen was informed of Anthony Blunt's treason when he confessed to MI5 in 1964 (though it was not made public till 1979). I am certain that she was, on the instructions of the Home Secretary, Henry Brooke.[†] Roy Jenkins confirms this in his memoirs. But Richard Thorpe's life of Alec Home, Prime Minister at the time,

---

[*] (1930–98), Poet Laureate 1984–98.
[†] Baron Brooke of Cumnor (1903–84), Conservative politician. MP for Hampstead 1950–66; Home Secretary 1962–4.

reveals that he was not told or consulted in case his acute sense of what was fitting led him to refuse to compromise the Queen with the secret.

22 May 2000

The Blairs have a baby. Much derision that he greets the Press with a mug of coffee in his hand – outside No. 10. No PR opportunity is left to chance with that hollow man.

25 May 2000

The *Telegraph* reports that as Lord High Commissioner to the General Assembly, the Prince of Wales is accompanied at Holyrood by Camilla Parker-Bowles. She even dined with the elders. Lord Reith must be turning in his grave. I suppose it is to prepare us for Queen Camilla.

To the Royal Box at Covent Garden at five for *Meistersinger* with Prince Eddie. First I have a look at the new Floral Hall, elegant and spacious, and perhaps a good place to lunch one day. The new enlarged amphitheatre is a triumph: worth every penny of what has been spent on it, compared to the Millennium Dome, which was a drain in every sense. Wonderful singers, orchestra and chorus and Bernard Haitink* continues to conduct with magic. The programme book too has a most interesting article on the marking of the prize songs and its elaborate list of penalties.

3 June 2000

I now see why I have frequently noticed a pair of jays in my garden. Hearing a rustling in the ivy today I notice the parent birds feeding four of their young in a roughly constructed nest.

Reports that the Queen and Camilla Parker-Bowles met at a lunch today at Highgrove given by the Prince of Wales for King Constantine's sixtieth birthday. It appears to be part of the Prince's plan to accustom the nation to accepting Camilla as part of the family. It contrasts with the only time Mrs Simpson met King George V – 'smuggled into Buckingham Palace' by the then Prince of Wales, as he described it. This was at a reception a few days before Princess Marina married Prince George.

4 June 2000

Torrents of gush about the meeting between the Queen and Camilla. It changes nothing. If the Prince marries Camilla, she will be Queen. If not, she will remain his mistress, though scarcely with the present Queen's encouragement.

---

* (b. 1929), Dutch conductor; Music Dir. of the Royal Opera 1987–2002.

7 June 2000

Ted Heath tells me, 'There is no debate in the Commons nowadays, just a braying rabble.' He is also annoyed at the frequent references in the *Telegraph* to his having promised that our entry into Europe would lead to no loss of sovereignty. He says he never made such a statement without qualification.

28 June 2000

In Oxford I meet the Vice-Chancellor, Colin Lucas,[*] who seems shell-shocked still by the monstrously unfair attack on Oxford's supposed 'elitism' by the Chancellor of the Exchequer, Gordon Brown.[†] Lucas tells me that one of the senior Treasury team told him: 'I don't know why you take the Chancellor so seriously. We never do.'

I go on to the Vice-Chancellor's garden party in New College. It turns out to be a charming spectacle – a lovelier garden than that of Buckingham Palace and the Mound now a thing of beauty. It is a thrilling spectacle to see a stream of guests, mostly in academic robes, climbing and descending the thirty-nine steps like colourful ants.

1 July 2000

The papers in their nasty way attack the Royal Family for not attending the opening of the playground in Kensington Gardens in memory of Princess Diana. The boys have chosen not to be there. Why should the others? There are fanciful accounts of Diana in love with Kensington Gardens, 'sitting under a tree reading a book'. Tosh.

3 July 2000

Breakfast at the Hyde Park Hotel with Charles Guthrie. He is disturbed by the judicial inquiry into the 'Bloody Sunday' events in Londonderry, which could last years and cost millions. Blair himself, Charles says, was against the establishment of the present inquiry, but could not resist the pressure of his Labour colleagues.

---

[*] Sir Colin Lucas (b. 1940), Vice-Chancellor of Oxford University 1997–2004; Master of Balliol Coll., Oxford 1994–2001.

[†] On 26 May 2000 Gordon Brown said in a speech to the TUC that it was 'an absolute scandal' that a pupil from a state comprehensive in the north-east was refused a place at Oxford University owing to 'an old establishment interview system'. Roy Jenkins, Chancellor of Oxford University, criticised Brown, saying that 'nearly every fact he used was false'. The controversy rumbled on for weeks with its tabloid-pleasing allegations of class prejudice.

11 July 2000

To St Paul's Cathedral for the Service of Celebration and Thanksgiving for the Queen Mother's 100th birthday (which is not till 4 August). Choose to wear a dark suit rather than a morning coat, as the invitation permits.

Arrive quite early, which is just as well. I am in a block of unnumbered seats in the South Nave, but get an aisle seat. I notice several self-important people like Roy Strong looking cross as they realise they have no reserved seats, but must take pot luck. The little York girls, without their mother, look charming. The two Wales Princes look rather awkward; Prince Harry now going as bald as his brother, and the livelier of the two.

The service is moving, not least the music of John Rutter.[*] The Archbishop of Canterbury, George Carey, delivers an excellent address, far more touching and witty than anyone could have expected.

Later in the day I have some talk with Prue Penn. She tells me that after the service the Queen Mother lunched with the Prince of Wales at St James's Palace, never having been there before – all of ten yards from the rear door of Clarence House.

12 July 2000

News of the death of Robert Runcie yesterday in St Albans. I shall always think of him with affection.

13 July 2000

An excellent obituary of Robert Runcie in *The Times* reviving something of the paper's former authority. It records affectionately all Robert's virtues, but also his failings such as a lack of decisiveness. It also recalls 'his Muggeridge[†]-type voice'. In fact, Robert had three voices: the strained parsonical tones of his sermons and addresses; the unremarkable voice of conversation with friends, and the Scots infusion when with old members of his regiment.

16 July 2000

At Walmer Castle the Queen Mother tells me that Robert Runcie stayed at Royal Lodge earlier this month, only a few days before his death. He slept much of the day but came to meals and reminisced about his army days. The QM always thought that his reference to the Argentine dead in his sermon at the Falklands service was appropriate – he having seen the dead in tanks when in the Scots Guards during the war.

---

[*] (b, 1945), composer, particularly of choral music.
[†] Malcolm Muggeridge (1903–90), author and media personality.

She again mentions her love of the 1662 Prayer Book, used at her church in the park here. 'It is difficult to get the parsons to stay. They go off to be deans. We allow the present incumbent one Sunday a month when he can use the modern liturgy. I was appalled by the service when I went to my old house, St Paul's, Walden Bury; such inappropriate words in the Holy Communion.'

18 July 2000

I ask Roger Holloway about Robert Runcie's attitude to the old and new Prayer Books. He regretted the loss of the 1662 beauty of language but bowed to the need for the new one to match the modern Church. He did not recognise the old Prayer Book as the Anglican equivalent of the universal Latin Mass.

19 July 2000

Andrew Roberts calls at ten and we go down to the Dome by Tube. It is an impressive structure, with spacious piazzas and a promenade running along the river. Polite, helpful staff too, hundreds of them, it seems. One initial drawback. There are hundreds and hundreds of schoolchildren excitedly running all over the place, bumping into each other and generally distracting. The Government, determined to doctor the poor attendance figures of paying customers, have brought in school parties free of charge. The catering is good.

The most ludicrous zone is Faith. It includes the ultimate in bathetic: 'Jesus died tragically young.' It also refers to his work on behalf of the 'marginalised'.

We watch a show of acrobats, trapeze artists, people on stilts, etc., old-fashioned fun in a big top. I used to do all that sort of thing at Sandhurst.

The Rest pavilion is ludicrous – people lying about listening to drooling music. National Identity has a mixed bag of slogans, including a tribute to the grey squirrel.

All in all, the Dome is imposing architecturally, but the contents reflect our yobbo culture.

20 July 2000

The Prince of Wales's office has just announced again that he will never marry Camilla. So why did he take her to Holyrood for the General Assembly?

2 August 2000

Read *Daring to Hope*, the diaries and letters of Violet Bonham Carter[*] from 1946 to her death in 1969. She filled those years with meetings, broadcasts and committee work on good causes: liberalism, Biafra, the anti-apartheid movement. Unlike most pinkish intellectuals, she hated the Soviet system. Many visits to W.S.C. in old age, when he had an increasingly clouded and impenetrable mind. She was a great hater and rejoiced over de Gaulle's ill-health. Consistently unfair to Tories too. A great batterer to the very end of her life. But how easy it is to be dogmatic when one has no responsibility for the consequences.

5 August 2000

On previous visits to Wales the Prince of Wales has been lent the flat in Powis Castle which Lord Powis[†] leases from the National Trust. The other day, however, Lord Powis told the Prince that he could not stay for the Royal Welsh Show if he brought Camilla. So the Prince had to stay elsewhere. If, as the Prince has announced on more than one occasion, he has no intention of marrying Camilla, why does he want to take her to official events, such as the stay at Holyrood as Lord High Commissioner? It is surely unusual for a member of the Royal Family to be accompanied by his maîtresse-en-titre, except on private travels. He seems to want her to be recognised as his mistress.

7 August 2000

I read a review by Raymond Carr[‡] of a new biography of A.J.P. Taylor. At a celebratory dinner once, Raymond proposed his health and referred to him as 'our great historian'. A.J.P.T. interrupted angrily, 'our greatest historian' – and never spoke to Raymond again.

Deaths announced of Alec Guinness and Robin Day. Poor Robin was always dejected at heart by what he thought a failed career – i.e. not Prime Minister.

12 August 2000

Charles Guthrie tells me that his patience with the Government is fraying. The Armed Forces are increasingly being used for supposed humanitarian

---

[*] Baroness Asquith of Yarnbury (1887–1969), politician and diarist; dau. of H.H. Asquith. President of the Liberal Party 1945–7.

[†] John Herbert, 8th Earl Powis (b. 1952).

[‡] Sir Raymond Carr (1919–2015), historian. Warden of St Antony's Coll., Oxford 1968–87.

campaigns, thereby stretching them beyond endurance and safety. On a visit to a large warship he lunched with the petty officers, who told him: 'Do get rid of the women from our ships.' There is one woman minister who wants a quota of disabled in each regiment or other unit.

He is gloomy about the future of the Armed Forces, with so many such pressures on them that should not exist: the humanitarian role, sex equality, race equality and recruitment of the disabled. Still, the job of soldiers and other public servants is to carry out the policies of the Government of the day.

John King sends me a pacifist poem on war, written by his nine-year-old granddaughter. The form may indicate poetic promise, but I suspect the content has been strongly influenced by a teacher. What can a nine-year-old know of 'the trenches' and Great War themes?

23 August 2000
To Kensington Gardens after lunch, where I sit for a while. I have changed my mind about the Diana park for children at the north end. It seems to be crammed with happy children and disturbs nobody else. So much better than a vast Diana memorial garden in the south front of Kensington Palace.

30 September 2000
A very tall Harrovian at a party tells me two contrasting things. He is about to start at Edinburgh University to read Portuguese and many of his former schoolmates have nits in their hair. How is this? 'Well, if you are playing rugger against an Eton side your heads rub together in the scrum. Washing the hair in itself does no good: nits like the clean Harrovian hair.' A new insight into a long-standing rivalry!

3 October 2000
The Times is serialising yet another volume of Alan Clark's diaries: trivial, self-serving and dirty-minded.

5 October 2000
I talk with Prue Penn about Malcolm Williamson,* Master of the Queen's Musick and a composer of no great merit. I show her his inordinately long entry in *Who's Who*. Prue tells me that the Queen's choice as Master of the Queen's Musick in 1975 was Benjamin Britten, but he was too ill and turned

---

* (1931–2003), Australian composer who was Master of the Queen's Musick 1975–2003.

it down. She then thought of William Walton, but realised this would make Britten jealous. So she appointed the obviously inferior Williamson. At least it pleased the Australians.

13 October 2000
John Wilsey* sends me his draft chapter on Eton for his biography of Colonel 'H.' Jones VC.† He seems to me to paint too kind a portrait of Jones's house-master, Tom Brocklebank,‡ and also of Robert Birley. So I talk to Giles St Aubyn in Guernsey. He agrees. Tom was dour, and Birley, although a great figure <u>outside</u> Eton, was not at all as good as Eric Anderson in actually running the school.

8 November 2000
To Westminster Abbey for the service of thanksgiving for Robert Runcie. A huge congregation, including the Prince of Wales and Prince Eddie. Surprisingly, in the order of service we are enjoined to stand for the arrival of the Lord Mayor of Westminster, but told specifically to remain seated for the arrival of the Prince of Wales and other representatives of the Royal Family.

9 November 2000
An exceptionally good lunch and much talk with John Wilsey at the Ritz. We go through the text of John's chapter on H. Jones at Eton. He is amused at the number of red-ink corrections I make; also vignettes I give him of Tom Brocklebank and Robert Birley. One chilling story he has heard from an Eton contemporary of H. is that H. said to a 'guinea pig' one day: 'You should not be at Eton at all, coming from a grammar school.' John asks me whether he should put in this example of H. and the 'guinea pig'. I say that he certainly should. Eton could be a disagreeable place and Brocklebank should have seen that such things did not happen.

10 November 2000
To the annual dinner at Claridge's of what used to be called Arco, but is now Global Crossing Ltd. All sorts of people tell me how much they miss my 'Albany' column.

---

* Gen. Sir John Wilsey (b. 1939), Chief of Staff UK Land Forces 1988–9; GOC Northern Ireland 1990–93; C.-in-C. UK Land Forces 1995–6. His book *H. Jones: The Life and Death of an Unusual Hero* was published in 2002.
† Lt-Col. Herbert Jones (1940–82), awarded the VC after being killed in action during the Falklands War.
‡ (1908–84), schoolmaster at Eton 1934–61.

At dinner I sit next to Norman St John-Stevas, really rather an unappealing man. When the cigars come round he asks the waiter which is the most expensive, takes a huge one, puts it in his pocket, then says to me, 'I don't smoke but I shall give it to my butler.' He has been so rude and off-hand with me during the dinner that I reply in kind: 'Is your butler old enough to smoke?'

1 December 2000
Princess Anne made a Knight of the Thistle. A deserved honour, but it leaves Princess Margaret all the more isolated.

14 December 2000
George Bush finally beats Al Gore as the next President of the USA after a cliffhanging, exceptionally messy election which left the Supreme Court divided and discredited.

20 December 2000
Charles Guthrie gives King Constantine and myself breakfast at the Hyde Park Hotel. He now says publicly what he has told me in private about the way the Government treats the Armed Forces, and raises a political storm. Of course, it doesn't matter what Charles now says publicly as he is so near to retirement. He has made it his business to get on with Labour ministers, but is appalled by Blair's weakness in Cabinet, bearing the imprint of the last person who sat on him. 'He should have exerted his authority at the beginning of his term of office: just as a new Commanding Officer of a regiment should impose strict discipline which can later be relaxed.'

Once or twice Tino has asked to see Tony Blair at No. 10, but has always been refused. Tino has borne up well during his years of exile, but has become very introspective.

2001

A general election year. The age of consent for male homosexual acts was reduced to sixteen on 8 January. The architect Denys Lasdun died on 11 January. On 24 January the Secretary of State for Northern Ireland, Peter Mandelson, resigned from the Cabinet for the second time. Labour had a twenty-point lead over the Conservatives in a MORI poll on 25 January. The foot-and-mouth crisis began on 19 February. On 8 March the wreckage of Donald Campbell's speedboat Bluebird *was raised from the bottom of Coniston Water after thirty-four years, and a week later Campbell's body was recovered. The 2001 census of the UK was held on 29 April. During the election campaign, Deputy Prime Minister John Prescott punched a protester in Rhyl on 16 May. Labour won a second landslide general election victory on 7 June. Edward Heath retired from Parliament, having served there since 1950.*

On 29 June the government announced plans to build a £3 million fountain in memory of Princess Diana in Hyde Park. Jeffrey Archer was sentenced to four years in prison for perjury and perverting the course of justice on 19 July. Riots broke out in Brixton on 20 July. Frank Longford died on 3 August. Bernard Levin died on 7 August. Sir Fred Hoyle, astronomer, died on 20 August. On 11 September in a terrorist attack two planes flew into the Twin Towers in New York with the loss of 2,752 lives. Iain Duncan Smith was elected leader of the Conservative Party on 13 September. The US Armed Forces invaded Afghanistan on 7 October. Lord Hailsham died on 12 October. Sir John Plumb died on 21 October. A MORI poll put Labour thirty-one points ahead of the Conservatives on 22 November. David Astor died on 7 December. Field Marshal Carver died on 9 December.

2 January 2001

I drive up to London with Prue Penn after a happy reunion weekend at our traditional New Year Party, shadowed only by Princess Margaret's absence and illness this year.

Prue tells me that at Sandringham in the summer the Queen invited her to attend a little service in one of its rooms conducted by the local parson.

The only other person present was the Queen Mother. Some of the servants had complained that the room was haunted and did not want to work in it. The parson walked from room to room and did indeed feel some sort of restlessness in one of them. This the Queen Mother identified as a ground-floor room which had been turned into a bedroom for King George VI during his last months. So the parson held a service there not exactly of exorcism, which is the driving out of an evil spirit, but of bringing tranquillity. The congregation of three took Holy Communion and special prayers were said, I think for the repose of the King's soul in the room in which he died. The parson said that the oppressive or disturbing atmosphere may have been because of Princess Diana: he had known such things before when someone died a violent death.

18 January 2001
I ask Nico Henderson whether it is true that his friendship with Donald Maclean, the spy, put back his career for six years. He says there is something in it, but that the postings he was given during those six years, although not high-flying, were respectable and responsible: Vienna and Santiago.

19 January 2001
Dukie Hussey tells me he has had a letter from someone inviting him to put his name to a round robin to No. 10 asking that Jeremy Thorpe should receive a life peerage. Dukie said no. It sounds a wrong and useless quest.

The news is announced that Peter Mandelson has resigned as Northern Ireland Secretary. It is his second resignation in the present Parliament. The main benefit is the harm it will do to Blair's reputation.

24 January 2001, Letter to James Douglas-Hamilton*
I much enjoyed our talk at Deene, and have now read your book *Motive for a Mission: The Story Behind Hess's Flight to Britain* with great interest. You must have found peculiar satisfaction in proving beyond all doubt that your father had had no contact with Rudolf Hess before the war or the faintest trace of Nazism. It was a tragedy that his name was ever dragged into so unsavoury a drama, and your book performs a public as well as a filial service.

If Hess was in search of a Scottish duke with whom to initiate peace negotiations, it is a wonder he did not choose Walter Buccleuch,† who did have a

---

* Baron Selkirk of Douglas (b. 1942), Scottish Conservative politician. MP for Edinburgh West 1974–97; Member of the Scottish Parliament for the Lothians 1999–2007.
† Walter Montagu Douglas Scott, 8th Duke of Buccleuch (1894–1973).

trustful tenderness for the Nazis. As late as April 1939, as you probably knew, he flew to Berlin to attend Hitler's fiftieth birthday celebrations, but was ordered back to London by the King and in the following year was relieved of his office of Lord Steward of the Household – to which of course your father succeeded.

Jock Colville's diary for February 1940 reveals that Walter tried to persuade Alec Home to press for peace with Germany in that month. Johnnie Buccleuch,* an old friend of mine, was much upset a few years ago when several historical works referred to his father's activities and he asked me how he could clear his father's name. After examining the evidence, I had to tell him with sorrow that this would be difficult, even though Walter did not believe that he was acting other than with a sense of patriotism. So Johnnie wisely took no action, which would only have inflamed controversy.

On another point, it does seem amazing that Hess's preparations for his flight to Scotland did not evoke alarm anywhere in Germany – not least the filling of extra fuel tanks. The Gestapo must have kept a watch on him and other prominent Nazis, if only for their protection.

I do have a fleeting recollection of Hess. When Nico Henderson was our Ambassador to Germany in 1972–75, I was asked to spend a weekend at our Embassy in Berlin, which we maintained as well as the one in Bonn, with the Carringtons as fellow guests. On the Sunday morning we were given a flight in a British Army helicopter over the city and flew fairly low over Spandau Prison. And there below us in the garden was Hess, apparently alone, looking much as he does in the photograph in your book. He wore a long coat and resembled Boris Karloff: I noticed that his arms and legs did not quite co-ordinate.

I like Alan Bullock's foreword. He was one of my tutors at New College.

25 January 2001

Huge newspaper coverage of Mandelson's resignation. It is universally agreed that it has diminished Blair's reputation, particularly for having restored him to the Cabinet only ten months after his first resignation. Both episodes were ignoble.

12 February 2001

Wet, yellow clouds hang over London.

I ask Oliver Millar whether he has ever heard the story about Tommy Lascelles catching sight of Anthony Blunt in the passage at Buckingham

---

* John Douglas Scott, 9th Duke of Buccleuch (1923–2007).

Palace and saying to Philip Hay: 'That's our Russian spy.' Oliver says that Mark Milbank* made exactly the same remark to him when Oliver arrived at the Palace as Deputy Surveyor of the King's Pictures.

12 March 2001

Prince Eddie calls for me with car and driver at 6.15. Early dinner at La Rueda. Then to the Wigmore Hall to hear Ian Bostridge† singing Schubert's *Winterreise*. He has an enchanting voice and his control of hands, gestures and facial expression is most accomplished. Eddie tells me, as I expected, that this is the work of a specialised coach. He is tall, fresh-faced, like a well-scrubbed school prefect who stands no nonsense.

The Queen, Eddie says, gave a party at Windsor the other day for her retiring head keeper at Sandringham, just the sort of gesture she makes from the heart.

20 March 2001

A fascinating account of what happened when Peter Mandelson, as Secretary of State for Northern Ireland, went on Irish TV and referred to the Brigade of Guards as 'chinless wonders' – a relic of his left-wing youth. When the Ministry of Defence Press Officer telephoned Charles, he told them to tell Mandelson's Press Office that he was seething with rage. As Charles expected, Mandelson then tried to telephone him, but Charles went to ground and would not take his call. 'I made him sweat for twenty-four hours.' When Charles did eventually talk to him, Mandelson apologised.

22 March 2001

To Buckingham Palace at 5.30 for a big party given by the Queen for 'British Book World', writers, publishers, booksellers, librarians, etc. As always I am struck by the elegance of the rooms for such an occasion. I enjoy a talk with Roy Jenkins. He is most amiable. I had hoped to see him here as I wanted to know more of his dining with Noel Annan as Home Secretary in 1966, at which Victor Rothschild brought Anthony Blunt, two years after he had secretly confessed to being a traitor. Roy does not seem to think it mattered that his civil servants had not yet told him of this, some six months after he had become Home Secretary. I think it remiss of them. What does amuse him is that Blunt made so little impression on him that he forgot the occasion until reading his diary when writing his autobiography years later. 'If I

---

* Sir Mark Milbank (1907–1984), Master of the Royal Household 1954–67.
† (b. 1964) tenor renowned in both opera and Lieder.

had been asked in a witness box whether I had ever met him, I would have
sworn I had not.'

1 May 2001

Prue Penn produces a delectable bit of gossip. Ludo Kennedy was among the
thousands of would-be 'people's peers' who applied unsuccessfully to go to
the House of Lords. I bet he had his title all worked out.

2 May 2001

I have a most useful talk with Robert Armstrong about Victor Rothschild
and the *Spycatcher* affair. Bits of the jigsaw are invaluable. Victor was anxious to safeguard the Rothschild name and wanted to bury all memory of the
Blunt episode. Yet he went on seeing him.

Victor desperately wanted to become Mrs Thatcher's intelligence adviser
in July 1980. She discussed it with Robert. Not a hope for Victor.

7 May 2001

One most interesting piece of news. The Queen is being painted by Lucian
Freud, at the suggestion of Robert Fellowes. The sittings take place in the
studio at the corner of St James's Palace. How extraordinarily daring of the
Queen.

8 May 2001

A day of cloudless skies and hot sun. Use my deckchair pass for the first time
by the Round Pond. Listen to the music of a tireless blackbird.

Prue Penn has some depressing but not unexpected news. She managed to
get hold of William Tallon[*] alone this morning and asked him what exactly
had taken place when Princess Margaret descended on Clarence House six
or seven years ago to 'tidy up Mummy's sitting room'. She spent a week going
through every drawer, wearing white gloves and stopping only for a picnic
lunch, throwing away most of her mother's personal correspondence. She
filled no fewer than thirty black bags with the papers, which William thinks
were shredded. (Princess Margaret told me about this with some pride,
soon after it happened.) Certain letters were not destroyed, mostly family:
the King, Queen Mary, the Queen and the Prince and Princess of Wales.
William was not allowed near. Since this happened, the Queen Mother has
no longer kept the letters of her friends, but tears them up when read and
answered.

---

[*] (1935–2007), steward and member of the Queen Mother's staff at Clarence House.

What a terrible act of destruction, and how much more difficult it will be for a biographer to recapture her life.

20 May 2001

To Glyndebourne. The opera is *Fidelio*, conducted by Simon Rattle,[*] with the Orchestra of the Age of Enlightenment. That is perfection. The production, as almost always nowadays, strives for an otiose novelty. The prisoners wear modern civilian clothes, as do the prison staff. So there is none of the spine-chilling contrast between haggard prisoners in rags and brutal guards in uniform. The prisoners, too, are hemmed in with chicken wire; so none of the haunting drama of the prisoners emerging from the dungeons blinking in the sunlight, with their later, despairing return to the depths. Why must producers mess things up?

23 May 2001

A really good party in the Ritz to mark its ninety-fifth birthday. I have a few minutes' conversation with Margaret Thatcher. I mention that my book on Victor Rothschild is getting on well. Margaret is just a tiny bit uneasy, I suppose in case I ask her why she did not give Victor more support when he was accused in the Press and Parliament of being a Soviet spy.

7 June 2001

General Election day. To the polling station in Kensington Library and cast my vote for Michael Portillo. No excitement about today's election: the quietest I have ever known, almost certainly because the result seems a fore gone conclusion. *The Times* tells its readers to vote Labour.

8 June 2001

Blair has won another landslide victory, losing only six seats and the Conservatives gaining only one. William Hague resigns as Tory leader, so I suppose the new leader will be Portillo – although he does not inspire universal trust. Perhaps the pro-European Kenneth Clarke would be more suitable.

9 June 2001

Some election results of interest. Peter Mandelson has swept back in Hartlepool with 22,5000 votes against Arthur Scargill's 912. Ludlow has been lost by the Conservative candidate.

---

[*] Sir Simon Rattle (b. 1955), Principal Conductor and Artistic Dir. of the Berlin Symphony Orchestra 2002–18; Music Dir. of the London Symphony Orchestra since 2017.

Overall Labour won 413 seats, the Conservatives 166 and the Lib Dems 46. So another full term of what is now not so New Labour.

12 June 2001

I go to *Zauberflöte* at Garsington Opera with the Carringtons. The way to hear it is the way that George Bernard Shaw, a better music critic, under the pseudonym of Corno di Bassetto, than he was a playwright, used to listen to the *Ring*: at the very back of the box with his feet up. I cannot take productions of Mozart's operas, or any other great operas, when smothered by the conjuring tricks of an ambitious director. Why that by now stale cliché of dictatorial uniforms and jackboots? Why an operating table? Why dress little boys in their suits from the school shop? Especially when so much of the music was so haunting?

19 June 2001

Dine at Eton to mark the publication of Tim Card's new history of Eton. We begin in the Provost's drawing room, where Eric and Poppy Anderson are now well installed, and most hospitable. I hear an amusing story about Martin Charteris as Provost. When Prince Philip was coming on a visit, Martin would give boys lessons on how to answer back his rudeness.

20 June 2001

To Oxford for Encaenia. Oxford looks terrible today: the pavements choked with people and the streets with gridlocked traffic. The Vice-Chancellor's lunch is in Univ., where I have some talk with Robin Butler, Master of his *alma mater*. Talking of the *Spycatcher* case in Australia, he says that Robert Armstrong did well in the witness box except for the one error about 'economical with the truth'.

One of my neighbours at lunch is a shy girl who works in the development office. She began her career by teaching, but the children were so disorderly that she could stand it no more and resigned. This saddens me.

23 June 2001

Lunch with William Shawcross at Café Flo. Hartley is now in a remote state, although there are intervals of clarity. William is at work on a big TV programme about the Queen, to coincide with her Golden Jubilee next year. Someone told him that there is not a single monarchist in Blair's Cabinet. When William told this to John Major, John said that in his Cabinet there was not a single republican.

11 July 2001

I much enjoy sitting next to Jennifer Jenkins at Drue Heinz's[*] annual lunch. She is as angry as I am that a memorial fountain to Princess Diana is to be built by the Serpentine at a cost of millions. I thought we had seen the last of such projects when the residents of Kensington voted down plans for a large memorial garden and fountain in Kensington Gardens. Roy is finishing his life of Winston Churchill. I bet Leonard Wolfson tries to get him a Wolfson Prize for it, having failed with Roy's book on Mr Gladstone.

15 July 2001

To Walmer Castle to dine with the Queen Mother. She looks lovely in pink silk. A short walk on the terrace with Alastair Aird. He says that when the QM is not in residence, the castle should fly the flag of the Cinque Ports, certainly not that of English Heritage. The Union Flag? No, says Alastair, Walmer is not a saluting point, as is Dover.

Prue tells me of the QM's astonishing programme on the approach of her 102nd year. To London tomorrow by helicopter, and on to Sandringham for a week on Thursday. The Royal Lodge for a race meeting, and back to Clarence House for her birthday. Up to the Castle of Mey, then down to Balmoral for a couple of days and so to Birkhall for the rest of the summer, with a perpetual succession of guests.

The Queen Mother turns to me before the pudding and we have much good talk and laughter. She tells me that Dickie Mountbatten in his bumptious way drove his motorboat too fast at Cowes, disturbing all the small boats. The King was furious with him. As a result of what the King said to him, he mended his ways. She admired his leadership in the Far East. It is interesting that in telling me all this, she refers not to 'the King' but to 'my husband'. I am not sure I have heard that informal note before. On Edwina she says: 'She never did a thing until the war, and then she never stopped.' On Christopher Soames in Paris: 'He barged his way about.' We bemoan the loss of the Royal Yacht, which I insist was a populist not a financial measure. When we talk of the robust character of the North-East she sings a few lines of the 'Blaydon Races', before buttering some biscuits for the corgis.

19 July 2001

The BBC ask me to be interviewed for a programme on the monarchy, written and presented by Tony Howard. Certainly not.

---

[*] (1915–2018), American patron of the literary arts.

20 July 2001

The papers bring an unpleasant tone of gloating to the conviction of Jeffrey Archer* for perjury and perverting the course of justice and his sentence to four years' imprisonment, though I have always found him a bad hat. Thatcher made him Deputy Chairman of the party, Major created him a peer and Hague chose him to be the Tory candidate for the election of the Mayor of London.

21 July 2001

Today would have been my brother Toby's eightieth birthday. I feel sad at his being deprived of fifty years of what would have been a fruitful life. As it was he had less than ten years after the navy in which to spread his wings. But he managed much on little money, with a sure taste in books and the arts. He had more goodness in him than I have, and I remember him with affection and admiration.

John Wilsey telephones to enquire about the treatment of my eyes. He says that when talking about his life of 'H.' Jones to David Fraser,† that fellow biographer said: 'Avoid writing about the living, or even about those whose children are still alive.'

25 July 2001

I hear that the new HM of Eton to succeed John Lewis is Anthony Little,‡ a former HM of Chigwell, and now of Oakham. He is the first OE headmaster since Claude Elliott.

3 August 2001

Jonathan Aitken has been advising Jeffrey Archer on how to behave in prison; Jonathan himself, before starting his sentence, was given similar advice by two prison governors.

4 August 2001

I am sad to hear that Frank Longford died yesterday – at the age of ninety-five. My affection and admiration of his courage in embracing unpopular causes grew with the years, even though sometimes his motives seemed ambiguous.

---

* Baron Archer of Weston-super-Mare (b. 1940), author and former Conservative politician.
† Gen. Sir David Fraser (1920–2012); Vice-CGS 1973–5; biographer of Alanbrooke (1982).
‡ (b. 1954), Head Master of Eton 2002–15.

The Queen Mother's 101st birthday. She receives flowers outside Clarence House. Alastair Aird looks worried by it all.

5 August 2001

Deeply shocked by pictures in all the Sunday papers of Princess Margaret in a wheelchair at the Queen Mother's birthday celebration yesterday. In a wheelchair, she is scarcely recognisable, wrapped in a rug, her arm in a sling, wearing huge dark spectacles against the sun and, worst of all, a face grotesquely swollen. Oh, the pity of it.

8 August 2001

Work on my biography of Victor Rothschild goes well today, carrying the story up to his decision to send a letter to the *Daily Telegraph* asking to be cleared of the allegation that he was a Soviet agent.

10 August 2001

Peter Carrington represents the Queen at Frank Longford's funeral. The service is inspired and is dominated by the Cardinal Archbishop, Cormac Murphy O'Connor,* a tall, handsome man with a strong yet benevolent voice. But there is far too much incense, like Peter Hall's production of the *Ring*. Some beautiful passages from Fauré's Requiem. There is a note in the order of service that those who are not Catholics may during the Communion receive a blessing. I do not take advantage of this. The Catholic Church <u>should</u> give Communion to Anglicans. There is a robust singing of Blake's *Jerusalem*, now being banned from some Anglican churches for its apparent secularism – what nonsense.

Read Anne de Courcy's *The Viceroy's Daughters*: Irene, Cimmie and Baba.† Lots on Curzon, Tom Mosley,‡ the Prince of Wales and his mistresses. A lot on Curzon's finances. Curzon was in deep despair about his finances, yet never countenanced giving up even one of his great houses.

31 August 2001

I read J.K. Rowling's *Harry Potter and the Prisoner of Azkaban*, the third in a series that is selling millions: ostensibly for children but sophisticated

---

* (b. 1932), Archbishop of Westminster 2000–09.
† Anne de Courcy (b. 1937), biographer and journalist. Lady Irene Curzon, later Lady Ravensdale (1896–1966). Lady Cynthia ('Cimmie') Curzon, later Lady Mosley (1898–1933). Lady Alexandra ('Baba') Curzon, later Lady Metcalfe (1904–95).
‡ Sir Oswald Mosley of Ancoats, 6th Baronet (1896–1980), politician. Leader of the British Union of Fascists 1932–40.

enough for all ages. It is a blend of public-school life and wizardry, most ingenious and full of jokes. But I am not sure I want to read another.

11 September 2001
Reports of an appalling, widespread terrorist attack on New York by several hijacked aircraft deliberately smashing into public buildings with huge casualties.

12 September 2001
Worldwide shock at the terrorist explosions in New York by hijacked planes crashing into the Twin Towers of the World Trade Building (both of which later collapsed) and also into the Pentagon. Huge casualties. It will make pleasurable air travel impossible for many years. And the retaliation will prove horrifying and messy. Why were the preparations not detected by US intelligence, supposedly the best in the world?

Conrad Black's peerage announced today attracts almost no interest. He has had to renounce Canadian citizenship to receive it.

20 September 2001
I ask Prince Eddie what he would like for his birthday. He suggests the new edition of Nigel Hamilton's* life of Field Marshal Montgomery, now being serialised in *The Times*. I say no: I will not support an author who writes such tosh about Monty having been a sublimated homosexual whose qualities of leadership sprang from 'bonding' with young men.

25 September 2001
I begin the last chapter of my book on Victor Rothschild with an account of how he spent the last years of his life destroying personal papers. I have a walk in Kensington Gardens and see a lady in a tartan skirt wheeling old Princess Alice on her outing with her set little face and no hat – in her 100th year. All round are Japanese tourists. I wonder what they would make of it if they knew that the old lady is the widow of the Prince who went out to give their Emperor the Garter some seventy years ago?

28 September 2001
I look at the typescript of William Shawcross' book on the Queen, to accompany a four-part TV series for her Golden Jubilee. It strikes me as

---

* (b. 1944), academic and biographer; his *Monty: The Making of a General* (1981) won the Whitbread Prize.

commonplace, without a gleam of new thought. He is uncertain on titles; does not know such elementary usage as being 'in' a warship, rather than 'on'. More importantly, he does not quote what I told him of my conversation with Michael Adeane at the time Alec Home became PM in October 1963 – that it is the Queen's duty to find a PM who can command a majority in the Commons, not one who will necessarily win the next General Election.

29 September 2001

To St Andrews, such a handsome city. But what a prospect for Prince William, who has just begun four years here, reading History of Art. He will surely not see it out.

Walk on past the Royal and Ancient Clubhouse to an immensely long, wide beach, with the breakers rolling onto it. Such a good walk. Three oystercatchers marching in step.

7 October 2001

The *Sunday Telegraph* has a good story, though I wonder if it can be true. Apparently the Queen visited Eton with Prince Philip to thank the beaks for teaching Prince William so well. She referred to 'the Head Master, Peter Jones'. He is in fact called John Lewis. She had the wrong store.*

I hear Tony Blair announce that we are bombing Afghanistan as punishment for the terrorist attack on New York and Washington. I cannot feel elated.

14 October 2001

Quintin Hailsham dies at ninety-four. He could be utterly charming, but also infuriating. I had several brushes with him – on the secrecy enjoined on a Privy Councillor (Tony Nutting after Suez), on the first use of the term Prime Minister (he wrongly said not until Stanley Baldwin), and on other issues on which he was dogmatic and wrong. He was also frivolously indulgent about Lord Devlin's book on the Bodkin Adams trial.

19 October 2001

Very near the end of my Victor Rothschild book. I have a last thought: how rarely he did anything for anybody else that disturbed his own life. He was an essentially selfish man.

---

* John Lewis's nickname among the Eton pupils was in fact Peter Jones.

21 October 2001

Pouring rain all day. Work away on Victor Rothschild and write the final page, which had been worrying me, at 11.15 p.m. A Trafalgar Day victory.

22 October 2001

I hear quite late that Jack Plumb died yesterday aged ninety-four. Somebody told me not long ago that he was annoyed that Victor Rothschild had asked me and not Jack to write his life. And now he dies as I am completing the last sentences of the book. What an odd turn of fate. Jack was kind to me in reviewing *KGV*, helping to get me the Wolfson Prize for the book, and then appointing me as a Wolfson judge. But he became bad-tempered and jealous in his last years. His behaviour to the other Fellows of Christ's was abominable, even worse to the servants. Isaiah Berlin called him an ignoble character.

27 October 2001

Read James Lees-Milne's *Holy Dread*, his diaries from 1982 to 1984, edited by Michael Bloch. As in the last volume, the prurience diminishes its enjoyment. Too many indiscreet references to Jim's homosexual adventures, including Alan Lennox-Boyd. Yet there are some interesting bits of gossip from Jim's journals. Elizabeth Jane Howard* says she expects to write the official life of the Queen Mother. About half a dozen references to me, some friendly and even flattering, others impatient of my supposed conceit and snobbishness. One sad feature: he is tortured by jealousy at the prizes I won for *KGV*.

John Murray told me a few months ago that if the present volumes – there are still several to come – do not sell well, he will fold up the publication.

2 November 2001

I tell Ion Trewin† at Weidenfeld & Nicolson that I have finished Victor Rothschild. He is delighted. I suppose he thought it would never arrive.

To St James's Palace at 12.30 for a reception given by the Prince of Wales to launch a memorial fund for Martin Charteris based on his affection and respect for the old Prayer Book. As always at meetings concerned with the Prayer Book, there are several Cecils and a crowd of rather frowsty High Anglicans. Some good talk, as always, with Richard Chartres, Bishop of London. While talking to Richard Chartres about Martin,

---

* (1923–2014), novelist; author of *The Cazalet Chronicles*; m.to Kingsley Amis 1965–83.
† (1942–2015), editor, publisher and author.

I mention his revival of the leaving portraits at Eton and mention that I commissioned Derek Hill to paint a scholarship boy of Martin's choice, Stephen Layton, who has now done so well in the world of modern choral music. Richard knows him well and says that he is already a dominating figure.

Philip Ziegler presses me to hurry up publishing my Journals. 'I thought the piece you showed me about dining with the Windsors in Paris was most illuminating.'

4 November 2001
William Waldegrave comes at 1 to collect the typescript of Victor Rothschild. He has been electing new Fellows of All Souls. He should be able to finish reading the book by next weekend. Talking of Anthony Blunt, William mentions that the man who so vehemently wanted him expelled from the British Academy in 1979 was Jack Plumb, himself an ex-Communist.

7 November 2001
Robert Lacey sends me part of his chapter on KGV for a revised edition of his book on the Queen. He has a rather too sensational account of how Philip Moore, the Queen's then Private Secretary, tried to censor my chapter on the King and the Tsar in *KGV*. I tone it down.

Listen to a little of Benjamin Britten's comic opera *Albert Herring*. It is terrible stuff. He should stick to paedophilia and sadism. I remember seeing a rehearsal of it at the Maltings in Snape once.

8 November 2001
I am reading the third and fortunately last volume of Woodrow Wyatt's diaries. How nimbly he switched as a confidant to Margaret Thatcher to John Major. He thought of asking Andrew Roberts to edit them, but was deterred by Andrew's supposed wealth – which Woodrow assumed would not make him an assiduous editor.

10 November 2001
Read the new, huge edition of the war diaries of Field Marshal Alanbrooke,[*] edited by Alex Danchev,[†] not altogether different from the original edition,

---

* FM Sir Alan Brooke, 1st Viscount Alanbrooke (1883–1963), CIGS 1941 and principal military adviser to Winston Churchill.
† Prof. Alex Danchev (1955–2016), Professor of International Relations at St Andrews University 2014–15.

but more vitriol about Winston, Field Marshal Alexander, General Marshall*
and Eisenhower.† How on earth did he have the strength to write so much
late at night or early in the morning when CIGS?

8 December 2001
David Astor‡ dies in his ninetieth year. He was always grateful for my having
helped Bill Astor§ when he had the world against him during the Profumo
scandal.

11 December 2001
Field Marshal Mike Carver¶ dies. A soldier of flair and brilliance; but acerbic,
which made him enemies.

A large parcel arrives from the Duchess of York. I shall keep it till
Christmas.

21 December 2001
The papers publish the appalling portrait of the Queen by Lucian Freud.

28 December 2001
I am reading through the 600 pages of Christopher Tyerman's *A History of
Harrow School*, primarily for the years that Victor was a boy there under
Edward Ford and later Cyril Norwood.** The whole book is enthralling and
far more forthcoming than any other school history I have ever read. Lionel
Ford†† comes badly out of it all and was virtually sacked. Ford's Headmaster's
House was what the author calls a hotbed of 'ferocious buggery'. No wonder
Edward was very upset with the book.

---

* Gen. George Marshall (1880–1959), creator of the Marshall Plan for post-war rebuilding in
Europe.
† Dwight Eisenhower (1890–1969). A five-star General in the US Army, in World War II he
served as Supreme Commander of the Allied Expeditionary Forces in Europe; President of the
US 1953–61.
‡ (1912–2001), newspaper publisher and editor. He was responsible for arranging the burial
of George Orwell in All Saints Churchyard, Sutton Courtenay, when he learned that Orwell
wanted to be buried in an English country churchyard. He bought two plots and his own
headstone is now next to Orwell's.
§ William Astor, (1907–66), businessman.
¶ FM Michael Carver, Baron Carver of Shackleford (1915–2001), Chief of the Defence Staff
1973–6.
** Sir Cyril Norwood (1875–1958), Headmaster of Harrow 1926–34; President of St John's
Coll., Oxford 1935–46.
†† (1865–1932), Anglican priest. Headmaster of Repton 1901–10; Headmaster of Harrow
1910–25; Dean of York 1925–32.

2002

End of foot-and-mouth disease in the UK after eleven months. Princess Margaret died at the age of seventy-one on 9 February; her funeral took place in St George's Chapel, Windsor, on 15 February, the exact fiftieth anniversary of her father's funeral there. Queen Elizabeth the Queen Mother died at Royal Lodge, Windsor, on 30 March at the age of 101. To mark her Golden Jubilee the Queen dined on 29 April at 10 Downing Street with the five living Prime Ministers who served under her: Edward Heath, James Callaghan, Margaret Thatcher, John Major and Tony Blair, together with the Countess of Avon, the widow of Anthony Eden. Margaret Thatcher's statue was decapitated at the Guildhall Art Gallery on 3 July. Rowan Williams, Archbishop of Wales, was elected to succeed George Carey as Archbishop of Canterbury on 23 July. A MORI poll on 12 December put Labour four points ahead of the Conservatives.

1 January 2002

Another lovely sunrise. The newly released Public Record Office documents reveal that in 1968 the Queen offered to give up the Royal Yacht as an economy measure. The Labour Government declined to accept this gesture and Denis Healey, as Chancellor, gave orders that it was not to be made public. The inference is that Labour wanted to encourage the image of the Queen as rich, privileged and selfish.

I hear that John Grigg died yesterday. He behaved heroically during his last illness. I wonder whether the Queen still resents John's supposed attacks on the monarchy in the 1950s. Listen to the annual New Year's Day concert from Vienna. I recall with sadness how, at one of our New Year's gatherings at Sutton Courtenay, Princess Margaret used to dance to this Strauss concert all the morning.

A vile documentary on television on the Queen. It is poignant to see extracts of John Grigg explaining just what he had said of the Queen and her court forty-five years ago.

William Shawcross is not happy with Anthony Howard as obituaries editor of *The Times* (a post which John Grigg once held). He would put a left-wing slant on those already written, telling William once: 'The stock obituary of your father is far too kind, and I am going to sharpen it.'

2 January 2002
A troubled night, thinking of John Grigg and of all my other friends facing cancer and other perils. There are obituaries of John in the *Telegraph* and *Times*. The first is a bit scrappy, the second patronising.

3 January 2002
William Shawcross telephones. He wrote to Robin Janvrin, the Queen's Private Secretary, telling him of John Grigg's admiration of the Queen and asking whether some sort of message could be sent to him in his final illness. Janvrin was away, but the letter was opened by an assistant secretary who showed the letter to the Queen. A message was then sent. I am pretty sure it cannot have reached John before his death. But how marvellous of the Queen.

7 January 2002
Sad to hear that William Rees-Mogg lost a great deal of money in Lloyd's – as only a clever economist could. He kept quiet about it, but had to sell his country home.

10 January 2002
Clarissa Avon tells me that Richard Thorpe is producing an enormous book about Anthony Eden. She is well pleased with what she has seen so far.

12 January 2002
I continue reading the early volume of Alan Clark's diaries. What a mess he was in *c*.1979: a troublesome constituency, severe financial problems, including a crippling overdraft and losses from compulsively playing backgammon at Brooks's, and disappointed at not receiving office.

I hear that Norman St John-Stevas, when staying at Royal Lodge once, said to a lady fellow guest, a countess, at bedtime: 'Gute Nacht, meine Frau.' She replied very strongly: 'I am not your Frau. In any case it should be "meine Gräfin."' What a bounder.

14 January 2002
Charles Guthrie telephones for a gossip. He wishes to ease himself out of his quasi-diplomatic life. He has declined to attend confidential briefings for senior officers at the Ministry of Defence and will not speak regularly in the House of Lords.

He is interested in what I tell him about Christopher Tyerman's new history of Harrow School: some of the beaks there, and Old Harrovians, are very annoyed by it, details of recent wife-swapping and the like. When Charles was a boy there some fifty years or so ago it was a harsh place: bad food and sanitation and much beating. He refused to be Chairman of the Governors a year or two ago.

16 January 2002
Indifferent reports on the health of both the Queen Mother and Princess Margaret. The QM keeps mostly to her room at Sandringham, and I hear that PM remarked to her maid the other day, 'If only I were a dog, I could be put down.'

22 January 2002
Prue Penn tells me there is much concern at Sandringham about the condition of the Queen Mother. She has been in bed for the past few days and before that she hardly left her room. As Prue puts it: 'The batteries are running down.' It would not surprise her if the Queen Mother wanted to die on or about the anniversary of the King's death, 6 February. Nor would she want her death to cast a shadow over the Queen's Golden Jubilee later in the year: so like Queen Mary in 1953 as the Coronation approached.

26 January 2002
Another extraordinary confidence from Prue: that the Queen Mother wanted me to have a KCVO for all I had supposedly done for the Royal Family over the years, including the writing of *KGV*. 'But it did not work,' she told Prue, 'I am the kiss of death.' I can hardly believe it, but Prue says that she and the Queen Mother discussed it quite seriously. I suppose the courtiers stamped on it – 'thin end of the wedge'.

9 February 2002
Charles Moore tells me that Princess Margaret died early this morning in King Edward VII Hospital, having had a stroke followed by a heart attack. One could not have wanted her ghastly existence to be prolonged.

The telephone rings all day with the *Telegraph*, as Charles forecast, asking me for an article. I turn them down, as well as requests from many other papers and TV stations.

10 February 2002
The *Sunday Telegraph* has gone to town on Princess Margaret's death, mostly

ill-informed. Hugo Vickers alone is satisfactory. One article says PM could never stop smoking. What tosh.

13 February 2002
Tony Snowdon also telephones. He says: 'People forget how incredibly happy we were in the first years of our marriage.' He goes on to say how sad he is.

14 February 2002
The Queen Mother has flown to Windsor in a helicopter for Princess Margaret's funeral tomorrow – in spite of being 101, suffering from a virus on the chest and having cut her arm at Sandringham in a fall two days ago.

25 February 2002
To the presentation of the Duff Cooper Prize at the Mayfair Hotel. It is won by Margaret MacMillan for her book on the Treaty of Versailles, *Peacemakers*, which has been well received and is just the sort of book Duff himself would have welcomed. Some fearful TV presenter makes the award, but can scarcely be heard through laughing at his own 'jokes'. He also misses the point that the author is a great-granddaughter of Lloyd George.

12 March 2002
Graham C. Greene telephones unexpectedly. He knows of my uncertainties as to who should edit my Journals, a task which will take some considerable time. In my absence, through death or otherwise, the drudgery of editorial and biographical notes will be a massive undertaking. He suggests I might consider Richard Thorpe, after he has finished his vast book on Eden. I tell him I must not have an editor with <u>views</u>, but someone who knows and appreciates my own mind and style. I do not want a sensational book, or one permeated by political distortions. Thorpe could well manage all the notes and could act on my behalf.

13 March 2002
Lunch with Peter Carrington. He is depressed by the sinking of Zimbabwe into anarchy and dictatorship under Mugabe. It was Peter who negotiated the Rhodesian settlement. He is no less daunted by President Bush's determination to launch a military attack on Iraq, with Blair prepared to commit British Armed Forces as a US ally.

30 March 2002
The *Sunday Times* telephones to tell me that they have heard from St James's

Palace that the Queen Mother has died, but that no official announcement has yet been made. It comes half an hour later at 5 p.m.: the old lady died at 3.15 this afternoon with the Queen at her bedside. So ends an epoch of history.

3 April 2002

The debate continues on the scandalous behaviour of the BBC mandarins in ordering its newsreaders and presenters <u>NOT</u> to wear a black tie when announcing and commenting on the Queen Mother's death.

9 April 2002

Queen Mother's funeral on TV is perfectly done, polished ceremonial yet moving beyond belief. Spoilt by pointless comments at the end by BBC people, nitpicking. William Shawcross later tells me that a BBC man said to him: 'Don't you think this marks the decline of the monarchy?' William replied, pointing to the huge, reverent crowds: 'Just look about you.'

27 May 2002

Roy Jenkins has won the Wolfson Prize for his life of Churchill. He made an interminable speech at the awards ceremony all about himself. I am not sure that a biography with <u>no</u> original research ought to have won the Wolfson. I blocked his book on Gladstone for the same reason when I was a judge of the Wolfson. There are plenty of other prizes for middlebrow books such as his.

George Carey, the Archbishop of Canterbury, on being told he is to be made a life peer on his retirement later this year, declares himself 'honoured and humbled'. Who could be humbled by joining that assembly of political trash?

4 June 2002

The Queen's Golden Jubilee celebrations. At 5.30 there is a fly-past of every sort of plane, including Concorde. The sinister bombers are escorted by gnat-like fighters. It is impressive in spite of our small air force.

13 June 2002

James Hughes-Onslow[*] telephones from the *Evening Standard* to ask me whether I know who will write the official life of the Queen Mother. I don't know that it will have been decided yet. James mentions Eric Anderson as a possibility. He once recorded a series of interviews with the Queen Mother

---

[*] (1946–2016), City financier and journalist.

and of course he is a Scot. Perhaps no decision will be taken for some time – though an official biographer ought to be given the chance to interview her elderly friends before they too follow her to the grave.

7 July 2002

Michael Jenkins[*] says that Philip de Zulueta made only one big mistake when with Harold Macmillan. During a visit to General de Gaulle at Rambouillet he allowed Macmillan to talk in French to de Gaulle when accompanied only by Philip himself and de Gaulle's Russian-born French interpreter; and he failed to keep a record of it. Hence Harold's mistaken impression that de Gaulle would not obstruct Britain's application to join the EEC in December 1962 and his sense of devastation when Britain's plea was rejected. Neither man spoke the language of the other well enough to discern nuances of meaning.

5 August 2002

John King is rather worked up that his local MP, Alan Duncan,[†] has publicly declared himself homosexual – which everybody knew but did not bother about. At his selection meeting, attended by John, he was asked about his failure to marry and gave an evasive answer. Of course he did – in Rutland of all places. He should not be in a stuffy constituency: better Hampstead or some such place. I warn John against taking part in any campaign to deselect Duncan. The constituency could well end up with a Liberal.

6 August 2002

Jack Plumb's will proven at £1.3 million. He leaves some money for college servants to have a party. It would have been better had he not snarled at them in his lifetime: one of his least attractive traits. He also gave Christ's £1 million before he died.

Lunch with Charles Moore at the Savoy. I do not envy his task of writing Mrs Thatcher's life in three volumes. I ask him whether he could not do it in two – and ensure that they both come out together: separately published volumes never sell as well. He tells me that Mrs T. suffers from a common delusion among the old, that she has no money. In fact, she earns millions from lecturing alone.

Princess Alexandra tells me that Prince Eddie is loyal to his father's memory. The Queen Mother once observed to her how his long-striding

---

[*] Sir Michael Jenkins (1936–2013), Ambassador to the Netherlands 1988–93.

[†] Sir Alan Duncan (b. 1957), Conservative politician. MP for Rutland and Melton since 1992.

walk was exactly like Prince George's. There is always a memorial service for him in August. Last year they took Nick Ullswater* with them to Scotland. His father, John Lowther,† Secretary to Prince George, died in the air crash with him in 1942.

7 October 2002
What a tragedy it was that it took John Grigg seventeen years from the publication of Volume Three of his Lloyd George biography to that of the almost completed Volume Four, the last chapter of which was completed by Margaret MacMillan, a great-grand-daughter of L.G. Among the causes of the delay were John's need to make money, especially by writing his volume of the history of *The Times*; illness; and writer's block, from which we all suffer Penguin Books will not commit themselves to commissioning an author to produce a final volume, from 1918 until his death in 1945. The firm wants to see how the present volume sells.

John was an exceptionally courteous man. Once, during a holiday in Northern Ireland, John and one of the boys had to be rescued by an RAF helicopter when lost on a misty mountain top. John afterwards thanked the crew and sent them presents. The pilot told him that he had rescued 490 people in a helicopter over the years, and that John was the only one ever to thank him.

12 October 2002
I hear Richard Strauss's *Die Liebe der Danae*, his penultimate opera, full of rich themes.

12 November 2002
Lunch with Peter Carrington at the House of Lords. The place is in some turmoil, preparing for the State Opening of Parliament by the Queen tomorrow, with innumerable rows of little gilt chairs in the Royal Gallery.

Peter in exceptionally cheerful mood, which is exactly what I need. We agree that the Prince of Wales does good with his charitable work, but is no judge of character in choosing his staff. We are both desperately sorry for the Queen, burdened at her age by worries.

21 November 2002
Brian Rees was commissioned by the governors of Stowe to write the school's

---

* Nicholas Lowther, 2nd Viscount Ullswater (b. 1942), PS to Princess Margaret 1998–2002.
† (1910–42), PS to Prince George, Duke of Kent.

history to mark the seventieth anniversary in 1993 of the school's foundation. No limitations were placed on his treatment of the material from the
archives. When the governors saw the script they cancelled the commission
without explanation. Brian still resents Stowe having suppressed the history
of the school they commissioned him to write – particularly in the light of
Christopher Tyerman's recent uninhibited history of Harrow School, for
which the author demanded complete freedom from the governors.[*]

4 December 2002

I lunch at the Savoy with John Riddell.[†] We talk about the mess that the
Royal Family continues to be in, after the break-up of Charles and Diana's
marriage and her tragic death. Both of whom led separate lives almost from
the moment of marriage. John tried to jolt the Prince out of his self-absorbed
life by telling him that he ought to learn how ordinary people live by talking
to Diana more; she, after all, had lived an unsheltered life with her friends
in a London flat. Charles replied: 'I prefer to talk to Laurens van der Post.'[‡]

6 December 2002

No decision has yet been taken, or at any rate announced, as to who will
write the official life of the Queen Mother. I have a hunch that Eric Anderson
could be chosen. He writes well and he did some recorded interviews with
her. Of course, Hugo Vickers would very much like to do it. He probably
wrote his life of Prince Philip's mother to show he could handle the material.

21 December 2002

A glorious performance of Richard Strauss's *Elektra* from the Met, surely his
greatest opera.

---

[*] The Governing Body of Stowe later changed their minds and allowed the publication in
2008 of *Stowe: The History of a Public School, 1923–1989*, with the proviso that Rees made it
clear that the views and judgements expressed in it were his own and not those of the school
authorities. The book was very well reviewed and was sold in the school shop at Stowe.
[†] Sir John Riddell, 13th Bt (1934–2010), PS to the Prince of Wales 1985–90; Lord Lieutenant
of Northumberland 2000–09.
[‡] Sir Laurens van der Post (1906–96), author and close friend of the Prince of Wales.

2003

On 15 February more than two million people in London demonstrated against the Iraq War, the largest demonstration in British history. The congestion charge levied on motorists driving into central London came into force on 17 February. On 27 February 122 Labour MPs voted against the government in a debate on the Iraq War. On 27 February Rowan Williams was enthroned as Archbishop of Canterbury. On 29 March British land troops joined US troops in the invasion of Iraq. On 9 April it was confirmed that Saddam Hussein's rule had ended and his statue was toppled in Baghdad. The BBC Radio 4 Today programme broadcast a report on 29 May that the government's claim in a dossier that Iraq could deploy weapons of mass destruction in forty-five minutes was known to be dubious. On 24 June President Vladimir Putin became the first Russian leader to make a state visit to Britain since Tsar Alexander II in 1874. On 26 June a MORI poll put Labour and the Conservatives level on 35 per cent. On 24 October Concorde made its final commercial flight after twenty-seven years. On 29 October Iain Duncan Smith resigned as leader of the Conservative Party. President George Bush made a state visit to London on 18 November amidst massive protests.

6 January 2003

Roy Jenkins dies at eighty-two. Although for some years we had a guarded, even frosty relationship, it thawed considerably in the last decade or so. He consulted me on his book about Chancellors of the Exchequer and we corresponded about Mr Gladstone. In particular, I recall the long and amiable talk we had at Buckingham Palace two or three years ago at one of the Queen's evening parties: each of us in a vast gilded *fauteuil* in an otherwise completely empty, enormous room. I think one reason for our friendship, or at least cordiality, was his becoming less touchy and me being ready to laugh at his own foibles. I cannot imagine who could make as able a Chancellor for Oxford – certainly not Chris Patten.

I learn a new word from his obituary in the *Daily Telegraph* – 'rhotic': the substitution of a 'W' for an 'R' in speech, e.g. 'Woy'.

10 January 2003

Roy Jenkins' death has left the Chancellorship of Oxford vacant. All the candidates mentioned so far fill me with dismay: ex-President Clinton, Shirley Williams, Chris Patten.

22 January 2003

Peter Carrington gave Ted Heath dinner at the Ritz last night to cheer him up. Poor Ted has had a horrible time recently giving evidence to the judicial inquiry into 'Bloody Sunday' in Londonderry, when he was Prime Minister. There were allegations that he approved a shoot-to-kill policy, which he didn't. Evidently Ted spoke little during dinner except to bemoan that he should be hounded at this time of his life.

27 January 2003

Death yesterday of Hugh Trevor-Roper, always a good friend. I so regret that I could never persuade my Wolfson Award colleagues to give him a prize. It is so sad to read all the newspaper headlines recalling his blunder in authenticating the forged Hitler diaries.

30 January 2003

Documents have just been released relating to the Abdication of Edward VIII. With the death and funeral of the Queen Mother still vivid in public memory there will be much interest, though they largely confirm what has long been known. There are, however, a number of titillating footnotes. The newly released papers, for instance, shed some light on Ernest Simpson, the British businessman whom the future Duchess married in 1928 and divorced in 1936. His wife was under surveillance by Special Branch police officers. Long after his divorce and own remarriage, I often used to see Mr Simpson at the bar of the Guards Club, though I never spoke to him. He was an unattractive-looking fellow, rather overweight with a small moustache, double-breasted waistcoat and a watch chain. One day I pointed him out to my guest, Anthony Powell, who could not take his eyes off this living legend. I always hoped that the novelist would one day immortalise Simpson as a second Widmerpool. Perhaps he did.

15 February 2003

A vast number of people have been demonstrating today, mainly in London, against war with Saddam Hussein. It is a devastating blow against Blair's backing of American policy and could split the Government. I am unconvinced of the need for war.

18 February 2003

Michael Brock* asks me to nominate Tom Bingham,† the Senior Law Lord, to stand against Chris Patten for the Chancellorship of Oxford in succession to Roy Jenkins. I shall do so.

22 February 2003

The election for the Oxford Chancellorship seems to rest between Chris Patten and Tom Bingham, though the list is not yet closed.

26 February 2003

There are four nominees for the Oxford Chancellorship: Chris Patten, Tom Bingham, Pat Neill‡ and someone I have never heard of, a woman comedian called Sandi Toksvig,§ campaigning for women's rights. The bookmakers go 7–4, 9–4, 11–4 and, surprisingly, since students do not vote, 3–1. I am of course for Bingham. It is a pity that Bingham and Neill, both eminent lawyers, should be pitted against each other: a distinct advantage to Patten.

8 March 2003

My biography of Victor Rothschild and Richard Thorpe's new life of Anthony Eden have both come out.

The stupid *Sunday Telegraph* has given Richard's book to A.N. Wilson¶ to review. His ignorance of the subject is stupendous. After reading the book he writes that Eden resigned from Neville Chamberlain's Cabinet in protest at the Munich Agreement. Eden's resignation was in February 1938, Munich in September. Wilson also writes that Eden was 'Deputy Foreign Secretary in the late 1940s'. It really is not fair on Thorpe to have years of labour judged by so lazy a reviewer.

11 March 2003, Letter to D.R. Thorpe

I hear your Eden biography praised everywhere and thought highly of it myself. I was delighted to see good reviews. All my congratulations on a

---

* (1920–2014), Vice-President and Bursar of Wolfson Coll., Oxford 1967–76; Warden of Nuffield Coll., Oxford 1978–88.
† Sir Thomas Bingham, Baron Bingham of Cornhill (1933–2010), Master of the Rolls 1992–6; Lord Chief Justice 1996–2000; Senior Law Lord 2000–08.
‡ Sir Patrick Neill, Baron Neill of Bladen, Dorset (1926–2016), Warden of All Souls Coll., Oxford 1977–95.
§ (b. 1958), Danish-born writer and broadcaster.
¶ (b. 1950), biographer, novelist and journalist; *The Healing Art* won the 1981 Somerset Maugham Prize.

triumphant conclusion to your years of labour. My own work on Victor Rothschild is a pamphlet by comparison.

17 March 2003

The result of the second round of the Oxford Chancellorship vote:

    Patten 4,203

    Bingham 2,483

    Neill 1,470

    So even if Neill had not divided the lawyers' vote Patten would still have been elected.

23 March 2003

Reports of the opening skirmishes of the Iraq War are depressing, not least the deaths inflicted on our forces by so-called friendly fire.

31 March 2003

Waterstones at Notting Hill have sold out of their copies of *Victor Rothschild* and their shelves are now bare of the book. But my spirits are restored by the *Evening Standard* feature on London's current bestsellers, in which I am number four in the non-fiction list and Richard Thorpe's *Eden* is number five.

2 April 2003

Before he died Bobbety Salisbury made Robert Cranborne promise never to commission a biography of him, although all his papers have been put in order. Bobbety is one of the great gaps of modern political biography. So whom to choose? As Bobbety had so much to do with Eden in the 1930s, I wonder whether Richard Thorpe could handle the social nuances and the Christianity, as well as the deviousness?

12 April 2003

Roy Jenkins' last words are reported in the papers: 'I could manage two lightly poached eggs.' I like <u>two</u>.

7 June 2003

Mary Soames telephones me from Churchill College, Cambridge, where she is spending a week in the archives researching for her memoirs and being treated with much deference. Her parents kept every scrap of paper, including school bills and reports that bring the past to life.

26 June 2003

Denis Thatcher's death is announced in the course of the day.

8 July 2003

William Shawcross calls with a fascinating piece of news: he is to write the official life of the Queen Mother. I am so pleased for him, although his prose does not exactly sing. I suppose the TV programme he did on the Queen, showing himself to be a romantic Royalist, must have helped. Hugo Vickers will be chagrined not to be chosen. I would not be surprised if he presses ahead with an 'unofficial' life.

There will be difficult problems to be solved – how sincere was she in enchanting all those she met and how much influence did she have on the King, particularly on political and constitutional matters? I have a mass of material, journal entries and letters, which I must let William see.

10 July 2003

Bad news follows good news. William Shawcross telephones to tell me that Hartley died last night.

12 July 2003

Death of Robert Salisbury at eighty-six. He was always kind to me during my writing of *The Later Cecils*, and in some ways easier to deal with than Bobbety. I am so glad I went back to see him at Hatfield a year or so ago.

18 July 2003

Hugo Vickers tells me he is deeply disappointed not to have been asked to write the official life of the Queen Mother. So many people had assumed that he would do so that he had been lulled into thinking that it was more or less settled. In retrospect he now sees that his chances vanished with the retirement of Robert Fellowes. His relations with Robin Janvrin are chilly but civil. Oliver Everett would also probably have backed Hugo when Royal Librarian.

20 July 2003

William Shawcross tells me he wants to begin work on the QM book immediately by interviewing the dwindling band of those who knew her intimately.

23 July 2003

Pleasant gossip with Richard Thorpe, pleased by his reception of his book on Eden. He tells me that Jessica Rees, daughter of Brian, who has brilliantly overcome the handicaps of her profound deafness, earns a lot of money from Arsenal Football Club by being able to lip-read alleged comments made by players to referees when disciplinary proceedings are brought.

4 August 2003

Prue Penn has increasing doubts about how Willie Shawcross will fare in writing the Queen Mother's official life. He thinks he can write it in two years, so that it appears in 2006, the Queen's eightieth birthday.* But he will simply not be able to read and digest all the material in that time.

7 August 2003

I pick up some essays of J.T. Christie,† one-time Headmaster of Repton. He relates how at Repton, his predecessor, Geoffrey Fisher, used to come down from his see of Chester unannounced. Christie would find him talking to the boys in the bedders. What a horrible man.

15 August 2003

There is a story in the *Daily Telegraph* today that Willie Shawcross is to receive an advance of £1 million for his life of the Queen Mother. That is quite possible, but will the book ever earn as much? Dearly loved figures, even as dearly loved as the Queen Mother, fade from public memory quite quickly.

21 August 2003

Watch a video of a rather moving, clever film called *Billy Elliot*, about the son of a miner who against all the odds, and his father's opposition, becomes a ballet dancer. It is set against the violence and bitterness of the miners' strike, which adds to its poignancy.

30 August 2003

A lovely day of sun and breeze. To Kensington Gardens in the afternoon. The sixth anniversary of Diana's death in Paris is tomorrow and there is a display of flowers on the gilded gates of the Palace brought by the faithful. There are also on the railings a display of little broadsheets criticising Camilla Parker-Bowles and the Prince of Wales.

---

* The book appeared in 2009.
† John Traill Christie (1899–80), Headmaster of Repton 1932–7; Headmaster of Westminster 1937–49; Principal of Jesus Coll., Oxford 1950–67.

2 September 2003

William Shawcross comes in for a drink. He is annoyed with the *Daily Tele-graph* for running a story that he will receive a £1 million advance on his official life of the Queen Mother. He could perhaps earn that from selling the rights to a tabloid paper, but they would want a lot of sensationalism for such a sum, and William is too honourable to do so. It will not be an easy book to write if he is to detect how far the Queen influenced the King against the wishes of Tommy Lascelles.

On Friday, William is going up to stay with the Queen at Balmoral. Tony and Cherie Blair will be there on what has become an almost statutory Prime Ministerial annual visit. William is not being asked to familiarise himself with Balmoral, but to help create a more informal atmosphere, where people can help to talk to the Blairs. William gathers it will be a deliberately low-key visit: no traditional dinner each night with grouse and bagpipes, but a barbecue.

10 September 2003

Lunch off remarkably good roast beef with Peter Carrington at White's. He and Iona had Margaret Thatcher to lunch at Bledlow recently. Although diminished in health, she said she would never have invaded Iraq. Nor of course would Peter have done so. Peter tells me a story about President Gis-card d'Estaing* when taken to see Blenheim. He said: 'What a large house for such a small victory.' Robert Southey† thought that too.

11 September 2003

A poignant story of Margaret Thatcher, who, a few weeks after Denis' death, braced herself to go through all his clothes and sent most of them to Oxfam. The next day their son Mark arrived and said: 'What happened to all the clothes I left here?' Margaret had gone to the wrong room and thrown out his clothes.

17 September 2003

The Queen has told William Shawcross that she does not want him to write a political book, 'as my mother had no interest in politics'. She was in fact deeply interested in politics and firmly Conservative in her views. The interesting question is, how far did she influence the King in his relations with the post-war Labour Government?

---

* Valéry Giscard d'Estaing (b. 1926), President of France 1974–81.
† (1774–1843), poet of the Romantic School and a Lake Poet; Poet Laureate 1813–43.

23 September 2003

Robert Blake's death is announced; he was a good historian, though not as brilliant a biographer of Disraeli as the *Daily Telegraph* proclaims. Nor should he have split the Conservative vote for a new Chancellor of Oxford by standing against Ted Heath and so allowing in Roy Jenkins.

5 October 2003

Edward Ford telephones for a chat. He thinks the Queen should have lent the Royal Yacht *Britannia* for the talks between Harold Wilson and Ian Smith on Rhodesia. As it was, Smith had a rather meagre cabin of the ship's surgeon in a British cruiser. It might have made a difference to the outcome of the talks – and even the future of the Royal Yacht.

14 October 2003

I regret that Richard Chartres, the Bishop of London, ruled himself out of being translated to Canterbury by his opposition to women priests. This is a pity, as I would have liked an Archdeacon Grantly at Lambeth.

24 October 2003

Re-read the third volume of Woodrow Wyatt's diary. He was a tremendous toady, flitting between Margaret Thatcher and John Major, an appallingly weak PM, however kind a man.

29 October 2003

The evening news announces that Iain Duncan Smith has lost a vote of confidence among Tory MPs by 75 votes to 90, and has resigned as leader of the party. His successor seems likely to be Michael Howard, an able man. It is characteristic of our contemporary culture that he feels obliged to announce which football club he supports.

12 November 2003

Lunch with Peter Carrington at a good fish restaurant. Cherie Blair, with Cate Haste, wife of Melvyn Bragg,[*] is writing a book on Prime Ministers' consorts and invited Peter Carrington to No. 10 to talk about those he knew. She simply couldn't understand Peter's admiration for Dorothy Macmillan

---

[*] Cate Haste (b. 1945), author, biographer and documentary film-maker. Melvyn Bragg, Baron Bragg of Wigton (b. 1939), broadcaster and author; Chancellor of the University of Leeds 1999–2017. Cate Haste researched much of *The Goldfish Bowl: Married to the Prime Minister 1955–1997*, published in 2004. She visited me to discuss Clarissa Avon, Dorothy Macmillan and Elizabeth Home.

– 'a real Duke's daughter', as he calls her. When Peter arrived at No. 10 and announced his business, the doorkeeper said: 'Oh yes, you have come to see Cherie?' 'No,' Peter responded, 'I have come to see Mrs Blair.'

1 December 2003

During the clearing out of a cupboard I find a tile from the floor of the old Guards' Chapel which I picked up from the debris of the flying bomb on Sunday 18 June 1944. It is magenta in colour and on it is superimposed a Brigade star in buff with the original motto, '*Tria Juncta in Uno*'. It is pitted, either by the bomb or by hobnailed boots. I shall set it into a wall or pavement in my garden.

4 December 2003

I give a lecture on King George V at Dulwich College. An intelligent audience and lively questions. I am mildly annoyed by one well-upholstered boy who occupies one of the few armchairs in the front row, then composes himself for what is doubtless a well-deserved sleep throughout. The poster advertising the talk quotes Lord Dawson of Penn:[*] 'Death came peacefully to the King at 11.55 tonight.' This allows me to expand on the misleading use of the word 'peacefully' – in fact a lethal dose of cocaine through the King's distended jugular vein.

5 December 2003

A long talk with Edward Ford. His principal concern is whether, as the surviving literary executor of Tommy Lascelles, he should ask the Queen whether she would object to the publication of the diary which Tommy kept from 1942 to 1946, when he was the King's Private Secretary. Tommy himself was adamant that it should never be published except with the consent of the Sovereign. [†] Edward's co-executor, Michael Adeane, would never have given his consent for publication. Edward agrees with me that it is not a good moment to decide the matter in view of the sneaky books which have recently been published by former servants of the Royal Family – and even worse articles in the newspapers. I tell Edward of the letter the Queen wrote to Jock Colville when he asked her permission to include in his published Churchill diaries his account of the time when he served her as Private Secretary.

---

[*] 1st Viscount Dawson of Penn (1864–1945), physician to the Royal Family; President of the Royal Coll. of Physicians 1931–7.

[†] The third volume of Lascelles' diaries, *King's Counsellor: Abdication and War*, was published in 2006.

Having read his proposed extracts, the Queen told him that she could not allow him to publish them, however innocuous, when she had forbidden her footmen to publish their recollections.

Meanwhile Tommy's diaries are in Churchill College, Cambridge, and Edward thinks I would be able to read them under certain conditions.

Edward thinks that Bill Heseltine* had a dangerous effect on the monarchy by sponsoring at least one film that contained much about the private life of the Royal Family. He had previously served with Bob Menzies in Australia, whom he had 'promoted' in a PR exercise, and thought it his duty to 'promote' the Royal Family.

Turning to William Shawcross' book on the Queen Mother, Edward wonders whether there is enough material for a book the size of which the public expects. Tommy's diaries, for instance, are restrained in comment on her.

Edward does not know who chose William to do the QM book. Hugo Vickers may have expected to get it, and he is now going ahead with his own book on the QM,† for which he has been collecting material in the expectation of being appointed official biographer. He is still bitter about his exclusion.

22 December 2003

The papers say that David Blunkett‡ has been taking part in a broadcast quiz. Of all things he chose as his special subject the Harry Potter books – and was beaten by a pop star. What an epitome of the Blair Government.

---

* Sir William Heseltine (b. 1930), PS to Elizabeth II 1986–90.
† His *Elizabeth, the Queen Mother* was published in 2005.
‡ Baron Blunkett (b. 1947), Labour politician. MP for Sheffield Brightside and Hillsborough 1987–2015; Sec. of State for Education 1997–2001; Home Secretary 2001–4; Sec. of State for Work and Pensions May–Nov. 2005.

2004

On 1 January papers released under the thirty-year rule revealed that Princess Margaret would not have lost her title or her Civil List had she married Group Captain Peter Townsend in the 1950s. On 6 January the coroner's inquest into the death of Princess Diana was opened. An independent inquiry, to be chaired by Lord Butler, to examine the reliability of intelligence on weapons of mass destruction in Iraq, was announced on 3 February. The Gherkin office building designed by Norman Foster was opened in the City of London on 28 April. Ronald Reagan died on 5 June. The sixtieth-anniversary commemorations of D-Day took place on 6 June. UKIP won twelve MEPs in the European elections on 14 June. The Queen unveiled a memorial fountain to Princess Diana on 6 July. On 14 July the Butler inquiry criticised the government intelligence over weapons of mass destruction. Bernard Levin died on 7 August. Tony Blair announced on 1 October that he would not stand for a fourth term as Prime Minister if Labour won the next general election. The Hunting Act banning fox-hunting in England and Wales was passed on 18 November. The Wales Millennium Centre was opened in Cardiff on 28 November. David Blunkett resigned as Home Secretary on 15 December. A tsunami in the Indian Ocean on 26 December killed 225,000 people, including several Britons.

7 January 2004

The circumstances of Princess Diana's death surface again. The coroner, who opened his inquest on her yesterday, referred to her as Diana Frances Mountbatten-Windsor. But that name was not hers. The declaration by the Queen in 1960 said that the name Mountbatten-Windsor was to be borne only by those descendants of George V 'who will enjoy neither the style, title nor attributes of Royal Highness, nor the titular dignity of Prince, and for whom a surname will be necessary'. As the former wife of the Prince of Wales, she bore the style and titles, except for HRH, which she abandoned. Her title was Diana, Princess of Wales; she thus needed no surname.

23 January 2004

Prue Penn to lunch with me at Le Gavroche. She has heard that it was the Prince of Wales who chose Willie Shawcross to write the Queen Mother's official life – although of course the Queen approved.

29 January 2004

Some interesting talk with Edward Adeane about his father Michael's opinion of my *KGV*. He has come across a long letter from Michael in draft, but either Michael never sent it or I failed to receive it. Edward will send me a copy. Apparently, Michael thought it a good book, though Jock Colville told me otherwise (he would!).

6 February 2004

Read *The Macmillan Diaries: The Cabinet Years 1950–1957*, edited by Peter Catterall.* The details of Cabinet meetings are important, but not engrossing. Some splendid tirades against civil servants and the Duke of Edinburgh. Lord Salisbury was a dominating figure, although constantly threatening to resign. Winston treats Eden abominably by utterly refusing to resign until 1955. Macmillan shows affection for his oldest friend Harry Crookshank, such a prissy, spiteful figure. Macmillan loves walking and shooting: deeply upset at apparent impending dissolution of Chatsworth after 1950. Macmillan becomes teetotal, partly to lose weight. He suffers much from colds and sore throats, is frequently exhausted and spends mornings in bed. A voracious reader while in office: Victorian two-volume biographies, history, the whole of Bagehot, classical novels, Rousseau in French.

13 February 2004

William Tallon telephones me, and says he has heard I have had cancer and wants to congratulate me on my recovery. He himself seems to have recovered from his troubles following the Queen Mother's death and sounds his old cheerful, polite self. I will ask him to lunch. He quotes an interesting remark made to him by David Bowes-Lyon:† 'When my sister married the Duke of York, the gates clanged behind her and never opened again.'

---

* Dr Peter Catterall (b. 1961), Professor of History and Policy at Westminster University since 2016.
† The Hon. Sir David Bowes-Lyon (1902–61); during World War II he was a member of the Political Warfare Executive propaganda dept.; Lord Lieutenant of Hertfordshire 1952–61.

27 February 2004

William Tallon lunches with me at the Ark. During the past two years I heard that he had suffered a complete nervous collapse after the deaths, first of his lifelong friend Reg Wilcock,[*] a fellow butler at Clarence House, then of Queen Elizabeth herself. It is a pleasant surprise to see him smartly turned out and apparently in good heart and displaying that blend of impish humour and deference that made him such an institution.

Although he has a Duchy of Cornwall flat near the Oval, arranged by the Prince of Wales, he cannot get over being ejected from his little classical temple at the gates of Clarence House. He was told it was to become a souvenir shop when the house was open to the public, but it remained empty.

Although I make no attempt to 'pump' him on Royal life, he volunteers many details. When Queen Elizabeth was not dining out, she would always change her clothes and jewellery for her solitary dinner with the two corgis, then TV and early bed.

Of her early life she said: 'I think of my twenty best friends in 1914. Only five came back.'

William was obviously thought to have too privileged a position at Clarence House by the senior courtiers. When Reg died he managed to have the service at the Chapel Royal, but several details William wanted were initially turned down: a choir, a Purcell anthem, the Union Flag on the coffin and the National Anthem at the end. So William approached the Queen and all were granted. But in allowing the National Anthem, the Queen characteristically added: 'Only the first verse.'

5 March 2004

Re-read the letters of Herbert Asquith to Venetia Stanley,[†] edited by Michael Brock. An astonishing tale: a Prime Minister in his sixties becoming utterly besotted by a girl thirty-five years his junior. He wrote to her every day, and was cast into depression if a day went by without his receiving a letter from her. Even after the outbreak of war he managed to take her out for a drive in his car most days, and included her in many weekends at The Wharf in Sutton Courtenay or at Walmer Castle. In his letters he told her every detail of military intelligence and Field Marshal French's[‡] plan, as well as the political relationship of Winston and Kitchener. Asquith even postponed an audience

---

[*] Reginald Wilcock (1934–2000), Deputy Steward to the Queen Mother 1978–2000.
[†] The Hon. Venetia Stanley Montagu (1888–1948), aristocrat and socialite.
[‡] FM Sir John French, 1st Earl of Ypres (1852–1925), C.-in-C. BEF 1914–15 and Home Forces 1916–18.

with the King in order to see her. It infuriated him that Venetia chose to be a nurse – looking after working-class people. He would sometimes send her letters through the post rather than by special messenger: what if one had been lost or turned up in a newspaper office! An hour every evening reading a novel in the Athenaeum, then a dinner party and bridge. There was probably little physical contact between them, though some suspect that there was. It is uncomfortable to read the statesman writing such phrases as 'we had a <u>divine</u> time.'

In May 1915 she agreed to marry Edwin Montagu.* All this was a shattering blow to Asquith: it probably affected his judgement and ultimately cost him the premiership.

Michael Brock is an exemplary editor.

12 April 2004

Ben Pimlott has died of leukaemia at only fifty-eight. A really tragic loss. He was a sound, leftish historian and a charming man.

20 April 2004

William and Caroline Waldegrave give a most jolly party at Christie's Gallery in the Old Brompton Road. I talk cricket with Harold Pinter. I tell him to read my Rothschild book, which describes Victor's 'gem of an innings' for Harrow v. Eton at Lord's in 1929, with Terence Rattigan† at the other end quite overshadowed. It was one of the few occasions on which Rattigan found himself out of the limelight. Pinter says he will get the book.

I talk with Robin Butler about the inquiry he has been asked to chair into the end of the Iraq War. I say: 'You are a great public servant. You are also barmy to take it on.' He says: 'That seems to be the accepted view.'

27 May 2004

Dukie Hussey tells me that before the Queen's State Visit to Germany, the German Ambassador gave a dinner to which Dukie was invited. But he was late because while dressing, Dukie, who of course lost a leg in the war, had a misfortune. His foot fell off and it had to be fastened into place with sticking plaster and bandages. When Christopher Soames heard this, he said: 'Serves the Ambassador right. He was probably the bugger who shot it off in the first place.'

---

* (1879–1924), Liberal politician. Sec. of State for India 1917–24.

† Sir Terence Rattigan (1911–77), one of the most popular dramatists of his time; his works have enjoyed a recent revival.

1 July 2004

Lunch at the Beefsteak. I sit next to Michael Cecil.* I ask him whether any progress has been made towards commissioning a biography of his grandfather, Bobbety. He says that his own father, who died not long ago, suggested that David Gilmour should be asked, but he had other projects. I wonder why Bobbety did not want a biography of himself to be written. Michael suggests both a natural modesty, but even more a fear of what might emerge about his private and family life.

7 July 2004

The *Daily Telegraph* has pictures of the Queen unveiling the Princess Diana memorial fountain in Hyde Park, a rather absurd waterway which has cost £3.6 million. But the Queen takes the opportunity to heal the breach between Lord Spencer and the Royal Family that began with his cruel address in the Abbey at Diana's funeral, a malignantly hostile performance.

15 July 2004

Robin Butler's report into the false intelligence that led Blair to declare war on Iraq clears him of dishonesty, but points to a flawed system at No. 10 that diverts such action from the Cabinet to cronies.

Read Andrew Devonshire's posthumously published memoirs, *Accidents of Fortune*. Good-humoured and modest. No mention of his MC, but that is not at all uncommon among brave men. He remarks on Harold Macmillan: 'He liked to think of himself as a figure out of Trollope – in fact he was pure Galsworthy.'†

10 August 2004

Death of Bernard Levin after a distressing period as a victim of Alzheimer's disease. He was brilliant at his best, but could easily succumb to self-indulgence in his articles. The last time I heard from him was after an outlandish production of the *Ring* at Bayreuth, when I said I would go there no more. Bernard sent me a card saying: 'We all feel like that sometimes. But you will be back.'

---

* Michael Gascoyne-Cecil, 7th Marquess of Salisbury (b. 1946), Conservative politician. MP for South Dorset 1979–87.
† John Galsworthy (1867–1933), novelist, renowned for *The Forsyte Saga* (1922); winner of the Nobel Prize in Literature 1932.

31 August 2004

It is the anniversary of Princess Diana's death seven years ago, and the railings in front of Kensington Palace are once again hung with flowers, photographs and messages: it has become an annual cult. One message reads: 'No to Queen Camilla.'

1 September 2004

Lunch with James Stourton. He wonders what sort of book William Shawcross will write about the Queen Mother. William never knew her, and so cannot be aware of her Edwardian way of life: mounds of baggage and troops of servants. James wonders whether disobliging details will be made known in an authorised biography? Yes, they should to give balance.

2 September 2004

Prue Penn tells me that William Shawcross has been working on the Strathmore papers at Glamis. William will then go on to Balmoral, but to stay with the Factor, not with the Queen.

13 September 2004

Hugh Cecil[*] sends me his monograph on Lord Lansdowne,[†] delivered as a lecture at the British Embassy in Paris to celebrate the centenary of the Entente Cordiale. When I was a boy Lansdowne was despised almost as a traitor for having advocated peace in 1917. Today he is seen as a visionary, and rightly so.

16 September 2004

The papers report amazing scenes both inside and outside the Palace of Westminster. To coincide with Blair's steamroller tactics in passing through a Bill to abolish hunting, a group of hunt supporters penetrated the Chamber of the Commons, demonstrated and were arrested after scuffles. There was also a mass demonstration outside Parliament, during which the police waded into some fairly pacific countrymen with truncheons causing much loss of blood. The pictures really do reveal that charge, usually on the lips of the left – 'police brutality'. It is perhaps another aspect of the class war that lies behind Labour's determination to outlaw fox-hunting.

---

[*] (b. 1941), author of *Lord Lansdowne: From the Entente Cordiale of 1904 to the 'Peace Letter' of 1917*. International political adviser; Under-Sec. at the Foreign and Commonwealth Office 1992–5.

[†] Henry Petty-Fitzmaurice, 5th Marquess of Lansdowne (1845–1927), Gov. Gen. of Canada 1883–8; Viceroy of India 1888–94; Foreign Secretary 1900–05.

2 October 2004

The PM has bought a house for his retirement in Connaught Square, a few yards round the corner from where I lived in Connaught Place. He has paid £3.6 million for it, which the papers seem to think is too much. House prices in general are likely to fall, and this one is too near the Bayswater and Edgware Roads, without a view of the park or a garden.

Read *Robert Byron* by James Knox.* His style is rather dense, but fortunately there are copious quotations from Byron's own travel books. How tough Byron was; and how he worked to earn a living, scarcely ever having had any money. It is now obvious how much Bruce Chatwin modelled his life and style on Byron.

27 October 2004

Lunch at the Beefsteak. I sit next to a large, amiable man who turns out to be Hugh Montefiore,† formerly Bishop of Birmingham, who stirred up much controversy by asserting that Jesus Christ may have been homosexual. He owed his preferment, he says, to Rab Butler, who encouraged Mervyn Stockwood‡ to make him a suffragan bishop. He was vicar of Great St Mary's, Cambridge, when Rab was Master of Trinity. After Kingston, he was translated to Birmingham by Jim Callaghan.

8 November 2004

Hugo Vickers calls for a gossip, mostly on Royal topics. He was on duty in St George's, Windsor, for the old Duchess of Gloucester's funeral, much impressed by the way her medals and decorations were displayed on the altar. With his eye for such things he even noticed that she was awarded King George V's Silver Jubilee medal some months before she married Prince Henry.

He seems quite calm about Willie Shawcross' book about the Queen Mother. His own will certainly come out first. What really puzzles Hugo is why Willie wants to write the book. He never even met the QM and, apart from doing a TV programme on the Queen, has no background knowledge of the Royal Family and the court.

By chance, Willie himself rings me later. He goes on to talk about his book,

---

* Robert Byron (1905–41), travel writer, best known for *The Road to Oxiana* (1937). James Knox (b. 1952), author and publisher of the *Spectator* 1983–92; Dir. of the Fleming Wyfold Art Foundation since 2015.
† Rt Revd Hugh Montefiore (1920–2005), Bishop of Kingston 1970–78; Bishop of Birmingham 1977–87.
‡ Rt Revd Mervyn Stockwood (1913–95), Bishop of Southwark 1959–80.

and hopes Hugo's will come out soon, allowing a decent interval before his own.

13 November 2004
Michael Howard, the Conservative leader, has sacked Boris Johnson[*] from his front bench after tabloid newspapers revealed details of Boris' private life. How utterly stupid. The Tories are really no longer worth a vote.

14 November 2004
I go to the Welsh Guards' Chapel, a site with so many memories, for the Remembrance Day service. The service is well done. My thoughts go back to the ruins, dust and corpses of June 1944. The Prince of Wales is here, and afterwards when he is doing his rounds I tell him that I shall be eighty tomorrow; he toasts me with a little glass of cherry brandy. So he is still on cherry brandy after all the years since he was caught drinking one at Gordonstoun. He says: 'Ah, you are another Scorpio.' It is his fifty-sixth birthday and he goes on to tell me that he is now the same age as his grandfather, King George VI, when he died in 1952.

15 December 2004
I finish reading the new expanded edition of Harold Nicolson's diaries. Towards his last decade he became almost stilted with elaborate tirades of various sorts. I become increasingly certain that he wrote the diaries for publication. There is a note of 'Look how clever I am, how amusing, how original.' But simultaneously he would repeatedly declare himself a failure.

19 December 2004
The papers are full of the resignation of David Blunkett as Home Secretary after his office was detected in having tried to fast-track a residence permit for his mistress's nanny. He also gave his mistress a railway warrant, issued to him as an MP, so that she could travel free to his cottage on the Chatsworth estate. He claimed she was his 'spouse'. The civil servants at the Home Office should have warned him against this sort of misdeed. But today's senior civil servants have been so politicised by the Blair Government that they are reluctant to uphold old-fashioned principles of ministerial integrity.

---

[*] (b. 1964), Conservative politician. MP for Henley 2001–8; Mayor of London 2007–16; MP for Uxbridge and South Ruislip since 2015; Foreign Secretary 2016–18. Became Prime Minister in 2019.

2005

On 1 January the Freedom of Information Act came into effect. On 6 February Tony Blair became the longest-serving Labour Prime Minister with 2,838 days in office, exceeding the combined record of Harold Wilson in his two terms. On 10 February Clarence House announced that the Prince of Wales was to marry Camilla Parker Bowles. On 11 February Tony Blair had a whistle-stop tour of marginal constituencies. The hunting ban came into effect on 18 February. On 24 March the Constitutional Reform Act came into effect, providing for the creation of a Supreme Court. James Callaghan, the former Prime Minister, died on 26 March, eleven days after his wife, Audrey. Pope John Paul II died on 2 April. On 5 April Tony Blair asked the Queen for a dissolution of Parliament for a general election on 5 May. The civil wedding of Prince Charles and Camilla Parker Bowles took place in Windsor Guildhall, followed by a service of blessing in St George's Chapel, on 9 April. On 19 April Cardinal Joseph Ratzinger was elected Pope Benedict XVI. On 3 May the last MORI poll before the general election put Labour five points ahead of the Conservatives. The general election of 5 May returned the Labour Party to power with a reduced majority of 66. On 6 May Michael Howard announced that he would resign as Conservative Party leader 'sooner rather than later'. The Ugandan-born Bishop of Birmingham, John Sentamu, was named the new Archbishop of York on 17 June. On 23 June Prince William graduated from St Andrews University. London was chosen as the host city for the 2012 Olympic Games on 6 July. On 7 July co-ordinated bombings in London by Islamic terrorists killed fifty-two people and injured over 700. Edward Heath, the former Prime Minister, died on 17 July. Robin Cook, formerly Foreign Secretary, died on 6 August. On 21 August a service was held at the Cenotaph to mark the sixtieth anniversary of the end of World War II. On 17 October the Conservative Party began voting for a new leader following the resignation of Michael Howard, and on 6 December David Cameron was elected. Harold Pinter won the Nobel Prize in Literature on 10 December. On 12 December a MORI poll put the Conservatives two points ahead of Labour. The Civil Partnership Act came into force on 19 December.

5 January 2005

The *Daily Telegraph* has a vivid obituary of Humphrey Carpenter, who died yesterday at the age of fifty-eight of Parkinson's disease. He caused much distress to an incautious Robert Runcie by including in his biography of him much material which Robert had spoken, obviously, off the record.

I talk with Jean Trumpington. We speak of Jeremy Thorpe. She says that George Harewood apparently behaved very generously at the time of the trial, giving Marion some silver which she could sell to help pay for Jeremy's defence.

6 January 2005

Willie Shawcross is about to retreat to Friston to make a start on writing his life of the Queen Mother. He will be alone, without even someone to clean and cook for him. He will get up at six and go to bed at nine. He has apparently accumulated a mass of material.

So far Willie has not consulted me, either on what form I think the book should take or to hear my memories of the QM. What I dread is to be asked to read the typescript; for if the present book is anything like the book on the Queen he produced for his TV programme, it may need drastic polishing. That could take a lot of time and possibly ruffle his feathers. I would rather forge ahead re-reading my own Journals with a view to publication.

19 January 2005

Paul Potts celebrates his fifty-fifth birthday and we have some talk. I explain why I cannot hang the two marvellous photographs of King George's funeral cortège which he gave me for my birthday. Although I have no fear of death, I do not wish to be forever reminded that the end could come fairly soon. I go round to discuss what I should like him to say about me as an introduction to my speech at Westminster Abbey on Wednesday. I should like him to touch on my friendship with Hartley over the years.

Willie Shawcross is exercised about the numerous letters Hugo Vickers says that he has been lent, all written by the Queen Mother. As he does not own the copyright, can Vickers publish them, or extracts from them, without permission from the Queen? Technically not. But as Willie says, the Palace is unlikely to withhold permission lest Vickers publicly complains of being censored. On the other hand, Willie was appointed to write the official life, and now finds himself at a disadvantage to a freelance biographer. He has every reason to feel aggrieved, particularly as Vickers is in a position to bring out his book at least a year before Willie's.

30 January 2005

William Hague talks well on Michael Berkeley's *Private Passions* programme. I am impressed that the moment he ceased to lead the Tory Party he set about writing the life of William Pitt the Younger.

10 February 2005

It is officially announced that the Prince of Wales is to marry Camilla Parker Bowles at Windsor in April: a civil ceremony followed by a service of blessing in St George's Chapel. She will be called HRH the Duchess of Cornwall; but when Charles becomes King it is said she will be known as the Princess Consort. So Charles will have the morganatic marriage denied to Edward VIII. It will certainly not strengthen the monarchy. I refuse all Press comment.

12 February 2005

The Camilla engagement rumbles on. Press comment extends from the mildly approving to the vindictively hostile. Much nonsense too about whether Princess Anne and the other Royal ladies will have to curtsey to Camilla. Only the Queen would receive a curtsey in public from her family. There seems to be general dislike of the proposed title of Princess Consort once Charles becomes King.

13 February 2005

I ask Edward Ford whether he will give a Royal bow to Camilla once she becomes the Duchess of Cornwall. He says: 'I shall look at my shoes, as if they need cleaning.'

17 February 2005

William Shawcross has been talking to Robin Janvrin about Hugo Vickers' rival, unofficial life of the Queen Mother. He is annoyed that Vickers, whose book will be published first, will almost certainly receive *carte blanche* copyright permission from the Palace to reproduce all the Queen Mother's letters which he has garnered from here and there over the years. The Palace will almost certainly be unwilling to withhold copyright permission from Vickers in case he stirs up the popular Press with the cry of 'Royal censorship'. I advise him to make it clear to Janvrin that Vickers must not use <u>any</u> unpublished material in the Royal Archives duplicates elsewhere which Willie wants to include.

2 April 2005

The poor Pope clings to life. His death is announced in the evening to universal sorrow.

Willie Shawcross tells me that when Cherie Blair interviewed Clarissa Avon for her book on the Prime Ministers' consorts, they took to each other hugely.*

28 April 2005

The General Election on 5 May seems to be going Labour's way, in spite of Blair being exposed for going to war against Iraq without the full legal support of the Attorney General, Lord Goldsmith.†

6 May 2005

Blair's Government is returned in the General Election for a third term, but with a majority in the Commons cut from 161 to 66: workable but humiliating. And a corresponding gain for the Conservatives in spite of all the forecasts that there would be a Labour majority of more than 100. Already the old Labour MPs are beginning to snarl. The Conservatives increased their number of seats from 166 in 2001 to 198. The Lib Dems went up from 52 to 62. Labour went down from 413 to 356.

7 May 2005

Michael Howard, having led the Tories to a General Election result better than most can have forecast, nevertheless now announces that he will soon retire as leader of the party on grounds of age. He is sixty-four, so would be approaching seventy by the probable time of the next General Election. Nevertheless, a blow to the party.

14 May 2005

I hear a story about William Shawcross and Tony Blair. A while ago, when he was researching his TV programme on the Queen, William was on the train from Cornwall to London when his seaside hotel, Tresanton, telephoned him to say that Blair was coming to dine. William was at first inclined to continue his journey. But on changing trains for London at Plymouth, there was a St Austell-bound train on the other side of the platform. So he thought it would be courteous to return to Tresanton in case there were any difficulty. When William asked the PM if everything was all right, Blair asked whether he was

---

* Clarissa Avon also told me how well they had got on together.
† Peter Goldsmith, Baron Goldsmith of Allerton (b. 1950), Att. Gen. 2001–07.

the manager. 'No,' replied William, 'I own the hotel, Prime Minister. I am making a film about the Queen, and you are the only person who has refused to take part in it.' PM: 'And do you think I should?' 'Yes, I do.' So Blair did agree to be interviewed.

19 May 2005

To Oxford for the day to lunch with Alan Ryan,[*] Warden of New College – probably the nicest and most distinguished in living memory. We have a good talk in the Warden's Lodging. Alan enthuses about Chris Patten as Chancellor, who he thinks even more successful than Roy Jenkins in keeping in touch with every aspect of the university. One striking statistic: only seven heads of houses are professional academics.

My Mound steps are mellow in the afternoon light, and look as if they had been here for centuries. Alan says that at night the undergraduates go there to smoke. It then looks like the haunt of glow-worms.

In the evening I have a long talk with Edward Ford on the telephone. Recalling that until a year or two ago he was Secretary and Registrar of the Order of Merit, I tell him how surprised I was by the OM for Michael Howard. Edward talks of his relations with Robert Fellowes, his successor as Registrar of the OM.

Edward says: 'I told Robert that I did not think Betty Boothroyd[†] should have had the OM; and that Tom Bingham should have had the OM rather than the Garter.' Edward also agrees with me that Howard and others should not have both the CH and the OM, particularly with only a very few years separating the two. 'In the OM testament I left for Fellowes, I urged close co-operation between the Palace and No. 10, to ensure that this did not happen.'

25 May 2005

Lunch with David Dilks at Brooks's. As always he is a generous host. He is in London to give a talk at the Canadian High Commission tomorrow on his new book on Churchill and Canada. It consists of extracts from political sources including Winston's own works. David's linking passages are clear and exemplary.

One interesting passage is on how much of the Commonwealth Winston failed to visit: Australia, New Zealand, Hong Kong, Malaya, Singapore,

---

* Prof. Alan Ryan (b. 1940), Warden of New Coll., Oxford 1996–2009.
† Baroness Boothroyd of Sandwell (b. 1929), Labour politician. MP for West Bromwich West 1973–2000; the first female Speaker of the House of Commons 1992–2000.

West and Central Africa, India after 1899 and South Africa after 1900.

David also dwells on the greed of the Churchill family in taking every advantage of copyright law. They charge a fee even for reproducing his speeches in *Hansard* – surely stretching it beyond what is reasonable.

We talk about the forged Hitler diaries and why Trevor-Roper failed to spot that they were forgeries. The first reason was that his German was adequate but not good. Nor had he read widely on Hitler, so failed to spot that everything in the diaries came from published sources. Nor was he given enough time to examine the diaries, much less to have chemical tests done on the paper and ink.

26 May 2005
Prince Eddie to lunch at Le Gavroche. We talk about Churchill wanting the Treasury to make an allowance to Princess Marina when Prince George's Civil List ceased on his death in the air crash in 1942. It was refused by the Treasury and the King did not want to make a fuss in case there should be attacks from the left on the tax-free Civil List of the Royal Family at a time of oppressive taxation throughout the rest of the country. What is not realised is that both the King and Queen Mary made Princess Marina an allowance out of their own money.

5 June 2005
After a tedious week of Leonard Bernstein, Radio 3 has now embarked on a glorious week of Beethoven, playing much of his output. I devour this feast, particularly the chamber music.

9 June 2005
To the annual Wolfson party at Claridge's. Some talk with Keith Thomas,[*] still Chairman of the judges. I manage to tell him with some tact that he should have had the OM that went to Michael Howard, which does not seem to displease him. He agrees with me that Tom Bingham should have had the OM rather than the Garter.

Also chat with Mary Soames, still scarcely able to come to terms with having been made a Lady of the Garter at eighty-three. This morning she went to the Palace to receive the insignia from the Queen. With a splendid touch of imagination, the collar of the Order turned out to be the one worn

---

[*] Sir Keith Thomas (b. 1933), Professor of Modern History at Oxford University 1986; President of Corpus Christi Coll., Oxford 1986–2000; Pro-Vice-Chancellor of Oxford University 1988–2000.

by her father, which has been on display at Chartwell and retrieved for Mary to swear at her installation on Monday.

15 June 2005
William Shawcross telephones with an astonishing story. Dominic Lawson has been sacked as editor of the *Sunday Telegraph*. Apparently, he was not even allowed to return to his office to collect his personal possessions, but escorted out of the building by security guards. The whole episode has been managed inelegantly, as was my own departure from the paper in 1997 at the hands of Dominic.

18 June 2005
Guards' Chapel Day in 1944.

Christopher Morgan[*] of the *Sunday Times* tells me how depressing it is to work for that paper. He is their religious correspondent and was best man at Rowan Williams' wedding. In the last months he has correctly forecast the names of the new Archbishop of Canterbury, the new Archbishop of York and the new Pope. Yet all three stories were sidelined in the inside pages.

24 June 2005
Martin Gilbert telephones to say he enjoyed my life of Victor Rothschild. He also tells me that in the Public Record Office he found the minutes of a committee some years ago to decide how much we could safely tell the Russians without compromising Britain's own security. One member of the committee was Anthony Blunt.

4 July 2005
Robert Lacey takes me as his guest to the Biographers' Club meeting in the Savile Club. After a talk on Queen Victoria's letters there is a discussion. One or two writers resent all censorship on the part of the Royal Archives. I do not agree. They are the Queen's archives and she is entitled to withhold inappropriate material. The trouble is that courtiers try to censor important material in the belief that they are meeting HM's wishes.

6 July 2005
As I am leaving a gallery in Cork Street, I hear the cabbies blowing their horns and shouting. I realise with disappointment, even despair, that London has been preferred to Paris, Madrid and New York for the 2012 Olympic Games:

---

[*] (1952–2008), religious affairs correspondent for the *Sunday Times* from 1997.

hugely expensive for the taxpayer, much disturbance from new building sites and an unpleasant air of triumphalism. The only pleasing feature is the discomfiture of President Chirac.* As I reach Piccadilly, RAF planes fly over releasing streams of red, white and blue smoke.

10 July 2005

To an exhibition and dinner at Eton. Afterwards Poppy Anderson thought-fully asks another guest to drive me back to London, which is a great blessing as the night is cold and I am beginning to wilt. As we wait for the car at the Burning Bush, I see a memorable sky, very dark blue with a sickle moon and the walls of College Chapel a gloomy grey, like the setting of a Verdi opera. How I love that place, but how grateful I am not to have spent my life there.

18 July 2005

News that Ted Heath died yesterday in Salisbury. His churlishness, which the obituarists do not attempt to conceal, was so monumental as to become almost attractive. I particularly remember him coming to dine with John Wilsey near Salisbury, where I was staying. As we went in to dinner I heard John ask Ted whether he knew me. 'Yes, good journalist; bad paper.' Which was better than the other way round. I also recall a good long talk with him at a Buckingham Palace evening party.

2 August 2005

I re-read David Newsome's *On the Edge of Paradise*, the life of A.C. Benson,† whose prolonged bouts of depression make one's own moments of gloom seem trivial by comparison. Newsome shows that his ailment sprang from the impossibility of having any sort of sexual relationship with the Eton boys he desired and worshipped – and hardly less so, the Cambridge undergrad-uates after he had moved to Magdalene.

I should like to have known more about the problems and possible Royal censorship of his editing of Queen Victoria's letters.

7 August 2005

Robin Cook, Labour's former Foreign Secretary, who resigned in protest at the Iraq War, died yesterday while mountain-walking in Scotland. He had

---

* Jacques Chirac (b. 1932), President of France 1995–2007.

† (1862–1925), author and academic. Schoolmaster at Eton 1885–1903; Master of Magdalene Coll., Cambridge 1915–25.

a sharp wit, but was handicapped by his pixie-like appearance. But he did stand up to Blair in a courageous way.

15 August 2005
The sixtieth anniversary of the end of the war against Japan after the dropping of the first atomic bombs. I was at Pembroke Lodge, Richmond Park, and did not at once take in what a reprieve it was as we trained to land in Japan. High casualties would have been enormous.

11 September 2005
Re-read Somerset Maugham's* *Cakes and Ale.* It is a brilliant novel with a wicked caricature of Hugh Walpole† and a charming, shrewd portrait of Thomas Hardy, though Maugham at first denied both attributions. Maugham makes himself rather unattractive as the narrator.

3 October 2005
There is a report in the papers that a critic thinks Hugo Vickers' book on the Queen Mother to be the best Royal biography he has ever read – the critic is in fact A.N. Wilson, clever but capricious. That must be bad news for Willie Shawcross, to whom I do not mention Wilson when he telephones me.

5 October 2005
Some talk with Chris Morgan about the new Archbishop of York, John Sentamu, originally from Uganda and the first black Archbishop in England. A radical, of course.

16 October 2005
The surprising award of the Nobel Prize in Literature to Harold Pinter has been received with too much obsequiousness. His Americanisms and use of filthy language puts him beyond the pale.

20 October 2005
The election of a new Tory leader is getting under way; whoever is chosen is unlikely to win the next election. I mildly incline to the youngish Etonian, David Cameron.

---

* William Somerset Maugham (1874–1965), playwright, novelist and writer of short stories; one of the most popular authors of his era.
† Sir Hugh Walpole (1884–1941), novelist and writer.

22 October 2005

Hugo Vickers tells me he is furious at the way the *Daily Mail* has serialised his book on the Queen Mother. I tell him that no newspaper pays many thousands of pounds to serialise a book unless it is given a completely free choice. Presumably the *Daily Mail* has done some editing and compressing. But from dipping into the book here and there, I find that he has written unkindly about all sorts of people, including Martin Gilliat, Ralph Anstruther and David Bowes-Lyon.

28 October 2005

Willie Shawcross does not propose reading Hugo Vickers' life of the Queen Mother. He tells me that A.N. Wilson has written three reviews of the book, all very favourable: *Evening Standard*, *Daily Telegraph* and *Country Life*. I think it wrong for a leading critic to do this.

31 October 2005

I read Ben Pimlott's life of Harold Wilson, an impressive personal and historical assessment. What a loss Ben's death has been.

Hallowe'en. In this affluent street, children pour out of their parents' 4x4 cars, dressed in very expensive costumes, masks and headpieces. By contrast I notice a mother and two children, hardly dressed up at all, except that each wears a single witch's hat. I find this divergence moving.

7 November 2005

I hear that Hugo Vickers' book on the Queen Mother has not sold at all as well as expected. It is because the sort of people whom he expected to buy it are waiting for Willie Shawcross. By contrast Andrew Roberts' book on Salisbury sold 6,000 copies, a respectable figure for a large book of its kind.

10 November 2005

Blair's Government was last night defeated by 31 votes in a Labour backbench revolt against his determination to extend to ninety days the time during which terrorist suspects may be held without trial. Several factors have brought this about: (a) Labour's mistrust of the PM at the way in which he carried the nation into war against Iraq on false evidence, allying himself with the ruthless belligerence of President Bush; (b) a growing preference for Gordon Brown to be installed at No. 10; (c) a mistrust of the police; and (d) a genuine outrage at the growing infringement of liberty of the subject. The Commons defeat does not require Blair to resign, but his authority is impaired.

1 December 2005

The *Daily Telegraph* reports that at the enthronement of Dr John Sentamu, the first black Archbishop, in York Minster yesterday, 'members of the congregation were handed Sudoku puzzles to amuse themselves as they waited for the arrival of Dr Sentamu'. No prayer books in the Minster, presumably.

3 December 2005

The *Sunday Telegraph* telephones to ask for a comment on the Queen's decision that Camilla, unlike Diana, should not be prayed for in church. I think this is wrong, and that the wife of the Prince of Wales should be prayed for. I deplore the various ways in which Camilla is not allowed to take the same status as her husband, e.g. the present proposal that when Charles becomes King, she would become not Queen but Princess Consort.

7 December 2005

I finish reading the life of the Queen Mother by Hugo Vickers. I enclose for him a list of factual corrections to have for the paperback. I also praise him for his industry and other qualities, without going overboard. He covers much of the ground that Willie Shawcross must cover, but disparages figures such as David Bowes-Lyon and Ralph Anstruther. I wonder if he would have done this if his book had been the official one?

9 December 2005

David Cameron, elected the new Conservative leader in succession to Michael Howard, seems determined to introduce Blairite policies rather than to maintain traditional Tory policies. Has he at thirty-nine the experience and strength of character to survive?

13 December 2005

Read Christopher Meyer's* *DC Confidential*, his memoirs as Ambassador to the United States, during the 9/11 disaster and the Iraq War. Meyer is immensely able, but conceited beyond belief. The book has raised a storm not because of any controversial diplomatic revelations, but because he has salted his memoirs with offensive personal remarks about the Labour politicians who stayed in the Washington Embassy in his time, particularly

---

* Sir Christopher Meyer (b. 1944), British Ambassador to the US 1997–2003.

Jack Straw* (Foreign Secretary) and John Prescott† (Deputy PM). With more justification he pitches into Blair's entourage at No. 10. What he cannot grasp is that the centre of gravity of foreign policy has passed from the FO to No. 10. He is sharp about Cherie Blair's hostility to the Republicans.

A particular cause of hostility to him from No. 10 and others is that he has since become Chairman of the Press Complaints Commission, thus responsible for considering complaints from those who feel they may have been disparaged in the memoirs of Meyer and others.

14 December 2005
Hugo Vickers answers my long letter about his life of the Queen Mother with good temper. He thanks me for pointing out mistakes. And when I remonstrate with him for irrelevantly disparaging characters – especially David Bowes-Lyon and Ralph Anstruther – he says: 'If I am to be really honest, I suppose that in writing a "rogue" book rather than the official version, I put those things in whereas I might not have done otherwise.' That is honest of him. He suggests that we meet to talk about that and allied topics, to which I readily agree.

23 December 2005
Prince Eddie tells me about the Royal Family Christmas lunch. 'I was lucky enough to sit next to Camilla. She is one of the best things to have happened for years. I like her down-to-earth good sense, total lack of airs, warmth, friendliness and sense of humour. She told me she loves Birkhall more than anywhere (good girl), though is not so keen on the Castle of Mey.'

---

* (b. 1946), Labour politician. MP for Blackburn 1979–2015; Home Secretary 1997–2001; Foreign Secretary 2001–6.
† (b. 1938), Labour politician. MP for Hull East 1970–2010; Deputy Prime Minister 2001–7.

2006

On 7 January Charles Kennedy resigned as leader of the Liberal Democrats, citing a drink problem. On 22 February the Prince of Wales's lawyers continued a High Court action against the Mail on Sunday to prevent further details from his journal from being published, such as his opinion that government officials in Peking are 'appalling old waxworks'. Sir Menzies Campbell was elected leader of the Liberal Democrats on 2 March. John Profumo died on 9 March. On 21 March a MORI poll put Labour eleven points ahead of the Conservatives. The Queen celebrated her eightieth birthday at Windsor on 21 April. On 5 May Tony Blair reshuffled his Cabinet: Jack Straw was replaced as Foreign Secretary by Margaret Beckett and Charles Clarke was sacked as Home Secretary and replaced by John Reid. George W. Bush greeted Tony Blair with the phrase 'Yo, Blair' on 17 July. On 19 November John Reid attacked Gordon Brown for openly campaigning to replace Tony Blair as Prime Minister. Marmaduke ('Dukie') Hussey died on 26 December. On 29 December the British government paid off the Anglo-American loan of 1946. Antony Lambton died on 30 December.

1 January 2006

The New Year opens damply in every sense. David Cameron announces a radical Conservative policy scarcely different from that of Tony Blair. I am also alarmed by the Government's giving the police power to arrest on even trivial charges such as dropping litter. One by one our liberties are eroded.

Re-read Aldous Huxley's *Antic Hay* with much enjoyment.

11 January 2006

Birgit Nilsson's[*] death announced. In fact she died last Christmas Day. I often heard her incomparable voice in my palmy days of opera in those great dramatic roles – Brünnhilde, Turandot, Elektra and of course Isolde. To

---

[*] (1918–2005), Swedish dramatic soprano.

commemorate her, Radio 3 plays a recording of her singing the 'Liebestod' from *Tristan*. I melt.

19 January 2006
To the Imperial War Museum for the exhibition of T.E. Lawrence. It is well done except for a perpetual noise of Arab music. The motorbike on which he crashed has been superbly restored and is a striking symbol of power as well as a thing of beauty. The charlatan as well as the man of action emerges well from the innumerable photographs. A brilliant Augustus John portrait. Why did Lawrence, as Aircraftsman Shaw, not wear any medal ribbons on his uniform?

23 February 2006
The Prince of Wales really does seem to have got himself into a mess by suing the *Mail on Sunday*, however nastily that paper has behaved in printing his private journal.

1 March 2006
Lunch with Peter Carrington in the House of Lords. Peter is taking a deep interest in my Journals. We never talk but he urges me towards publication. But he has never seen any of it and I promise to remedy this soon: probably one or two set pieces, e.g. Macmillan, the Queen Mother, etc., together with three months' continuous Journal chosen more or less at random.

We talk of the dottiness of Rowan Williams ('The Druid') as Archbishop of Canterbury, and his folly in publicly agreeing with the vote of the Synod to disinvest in companies which trade with Israel. I say how much I should have liked Richard Chartres as Archbishop, but that he ruled himself out by opposing women priests tooth and nail.

Peter also has reservations about Christopher Soames. When Peter appointed Christopher to be Governor of Rhodesia, Christopher took the job but insisted on putting on record that he thought it was too early – so that if things had gone wrong, he could have put the blame on Peter. As Peter says, he always looked after his own interests.

We run into Patrick Wright, former head of the Diplomatic Service, who says: 'I never know what is going on in the Foreign Office now Kenneth's column is no more.'

As we leave, Peter says with deep feeling: 'I have spent sixty years in this place and now it means nothing to me.'

10 March 2006

John Profumo died yesterday at the age of ninety-one. His exertions on behalf of Toynbee Hall earned him much praise during the last saintly forty years of his life after his days as a dashing minister. I am pleased to have given a party for him during his early disgrace, to which Alec and Elizabeth Douglas-Home and Selwyn Lloyd came. How piquant that his downfall should have been caused by lying to the House of Commons about his affair with Christine Keeler. Who does not lie to the House of Commons nowadays? And how inane of him to think that his 'guilt' could be covered up indefinitely; even more insane of him to sue two foreign papers for doubting his innocence. He showed astonishing robustness. Immediately after making his untrue profession of innocence to the Commons one Friday morning in March 1963, he went off to Sandown Park races with the Queen Mother.

12 March 2006

I rarely listen to Radio 4 plays, but tonight I tune in to Alan Bennett's *The History Boys*, which has had a triumphant run at the National Theatre. Most amusing, though surely the sixth-form boys of the grammar school would not talk to their History beak in such uninhibited language – nor discuss sexual experience and problems so frankly.

16 March 2006

I lunch at Boodle's with Hugh Leggatt. We discuss the revelations about the way in which Blair and his inner advisers create peerages: candidates have been handing over 'loans' to Labour Party funds of several million pounds. Fortunately, the committee of the House of Lords responsible for examining such nominations to peerages have blocked them. I compare it all to the shady manoeuvres of Lloyd George, though in those days the Tories sold honours just as freely as did the Liberals.

18 March 2006

To the Science Museum, South Kensington, for William Waldegrave's premature sixtieth birthday party. He is the Chairman of the Museum, so is able to have a dinner party for several hundred people in one of the best toyshops in the world. I have a pleasant – and useful – talk with Richard Chartres, the Bishop of London – who assures me that as a CBE I can have my memorial service in the Chapel of the Order of the British Empire in St Paul's. I must warn William to remember this when the time comes.[*]

---

[*] K.R.'s memorial did take place there on 8 May 2014, with William Waldegrave giving the address.

I also see Michael Howard, the recent leader of the Conservative Party, both clever and amiable. I am not sure the party should have deposed him. I also meet tonight George Osborne, Shadow Chancellor of the Exchequer, who will make a fine young leader when David Cameron is inevitably stabbed in the back.

22 March 2006

I give breakfast to Prince Eddie and Charles Guthrie. Our little club of three is most enjoyable. If anything, Prince Eddie is the most enthusiastic of all. Charles is very steamed up about the decision of the Government to send troops to Afghanistan, but he thinks it would not be right to criticise publicly his successors on the General Staff for being so lukewarm in opposing the Government's hawkish attitude.

23 March 2006

Lunch at the Garrick with Simon Heffer.* He has a deep love of music but, surprisingly to me, he considers the completion by another hand† of Elgar's unfinished Third Symphony a masterpiece.

Simon talks well about Enoch Powell, whose official life he wrote. Among the material he used were the many letters Enoch had written to his mother. Enoch was also apparently deeply ashamed of having become a brigadier on the Staff, yet never having fought. He would really have liked to have been killed in battle. Another deep romantic love was for India.

27 March 2006

The Bow Group has produced some so-called research on political honours, giving the alleged sums paid under Blair. It says a barony can be had for £2,651,250, a knighthood for £747,638 and a CBE for £611,000. Ridiculous.

21 April 2006

The Queen is eighty today. The 8 a.m. news churlishly places this item way down the list, preceded by David Cameron's visit to Norway to study global warming, and Iraqi politics, etc.

---

* Professor Dr Simon Heffer (b. 1960), journalist, author and political commentator; official biographer of Enoch Powell (1998); biographer also of Thomas Carlyle (2012) and of Ralph Vaughan Williams (2014).

† Elgar's unfinished Third Symphony was completed by the composer Anthony Payne for performance in 1998.

29 April 2006

Edward Ford consults me about a problem he faces as the only surviving executor of the will of Tommy Lascelles. Tommy left his diaries to his daughter,
not to the Royal Archives. The daughter allowed Duff Hart-Davis to produce
two volumes of them, up to 1936. Now Duff has prepared a third volume for
publication, covering Tommy's years in the Palace in wartime. Under Duff's
discreet editing this wartime volume is unlikely to contain anything offensive
to the Royal Family. But Edward feels strongly that whatever its contents, the
diary of a Private Secretary to the Sovereign should not be published; indeed,
he thinks it wrong that Tommy even kept a diary. The Queen has consulted
Edward, and he asks me what he should say to her. I tell him that in my own
personal opinion, there can be no objection if the Queen has the right to
remove any passage which she feels objectionable or embarrassing; in fact,
Duff has already told me that it is an anodyne document. On a technical
point, Tommy became Private Secretary before the days when all members
of the Household had to sign a pledge not to reveal material gained while in
the Queen's employment. In any case, Dick Crossman's diaries blew away
any lingering constraints of discretion. And Jack Wheeler-Bennett included
in his fairly discreet official life of King George VI that the King was opposed
to Churchill's becoming PM in 1940. I don't think I convince Edward Ford,
but he will think about it.

3 May 2006

Lunch with Prince Eddie at Boodle's. He enjoyed all the parties for the Queen's
eightieth birthday. He, Alexandra and Michael have given the Queen some
ornamental trees as a birthday present. Prince Andrew and Prince Edward
were both made Knights of the Garter. Apparently, Hugo Vickers, with his
knowledge of these things, told Prince Edward that he was the 999th Knight
of the Garter. Who will be the 1,000th?*

1 June 2006

The Prime Minister is in further trouble. After the Deputy PM, John Prescott,
had been detected in an open affair with his Civil Service secretary, Blair
refused to sack him. Instead he removed him from running a ministerial
department but allowed him to retain a full Cabinet minister's salary as well
as two grace-and-favour residences, an apartment in Admiralty House and
Dorneywood. This provoked such hostility, not least from Labour MPs, that
Prescott has now relinquished Dorneywood. The piquancy of it all is that

---

* Prince William, Duke of Cambridge, became the 1,000th Knight of the Garter in 2008.

he was forced to give up Dorneywood not because it was wrong for him to continue to use it, but because he was photographed playing croquet there on a Thursday afternoon when he should have been at his desk deputising for Blair, who is having a holiday. It is the supposedly upper-class pastime of croquet that did him in. Had he been at a football match, he would have escaped much criticism.

8 June 2006

Hugh Thomas tells me that Black Rod, in the House of Lords, has a disconcerting habit of asking a new peer: 'How much did you pay for it?' There are three sorts of response: (a) outraged silence; (b) a nervous giggle, and (c) a bold, ironic '£200,000'.

23 June 2006

Death of David Jewell at seventy-two. He was headmaster of Repton, 1979–1987. He made chapel compulsory and abolished corporal punishment. His obituary in the *Daily Telegraph* speaks of the school as being popular with Derbyshire farming families and Midlands industrialists. He went on to be Master of Haileybury, which the obit calls 'one of the great schools'. Was it? I should have thought a sideways move on a par with Repton, certainly in my own day. My relations with Jewell were warm. He invited me to become President of the Old Reptonian Society, but I declined; those bonhomous assemblies of footballers, golfers and Freemasons were not for me.

By chance, as I am writing about Repton, the wireless plays Richard Addinsell's* haunting school song composed for the film *Goodbye, Mr Chips*, filmed at Repton. I have not heard it for years. It almost brings tears to my eyes.

25 September 2006

I see the film *The Queen*, with Helen Mirren utterly brilliant in the title role. It <u>is</u> the Queen one is watching, in every nuance. The film is set in the days between the death of Diana in Paris and her funeral. It strains the truth in one way: the determination of Tony Blair to stick to his own plan of sharing the grief of the nation for the death of 'the People's Princess' – against the supposed cold-hearted Queen and Royal Family. There is one devilishly clever sequence in which the Queen is upset at the killing of a fourteen-pointer stag – even more so because it was shot by a paying visitor to a neighbouring estate to Balmoral. On the same theme, a depressed Queen, watching the

---

* (1904–77), composer renowned for his film music.

crowds in London on TV, instantly cheers up as her dogs come tumbling into the room. Another brilliant sequence is the Queen's visit to the mourning crowds once she has decided to fly south and make a broadcast about Diana.

The other roles are less good. There is a bad-tempered, unattractive Prince Philip; a wet, troubled Prince Charles – particularly his nervous hand gestures; a grotesque Queen Mother, watching TV with a <u>tumbler</u> of dry martini complete with olive, and pronouncing 'gone' as 'gorn' – which she did.

All the rage I felt at Diana's funeral surfaces again: loathsome showbiz people crowding into the Abbey to make an 'appearance' and applauding Spencer's shameful attack on the Royal Family.

4 October 2006

I lunch at the Beefsteak with John Freeman,[*] now in his ninety-second year, but well turned out, sparkling in conversation and with beautiful manners. I recall how kind he was to me when he was Ambassador in Washington and how utterly un-pompous. 'I always regarded myself as a functionary, not an initiator of policy.' Hence his admiration of Denis Greenhill, who was similarly restrained.

He quotes with appreciation Harold Macmillan in conversation about President Kennedy's 'Camelot'. Harold compared it to a small medieval state, self-contained and industrious. 'I should not be surprised,' Macmillan added, 'if one day there were to be a Cardinal Kennedy.'

On Dickie Mountbatten: 'He was in too much of a hurry to return home from India at the time of independence to resume his naval career and ultimately become First Sea Lord.' I ask John how much blame should attach to Cyril Radcliffe[†] in India for provoking civil war by drawing unsatisfactory boundaries. John says: 'He came on the scene too late, then drew thick lines on small maps.'

John admired Lord Chelmsford. 'Had the Montagu-Chelmsford Reforms[‡] been put into operation, India would have become independent ten years earlier and without bloodshed.'

---

[*] (1915–2014), journalist, broadcaster, diplomat and Labour politician. MP for Watford 1945–55; High Commissioner to India 1965–8; Ambassador to the US 1969–71; Chairman of London Weekend Television 1971–84.
[†] 1st Viscount Radcliffe (1899–1977), Law Lord; Chancellor of Warwick University 1965–72.
[‡] Sir Francis Thesiger, 1st Viscount Chelmsford (1868–1933), Viceroy of India 1916–21. The Montagu-Chelmsford Reforms of 1918 outlined the introduction of self-governing institutions to India.

17 October 2006

Duff Hart-Davis tells me that his third volume of Tommy Lascelles' diaries is coming out at the end of the week.

See the film of *The History Boys* by Alan Bennett. It is very funny with touches of brilliance and without any inhibition in referring to homosexual attraction between boy and boy, and boy and master. One line by a downcast boy: 'I'm small, I'm Jewish, I'm homosexual and I come from Sheffield. I'm fucked.' Not quite sure the old beak's melodramatic death on a motorcycle, with sentimental memorial service, quite comes off.

18 October 2006

Talk to Duff Hart-Davis about the third volume of Tommy Lascelles' diaries he has edited and which is about to come out. Considerable difficulty with the Palace, which received the manuscript in February last year, but have only now cleared it for publication. They insisted on the removal of a remark by Tommy on the then Queen's lack of punctuality: 'We left at 10 o'clock, or rather 10.12 – all the same to Her Majesty.' Robin Janvrin also insisted on maintaining the fiction that the Sovereign writes his or her own speeches. And Duff was not allowed to use Tommy's letters home to his wife during the King's tour of South Africa in 1947, when he suspended writing his daily dairy. Quite absurd restrictions.

11 November 2006

My review of the third volume of Tommy Lascelles' diaries appears in the *Daily Telegraph*. But various bits have been cut out, including the account of the King, irritated by his Labour ministers, exclaiming as he drives past Runnymede: 'That's where it all began.'

For the first Remembrance Day I can recall, I am not wearing a red poppy. There are no sellers in the street or in any shop I know. Apparently, it is difficult to enrol volunteers.

12 November 2006

I talk with Mary Gordon Lennox.* We discuss David Cameron, who Mary thinks is not as clever as the deposed William Hague. Cameron is unwilling at present to court the traditional Tory voter. Why did the party get rid of Hague as leader? 'Because he has no hair,' Mary says.

She has an interesting point about Eton. There are now so many boys from

---

* Lady Mary Gordon Lennox (b. 1934), Lieutenant of the Royal Victorian Order (DATE APPOINTED?).

all over the world that boys like her grandsons cannot be certain to make lifelong friends, as in Nicky's day.

20 November 2006

Gay Charteris telephones with the sad news that Edward Ford died yesterday. He seemed to have declined a lot when I last saw him on 7 November at the launch party for Tommy Lascelles' diaries. We had some good talk over the years. I pleaded the loss to history if Tommy's wartime diaries were not published. He came round to my view.

24 December 2006

I lunch with Philip Goodhart. He says that Peter Rees,* when Chief Secretary to the Treasury, inadvertently helped to bring down Margaret Thatcher. There was a meeting at Chequers to discuss the Poll Tax, which I record in my life of Victor Rothschild, to which Nigel Lawson should have come. Instead he sent Peter with instructions to deter Margaret from going ahead with what was bound to be a most unpopular measure. But Peter did not carry the big guns necessary, so the Poll Tax came into being and ended in disaster.

During the past few days I have read Philip's 100-page book *A Stab in the Front: The Suez Conflict, 1956*. An exemplary work. The political and military themes are clearly set out, with some fascinating sidelights. John Foster Dulles† must carry much blame for goading Nasser into nationalising the Suez Canal Company by withdrawing US aid for the Aswan Dam, then refusing to support the UK-French expedition. The logistics were difficult: Cyprus was 300 miles from Port Said and Malta 1,000 miles. Our planes and weapons were out of date. Macmillan used colourful metaphors which Ike misunderstood.

30 December 2006

Saddam Hussein is hanged, while Tony Blair spends the New Year as usual spongeing on a very rich pop star in the Caribbean.

Richard Thorpe, now writing a big book on Harold Macmillan, completing a triptych of biographies of Tory Prime Ministers, asks me if I know the truth about widespread rumours that he was sacked from Eton for some homosexual behaviour. I doubt it, more likely to have been on health grounds.

---

* Baron Rees of Goytre (1926–2008), Conservative politician. MP for Dover 1970–87; Chief Secretary to the Treasury 1983–5.
† (1888–1959), US Sec. of State 1953–9.

Would, or could, Macmillan have tried to become Provost if this allegation had been in the background, or won the affection of people like Bobbety and Oliver Lyttelton? Perhaps Richard could ask Alexander Stockton if the traditional leaving book given to Etonians, but never to those expelled, of Thomas Gray's poems is or was in Harold's library.*

---

* K.R.'s advice was exemplary. Harold Macmillan was given a leaving copy of Thomas Gray's poems. For the story of his withdrawal, not expulsion, from Eton see D.R. Thorpe, *Supermac: The Life of Harold Macmillan*, pp. 26–9.

2007

The Bank of England increased interest rates to 5.25 per cent on 11 January. On 7 March in a House of Commons vote a majority of MPs supported a fully elected House of Lords. On 14 March the Commons gave its approval to the updating of the Trident missile system. The rebuilt Wembley Stadium opened to the public on 17 March. On 17 April inflation was 3 per cent. An earthquake of 4.3 on the Richter Scale hit Kent on 28 April. Boris Yeltsin, the former Russian President, died on 23 April. On 19 May Tony Blair announced that he would step down as Prime Minister on 27 June. The Cutty Sark was severely damaged by fire in Greenwich on 21 May. On 24 June Gordon Brown was elected Labour leader and on 27 June became Prime Minister. Jacqui Smith became the first female Home Secretary on 28 June. On 1 July a smoking ban came into effect in all enclosed public places in England. On 22 July severe floods, particularly in the Midlands, left hundreds homeless. William Deedes died on 17 August at the age of ninety-four. On 14 September Northern Rock Bank received support from the Bank of England. On 26 September Labour had a twenty-point lead over the Conservatives, but Gordon Brown declined to call a general election. Sir Menzies Campbell resigned as leader of the Liberal Democrats on 15 October and on 18 December Nick Clegg was elected as the party's leader.

2 January 2007

Tony Lambton has died at the age of eighty-four. Staying at Cetinale was always a memorable aesthetic experience and I shall always be grateful for his hospitality. Of course, one had to sing for one's supper by entertaining him with gossip and reflections on history. Never having learned Italian during all his years there, he had little social life outside English expatriates and his own visitors. But he had a cruel and malicious streak which led him not only to disparage friends behind their backs, but also to their faces. Nor did I emerge entirely unscathed, though I am glad we made it up at the Channons' a year or two ago, the last time I saw him.

20 January 2007

Talk to Richard Thorpe about the OM and the CH. He is hugely knowledgeable on political gossip. While researching his Macmillan biography he has
seen a copy of a letter from Macmillan recommending A.L. Rowse for the
OM. He also tells me a story of Lord Midleton (St John Brodick),* Chairman
of the Charterhouse governors in the 1930s. He came over to Charterhouse
to hear Robert Birley preach his first sermon as Headmaster in September
1935. Birley was concerned that his churchmanship might not pass muster
and put a considerable amount of preparation into his sermon. At the end of
the service Midleton was waiting for him outside the West Door. His only
comment to Birley was: 'Never preach again in brown shoes.'

24 January 2007

A *Sunday Express* journalist asks me what I thought of Helen Mirren as
the Queen in the film about the events surrounding Diana's death. I try
to be helpful. 'And do you think the Queen has seen it?', he asks. I say, 'I
don't know, but probably not. She doesn't really care what people think
about her.'

I hear that poor Lady Thatcher spent Christmas alone with her carer and
had some 'fast food' for dinner. Can it be true?

6 February 2007

I am much enjoying Noël Coward's diaries, which I have read before. How
impressive a worker he was, in spite of exhaustion and unreliable health. He
loved solitude with books and music. Otherwise a frenetic social life, lived
under perpetual Press disparagement. Rather sad how at grand parties he
was 'persuaded' to sit down at the piano and sing his songs.

8 February 2007

Peter Carrington returns the specimen extracts of my Journals that I lent
him. He likes them very much, even an account of our talk over lunch in
1982, after his resignation from the Thatcher Government, which he says is
an accurate account.

20 February 2007

I give Mary Soames lunch at Le Gavroche. Although we both found Duff
Cooper's diaries disappointing, Mary speaks with admiration of Duff

---

* William St John Brodrick, 1st Earl of Midleton (1856–1942), Conservative politician. MP
for West Surrey 1885–1906; Sec. of State for India 1903–5.

Cooper's legacy: (a) his courageous resignation in 1938, with the loss of a much-needed salary, an agreeable ministerial job as First Lord, Admiralty House and the yacht *Enchantress*; (b) he was the link between Winston and de Gaulle, and worked to prevent a final breach that could so easily have taken place. A new Churchillism. When preparing the material for a book he would say: 'It is never a waste of time winding one's spools.'

27 February 2007

Lunch with Charles Guthrie. He has a story about a conference on the collapse of our defence of Crete in the war, with Wavell in the chair. A junior officer, called on to speak, said: 'There were many mistakes made and they are all sitting in the front row.'

Re-read C.P. Snow's *The Light and the Dark*, an early novel about a Cambridge College. The hero is a young man called Roy Calvert, haunted by melancholia, who is eventually killed in the war as a bomber pilot. Good in the Cambridge scenes, but not so good when he writes of an aristocratic family. I remember Harold Macmillan dwelling on this gap in Charles's novels. He should have stuck to dons and civil servants, about which he wrote so well.

26 March 2007

Peter Carrington has admitted to me that when he helped to negotiate our entry into Europe in 1972 he thought we would be joining no more than a free-trade area, not a relentless machine for imposing uniformity on every facet of European life. An extraordinary confession from a former Foreign Secretary. But of course that is exactly what I, and many others, believed at the time. So I keep quiet about my place on the committee that co-ordinated national celebrations of the event.

2 May 2007

Lunch with Peter Carrington at White's. He dined with Eric and Poppy Anderson at Eton the other day to meet the Queen and Prince Philip. The Shawcrosses were there. Willie told him that he had finished his book on the Queen Mother and that the Queen had read it and approved.

William Waldegrave, Peter says, will follow Eric Anderson as Provost, though there is no immediate plan for Eric to retire.

Peter does not regret resigning as Foreign Secretary as a point of honour when the Argentine invasion of the Falklands took his department by surprise. Mrs Thatcher of course tried to dissuade him. He asked her whom she would appoint as his successor. She said Francis Pym.* Peter: 'But you can't stand him.' M.T.: 'Yes, but he is the best of a bad bunch.'

11 May 2007

Blair announces that he is to retire as Prime Minister on 27 June. The long-expected news is received with ill-veiled mockery. The invasion of Iraq at President Bush's coat-tails, and all that has followed in loss of British lives and reputation, will cloud his reputation for ever.

Wanda Boothby telephones me. She finds herself rather in need of money and wants to sell Bob's papers. She has already somewhat diminished their value by letting Robert Rhodes James have those on the Czech assets scandal and Richard Thorpe on Bob's correspondence with Harold Macmillan. Bob destroyed all the letters he received from Dorothy Macmillan. She approached the Bodleian, but they did not seem to be enthusiastic. She asks my advice. I tell her I will talk to the Bodleian to elucidate their attitude. And if the library does not make an offer, I suggest that she writes a letter to the *Daily Telegraph*, asking whether any friend or acquaintance of Bob's or any historical archive would be interested in acquiring them. Christie's have apparently put a valuation of £80,000 on them.

18 August 2007

Death of Bill Deedes yesterday at ninety-four. My own memories centre on the talk and laughter we shared in Peterborough Court when I first joined the *Daily Telegraph* in 1952. On his joining Churchill's last Government in 1954 as Under-Secretary for Housing, I took over the exceptionally interesting role of writing the political pieces in the 'Peterborough' column: an invaluable introduction to both Houses of Parliament and its denizens. Bill must have shown great courage when fighting from Normandy to the Baltic, and winning the Military Cross.

3 September 2007

Crowds are still flocking to the railings outside Kensington Palace and putting up flowers and other tributes to Diana. It was foolish of Dodi Fayed during those last hours in Paris to show Diana the Windsors' home in the Bois, for the Windsors epitomised exile, failure and rejection.

---

* (1922–2008), Conservative politician. MP for South East Cambridgeshire 1961–83; Sec. of State for Defence 1979–81; Foreign Secretary 1982–3.

15 September 2007

We are in the middle of a very serious financial crisis, triggered by the near-collapse of Northern Rock. Its share price has dropped by about a third and investors are besieging its offices to withdraw their money.

1 December 2007

Hugo Vickers telephones me. He has been taking part in a BBC programme at Sandringham on John Betjeman's poem on the death of King George V, and wonders how I came to print 'Mrs Simpson' in the version used as an epilogue to my biography of the King. It was Owen Morshead who drew my attention to it in the late 1970s, and I corresponded with John Betjeman who explained that 'Mrs Simpson' was in the original version.

William Tallon is to have his funeral service next Thursday in the Queen's Chapel, St James's Palace. Soon after he died the 'authorities' descended on his Duchy of Cornwall flat in Kennington and removed some or all of his papers. They apparently included self-pitying letters from Prince Charles about his lot; also stocks of unused Christmas cards of the Queen Mother. As he was found dead in his flat, there had to be a post-mortem. So his wish to bequeath his body for medical research could not be met. Only whole bodies are acceptable.

7 December 2007

Prince Eddie's heart sinks each Christmas at the prospect of sending out cards. He doesn't reply to all those he receives. For instance, one came today from the Mayor of London and he doesn't even know his name.

Eddie describes how the Queen plans the annual family Christmas lunch down to the last detail. The grown-ups are in one big room, the children in another. Towards the end of lunch, the doors are flung open and in rushes the horde.

18 December 2007

I went to replenish my stock of picture postcards at the National Portrait Gallery shop, but they no longer sell the usual postcard size, only bigger ones with a special envelope. The sort of irritation that occurs constantly these days.

Lunch at the Beefsteak. Douglas Hurd is in ebullient form. He is writing a book on British Foreign Secretaries and asks me if I know where he can find Edward Grey's* papers. It has long been a mystery. Michael Brock once

---

* 1st Viscount Grey of Fallodon (1862–1933), Liberal politician. MP for Berwick-upon-Tweed 1885–1916; Foreign Secretary 1905–16; Ambassador to the US 1919–20.

told me that they were lent to G.M. Trevelyan for his book *Grey of Falloden*, then dumped in an outhouse in Wallington. When next discovered they had rotted completely, so were surreptitiously destroyed. A terrible story.

19 December 2007

Gordon Brown, the PM, had no idea how to talk to soldiers during his visit to Iraq and Afghanistan, nor was David Cameron any more at ease. After Brown's visit, someone out there heard him say: 'Well we need not go there again. They will all vote Conservative.'

31 December 2007

I have a talk with Patsy Grigg. She asks me if I know who could write the official life of Roy Jenkins. Apparently, the Labour man Andrew Adonis[*] (now a peer) began it but has now withdrawn. I suggest Richard Thorpe could do it.

Patsy has been reading a new book on the British Empire by Piers Brendon[†] in which he asserts that Ned Grigg[‡] was so taken by Mussolini that he had a Blackshirt uniform made to wear. It sounds utterly out of character. Could I ask the author for his reference, which the book does not include? I shall do so.

---

[*] Baron Adonis of Camden Town (b. 1963), Labour politician and author. Sec. of State for Transport 2009–10.
[†] Dr Piers Brendon (b. 1940), historian. Fellow of Churchill Coll., Cambridge since 1995; keeper of the Churchill Archives Centre 1995–2001.
[‡] Sir Edward Grigg, 1st Baron Altrincham (1879–1955), Governor of Kenya 1925–30.

2008

On 18 February Mohammed Al Fayed claimed at the inquest into the death of Princess Diana that she and Dodi Fayed were murdered in a conspiracy arranged by the Royal Family. Northern Rock was nationalised by the British government on 22 February. On 28 March the new Terminal 5 at Heathrow Airport opened with many IT problems that caused 500 flights to be cancelled. On 7 April the inquest into the death of Princess Diana recorded a verdict of accidental death. Boris Johnson was elected Mayor of London on 1 May. On 27 May construction work began on the Olympic Stadium for the 2012 London Games. On 18 July a MORI poll put the Conservatives twenty points ahead of Labour. The government announced a bank-rescue package of £500 billion on 8 October. On 18 December Woolworths stated that it would close its 807 UK stores by 5 January 2009, putting 27,000 people out of work. Harold Pinter died on 24 December.

1 January 2008

I telephone Andrew Elgin[*] with New Year greetings. He has not been well. I remind him that it is exactly sixty years to the day since I stayed at Broomhall for the first time as a guest of his father, and what a gloomy place it looked in the sleet that morning, I having come up by night train, although there was much good cheer within. It was on that first visit, during a pheasant shoot, that his father's butler came running through the fields with a telegram from Claude Elliott, inviting me to become a temporary History beak at Eton while Kenneth Wickham had a lung removed in hospital. This gave me an abiding love of Eton and had other consequences.

3 January 2008

There has been a fierce fire at the Royal Marsden Hospital, with the roof of

---

[*] Andrew Bruce, 11th Earl of Elgin (b. 1924), Chief of Clan Bruce; Lord Lieutenant of Fife 1987–99; Lord High Commissioner to the General Assembly of the Church of Scotland 1980–81.

one wing destroyed. I wish the financial world was not in such turmoil as a result of the Northern Rock collapse and other disturbances, otherwise I would send them an instant cheque. As it is, I shall wait a week or two, then send a bequest.

5 January 2008
Recalling that Graham C. Greene suggested that Richard Thorpe would be a good person to edit my Journals, I telephone Richard at his home in Banbury. I find him enthusiastic for the task, once his Macmillan biography is finished. I do not promise him the task on the spot, but pave the way for future detailed talks. I have long been apprehensive about Andrew Roberts as editor. Richard has proved he knows the political world of the last century intimately. He says it would be 'a great honour' to edit my Journals.

The Stock Exchange continues to wilt – rather worrying.

10 January 2008
Patsy Grigg sends me a photocopy of a page from a new book by Piers Brendon called *The Decline and Fall of the British Empire*, in which he writes: 'Sir Edward Grigg so admired Mussolini that he publicly appeared in a Blackshirt uniform of his own design.' It is hugely improbable that Ned ever did any such thing. The author gives no reference. So I write to him care of his publisher to ask for his source.

11 January 2008
I read some of Alastair Campbell's[*] diaries of his time as a principal adviser to Tony Blair at No. 10. Fascinating to see how decisions were taken.

12 January 2008
I meet David Starkey[†] at a dinner party with the Northbournes at Coldharbour. He asks cautiously what I thought of Tommy Lascelles. I reply that it is difficult wholly to respect a man who so deeply regretted having gone to Marlborough instead of Eton, because he thought the Marlborough parents were county cricketers whereas the Eton parents were Masters of Foxhounds. He is delighted by this.

---

[*] (b. 1957), journalist; Downing Street Press Sec. 1997–2000.

[†] (b. 1945), historian and well-known radio and television personality. Lectured in History at the LSE 1972–98; his documentaries on the Tudors were big ratings successes.

17 January 2008

I write to Quincy Adams[*] about his new life of A.J. Balfour, which is able. I am pleased that he takes my side in the dispute on how far King George V allowed a supposed dislike of Curzon to affect his judgement in favouring Baldwin as PM in 1923, i.e. not at all. It was entirely because Baldwin was in the Commons, Curzon in the Lords. Obtusely, David Gilmour takes the other side, as did Roy Jenkins.

3 February 2008

Hugo Vickers told Prue Penn that he thought Willie Shawcross' book on the Queen Mother would be too late, as interest in her swiftly fades. Prue unwisely passed this on to Willie, who replied: 'Thank you. That is just what I wanted to hear.' Yet what Hugo says is nevertheless true – Willie's delay has probably caused him to miss the boat.

5 February 2008

I have lunch with Robert Lacey. He is much encouraged by my proposal to ask Richard Thorpe to edit my Journals. They were at Selwyn College, Cambridge, together in the early 1960s. Robert thinks Richard would be ideal.

5 March 2008

Lunch with Peter Carrington at White's. Both of us are rather depressed by the economic decline of the country, the flagging stock market and the monumental incompetence of the Blair Government.

Richard Thorpe has been to see him about his new book on Macmillan. Peter says, 'He will write a thorough and accurate book.' This prompts me to tell Peter that I will ask Richard to edit my Journals, and that his literary qualities are exactly what is needed.

8 April 2008

The inquest on Princess Diana has ended. Although the verdict of the immensely long and expensive inquest on Princess Diana is, predictably, unlawful killing against the drunken driver of the car, hired by Fayed's Ritz Hotel, and the paparazzi who chased it by car and motorbike, there are two factors which cast a shadow over it:
1. Two of the jurors disagreed.

---

[*] Prof. R.J.Q. Adams (b. 1943), American historian; biographer of Balfour (2007) and Bonar Law (1999).

2. Of a popular poll, about one-third thought that Diana had been murdered as part of a plot, by persons yet unknown.

18 April 2008

Willie Shawcross is on the last chapter of his biography of the Queen Mother and it will appear not this autumn but that of 2009. I suspect that the Royal Archives people will go through it for him, always a long undertaking. I shall be glad when the book is out of the way and the two of us can talk of other things.

8 May 2008

I re-read Cyril Connolly's *The Rock Pool*, published in 1937, and bearing the strong influence of Aldous Huxley. I surmise that his anti-hero, an introspective Wykehamist, full of self-hatred, contains many traits of his own.

5 June 2008

Hillary Clinton is out of the race for the US Presidency, thank goodness.

19 June 2008

I read the last volume of Alan Clark's diaries, published in 2002. I dipped into this at the time, but have never read the whole volume. It records his abrupt changes of mood. First, Alan's misery at being retired from the Commons in 1992; then his euphoria at being returned as Member for Kensington and Chelsea; finally, after years of hypochondria, the growth of what turned out to be a brain tumour and his horrible death. He was much put out by his failure to be made a peer or even to be knighted. Deep love for his wife, though he did not always show it. It is horrifying how he recorded his own physical decline, pages and pages of distressing symptoms. There is a charming handwritten note from Tony Blair three months before Alan died in September 1999: 'Come back soon and give me a hard time.' One of the nicest things I have ever heard of Blair.

6 August 2008

Lunch with Peter Carrington at the Belvedere. He saw Kissinger the other day, who told him that Barack Obama,* the Democratic candidate for the White House, may win the election but will be a disastrous President. He is not very knowledgeable or wise, and will find an empty White House from

---

* Barack Obama (b. 1961), President of the US 2009–2017.

which all Bush's advisers will have fled. On British politics Peter agrees with me that Gordon Brown will probably survive the plots against him.

25 August 2008

Olympic fever at the UK's having won a big bag of medals at the Games in China. Our miserable PM Gordon Brown claims quite a lot of credit for it.

The fiftieth anniversary of Ralph Vaughan Williams' death this week has brought an outbreak of his music on Radio 3, not much of which brings me much pleasure. But I listen to a 1950 recording for the BBC archives of a talk by him on how Bach's music should be performed. He has an attractive, forthright patrician voice and intonation. His theme is that in performing Bach today it is permissible to vary Bach's original score a little to enhance the use of the Authorised Version of the Bible. Quite convincing.

28 August 2008

Another delightful talk by Vaughan Williams from the BBC archives of 1955, on his friend and teacher, Sir Hubert Parry.* He was generous towards his pupils, and even criticism was charmingly delivered. Of a composition of V.W.'s, Parry said to him: 'I cannot decide whether that passage was a mistake or whether there was something characteristic about it.' Parry told all his pupils to study the late Beethoven quartets. V.W. says that Parry's *Blest Pair of Sirens* – from Milton – is 'the best music that ever came out of these islands'.

Not surprisingly, V.W., with his brisk military speech, does not fail to mention that Parry had 'the mind of a country squire'. On the bench, having fined a poacher five shillings, he rushed out through the back of the court to pay it back to him.

3 September 2008

I give Ferdy Mount† lunch. We talk about his recent memoir *Cold Cream* and his account of how, as a Praepostor at Eton, he had to witness Robert Birley flogging a miscreant with a birch on his naked buttocks, having taken a run before delivering each stroke in order to increase its force. 'It may not have been a long run,' Ferdy said, 'but it was certainly a run.' I find this degrading in a Head Master.

---

* 1st Bt (1848–1918), composer and teacher. Head of the Royal College of Music 1895–1918; Professor of Music at Oxford University 1900–08.

† Sir Ferdinand Mount, 3rd Bt (b. 1939), writer, novelist and columnist for the *Sunday Times*.

5 September 2008

I write to congratulate William Waldegrave on his appointment as the next Provost of Eton, which has been announced publicly. I tell him to remember the wise words of a former Provost: 'Be a reformer, but don't be found out.'

10 September 2008

I hear a story from Patsy Grigg of how Mannie Shinwell, in old age, had to make a speech to an Australian audience, but at the last moment broke his false teeth. His hosts took it calmly and promised him that a man would arrive within a few minutes to mend them. Sure enough, the man turned up and did a superb repair. Mannie thanked him and said: 'I suppose you're a dentist?' 'No,' the man replied, 'I'm an undertaker.'

I have an amusing letter from William Waldegrave in reply to my letter of congratulation. On my advice to him, 'Be a reformer, but don't be found out', he writes: 'An excellent slogan. I shall get a King's Scholar to put it into Latin so that the other Fellows will not understand.'

13 September 2008

I met an interesting QC, Philip Havers,* son of the Lord Chancellor. I ask him in what fields he practises. Among them are medical cases. So we discuss Lord Dawson of Penn and King George V. When I tell him that the King was in no pain but that Dawson hastened his death by large doses of morphine and cocaine, Havers declares emphatically that it was <u>murder,</u> whatever Dawson's views on euthanasia. I am interested to have this confirmed by a specialist.

14 September 2008

I sit next to Bob Worcester† of MORI, very agreeable. He tells me that when he met the Queen Mother, she complained to him that <u>she </u>had never been polled by his MORI investigators.

We also agree that in spite of the current hostility and contempt provoked by Gordon Brown among his supposed Labour supporters, he will still be PM in six months' time.

28 September 2008

Another beautiful day, with warm golden sun. I sit by the Round Pond and

---

* The Hon. Philip Havers (b. 1950), barrister.
† Sir Robert Worcester (b. 1933), founder of MORI.

read more of Alastair Campbell's diaries of his years at No. 10 with Tony Blair. What a nest of vipers.

The old deckchair attendant in Kensington Gardens, as always, comes up to shake my hand.

3 October 2008

Astonishing news in the evening that Gordon Brown, in a melodramatic attempt to strengthen his failing Government, is bringing back Peter Mandelson as Secretary of State for Business. The two men have loathed each other since 1994, when Mandelson abandoned Brown in the election of a new leader of the Labour Party in favour of Blair. Mandelson, moreover, is a shady, discredited politician, twice required to resign from a Blair Cabinet. By chance I am reading about Mandelson in Alastair Campbell's diaries: a horror chronicle of political manipulation and a hatred of the Press more than is reasonable.

4 October 2008

Peter Mandelson's appointment to the Cabinet is received with universal disgust and derision. The headline in the *Daily Telegraph* is 'Lord of darkness returns', but in the *Daily Mail* 'Lord of sleaze'. That such a man should now be made a peer.

While out shopping, I pause to watch a military band and a detachment of Chelsea Pensioners go by – and I confess that my eyes fill with tears. Then I look again, and see that I could give many of them twenty years.

9 October 2008

The *Daily Mail* picks my brains about the problems facing the Prince of Wales, sixty next month, when he ascends the throne. I point out that most Sovereigns, though not the present Queen, began unpromisingly but turned out well. Camilla <u>must</u> be Queen. We don't want what would in effect be a morganatic marriage if she is to be called Princess Consort.

27 October 2008

Andrew Roberts refers to me in a newspaper article as 'the distinguished historian Kenneth Rose'. I wish he hadn't. Epithets, like dogs, should be kept under control.

6 November 2008

Barack Obama becomes the first black President of the United States. He comes over as being articulate, with much charm.

11 November 2008

Ninetieth anniversary of Armistice Day. In the years before the commemoration was switched to Remembrance Sunday, 11 November was a hallowed day, treated with respect, even reverence – in our family not least because my father had served in the Great War and my mother was in the Voluntary Aid Detachment. So I ponder this Tuesday the passing of friends and my own survival.

12 November 2008, Letter to Brian Rees

I have been reading your history of Stowe with immense pleasure and admiration. The introductory chapter, you will recall, so impressed me that I could not read on without first telephoning you with my congratulations. All that follows delighted me no less.

Only once have I been to Stowe. The beauty of the architecture in a sylvan setting left its imprint on me, and reminded me of my own schooldays at Repton, founded in 1557 on the ruins of church and monastery. But there are differences in their development. Stowe has held its place as a national institution; Repton, alas, has taken a less exacting path into regionalism. In my day Repton drew its boys from the same social and geographical strata as Stowe – in particular the country clergy and the professions. Today Repton is primarily – or so it seems to me on my rare visits – for the sons, and daughters, of successful businessmen, Sheffield steelmakers and executives of Rolls-Royce at Derby. This I regret: the horizons of the school have shrunk and Repton's contribution to the life of the nation is minimal.

20 November 2008

Hugo Vickers rings with news about his perusal of James Pope-Hennessy's[*] papers. On James's life of Queen Mary, Hugo says it would never have escaped drastic censorship had not Tommy Lascelles carefully guided it through all difficulties.

Also an important remark if true, as it probably is: 'The Queen has refused to say anything to any Royal biographer, including Willie Shawcross.' I certainly heard she was not helpful to Philip Ziegler when he was writing his life of Edward VIII.

2 December 2008

I dine with Charles Guthrie at White's. While we are eating, a tall, youngish man with a very pink complexion and curious ridge of hair high up on his

---

[*] (1916–74), biographer and travel writer.

forehead walks through to the other room. 'Is that David Cameron?', I ask Charles. It is – I think it is the first time I have ever set eyes on him. He looks extraordinarily young, with unlined features and the complexion of an undergraduate or even a schoolboy.

3 December 2008
Willie Shawcross sends me a couple of typed pages from his biography of the QM in which he quotes from my letters to her, found in the Royal Archives – so fortunately Princess Margaret did not manage to destroy <u>all</u> her mother's correspondence at Clarence House as she once told me. The main reference is to our standing together on the terrace at Walmer Castle gazing across to France.

14 December 2008
I have a long talk with Richard Thorpe during which I confirm that I should like him to edit my Journals. He looks forward to it, although he will still be working on his life of Macmillan until well into 2009. I am relieved to have got all this finalised, though I suspect the Journals will not come out in my lifetime. Richard has been invited to give the annual Sir Robert Birley memorial lecture at Charterhouse on 7 October. His subject is 'Writing Biography', and he suggests that I might like to hear it. He says that all past Birley lecturers (I gave the third one some years ago after William Rees-Mogg and Hugh Trevor-Roper) are welcomed back as guests. I shall look forward to that.

Richard also tells me an amusing story about a white-tie dinner at All Souls on 3 November 1956, the evening Eden broadcast to the nation about the Suez Crisis. The dinner was delayed for half an hour so that the Fellows and guests, including Lord Halifax, could watch Eden delivering his momentous speech on Suez on TV. The only television set, as it happened, was in the butler's pantry, into which everybody crowded in full fig. Eden declared, 'I am utterly convinced that the action we have taken is right.' The broadcast was followed by a long silence in the pantry, broken eventually by Halifax saying, 'Anthony always did have this thing about dictators.'

2009

On 5 January cold weather caused widespread disruption across the UK. Woolworths completed the closure of its UK stores on 6 January. On 8 January the Bank of England cut its base rate to 1.5 per cent, the lowest in the bank's 300-year history. Further snow caused fresh disruption on 3 February. On 5 February the Bank of England reduced its base rate to 1.0 per cent. On 13 February shares in the Lloyds Banking Group closed 30 per cent down and the Chancellor of the Exchequer, Alistair Darling, refused to rule out full nationalisation. The Bank of Scotland announced losses of £24.1 billion on 26 February. On 5 March the Bank of England reduced the base interest rate to 0.5 per cent, its lowest ever level. The Speaker of the House of Commons, Michael Martin, announced his resignation on 19 May. On 1 June a MORI poll put the Conservatives 22 per cent ahead of Labour. Gordon Brown reshuffled his Cabinet on 5 June. On 22 June John Bercow was elected as the 157th Speaker of the House of Commons. On 29 September the Sun *newspaper withdrew support from the Labour Party and backed the Conservatives. The Supreme Court of the UK opened on 1 October. On 16 December ITV closed its Teletext service.*

20 January 2009

Richard Thorpe comes to Brunswick Gardens in the morning to look through quite a lot of my Journals for when he becomes the editor once he has completed his life of Macmillan in June. He is most encouraging about what I have written about Rab Butler and that generation of politicians. 'Gold dust, gold dust,' he murmurs to himself. He, I and Graham C. Greene will meet soon to formalise all the details. I shall have to write an introductory essay on childhood, Repton, the war, Oxford, and working in Italy. Richard is a well-balanced, decent man who will not, I think, edit the Journals other than unobtrusively. He has a good sense of humour, which is essential, and likes an old story, as I do. He tells me today the story of Ursula Vaughan Williams' funeral in St John's Wood. After the coffin had departed to the crematorium, the congregation were invited to the Long Room at Lord's for a reception. As the gathering was breaking up, an MCC committee member, trying to be helpful for cricketing fans, said: 'Before you go, would anybody like to see the Ashes?' It was a pure H.M. Bateman moment, which Ursula would have much enjoyed.

We go on to talk about Eton, particularly the snobbishness which so appalled John le Carré when a beak. Richard tells me of an Eton boy being invited out to tea by a new beak. 'What sort of tea did he give you?' the boy was later asked by those who messed with him. The boy replied: 'Milk in first, and Indian.'

When on our way to my local restaurant for lunch, I point out to him a shabby figure creeping along Kensington Church Street: Lucian Freud. I quote Browning to Richard: 'Ah, did you once see Shelley plain?'

22 January 2009

There is conjecture as to whether Tony Blair will get the Garter. I doubt if he would want it. Hugo Vickers has suggested that the Queen could strike a compromise by offering him the Order of the Thistle. There is a mistaken implication here that KT is in some way inferior to KG. No Scot would agree.

29 January 2009

The *Daily Mail* asks about the relationship between the Queen Mother and Anthony Blunt. Wilfrid Blunt calls them distant cousins in his autobiography, but Anthony never established a family intimacy with her; he was interested in Royal collections, but not their owners. I remember Martin Gilliat telling me that the Queen Mother did not like to hear Blunt disparaged even after he had been exposed by Mrs Thatcher as a Soviet spy.

5 February 2009

I lunch at the Garrick with Graham C. Greene, who is to act as my agent for the publication of my Journals.

We enjoy much gossip about friends in common. Graham has a high regard for Arnold Weinstock. When Graham was Chairman of the Trustees of the British Museum, Arnold was most generous in dipping into his own pocket to help various projects for which there was no public money available. This help was forthcoming on the understanding that there should be no publicity.

11 February 2009

I lunch with James Stourton. He makes a remark which is perceptive: that he infers from reading it that I was unhappy in writing the life of Victor Rothschild. He is right: for some of the time I was suffering from cancer and

Weidenfeld & Nicolson presumed that there was little hope of my producing any lucrative book in the future. And above all I came to realise that neither Victor's character nor achievements were as admirable as I had presumed on embarking on my biography of him. He bullied or bribed endless people, including myself, into doing work for him – particularly in completing his two-volume catalogue of his eighteenth-century collection of manuscripts, books and bindings. Even some of his medical work is now thought to be over-rated.

Talking of schools and schoolmasters, James tells a curious story of Eton in days gone by. A very bright and agreeable beak had a house. Some years later he confessed to the Head Master that he had fallen in love with one of his boys – though there had been no physical relationship. As he found this distracting, he wished to be relieved of his house. This was quietly done and he remained a beak. What a civilised way of solving an awkward problem.

19 February 2009

Mollie Butler has died at the age of 101. We last spoke on the telephone about a year ago, when she still retained her lovely silvery voice and always laughed at my imitation of Ted Heath talking about music, especially 'Braaahms'. How I loved Mollie and Rab, and what kindness they showed me over the years.

Graham Greene telephones me after reading the thick folder of typed extracts from my Journals and some in MS. As he is not given to hyperbole, I am moved by his verdict. I listen to *The Creation* in a contented state of mind.

9 March 2009

Year after year when I was a judge for the Wolfson Prize for History, one or two of my fellow judges put forward that unrepentant Stalinist Eric Hobsbawm[*] for a prize, and year after year I saw to it that he was not successful. I retired as judge in 1995, having secured the prize for Colin Matthew's scholarly and illuminating edition of the fourteen volumes of Mr Gladstone's diaries. In 1996 my fellow judges gave the prize to Hobsbawm 'for his distinguished contribution to the writing of history'. The citation should have been for the perversion of history. None of my fellow judges was either a Communist or an ex-Communist: all were liberals and no doubt thought they were being enlightened and broad-minded in their choice of a Stalinist.

---

[*] Eric Hobsbawm (1917–2012), Marxist historian. His best-known works include his nineteenth-century trilogy: *The Age of Revolution* (1962), *The Age of Capital* (1975) and *The Age of Empire* (1987). President of Birkbeck College, London University 2002–12.

17 March 2009

Nico Henderson has died in his ninetieth year. He has been in poor health for some time. Although a friend of many years with whom I stayed in Paris and Berlin, he was always a shade suspicious of what I might write about him. I laid his doubts to rest by writing a rave review of his last book, *Old Friends and Modern Instances*, in 2000. For the most un-stuffy of ambassadors, he could be touchy about criticism. He did not like at all the reason which Peter Carrington gave for calling Nico out of retirement to become our Ambassador in Washington: 'Because you are so eccentric.'

22 March 2009

The financial outlook becomes bleaker, with a load of debt that will oppress the nation for years to come. The banks, having been given billions of pounds by the Government to stay afloat, are spending part of it in giving bonuses to the directors and other staff responsible by their greed for causing the crisis and reducing the value of individual bank shares to a few coppers. Reward for failure is the order of the day.

29 March 2009

The Government is again discussing whether to change the Act of Settlement and so allow members of the Royal Family either to be or to marry Roman Catholics; also to allow female members of the Royal Family to take precedence over males according to date of birth in the line of succession. Had this been so in the nineteenth century the Kaiser would have become King of the UK.

6 April 2009

The scandal of MPs' expenses grows daily in its shocking detail. Hardly any of them seem to have broken the rules. If so, it is the rules which are wrong, allowing MPs to fiddle their declaration of second homes in order to claim thousands of pounds on maintaining and furnishing them – the husband of the Home Secretary, whom she pays £40,000 a year to act as her assistant, has even put down pornographic videos as a parliamentary expense. And ministers with grace-and-favour houses in London continue to claim on a private London house (which can be let) as well as one in the constituency. MPs should receive more salary and fewer expenses.

7 April 2009

Lunch with Peter Carrington at White's. He tells me of the worst row he ever had with Mrs Thatcher when he was Foreign Secretary. In front of Robert

Armstrong and Michael Palliser, she rebuked him for his policy on Israel, which she said was much resented by her Jewish constituents in Finchley. Peter replied: 'I thought it was the policy of the Government, not mine alone. But if you think that our policy should be based on whether or not it satisfies your Jewish constituents, you had better get yourself another foreign policy and another Foreign Secretary.' And he went out, slamming the door. Later in the day he passed the PM in a corridor, who said: 'That didn't go very well this morning.' As Peter says to me: 'That was as near as she ever got to an apology.'

10 April 2009
Good Friday. I listen on Radio 3 to Tony Blair being interviewed about his faith and beliefs. Joan Bakewell[*] puts her questions with clarity and authority, which makes Blair less evasive than usual. I don't believe he is a true Catholic at all. When asked about what drew him to Mass, he says 'the idea of doing things together'. I doubt whether he accepts transubstantiation.

14 April 2009
In four days' time, Prince Philip will become Britain's longest-serving consort, passing the fifty-seven years and seventy days of Queen Charlotte, the consort of George III. The *Daily Telegraph* says the Queen has coped so wonderfully owing to the support he has given her over the years. In fact, the Queen has done it by virtue of her own remarkable strength and character.

17 April 2009
Hugo Vickers tells me he will not review the Shawcross book on the Queen Mother. Nor shall I: too many pitfalls.

8 May 2009
VE Day in 1945, which found me in Cuxhaven.

13 May 2009
The scandal of MPs who have milked the expenses system of the Commons, ministers and backbenchers alike of all parties, continues. The *Daily Telegraph* has done a tremendous public service in printing a mass of detail leaked by a Commons insider. Michael Martin,[†] the Speaker of the House,

---

* Baroness Bakewell of Stockport (b. 1933), journalist and television presenter. President of Birkbeck Coll., London University.
† Baron Martin of Springburn (b. 1945), Speaker of the House of Commons 2000–09.

has become an object of ridicule and contempt for having tried to block publication. He has further damaged his reputation by rebuking a woman Labour MP who urged that Parliament should now try to launch a criminal investigation against whoever leaked the material to the *Telegraph*.

18 May 2009

The continuing exposure in the *Telegraph* of fraudulent or exaggerated claims by MPs indicates that the officials of the Commons fees office have failed to police the system. The Speaker, Michael Martin, who has consistently resisted newspaper demands for the expenses of individual MPs to be made public, has made an inadequate apology to the nation, but refuses to accept responsibility, much less resign. He is heckled and treated with disrespect to his face. Of course, he should never have been elected Speaker by Labour – a move designed to teach the Tories a lesson. But those who did elect him should not now turn on him in so uncouth and brutish a manner.

19 May 2009

Speaker Martin has finally bowed to the inevitable and resigned.

3 June 2009

I lunch with David Hirst.* We talk of the Bodkin Adams case. David emphatically agrees with me in criticising Lord Devlin's book on the case, on two grounds: (a) he retried the case in the book, finding Bodkin Adams guilty; (b) it was a sustained mocking attack on Reggie Dilhorne. David also agrees with me that it was frivolous of Lord Hailsham not to condemn the writing of such books by judges. Instead, when I complained about Devlin's book to Quintin Hailsham, he replied, with a merry laugh, 'Oh, but it was such a good read.'

22 June 2009

John Bercow, who calls himself a Conservative MP but is Labour at heart, is elected Speaker by secret ballot, though it is widely believed that scarcely any Conservative voted for him. Thus does the Labour Party continue to play a spiteful political game when outside Westminster the country calls for a strong Speaker to reform Parliament and curb the expenses scandal.

9 July 2009

I give Peter Carrington lunch at Le Gavroche. He looks surprisingly well

---

* The Rt Hon. Sir David Hirst (1925–2011), Lord Justice of Appeal 1992–9.

for any age, amazingly so for a recently widowed nonagenarian. He tells me he has answered 400 letters on Iona's death in his own hand, with sixty remaining to be written. 'So please forgive me if I do not write to thank you for this lunch.'

We talk of our dismay at the recent deaths in Afghanistan of two senior Welsh Guards officers and others. And I quote Lord Derby on the difficulty of conducting military operations in Afghanistan. 'The trouble is', Peter truly observes, 'that today's ministers know no history.' He recalls how as Foreign Secretary he went to Moscow on behalf of the European Community to deplore the Soviet occupation of Afghanistan. Gromyko replied to Peter's reminder that of a population of nineteen million Afghans, three or four million were now refugees in Pakistan, 'They are not refugees,' the Russian Foreign Minister said. 'Afghans have always been a nomadic people.'

Peter worries that the revelation by the *Telegraph* of the way in which nearly all MPs have fiddled their parliamentary expenses has brought Parliament into almost universal contempt. One can trace it back, he says, to Mrs Thatcher's refusal to increase the salaries of MPs at a time of austerity. Willie Whitelaw then came up with the wheeze of generous parliamentary allowances.

22 July 2009

I talk to Richard Thorpe, who tells me, as I expected, that he is running a little late with his big book on Macmillan, but hopes to embark on the Journals in the autumn. He speaks of a recent book on Macmillan, full of errors and misinterpretations. The writer says that during the Night of the Long Knives, Harold had hoped to avoid an extensive Cabinet reshuffle by moving Selwyn Lloyd from the Treasury to the Home Office. But, according to the recent book, Selwyn refused 'because of his private life'. That is a most infamous and damaging statement. As Richard discovered when writing his life of Selwyn Lloyd, the real reason he refused the Home Office was that he detested capital punishment.

12 August 2009

Lunch with Richard Davenport-Hines.* I successfully pressed his claim to the Wolfson Prize in 1985. He is writing a book on the sinking of the *Titanic*,

---

* (b. 1953), historian and literary biographer; his books include *The Macmillans* (1992), a biography of W.H. Auden (1995) and *An English Affair: Sex, Power and Class in the Age of Profumo* (2013).

in which he will doubtless be obliged to show that the first-class passengers behaved as cravenly as the steerage ones behaved heroically. We agree that David Cannadine's book on the decline of the British aristocracy is outdated: the book to be written is the resilience of the British aristocracy, and Richard Davenport-Hines is the man to do it. We agree on all sorts of other themes, particularly the pre-eminence of the under-rated Alec Home over most other PMs of our time.

17 September 2009

The papers are full of extracts from Willie Shawcross' book on the Queen Mother. As far as I can see there is nothing much new. It becomes increasingly clear that he could have reduced the 1,000 pages-plus by half had he omitted detailed accounts of overseas tours and other stuff.

20 September 2009

Sarah Bradford, biographer of George VI, telephones to sound out my opinion of Willie's Queen Mother. I have to confess that I have not yet seen it, and am unlikely to read its 1,200 pages for some time. She seems to think that Willie has been sat upon by the Royal Archives and pressed to include all the boring details of Royal tours for the record. A sniffy review in the *Sunday Telegraph* regrets the absence of her sense of mischief.

Prue Penn regrets Willie's lack of both enquiry and insight into the QM's lively mind. She says she was responsible for the passage in the book about Princess Margaret burning Princess Diana's letters to the QM.

22 September 2009

Hugo Vickers telephones to give me his opinion on Willie Shawcross' official life of Queen Elizabeth the Queen Mother. He went to the launch party at the Queen's Gallery, Buckingham Palace. Hugo says: 'My book on her was braver and funnier and I wrote to inform. There is not a drop of humour in Willie's book or any character sketches of courtiers. He does not explain what inspired her and how she kept going.' Hugo still sounds bitter at not having been chosen to write the official life himself. Later I go out and buy a copy. It is uncomfortably heavy to lift and impossible to take on a journey. The lady in the shop says: 'We have some copies with wheels on!'

11 November 2009, Letter to the Prime Minister, Gordon Brown

I feel moved to send you a line of sympathy and support over the abominable way in which you have been treated by the Press and others over your letter to the mother of Guardsman Janes,* 1st Battalion Grenadier Guards.

It seems to me that from kindness of heart you went far beyond what was required of a Prime Minister to write to Mrs Janes in your own hand; and having made that generous gesture, you ill-deserved trivial criticism of handwriting and supposed errors of style. The alleged inadequacy of the supply of arms to our troops in Afghanistan is a matter that invites debate. But I am sure I speak for many in regretting that it has become confused with your intention of bringing some comfort to the mother of a dead soldier.

24 November 2009

I talk to Peter Carrington and seek his opinion on my proposed life of Bobbety Salisbury. Peter found him a most able Leader of the Opposition in the House of Lords when the Parliament Bill of 1949, limiting the peers' veto, was being debated. But he sees many difficulties for any biographer in writing truthfully about Bobbety's craftiness and the conceit of the family. What, for instance, would the family make of the remark of a Labour peer: 'The noble Marquess talks of our kith and kin in Rhodesia. But not many of them would get through the gates of Hatfield House without paying half a crown.'

Peter tells me that during the debates of 1949 the then Duke of Marlborough† accosted Bobbety outside the Chamber and harangued him for being too accommodating to Labour. Bobbety listened courteously, then said: 'In order that I might write you a letter on the subject, would you be kind enough to tell me your name?'

9 December 2009

William Waldegrave, who, at my request, wrote to Richard Chartres, the Bishop of London, to confirm that my memorial service may be held in the crypt Chapel of the Order of the British Empire in St Paul's, sends me the Bishop's charmingly expressed consent. Richard, who is Prelate of the Order, has consulted the Dean. So that is one melancholy task fittingly achieved.

15 December 2009

I talk to William Waldegrave about appointing a second or joint executor alongside him. I tell him I have in mind to appoint one of the partners in Wrigleys, my solicitors in Leeds.‡

---

* Jamie Janes (1989–2009), killed as the result of an explosion in Helmand province.
† John Spencer-Churchill, 10th Duke of Marlborough (1897–1972).
‡ This is what happened.

Richard Thorpe tells me a sad story about Churchill College. The historian Piers Brendon, with whom I had a row about his accusing Ned Grigg of wearing a Blackshirt uniform of his own design when Governor of Kenya, gave a controversial lecture on 'The Decline of Politics', which was humorously reported in the Churchill College annual *Chronicle*. In the lecture he sneered at Eden, saying that Clarissa used to blacken his moustache to hide the grey hairs when he was going on TV, and other absurdities. Clarissa was furious that the *Chronicle*, which is widely circulated, should go out under Churchill College's name, and asked Richard to write to the Master pointing this out. He duly did so, but the Master did not even reply.

The 2010s

2010 was a general election year that brought to an end thirteen years of Labour government, first under Tony Blair, and from 2007 under Gordon Brown; the coalition government under David Cameron with the Liberal Democrats was the first since Churchill's in 1940.

In the last few years of his life, Kenneth's activities inevitably declined in number, though he never liked a day to pass by without hearing a good story. Increasingly his attention turned to how his journals should be presented for publication. He reluctantly accepted that his involvement in their preparation would be less than he had planned and anticipated.

On 27 March 2011, the year in which Kenneth's journals end, the UK census took place. From 17 to 20 May the Queen made her first state visit to Ireland. On 11 July George Lascelles, 7th Earl of Harewood, died. The artist Lucian Freud died on 20 July. On 15 September the Fixed Term Parliament Act was passed.

29 January 2010

More work on the Journals. Richard Thorpe comes for tea. Richard had come on from lunching at the Oxford and Cambridge Club. I ask him who proposed him some years ago. He says simply that his sponsors were Roy Jenkins and Owen Chadwick, his Master at Selwyn College. To be proposed by two members of the Order of Merit must have impressed the Secretary of the club, as it does me!

26 February 2010

Sorting some papers, I am amused to come across a brief note from Colin Matthew at the time that Roy Jenkins' book on Gladstone appeared, much of it taken directly from Colin's monumental edition of the Gladstone diaries. It reads: 'W.E. Gladstone: I was touched to see how Lord Jenkins simply took my research on Gladstone's finances as correct!'

2 March 2010

Death of 'young' Winston Churchill. I always liked him, though was shocked by the ruthless greed with which he and other members of the family pocketed £12.5 million of taxpayers' money (through the National Heritage Fund) from the sale to the nation of his grandfather's personal papers. He also levied a copyright fee on those authors who used the papers in Churchill College, Cambridge.

I have been enjoying Frank Johnson's book of collected articles and parliamentary sketches, not least his account of how as a boy at Covent Garden he lay in Maria Callas' arms during a performance of *Norma*, one of his eyes pressed into her nipple.

3 March 2010

Receive an invitation to a Repton Gaudy, which I shall decline. I am amused to read in their newsletter that there will be a cricket match against WORKSHOP.

Michael Foot has died in his nineties. I admired his love of English literature, but what a lightweight he proved in politics.

7 March 2010

Peter Carrington tells me an interesting thing. The meeting of the victorious powers after the end of the European War in 1945 was held at Potsdam, because all the buildings in Berlin had been destroyed. But in Potsdam the house where the Crown Prince had lived was intact, fully furnished and with servants.

Peter was talking to Margaret Thatcher the other day and said: 'I had no idea you were going to turn out as you did.' She said: 'Nor did I.'

30 April 2010

The papers are full of an extraordinary gaffe by Gordon Brown who, while electioneering, was accosted by a Labour voter on various contentious issues including immigration. Having politely argued with her, he got into his car. But, forgetting that he still had a live microphone in his lapel, he remarked to a member of his staff: 'What a bigoted woman.' The episode has been plastered all over the Press and is said to have lost him the election. Surely it is a relatively trivial matter, but Britain is in a state of hysteria on many matters.

1 May 2010

Now that all the nonsense of the Brown-Cameron-Clegg TV debate has died down, Cameron is not only ahead of the other two in the polls, but looks as though he could be the next PM without depending on Clegg's support. Whoever wins will be burdened by the poisoned chalice of an enormous economic debt to be reduced only by penal taxation.

4 May 2010
The country awaits the General Election in two days' time as a chance to evict Gordon Brown as Labour PM. I think that David Cameron will just scrape an overall majority, though his Conservatism is rather too close to Labour for an old man like me. If no overall majority, he may nevertheless become PM of a Con–Lib Dem coalition. Whoever wins will have a huge financial deficit to clear caused by the profligate spending of Labour since 1997.

7 May 2010
Quite a good night's sleep in hospital. Awake at 7 for BBC news. David Cameron seems to be heading for an overall majority, but it does not last. Eventually a hung Parliament:
   Conservatives 307 seats (36 per cent)
   Labour 258 seats (29 per cent)
   Lib Dem 57 seats (23 per cent)
   The Conservatives have failed to win some of the expected marginals, and the Lib Dems have actually lost a few seats overall. So there is the ghastly prospect of a Labour–Lib Dem coalition to keep out the Conservatives. Cameron should have fought a more traditional campaign rather than whoring after 'progressive' votes.

8 May 2010
The political negotiations continue, with Gordon Brown still at No. 10 and Clegg apparently negotiating with both the PM and Cameron. Meanwhile Europe is in the grip of a severe financial crisis caused by the collapse of Greece's currency.

11 May 2010
The political negotiations continue all day, looking at first as if the Lib Dems and Labour will form a coalition. Then at 9 p.m. I hear that Nick Clegg has dropped Labour as an ally and agreed to form a coalition with David Cameron. But what a dirty game Clegg has played.

12 May 2010
The Conservative–Lib Dem coalition looks fragile in the long term and seems

sure to splinter later in the year and precipitate a second General Election in favour of a wholly Conservative Government. It is absurd that these devious Lib Dems, who in the past few days have been willing to sell themselves with equal alacrity to Conservatives and Labour alike, should have several plum jobs in the new coalition. But William Hague will be a good Foreign Secretary and George Osborne perhaps a better Chancellor than the Press expects. As Derby told a reluctant Disraeli: 'They give you the figures.'

An amusing letter, as always, from Brian Rees. He tells me that when his father-in-law Robert Birley got engaged to be married, he celebrated by taking his bride-to-be to the theatre. And what did he choose? *Othello!*

Kenneth's medical treatment in the second half of 2010 became more complex, including a heart bypass operation. His Journals did not resume until December.

20 December 2010

Very sudden death of the left-wing journalist and author Anthony Howard, about ten years younger than I am. He was a competent reviewer, but could not always resist an unfair barb. 'Albany' and the *Sunday Telegraph* were not his scene at all. Rab Butler chose Howard to be his official biographer, characteristically saying to me shortly afterwards: 'We thought of you, you know.'

4 January 2011

To the Chelsea and Westminster Hospital for a three-month review of my post-stroke condition by a very amiable specialist.

6 January 2011

Richard Thorpe tells me about Anthony Howard's funeral yesterday. Robert Harris* gave a daring but funny address. He spoke of Howard's sense of mischief as obituaries editor of *The Times*. Howard would go over those already written, diluting the eulogy by the insertion of a paragraph beginning, 'However . . .'. Patsy Grigg was affronted by the obit of John which Howard doctored.

I am amused by Richard's gossip. He hears news of Charterhouse from his former colleagues. Not long ago a master there had a sex-change operation, which was splashed across all the national papers. It was thought that form

---

* (b.1957), broadcaster and author of the bestselling *Fatherland* (1992); also *Enigma* (1995) and *Pompeii* (2003).

masters, particularly of junior forms, should be encouraged to have uninhibited question-and-answer sessions about sexual matters as counselling. The boys soon demonstrated that they knew far more than the masters, and far from being puzzled took delight in embarrassing their elders. The master in question had been an Oxford rowing Blue. When it came to questions one junior boy asked: 'Is he now in the coxless fours?'

11 January 2011
A rare visit to the Gate Cinema, Notting Hill, to see *The King's Speech*, the story of how the speech therapist Lionel Logue, about whom I wrote in *Kings, Queens and Courtiers*, cured King George VI of a stammer that mingled pity and embarrassment in all who heard him on public occasions. As in so many films about historical events, particularly about the Royal Family, accuracy has been sacrificed to drama. A grotesque portrait of Churchill.

17 January 2011
I talk to Michael Meredith, Librarian at Eton, to ask him whether he would like the twenty to thirty of my books on Eton matters for College Library. The answer is a grateful 'Yes', to illustrate one man's interests and tastes. I ask Michael whether he wants some of them as duplicates. No, he says, the Eton Library does not possess any of those on the list. I find this odd, particularly regarding Curzon. I do not, however, feel bound to let him have all those on the list. I should give Curzon's *Persia and the Persian Question* to Richard Thorpe, the first-edition two-volume Panshanger copy that belonged to Lord Cowper. After all, it was through our joint interest in Curzon that we first met nearly forty years ago.

I do have one disturbing thought about leaving books to Eton College Library. They will be placed on the beautiful new shelves in Lupton Tower, but beyond the reach of most boys, who will not be allowed to browse. Much of my own education depended on browsing in libraries, especially at Repton. For Meredith, I fear, they are valuable objects to be hoarded. At best he will only use them for the occasional special exhibition or seminar.

12 April 2011, Letter to the Duke of Kent
It was generous of you to include me in your party to Covent Garden. *Fidelio* is always a joy, although my sheltered life does not make it easy to find my way through its sexual maze. The opera has a noble theme and I should like one day to see a production – minus Covent Garden's ironing board and gangster suits – as Wieland Wagner might have done it. I was nevertheless enchanted by the music, and particularly enjoyed hearing it with you and

your family. Our friendship of well over half a century has been – and continues to be – one of the joys of my life.

21 April 2011
The PM, who still displays the mind of a PR man rather than a statesman, has again made a fool of himself. Having stupidly announced a few days ago that he would attend Prince William's wedding in a suit rather than a morning coat, he now changes his mind in the face of universal derision, and will after all dress as he should for a Royal wedding. Democratic gestures are rarely rewarding.

6 May 2011
Osama bin Laden's[*] assassination disturbs me, as it does the Archbishop of Canterbury. The Americans tend to overact. When they hanged the German war criminals at Nuremberg, the heads of some of the victims were torn off and a lot of mopping-up was necessary.

28 May 2011
Manchester United 1 Barcelona 3.
    I can't weep for Alex Ferguson.[†]

11 June 2011
Honours List. Bruce Forsyth[‡] is given a knighthood. So public pressure <u>does</u> work.

13 September 2011
I am deeply disturbed by the conduct of David Cameron, the PM, who has declared a planning free for all in the construction industry, apparently in return for huge donations to the Conservative Party. He is not a true Tory at heart but a spivvy Etonian entrepreneur.

6 October 2011, Letter to Lady Soames
The bomb that destroyed the Guards' Chapel in 1944 was a terrible episode. I was among those who for two days helped to extricate the bodies, a few of whom we brought out alive from under tons of rubble. The corpses were not,

---

[*] (1957–2011), 1st General Emir of Al-Qaeda 1988–2011.
[†] Sir Alex Ferguson (b. 1941), Manager of Manchester United 1986–2013; regarded as one of the greatest managers of all time.
[‡] Sir Bruce Forsyth (1928–2017), popular entertainer.

as we expected, objects of horror, but had a strange beauty, each covered by a film of white dust that turned it into a Greek or Roman sculpture. Such are the paradoxes of war.

27 October 2011
Derek Hill, the artist, has had a huge biography written about himself. At my home the other day, the author met Peter Carrington and asked: 'Were you ever painted by Derek Hill?' Peter: 'No, but he painted my dogs.'

31 October 2011
Hallowe'en. How I dislike hordes of well-heeled local middle-class children knocking on doors and demanding: 'Trick or treat', a far from sophisticated form of blackmail and thuggery they have presumably learned from their rich parents.

On this note Kenneth's journals end. There are no entries for 2012 or 2013. There is, however, one last letter at Christmas 2013 to Sarah, Duchess of York and her two daughters:

22 December 2013
I do hope the girls are as high-spirited as usual. I have never forgotten that time I came to tea with you in the country, when the tomato ketchup for the girls' fish fingers was brought to the table in a pretty Spode sauce boat. And they sweetly said grace before their meal, which is hardly done in private houses nowadays.

EPILOGUE

Where are the kings, and where the rest
Of those who once the world possessed?

They're gone with all their pomp and show,
They're gone the way that thou shalt go.

O thou who choosest for thy share
The world, and what the world calls fair,

Take all that it can give or lend,
But know that death is at the end.

Henry Wadsworth Longfellow

Throughout 2013 Kenneth discussed with me how he would like his journals edited and presented. His original idea had been that we would work on the selection, editing and compiling footnotes together, but by 2013 he had tacitly accepted, even though he had at the time remission from his cancer, that he would not be able to contribute in the long term as he had originally intended. His journals would be a posthumous legacy. This made our talks all the more valuable. He began thinking more in his book-lined home in Brunswick Gardens about the bequests and mementoes that he would like his friends to have by way of remembering him. Valediction was certainly the watchword.

Our first contact had been in 1984 over Lord Curzon, and Kenneth suggested that I might like his first edition from 1892 of the two leather-bound volumes of George Curzon's *Persia and the Persian Question*. He had searched for this rare literary treasure for a long while, finally tracking it down, as he recorded in his Journals, in March 1955 at Forbes and Francis, booksellers by Windsor Bridge, for £15. The volumes had come from the library at Panshanger and had originally belonged to the 7th Earl Cowper

(1834–1905), Government Chief Whip in the Lords under Gladstone, and later Lord Lieutenant of Ireland. The volumes contain Earl Cowper's own bookplate. I had seen and studied Curzon's original meticulous, handwritten manuscript of the great work in the Old India Office Library forty years earlier, so this was a thoughtful and much-appreciated gesture. The two volumes now sit on my own bookshelves next to all Kenneth's own books.

The last time I saw Kenneth was at a lunch at the Athenaeum Club with Eric and Poppy Anderson on 9 October 2013. The Andersons had been important people in both Kenneth's life and mine: in Kenneth's case, sparking off memories of his days after the war in what he called 'that enchanted valley'; and in my case from 1959, when I had been Eric Anderson's first Oxbridge pupil at school in Edinburgh.

That day Kenneth was in his characteristic mood of reminiscence, especially about his time at Eton and Oxford; 9 October, he mentioned, was the fifty-fifth anniversary of Harold Macmillan re-entering 10 Downing Street after his triumph in the 1959 general election. His conversation was its customary blend of sparkling variety. When we parted in the great pillared hall of the Athenaeum, Kenneth pointed out that this was the exact place where Dickens, coming out of the Morning Room on his way to the staircase, had met Thackeray, with whom there had been so much antipathy. Thackeray reached Dickens just as he had put his foot on the great staircase and said, 'It is time this foolish estrangement should cease and that we should be to each other what we used to be. Come, shake hands.' They did so, a touching moment of literary history. We too then shook hands and Kenneth's final words to me were, 'I will see you in the New Year.' It was not to be.

On 24 January 2014 Graham C. Greene rang me up with the sad news that Kenneth had died that day at the Chelsea and Westminster Hospital. He had had a serious fall at home a few days earlier and had been in a coma ever since. Shortly afterwards I attended a meeting at Brunswick Gardens with his solicitor from Leeds and various archivists from the Bodleian Library to assess his papers. The house seemed very empty without his laughter and merriment. The Christmas decorations were packed away, but there was one touching detail. Alone on the chimneypiece was a single festive card – from Sarah, Duchess of York and her daughters, thanking him for all his support of them.

Although in his will Kenneth had stated that all the journals should come to myself first and then go to the Bodleian Library after I had finished with them, it was quite clear as we toured every nook and cranny of the rambling house, finding filing cabinet after filing cabinet filled with numbered and dated wallets, that this would be impractical. It would be far better in every way for the Bodleian archivists to take all the material into safe storage at their depot in Swindon and to store the papers in acid-free boxes. When this was done I then collected ten of the 400 boxes at a time from the New Bodleian Library to take them home for scrutiny and photocopying. This process took two years, before I began selecting and footnoting the Journals.

Lengthy obituaries of Kenneth appeared in both *The Times* and the *Daily Telegraph*. Kenneth had not wanted the fuss of a funeral, but practicalities necessitated a dignified farewell before the memorial service that was arranged for 8 May at the Chapel of the Most Excellent Order of the British Empire in the crypt of St Paul's Cathedral, where readings were given by the Duke of Kent and Lord Carrington and an address by Lord Waldegrave to a packed congregation. The service previously at the West London Crematorium on 11 February was very short and was attended by just five people – Lord and Lady Waldegrave, Sir John Nutting, Graham C. Greene and myself. As the simple ceremony ended I thought of the final stanza of one of Kenneth's favourite poems, 'The Rolling English Road' by G.K. Chesterton:

> My friends, we will not go again or ape an ancient rage,
> Or stretch the folly of our youth to be the shame of age,
> But walk with clearer eyes and ears this path that wandereth,
> And see undrugged in evening light the decent inn of death;
> For there is good news yet to hear and fine things to be seen,
> Before we go to Paradise by way of Kensal Green.

INDEX